JIHĀD IN WEST AFRICA DURING THE AGE OF REVOLUTIONS

JIHĀD IN WEST AFRICA DURING THE AGE OF REVOLUTIONS

Paul E. Lovejoy

Ohio University Press
Athens

Ohio University Press, Athens, Ohio 45701
ohioswallow.com
© 2016 by Ohio University Press
All rights reserved

Printed in the United States of America
Ohio University Press books are printed on acid-free paper ⊚™

26 25 24 23 22 21 20 19 18 17 16   5 4 3 2 1

Library of Congress Cataloging-in-Publication Data

Names: Lovejoy, Paul E., author.
Title: Jihād in West Africa during the Age of Revolutions / Paul E. Lovejoy.
Description: Athens, Ohio : Ohio University Press, 2016. | Includes bibliographical
    references and index.
Identifiers: LCCN 2016040522| ISBN 9780821422403 (hc : alk. paper) |
    ISBN 9780821422410 (pb : alk. paper) | ISBN 9780821445839 (pdf)
Subjects: LCSH: Islam—Africa, West—History—18th century. | Islam—Africa,
    West—History—19th century. | Jihad. | Usuman dan Fodio, 1754–1817. |
    Sokoto Jihad, 1803–1830. | Islam and state—Africa, West. | War—Religious
    aspects—Islam.
Classification: LCC BP64.A38 L68 2016 | DDC 297.096609033—dc23
LC record available at https://lccn.loc.gov/2016040522

*Dedicated to Rina for her inspiration, encouragement,
and support*

CONTENTS

TABLES

MAPS

PLATES

Following page 132:

1. Muslims in Asante, 1820
2. Muslim Fulbe in Senegambia, 1853
3. Gobarau Mosque in Katsina, Eighteenth Century
4. Jenne Mosque, restored 1906–7
5. Timbuktu in the 1850s
6. Muhammad Kabā Saghanughu, *Kitāb al-ṣalāt*
7. Ayuba Sulaymān Diallo of Fuuta Bundu
8. *Bori* Ceremony
9. ʿAḥmad b. al-Qāḍī b. Yūsuf b. Ibrāhim al-Timbuktāwī.
   Hatk al-Sitr ʿAmmā ʿAlayhi Sūdani Tūnus min al-Kufr, 1813
10. Shehu al-Kānimī
11. Kano Cavalry
12. Tomb of ʿUthmān dan Fodio
13. Walls of Kano, 1905
14. *Ribāṭ* at Wurno
15. Kano City in 1850
16. Kano Mosque, 1890
17. Sokoto Market, 1853
18. Kofar Mata Dyeing Center, Kano

Following page 258:

19. ʿUmar ibn Saʿīd of Fuuta Toro
20. Ibrahima ʿAbd al-Raḥmān
21. So Allah
22. Tripoli Slave Market
23. Salvador, Bahia, 1826
24. Muslims in Bahia
25. Hausa Porters in Bahia
26. Mahommah Gardo Baquaqua
27. Bello's Map of the Sokoto Caliphate

Plates

ACKNOWLEDGMENTS

I owe a debt to various scholars, students, and former students with whom I have worked and published throughout my career. Without their enthusiastic involvement and intellectual interaction, my work would never have attained the level that it has. I specifically want to recognize the contributions of Steven Baier, with whom I first developed the argument relating to the desert-side economy of the Bilād al-Sūdān. Jan S. Hogendorn and I together recorded oral testimonies in Nigeria and analyzed British colonial policy on the slave societies of what became Northern Nigeria. David Tambo and Louise Lennihan were part of a team that copied many documents in the Nigerian National Archives in Kaduna, which have subsequently been digitized and cross-referenced to the digital collection made by Mohammed Bashir Salau, whose work on plantations in the Sokoto Caliphate has elaborated my early conceptions of plantation slavery in West Africa. Sydney Kanya-Forstner and I undertook several projects that inform this book, including the study of the conquest of the Sokoto Caliphate, French policy on slavery, and the travels and impact of Ahmad el-Fellati ibn Dauda ibn Muhammad Manga. Yacine Daddi Addoun and I studied the life and works of Muhammad Kabā Saghanughu, as well as the Katsina merchant Ahmad Abu al-Ghaith and the account of Islam in Brazil of 'Abd al-Rahman al-Baghdadi. Jennifer Lofkrantz and I worked on Islamic law and commerce in West Africa. Jamie Bruce Lockhart and I published an annotated version of the journals of the second expedition of British diplomat Hugh Clapperton, whose accounts of Oyo, Sokoto, and Borno in the 1820s are crucial in understanding the jihād. I first undertook the study of the life of Mahommah Gardo Baquaqua with Robin Law and have continued it with Bruno Véras and Danielle Brouwer. Various people have helped with the oral data that underlie the study of slavery in the Sokoto Caliphate, including Mohammed Bashir Salau, Ibrahim Hamza, Saude Hamza, and of course the various students and research assistants who were involved in the collection of oral interviews when I was a lecturer at Ahmadu Bello University in Nigeria. David V. Trotman and I analyzed the Muslim immigrants to Trinidad in the early nineteenth century and by extension developed the idea that the experiences of individuals in Africa shaped their responses to enslavement and emancipation in the Americas. Moreover, over the years I have benefited from extensive intellectual interaction with Martin A. Klein, Ann O'Hear, M. B. Duffill, Toyin Falola, Boubacar Barry, Suzanne Schwarz, David Richardson, and Bruce Mouser and more recently with Benedetta Rossi, Manuel Barcia, Ibrahima Seck, and Gwendolyn Midlo Hall. Carlos da Silva Jr., Neilson Bezerra, Myriam Cottias, Elaine Moreira, Mariana Candido, Feisal Farah, Henry B. Lovejoy, Jennifer Lofkrantz, Vanessa Oliveira, Olatunji Ojo, Tim Soriano, Bruno Véras, and Katrina Keefer have also assisted in various ways and therefore require an expression of my appreciation. Various colleagues have commented on all or portions of the manuscript, including Yacine Daddi Addoun, Michael La Rue, Bruno Veras, Bruce Mouser, Jennifer Lofkrantz, and Sean Kelley. David Eltis has helped me in many ways, often challenging me to refine my arguments, and especially through his patience in deciphering the Voyage Database. Yacine Daddi Addoun corrected the Arabic. Henry Lovejoy deserves additional recognition for constructing the maps for this study and providing essential feedback on the Yoruba dimension. Charles Eberline undertook the painstaking task of copy editing the manuscript, for which I am grateful.

Various aspects of my arguments in this book have been presented at conferences too numerous to list, as well as in many publications that are identified in the introduction. I fully acknowledge this lengthy progression of my thoughts that have been shaped over the years since I conducted my Ph.D. research in Nigeria in 1969–70 and subsequently developed my thoughts while I was teaching at Ahmadu Bello University in 1974–76. The Social Sciences and Humanities Research Council of Canada has provided generous funding for my research over the years. Moreover, the research for this project was completed under the auspices of the Canada Research Chair in African Diaspora History. The need to discuss the issue of jihād in the context of the Atlantic world and the contemporary political scene derives from numerous conversations I have had with Rina Cáceres Gómez, to whom this book is dedicated.

GLOSSARY

ajami—Languages other than Arabic written in Arabic script

al-ḥājj—Honorific title for someone who has performed the pilgrimage to Mecca

alkali (Hausa)—Judge

Bilād al-Sūdān—Land of the blacks, that is, sub-Saharan Africa and specifically the Sahel and savanna

birni (Hausa)—Walled town

bori (Hausa)—Spirit-possession cult

caffa (Hausa)—Land grants based on clientage

ceddo—Warlords, military governments of the western Bilād al-Sūdān

diwal—Provinces of Fuuta Jalon

fadama (Hausa)—Irrigated land

Fulani (Hausa)—Fulbe

gandu (Hausa)—Plantation, depending on context; land worked collaboratively on the basis of kinship

gona (Hausa)—Farm

Ḥadīth—Oral traditions of the Prophet Muhammad

hijra—Flight, withdrawal of the Muslim community to a sanctuary

hurumi (Hausa)—Land grants based on clientage

imām—The leader in prayer at mosques; by extension, the leader of the Muslim community

jamāʿa—Muslim community

jihād—Muslim holy war

ribāṭ—Fortified town, often on a frontier

rinji (Hausa)—Plantation

rumde—Slave estates, plantations; also *rimaibé*

salafi—Adherence to strict interpretation of Islamic law and rejection of innovation

sarki (Hausa)—King, chief; but when used with a specific title, *sarkin*, as in *sarkin gandu*

sarkin bori (Hausa)—Chief of the *bori* spirit possession cult

sarkin gandu—Overseer of a plantation, i.e., "chief of the *gandu*," i.e., plantation

Sayfawa—The dynasty of Borno

Sharīʿa—Islamic law

shurfa—Claiming descent from the Prophet Muhammad

ṣūfī—An adherent of Sufism, a mystical approach to Islam

ṭarīqa—*Sūfī* brotherhood, for example, Qādiriyya, Tijāniyya

tawaye (Hausa)—Rebellion, specifically in 1817

tungazi—Plantation in Nupe

wathīqat—Document

zane (Hausa)—A woman's body cloth

zawāyā—Muslim clerical communities in the southern Sahara

ORTHOGRAPHY

The way of writing names, places, and things is a complicated matter. I have attempted to follow a set of procedures that are not necessarily always logical but that I hope are consistent. For names and terms, I have preferred Arabic renditions, such as 'Uthmān rather than Uthman or Usman, but in the case of Muḥammad I have generally chosen Muhammad, except when individuals have preferred Mohammed or some other form. I have adopted the Hausa form, 'Abdullahi, rather than other forms of 'Abdullāh.

With respect to Hausa names, I have avoided implosive distinctions, thus dan Fodio, not the hooked "d" for ḋan (son of). In cases where names were historically written in Arabic, Fulfulde, and Hausa, for example, I have arbitrarily selected one designation, as in 'Uthmān dan Fodio, rather than Usuman or Usmanu ḋan Fodio or Uthman ibn Fūdi. I have chosen to use *jihād* throughout, but in roman type, rather than to anglicize the term as *jihad*. When I refer to primary texts in Arabic, I have employed diacritics, as I have with sources in French, German, and Hausa, although I apologize for any lapses or mistakes. It should be noted that Hausa names and words sometimes have an apostrophe, which is not to be confused with Arabic diacritics.

As for the names of places, I have preferred the present spellings of names as they occur in modern countries, hence Borno rather than Bornu or Bornou and Ouidah as opposed to Whydah.

In the case of Fulfulde names, I have adopted Fuuta Jalon, Fuuta Toro, and Fuuta Bundu rather than Futa Jallon, Futa Toro, and Futa Bondu and other variations. For ethnic terms, I have avoided adding the English plural form "s" or "es" and have instead used the same term for both singular and plural, hence Hausa, not Hausas. Fulbe, Fulani, Pulo, Fula, and other variations are a problem, but I have tended to use Fulbe except when the context is clearly one in which the Hausa form, Fulani, seems warranted.

With respect to distances, I have used kilometers rather than miles except in quotations.

INTRODUCTION

This book had its genesis in the realization that scholarship has not necessarily been crossing boundaries, particularly in the incorporation of African history into mainstream global history, and therefore the nature of the discourse on important subjects has frequently been neglected.[1] This is a particularly serious problem in the contemporary world, when militancy and aggressive confrontation have characterized the relations between Muslims who refuse to accept complacency and toleration when global capitalism and Western domination perpetuate inequities and injustice. Ignorance and simplistic interpretation characterize the CNN approach to the coverage of the news. Efforts to control resources—petroleum, minerals, agricultural production, labor migration—reinforce the wealth of the few who control companies and receive the support of countries who advance the interests of capitalist resources in the name of free enterprise in what is factually restrictive and monopolistic concentration of wealth in the elites that profit from corruption and secret arrangements that benefit the few, whether or not altruistic motives or occasional acts of generosity are implemented through donations that cleanse dirty money by attaching the names of the rich to institutions that guarantee a place in history.

The role of Islam in the modern world is often misunderstood, and the role of Islam in West Africa even more so. The terrorism of al-Qaeda and its affiliates in northern Mali and southern Algeria is attributed to an infusion of foreign ideas from the Middle East without recognition of the long tradition of Muslim resistance and political fervor in the region itself that stem from the poverty imposed by political decisions. Similarly, the murderous path of Boko Haram and the earlier Maitatsine movement in Nigeria, Niger, and Cameroon is approached with a shocking sense of discovery that fails to recognize a long tradition of homegrown Islamic radicalism, despite any role played by pan-Islamic influences.[2] The dynamic forces that have arisen as a response to globalization and military solutions that are far more devastating than the evil that is targeted are not necessarily revolutionary in what they prescribe. One has only to look at the attitudes toward women to see that misogyny is a central feature of the response. In a postsocialist world, polarization has produced a new dialectic whose outcome is far from certain. That dialectic is associated with the Muslim concept of jihād as justifiable holy war against non-Muslims and indeed against Muslims who are considered lax and unsupportive of a strict adherence to Islamic law as understood in reference to the Sharīʿa.

The focus of this book is on the past, not the current manifestations of jihād and the global contradictions of enormous population growth, the tremendous advances in technology and scientific discovery, and the increasing concentration of wealth and power in the hands of tiny elites who have the means to perpetuate their position. Understanding the past jihād movement in West Africa is essential because the evolution of human society seems determined to find new ways of not learning from the past and relying on ignorance and subterfuge when the amount of new knowledge that has emerged is actually accelerating without any significant corresponding impact on the body politic. The more we learn through scientific enquiry, the less we seem to understand. The exposition of past jihād is essential in understanding how jihād continues to have strong appeal in West Africa, as does the intensive militancy of Islam in other contexts in the Middle East, in East Africa, and indeed in Great Britain, North America, and elsewhere.

This book attempts to situate the historical attraction of jihād in the context of the late eighteenth century and the first half of the nineteenth century in West Africa, and specifically in the region south of the Sahara that is often referred to as the western and central Sudan and here is referred to as Bilād al-Sūdān, from the Arabic, the "land of the blacks." This period is often labeled the age of revolutions in western Europe and the broader Atlantic world to highlight the series of revolutionary movements that produced the political and economic configuration of the modern world. The corresponding changes in Africa, and specifically in Islamic Africa, are almost entirely ignored or silenced. Whether or not the age of revolutions is thought to have begun with the independence of North American colonies from Great Britain in the 1780s or the outbreak of the French Revolution after 1789, the momentous events of the era resulted in the slave uprising in St. Domingue and the formation of independent Haiti in 1804, the Napoleonic Wars and subsequent attempts at restoration of monarchies in Europe, the independence of the mainland colonies of the Spanish Empire, the emergence of Brazil as an American nation, and the equally important and numerous slave uprisings and acts of resistance that followed Haitian independence. Notably absent from this focus on the age of revolutions are events and transformations that occurred in Africa, particularly Africa south of the Sahara. The focus here is on Islamic West Africa, not other parts of Africa, but the same questions of why we do not understand more when we know more can be directed at changes that occurred elsewhere on the continent. I argue in this book that the global transformations associated with the age of revolutions have to be reconceptualized to include other movements that were contemporaneous with the transformations that occurred in western Europe and the move toward independence of the European colonies in the Americas.

In examining Islamic West Africa and the background to the contemporary spread of al-Qaeda, al-Shabaab, Maitatsine, and Boko Haram, I draw heavily on my earlier work, in which various aspects of my argument in this book have been elaborated.[3] The orientation of my many publications has been directed at overcoming the neglect of African history that underlines this book. The proposition that is pursued here is simple: how are we to understand the age of revolutions from the end of the eighteenth century through the middle of the nineteenth century without considering the course of jihād in West Africa during the same period? Why is it that parallel developments are not examined? Why do scholars continue to interpret the West African experience in simplistic terms, unless they are specialists, when there is a vast literature that is accessible and easy to understand? Why do scholars talk about people in Senegambia as "converts to Islam" when they were simply Muslims who had not converted from anything because they were born into societies that had been Muslim for centuries and when there is no proof of any "conversion"? Why do scholars refer to "Islamicized Africans" who were actually Muslims when the same scholars do not use the same conceptual framework and do not refer to "Christianized Europeans" when they discuss Europeans who not only might be Christians but also might be Jewish? Why is such conceptual weakness tolerated when the same scholars make sure that sound historical standards are applied in accepting articles for learned journals like the *American Historical Review* or the *William and Mary Quarterly*? Common sense dictates that such biased, terminological slippage should not be allowed to determine the achievement of tenure and promotion when in fact such bad scholarship and inept thinking have impeded scientific advancement. Somehow, breaking through the conceptual blockages of perceiving the Atlantic world as a framework that does not incorporate Africa into the picture has to confront the failure of scholarly discourse.

The age of revolutions in Europe and the Americas transformed political structures and laid the foundations for economic development in western Europe and the Atlantic world, but also, despite the failure to include an analysis of Africa in the Eurocentric paradigm, it was challenged and transformed from within Africa. These transformations emanating from Europe and the Americas led to European colonial imperialism and imposed racialized interpretations of history that prevail to this day through the terminology that is employed in discussing the "other" and the means of verifying distorted methodology. The changes that emerged during the age of revolutions introduced what has been called a "second slavery" in the Americas, particularly in the United States, Brazil, and Cuba, despite revolutionary changes that undermined monarchies, sometimes promoted more representative governments, and propelled economic change and technological advancement. Yet the analysis stops abruptly when a global view is required. How are we to understand the contradiction between revolution and intensified exploitation without examining what can also be called a "second slavery," to use a term coined by Dale Tomich,[4] which emerged in the jihād states of West Africa in the same period? How can we explain the contradictions of political reform and restorative reaction in Europe and the Americas without considering Muslim countries and the parallel and equally contradictory movements that prevailed in the regions dominated by Islam? The impact of industrialization and economic growth was indeed global, but there were countervailing forces at work in the world that attempted to achieve similar intensified economic growth, as outlined in this book with respect to the many Muslim countries of West Africa. To the extent that such transformations occurred during a time at which political revolution was current throughout the broad Atlantic world that includes West Africa, one has to account for the expansion of economies in areas dominated by Muslim governments in West Africa and elsewhere. This is not to say that the various trajectories were the result of the same causes or shaped the course of events in a common global pattern, but any attempt to understand contemporary Muslim extremism has to consider that there was a period in the past when the age of revolutions was shadowed by the age of jihād.

A number of articles and book chapters that I have previously published have prompted particular arguments in this book. I want to fully acknowledge the extent to which this analysis draws on my previous and ongoing research that has been central to my scholarly career. Moreover, a number of my students have been influential in the development of my thinking. Their research has expanded on some of my ideas, and I have drawn considerable inspiration from working in the collegial atmosphere that graduate teaching promotes. In some cases I have published essays in collaboration with students and former students, as well as editing collections of essays that draw on co-operation and intellectual discussion. I have also developed my ideas in concert with colleagues with whom I have long interacted and with whom I have sometimes published, if not always agreed. It is often difficult to distinguish the sources of ideas and the specific contributions of primary materials that underlie this book. I have shared rare source materials and have borrowed from others in ways and at times that would require a detailed autobiography to uncover. The primary materials that I have amassed over the past forty years, which are on deposit at the Harriet Tubman Institute for Research on Africa and Its Diasporas at York University, amount to an enormous quantity of data. Rather than cite the various articles, chapters, and sections of my books that have influenced the writing of this book, as well as the extensive materials from archives in more than twenty countries, I refer instead to the bibliography and the discussion in the book itself. Similarly, the publications of my students, where relevant, are also referenced in the bibliography and in the annotations.

My approach relies on a methodology that I have characterized as an alternative perspective to a Eurocentric bias that can discuss Muslim converts when there is no proof of any conversion or "Islamized" structures and people when nothing was "Islamized" in the way that is intended in such descriptions, because things, institutions, and people were already Muslim. There was no process under way that can be described as "Islamization," even if what was emanating from Europe was justification of imperial ambitions through claims to "Christianization" and "Europeanization" that were intended to justify subjugation and domination. It was and is easy to determine who was a Muslim and who was not, even if Muslims disagreed over whose interpretation of Islam was legitimate and whose was not. People did convert. That is not the issue, but when, where, and why conversion occurred requires an understanding of historical context.

The relevant historical questions relate to interpretation of the impact of Islam, not to conversion. In West Africa, the Qādiriyya *ṭarīqa* or brotherhood that adhered to a *ṣūfī* or mystical order of interpretation became dominant during what can be called an era of jihād, at least until the emergence of Tijāniyya and then the Mahdiyya extended the influence of jihād beyond the period that was contemporaneous with the European age of revolutions.

The primacy of Sufism does not mean that everyone was an adherent of the Qādiriyya or accepted its *wird* or path. Depending on context, people behaved as Muslims in some contexts and might not in others. Behavior was defined by prayer in Arabic, profession of monotheism, and recognition of the Prophet Muhammad, as well as the practice of certain customs relating to Ramaḍān, fasting, and communal celebration. Religious leaders who were literate in Arabic and taught children and adults the rudiments and advanced sciences had to be acknowledged as leaders of the community, whether it was seen locally in the specific context of a town or section of a town or broadly in terms of the world of Islam. Relations between males and females were subject to norms that were written and based on the Sharī'a. Local customs and practices were also respected, however, although there was a strong tendency to condemn human sacrifice, the veneration of spirits associated with trees, rocks, hills, and other natural phenomena, the eating of pork, drinking, smoking, and human greed through the collection of interest, speculation, and hoarding. Individuals in situational contexts sometimes acted in ways that others might condemn as unorthodox. Slavery was a complicating factor in understanding how Islam was understood because of the emphasis on the status of freeborn Muslims as being inherently protected from enslavement and the social ostracism associated with the lack of kinship. However, to discuss societal relationships in terms of conversion or a process of "Islamization" does not grasp the historical context and only imposes a discourse that is foreign and that cannot be documented.

The jihād movement was revolutionary, as I document in this book. Interpretations of Islam were fundamentally changed as a result of jihād. Not only were existing governments overthrown and new states established, which were revolutionary acts in themselves, but also the centrality of Islam to society and social relationships was consolidated in ways that had not been the case previously. Most of the savanna and the Sahel had long been part of Dar al-Islam, the world of Islam, but the establishment of the jihād states intensified the practice of Islam among elites, merchants, and the general population in ways that affected the meanings of ethnicity. I have previously attempted to present a more sophisticated analytical approach and perspective on understanding identity in the context of West Africa, which I have characterized as a "methodology through the ethnic lens." As I have explained, ethnicity is a complicated phenomenon that is situational. References in the sources to what is considered "ethnic" require explication to discover what is meant and what is not. Ethnicity is complex, both changing and not changing.

Hausa and Mande had existed as identities related to language and culture for hundreds of years before the period that is the focus of this book. Patterns of scarification and cultural upbringing reinforced these identities over very wide geographical regions involving very large populations. Recognition of the ethnic factor is only the first step in understanding the revolutionary impact of the jihād movement on political structures and economic underpinnings that once may have been referred to as modes of production and social formations.

Many scholars have attempted to confront the perplexing dilemma of ethnic terminology that sometimes seems to confuse attempts to understand African history. This perplexity especially applies to scholars of the Atlantic world and scholars of slavery in the Americas; a comparable dilemma of ethnic terminology does not seem to affect the analysis of European history, when there was no such identification in the ongoing frictions among France, England, Spain, Portugal, and other "European" countries. The origins of people, how they have identified in different contexts, and the languages individuals have spoken are repeatedly confused and often fused. The same methodology should be employed in the disaggregation of context and the explanation of relationships for people of European and African background. If we examine the age of revolutions as a unifying feature of history in the world of western Europe and the Americas, we need to understand the age of jihād in West Africa during the same period. The implications for appreciating the seriousness of contemporary jihād in the Islamic world, whether in West Africa or elsewhere, are profound.

1 THE AGE OF REVOLUTIONS AND THE ATLANTIC WORLD

Eric Hobsbawm described the period between around 1775 and 1850 as the "age of revolution" that marked a turning point in modern history.[1] For Hobsbawm and subsequent historians, revolution altered the course of world history, or at least the history of that part of the world centered on Europe and by extension the Americas and what has come to be known as the Atlantic world. The political transformations that undermined autocratic and aristocratic governance were matched by economic change, especially the intensification of industrialization and the emergence of the modern global economy. The powerful arguments supporting this view of historical change challenge scholars of Africa and the African diaspora to understand how people of African descent fitted into this period of history. Clearly, the St. Domingue revolution and many slave revolts that occurred during the age of revolutions can be understood to be part of the historical trend identified by Hobsbawm. Indeed, Eugene Genovese has argued as much, envisioning the St. Domingue revolution as a turning point in the history of resistance to slavery. According to Genovese, resistance before the St. Domingue uprising idealized a politically independent African past, while subsequently the enslaved population concentrated on overthrowing the system of slavery rather than on establishing enclaves of restoration of some reconstructed African past.[2] As David Armitage and Sanjay Subrahmanyam have noted, the identification of the "age of revolutions" is one of "the most enduring period markers known to modern historians and has often been used by scholars invested in identifying pivotal moments in the emergence of a putatively modern world."[3]

What is not clear is how the African regions that bordered the Atlantic and the people who constituted the African diaspora in the Americas related to the global pattern that is identified as the age of revolutions in the Atlantic world. According to Joseph C. Miller, the age of revolutions was only "one phase in a longer cycle of militarization and commercialization in the greater

Atlantic world that becomes visible when the dynamics of African, rather than Euro-American, history are used to define and calibrate the dimensions of transformation."[4] My purpose is to expand on Miller's conception of the *longue durée* by focusing on jihād in West Africa as a means of establishing a clearer outline of the periods in African history. In this perspective, a large part of West Africa witnessed revolutionary changes at the same time as the age of revolutions in Europe and the Americas, which help establish how the homelands and regions of origin of the enslaved were affected by transatlantic historical forces. It is surprising that Africa has largely been excluded from the discussion of the Atlantic world and the era of revolutions, except when enslaved Africans were taken to the Americas and expressed their resistance to slavery.[5] In introducing African history into this discourse of revolutionary change, the aim is examine how the homelands of enslaved Africans can be brought into the discussion. The period of revolutions in the narrowly defined "Atlantic" world of western Europe and the Americas coincided with an era of jihād that was part of Miller's "longer cycle of militarization and commercialization."

Clearly, the economic consequences of the Atlantic slave trade in the development of the global economy were profound, as was long ago recognized by Eric Williams. Barbara Solow, who provides one of the best overviews, has outlined many issues relating to the relative importance of slavery in the economic transformation of the Atlantic world and western Europe, but without any consideration of the African dimension of slavery. Her complete silence on African history, not just the jihād movement, suggests that her analysis has to be taken much further than she dared to go.[6] What constituted the Atlantic world in this period, and why is most if not all of Africa excluded from discussion of that conception? It is perhaps not surprising that the idea of Atlantic history has received considerable criticism, but the place of Africa in a global perspective is still largely ignored. As David Armitage has proclaimed, "We are all Atlanticists now," and an examination of the jihād movement shows how this pronouncement can extend into the interior of West Africa.[7] James Sidbury and Jorge Cañizares-Esguerra have challenged what is meant by "Africa." They have shown that various parts of Africa have to be distinguished from each other, and I would add that it has to be determined how different regions fitted into the Atlantic world, if they fitted at all.[8] Despite the asymmetrical relationships that characterized the regions that bordered the Atlantic Ocean, it can still be asked what those relationships entailed, even though many scholars have avoided a meaningful discussion. The considerable interest in the origins of enslaved Africans and their influence on the development of the "creole" societies of the Americas might suggest that the study of the Atlantic world would have corrected this distortion, but it has not. In fact, this interest in the origins of enslaved Africans rarely includes an understanding of the historical context in which people were enslaved in Africa, marched to the coast, and sold to the captains of the ships destined to cross the Atlantic. Yet this migration occurred during the age of revolutions, and Africans and people of African descent played a major role in the events of the Caribbean, North America, Brazil, and Hispanic America, and indeed in the abolition movement against the slave trade and slavery.

Cultural influences, such as the religious practices and beliefs of the Yoruba; the resistance of slaves and the assignment of ethnicity to resistance, as with Akan in Jamaica; and the cultural links between Brazil and Angola, as expressed in capoeira, have been central in the study of slavery. Although we know the regions of Africa from which people came, too often the African component is amorphous, timeless, and devoid of the rigorous methodology of historical analysis, except among specialists who have not been concerned with how African regions fitted or did not into the age of revolutions. My contention is that historians of slavery in the Americas and the resistance to slavery in the age of revolutions have sometimes ignored and often misinterpreted and misrepresented the historical context to which a significant proportion of the population of the Americas traced its origins. My aim is to draw attention to the fruits of African historical research so that information on the jihād movement can be incorporated into the historical reconstruction of the Atlantic world. Any conception of the Atlantic world has to include those parts of Africa that actually bordered the Atlantic and thereby helped define the geographical boundaries of analysis. The Atlantic world does extend to the Americas from England, France, Spain, and Portugal, but the connections are not just to Brazil, the Caribbean, Hispanic America, and North America but also to various parts of West Africa and indeed to Angola and Mozambique, whose involvement in the era of revolutions should be considered because of the links of these areas to the Atlantic world. Indeed, without the forced migration of Africans to the Americas, there would not have been an Atlantic world.

My focus here is on the jihād movement of West Africa and specifically the consolidation of states that were founded in jihād and that came to dominate much of West Africa during the same period as the age of revolutions. I argue that, as with western Europe and the Americas, the history of West

Africa was also characterized by an age of revolutionary change. Although jihād was not inspired by the same sentiments and forces that characterized the history of Europe and the Americas, there were important similarities and interactions that provide a new perspective on the Atlantic world and the age of revolutions. The jihād movement affected the forms and intensity of slave resistance in the Americas, particularly in Bahia and Cuba. Jihād was also responsible for the continuation of slavery in West Africa on a massive scale. My intention is to demonstrate how the West African jihāds helped shape the Atlantic world and therefore why this history should be incorporated into the analysis of the age of revolutions. Muslims were found in all parts of West Africa except in the coastal forests inland from modern Liberia and Côte d'Ivoire and the interior of the Bight of Biafra (plate 1). Their political control of the interior and their commercial domination of trade almost everywhere were factors that affected the Atlantic world.

When the jihād movement was first identified as a "neglected theme" in West African history in the 1960s, the focus of African historical research was on Christian missions, European colonialism, and the nationalist thrust toward independence. It can be legitimately claimed that since then, the study of Islamic Africa has become a major theme of historical research and analysis, but unfortunately that analysis has often been ignored in the historiography of the Americas. The extensive research that has been undertaken in the past generation has radically transformed our understanding of African history, especially those areas where Islam was predominant. Moreover, with access to the huge libraries of Timbuktu and many other centers, the amount of available documentation has mushroomed, with the result that the study of Islamic West Africa will continue to be subjected to revision and further analysis. Islamic Africa, specifically including sub-Saharan Africa, has come into its own, even without the attention that radical Islam in the form of al-Qaeda, Boko Haram, and other manifestations of contemporary jihād has generated. Despite the recognition that the Islamic presence is substantial, the history of Islam in West Africa has not entered the mainstream of historical analysis. Nowhere is this more apparent than in the silence of historians on West Africa during the age of revolutions, which is seen as focused on Europe and the Atlantic world to the exclusion of Africa and Asia.

There is a long tradition of jihād in the history of the Islamic world, beginning with the initial jihād led by the Prophet Muhammad. Subsequent jihāds of later eras referred back to the founding of Islam and favored strategies and ways of legitimization with reference to the original jihād. The power of this tradition was realized in West Africa, beginning in the last decades of the seventeenth century and becoming manifest in the eighteenth century with the establishment of Fuuta Bundu in the 1690s, Fuuta Jalon in 1727–28 and especially after 1776, and Fuuta Toro in 1775 and most especially in the nineteenth century with the establishment of the Sokoto Caliphate after 1804, the reform of Borno after 1810, and the establishment of Hamdullahi in Masina in the middle Niger basin in 1817. It can be said that by 1835 West Africa had come under the dominance of jihād regimes that would then be expanded further with the launch of the regime established by al-Hājj 'Umar (map 1.1). As an ideology, a military strategy of conquest, and an intellectual reformation, the jihād movement shaped West Africa and laid the foundation for the conversion of the majority of people in West Africa who were not already Muslims to Islam.

Not only was the region of West Africa transformed, but the influence of the movement that materialized in West Africa eventually reached as far east as the Nilotic Sudan, where the Mahdist state was established after 1884. The Mahdist movement in turn reverberated back westward, challenging the continued legitimacy of the Sokoto Caliphate, Borno, and other Muslim states that had been founded or reformulated as a result of jihād. The incursions of the Mahdist leader, Rābih ibn Fadl Allāh, into the Lake Chad basin and his conquest of Borno in 1893 threatened the stability of the Sokoto Caliphate as Hayatu, a direct descendant of 'Uthmān dan Fodio, rallied to Mahdism and claimed legitimacy as the leader of the Mahdist cause there. Mahdist resistance to the colonial occupation in the Sokoto Caliphate in the early twentieth century proved particularly threatening until the Mahdists were crushed at Satiru, near Sokoto, in 1906.[9] Hence the tradition of jihād that began with the Prophet Muhammad intensified first in West Africa, and its influence was spread through migration and propagation of the ṣūfī message of the Qādiriyya. In turn, the Qādiriyya presaged the Tījāniyya movement of al-Hājj 'Umar and the Mahdiyya of the Nile and its subsequent offshoots to the west as far as Lake Chad and beyond.

Many Muslim jurists have characterized jihād as an obligation of all believers. As 'Uthmān dan Fodio established in his *Bayān wujūb al hijra 'alā 'l-'ibād* (The exposition of obligation of emigration upon the servants of God), based on references to the interpretations of earlier Muslim scholars, jihād was defined as an effort to confront impure acts or objects of disapprobation through the use of the heart, the tongue, the hands, and military action. John Ralph Willis has characterized these four manifestations of jihād as follows:

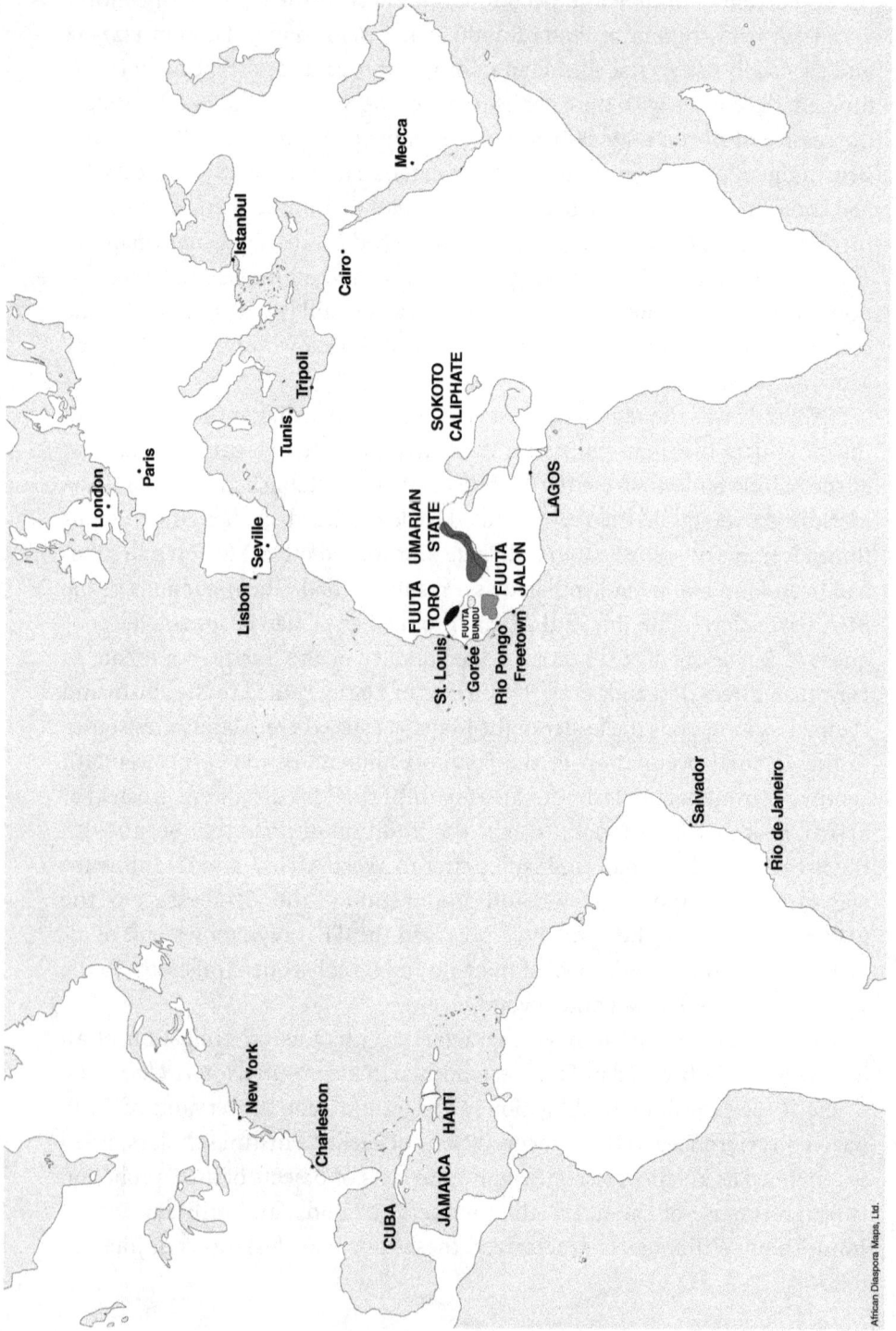

MAP 1.1. The Jihād States in the Atlantic World, 1850.

African Diaspora Maps, Ltd.

The *jihād* of the heart was directed against the flesh, called by the Sufis the "carnal soul." It was to be accomplished by fighting temptation through purification of the soul. The *jihād* of the tongue and hands was undertaken in fulfilment of the Qur'ānic injunction to command the good and forbid the bad. And the *jihād* of the sword was concerned exclusively with combating unbelievers and enemies of the faith by open warfare.[10]

The reflections of 'Uthmān dan Fodio in his commitment to jihād were based on these distinctions. He was preoccupied with the personal purification of the soul and with prescriptions that upheld good behavior and condemned what was considered to be immoral. His call for *jihād fi sabīl Allāh* (jihād in the path of Allah) through military confrontation and conquest was a last resort, not the sole aim of his dedication to Islam. Moreover, his commitment was based initially on withdrawal and the avoidance of confrontation, which in the classic interpretation of Islam was the *hijra*, in imitation of the Prophet's withdrawal from Mecca to Medina in 622 CE. As Willis has explained, "Turning one's mind from evil and things temporal was *hijra* of the heart. Withdrawal of verbal or physical support for actions forbidden by Qur'ān, Sunna, or Ijma' realized *hijra* of the tongue and hands." The *Sunna* refers to the social and legal customs and practices of the Muslim community, while Ijma' is the consensus of the Muslim community, especially jurists, on religious issues. Finally, jihād of the sword only followed after Muslims removed themselves from the world of unbelievers and those who would harm Islam, explicitly because of the threat against their survival as a community. As is clear, the doctrines of jihād were revivalist, calling for a return to the customs and actions of the Prophet and rejecting reforms and changes that deviated from the original traditions of Islam.

An understanding of the jihād movement during the age of revolutions is relevant to contemporary politics in West Africa, particularly the uprising in northern Mali and southern Algeria in 2012–13 and the reign of terror in Nigeria perpetrated by Boko Haram since 2002. However the long tradition of jihād is assessed, its impact in terms of consolidating Islamic governance continues to this day, including efforts at the establishment of Sharī'a jurisdiction in northern Nigeria and the inclusion of all countries in West Africa in the Islamic fold of nations today, even if there are many Christians in Nigeria, Ghana, Côte d'Ivoire, and Sierra Leone, as well as Muslims. The spread of the al-Qaeda movement in Mali and southern Algeria and the role of Boko Haram in Niger and Nigeria demonstrate the continued power of jihād. But there is a fundamental difference between the nature of jihād as discussed in this book and the contemporary manifestation of jihād by Islamists associated with Boko Haram. Whereas the jihād of the past was associated with the ṣūfī brotherhoods, particularly the Qādiriyya, the contemporary movement is *salafi*, which is associated with literal, strict, and puritanical approaches to Islam and is in line with the anti-ṣūfī tradition of Wahhābism. This history can be recognized as a major theme in historical change in West Africa since the eighteenth century, when radical, Islamic forms of government, society, and law evolved as a parallel movement to the age of revolution in Europe and the Americas of Hobsbawm and Genovese.

Islam in West Africa and the Context of Jihād

One of the reasons that Africa is usually not included in a conceptualization of the Atlantic world arises from a failure to appreciate the long history of Islam in Africa, other than the region along the shores of the Mediterranean and the desert oases of the northern Sahara. A false division is thereby thrust on Africa that sees the Sahara Desert as a divide between the Mediterranean and "black" Africa, as is forcefully argued by Ann McDougall, among others. According to McDougall, the people who inhabited the Sahara might identify with communities south of the Sahara, in North Africa, or in the Sahara itself.[11] I have argued elsewhere that the "desert-side economy" was characterized by the flow of people between the Sahara and the savanna, as well as trade into and across the Sahara.[12] In the Muslim context, the region south of the Sahara was identified as the Bilād al-Sūdān, the land of the blacks, but it was long recognized that the major states of the region, from Ghana in the eleventh century to Mali in the fourteenth century to Songhay in the sixteenth century, were Muslim states, as confirmed by the allegiance of the ruling aristocracies of these states to Islam. Kanem, in the Lake Chad region, and its successor state of Borno were identified with Islam; its ruling dynasty, the Sayfawa, was recognized as Muslim for a thousand years until its final demise in the nineteenth century during the era of jihād. The Senegal River valley was solidly Muslim from the eleventh century, while the Hausa states between the Niger River and Lake Chad were Muslim by the thirteenth century, if not earlier. Paulo F. de Moraes Farias has documented the long-standing interactions across the Sahara from Andalusia in what is now Spain to the Niger River valley, as reflected in Arabic texts, archaeological artifacts, and inscriptions on tombstones.[13] Even the so-called non-Muslim Bambara states of Segu and Kaarta, located between the Niger and the Senegal Rivers, have been mistakenly associated with "paganism" because the ruling elites were warriors who violated many of the precepts of Islam, but many Muslims, especially merchants, resided there, and to some extent the term "Bambara" was used conveniently to justify the enslavement of people from these states, whether or not they were Muslims.

The antiquity of Islam in West Africa and its persuasive influence are not in question, therefore, which raises a number of issues of interpretation and misinterpretation that are sometimes to be found in the scholarship of historians who are not specialists in West Africa and even more frequently in public discourse that treats Islam as if it were a recent introduction. One false conception relates to the idea of conversion: that somehow the people there converted to Islam at various times when in fact people had been Muslims for generations. When this mistake is applied to the seventeenth, eighteenth, and nineteenth centuries, it takes on a peculiar meaning, as if Islam were a new introduction, although the Gambia River societies had been associated with the broader Muslim world since the incorporation of the valley into the Mali Empire in the fourteenth century.[14] It is true that people did convert to Islam during this period, but the way in which conversion is often used as a descriptive term suggests that Islam was a foreign, alien religion of recent intrusion. Nothing could be further from the historical context, however. When the reference to conversion is made, moreover, there is usually no documented proof that individuals actually became Muslims through conversion. References to contemporary European accounts that assess the religion of local societies at the time have to be treated with caution. There certainly were people along the Atlantic coast who were not Muslim, but the identification of people and places as "Mandingo," Jolof/Wolof, and other ethnic labels almost always implied some kind of association with Islam.

Another misconception that has to be confronted in understanding the importance of Islam in the West African savannah and the Sahel relates to the extent of urbanization that was characteristic of the region well before the emergence of jihād as a factor in the late seventeenth century and certainly during the eighteenth and nineteenth centuries. Beginning with the medieval empires and continuing through the fall of Songhay in the last decade of the sixteenth century, West Africa was heavily urbanized, although by modern standards the size of towns and cities was small. This urbanization was identified frequently with city walls that were constructed for defensive purposes and with public spaces associated with mosques and city markets. The governments of these urban spaces built palaces, as well as overseeing the maintenance of mosques, markets, and defensive walls. These towns and cities were connected through long-distance trade, commercial networks that were Muslim, and locations of craft production, especially cotton textiles, leather goods, and ironware. Well before the spread of the jihād movement, these centers were closely associated with Islam and Muslims who had migrated from elsewhere but had settled to pursue economic opportunities. Wherever there was an indigenous, non-Muslim society, the urban centers were usually divided into twin cities, one that housed the local community and the other that was home to Muslims and the center of trade and craft production. As Paulo Farias has emphasized, the separation between Muslims and non-Muslims that was realized through distinct urban quarters spatially separated from each other was more than symbolic. Muslims honored a tradition that tolerated non-Islamic practices and religious worship but specifically avoided syncretism and insisted on orthodoxy with respect to the basic tenets of Islam.[15]

The Muslim networks were tied together through commercial interaction and also education and religious study that were common features of Muslim society not only in West Africa but throughout the Islamic world. Travel and distant learning were valued in the Muslim context because of the emphasis on pilgrimage and the obligation to visit the holy places of Mecca and Medina if possible. The glorification of this tradition was symbolized in West Africa by the legendary pilgrimage of the Malian emperor Mansa Mūsā, whose famed visit to Egypt and the Holy Lands is remembered because of the vast quantities of West African gold that he took with him. Similarly, the coup d'état that brought Askia Muhammad Ture to the throne of Songhay in 1493 was sanctified through his pilgrimage to Mecca as a step in the imposition of Muslim government and adherence to Islamic law. Study abroad (taghrīb) was encouraged as a means of acquiring an education and also promoted connections among Muslims, sustained orthodoxy, and linked communities.[16]

The Islamic sciences flourished in West Africa for many centuries before the advent of the jihād movement.[17] This can be seen with respect to historical scholarship, which flourished in such places as Timbuktu and is displayed in such histories as 'Abd al-Raḥmān al-Sa'dī's Ta'rīkh al-Sūdān (History of the Sudan) (ca. 1655) and Ta'rīkh al-fattāsh fī akhbār al-buldān wa 'l-juyūsh wa-akābir al-nās (The chronicle of the researcher into the history of the countries, the armies, and the principal personalities), attributed to Maḥmūd Ka'tī (d. AH 1 Muḥarram 1002; 27 September 1593) and continued after his death, with the surviving version ending in AH 1074 (1654–55 CE).[18] The legal tradition was historical in orientation because of the practice of citing previous fatwa in issuing opinions on contemporary legal questions. The intellectual tradition of quoting the Qur'ān and the Ḥadīth privileged historically documented chains of authority in the construction of arguments and establishing legitimacy. Among Muslims there was the scholarly tradition of *isnād*, which traced an individual's intellectual and religious pedigree with reference to one's teachers and in turn their teachers. The identification with a chain of authority (*silsila*) that was historical established specialization and knowledge of a specific curriculum. The extensive bibliography that has been assembled of indigenous writings and the distribution of books brought from North Africa and other parts of the Islamic world further attests to the level of Islamic scholarship of long standing, to which the jihād tradition owes its origins.[19] By the late seventeenth century this literate component of Islam had been consolidated in West Africa, largely under the leadership of the Qādiriyya brotherhood and its standardized curriculum. Children, particularly boys, learned the rudiments of Arabic from Muslim scholars wherever there was a Muslim community in West Africa. Those students who showed particular promise were encouraged to study further. Commercial households and the political elite were most seriously committed to assuring that the literate tradition was sustained.[20]

That Islam was deeply rooted in West Africa is occasionally questioned because of the presence of certain practices that some people who are not Muslims have considered non-Islamic, including the widespread use of amulets, divination, and spirit possession. Amulets were small leather pouches that contained excerpts from the Qur'ān written in Arabic and sometimes have mistakenly been thought to be charms or survivals of non-Muslim practice. Rather, they were associated with writing and the mysticism associated with the Qur'ān. Those who made these amulets were usually Muslim scholars and teachers who sold them as a way of securing an income, and the people who bought them included both Muslims and non-Muslims because of the mystical powers that were attributed to them.[21] Similarly, divination was a recognized Islamic science and was studied at mosques and with scholars along with other subjects, like jurisprudence (*fiqh*), the study of the sayings of the Prophet (*Ḥadīth*), theology (*kalām*), and astrology. Forms of Islamic divination are thought to have influenced the spread of divination among non-Muslims, including the Ifá divination of the Yoruba and the river-pebble divination (*aŋ-bere*) of Poro society in the interior of Sierra Leone and Liberia.[22] Finally, spirit possession (*bori, gnawa, zar*), which is sometimes thought to be in violation of Islamic practice and hence a remnant of pre-Islamic belief or non-Muslim behavior, was in fact very much a part of Islamic tradition and was found throughout West Africa, North Africa, and the Middle East.[23] Rather than perceiving the use of amulets, divination, and spirit possession as deviant features of Islam or evidence of non-Muslim syncretism, it is more accurate to consider that these mystical expressions and practices were integral to Islam in West Africa.

The tradition of jihād was closely associated with the Qādiriyya brotherhood, which was predominant among Muslims in West Africa by the late seventeenth century and particularly in the eighteenth century. The brotherhood (ṭarīqa) traces its origins to the teachings of ʿAbd al-Qādir Jīlānī (1077–1166) of Baghdad, a respected scholar and preacher originally from the Iranian province of Mazandaran. The order relies strongly on adherence to the fundamentals of Islam, particularly to the outward practices of Islam as determined by the Sunna, that is, the documented practices and customs of the Prophet Muhammad. Those who adhere to the Qādiriyya are very well disciplined, are known for a commitment to the "inner" jihād, and attempt to display saintly living. Jīlānī specifically emphasized what he described as the desires of the ego, the "greater struggle" or jihād against greed, vanity, and fear. Although the brotherhood has had a strong influence across the Islamic world, my concern here is with its influence in West Africa. By the end of the eighteenth century, the most prominent Qādiri intellectual was Sīdī al-Mukhtār al-Kuntī (1729–1811), who was based in Azawad, in the Sahara, northwest of Timbuktu. Al-Kuntī was associated with the caravan towns (qṣar) of the Sahel, especially Walāta, Tichitt, Timbuktu, Wadan, Asawan, and Shinqīt, where the Ḥassāniyya had established centers of education focused on a core curriculum that emphasized jurisprudence (uṣūl) and syntax (Arabic-language study). Through the scholars at these centers, the Qādiriyya was transformed from an essentially private commitment into a corporate identity that emphasized public membership.[24] Although the emphasis on jihād was personal and peaceful, and al-Mukhtār was respected for his ability to negotiate among Muslims in dispute, especially the Tuareg of the desert, this commitment could extend to violent confrontation. Indeed, al-Mukhtār al-Kuntī clearly reached this conclusion in extending his support to the jihād of ʿUthmān dan Fodio, one of his former students, in 1809, thereby providing his blessing for the formation of the Sokoto Caliphate as a jihād state.

Finally, there is a common misconception that jihād is a movement directed against non-Muslims, not Muslims, although it should be clear that the different meanings of jihād, as described by Willis, concern purification, including the purging of evil among Muslims.[25] Indeed, the jihād movement, which is the subject of this book, often targeted governments that were at least nominally Muslim, but that proponents of violent jihād considered lax in their commitment to Islam, often tolerating practices that were sometimes considered unorthodox, such as the use of amulets, as condemned in the teachings of Sīdī al-Mukhtār al-Kuntī. The arbitrary incursions of warrior elites who were known locally as *ceddo* in Senegambia, as well as the Bambara states of Segu and Kaarta, were pervasive. The Hausa governments and even the Sayfawa dynasty of Borno were also subject to criticism, although these governments often claimed allegiance to Islam and usually supported the Muslim scholarly community, even being educated by it. As I will discuss later, one of the most serious grievances was the failure of governments to protect the status of freeborn Muslims and otherwise allow Muslims to congregate more publicly, as the Qādiriyya brotherhood was increasingly advocating under the spiritual leadership of al-Kuntī.

Slave Resistance, the Age of Revolutions, and Islamic West Africa

The question of the resistance of slaves is at the heart of the social and cultural history of slavery. Specifically, historians have been preoccupied with a comparison of resistance among the different European colonies in the Americas, with a particular focus on the significance of revolt in St. Domingue and the establishment of the revolutionary state of Haiti for subsequent events of resistance in the Americas. Undoubtedly, as Hobsbawm characterized the period from 1789 to 1848, an "age of revolution" resulted in "the transformation of the world," what he referred to as the "dual revolutions," that is, the French Revolution of 1789 and the contemporaneous British Industrial Revolution.[26] Although Hobsbawm focused on transformations in northwestern Europe and by extension the global dependencies of Britain and France and the emerging independent countries of Latin America, he was aware of possible reverberations in Africa and elsewhere. However, there is no indication in his work that he appreciated that revolution and transformation might occur largely independent of western Europe, as in the case of the jihād movement of West Africa, and thereby have an impact on shaping the modern world in ways that intersected with the age of revolutions in Europe and the Americas. Moreover, there can be little doubt that forms of resistance to slavery were different before 1793 from those after that date, the separation being marked by the revolutionary events in St. Domingue and the establishment of independent Haiti, as Genovese first suggested.[27] Their pioneering insights have shaped historical discourse for the past half century. Genovese's analysis of the changing nature of slave resistance has resonance in Africa through the impact of the British abolition movement and the founding of Sierra Leone, although he did not venture to explore these implications. The intersections of the ages of revolution in Africa and the Atlantic world have yet to be explored. This chapter is intended to demonstrate the ways in which West Africa did and did not fit into the pattern elsewhere, as suggested by Hobsbawm and Genovese.

Despite the significance of the dual revolutions of industrializing Britain and political change in France that helped shape the world, Hobsbawm was mistaken in thinking that "the Islamic states were convulsed by crisis; [and] Africa lay open to direct conquest" in the period 1789–1848.[28] Hobsbawm may have been correct for the Ottoman state during the Napoleonic era and the resulting reform in Egypt, as well as the British conquest of Islamic areas of India, but his observations do not extend to West Africa. Rather, Africa did not lie open to "direct conquest," at least not before the French conquest of Ottoman Algeria in 1830–47 and its continued occupation of St. Louis and Gorée, although direct conquest of the Senegal River valley occurred only after 1854. The British blockade of the West African coast after 1808 may have shaken the coastal states of Africa, but it had virtually no impact in the interior other than to reinforce the goals of the Islamic jihād movement in isolating Africa from the Atlantic world of slavery without undermining slavery itself. In southern Africa the Great Trek of the Boers after 1834 was a response to British policies of abolishing slavery and efforts to govern an unwilling settler population, not conquest. Although Genovese recognized the importance of Muslim resistance to slavery and the Malês uprising in Bahia in 1835, he did not notice a similar uprising among the Muslim Yoruba in the British colony of Sierra Leone in 1831–32 at virtually the same time or the connections between Yoruba resistance in Cuba in the 1830s and events in West Africa arising from the jihād movement.[29]

The arguments in this book are directed at Eric Hobsbawm and Eugene Genovese largely in symbolic fashion, not because they neglected the scholarship of the jihād movement of the late eighteenth and early nineteenth centuries, which they did, but because their enormous contributions to an understanding of the age of revolutions have achieved a level of orthodoxy that overshadows the wealth of scholarship on a missing component of that era. The scholarship on the age of revolutions has evolved greatly since Hobsbawm and Genovese published their pioneering works half a century ago. Among the many studies that have broadened the conception of the Atlantic world to include Africa, one can highlight the various biographical studies, such as James Sweet's account of Domingoes Álvares, African healing, and the intellectual history of the Atlantic world and Walter Hawthorne's examination of the links between the upper Guinea coast and northeastern Brazil, which serve as models for a transatlantic perspective.[30] Most especially, Jane Landers offers new insights on the shaping of an Atlantic world that attempts to integrate the West African backgrounds of people who were associated with the development of an Atlantic-wide "creole" society. As Landers has argued, biographical accounts provide "a prism through which to examine the active participation of Africans and their descendants in the age of Atlantic revolutions."[31] Landers demonstrates that such stories "make possible a more complex understanding of the traditional narratives and popular views of the Age of Revolutions, and demonstrate their active political and philosophical engagement in the most important events of their day."[32] Following the approach of these scholars, this study also relies heavily on biographical accounts.

The historiography of slavery during the age of revolutions has recognized influences emanating from Africa in shaping slave society in the Americas, although this was not a concern of Hobsbawm, whose age of revolutions focused on social and economic change in Europe and the Americas in a way that had little room for influences originating in Africa. Yoruba influence in particular is a feature of the African diaspora that emerged in the nineteenth century, particularly in Cuba and Brazil, but also in Sierra Leone and Trinidad because of the extension of British abolitionist policies to those states. Although Genovese's insight into the importance of St. Domingue as a turning point from rebellion as a form of resistance to one of revolution fits neatly into Hobsbawm's paradigm, Genovese's understanding of African influences was seriously flawed. There can be no argument about the importance of both scholars in understanding revolutionary change or the importance of St. Domingue in that process, but their contributions ignored the Atlantic world of Africa.[33] Despite the limitations that can be identified, both Hobsbawm and Genovese can be credited with influencing the study of slave resistance as a part of the age of revolutions, and here my intention is to place jihād in West Africa in this context.

My aim, therefore, is to extend the discussion of the age of revolutions beyond Hobsbawm's identification of a twofold industrial and political transformation and Genovese's recognition of the St. Domingue uprising as a turning point from rebellion to revolution to ask how Africa fitted into their paradigms. The consolidation of a field of research that focuses on the Atlantic, especially the black Atlantic, has neglected issues of how the regions of Africa that interacted with the Atlantic world helped shape developments. Although we recognize the development of ethnic-based "nations" in the Americas and distinguish between African-born populations and creole/mulatto/mestizo societies that variously emerged in Brazil, the Caribbean, mainland Hispanic America, and North America, there has been a neglect of how the processes of change that were unleashed by the expansion of slavery in the Americas altered the course of history in Africa. The challenge of this book goes beyond Hobsbawm and Genovese to address the field of Atlantic studies. My intention is to elaborate on the contributions of Paul Gilroy, Ira Berlin, Gwendolyn Midlo Hall, Jane Landers, and others in understanding how the emergence of a "black Atlantic" was shaped by influences from the deep African interior.[34] Similarly, a transnational and global perspective suggests modifications of the approach of Bernard Bailyn and David Brion Davis in examining European and European settler control of the Atlantic world.[35] Although scholars studying Atlantic history recognize that the overwhelming number of people who crossed the Atlantic before the middle of the nineteenth century came from Africa, not Europe, and that this demography had a significant impact, especially as a contributing factor in slave resistance, sense of community, and commercial interaction, the connection with historical developments in Africa deserves fuller attention. A focus on the black Atlantic has to address why parts of Africa, at least Muslim areas, were able to retain a degree of autonomy.

Central to the argument of this book and my dialogue with Hobsbawm, Genovese, and other scholars who analyze the age of revolutions without reference to Islamic West Africa is that the age of jihād has been largely overlooked. I suggest that locating jihād in the interpretation of the age of revolutions and the Atlantic world challenges our understanding of the modern era and provides a corrective that parallels a recognition of Haiti's place in that analysis. The jihād movement shaped the slave trade from the late eighteenth century through the nineteenth century and reveals the importance of Islam in explaining the supply of slaves, a crucial insight with profound implications for our understanding of the trade, the origins of Africans sent to the Americas, and ethnicity in the Americas. I maintain that a fuller understanding of the age of revolutions requires the application of historical methodology that seeks out sources and interpretations that can test conceptual hypotheses and intellectual insights. The main problem is that both Hobsbawm and Genovese, and much of the scholarship since they set the direction of research, shaped a model for the modern world that provides a European focus on the history of the Western world, despite the opposition of many scholars to such a Euro-centric perspective. The question to be addressed is whether it is possible to ignore Africa, in this case West Africa, in the reconstruction of the history of the Atlantic world during this period.

Of course, the chronological framework of the age of revolutions shifts from scholar to scholar; Hobsbawm emphasized the years 1789–1848, while Wim Klooster begins the period earlier with "civil war" in the British Empire and the independence of the United States. The Age of Revolution of David Brion Davis begins in 1770 and ends in 1823. Jane Landers associates the age of revolutions with resistance to slavery from the second half of the eighteenth century to the middle of the nineteenth century. Whether or not the era is considered to have begun in the 1770s and to have ended with the American Civil War of the 1860s depends on the focus of analysis, but the general idea of an "age of revolutions" has become Atlantic-wide in its orientation.[36] For Landers, the age of revolutions is more concerned with the international quest for liberty coming from slaves and free blacks than with nationalist discourse, and hence her analysis ends in 1850, while Manuel Barcia ends his study in 1844.[37] The jihād movement fits into this chronology regardless of whether the period is thought to begin in the 1770s or 1789 and end in 1848 or the 1860s. During this era virtually the whole of the interior of West Africa from Senegambia to Lake Chad came under the rule of jihād states that swept away the preexisting political structures, with quite significantly different results that help expand the concept of the Atlantic world to include West Africa.

Perspectives on History

What was common in West Africa was the Islamic context, not the identification as Hausa, Yoruba, Mandingo, Juula, Fulbe, and so on. I contend that ethnicity was an extension of political identity, and its meaning has to be deconstructed. Ethnic labeling was transferred to the Americas, often buttressed with identification with a common language, like Yoruba, Igbo, Kimbundu, or Kikongo. In the context of the jihād movement in West Africa, Fulfulde and Arabic were the primary languages of the religious and political elite, but Hausa and Mandinke were dominant over wide regions and were closely associated with trade. Hence these languages and their corresponding labeling in the Americas as Hausa or Mandinga/Mandingo reflected African backgrounds that need to be tied more closely to our understanding of Atlantic history. The role of Fulbe clerics was particularly important in spreading jihād ideology (plate 2). These distinctions were important in Bahia and helped shape resistance. In other words, if the Bahia uprising is to be considered within an Atlantic perspective during the age of revolutions, it has to be seen in the context of events in West Africa. To a great extent the transatlantic dimension is missing this perspective, particularly with reference to the jihād states of those portions of the interior known as the western and central Bilād al-Sūdān. By the eighteenth century "Bilād al-Sūdān," the Arabic term for "land of the blacks," had come to designate the savanna and Sahel regions bordering the southern Sahara and specifically identified the Islamic states that dominated this region. Indeed, in some sources from the nineteenth century, the term "Soudan" is the name used for the Sokoto Caliphate, as distinct from Borno, for example.

The presence of enslaved Muslims in the Americas is well established, although the connection or lack thereof with the jihād movement depended on a number of factors that reveal the intersection between the jihād movement and the age of revolutions and the major transformations in slave resistance in the Americas. The experiences of Muslims in Bahia, where Yoruba became the common language of the Muslim community, even though that community also included other Muslims who were not Yoruba in origin, helps us understand the age of jihād. As I examine in this book, there are many accounts of individuals whose lives relate to the jihād movement, including Richard Pierpoint, who was enslaved in Fuuta Bundu and fought on the side of the British in the American War of Independence and then with Canadian troops who repulsed the American invasion of the Niagara Peninsula in the War of 1812. Similarly, Muhammad Kabā Saghanughu, enslaved in 1777 near Fuuta Jalon, subsequently led a Muslim community in Jamaica until his death in 1845, while Mahommah Gardo Baquaqua was enslaved near Djougou in the year of Kabā's death and, after being in Brazil for two years (1845–47), was able to escape in New York; Baquaqua subsequently wanted to head a Baptist mission to Africa, but this never happened. Finally, Muhammed ʿAlī Saʿīd, who was enslaved in Borno in 1851, when Baquaqua was at Central College in upstate New York, traveled through the Ottoman Empire and then to Europe, the Caribbean, and North America before joining the Union army in 1863, although he had never been enslaved in the United States. All were Muslims, and their stories help connect the worlds of revolution and jihād.

The problem is one of perspective. A consideration of slave resistance and revolution in the Atlantic world has tended to focus on the Americas and

Europe without attempting to understand what was happening in Africa. The "age of revolutions" as a concept and a chronological period of history owes a great debt to Hobsbawm, Genovese, and other scholars. The chronicle of historical change from the last decades of the eighteenth century until the middle of the nineteenth century has been isolated as a phase in the history of slavery and specifically its demise that was associated with revolutionary change in western Europe. As we are all aware, the abolition movement in Britain, the French Revolution, the uprising in St. Domingue, the independence of Haiti, and slave resistance from the United States to Brazil figure prominently in our understanding of this period of history and its interface with the emerging Industrial Revolution and the constitutional restrictions or outright elimination of monarchal rule in western Europe. Consequently, this book is a dialogue with Hobsbawm and Genovese, and by extension with the dominant literature on slavery and resistance in the Americas, Atlantic studies, and comparative history.

My dialogue with these scholars and the trend in historiography that derives from their inspiration, especially the emergence of Atlantic studies and the "black Atlantic" paradigm, concentrates on the events in Africa that occurred during the period of the age of revolutions and how these events in Africa might or might not have helped shape the patterns of change in the Americas that led to the destruction of slavery as the dominant institution there. How are we to conceptualize African history and the origins of people from Africa who were involved in the revolutionary events of the Americas? I contend that influences emanating from Africa and specifically the jihād movement in West Africa had a profound impact on the shaping of revolutionary forces in the Americas. The jihād movement clearly helped shape events in Bahia, specifically the Malês uprising of 1835, and also the consolidation of Yoruba influence in Cuba. Implicitly, I am raising questions about the scope of the age of revolutions and revolutionary action among enslaved populations in the Americas, and I am challenging Atlantic studies to broaden the conception of the Atlantic world to include events in Atlantic Africa and its interior. Hobsbawm's interest in the transformation of government in the age of revolutions, with the challenge to despotic monarchy and the emergence of more democratic regimes, might lead us to a consideration of how the jihād movement transformed government in West Africa at the same time. In parallel with the changing nature of slave resistance in the Americas and the emergence of a "second slavery" in the Americas in the nineteenth century, moreover, the jihād movement resulted in a great increase in the number of slaves in West Africa that can be placed alongside the increase in slavery in Brazil, Cuba, and the United States.

Specifically, João José Reis has demonstrated the complex nature of the Muslim uprising in Bahia in 1835 in terms of the identification of participants along class lines (slave/free), on the basis of ethnicity (Yoruba, i.e., Nagô, Hausa, and so on), and according to religious divisions (Islam, *orişa* worship, and so on). Stuart Schwartz earlier drew attention to the various Hausa revolts and conspiracies in Bahia from 1807 onward.[38] Admittedly, Michael Gomez has recognized the importance of Islamic influence in the Americas. Moreover, Sylviane Diouf has examined resistance and revolution in the context of African influences on events in the Americas, but Gomez and Diouf do not base their works on the Sokoto Caliphate and its role in West Africa, which is the focus here.[39] It is my contention that these contributions fall short of placing the events of the Americas during the age of revolutions in the context of the jihād movement and specifically events that created the Sokoto Caliphate. In fact, Diouf contends that the conditions for jihād were not present in Bahia in the 1830s, an interpretation that Reis has accepted.[40] Similarly, Manuel Barcia has drawn attention to the presence of Muslims in Cuba as a result of the traffic from the Bight of Benin to Cuba and has correctly recognized the role of jihād in their enslavement and the enslavement of many non-Muslims as a result of the jihād. Barcia has identified fifteen revolts and conspiracies in Cuba between 1832 and 1844 that were associated with Yoruba who had been enslaved in the context of the jihād, although most of the participants, if not all, were not Muslims.[41]

The fact that Muslim slaves were common along the routes stretching through Yorubaland to Bahia by the early nineteenth century has prompted Humphrey Fisher to argue that the jihād erupted "precisely *because* Muslim slaves were arriving in Yorubaland and Bahia, torn from Hausaland and *dar al-Islam*. . . . The shock waves, flowing into Hausaland, helped ignite the *jihād*; then, flowing out again, spread that example."[42] Fisher's conclusion is supported by the writings of Muhammad Bello and the analysis that the enslavement of Muslims was a major factor that prompted the outbreak of jihād in 1804. Although the role of Hausa and other Muslims in the uprising of 1835 is subject to different interpretations, my understanding of the Malês uprising places a heavy emphasis on the role of Islam as a unifying force. The uprising and, even more threatening, the possible appeal to the population outside Salvador rested on its appeal to Islam, in which Yoruba was used as the common language of communication because most Muslims were Yoruba or at least spoke the language. However, the historic importance of the Hausa cities and their mosques, such as the Gobarau Mosque in Katsina, has to be emphasized (plate 3). Individuals originally from Borno or one of the Hausa centers most certainly would have spoken Yoruba as well and in some contexts would have been identified as such. The odyssey of ʿAlī Eisami demonstrates this complexity. ʿAlī was from Borno, had been sold as a slave because he was captured in the jihād, and had been taken south through the Hausa towns, ending up in the capital of Oyo. On the outbreak of the Ilorin uprising in 1817, ʿAlī was sold south because it was feared that he would flee to the cause of Islam. Instead, ʿAlī became a Christian in Sierra Leone and took the name William Harding. Depending on context, ʿAlī would have been considered Yoruba if language was the determining factor, since he was fluent in Yoruba. Nonetheless, he was Kanuri by origin, was a Muslim, could also speak Hausa, and became a principal informant for Sigismund Koelle in his linguistic studies in Sierra Leone in the late 1840s.

Although Barcia has correctly noticed the presence of Muslims in Cuba, his study also shows that the number of Muslims was actually very small.[43] In Cuba people whom we now refer to as Yoruba were known as "Lucumí," while in Brazil they were known as "Nagô." In both cases their presence was closely associated with the jihād movement.[44] As Henry B. Lovejoy has demonstrated, those identified as Lucumí in Cuba very largely came from Oyo and its dependencies, and most were not Muslims, a profile that is the reverse of the demography of Bahia, where Muslims were heavily concentrated.[45] Lovejoy contends that there was a conscious attempt to reconstitute elements of the Oyo state in Cuba, including the promotion of Shango as the principal orişa in the Yoruba pantheon and the identification of Shango with Saint Barbara among the Catholic saints. Because of the timing of the Yoruba influx into Cuba, Oyo Yoruba were predominant in both rural and urban communities and therefore were involved in uprisings, conspiracies, and disturbances that have been associated with their presence in Cuba.[46] By comparison with Bahia, it seems that very few Muslims were sent to Cuba.[47] Although Atlantic merchants may have consciously directed enslaved Muslims and non-Muslims toward different destinations in the Americas, it also seems clear that the distribution reflected different migration patterns. Muslims were sent to Bahia in disproportionate numbers during the 1820s, while the overwhelming majority of arrivals in Cuba occurred in the 1830s, when relatively few enslaved Muslims left from Lagos. Oyo Yoruba emerged as dominant among the Yoruba population in Cuba, which was reflected in membership in religious brotherhoods (*cabildo*) and the importance of Shango as a deity of reverence. All the *oriṣa*, including Shango, were important in Bahia, too, but so was the concentration of Muslims. A comparison of Cuba and Bahia within the framework of black Atlantic history shows different forms of political and religious mobilization in response to slave society.

How does the question of slavery in the jihād movement in West Africa inform the comparison of resistance among the different European colonies in the Americas? What similarities and differences characterized revolt in St. Domingue in the 1790s, the establishment of the revolutionary state of Haiti in 1804, and the revolutionary movement of jihād in West Africa in the same years? How did the influences of these two movements affect subsequent events of resistance in the Americas and the consolidation of Islam in West Africa? When the history of West Africa and, by extension, of west central Africa and southeastern Africa is included in an analysis of the Atlantic world, the history of people of African descent assumes a more influential role in the history of the modern world. The demography of transatlantic migration and the influences emanating from Africa on modern culture, particularly music and art, are obvious examples.

Slavery was a factor in the jihād movement, specifically in regard to complaints that freeborn Muslims were being enslaved and that such enslavement was illegal under Islamic law and was condemned as a violation of the rights of Muslims. The concern was directed at protecting Muslims, not at opposing slavery, which became a core institution underpinning the society and economy of the Sokoto Caliphate as it expanded in the course of the first half of the nineteenth century. Hence the revolutionary movement of jihād that swept West Africa in the period of the age of revolutions in Europe and the Atlantic world had a far different impact on the course of slavery, but nonetheless the revolutionary dimensions of the jihād were profound and require analysis of it as a parallel movement to the forces with which Hobsbawm and Genovese were concerned. The jihād movement served further to impose a level of autonomy on West Africa at the same time at which the incidence of slavery in the region expanded enormously, most especially in the central Bilād al-Sūdān and Oyo, from where many of the enslaved who went to Cuba and Brazil actually came. The interconnectedness and contradictions that emerged require fuller treatment than they have been given by most scholars who have examined slave resistance during the age of revolutions. Other topics of considerable importance include the debate within Muslim circles over the legitimacy of enslavement, as revealed in the diplomatic exchanges between Muhammad Bello and Muhammad al-Kānimī, the heads of state of the

Sokoto Caliphate and Borno, respectively, and the open warfare that erupted between these states in consequence of the failure to reach an acceptable accord over the course of jihād.[48] Similarly, the little-known diplomatic negotiations between Caliph Muhammad Bello, supreme ruler of the Sokoto Caliphate, and Captain Hugh Clapperton, the official representative of the British government, over the abolition of the slave trade in the 1820s bring into focus contradictions in understanding the age of revolutions.[49] Their discussions and resulting accord demonstrate that abolition has to be examined from broader perspectives than a British focus.

I contend that the relative importance of Islam as an inhibiting factor in the provision of slaves for the Americas is underestimated. Limitations arising from controlled efforts to isolate West Africa from slavery in the Americas related to Muslim prohibitions.[50] First, let us consider that the Muslim states of the region engaged in a conscious attempt within West Africa to establish autonomy. In this regard, there was a relatively clear break in patterns of trade, so that we can talk about at least two phases in the transatlantic migration. The first period was the period before around 1800, and the second was the nineteenth century. The jihād that resulted in the creation of the Sokoto Caliphate after 1804 effectively marked a break in the trade and politics of the deportation of slaves to the Americas between these two phases. Although there was involvement in the transatlantic and trans-Saharan slave trades, the jihād movement undermined the deportation of enslaved Africans to the Americas from West Africa. Even so, there was a recognizable Muslim cohort both in the period before 1804 and after. The second period was also marked by the British campaign to abolish the slave trade after 1807, which initially attacked the trade of West Africa and thereby reinforced the political aims of the Muslim states of the interior to limit participation in the transatlantic slave trade, although unintentionally. The combined impact of Muslim jihād and British abolition reinforced a trend that pushed the slave trade from West Africa to west central Africa and Mozambique, the Bantu-speaking region from where approximately half of all Africans who went to the Americas trace their origins. After 1807, 1.9 million out of 2.78 million Africans came from the Bantu regions, amounting to 68 percent of total arrivals in the Americas, and if the Bight of Biafra is included, 80 percent of the forced migration after British abolition targeted Africans from regions where the jihād movement was not a factor.

The significance of where enslaved people came from has been recognized as an important factor in the slave trade, but analysis so far has not appreciated why Muslim regions were marginal and underrepresented despite their relative importance in Bahia and North America and their limited impact in Jamaica, Trinidad, and St. Domingue. I suggest that during the age of revolutions west central Africa and southeastern Africa were constituted as the principal regions of slave origin, while West Africa was transformed from within by changes that resulted in the consolidation of Islamic rule and were as effective as British abolition in removing the region from the transatlantic slave trade. The basic thrust of this argument is not new.[51] However, the argument has either been misunderstood or largely ignored or both, and my aim here is to make the argument explicit.

My challenge is methodological. I am identifying what can be termed "the methodology of the tabula rasa" or can also be called the "argument in empty space," in which the scholarship of the "other" is overlooked, but its exclusion in the end has to be recognized as a particularly challenging inhibition to historical reconstruction.[52] When much of the historiography and readily available source material that underpin historical change is not incorporated into historical analysis, as I am claiming here, it is possible to propose interpretations that are isolated and distorted through a limiting perspective. Much of the scholarship that is associated with "Atlantic studies," including the attempt to understand slavery and resistance during the age of revolutions, falls into this trap. Although it may not be clear why certain knowledge is overlooked, whether from naïveté, ignorance, or design, we have to assess responsibility for such an approach that shortchanges innovation and hard work. We have to recognize that the aim of scholarship is to overcome the limitations of specific perspectives and to broaden interpretations to take into account new sources, innovative uses of new knowledge, and the inevitably widening circles of inclusion. A methodology of designed ignorance is prevalent in certain studies and historical approaches, in my opinion, and this is the case with an understanding of the jihād of West Africa. In Latin America, this approach of privileging some scholarship by subjecting that of others to silence and nonrecognition is sometimes referred to, informally, as the "methodology of the gringos," in which North American scholars blitz local archives and subsequently claim to have made intellectual and scholarly breakthroughs that completely bypass the research of scholars in Latin America, especially if scholars write only in Portuguese or Spanish and hence conveniently can be ignored, or if it might require too much extra work and interaction to uncover what is often a wealth of research that has previously been completed or is currently under way. The same observation applies to scholars in Nigeria, such as Yusuf Bala Usman, H. Bobboyi, and A. M. Yakubu.[53]

These scholars are often ignored in "western" scholarship. The same curtain of silence through nonrecognition is lowered on the intellectual contributions of scholars in Africa and indeed even on scholars who focus on Africa but who are not at universities in Africa. The avoidance of the rich documentation on the jihād movement is even more glaring than I am suggesting, since I have specifically not referred to many of the primary source materials that are readily available in published form, let alone the enormous amount of relevant material that is to be found in archives in Nigeria, Mali, Morocco, France, England, the United States, and elsewhere. Nonetheless, it is central to the argument of this book that a fuller understanding of the age of revolutions requires a revolution in the application of historical methodology that seeks out sources and interpretations that can test conceptual hypotheses and intellectual insights. The question that has to be addressed is whether it is possible to ignore Africa, in this case West Africa, in the reconstruction of history during this period.

Despite the increasingly detailed research on African cultural and social impact in the Americas, the focus on slave resistance and revolution still omits the important components of the period that derive from the African background of the enslaved. I am arguing that the historical trends in the consolidation of Islam in Africa favored the emergence of west central Africa as the dominant region of origins of enslaved Africans, even though it will seem to some scholars that West Africa was a major source of slaves. In fact, hundreds of thousands of enslaved African did come from West Africa, but relatively few came from the Muslim regions of the interior. There is an apparent contradiction, therefore, that has to be explained. Most of the deported enslaved population from West Africa came from near the coast, and hence the region as a whole was underrepresented as a source of slaves.

I contend that the regional origins of Africa have to be contextualized within Africa, just as the destination of slaves and the resulting slave societies in the Americas and within Africa have to be understood in the context of the specificities of the Americas and influences that originated in Europe, particularly western Europe, as well as the historical context of West Africa. The forces that were unleashed in Africa were global, shaped to various degrees by events outside Africa as well as regional and local conditions therein. Theoretically, in terms of demography, I contend, West Africa could have supplied all the slaves that went to the Americas during the age of revolutions, but this did not happen, even though many slaves did come from there. Moreover, just as events in the Americas reveal a struggle between resistance to slavery and efforts to sustain what some had thought a dying institution, events in Africa reflect the great expansion in slavery, not its demise, so that the focus on revolutionary change in relation to resistance to slavery has to take into account the destination of the enslaved population, whether that population remained in Africa or went to the Americas. The West African experience has a bearing on another important debate. Sociologist and historian Dale Tomich has suggested the concept of "second slavery," in which slavery in the Americas was not a dying institution.[54] Rather, in Tomich's view, slavery was increasing in the early nineteenth century thanks to a new political order imposed by the British after the fall of Napoleon. Hence the parallel to the great expansion of slavery as a result of the jihād in West Africa should be noted.

As Murray Last has suggested, the Sokoto jihād was analogous to the French Revolution and just as the French Revolution had a sweeping impact in Europe and the Americas, the Sokoto jihād had repercussions across West Africa as far as the Nile River.[55] Sokoto was preoccupied with spreading the jihād and providing the intellectual inspiration and tactical training for future jihād participants, many of whom came to Sokoto for training and education. Al-Ḥājj ʿUmar was one such cleric, who joined the Tījāniyya brotherhood in Mecca when he was on pilgrimage and subsequently returned to sub-Saharan Africa via Borno and then settled in Sokoto as the leader of the Tījāniyya.[56] Hence, there was a strong tradition of such learned leadership. As the book market of the Sahel shows, scholars in the western Bilād al-Sūdān would have read some of Sokoto's works just as the dan Fodios read Algerian and Songhai texts.[57] The book trade establishes clearly the intellectual background of the jihād movement, which involves a long written debate, just as the age of revolutions did in Europe and the Americas.

According to Voyages: The Trans-Atlantic Slave Trade Database, at the time of the consolidation of the Sokoto Caliphate, west central Africa was already a dominant source of slaves for the Americas. This fact is crucial in recognizing the caliphate's self-imposed withdrawal and failure to participate in the transatlantic slave trade, despite price incentives in the interior of West Africa that could have resulted in the supply of many more slaves than was the case. The relatively high rate of slave resistance near and onboard slave ships in the Senegambia ports in the eighteenth century may have had an influence on the reluctance of European slave ships to visit the area.[58] Such resistance reinforces the argument here with respect to the influence of Islam on commercial patterns. The consolidation of Islam, ironically, at first increased the number of enslaved West Africans sent to the Americas, especially to Bahia and Cuba. These conclusions confirm some of the arguments suggested in this book that the history of the diaspora has to start in Africa, not in the Americas, especially with regard to resistance and efforts to establish reconstituted social, religious, and cultural manifestations.

2 THE ORIGINS OF JIHĀD IN WEST AFRICA

The chronology of the jihād movement spans a period of almost two hundred years, from the end of the seventeenth century through the end of the nineteenth century. Although the focus of this book is on the same era as the age of revolutions from the last quarter of the eighteenth century to the middle of the nineteenth century, this chapter provides an overview of the main events of the late seventeenth through the late eighteenth century. The idea of jihād was rooted in the confrontation of established political authority through the purification of Islamic practice and the imposition of governments that were forcefully committed to governance on the basis of Islamic law and tradition. Dedication to holy war and adherence to orthodoxy were not new, but the pattern of change that was determined through self-proclaimed jihād and the ways in which orthodoxy was interpreted through allegiance to the ṣūfī brotherhood of the Qādiriyya were unique and hence the reason that it is possible to refer to a jihād movement.

The major features of the historical trajectory of jihād are well established and are outlined in table 2.1, which is included here for purposes of reference and as a means of guiding readers through the necessary detail that has to be included as one means of demonstrating that the jihād movement was comparable in scale and impact to the age of revolutions of Europe and the Americas. The spread of jihād in West Africa occurred well after the collapse of the Muslim empire of Songhay in 1591–92 and the subsequent period that was perceived by many Muslim scholars as a century of political decadence and the emergence of military elites that dominated the numerous small states of the western Bilād al-Sūdān. The dispersed commercial diaspora of Muslim merchants and various centers of Islamic learning across West Africa sustained a vision of a more unified community, however. That vision ultimately brought forth a political movement.

The jihād movement can be traced to the campaigns of Awbek Ashfaga, better known as Nāṣir al-Dīn (protector of the faith), in the western Sahara,

TABLE 2.1. The Jihād Movement in West Africa: Major Events, Places, and Personalities, ca. 1670–1850

Dates	Jihād state	Location	Principal events	Major personalities	Characteristics	Political title
1673–74	"Shurrbubba" or Char Bouba	Senegal valley	Invaded Fuuta Toro and Wolof states	Nāsir al-Dīn (d. 1674)	Defeated and killed in 1674; followers dispersed	Imam
1698–99	Fuuta Bundu	Upper Senegal valley	Battle of Arondou in Gajaaga	Mālik Sy (d. 1699)	Founded with support of refugees from Nāsir al-Dīn	Eliman
1726–27	Fuuta Jalon	Highlands of Fuuta Jalon	Political capital established at Timbo	Ibrahima Karamokho Alfa (d. 1751)	Immigration of Torodbe clerics associated with Nāsir al-Dīn	Almami
1769–76	Fuuta Toro	Senegal Valley	Establishment of almamate (1776)	Sulaymān Baal (d. 1776)	Succeeded by ʿAbd al-Qādir	Almami
1776	Fuuta Jalon	Highlands of Fuuta Jalon	Defeat of Sankaran (1776)	Ibrahima Sory Mawdo (ruled 1751–91)	Second phase	Almami
1789–91	Moria	Upper Guinea coast	Defeat of Yangekori (1796)	Mahdī Fatta (d.1791)	Mahdist uprising crushed	
1804–8	Sokoto Caliphate	Hausaland, Nupe, Northern Yorubaland, Adamawa	Collapse of Hausa states, Gobir, Kebbi, Kano, Katsina, Zaria	ʿUthmān dan Fodio (d. 1817); Muhammad Bello (d. 1835)	Establishment of 33 emirates, with twin capitals at Gwandu and Sokoto, 1817	Sarkin Musulmi

(continued)

TABLE 2.1. (*continued*)

Dates	Jihād state	Location	Principal events	Major personalities	Characteristics	Political title
1810	Borno	Lake Chad basin	Construction of Kukawa, 1814	Muhammad al-Kānimī (d. 1837)	Replaced Sayfawa dynasty	Shehu
1818	Hamdullahi	Masina in Middle Niger	Construction of capital near Mopti, 1819	Ahmad b. Muhammad Lobbo (d 1853)	Captured Jenne and Timbuktu	Seku
1848	Toucouleur State	Between Fuuta Jalon and Middle Niger River	Establishment of fortress near Kayes	'Umar ibn Saʿīd al-Fūtī Tal (d. 1864)	Conquered Segu and Kaarta	al-Hajj

who allied various clerical factions of nomads (*zawāyā*) against militarized nomadic clans, particularly the Banī Ḥasan Arabs who had migrated to the region. Rather than confront the Banī Ḥasan directly, Nāṣir al-Dīn launched a campaign against the states of the Senegal River valley in the 1670s, which he proclaimed was a jihād. He successfully conquered the states of Waalo, Fuuta Toro, Kajoor, and Jolof, but the movement was stopped by Nāṣir al-Dīn's death in 1674, and the old order was virtually reestablished by 1677. Nonetheless, as Boubacar Barry has argued,

> Nāsir al-Dīn's movement was an attempt to regulate political and social life according to the teachings of the *sharī'a* (Islamic law) in its purest orthodox form, by putting an end to the arbitrary power of the Hasaniyya warriors and establishing a Muslim theocracy. The proclamation of a *djihād* [sic] in the kingdoms of the river valley was motivated by both economic and religious considerations, to conquer the trade in grains and slaves and to convert the peoples and purify the practice of Islam.[1]

Hence the idea of jihād and revolutionary change first emerged with Nāṣir al-Dīn in the Senegal River and was associated with the religious communities that were *ṣūfī* and associated with the Qādiriyya brotherhood, which emphasized piety and obedience to the authority of the religious community.

Rudolph Ware has argued that the Qur'ānic schools became striking symbols of Muslim identity and powerful channels for political expression in Senegambia. Because Muslim scholars traveled widely, Ware has characterized them as "walking Qu'rans" whose epistemological embodiment gave expression to classical Islamic frameworks of learning and knowledge.[2] The center of learning at the grand mosque of Pire in Saniakhor attracted many students who later went on to political careers, including Mālik Si, the founder of Fuuta Bundu, and 'Abd Qādir Kane, who led the clerical revolution in Fuuta Toro in 1776. The descendants of Demba Fall pursued his work in propagating Islamic learning and teaching the Muslim leadership that waged jihād in Fuuta Toro and elsewhere.[3] Besides the Fall family, other families, in particularly the Cisse, also studied at Pire. One of the Cisse of Pire, Tafsīr Abdou Cisse, was the *muqaddam* (spiritual guide) of Mālik Si. The grand mosque of Pire-Gourèye was virtually a university.[4] Another center at Koki, also founded in the seventeenth century by clerics, had close relations with the king of Kajoor. Pire and Koki dominated Muslim intellectual life throughout the eighteenth century, as students and teachers from many clerical lineages traveled to these towns to study. Koki was in Ndiambour and even opened branch schools at Koki-Kad, Koki-Dakhar, and Koki-Gouy in the neighboring province of Mbacol. In fact, there were such centers of learning at all the major mosques in West Africa, such as the ones at Timbuktu, Agades, Katsina, Yandoto, and elsewhere. The mud-brick mosque at Jenne was particularly impressive (plate 4).

In the 1690s some refugees from Nāṣir al-Dīn's movement settled in Gajaaga and the area further upstream along the Senegal, where under the leadership of Mālik Si they established the Muslim state of Fuuta Bundu near the gold fields of Buré; upon Mālik Si's death, leadership passed to his son Bubu Mālik Si.[5] Thus the idea of Islamic-inspired political reform and military conquest developed as a powerful tradition in West Africa, in particular under the leadership of the Muslim clerical class of Torodbe, whose members were of diverse origin but who identified with the Fulbe pastoralists who dominated cattle herding in the Senegal River region and elsewhere. The Torodbe clerical families inhabited their own communities, zawāyā, which were scattered along the Senegal River, especially in the central parts of the flood plain. The Torodbe had strong links with Kajoor and the religious centers of Pire and Koki, as well as other religious centers in the southern Sahara.

In the eighteenth century and even earlier, many Muslims in West Africa lived peacefully among non-Muslims. The followers of al-Ḥājj Sālim Suwari from Ja in Masina, in the middle Niger delta, who had settled at Jahaba in the gold fields of Bambuhu in the late fifteenth century, were also associated with advocacy of nonconfrontation. On similar lines, Suwari's disciples, namely, Muhammad al-Būnī and Yūsuf Kasama, spread his ideas among the Juula and Jakhanke merchant communities, respectively, while another follower, Shaykh 'Abd al-Raḥmān Zaghaite, did the same in the Hausa cities. As Ivor Wilks has argued, this Suwarian tradition openly rejected the idea of jihad: "The principal dicta of al-Ḥājj Sālim had to do with relations with unbelievers," and jihād was "permissible only in self-defense should the very existence of the community be threatened by unbelievers."[6] Adherents of the Qādiriyya brotherhood, especially the Kunta clerics under al-Mukhtār, were particularly noted for their advocacy of peaceful integration and toleration and respect for multicultural settings, which was the basic premise for commercial interaction across West Africa. In the second half of the eighteenth century the clerics in the caravan towns (qṣar) of Walāta, Tichitt, Timbuktu, Wadan, Asawan, and Shinqīt, which were located in the Sahel and the southern Sahara, concentrated on teaching jurisprudence and syntax, not the promotion of jihād.[7] Timbuktu stands out in the popular imagination as both a mysterious and distant place and a great center of learning with its Sankore mosque (plate 5), but it was only one of many such centers.

Over time, however, many Muslims came to believe that their community was being threatened and began to advocate jihād, the implications of which started to become apparent in West Africa in the form of opposition to the transatlantic slave trade. In general, Muslim principles condemned the enslavement of freeborn Muslims and the sale of slaves to non-Muslims; however, this prohibition failed to address slavery as an institution. For instance, there were no attempts to prevent domestic slavery; quite the contrary, the appeal to jihād transformed the appeal to Islam, as Barry has argued, "from the religion of a minority caste of merchants and courtiers in the royal courts [to] . . . a popular resistance movement against the arbitrary power of the ruling aristocracies and against the noxious effects of the Atlantic trade."[8] This popular resistance led to the call for jihād in Senegambia, which was a reaction to the consolidation of military regimes in the various states of the region that were considered oppressive because they were supplying slaves as part of the transatlantic slave trade. The military elite, *ceddo*, were preoccupied with slave raiding and expressed disdain for Muslim scholarship and the status of freeborn Muslims. The memory of Nāṣir al-Dīn's movement and the survival of the idea of jihād in Fuuta Bundu presaged a far more significant movement.

In 1727–28 jihād spread to the highlands of Fuuta Jalon, from where the Senegal and Gambia Rivers flowed, and where Karamokho Alfa established an imamate that was also connected with Fulbe pastoralists and Muslim clerics (see Map 2.1).[9] As the head of the Sediyanke lineage of the Barry family of Timbo, Karamokho Alfa formed a confederation that initiated jihād, earning the title *almami*. The confederation was divided into nine provinces or *diwal* (sing. *dime*), whose chiefs bore the title of *alfa* and were appointed from among the leaders of the jihād. From the beginning, the power of the *almami*, with his seat at Timbo, was limited by the wide autonomy assumed by the chiefs of the provinces of Labe, Buriya, Timbi, Kebaali, Kollade, Koyin, Fugumba, and Fode Haaji. The *almami* governed through a council of elders acting as a legislature at Fugumba, the religious capital. With the death of Karamokho Alfa about 1751, jihād entered a new phase that affected trade along the coast. Ibrahima Sori became *almami* and subsequently instituted an aggressive policy against neighboring countries under the pretext of waging jihād. According to Barry, Ibrahim Sori, in alliance with the Jalonke kingdom of Solimana, engaged in a series of wars to procure slaves and booty. The jihād was far from secure, however. In 1762 Konde Burama, king of Sankaran, was

The Origins of Jihād in West Africa

able to occupy Timbo after the defection of Solimana. Only in 1776 was Ibrahima Sori finally able to eliminate the threat, consolidate Fuuta Jalon domination of Solimana to the east of Timbo, and end the threat of Sankaran.[10]
Even then, a slave uprising challenged the jihād state in 1785. The enslaved
populations of a number of plantations (*rimaibé*) took advantage of war between Fuuta Jalon and the Susu to the south of Fuuta Jalon to revolt. The leaders (*alfa*) of the various *diwal* that constituted Fuuta Jalon combined to crush
the uprising; three thousand were reported killed, and many refugees fled to
Susu territory. The refugees, particularly those at Yangueakori, remained
defiant. Eventually, however, the Susu came to terms with Fuuta Jalon, and a
combined expedition destroyed Yangueakori in 1796.[11] Thus what can be considered as opposition to jihād was crushed.

The appeal to jihād as a means of political change attracted adherents
other than the Fulbe clerics and scholarly Muslims of Fuuta Jalon. To the
south, a Muslim holy man from the interior named Fatta declared himself
Mahdī and, as the messianic redeemer who according to prophecy was destined to make the entire world Muslim, led a jihād in 1789 to achieve that result. With fifteen thousand followers, mostly recruited among Susu and the
enslaved population of the area, he invaded Moria, a Muslim state on the
coast that was already weakened by war and a succession crisis. Local rulers
and elders prostrated themselves before Mahdī Fatta, and massive numbers
of fugitive slaves joined his army. Among his targets were the British and
mixed-race traders along the coast. He required his followers to wear yellow
garments, and even some of the European and mixed-race traders did so to
try to save themselves. The traders on the Rio Pongo felt the threat, as did the
Muslim elites of Moria and neighboring Sambuyo, who temporarily put their
differences aside to deal with the jihād in their midst and crush the slave uprising that the jihād sanctioned.[12] Fatta was executed in the early 1790s, and
the jihād and slave revolt came to an end. The Fuuta Jalon military that was
concentrated in the various *diwal* asserted its authority in Fuuta Jalon, but
Almami Sori's death in 1791 prompted a succession crisis when Sori's son,
Sadu, attempted to claim the position of *almami*. Bademba, son of Almami
Karamokho Alfa, challenged Sadu, who was assassinated in 1797/98.[13] Thereafter the two factions agreed to alternate the succession, thereby institution-
alizing the internal rivalry within Fuuta Jalon.

The jihād in Fuuta Toro evolved during the disorder along the middle
Senegal River valley after the great drought that hit most of West Africa in
the middle of the eighteenth century.[14] The ruling Denyanke dynasty was subjected to internal strife and open harassment from the Maure of the Brakna

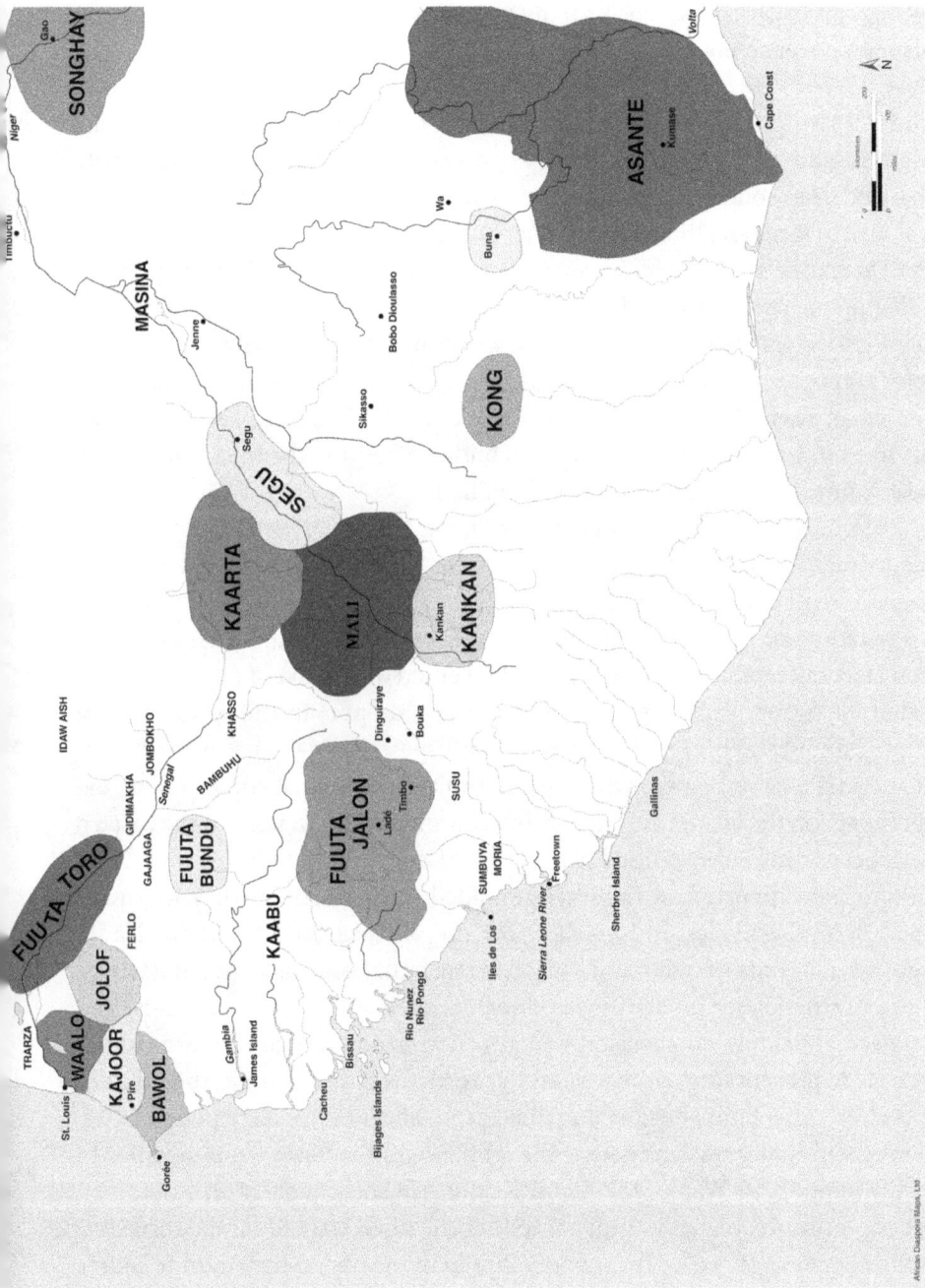

MAP 2.1. Fuuta Jalon and Fuuta Toro, 1795.
Source: Henry B. Lovejoy, African Diaspora Maps

region north of the Senegal River, who dominated the central and western parts of Fuuta Toro, while the Denyanke were confined largely to the eastern parts of the Senegal flood plain. This situation made it possible for the Torodbe to stage an organized offensive that eventually resulted in the establishment of a new government that became committed to jihād. First under Sulaymān Baal, the Torodbe consolidated their position in central Fuuta Toro, where the fords crossing the Senegal River could be defended against raids by the Maures, and by the early 1770s they had stopped paying the annual tribute that had been collected. Together with clerics from Pire in Kajoor, Sulaymān was able to forge an alliance with other Torodbe in western Fuuta Toro, where the Denyanke rulers held sway, in an attempt to stop the Denyanke from pillaging the central valley. Unfortunately, in 1776 Sulaymān Baal and several key Pire clerics were killed in battle, which marked a turning point in the reform movement. Through the intervention of Fuuta Jalon, a successor to Sulaymān was selected in Abdul Kader Kan, who had not previously been involved in the struggle in Fuuta Toro but who became the first almami of a new regime that became committed to jihād.

Abdul Kader had been educated at Pire and Koki, as well as at centers in Mauretania. Sharing Sulaymān's commitment to education, he had been teaching in a small village in Fuuta Bundu because the *almami* of Fuuta Bundu had a reputation for supporting the Torodbe clerics. With Abdul Kader's installation at a new capital at Thilogne, the jihād entered a period of expansion that lasted for twenty years. He clearly had strong support in the royal court of Fuuta Bundu, and his reputation in Kajoor, especially at Koki, was very great. He negotiated a settlement with the Denyanke dynasty that conferred virtual autonomy on the former ruling elite but confined their territory to the eastern periphery of the Senegal flood plain. Abdul Kader then set out to redistribute land to the supporters of the jihād, founded some thirty to forty mosques, and appointed judges and teachers for the villages. In 1785 Abdul Kader negotiated a commercial treaty with the French that generated an annual tribute. In 1786 a major offensive was launched against the Trarza Maures, and between 1789 and 1791 garrison villages were established at the fords of the Senegal to prevent further incursions by the Maures. By this time Abdul Kader was clearly invoking allegiance to jihād as justification for state policies.[15] By 1790 Abdul Kader was able to use his influence in the lower Senegal valley to secure support in Waalo, Jolof, and Kajoor. He subsequently also obtained the recognition of Khasso in 1796, so that the jihād state of Fuuta Toro controlled the Senegal valley from Fuuta Bundu in the east to the Atlantic shores in the west.

However, Fuuta Toro suffered a crushing defeat in Kajoor in late 1796 at the battle of Bunguye, which reasserted the independence of the Wolof states. Abdul Kader was captured and held prisoner for several months before being allowed to return to Fuuta Toro. Waalo, in turn, revoked its allegiance to Fuuta Toro. The Islamic center at Koki became embroiled in the struggle promoted by the jihād in Fuuta Toro, and its scholarly reputation suffered as a result.[16] In 1797 Fuuta Jalon intervened in a succession crisis in Fuuta Bundu after the execution of Almami Sega Gaye. Subsequent difficulties with Fuuta Bundu and Khasso further reduced Fuuta Toro hegemony, and in 1807 Abdul Kader was killed in battle against Fuuta Bundu, which had secured the support of the Bambara state of Kaarta. Thereafter the jihād was effectively undermined, and French influence along the Senegal River steadily extended further into the interior.[17]

Nonetheless, by the end of the eighteenth century the jihād movement was clearly established from the Senegal River valley in the north to the highlands of Fuuta Jalon and the coastal zone to the south, but with somewhat mixed results. Jihād had become fully associated with the Fulbe, particularly with the scholarly and religious elite who were spread across the savanna and the Sahel of West Africa because of the transhumance migration patterns of the cattle herders and the elite who owned the cattle. The Muslim and learned leadership was allied with and often related to the clan heads who managed the cattle herds that traversed West Africa. Ethnically related pastoralists, who were variously known as Peul, Ful, Fulbe, Fula, or Fulani depending on their location in West Africa and spoke a shared language, Fulfulde, became particularly influential in the jihād movement. As the jihād of Mahdī Fatta in Moria demonstrates, the idea of jihād also appealed to other Muslims, although in his case jihād was not successful. Perhaps because Fatta's uprising was linked to what amounted to a slave revolt in Moria, the supernatural powers that he claimed protected him from death were openly challenged, and his appeal was undermined when it was proved that he had no such powers.[18]

Ethnicity played a significant role in all the successful jihād movements. Except for the jihād in Moria, Fulbe/Fulani were involved in all the jihāds from the 1690s to the middle of the nineteenth century. Nonetheless, it is important to emphasize here that the jihād movement was not an ethnic phenomenon. Muslims came from many different ethnic backgrounds and included the merchants of the extensive Muslim commercial networks that linked West Africa in a common economic market. The Qādirī shaykh Sīdī al-Mukhtār was not Fulbe, nor was Jibrīl ibn 'Umar, one of 'Uthmān dan Fodio's teachers.[19]

Those Fulbe who were well learned in the classic scriptures of Islam and were fluent in Arabic were of the Torodbe clan, whose members were not pastoral nomads. In many cases they were able to appeal to pastoral Fulbe and in the process secure their commitment to an aggressive Muslim agenda. In the central Bilād al-Sūdān the Fulbe were known by the Hausa term "Fulani," and their ethnic allegiance was fundamental to the consolidation of the Sokoto Caliphate.

In the context of explaining why jihād began in the far western Bilād al-Sūdān, two underlying factors are significant: first, the organization of Muslim trade in West Africa, and second, the transhumance patterns of the cattle-owning Fulbe. Muslim merchants, craftsmen, and scholars were found in virtually every town in West Africa, providing an interlocking network of communities from Senegambia to Lake Chad. Fulbe cattle herders followed migratory trails that took them from the Senegal River southward into the hills where the Gambia, Senegal, and Niger Rivers begin. The resulting migratory drift of nomads followed north/south transhumance patterns that led to the progressive eastward movement of the Fulbe across West Africa as far as Lake Chad.

The headwaters of the Senegal, Gambia, and Niger Rivers and the gold fields of Bambuhu and Buré encompassed a region traversed by cattle nomads whose ethnicity as Fulbe, Ful, and Peul meant an underlying common tie to ecologically based production and marketing. Their language, Fulfulde, was akin to Wolof, and in a certain sense the only difference between Wolof and Fulbe was whether a person owned cattle or not. The reality was far more complex, however, because evidence of the presence of Fulbe existed virtually everywhere in West Africa north of the forest where cattle could be bred. Transhumance migration, whereby herds followed the pattern of the seasons, moving north during the rainy season and toward groundwater or wells for the herds in the dry season, often resulted in a north/south migratory pattern. Herds were taken to pastures and sources of water rather than being watered and fed in restricted spaces. The owners of the herds were powerful men who also controlled settled slave plantations where grain could be secured and where herds could be pastured during the dry season, thereby fertilizing fields and increasing crop production.

An initial explanation for the spread of the Fulbe across West Africa is both religious and ecological, in which people from the Senegal River valley moved across West Africa, filling a niche in the economy through specialization in pastoralism. Islam and ethnicity were factors in the formation of a diaspora conception of identity as Fulbe, Fulani, Pula, Ful, and Fula who spoke a common language, Fulfulde. As reflected in the names Fuuta Bundu, Fuuta Jalon, and Fuuta Toro, the prefix *Fuuta* indicates the ethnic association with Fulbe. Since the sixteenth century, at least, the Fulbe had been considered Muslims, with the exception, according to Aḥmad Bābā of "a certain section of the Fulbe south of Jenne."[20] The Toronkawa clan, in particular, was associated with Islamic learning and with sedentary communities that provided an anchor to the migratory patterns of the pastoralists. The Toronkawa, affiliated with the Qādiriyya *ṣūfī* brotherhood, was one of a number of clans who built their influence and authority on the basis of belonging to the Qādiriyya brotherhood. The Kunta and the Saghanughu were two other such clans: the Kunta were centered on Timbuktu and the region to the northwest, and the Saghanughu were scattered in communities throughout the region of the upper Niger. The Kunta were ethnically Arab by descent, while the Saghanughu were Soninke in origin, as was al-Ḥājj Sālim Suwari; however, by the seventeenth century the Saghanughu and other Jakhanke were often considered Mandinke, as in the case of Muhammad Kabā Saghanughu, who came from Bouka in the Tinkisso River valley, one of the tributaries of the Niger River, approximately twenty kilometers south of Dinguiraye, which was also on the Tinkisso.[21]

The enforced travels of Muhammad Kabā Saghanughu provide an insight into the age of jihād in what is sometimes called "greater Senegambia," which includes Fuuta Jalon and its borderlands to the south and east of the highlands. In his *Kitāb al-ṣalāt*, written in Jamaica around 1820, Kabā Saghanughu reveals the range of knowledge of the literate elite of West Africa (plate 6). Indeed, Kabā's association with the Saghanughu connects him with one of the most scholarly families in the western Bilād al-Sūdān.[22] He had studied the basic subjects, the Qur'ān, Ḥadīth, and *fiqh*, and referred to the *Ṣaḥīḥ*s of Muslim and Bukhārī, both books on *hadīth*, and to the anonymous commentary *Kitāb al-Munabbihāt*. He also cited Shaykh Bābā al-Fakiru, who seems to have been one of his teachers, besides his uncle, Mohammed Batoul.[23] The style of scholarship to which Kabā was exposed was the standard education taught by the Qādiriyya, which focused on a core curriculum consisting of the *Muwaṭṭa'* of Mālik, the *Shifā'* of Qāḍī 'Iyaḍ b. Mūsā, and the *Tafsīr al-Jalālayn*.

Because it is very clearly evident that Muhammad Kabā was a Muslim, it is reasonable to speculate that his enslavement was connected with the resistance to Islam. It is likely that he was enslaved by non-Muslims who did not have access to ransoming circuits. He clearly fell into the hands of enemies of Fuuta Jalon. Kabā does not seem to have passed through the Muslim

The Origins of Jihād in West Africa

commercial networks and hence was likely traded south of Fuuta Jalon to Bunce Island on the Sierra Leone River or possibly the islands off the shore of the Sierra Leone Peninsula, either the Bananas or Sherbro. In any event, he ended up in Jamaica in 1777 on one of the several ships that went from the upper Guinea coast to Kingston in that year. The friction on the frontiers of jihād that exposed Muslims to enslavement impelled people to travel in caravans; there is no evidence about what happened to the caravan that Kabā must have been in, but it must have suffered more than his enslavement. He was on his way to Timbuktu to study law, following a route from the Tinkisso River to the northeast. The caravans from southern Fuuta Jalon that were going north and northeast were usually laden with kola nuts and at least some gold from the alluvial deposits of the tributaries of the Niger River. The merchants in the region passed between towns that connected with the kola producers of the forest region, and Kabā's enslavement most probably occurred in one such area, among people who were apparently not Muslims and who would have had commercial contacts along the Sierra Leone River or at departure points farther south as far as the Gallinas.

Someone of Kabā's stature usually would have been ransomed. Why he was not is a mystery; however, he was not the only freeborn Muslim who was not thereby rescued from slavery. Ransoming was common because the ransom price was usually higher than the purchase price of a slave—often twice the price—and ransoming was favored under Islamic law and practice.[24] Ayuba ibn Sulaymān Diallo of Fuuta Bundu, known to the Europeans as Job ben Solomon, was probably the best known of the early Africans in the Americas (plate 7). He was captured during a commercial venture to the Gambia in 1731 and was sold as a slave to Maryland before he could be ransomed. He learned only after he arrived in North America "that his father sent down several slaves, a little after Captain Pike sailed [from the Gambia River], in order to procure his redemption; and that Sambo, King of Futa [Bundu], had made war upon the Mandingoes, and cut off great numbers of them, upon account of injury they had done to his schoolfellow."[25] In a letter that Ayuba wrote to his father after his capture, he stated that "there is no good in the country of the Christians [for] a Muslim."[26] There were other instances, too, of important individuals ending up in slavery and failing to be caught by the ransoming net. It is likely that Big Prince Whitten, studied by Jane Landers, was another example. Enslaved in the Gambia valley, apparently, he was taken to Charlestown in the 1770s, although he subsequently escaped and made his way to St. Augustine in Spanish Florida, where he served in the Spanish militia for 26 years under the name Juan Bautista after his conversion and baptism. He was identified as "Mandinga," which meant that he was Muslim by origin and probably a Mandinke from Kaabu or one of the principalities along the Gambia.[27]

The impact of the transatlantic slave trade can be assessed in terms of the number of people who left from ports of the upper Guinea coast, from roughly Cape Mount and the Gallinas to the Senegal River. The peculiarity of this coast hid the Muslim interior from the eyes of the ships trading along the rivers and lagoons behind the bar along the Gallinas coast, the swampy island of Sherbro stretching northward to the Sierra Leone Peninsula, and the islands of Bananas and Plantain offshore from the Sierra Leone Peninsula; however, the coast provided convenient bases of operations for such non-Muslim merchant families as the Clevelands and the Corkers.[28] The Sierra Leone River was an ideal anchorage on an African coast that has few natural harbors; however, the river could not be navigated farther inland beyond Bunce Island. The main river was only an inlet of the sea that was fed by several small rivers that provided minimal transportation links with the interior. Kabā probably would have been brought to the coast south of Fuuta Jalon, or he might have been ransomed, but in any event, his path avoided Muslim centers where his status might have secured his freedom.

There are reports of Muslims in the Americas who came from Senegambia in the eighteenth century that arose because of the enslavement of Muslims and in turn the response of the Muslim reformers in calling for jihād and in propagating the consolidation of Islamic states based on Sharī'a law.[29] Bilali Mahomet had come from Timbo in Fuuta Jalon, probably in the 1790s. In 1813 he was assigned as head driver on a plantation on Sapelo Island.[30] Other examples of Muslims who reached the Americas in the eighteenth century include Ayuba, who came from Fuuta Toro, and Richard Pierpoint, whose Muslim name is not known, but who came from Fuuta Bundu sometime around 1760. Pierpoint was apparently captured in a war that involved an invasion of Fuuta Bundu from Kaarta or Segu. He almost certainly was Fulbe, but most references that have survived refer to him as Mandingo, that is, Mandinke.[31] Similarly, Muhammad Kabā Saghanughu, who was of Soninke origin, was referred to as Mandingo in Jamaica, as were other Muslims from West Africa, such as a man called "London" and others from St. Domingue, Antigua, and elsewhere.[32] Samba Makumba from Fuuta Toro reported in Trinidad that

the Mahometans are forbidden to make slaves of those of their own faith, and when any of their people are concerned in this traffic, they believe their religion requires them to put a stop to it by force. It was for this purpose a war was commenced by the Fullahs against these other tribes, and in this war Samba was taken prisoner and sold as a slave.[33]

Samba, who was sixty in 1841, observed that "he belonged to the tribe Fullah Tauro [Fuuta Toro], which engaged in a war with six other tribes in Africa to prevent them, as he said, from carrying on the slave trade." Ṣāliḥ Bilali of Timbuktu, who was born in Masina around 1770, had been enslaved by Bambara and sold from Segu to Asante; subsequently, from Anamobu he went to the Bahamas before arriving finally in South Carolina.[34] Rosalie of the "Poulard Nation," which indicates that she was Fulbe, is another example of a Muslim who was enslaved in this period.[35] According to Rebecca Scott and Jean-Michel Hébrard, she was probably born around 1767 and enslaved sometime after 1780. Rosalie was unusual in being one of the very few Fulbe females reported to have been enslaved. It is also possible that she was actually enslaved as early as 1775 or 1776, when the Moors invaded Waalo and enslaved many people, and when the jihād state of Fuuta Toro was being founded.[36] Although there were Fulbe women reported in the Americas, they represent only a small portion, except in Louisiana, where they constituted about 25 percent, and in Maranhão, where they were about half the total.[37]

In the case of Fuuta Jalon, the Islamic state attempted to control the course and direction of the slave trade, not only because it dominated the highlands inland from the coast but also because it forced trade to flow to the north via the Gambia River or southward toward the Sierra Leone River. The relatively few Muslims who reached the Americas included those from Fuuta Jalon, but overall, the Muslim interior of West Africa was underrepresented in terms of the numbers of slaves who moved as part of the transatlantic migration. In fact, Zachary Macaulay reported in 1793 that there was strong opposition in Fuuta Jalon to involvement in the transatlantic slave trade and that the succession crisis after the death of Almami Sori was a consequence of this opposition, which is probably an exaggeration but is nonetheless significant as an indication of attitudes toward the enslavement of Muslims.[38] With the onslaught of jihād, there were attempts to suppress the sale of slaves who might be Muslims to non-Muslims. Fulbe clans established their political dominance over the Jalonke population in the highlands to which the Senegal, Gambia, and Niger Rivers trace their origins. Centered at Labe and Timbo, the Fulbe developed a vibrant plantation economy based on slave labor and otherwise maintained commercial links with the Muslim interior through connections with the Mandinka towns, such as Dinguiraye, Kankan, Sikasso, and others that were on the route to the inner Niger basin. In Fuuta Toro, Almami Abdul Kader reached an accord with the French at St. Louis in 1785 that allowed French merchants to pass up the Senegal River to obtain gum arabic and slaves upon payment of a tax but prohibited the purchase of slaves in Fuuta Toro itself.[39]

The jihād leadership was conscious of tradition and hence was preoccupied with analyzing whether the conditions for jihād were present. The signs were discussed, events and motives were justified through reference to tradition, and a template for jihād was mythologized. There were recognizable building blocks that had to be in place, most especially conditions in which Muslims were being oppressed and were forced into a retreat where war was initially justified as defensive and unavoidable. Indeed, when such conditions prevailed in the Hausa state of Gobir and elsewhere, Muslims flocked to the camp of ʿUthmān dan Fodio and his supporters, which was established at Degel in the 1790s. By following the events and statements of the jihād leadership, it is possible to discern what it took to undertake a jihād and how the movement benefited from an association with earlier jihāds, particularly in West Africa, that led to the establishment of three Muslim states, all dominated by Muslims who were also considered to be ethnically Fulbe. The tradition of jihād as developed in West Africa from Fuuta Bundu to Sokoto had a common feature in that the leadership was Fulbe, and this tradition continued. The same was true in the establishment of the Hamdullahi Caliphate, which initially was under Sokoto. Al-Ḥājj ʿUmar himself, being Fulbe, had pretensions to succeed Muhammad Bello as caliph of Sokoto upon Bello's death. Al-Ḥājj ʿUmar was married to Bello's daughter, but the succession went to Bello's brother. Even the Mahdist state of the Nilotic Sudan relied heavily on the Fulbe, who were known in the Nilotic Sudan as Fellata and formed the backbone of the Mahdist military. With the assassination of the Mahdi, the succession passed to Abdallahi, who was the head of the military.

This ethnic compatibility between the Fulbe leadership and the Muslim intellectuals of diverse backgrounds, combined with the success of jihād across Africa from the Atlantic to the Red Sea, facilitated the spread of ideas and justification through the rigors of Islamic scholarship. Indeed, the migration of young men who wished to be employed in armies or to study under teachers who were attached to the mosques of the principal towns was a major factor in consolidating the appeal of jihād and reform. This movement of students overlapped with commercial travel, and the distribution of slaves through long-distance trade meant that all the Muslim regions of sub-Saharan Africa were well integrated. This can be seen in the surviving biographical accounts of Muslims who somehow ended up in slavery despite the efforts to prevent such fateful loss of freedom. In general, trade and marketing were organized in a way that promoted regional integration. In the western parts of West Africa, Muslims who were identified as Juula and who spoke the same language (Malinke) were closely linked to the Qādiriyya. They controlled long-distance trade, with outposts from Senegambia as far east as the Hausa cities and Borno. A similar Hausa commercial diaspora radiated outward from the central cities of the Hausa states and later the Sokoto Caliphate, particularly Kano, Zaria, and Katsina, but in the case of this commercial system, the language of trade was Hausa. The network extended to the middle Volta basin and Asante, to the Yoruba coast of the Bight of Benin, and eastward as far as Wadai. Both Juula and Hausa merchant networks were linked across the Sahara and hence were tied to the extensions of trade from Morocco, whose immigrants to sub-Saharan Africa known as *shurfa* (Hausa: Sharifai) claimed to be direct descendants of the Prophet, whether or not the reality substantiated their claims. This overlapping series of networks also connected with the Ottoman domains from Algiers to the Hijaz and even the Jellaba merchants of the Nile River valley and the trade of Wadai and Darfur.

Specifically, the commercial interior of West Africa was controlled by Muslim merchants who operated along trade routes between dispersed towns where there were communities with which they identified.[40] These dispersed networks have sometimes been referred to as "commercial diasporas," following the lead of Philip Curtin and Abner Cohen.[41] The concept of diaspora is used to describe the social organization of the merchants who formed the layers of commercial networks that dominated the trade from the interior to the coast of West Africa. Traders operated over considerable distances and relied on agents and partners who were resident in towns and cities along the trade routes that were often far from the homelands of the merchants. The two principal diasporas included the "Juula" (also Dyula), which means "merchant" in the languages of the Manding, and the "Hausa," which was centered in the central Bilād al-Sūdān. Both ethnic terms reflected the use of a common commercial language, either the Juula dialect of Malinke or Hausa, as well as identification with Islam. This structure of trade became particularly significant after the Moroccan invasion of the Songhay Empire in 1591–92 and the ending of the hegemonic Muslim state that encompassed much of

JIHĀD IN WEST AFRICA DURING THE AGE OF REVOLUTIONS

West Africa from Senegambia to the Hausa cities of the central Bilād al-Sūdān. In the absence of a centralized state, these commercial networks, which constituted a complex diaspora, assumed the function of connecting the many towns and cities into an interlocking grid that relied on Islam as a unifying ideology.

The structure of trade and marketing provided economic linkages over a wide area and was centered on a commercial diaspora that depended for its operation on connections that nurtured an intellectual, scholarly, and religious hierarchy steeped, to a greater or lesser degree, in Islamic learning. For its functioning, the commercial system depended on the maintenance of links among communities based on kinship, personal friendships, and religious instruction, as well as business partnerships. The urban-centered commercial structure was matched by a rural structure based on transhumance migration and management of livestock and sedentary settlements of plantations and farms on which slaves worked. The jihād movement thus brought together a range of Muslims whose identities crossed ethnic boundaries and required knowledge of and fluency in more than one language, one of which was Arabic for the intellectual elite. All men had to have attended Qur'ānic school as boys and had to be more or less literate. They were expected to attend mosque on Fridays and to engage in communal prayers that highlighted this emphasis on literacy, the acquisition of knowledge, and travel, explicitly encouraged by the tenets of Islam that sanctified pilgrimage to Mecca and the many centers of learning along the routes to the Hijaz.

An example of the interlocking commercial and religious connections across West Africa can be gleaned from the biography of Abū Bakr al-Siddīq, who was born in Timbuktu around 1790 and was brought up in Jenne, farther south on the Niger River. Abū Bakr's life story is known from his autobiography and other documents that came to light in Jamaica, where he became associated with R. R. Madden, special magistrate at the time of the British emancipation of slaves in 1834.[42] Abū Bakr's father, Kara Mūsā, who traced his ancestry to Shaykh 'Abd al-Qādir, was of *shurfa* descent, that is, someone who claimed to be a descendant of the Prophet, which in turn traces his origin to Morocco. The family had been prominent among the Muslim learned class in West Africa for generations. Kara Mūsā was considered *tafsīr* (a West African grammatical corruption of *mufassir*, a scholar who specialized in Qu'ranic exegesis) and was a prominent merchant. Abū Bakr received his early education in Jenne and at age nine began an extended tour of Muslim centers in West Africa, first at the Juula town of Kong and then at Bouna, where, according to Ivor Wilks, 'Abd Allāh ibn al-Ḥajj Muhammad al-Watarawi presided over a community of scholars drawn from many parts of the western Bilād al-Sūdān. Indeed, Abū Bakr's teachers included not only al-Watarawi but also Shaykh 'Abd al-Qādir Sankari from Fuuta Jalon, Ibrāhīm ibn Yūsuf from Fuuta Toro, and Ibrāhīm ibn Abī al-Ḥasan of Silla, who was originally from Dyara, an important Soninke center near Nioro, north of modern Bamako. Moreover, Abū Bakr's mother, Ḥafsah, who was known as Nagode (Hausa: "I am thankful"), was from Katsina but also had family in Borno. Her father, Muhammad Tafsīr, had been on pilgrimage to Mecca, and he and her brothers were involved in trade with Borno and the middle Volta basin and Asante. Abū Bakr's trade with his father-in-law, Muhammad Tafsīr, included gold, as well as horses, donkeys, mules, and silks that had been imported from Egypt, and although Abū Bakr does not mention them, kola nuts were almost certainly sent to Katsina as well. Thus Abū Bakr was associated with the intellectual and commercial diaspora that stretched from Senegambia to Lake Chad in the eighteenth century.[43]

As Abū Bakr's account demonstrates, the interior trade of the western and central Bilād al-Sūdān constituted a diversified regional commerce that was to a large extent ecologically determined, and goods imported via the Atlantic and the Sahara supplemented this regional trade of West Africa.[44] The variety of goods that were traded reflected a pattern of commerce that was closely associated with ecological regions and localized niches of production. Commodities included agricultural products, livestock, minerals, and manufactured goods. Many towns and cities of the interior grew with the development of extensive regional markets. Trade across ecological zones from the desert through the Sahel and the savanna to the forested regions of the coast fostered economic exchange. For example, livestock and salt were produced in the desert and the Sahel, whereas agricultural products, such as grain, root and tree crops, cotton, and indigo, were prominent in the region, depending on local conditions. Moreover, such manufactured goods as cotton textiles and leather products were centered in the many towns and cities in the agricultural zones. In addition to kola nuts, various types of salt were also widely distributed that were used not only for culinary purposes but for various medicinal purposes for both people and animals and for industrial needs in textile dyeing, the tanning of leather, and soap production. Some salts were also mixed with tobacco for use as snuff or for chewing, stashed already prepared for ingestion in leather pouches. Kola nuts and gold were key commodities from the forested regions inland from the Sierra Leone River, the region south of Wagadugu, and the Akan forests.[45]

The Muslim commercial networks across West Africa comprised socially determined communities based on common origins. Merchants of these commercial networks were recognized as Hausa, Maraka, Yarse, Jakhanke, or Wangara or employed self-identifying names, such as Saghanughu, Kabā, and Ture, that associated individuals with particular towns and regions of origin.[46] Curtin actually studied one of these networks, the Jakhanke, on the basis of which he first developed the concept of commercial diaspora. His work was reinforced by the excellent study of the Jakhanke by Lamin Sanneh.[47] The recognition of Islam as the religion of community, the use of common commercial languages, either Hausa or Manding and its dialects, such as Juula, and the maintenance of social relationships and kinship over great distances formed the basis of layered and overlapping commercial diasporas that facilitated the operation of trading networks. The communities of the diaspora provided the infrastructure for the commercial networks and for the religious, marital, kin, and intellectual networks that constituted the diaspora and tied it to the homeland or a central town or city. Although the focus here is on the commercial and legal dimensions of the Muslim diasporas in West Africa, it should be recognized that these diasporas not only serviced trading networks but also, like other commercial diasporas, accommodated other kinds of networks that were religious, kinship based, educational, marital, and commercial. Diasporas operated across space over long distances and were based on communities that served as outposts for commercial and culturally specific interactions. The population associated with diasporas was used to traveling, often involving marriage to partners in towns along the trade routes. The constituents of commercial diasporas were instructed to travel for business, for an education, or to visit relatives and to engage in apprenticeship in trade and craft production. Mobility in the operation of long-distance trade was reinforced as a way of life through parallel migrations for other reasons.

The centrality of learning and hence basic education was a feature of the jihād movement. It was through teaching and the dissemination of historic texts that Islam was consolidated as the dominant religion in the interior of West Africa. The centrality of literacy was not new but had characterized the religious and political elite for generations and had predominated during the era of the Songhay Empire. By the end of the eighteenth century the importance of literacy lay in the means of focusing on the cause and course of jihād. The literary flowering of the jihād movement can be likened to the European Enlightenment's role in inspiring and directing the age of revolutions. In this sense the age of jihād finds a parallel with revolution elsewhere and was indeed linked with Muslims throughout West Africa, in the Maghreb, and elsewhere in the Islamic world.

Lamine Kabā, who was born in Fuuta Jalon about 1780 and arrived in the United States around 1807, provided a detailed account of education in the jihād states. According to his biographer, Theodore Dwight Jr.,

> Lamen Kebe . . . was born in the kingdom of Futa Jalloo [Fuuta Jalon], and travelled sufficiently during his youth to give much interest to the accounts he communicates. He performed two journeys, when quite young, to the Jaliba or Niger River, in one instance in company with an army of Mahomedans, in a successful war upon an idolatrous nation, to convert them to Islamism. His education, which commenced at fourteen, and was finished at twenty-one, was obtained chiefly at Bunder, the city in which a late and expensive English expedition of discovery met a fatal defeat from the natives. He was a school-master five years in the city of Kebe [Kangaba], which he left to travel to the coast, to obtain paper for the use of his pupils, when he was taken and sold as a slave.[48]

His father was "Serecule," that is, Sarakole; his mother was of the "Manenca" nation. He had originally lived north of Fuuta Jalon at Diafun or Jafunu and subsequently at Jaga (Diaga), but a plague of locusts drove the family to eastern Fuuta Jalon. According to what Dwight was told, teachers "devoted years to study and instruction," including women who "rivalled some of the most celebrated of the other sex in success and reputation for talent and extraordinary acquisition."[49] Dwight's report emphasized the importance of education:

> Schools in several countries of interior Nigritia are supported by the government, on such a liberal and judicious system, that all the children have the means of instruction in reading and writing at least, on low terms; while the poor are taught at the public expense, taxes being laid to pay the master or mistress. Private schools are also very numerous, particularly in the larger towns of some of the most learned nations. In some schools, boys and girls are under the care of the same master; but they are placed in separate rooms. Our informant had from fifty-five to fifty-seven pupils in his native town, after he had completed his education, among whom were four or five girls. His scholars, according to the plan pursued in his education, were seated on the floor, each upon a sheepskin, and with small boards held upon one knee, rubbed

over with a whitish chalk or powder, on which they were made to write with pens made of reeds, and ink which they form with care, of various ingredients. The copy is set by the master by tracing the first words of the Koran with a dry reed, which removes the chalk where it touches. The young pupil follows these marks with ink, which is afterwards rubbed over with more chalk. They are called up three at a time to recite to the master, who takes the boards from them, makes them turn their backs to him, and repeat what they were to do the previous day, which they have a decided interest in doing to the best of their recollection; because it is the custom to mark every mistake with the stroke of a stick upon the shoulders.[50]

Dwight thought that "the mind of our informant shows some of the traits of a professional school-master, and his opinions on pedagogy, claim some attention, as they are founded on experience, and independent of those current in other countries." Lamine told Dwight that

children should not be allowed to change school. In our country, no such thing is known or permitted, except when absolutely necessary. It is indeed permitted to a boy who has learnt all his master has to teach, to seek other teachers during the recess of his own school, if he does not neglect his own; and it is not an uncommon thing for an intelligent youth to attend the instructions of two or three teachers at different hours of the day.[51]

Moreover, education was closely associated with trade. Wherever Muslim merchants were found, there were schools.

The region in which Muslim merchants were operating between the Sahara and the West African coast encompassed several currency zones, including cloth strips, gold, cowrie shells, and silver, by the end of the eighteenth century. Merchants and their employees had to be adept at dealing with the various currencies, as well as the changing political circumstances. They used gold (based on the gold-dust measurement of the *mithqāl*, a unit of weight usually equivalent to 4.25 grams) of the western Sahel and Sahara, cowries in a wide zone in the savanna and the forest, and silver coins more extensively, beginning in the late eighteenth century. Concurrently, in some places various commodity currencies prevailed, such as strips of cloth and iron objects that resembled small hoes.[52] The landlord-brokers who were resident in the various towns and cities of West Africa were responsible for dealing with currency exchange and credit. Cowries were bulky and difficult to transport, and hence landlords vouched for sales and purchases of commodities, taking a commission on sales but also safeguarding both commodities and cash. Landlords were therefore essential to the operation of trade because of the vagaries of currency supplies and liquidity. They also warehoused the goods of long-distance trade, provisioned caravans, and provided other services to itinerant merchants, including feeding them and tending livestock.[53]

In addition to this dispersed commercial structure, the interior of West Africa was also held together through the transhumance migrations of Fulbe cattle herders and desert nomads, particularly the Tuareg and the Maure, which also helped integrate West Africa. Like the merchants, these nomadic peoples also relied on Islam as a means of unification, drawing on the Islamic legal system to regulate community relationships and to settle disputes in the absence of centralized states.[54] Although the Fulbe originated in the Senegal River valley, they came to monopolize cattle rearing across all of West Africa by the sixteenth century. Cattle were moved across the open savanna in a generally northerly and southerly pattern to follow pastures and available supplies of water, and in the course of this transhumance they gradually drifted eastward as far as Lake Chad and eventually even farther east. The Toronkawa, to which the family of ʿUthmān dan Fodio belonged, settled in the Hausa region before the eighteenth century, for example. Because they traced their origins to the Senegal valley, as other Fulbe did, they could rely on clan ties, linguistic compatibility, and other cultural traits to reinforce an ongoing interaction. The Fulbe leadership thereby amassed considerable resources that derived from the retention of common traditions arising from this economic niche. The elite controlled the herds of cattle, horses, goats, and sheep but also invested in landed estates that relied on slave labor to produce agricultural products and provide bases of operations for nomadic herds.

Similarly, desert nomads, whose dominance of tracts of land in the Sahara and the Sahel was based on the rearing of camel herds but also other livestock, followed their own transhumance patterns of migration. In the course of moving herds in search of water and pasture, they also took advantage of the transport capacity of the camels to move commodities to market, particularly various types of salt processed at desert and Sahelian locations, grain (especially sorghum and millet), textiles, leather goods, agricultural tools, and other commodities, including kola nuts. Like the Fulbe, the desert nomads also invested heavily in agriculture through the establishment of slave estates on often marginal lands that could be very productive in good seasons but risked poor harvests in years of little rain. Hence the Kel Gress, Itisen, and Kel Ewey, among other Tuareg, established economic corridors of trade and production that fed desert salt into savanna markets and moved agricultural output from areas of surplus to markets. They hired out transport services while their camel herds remained in the savanna during the long dry season. The nomads also supplied camels for trans-Saharan trade, which usually followed a relay network that involved other nomads who lived farther north in the Sahara to connect with Morocco and the Ottoman domains of the Mediterranean. These networks also facilitated the pilgrimage to Mecca and the Hijaz. The rearing of donkeys and horses was equally important; the donkeys were needed for transport, sometimes over considerable distances, while horses formed the military backbone of the many warlords who controlled the savanna.

This desert-side economy based on transhumance thereby encouraged migration and interaction over considerable distances, which meant that the cultural unity of West Africa was far more secure than the fragmentation of the political landscape might suggest. After the collapse of Songhay in 1591–92, the many walled towns across West Africa allowed local elites to hold sway over limited tracts of territory. Despite the criticisms of Muslim intellectuals that these elites did not promote Islam sufficiently and oppressed the peasantry, in fact, these states provided security for local peasant production of grain, cotton, and other agricultural commodities. The manufacture of textiles and the curing of leather goods enabled regional industrial output for markets that encompassed most of West Africa and even stretched across the Sahara. Ecologically, trade and production followed a gradient from desert to rain forest; the presence of tsetse flies limited where livestock were to be found, and the seasonal fluctuations in rainfall guaranteed a symbiosis between nomads and sedentary farmers.

The friction that inevitably existed in this political economy pitted the rulers of towns and states against the heads of the nomadic livestock herders because of claims to taxation and efforts to avoid exactions by nomadic herders. Wherever Fulbe clan leaders and desert nomads established agricultural estates, it was necessary to work out arrangements with warlords who controlled the territory. When these arrangements broke down, nomads could migrate, but in doing so, they might lose control of slaves who were settled on the land in any particular state. The risks of raiding, confiscation, and outright theft were therefore a constant impediment to political unification and consequently exacerbated the cultural divisions between nomads and sedentary populations. Once again, adherence to Islam became a means of addressing this friction, particularly when the call to jihād was directed at transforming the political landscape.

The early jihāds of Senegambia and the highlands where many of the rivers of West Africa originate addressed the perceived injustices of the established governments of the region, particularly the indiscriminate use of military force in the subjugation of the populace. The opposition to the non-Muslim governments of Segu and Kaarta in the region among the rivers has long been recognized. The interpretations in virtually all historical analysis pit Muslims against these Bambara states. In fact, the term "Bambara" as an ethnic category and their identification as non-Muslims reflected the tensions that moved West Africa toward jihād. Unlike governments closer to the coast, the ruling elites of the interior relied on military force based on cavalry and inevitably employed slaves to tend the horses and to staff the military. Bambara referred both to an ethnicity that was not considered Muslim and to the political authority of states that were also charged with harassing Muslims. Muslim merchants used the term to justify the purchase and sale of slaves who were implicitly identified as non-Muslims or who were classified as not being Muslims. The people of Segu and Kaarta, the "Bambara" states, were Bamana ethnically, their language was a dialect of the Mande languages of the region, which also included Malinke and Juula, and they were often recognized in the Americas as Mandingo or Mandinga if they were Muslims. This confusion in terminology has affected the study of slave culture in the Americas. Unpacking these terms and establishing their historical context is part of the task of figuring out how West Africa fitted into Atlantic history and the age of revolutions.

Slavery underpinned the confusion over ethnic, religious, and political terminology. To be "Bambara" in West Africa meant that a person could be enslaved as far as Muslims were concerned. The Muslims who held such views included the merchants of the Muslim commercial diaspora, the intellectual elite, and those who championed jihād. This ethnic labeling that was associated with slavery can be traced back to Aḥmad Bābā in the early seventeenth century and his predecessors before then. Aḥmad Bābās scholarship, which was influential in the jihād movement, was the culmination of a tradition that emphasized jurisprudence and syntax and was associated with the Baghayogho, a Soninke clan that spread throughout the Malinke regions of Mali and then the Songhay Empire and was also referred to as Wangara.[55] The term "Bambara" usually referred to those identified as Bamana who lived between the upper Niger River and the Senegal River and who became subjects of Segu and Kaarta and their non-Muslim governments in the seventeenth and eighteenth centuries. Linguistically and culturally, other than allegiance to Islam, they shared many features in economy and society with Mandinka and Soninke, whose affiliation with Islam was assumed on the basis of ethnicity.

Other distinctions of ethnicity were similarly ephemeral. Wolof and Fulbe in the Senegal valley shared allegiance to Islam and spoke mutually intelligible languages but were distinguished on the basis of economy. Wolof identified with the sedentary states of the Senegal region, including Waalo, while the nomadic population identified as Fulbe. The jihād movement changed this pattern; the states of Fuuta Bundu and Fuuta Toro emerged as states dominated by the Fulbe, as the designation "Fuuta" indicated. Various dichotomies characterized the cultural and political complexion of West Africa, including nomad versus sedentary and enslavable non-Muslims versus Muslims who under Islamic law were legally protected from enslavement. Language was often a signifier of identity, but most people spoke more than one language if they lived in contexts where such fluency was required, and Muslims by definition had to understand some Arabic, if only the daily prayers and the rudiments of education. Islam, and especially the consolidation of the Qādiriyya brotherhood, tended to transcend these dichotomies and to provide an alternate approach to identification. The Muslim commercial diaspora and the migrations of Fulbe and desert nomads propagated such affiliation within West Africa, that is, the region referred to in Muslim circles as Bilād al-Sūdān, "the land of the Blacks."

The situation in Borno and the Hausa states during the seventeenth and eighteenth centuries was similar. There, too, Fulbe cattle nomads, their clan leaders, and the many agricultural estates that they established were found throughout the region, and as elsewhere in West Africa, the friction between the Fulbe, who were known in Hausa as Fulani, and the established governments of the Hausa states and Borno was pronounced. The main Hausa states that had been tributary to Songhay before 1591 subsequently fell under the sway of Borno, but a prolonged and serious drought in the middle of the eighteenth century disturbed this political context. The Tuareg nomads (especially Kel Ewey, Itisen, and Kel Gress) asserted their autonomy even while maintaining crucial economic links with the Hausa states because of the market for desert salt, textiles, grain, and other commodities. It was among the Tuareg that the first rumblings of jihād were to be heard, although in the end the Fulbe led the way. The Tuareg cleric Jibrīl ibn 'Umar initially called for jihād in the late eighteenth century as a remedy for the injustices that he identified.

Inevitably the eighteenth-century wars among the Hausa states resulted in extensive enslavement (and reenslavement), and many captives were Muslims, some of whom ended up in the Atlantic world despite the efforts of some Muslims to prevent this fate, at least for freeborn Muslims. According to a Borno praise song dating to the late eighteenth century, "You can put chains around the necks of the slaves from other men's towns and bring them to your own town,"[56] but that did not warrant their sale to non-Muslims. The problem was that many Muslims were slaves, and in those turbulent times ʿUthmān dan Fodio, the leader of the Sokoto jihād after 1804, and other Muslim leaders were concerned with the protection of the Muslim community and the welfare of the enslaved who were Muslims. Indeed, in these wars it was difficult to establish who was being reenslaved and who should have been protected because of their previous status as free and therefore, if captured in war or in raids, should have been ransomed and restored to their freeborn status. By 1800 there were many complaints about the enslavement of Muslims. Jibrīl ibn ʿUmar, whose influence on ʿUthmān dan Fodio was considerable, wrote that "the selling of free men," by whom he meant Muslims, was forbidden, and he wrote this because he was aware that Muslims were being sold. For Jibrīl, this prohibition and similar ones on adultery, alcohol consumption, and manslaughter were the ways in which "our people are distinguished." Failure to enforce such prohibitions was reason for deep concern, if not open rebellion against established governments that were unable or unwilling to enforce such strictures.[57] Similarly, Muhammad Tukur, a Fulani scholar who was a contemporary of ʿUthmān dan Fodio, composed a song that castigated those "who reduce free people to slavery without a legitimate reason." Tukur charged that such actions were in discord with those of the Prophet, and indeed he classified such villains as "Unbelievers."[58]

Certainly non-Muslims were being enslaved, which was not a problem for Muslims if their status was clearly established. Ukawsaw Gronniosaw (ca. 1710–72), who came from Borno and hence from an area of strong Muslim influence, was enslaved sometime in the 1720s. Gronniosaw was apparently not a Muslim or at least not someone whose status as a Muslim could have protected him from enslavement.[59] He claimed that he was from Zara, which might be identified with Azare, a town located between Borno and Kano, or even possibly the Hausa city of Zaria, although the latter seems less likely because the details he provides do not suggest that he was Hausa. His references to religion show that he came from an area in which people decidedly mixed their Islam with local non-Muslim practices if they adhered to Islam at all.[60] Gronniosaw reflected an impurity in belief that was subsequently used as justification for jihād. As Muhammad Bello, the son and successor of 'Uthmān dan Fodio, claimed, many people worshipped spirits that were thought to inhabit trees and rocky outcrops where shrines were located. Many Muslims condemned such practices and even advocated repression and persecution of those who practiced rituals associated with these shrines. Unfortunately, what Gronniosaw recorded is not always clear. Among his claims, he bragged that he was wearing gold on his body when he traveled along the well-established trade route from Borno through the Hausa cities and Borgu to the middle Volta River basin and to Asante.[61] In fact, this was impossible, since gold came from Asante; it was not taken there. More likely, the reference to gold exaggerated his status and thereby made his fall from grace and sale into transatlantic slavery more tragic when in fact he probably was taken to Asante by kola merchants as a young slave for sale. Nonetheless, the sale of slaves to the coast was a complaint of the jihād leadership, even if Gronniosaw was not actually a Muslim. According to the interpretations of the jihād leadership, it was the responsibility of the master and the merchant to establish that someone who was enslaved was not a Muslim, rather than that of the individual slave to prove that he or she was illegally enslaved. The onus of proof also governed the sale of slaves to non-Muslims, including European slavers at the coast, since no one could ever be absolutely certain that an individual was not freeborn.

Muslims were enslaved, nonetheless, and individuals whose freeborn status might be questioned might find themselves enslaved. This was the case of the Hausa slave who became known as Pierre Tamata, who was purchased at Porto Novo or Ouidah by a French merchant sometime in the 1770s or perhaps earlier and taken to France, where he was educated. Tamata then returned to West Africa as an agent for French merchants from La Rochelle and subsequently became the principal merchant at Porto Novo in the 1780s.[62] Whether he was a freeborn Muslim or not, Tamata was a willing collaborator in the slave trade to the French Caribbean and profited from his involvement. Nonetheless, he continued to identify as Muslim, and his son became the imam of the Muslim community in Porto Novo. His descendants still reside in Porto Novo, where a handsome mosque stands as testimony to his historic importance. Very few enslaved Muslims were sent from Porto Novo to the French Caribbean while Tamata was involved in the trade. It is not clear

The Origins of Jihād in West Africa

whether Tamata was responsible for assuring this commercial pattern, but at the same time, Muslims and many others whose allegiance to Islam might have been questionable did leave Porto Novo and other ports in the Bight of Benin, principally for Bahia. Enslaved Muslims were living in Porto Novo in the 1780s and 1790s and apparently in Dahomey as well, where they were also frequently engaged in crafts and in the military.[63]

People who were identified as Hausa constituted a significant community in Bahia by the first decade of the nineteenth century, which confirms the criticisms of the jihād leadership in the interior that questionable sales of slaves to Europeans were taking place. The complaint was a fundamental objection of Muslims.[64] The extent to which slaves were Muslim at the outbreak of the jihād is difficult to establish, although information from Oyo and the Guinea coast, as well as the presence of enslaved Muslims, usually described as "Hausa," "Tapa" (i.e., Nupe), and "Borno" in the Americas, demonstrates that enslaved Muslims were traded south, apparently increasingly so after the 1750s and certainly by the 1780s, when Oyo opened a direct route to the Bight of Benin and established its hegemony over Porto Novo and Badagry as a means of bypassing the route through Dahomey to Ouidah. Trade developed rapidly after 1770, when merchants began to buy slaves at Porto Novo, Badagry, and Lagos as well, and then there were discussions of establishing a French fort at Porto Novo. It was never built, but nonetheless the proposal demonstrates French interest in the area.[65] According to Peter Morton-Williams, Oyo developed the route to Porto Novo by settling slaves in the largely deserted Egbado districts, thereby creating a safe outlet to the coast that bypassed Dahomey, which paid tribute to Oyo but limited Oyo profits from the sale of slaves.[66] As the foremost merchant in Porto Novo, Pierre Tamata was instrumental in promoting Oyo commercial operations in supplying slaves for St. Domingue and other French islands in the Caribbean.[67] In the 1780s and early 1790s Tamata took advantage of his Hausa origin and his education in France to turn his business into a profitable enterprise, his former master "granting him credit to a considerable amount."[68] Muslim merchants took their slave caravans south from the central Bilād al-Sūdān, crossing the Niger at Raka, which was located a few kilometers from the Niger River, near its confluence with the Moshi, and then went to Porto Novo, where Tamata served as their contact.

Many of the slaves who originally came from the central Bilād al-Sūdān were retained in Oyo, in Dahomey, or on the coast itself. By the end of the eighteenth century there was a large Yoruba population in Raka, even though the town was originally Nupe. According to Samuel Johnson, "Nearly all the children of influential Oyo chiefs resided there permanently for the purpose of trade."[69] By the early nineteenth century enslaved Muslims had become a recognized and significant element in the Oyo military, especially the cavalry stationed at Ilorin, and in certain crafts in the Oyo capital.[70] Even as late as 1804, after the demise of the French trade, Porto Novo remained a principal source of slaves coming from Oyo; in a letter from King Hufon to Prince João of Portugal, 16 November 1804, Porto Novo was described as "the port where there is the greatest abundance of captives; the Ayos [Oyo] and Malês [i.e., Muslims] bring them here," clearly along the route from Raka through Oyo.[71] In 1812 Muhammad Bello described this trade in his geographical description of the central Bilād al-Sūdān. "Yarba," by which he meant Oyo, was an

> extensive province, containing rivers, forests, sands, and mountains, as
> also a great many wonderful and extraordinary things. . . . By the side of
> this province there is an anchorage or harbour for the ships of the
> Christians, who used to go there and purchase slaves. These slaves were
> exported from our country, and sold to the people of Yarba [Yoruba],
> who resold them to the Christians.[72]

Bello's comments are instructive. They reveal that the learned Muslim leadership was aware that merchants who inevitably would have been Muslims, since all trade passed through a commercial network that was Muslim, were involved in the sale of slaves to Oyo and hence to Christian merchants on the coast. As reports from the early nineteenth century make clear, merchants traveled overland to Porto Novo from the "country of the Joos [Oyo]," which was "the principal negro nation," passing through the country of the "Anagoos [Anago] and Mahees [Mahi]" but avoiding Dahomey, along "rivers, morasses, and large lakes which intersect the countries between Haoussa and the coast," apparently referring to the lagoons between Porto Novo and Lagos.[73] Indeed, before 1807 Hausa traders "were continually to be met with at Lagos."[74] This was the trade with the Christians that Muslim reformers wanted to stop and that was one of the causes of the jihād in the central Bilād al-Sūdān.

In his discussion of "important matters" in *Masā'il muhimma* (1217/1802), 'Uthmān dan Fodio, also referred to as shaykh, wrote that the sale of any "Fulani" as a slave was strictly forbidden. Writing at Degel, which the Muslims had established in the face of political persecution, the shaykh based his ruling on the long-standing recognition that most Fulbe were Muslims. By this time tension between the followers of dan Fodio and the government of Gobir

The Origins of Jihād in West Africa

had reached an impasse. In a poem written in Fulfulde, *Tabbat hakika*, dan Fodio predicted that "one who enslaves a freeman, he shall suffer torment. The Fire shall enslave him, be sure of that!"[75] In another song he attributed the "troubles" of the central Bilād al-Sūdān to the disregard of freeborn status, condemning any actions that led to the "capture of a free man, not a slave; then follow this with enslavement." His definition of who was a "free man" referred to Muslims.[76] In response to the questions of al-Ḥājj Shisummas ibn Aḥmad, a Tuareg cleric, the shaykh reiterated the criteria for the enslavement of captives, specifically addressing the concerns of freeborn people who had been enslaved and therefore morally and legally could not be enslaved, although their ransom could be demanded and proof of their status required.[77] Similarly, Muhammad Bello in *Miftah al-sadād* also insisted that it was "not lawful to enslave the Fulani," despite the fact that in the Bilād al-Sūdān there were some Fulani living between Katsina and Kano and to the west of Katsina whom Bello did not consider Muslims.[78] Such frequent pronouncements appear to reflect a situation in which the Muslim leadership thought that there was a serious problem with regard to slavery, not specifically with respect to slavery as an institution but with efforts to distinguish who could be enslaved and who should not be enslaved and what had to be done to regulate enslavement.

The various testimonies of 'Uthmān dan Fodio, Muhammad Bello, and others apparently attest to the conditions of wide areas of West Africa. These complaints seem to have been common wherever Fulbe herded their cattle and Muslims like the Sulleibawa settled and began to teach. The inspiration of the Fuuta jihāds in Senegambia and the perceived transformation of political society in those states prompted the spread of resistance and criticism. As the level of education of many leaders demonstrates, there was a preoccupation with learning, political reform, and the demand for rights as Muslims. Protection from enslavement was considered the right of freeborn Muslims and recognition of the integrity of anyone who claimed that status. Slavery and the slave trade were factors in the jihād movement, as was autonomy from the European-dominated Atlantic world.

The first phase of the jihād movement that was concentrated in Senegambia had mixed results. On the one hand, the political boundaries of Fuuta Jalon and Fuuta Toro were relatively limited. Fuuta Toro controlled much of the Senegal River valley until 1796, but its territory was reduced thereafter. Fuuta Jalon was confined to the highlands from where the Senegal, Gambia, and Niger Rivers flowed. Political leadership in Fuuta Jalon was fractured among competing dynasties and rival claimants to succession to the position of *almami*. The regimes of jihād controlled land and concentrated enslaved populations for purposes of production, more so in Fuuta Jalon than in Fuuta Toro. On the other hand, the spread of Islamic education and the consolidation of Muslim societies were important achievements that had a wider impact than in the immediate states of jihād and laid the foundation for the later movement of al-Ḥājj ʿUmar and subsequent leaders who pursued a jihād model of social and political reform.

3 THE JIHĀD OF ʿUTHMĀN DAN FODIO IN THE CENTRAL BILĀD AL-SŪDĀN

The jihād led by ʿUthmān dan Fodio is sometimes called the Fulani jihād because of the predominance of Fulbe in the movement, although the ethnic designation underestimates the importance of Islam. At other times the jihād is referred to as the Sokoto jihād after the capital that was founded on the Rima River in 1809, but again this reference is problematic because Sokoto was often not the seat of government. It is where the tomb of ʿUthmān dan Fodio was located after 1817, but Muhammad Bello actually spent most of his time when he was head of government at his *ribāṭ* (fortified town) at Wurno, to the north of Sokoto, not in the nominal capital. Sokoto is the current site of the palace of the sultan, the direct descendant of the jihād leadership, as well as the capital of one of the states of modern Nigeria. ʿUthmān dan Fodio as *amīr al-Muʾminīn* (commander of the faithful), the *shehu* (Hausa), shaykh (Arabic), *sarkin Musulmi* (Hausa: leader or commander of the Muslims), and other titles of respect demonstrates that complexity in detail is a feature of the jihād and highlights the centrality of religion. How to do justice to this elaborate nomenclature and a political jurisdiction that included thirty emirates and over fifty subordinate emirates exacerbates the problem. Allegiance was initially focused on ʿUthmān dan Fodio as imām, who delegated authority to specific individuals who were given a flag (*tata*), although the actual number of flags that were issued is not clear. The plethora of leaders and their retinues can be confusing, which might explain why Murray Last initially designated the state that was established the "Sokoto Caliphate," a name that was not used at the time.[1] Heinrich Barth did refer to the "Empire of Sokoto" in his informative analysis of the 1850s but also referred to the "empire" as "Sudan."[2] Other accounts usually referred to "Sudan" or "Soudan," as distinct from Borno (Bornu, Bornou), Bagirmi, Wadai, and other sub-Saharan Muslim states.[3]

The centrality of Sokoto to the jihād movement is undisputed, and the date 1804 is considered a turning point in West African history. In the process of establishing an Islamic state, all the Hausa states were overthrown, Borno lost half its territory, and regions astride the Benue River extending into the mountainous districts beyond the headwaters of the Benue and its tributaries were incorporated, while the Oyo Empire collapsed. These dramatic changes can be seen through a comparison of maps of West Africa dating to around 1800 and around 1836 in which the revolutionary transformations are apparent (map 3.1 and map 3.2). As evident in map 3.1, Oyo dominated most of the coast of the Bight of Benin from Badagry and Porto Novo westward to Ouidah, with Dahomey, moreover, a tributary in this period. In 1800 there was a vibrant trade from the Hausa states and Borno to the south, as well as an east-west trade from the Hausa cities to Asante in the Volta basin in the southwest. By 1837 the area had been transformed as large areas were incorporated into the Sokoto Caliphate. Dahomey asserted its independence from Oyo in 1823, and with Oyo's final collapse in 1836, several city-states, including Ibadan and Abeokuta, emerged that successfully resisted further caliphate expansion from the north. Moreover, a reform regime under Muhammad al-Kānimī and his successors replaced the ancient Sayfawa dynasty in Borno, which had lost its western provinces and had to rebuild its capital at Kukawa after Birni Ngazargamu was occupied twice and then destroyed in 1810.

The jihād can be examined on the basis of the following chronological benchmarks: first, the initial phase in the Hausa states of Gobir, Zamfara, Kebbi, Kano, Daura, Katsina, and Zaria between 1804 and 1808 that led to the formation of the Sokoto Caliphate; second, the invasion of Borno in 1808 that was repulsed only in 1810; and third, the extension of jihād to Nupe in 1810, with the subsequent civil wars there and the ascendancy of Malam Dendo in 1819. [4] For comparative purposes, it should be noted that the outbreak of jihād in 1804 coincided with the emergence of Haiti as an independent state in the midst of the Napoleonic Wars. In 1817, upon 'Uthmān dan Fodio's death, the jihād entered a new phase that in many ways continued until 1837 and the end of the first generation of leadership. By then, twenty-eight emirates had been established, as well as the twin capitals at Gwandu and Sokoto. Table 3.1 summarizes key events, leadership, and important results up to 1837. The second benchmark of 1817 was significant because it was not only the year in which 'Uthmān dan Fodio died but the year of local rebellions (*tawaye*) and the

MAP 3.1 Bight of Benin and Central Bilād al-Sūdān 1800.

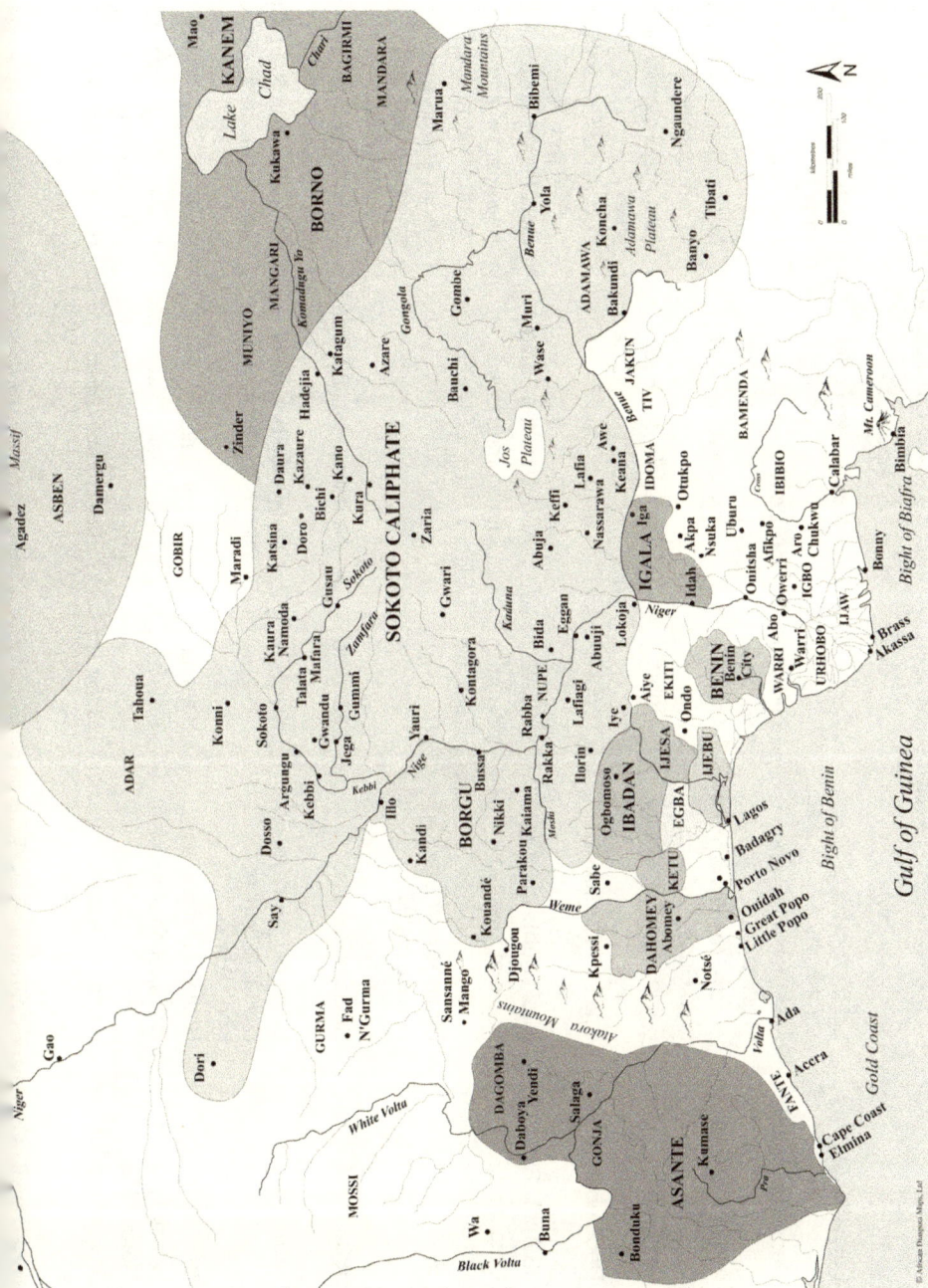

MAP 3.2. Sokoto Caliphate, Borno, and Bight of Benin, 1840.
Source: Henry B. Lovejoy, African Diaspora Maps

TABLE 3.1. **Selected Events in the History of the Sokoto Caliphate, 1800–1837**

Date	Event	Place	Personalities	Consequences
Late 18th century	Establishment of Muslim community	Degel	'Uthmān dan Fodio	Relations with Gobir become strained
December 1803	Gobir forces attack Muslims	Gimbana, Gobir	'Abd al-Salām	Dan Fodio intervenes to free prisoners
21 February 1804	*Hijra*—Muslims withdraw from Gobir	Gudu	'Uthmān dan Fodio	Notification of supporters of forthcoming jihād
June 1804	Battle of Tabkin Kwatto	Gobir	Abdullahi dan Fodio	First major victory of the jihād
December 1804	Battle of Tsuntsuwa	Gobir	'Uthmān dan Fodio	Severe defeat for jihād; siege of Alkalawa fails
13 April 1805	Birnin Kebbi captured	Kebbi	Abdullahi dan Fodio	Fall of first Hausa state
October–November 1805	Battle of Alwassa	Kebbi	Muhammad Bello	Reversal for jihād; allegedly 1,000 Muslims killed
1806	Birnin Yawuri attacked unsuccessfully			Birnin Yawuri agrees to peace, but with independence
1806	Battle of Yandoto	Yandoto	Muhammadu Namoda	Collapse of major Muslim center that opposed jihād
1807	Battle of Dan Yaya; Defeat of Sarkin Kano Alwali	Kano	Sulaymān becomes first Kano emir	Occupation of Kano City; Kano aristocracy dispersed
1807–8	Battle of Dankama	Katsina	'Umar Dallaji	Sarkin Katsina killed
February–March 1808	Occupation of Katsina	Katsina City	'Umar Dallaji becomes emir	Katsina forces withdraw north to Damagaram
3 October1808	Battle of Alkalawa	Gobir	Sarkin Yunfa killed	Gobir collapses

Date	Event	Place	Person/Office	Event
November 1808	Overthrow of Sarkin Zazzau Makau	Zaria	Malam Mūsā becomes emir	Independent Abuja founded
1809	Construction of Sokoto on Rima River	Gobir	Muhammad Bello	Sokoto becomes capital of the jihād state
1808–10	Extension of jihād	Borno	Goni Mukhtār leads jihād	Destruction of Birni Ngazargamu
1810–12	Occupation of Mokwa	Nupe	ʿAbd al-Rahmān (Dan Tsatsa)	Consolidation at Rabba
1817	Death of ʿUthmān dan Fodio	Sokoto		Succession of Muhammad Bello and Abdullahi dan Fodio
1817	Zamfara tawiya	Zamfara	ʿAbd al-Salām	Execution of ʿAbd al-Salām
1817	Ilorin uprising	Oyo	Are Ona Kakanfo Afonja	Muslims in military under leadership of Alimi Sālih
1817	Hamdullahi jihād	Masina	Ahmad Muhammad Lobbo	Established as an independent state, although inspired by the Sokoto jihād
1823	Defeat of Oyo and its allies	Ilorin	ʿAbd al-Salām, son of Alimi Sālih, becomes emir	Establishment of Ilorin as emirate
1836	Destruction of Oyo capital (Katunga)	Oyo	Emir of Ilorin Shiʿta	Final exodus of Oyo Yoruba southward
1837	Death of Muhammad al-Kanimī	Borno	Ibrāhīm becomes ruler of Borno	End of Sayfawa dynasty
1837	Death of Muhammad Bello		Aliyu becomes caliph	Al-Hājj ʿUmar moves west in protest

uprising at Ilorin. 'Abd al-Salām, one of the few jihād leaders who was not Fulbe or Fulani, and his supporters staged an uprising in Zamfara during the succession crisis after the shaykh's death. In crushing the revolt and executing 'Abd al-Salām, the Sokoto aristocracy became more firmly identified as Fulani, which was further reflected in the leadership of the revolt at Ilorin. The jihād continued for the rest of the century, with the establishment of all the emirates and the many subemirates in Fombina, also known as Adamawa, with a capital at Yola.

The jihād began in 1804 after a period of twenty years of increasing friction between 'Uthmān dan Fodio and the government of Gobir and indirectly between 'Uthmān's followers and the governments of the other Hausa states—Kebbi, Katsina, Daura, Kano, and Zaria. The issues concerned the insistence of dan Fodio on reforms in the treatment of Muslims and the promotion of an Islamic society. Initially, the king of Gobir, Sarkin Gobir Bawa Jan Gwarzo, conceded a number of measures to 'Uthmān dan Fodio at a public confrontation in 1785 at Magami that related to the guarantee of freedom to preach, the treatment of Muslims and prisoners, and taxation. This success resulted in further calls for reform in matters of marriage, inheritance, and other aspects of social relations.[5] Dan Fodio toured the upper Sokoto River area between 1788 and 1792 to preach and thereby spread his influence as a reformer. Bawa's death in 1789–90 and the succession of Bawa's brother Yakubu as Sarkin Gobir provided the context for dan Fodio's continuing appeal, but when Yakubu was killed in battle with Katsina in 1794/95, relations with the Gobir government deteriorated rapidly. Yakubu's successor, Nafata (1794/95–1801), revoked the concessions and instead enacted decrees that declared that no one could convert to Islam, but that everyone had to follow the beliefs of his or her parents. He prohibited the use of turbans and veils for women, and Muslims were not allowed to carry weapons. Nafata's successor, Yunfa (1801–8), went further in the attempt to curb the growth of the movement, even attempting to assassinate dan Fodio. In December 1803 Gobir forces attacked and occupied Gimbana, a settlement under 'Abd al-Salām, one of dan Fodio's foremost supporters. The Shehu, as dan Fodio was known, who lived at Degel, intervened and released the prisoners, effectively defying the Gobir government and committing an outright act of treason. On 21 February 1804 dan Fodio withdrew from Degel and moved to Gudu (Sokwai) near Kwonni, across the border and therefore technically outside Gobir.[6] The Muslims considered this migration the *hijra* that preceded jihād, following the pattern of the Prophet Muhammad's original jihād. Sarkin Yunfa sent emissaries requesting that the Shehu return, but negotiations broke down, and fighting began at Matankare on 21 June 1804. The Shehu's forces won a major victory against Yunfa at Tabkin Kwoto, after which the Shehu moved to Magabci, and shortly thereafter war spread to the other Hausa states.

The expanding conflict pitted the established governments of the Hausa states against dan Fodio's community and his sympathizers among Muslims throughout the region. Moreover, dan Fodio was able to gain the support of the major clan leaders of the Fulbe pastoralists on the basis of ethnic solidarity that appealed to dissatisfaction of the Fulbe with government taxation and regulation. Without this support, dan Fodio could not have sustained a military campaign. Dan Fodio formally pursued jihād, issuing flags (*tata*) to key supporters who were charged with undertaking the struggle against the ruling authorities. For example, Moyijo, leader of the Kebbi Fulani, and Muhammad Namoda, leader of the Zamfara Fulani, played major roles in a series of battles in the Sokoto area of the Sokoto, Rima, Kebbi, and Zamfara River valleys, including Matanakari (1804), Tabkin Kwatto (1804), Birnin Konni (1804), Tsuntsuwa (1804), Silame (1805), Kanoma (1805), Birnin Kebbi (1805), Gwandu (1805), Alwassa (1805), Yandoto (1806), Kamba (1806), Fafara (1806), Alkalawa (1808), Tanda (1809), and Illo (1811).[7] Birnin Kebbi fell on 13 April 1805, thereby toppling the first of the major Hausa governments, while the capital of Gobir, Alkalawa, was taken on 3 October 1808, and the city was destroyed. The defeated Hausa of Gobir regrouped first under the leadership of Salihu, then Gumki, and finally 'Alī (1817–35) and continued the struggle against the jihād. The Gobirawa, as people from Gobir are referred to in Hausa, eventually settled at Tsibiri after joining the defeated government of Katsina, thus establishing a pocket of resistance on the northern region of Gobir and Katsina. Nonetheless, the jihād spread northward into the region of Adar and secured the support of the main Tuareg confederations of nomads, particularly the Kel Gress, Kel Ewey, and Itisen, and thereby established hegemony over the region as far as Agadez in the Air Massif.[8] Similarly, the jihād spread eastward to the other Hausa city-states that were tributary to Borno, including Katsina, Daura, Kano, and Zazzau (Zaria).

At the time, the ruler of Kano was Sarkin Kano Alwali, who ineffectively tried to contain the movement but miscalculated the ability of Kano troops to isolate the various Fulbe communities and the clan leaders who controlled considerable resources, particularly horses.[9] The jihād community very early gained control of Rano, Karaye, Bebeji, Tofa, Aujara, Jahun, Dambarta, and Sankara. Similarly, the Fulbe clans who were settled in western and southern

The Jihād of 'Uthmān dan Fodio

Kano, notably the Jobawa at Utai near Wudil under Malam Bakatsine and his brother Malam Saʿīdu, joined the jihād. In the southwest the Fulbe joined the uprising. The Suleibawa clan, the strongest and most numerous Fulbe faction, was centered at Kiru under Malam Jamau, who was able to control the territory from Kiru to Recifa and Kwassallo in northeastern Zazzau. The Danejawa were centered around Zuwa under Yusufu, also known as Malam dan Zabuwa. Bebeji, due east of Kiru, was under Sarkin Fulani Bebeji. The Ba'awa, whose Yolawa segment was considered the most senior of all the Fulbe clans, were further north under Malam ʿAbdurraḥmān Goshi and Malam Jibir. Due north of Kano at Matsidau and Shiddar were the Dambazawa under Muhammadu Dabo Dambazau. The Yerimawa clan under Malam Mayaki dan Tunku was at Dambarta. Taken together, these clans were strategically located near all the main walled towns in the densely populated countryside of the region around Kano City. In Kano City itself several clerical lineages, including the Modibawa or Mundubawa under Suleimanu and the Gyenawa under Malam Dikoyi and Zarawa, were loyal to Shehu dan Fodio. Besides the strong Fulbe support for the jihād, there were also key Hausa supporters, including those under Malam Usuman. One of the leading Hausa judges (*alkali*), Yusufu, who was at Kura, the important dyeing center south of Kano, was another of the leading judges. Alkali Yusufu headed a Hausa faction known as Kunjiya.

The battle at Dan Yaya in early 1807 was a crippling defeat for Sarkin Kano Alwali's forces. Alwali's attempt to confront the Fulbe clans failed, although even then the jihād was far from victorious. Another battle at Burumburum in southern Kano also resulted in defeat for the Kano government. Alwali was forced to flee north toward Damagaram, where he joined the defeated rulers of Katsina and Daura, Sarkin Katsina dan Kasawa and Sarkin Daura Abdu. Even after Alwali's flight, large areas of Kano still were not under the effective control of the jihād armies, including the towns of Rano, Dutse, and Birnin Kudu, the districts of Gezawa, Gabazawa, Girke, Babura, Dambarta, and Kumbotso, and the area around Kura. Finally, in April–May 1807, the jihād forces occupied Kano City, and in 1808 Sarkin Kano Alwali died at Burumburum. Sulaymān became the first emir of Kano, succeeded in 1819 by Ibrāhīm Dabo, both of whom were leading Fulbe clan leaders.

In Katsina the jihād movement erupted under Sarkin Katsina Bawa dan Gima, who had succeeded Sarkin Katsina Gozo (1795–1801) upon the latter's assassination in 1801.[10] Bawa was particularly hostile to the jihād movement. After the Shehu's victory at Tabkin Kwatto in 1804, Sarkin Katsina Bawa openly rejected the Shehu's appeal for reforms and aggressively sought out the Shehu's supporters who had joined the movement. Bawa ordered attacks on the jihād supporters in Katsina, particularly targeting Malam Muhammadu na Alhaji, who had been with the Shehu at Kirari. Bawa's death in 1805 brought Maremawa Muhammadu Tsagarana to the Katsina throne, who continued the active campaign to crush the jihād. In March 1805 Malam Muhammadu na Alhaji, who had been with the Shehu, moved back to Katsina territory to lead the jihād there. Malam 'Umar Dallaji, who would become the first Fulbe emir of Katsina, joined the *jama'a* (the Muslim community) at Yantumaki in October 1805. Sarkin Katsina Maremawa Muhammadu and Sarkin Daura Abdu led expeditions into Kano in the dry season of 1805–6 to help confront the jihād there, but their forces were defeated by dan Tunku at Dawakin Girma near the Katsina border. As should be clear, the jihād was fought during the long dry season each year because of the difficulties of travel during the rainy season, when rivers were often swollen and extensive flooding occurred in many places.

In the dry season of 1806–7 the three Katsina leaders were Malam Muhammadu na Alhaji, who died in 1807, 'Umaru Dumyawa, and 'Umar Dallaji. Together they launched a campaign against Yandoto, located in southern Katsina between Kano and Zamfara and at the time the leading center of opposition among Muslims. Yandoto had long been a center of Islamic learning in the Hausa states, and the opposition of its *'ulamā'* (Muslim scholars) had been a serious problem in expanding support for the jihād. Its fall set the stage for the next phase in Katsina, when jihād forces from Zamfara and Kano came to Katsina to assist in defeating the reigning Katsina dynasty in the battle of Dankama, where the Sarkin Katsina was killed. By February–March 1808 'Umar Dallaji had moved into Katsina as emir. Nonetheless, the jihād was far from over in Katsina territory; Maska and Gozaki in southern Katsina were subdued only in 1809–10.[11]

After the protracted siege of Katsina City in 1807, the defeated *sarki*, Magajin Halidu, fled to Tsirkau in Daura, where he is said to have committed suicide. The new ruler was dan Kasawa, son of a former *sarki*, who led the Katsinawa north to Damagaram, where they met the defeated ruler of Daura, Abdu. Dan Kasawa spent two years in Zinder but then moved to Gafai, near the boundary between Damagaram and Katsina, where he remained for the next eight to ten years. While dan Kasawa was at Gafai, many Katsina Hausa joined him, although there is no evidence of counterattacks against Katsina during this period. At this time Maradi was the northern province of Katsina, under a Fulani official. Its territory stretched from Tsibiri to Damagaram, north of Fulani-controlled Daura.[12] About 1821 dan Kasawa staged a revolt in Maradi with considerable local support and took not only Maradi but also Garabi, Maraka, Ruma, and Zandam, thus freeing a large section of north-western Katsina from jihād rule. Dan Kasawa received help from Gobir, Daura, and some Tuareg. When he died in 1831, the independence of Maradi had been secured. In 1835 Muhammad Bello inflicted a severe defeat on dan Kasawa's successor, dan Mari (1835–43) and his Gobir allies, who had also set-tled at Maradi. The struggle centered on Ruma, which the jihād forces turned into a wilderness. Athough the Gobir forces were at Maradi, they agreed to move to a nearby location, Tsibiri, a few kilometers west of Maradi. Despite repeated attempts, Caliph 'Aliyu Babba (1842–59) of Sokoto failed to take Tsibiri and Maradi, and thereafter Maradi posed a continuing threat to the caliphate. Under the leadership of dan Baskore (1854–75), Maradi allegedly conducted eighty-three raids against caliphate territory.[13] This vulnerability to sudden raiding continued for the rest of the century, necessitating the maintenance of walled towns throughout Katsina, Zamfara, Kano, and northern Zaria.

In Daura, Malam Ishi'aku became the jihād leader; he had taught the children of the reigning Daura monarch, Sarkin Gwari 'Abdū, but when the jihād broke out, he went to Degel to be with the Shehu.[14] He was given a flag with instructions to pursue the jihād in Daura. When Daura fell in the dry season of 1805–6, Sarkin Gwari and the Hausa leadership retreated to Dam-agaram and eventually established two independent enclaves, one at Zango and the other at Baure. 'Abdū had been given the name Sarkin Gwari because he married a Gwari woman; it was a nickname of contempt. When the exiled Katsina *sarki* committed suicide at Tsirkau, a Daura vassal town, the Daura forces were forced to retreat to Damagaram with the exiles from Katsina. Sar-kin Gwari had appealed to Borno for aid, but none came, allegedly because of famine in Borno. Thereafter, 'Abdū's whereabouts are a bit confusing; he spent nine years at Miriya before moving to Falke, Babban Ruwa, and finally Kalgo, where he remained for four years. The court continued to migrate, settling at Sallewa ta Kuykuyo for six years and six months. Then 'Abdū moved to Yekuwa, about forty kilometers east of Daura City, where he marshaled sufficient support to reestablish control over much of Daura territory. He died there, probably in 1825–26, and was succeeded by his brother, Lu-kudi, who reigned from 1825 to 1854, initially jointly with Nūḥu, the son of Sarkin Gwari 'Abdū, who succeeded fully in his own right in 1854. As is clear from this chronology, the exiled government of Daura preserved the state structure but had no firm capital and no firm territorial base.

In Zaria, 'Uthmān dan Fodio's circular letter calling on the Hausa governments to reform reached Sarkin Zazzau Isiaku Jatau in July 1804.[15] Isiaku accepted the Shehu's appeal, but when he died in November 1806, his son and successor, Makau, repudiated the agreement. The Shehu then appointed Malam Mūsā to lead the jihād in Zaria with the support of troops from Zamfara and elsewhere. Malam Mūsā was a Fulbe cleric who came from the town of Malle, south of Timbuktu, and had studied under the Shehu. It was unusual for someone to receive a flag who was not from the area, but apparently the Shehu did not think that there was any local Fulbe leader in Zaria with the credentials to confront the Hausa dynasty. There were several Fulbe lineages located in Zaria territory; near present-day Kaduna were the Bornawa, led by Yamusa and his brother Bapaiyo and the Suleibawa, under Malam Kilba and his son Audusallami. There were other Suleibawa at Kwassallo and Ricifa to the northeast of Zaria. Mūsā was successful in fashioning a coalition and defeated Makau in December 1808, forcing the Hausa government to retreat southward, where Makau established a new base at Abuja. Malam Mūsā ruled at Zaria until his death in 1821.

The Zaria jihād affected a wide region largely to the south of Birnin Zaria. Vassal towns were conquered or established at Keffi, Jema'a, Doma, and later Kwotto, southeast of Keffi. Lere was founded to the east of Zaria, while the non-Muslim Gwari of Kuriga were subdued. Other vassal states in the south included Kajura and Kauru; in the west were Gwari at Lapai and Kusheriki. Karigi had a similar status in the north of Zaria. Zaria forces raided as far as Wukari in Jukun country. Initially Zaria ruled Lapai and Lafia, but at local request to Sokoto, Lafia was transferred to Bauchi, and Lapai was later placed under Bida.

The death of Malam Mūsā created a succession crisis that was resolved through the intervention of Sokoto. Over the course of the rest of the century, four different Zaria factions came to power, effectively rotating the emirship. The four lineages were the different Fulbe lineages, the Bornawa, Suleibawa, Katsinawa, and Mūsā's family, known as the Mallawa. Yamusa of the Bornawa, who ruled from 1821 to 1834, emerged as the strongest Fulbe leader under Mūsā, and by the end of Mūsā's rule they were running the state almost jointly. Mūsā never assumed the title of emir, governing simply as *malam*, or cleric, and shunning the title of emir or *sarki*. Yamusa continued this tradition, which differed from those in all the other emirates. The chief opposition was Jaye of the Suleibawa, who became *madaki*, and the presumed successor, and when he died, his son Hamada became *madaki* and the chosen successor. On the death of Yamusa, the succession had to go either to the

Mallawa or the Bornawa, but to avoid conflict, the decision on succession was referred to Sokoto, and Muhammad Bello selected 'Abdulkarīm of the Katsinawa lineage as a compromise candidate.

By attacking the Hausa dependencies of Borno, the jihād leadership was on a collision course with Borno itself, which had been the imperial overlord of Katsina, Daura, Kano, and Zazzau. As previously noted, Borno was ineffective in providing support for any of the regimes in those states and also was far from successful in stemming the eastward drift of jihād into Borno territory or to its south into Mandara and the Benue River basin.[16] A titled official, Galadima Dunama, located at Nguru, administered the western portions of Borno and the large district that would become portions of the emirates of Hadejia, Katagum, Jema'are, and Misau. There were three principal Fulbe leaders in the area: Bi Abdur, Lerlima, and Ibrāhīm Zaki. Bi Abdur was centered near Hadejia and was a functionary under Galadima Dunama, but he sent his brother to the Shehu to get a flag, probably in 1805. They attacked Hadejia and Auyo to the southwest of Hadejia and drove Dunama from Nguru in 1807. To the south, the Fulbe were centered at Deya under two learned men, al-Bukhārī, who died before hostilities began, and Goni Mukhtār, who then assumed the leadership of the southern Fulbe. Mai Aḥmad, the ruler of Borno, sent several expeditions under his official, the Kaigama, in an attempt to subjugate Goni Mukhtār, but the Borno forces were defeated each time. Mai Ahmad then issued a drastic decree ordering all Fulbe in Borno to be killed, which prompted a Fulbe exodus in great numbers toward the south and west. Other Fulbe from Borno joined Buba Yero, who had already been conquering larger areas of what became Bauchi and Gombe even before the jihād had begun. At this point, according to Louis Brenner, 'Uthmān dan Fodio was not fully aware that the Fulbe in western Borno had staged an uprising against Mai Ahmad.[17] In *Infāq al-Maysūr*, Bello's account of the jihād, Borno receives scant mention in this period.

Mai Ahmad sent repeated expeditions against those Fulbe under Bi Abdur and Lerlima and also against Goni Mukhtār. Lerlima was overcome, but Bi Abdur not only repulsed the Borno attacks but also succeeded in killing the Galadima. Thereupon the Fulbe forces made deep raids into Borno, spreading terror and destruction and creating countless refugees. When Bi Abdur died in early 1808, Ibrāhīm Zaki became the leader of the Fulbe forces and mounted a campaign to take the Borno capital at Birni Ngazargamu. Although the first assault was repulsed, he succeeded in taking the city late in 1808, ransacking the palace and sending an enormous amount of booty to Sokoto.

According to Brenner, "All the territory west and south of Birni Gazargamu had been laid waste."[18] Mai Aḥmad was forced to flee and regroup. In doing so, he turned to Muhammad al-Amīn b. Muhammad al-Kānimī, who was a respected scholar residing at Ngala, southwest of Lake Chad. Mai Aḥmad was now old, and unwisely going against the custom that prevented succession until after the death of the *mai*, he passed the kingship to his son, Dunama (not to be confused with the deceased Galidima of Nguru). Aḥmad died a few months later, but the consequences of the unusual transfer of power would affect Borno politics subsequently because it could be considered an illegal measure. In approaching Muhammad al-Kānimī, Dunama effectively admitted that his government could not survive without additional leadership. Al-Kānimī had spent the first years of his life in Murzuk in the Sahara and had studied in Tripoli. In the 1790s he went on pilgrimage with his father, who died before they could return. Al-Kānimī remained in the East for about ten years and returned to Borno through Wadai and Darfur. His ascendancy in Borno rested on the recognition of his status as an al-ḥājj, having returned from pilgrimage to Mecca, and as a learned scholar and teacher.

When al-Kānimī became involved in Borno politics in 1809, the jihād had already spread to the region of Ngala and Mandara, Borno's southern province. Muhammad Wabi was the Fulbe leader in the Ngala area and joined the jihād, but al-Kānimī defeated him in battle. Al-Kānimī was then asked to help liberate Birni Ngazargamu in early 1809, which was accomplished, and the Fulbe leader Goni Mukhtār was killed. Mai Dunama then had to pacify the countryside to the west of Birni Ngazargamu that had been destroyed. By then, Ibrāhīm Zaki's capital was at Katagum, now one of the emirates under Sokoto. Ibrāhīm Zaki not only repulsed Mai Dunama's army but also forced Borno's retreat eastward, while Goni Mukhtār's son and successor, Muhammad Manga, regrouped the Fulbe to the south. Nonetheless, by this time al-Kānimī had become the principal supporter of Mai Dunama and was given an extensive fief in the Ngurno area, with its largely Kanembu population, as a reward. Al-Kānimī also had wide appeal among Shuwa Arabs.

Because of Dunama's failure to stem the jihād, his court organized a coup d'état, claiming that his succession had been illegal, and instead installed his uncle, Muhammad Ngileruma, who then built a capital at Birni Kafela, only a few kilometers from Ngurno, al-Kānimī's stronghold. However, Ngileruma was on the throne for only three or four years before al-Kānimī deposed him and reappointed Dunama as *mai*. Al-Kānimī was then given even more land stretching from Ngala to Ngurno, which consolidated his position among a following that was largely non-Kanuri but included Kanembu, Shuwa, Tibu, Tuareg, and Bagirmi, the main subordinate populations in the Borno state. Under al-Kānimī's leadership, Borno was able to remain independent of the Sokoto jihād, but at considerable cost. The Sayfawa dynasty in the end was eliminated, with al-Kānimī and then his son becoming supreme ruler with the title of Shehu, the honorific by which 'Uthmān dan Fodio was also known. Moreover, the capital of Borno was eventually moved from Birni Kafela to Kukawa, which al-Kānimī had founded in 1814.[19]

The removal of the Zaria dynasty to Abuja to the south near the confluence of the Niger and the Benue Rivers coincided with the outbreak of jihād in Nupe in 1810–12. 'Uthmān dan Fodio recognized the Nupe cleric 'Abd al-Raḥmān al-Nufawi also known as dan Tsatsa (d. 1829), as the leader by issuing him a flag. 'Abd al-Raḥmān visited the Shehu and pledged his submission. In 1813 Muhammad Bello confirmed his support in *Infāq al-Maysūr*, noting after an early campaign that "there returned our people [to Sokoto] who had gone to Nupeland to help 'Abd al-Raḥmān al-Nufawi against the army of Nupe. And indeed they fulfilled their trust. We put forward our best endeavour and brought back what there was to bring [i.e., booty]."[20] Although 'Abd al-Raḥmân occupied the Nupe capital, Mokwa, for six months, he was unable to hold it and had to appeal for external assistance from Sokoto.[21] The Nupe king, Etsu Yikanko, was killed but was succeeded by Jimada. 'Abd al-Raḥmān supported Majiya for the position of *etsu*, however, and Majiya's appointment was eventually achieved after Jimada was killed at Gbara on the Kaduna River near the confluence with the Niger. However, after the death of 'Uthmān dan Fodio in 1817 and the division of the caliphate into two spheres, Malam Dendo, who was a Fulbe leader, rose to prominence among the Muslims. 'Abd al-Raḥmān owed his allegiance to 'Uthmān dan Fodio, but the Gwandu regime became the direct overlord of Nupe after 1817 and favored Malam Dendo. When British diplomat Hugh Clapperton was at Kulfo in 1826, he was in contact with 'Abd al-Raḥmān, the "learned malam," whose influence was much reduced, although he was still revered as a pioneer of jihād and a saint.[22] By then the shifting politics of Nupe had placed him at odds with Dendo, and 'Abd al-Raḥmān was murdered three years later. Michael Mason has established conclusively the complicity of Dendo in the assassination, suggesting a plot to undermine indigenous Nupe leadership.[23]

Because of shifting alliances, the course of the jihād was confusing. Nupe was now involved in a protracted civil war that lasted until 1857, when Bida was finally established as the capital of a Nupe emirate.[24] The various candidates for succession to the Nupe kingship sought the support of the jihād leadership but then attempted to limit the influence of the Muslim leadership, which prevented an easy transition. Majiya, who was located at Zugurma, had been Dendo's student and had initially supported ʿAbd al-Raḥmān in 1810–12. He consolidated his rule after Jimada was killed.[25] Majiya then established his capital at Raba on the Niger.[26] Jimada's son Idrīsu and the supporters of Jimada fled to Ilorin. Majiya attempted to consolidate his position as *etsu* between 1820 and 1824 by turning on his Muslim allies, who also moved to Ilorin. Malam Dendo then formed an alliance with Idrīsu and the exiled Nupe faction. Majiya attacked Ilorin in 1823–24 but was defeated and driven back across the Niger River. Malam Dendo occupied Raba, while Idrīsu was now recognized as *etsu*.

In the course of this uncertainty, the two small emirates of Lafiagi and Agaie were established on the south side of the Niger around 1824. To make matters even more confusing, Idrīsu then turned on the Muslims and after 1825 tried to drive them out of Raba, which forced Dendo to reestablish an alliance with Majiya. In early 1826 Gwandu sent an army to support Dendo, and the Gwandu forces returned with one thousand slaves and four thousand gowns, Nupe being a center of textile production.[27] When Clapperton entered Nupe in April 1826, Idrīsu had just been driven out of Raba, and it looked as if Majiya was firmly in control of the *etsu* throne at Jangi, with Dendo behind the scenes in Raba nearby. Although the allied forces of Ilorin Muslims had supported Idrīsu in defeating Majiya, forcing Majiya to withdraw to Tabria in 1825, Dendo changed his mind and apparently summoned his former student to Raba for his submission. Meanwhile, Idrīsu regrouped, with the support of Beni river traders who had access to firearms from the Niger River trade, and persisted in his bid for the throne. Nonetheless, Majiya reigned until his death around 1841.[28] Malam Dendo died in 1833, but the succession to the emirship was contested. Usman Zaki became emir at Raba, but his brother Masaba refused to recognize him and settled at Lade near Lafiagi on the south of the Niger. Civil war continued, now among the Muslims, not the claimants to the Nupe throne. A settlement was reached only in 1857 with the foundation of Bida as the capital of a united Nupe emirate.[29]

The uprising in the military at Ilorin in 1817 and the subsequent incorporation of Ilorin as an emirate into the Sokoto Caliphate in 1823 has special significance in linking the jihād movement as a major event in Atlantic history with the age of revolutions. The concentration of Muslims in the military undermined Oyo's hegemony in the interior of the Bight of Benin and made it clear that jihād was a continuous affair of expansion that combined

The Jihād of ʿUthmān dan Fodio

ethnicity and religion in a tenuous union. Ilorin formally became an emirate in 1823 when the son of Alimi Ṣāliḥ, ʿAbd al-Salām, became its first emir, reporting to Abdullahi dan Fodio at Gwandu and not Muhammad Bello at Sokoto. Meanwhile, Dahomey, tributary to Oyo since the 1730s, asserted its independence at the same time, thereby placing Oyo in a delicate position that relied on support from Borgu and involved Oyo in the confrontation in Nupe. The results were disastrous, as reflected in the emigration to the south of refugees who wanted nothing to do with Islam, founding new centers at Ibadan, at Abeokuta, and elsewhere.[30]

Ilorin was particularly important because of the role it played in the collapse of Oyo and the subsequent migration of Yoruba to Cuba and Brazil and indirectly to Sierra Leone and Trinidad, as well as the transformation of much of the interior of the Bight of Benin. The attempt of Are Anakamfo to achieve autonomy within Oyo by using his position as general of the *alafin*'s army to force the hand of the Oyo aristocracy at the capital unintentionally released the forces of jihād. Traditionally, the *alafin* could not personally go to war but had to depend on the titled officials of the Oyo Mesi, the council of state, which resulted in periodic tension and outright crisis. In the middle of the eighteenth century Basorun Gaha, the leading official of the Oyo Mesi, usurped power from the *alafin*. If the Oyo Mesi voted against the *alafin*'s continuation, the *alafin* had to commit suicide, a proviso that Basorun Gaha manipulated to his advantage several times until the rise of Alafin Abiodun, who reigned until 1789. Because the *alafin* could not appear on the battlefield, Abiodun promoted his military position through an army stationed at Ilorin under a subordinate official with the title *are ona kakanfo*, which Afonja held at the time of the uprising in 1817. However, Afonja's political ambitions backfired because the 1817 uprising was virtually a military coup d'état, so that Afonja remained in power, but power increasingly shifted to the proponents of jihād. Most of the military were enslaved young Muslims who had come from farther north and were Muslims and hence were susceptible to the appeal of ʿUthmān dan Fodio. Under the leadership of Alimi Ṣāliḥ, the Muslim faction steadily promoted the cause of Islamic uprising. Bands of Fulbe roamed the countryside, attacking villages and enslaving people. Conflict between Oyo and Ijesha over control of the trade routes to the coast erupted into warfare, known as the Owu wars, that led to the destruction of the Owu province and the migration of refugees to the south.[31]

Because of the jihād in Oyo, the capital district of Oyo was completely abandoned by 1836 through flight and slavery; the previously heavily populated region around the capital was transformed into a virtual desert, which it remains largely to this day. The conflict is often referred to as the Yoruba wars in the scholarly literature and is sometimes even characterized as a civil war; it is clear that the establishment of Ilorin as a recognized part of the Sokoto Caliphate was more than a civil disturbance, and, even more relevant, that the jihād was primarily responsible for the collapse of the Oyo state and the concurrent and subsequent warfare that resulted in the enslavement of the overwhelming majority of people who became part of the Yoruba diaspora.[32] Hence the resulting activities of Yoruba in both Cuba and Brazil have to be considered, in my opinion, as an outgrowth of the jihād movement of West Africa, not merely an extension of slave resistance that was associated with the age of revolutions. The complexities of ethnicity and the struggle that arose from religious conflict affect an interpretation of the Malês uprising in Bahia and also Yoruba resistance in Cuba and Muslim unrest in Sierra Leone.[33] By the time of Muhammad Bello's death in 1837, Ilorin had successfully established its supremacy over the northern Yoruba country under Fulani leadership, while opposition to jihād was firmly established at the new Yoruba centers to the south, especially at Ibadan. Where Oyo had once controlled an extensive part of Yorubaland that stretched to the sea at Porto Novo and Badagry and included Dahomey, its port at Ouidah, Mahi country, and parts of Borgu, its territory was steadily whittled away by 1836.

Bishop Samuel Crowther, himself of Oyo origin, attributed the destruction of Oyo towns in the 1820s to Muslims, whom he called Fulani even though many spoke Yoruba, and whose origins beyond that cannot always be determined.[34] Similarly, Clapperton and his servant, John Lander, reported the destruction of towns in the 1820s, which they attributed to Muslims, whom they also identified as Fulani. These accounts are based on their personal observations while traveling from Badagry to Katunga, the capital of Oyo, in 1826–27 and on observations by Lander and his brother in 1830. As Clapperton and the Lander brothers seem to have understood, the degree to which people spoke more than one language and the role of Islam as a revolutionary force in Oyo made ethnic labeling complicated. Their description of a corridor of destruction extending from the coast along the main commercial corridor to the heart of Oyo and the capital at Katunga included reports on Owu.[35] Other contemporary sources confirm the complexity of ethnic identification and the importance of religion as a decisive factor. Crowther met several "Yoruba" soldiers in 1841 and 1857 in the service of the Nupe emirates. They spoke fluent Yoruba but also spoke Hausa, Nupe, and Fulfulde, and because they were in the employ of the Muslim emirates, they were referred to as Fulani, as they were known in Hausa.[36]

There are two theaters of jihād that remain to be discussed: first, the regions of the Benue River basin to the east and south of the central Hausa emirates, which were under Sokoto after the division of the caliphate in 1817, and second, the Niger River valley and the area to the west of the caliphate's capital districts, which paid homage to Gwandu. The eastern portion included Gombe, Bauchi, and, above all in importance, Adamawa. The region was to the south of Borno and with some exceptions, especially in the Jukun area, had few centralized states and was largely devoid of a Muslim population except for itinerant merchants and wandering Fulani pastoralists. By contrast, the region under Gwandu to the west consisted of a series of small emirates, with the exception of Masina, which in any event became the independent jihād state of Hamdullahi after 1817, although it maintained diplomatic relations with Sokoto. Historically, most of this region had once been part of the Songhay Empire.

Buba Yero, leader of the Fulbe in the Gongola River valley, had already been conquering territory in what became Bauchi and Gombe even before the jihād.[37] There were no centralized states in this region, and hence when the jihād was declared in 1804, he quickly pledged his allegiance. He then continued his campaign to subdue the various decentralized ethnic groups in the region and fashion a state centered on the town of Gombe in the Gongola River valley. He also issued flags of his own, most notably to Hammarwa, the head of the Fulbe who had migrated from Kiri in the Gongola valley, in 1812. Hammarwa specifically targeted the Jukun state of Kona that straddled the Benue, with its capital at Akuro. Muri was founded as the capital of the Fulbe Kiri in 1817. Hammarwa's campaigns against the dispersed non-Muslim ethnic groups resulted in gradual expansion from Muri to the south and southwest. However, Hammarwa fell out with his overlord in Gombe, a punitive expedition was sent to Muri in 1833, and Hammarwa and his son were both executed. Thereafter, Sokoto intervened and established Muri as a separate emirate.[38]

Bauchi emerged as an emirate in the region east of the Jos Plateau, which, like Gombe, was an area without centralized states and whose population was almost entirely non-Muslim. In 1804 'Uthmān dan Fodio gave a flag to one of his students, Isiyaku, who was from the area where Bauchi would emerge as an emirate, but Isiyaku apparently died before reaching Kano on his way to implement the campaign. The question of who should succeed him was referred back to the Shehu, who opted to give the leadership to Isiyaku's student Yakubu (1753–1833), who had been with Isiyaku at Degel studying with the

JIHĀD IN WEST AFRICA DURING THE AGE OF REVOLUTIONS

Shehu. Yakubu was unusual in that he was not Fulbe but came from the Gerawa, who were generally not Muslims, although Yakubu's father and grandfather were Muslims and had been good friends of Isiyaku. Yakubu was the only person who was not Fulbe to become the head of one of the emirates; the other two leading non-Muslims, ʿAbd al-Raḥmān of Nupe and ʿAbd al-Salām of Zamfara, never attained that distinction. Yakubu raided as far as the Benue River, conquering Lafia Beriberi, the Wurkan hills, parts of the Gongola River valley, and Leri. His son Ibrāhīm succeeded him and had to face revolts of Ningi, Dass, and Duguri.

Shehu dan Fodio appointed Moddibbo Adama as the supreme leader for the region south of the Benue River, which was another region without centralized states, and in reference to his key role the emirate became known as Adamawa, although it was also known as Fombina, or the lands of the south in Fulfulde. Adama marshaled the Fulbe in this area to form military units and found towns that were then recognized as part of the emirate. In this way the Fulbe established Garoua, Maroua, Rai, Chebowa, and Gurin and later Ngaoundere, Tibati, Kontcha, and Banyo. Adama also had to navigate rivalries among the Fulbe clans that required the use of force, as in conflicts between Rai Bouba and Yola and of Tibati with Ngaoundere and Yola. Adama ruled from 1809 to 1847 and was succeeded by Lawal, who ruled from 1847 to 1872.[39] As head of Adamawa, Adama was referred to as *lamido*, Fulfulde for "ruler," rather than as emir.[40] Adama received his flag from the Shehu in March 1809 and in 1810–11 led the campaign against Mandara and Borno, but failing to consolidate his position there, he subsequently issued over forty flags himself and by 1825–30 was responsible for founding Ngaoundere, Banyo, Kontcha, and Tignere on the Mambila Plateau. In 1841 he established his capital at Yola on the Benue River.[41] Adamawa or Fombina, with an area of 100,000 square kilometers, had forty subemirates, the most important of which were Tibati, Ngaoundere, Rai-Buba, Maroua, Banyo, Garoua, and the capital at Yola.[42]

In contrast to the expansive extension of the jihād to the southeast of the Hausa heartland of the Sokoto Caliphate, the consolidation of the emirates to the west of Gwandu was small scale, although it nonetheless encompassed a territory along the Niger River and to the west of the Niger that was still of considerable size. Eight emirates were established west of Gwandu, mostly in the Niger River valley. Nine small emirates were established west of Gwandu, mostly in the Niger River valley, although Liptako, with its capital at Dori, was located 120 km west of the Niger River.

The Jihād of ʿUthmān dan Fodio

The deep concern expressed by the Sokoto leadership over the issue of slavery has prompted Humphrey Fisher to suggest that 'Uthmān dan Fodio may have been a "Muslim Wilberforce," which is a useful comparison in attempting to provide a perhaps shocking equation of thinking over the issues of slavery. According to Fisher, "One of the major causes of the *jihād* which began in Hausaland in 1804 was the increasing enslavement of free Muslims," which 'Uthmān dan Fodio and his son Muhammad Bello in particular found alarming.[43] Whether or not the incidence of enslavement had increased in the years before 1804 is uncertain, although slaves from the central Bilād al-Sūdān became more common in the export ledgers of the Bight of Benin in the last third of the eighteenth century than previously, which suggests such an increase.[44] Inevitably those who were enslaved included respectable Muslims who somehow had been enslaved. Whether or not Fisher's comparison of Wilberforce and dan Fodio stands up to scrutiny is another matter, considering that Wilberforce was hardly sympathetic to conditions in Africa or that dan Fodio wanted to abolish the slave trade with Christians and had very little interest in the Atlantic world otherwise.

'Uthmān dan Fodio explained the underlying principles of the movement in *Kitāb al-farq*, which were to eliminate social injustices introduced by oppressive governments, to combat *bid'a* (innovation), and to promote the full observance of Islam.[45] In his *Tanbīh al-ikhwān 'alā aḥwāl al-Sūdān* dan Fodio wrote, "As for the sultans [of Hausaland], they are undoubtedly unbelievers, even though they may profess the religion of Islam, because they practice polytheistic rituals and turn people away from the path of God and raise the flag of worldly kingdoms above the banner of Islam. All this is unbelief according to the consensus of opinions."[46] As the history of Fuuta Bundu, Fuuta Jalon, and Fuuta Toro demonstrates, the jihād of 1804 drew on earlier influences that covered a region from modern Dakar to Khartoum in the Nile valley. The model of Islamic rule was based on a form of government that owed inspiration to the *ṣūfī* brotherhood, or *ṭarīqa*, the Qādiriyya, and in turn inspired the Islamic states associated with the Tījāniyya after 1838 and, by the end of the century, the Mahdiyya as well. Of course, this model stands in sharp contrast to the tendency toward republicanism and constitutional monarchy that characterized the age of revolutions studied by Hobsbawm and others. Nonetheless, the revolutionary impact altered the political landscape, the basic components of society, and the economy in ways that fundamentally shaped West Africa.

The ideas that informed the jihād movement were widespread, as reflected in the writings of Aḥmad b. al-Qāḍī b. Abī Bakr b. Yūsuf b. Ibrāhīm, also known as al-Timbuktāwī, in 1813. Aḥmad al-Timbuktāwī was a Fulbe cleric from Timbuktu, as his name indicates, who performed the pilgrimage in the first decade of the nineteenth century. On his return home in 1813, he had occasion to observe the religious practices of the black African community in Tunis, which consisted primarily of enslaved individuals from south of the Sahara who were identified according to the towns and places from which they had been dispatched across the Sahara, such as Kano, Katsina, Timbuktu, and Borno. These identifications do not allow a determination of whether they had been Muslims before their enslavement, but as far as al-Timbuktāwī was concerned, they were not practicing Islam in a manner that met his approval. His comments, therefore, provide a perspective on how Muslims, especially Fulbe, viewed society in sub-Saharan Africa and thereby justified jihād. In his opinion, the blacks of Tunis were involved in spirit-possession cults, known as *bori* in Hausa, which warranted their enslavement (plate 8). He considered *bori* a form of religious practice that violated the tenets of Islam. On the basis of what he saw in Tunis, he asserted that:

> The it is disobedient to be silent on *fitna* [dissension] because that is among matters that require fulfilling conditions of *al-'amr bi'al-ma'arūf* [ordering what is good and forbidding what is evil] since that is plain polytheism, and resisting polytheism is a *jihād*, and *jihād* is incumbent even if it causes self-destruction or destruction of the wealth.[47]

Consequently, al-Timbuktāwī believed that the blacks of Tunis were rightly enslaved (plate 9).[48] Adhering to similar ideas, 'Uthmān dan Fodio in turn inspired a generation and more to oppose *bori*, and although *bori* were never eliminated, as al-Timbuktāwī and 'Uthmān dan Fodio might have wished, a Muslim state based on Sharī'a law was established.

The jihād movement provides the context for analyzing how political change in West Africa mirrored the Atlantic world. One of the legitimizing claims for the necessity of jihād was that political authorities were engaged in what was considered illegal enslavement and, in addition, were selling Muslims into the transatlantic slave trade. The complaints came to a peak in 1804 when the government of Gobir ordered the seizure of followers of 'Abd al-Salām, one of 'Uthmān dan Fodio's most fervent disciples, and thereby directly challenged the freedom of dan Fodio's followers. The government of Gobir alleged that many of those who were seized were slaves who had fled their masters, but from the perspective of the nascent jihād movement, the followers were Muslims whose freeborn status was assumed, although it is impossible to know whether this was true. The thin line between claims of freedom on the basis of adherence to Islam and status at birth were interpreted to the benefit of the claimant; it was the responsibility of slave masters to establish otherwise. As the scholarly literature on the jihād movement makes clear, slavery was a factor in discussions of religion and ideology and pervaded the standards of resistance and aims at reform. When ʿUthmān dan Fodio declared jihād in 1804, he could not have known about developments in Brazil and the Caribbean, and surely he could not have known that in the same year Haiti became an independent state. Nonetheless, there was deep concern among the Muslim intellectual and political leadership about the fact that enslaved Muslims were being sold through Oyo to the Bight of Benin for sale to Europeans, and that some of them actually were sent to St. Domingue because of the French trade at Porto Novo and the commercial involvement of Pierre Tamata as an agent for French merchants, as discussed previously.

The enslavement of freeborn Muslims and their sale to Christians who were involved in the Atlantic trade was of particular concern to Muhammad Bello. Bello specifically condemned the sale of slaves to Oyo, which was clearly articulated in his manifesto and history, *Infāq al-Maysūr*, which he finished in 1812. In his reference to Oyo, which he called "Yoruba," he noted, "The people of this country used to receive slaves from this country of ours, and they used to sell them to the aforementioned Christians. I am mentioning this affair so that you will not buy [or sell] a Muslim slave from anyone who brings one there. It is because of this that the calamity is general."[49] The preoccupation with the illegal enslavement of Muslims was clearly expressed in the debate between Muhammad Bello and Muhammad al-Kānimī of Borno (plate 10), as discussed in *Infāq al-Maysūr* and in an ongoing correspondence between the two rulers for another decade. The failure to resolve the issues in dispute ultimately resulted in war between Sokoto and Borno in 1826–27.[50] The debate over the enslavement of Muslims was one of legitimizing the necessity of jihād but did not extend to the enslavement of non-Muslims or of nonbelievers and apostates in general. The issues that Bello and al-Kānimī addressed related to Islamic law and the regulation of the institution of slavery. Far different from the issues behind resistance to slavery in the Americas, the concern in the Sokoto Caliphate was over the nature of the Muslim state and the role of the state in protecting freeborn Muslims. The jihād rapidly overthrew the principal Hausa governments of Gobir, Kebbi, Kano, Katsina, and Zaria by 1808 and then spread to Borno in the east after 1808[51] and to Nupe in the south by 1810.[52] From the central Bilād al-Sūdān the shock waves were sent south into Oyo and Yorubaland after 1817 and especially after Ilorin became an emirate within the Sokoto Caliphate in 1823. The issue of slave or free status preoccupied the jihād leadership.

In accusing the governments of the various Hausa states of enslaving free Muslims and thereby providing slaves for southern export, 'Uthmān dan Fodio encouraged slaves to escape or otherwise assert their Islamic identities.[53] Hence the proponents of jihād found justification for their actions in protecting Muslims and thereby directly challenged the authority of all the governments of the region. Many enslaved Muslims took advantage of the jihād to assert their freedom after 1804, often by fleeing to the camps of the jihād armies, where they sought protection. To enforce the Gobir decree, as 'Uthmān dan Fodio complained, "The Sultan of Gobir attacked the Sheikh's people; they fled, for they were afraid. The Gobir army followed them and captured some and slew others, seizing children and women, and selling them in our midst."[54] It is likely that many of those who were taken prisoner were in fact people who were considered by the Gobir authorities to have escaped from slavery. 'Abd al-Salām, one of the Shehu's Hausa supporters, led a raid on the Gobir detachment, freeing the Muslim captives and clearly demonstrating active rebellion against Gobir authority.[55] Although it was not always possible to prevent the sale of prisoners who were Muslims, Abdullahi dan Fodio criticized some of his fellow Fulani Muslims in Tazyīn al-waraqāt (1813) as "sellers of free men in the market."[56] This was one of the reasons that he became disillusioned with the jihād and emigrated eastward. He was particularly critical of excess, condemning the extent of concubinage, as well as ostentatious clothing and other displays of wealth.[57]

The flight of the enslaved to the cause of jihād is most noticeable in the case of Ilorin, probably because of the availability of documentation. The Ilorin garrison, which consisted of Hausa and other slaves from farther north, mutinied in 1817 in a bid by its commander, Afonja, to topple the Oyo government. Afonja lost his life in 1823 when he tried to rein in the jihād.[58] As 'Alī Eisami reported from his own experience, "All the slaves who went to the war, became free; so when the slaves heard these good news, they all ran away."[59] 'Alī, a Borno slave, was sold to merchants at the coast for sale overseas because his master feared that he would join the Muslims. The jihād continued into the 1820s, and the Muslims offered "liberty to all the Mahometen slaves, and

The Jihād of 'Uthmān dan Fodio

encouraged others to kill their pagan masters and join them."[60] Ilorin became virtually autonomous, which contributed to an ongoing crisis that resulted in the eventual destruction of Oyo in the early 1830s and the incorporation of much of its territory into the caliphate as the Emirate of Ilorin.[61] Similarly, in Nupe in 1831, "all runaway slaves are encouraged to join the ranks on condition of receiving their freedom; and they are joined by a vast number from the surrounding country."[62]

From the perspective of the caliphate's leadership, slavery was closely associated with issues of religion and required the recognition of Islamic law. Muslim forces were supposed to inquire into the religious status of slaves; those who had been born free were usually allowed to contact relatives in order to arrange ransom.[63] Muslims who owned slaves were supposed to instruct their slaves in matters of religion, and hence the ideal master-slave relationship involved a Muslim master whose trusted slave was committed to Islam, whether recently acquired or not.[64] The predominant reason for restricting the sale of slaves was to assure their inevitable conversion to Islam. Procedures for emancipation, including self-purchase and redemption by third parties, allowed for the integration of individuals, as Muslims, into free society.[65]

As far as Sokoto was concerned, enslaving free Muslims was not acceptable, although attacking enemy countries opposed to the imposition of Sokoto's authority was sanctioned. In *Sirāj al-ikhwān*, 'Uthmān dan Fodio justified "the legality of fighting those among the learned, the students, and the masses who aid the Unbelievers and the legality of fighting those who neglect to put themselves under the authority of a Muslim ruler."[66] At this time the status of Muslims in neighboring Borno was specifically in dispute. When the supporters of the jihād destroyed the Borno capital at Ngazargamu and laid waste a considerable district around the capital, they also enslaved many people who could not flee. The experience of 'Alī Eisami reveals the extent of destruction at this time. Son of a Muslim cleric, 'Alī attended Qur'ānic school until he was eleven, but he was enslaved in 1808 when the jihād forces sacked the Borno capital.[67]

Shehu Muhammad al-Kānimī, who rallied Borno against the jihād after 1808, accused the Sokoto leadership of hypocrisy on the slavery issue, elaborating on the arguments of Islamic scholarship, including the views of 'Uthmān dan Fodio himself, to demonstrate the illegality of enslaving the inhabitants of a Muslim country.[68] Since Borno was a Muslim country, al-Kānimī asked Bello, "Tell us therefore why you are fighting us and enslaving our free people?"[69] Between 1808 and 1812 al-Kānimī staged a series of counterattacks on Sokoto territory that delivered a punch in the diplomatic offensive against the jihād regime. Thereafter strained relations prevailed between Borno and Sokoto, and open war erupted again in 1826–27. The various letters between Bello and al-Kānimī, the paramount rulers of the two major states in the region, confront the issue of who was a Muslim and therefore should not be enslaved and who were opponents of the jihād and thereby were classified among those who could be enslaved. The biographical accounts of Muslims who were enslaved during the jihād demonstrate that many Muslims were in fact enslaved despite the intentions of the jihād leadership.[70]

Al-Kānimī's position on jihād provides the most serious critique of the necessity for jihād. According to his interpretation, there were four types of people in every state, namely, unbelievers, apostates, Muslims who cared little about the requirements of religion, and Muslims who "are completely immovable in their faith."[71] Brenner quotes al-Kānimī as saying that "every country in this region contains these four types. Anyone who gains control over them by aggression will inevitably have the difficulty of discrimination. And whenever the difficulty of discrimination has made all injury general, then the abandonment of the unbeliever is more acceptable than the killing of a Muslim."[72] In pursuing the jihād in Borno, Goni Mukhtār argued that Borno could be attacked for five reasons: sacrificing for alms was common at certain places, free women were failing to cover their heads, bribe taking was prevalent, money set aside for orphans was being squandered, and false judgments were being rendered in law courts. Al-Kānimī refused to accept these as constituting unbelief, although he considered these practices reprehensible. According to al-Kānimī, all countries suffered from the presence of sinful actions, but that did not constitute unbelief and warrant jihād.[73] The correspondence between Bello and al-Kānimī lasted from 1808 to 1812 and failed to resolve the differences in interpretation.

Predominance of Fulbe (Fulani) in the Jihād

The problem of succession to leadership upon the death of 'Uthmān dan Fodio was well understood and virtually arranged in 1813, four years before the Shehu's dealth. It was decided to govern through two spheres, one headed by the Shehu's brother Abdullahi and the other by his son, Muhammad Bello. There seems to have been no question about the continuation of the dominance of Fulbe intellectuals. Abdullahi was stationed at Gwandu, in the heart of the Hausa state of Kebbi, and intended to preside over the western emirates, which at the time may have appeared to be the most likely areas of political expansion. As things turned out, many small emirates were established, and although it could not have been known at the time the decision was made for the division, Ilorin would emerge as an important emirate, and Nupe would continue to struggle for stability until the establishment of Bida in 1857. Muhammad Bello officially resided in Sokoto, which was not far from the former Gobir capital of Alkalawa, now deserted, but in fact spent most of his years as caliph in his *ribāṭ* at Wurno, to the north of Sokoto. Bello's sway was over the principal Hausa states that had paid allegiance to Borno, and hence he continued the jihād against Borno and spawned emirates that derived from that campaign, the most important of which, as it happened, was the vast territory of Adamawa with its plethora of subemirates. Bello thereby gained responsibility for the most productive and extensive parts of the caliphate.

The year of dan Fodio's death marked the emergence of Masina in the far west as the independent state of Hamdullahi, which probably would have pledged its allegiance to the Shehu but chose not to recognize either Abdullahi or Muhammad Bello as its overlord. Equally significant, the Muslim uprising in Ilorin in 1817 undermined Oyo as a principal source of slaves in West Africa and began the migration of enslaved Yoruba to the Americas. Hence as Europe and the Americas were adjusting to the end of the Napoleonic Wars and the British were intensifying antislave patrols on the West African coast and eliminating Muslim corsairs in the Mediterranean, the jihād movement expanded in West Africa through the agency of the dan Fodio family. The final benchmark of 1837 was the death of Muhammad Bello and hence the end of the first generation of the jihād leadership; Abdullahi had died two years earlier and was succeeded by his son. Bello was succeeded by his brother. Bello's death occurred a year after the final collapse of Oyo, whose capital, along with the region around it, was abandoned in 1836, within a year of the Malês uprising in Bahia and various conspiracies in Cuba that were attributed to the Yoruba and only a few years after British emancipation of slaves in its colonies in 1834. In the interior of the Bight of Benin, the jihād undermined the stability of the whole of Yorubaland. The result was the massive flight of Yoruba to the south and the steady departure of enslaved Yoruba for Brazil, Cuba, and, because of British naval patrols, Sierra Leone.[74]

The jihād was based on Fulbe allegiance and ultimately the use of cavalry and therefore extended the appeal of the Fuuta states in the western Bilād al-Sūdān to areas far to the east (plate 11). The migrations that herders and clerics such as the dan Fodio family had earlier undertaken, the monopoly of cattle production as reflected in the domination of Fulbe clan leaders, and the policies that encouraged Fulani, as the Fulbe were known in Hausa, to settle in the states where they moved their herds reinforced Fulbe ethnicity; the diaspora provided the basis for the consolidation of the jihād aristocracy. The shaykh's clan, the Toronkawa, which traced its origin to Fuuta Toro and the clerical familes of Torodbe, was associated with an intellectual tradition, a sedentary lifestyle, and a multilingual environment; the dan Fodio family knew Hausa, Fulfulde, Arabic, and probably Kanuri and Tamachek, although apparently not Yoruba. Even as far away as the middle Niger valley this pan-Fulbe allegiance prompted the founding of Hamdullahi, south of Timbuktu, in the region of Masina. Aḥmad Muhammad Lobbo al-Māsinī launched the jihād there in 1816 and initially pledged support to 'Uthmān dan Fodio, which he renounced in 1817 on 'Uthmān's death.[75] Thereafter Hamdullahi was an independent jihād state until it was overthrown by al-Ḥājj 'Umar ibn Sa'īd Tal (1797–1864). If Hamdullahi had remained part of Sokoto, the caliphate would have stretched virtually from the upper Niger River to Lake Chad. At one point Sokoto even laid claim to the coast of the Bight of Benin, although attempts to push to the coast failed. The selection of Bello's successor pitted Bello's brother Abubakar Atiku against the Tījānī leader, al-Ḥājj 'Umar, who had married Bello's daughters, apparently Mariam initially and, upon her death, Ramatullah.[76] When Atiku was appointed, 'Umar left Sokoto for the western Bilād al-Sūdān, where he recruited an army in Fuuta Toro and Fuuta Jalon and also attracted many Hausa volunteers from the Sokoto Caliphate, which enabled him to extend jihād, now under the banner of the Tījāniyya rather than the Qādiriyya, as the previous jihāds had been. By the 1850s much of West Africa had been consolidated into one of the jihād states, and their influence extended throughout West Africa and beyond. The conquest of Hamdullahi created a caliphate of the Tījāniyya and also further consolidated Fulbe/Fulani aristocratic rule.

The model of reformed Islamic rule that Sokoto imposed, which was retained and modified under colonial rule, was based on a form of government that owed inspiration to ṣūfī brotherhoods or ṭarīqa, first the Qādiriyya, then, by the middle of the nineteenth century, the Tijāniyya, and by the end of the century, the Mahdiyya as well. The level and extent of Islamic scholarship on which this movement and its reverberations were based is well documented and has already undergone considerable analysis, as reflected in the bibliographic references to literature in Arabic that has been compiled by John Hunwick and his associates into a massive index of primary source materials

The Jihād of 'Uthmān dan Fodio

in Arabic and other languages written in *ajami* (Arabic script). The extent of such documentary materials is best epitomized by the enormous libraries of Timbuktu. From the writings of Aḥmad Bābā and his associates in the late sixteenth century and early seventeenth century onward, it is clear that the Muslim scholars and clerics of West Africa were fully aware of transatlantic slavery and had developed a response to what for some appeared to be an attractive means of making money. The resulting limitations on Muslim involvement in trade with Europeans, that is, Christians, effectively undermined the participation of Muslim regions in the sale of slaves to the Americas, although participation was not entirely eliminated. Muslims were nonetheless sold to the Americas, but the circumstances under which they were sold are very important and instructive. Muslims were indeed taken as slaves across the Atlantic, which demonstrates that some of the enslaved did come from areas of Muslim influence and control, but proportionately, the numbers were relatively few, as is argued in chapter 5, and there was strong resistance to more serious involvement that was effectively enforced, as can be seen by the extent to which West Africa supplied relatively fewer slaves to the Americas than west central Africa.

The triumvirate of ʿUthmān dan Fodio, his brother Abdullahi, and his son Muhammad Bello should be included in the list of major figures of the age of revolutions, comparable in terms of the significance of their leadership to that of William Wilberforce and Simón Bolívar. The dan Fodio triumvirate inspired jihād and provided unbroken leadership from the outbreak of hostilities with the government of Gobir in 1804 to the death of Muhammad Bello in 1837. The scholarly tradition associated with the jihād movement and the great outpouring of literary masterpieces in law, government, history, and mysticism, including poetry, is noteworthy. The three leading intellectuals of the Sokoto jihād, ʿUthmān dan Fodio, Abdullahi dan Fodio, and Muhammad Bello, composed numerous pamphlets, treatises, legal opinions, and other texts in the course of their lives.[77] ʿUthmān dan Fodio died in 1817, his brother in 1828, and his son in 1837. The outpouring of literary texts is astonishing. In fact, it should be considered the product of a leadership of four, since the Shehu's only daughter, Nana Asma'u (1793–1864), also wrote extensively.[78] Nana was married to Gidado Junaidu al-Bukhārī, himself a prolific writer who held the title waziri under the Shehu and along with Muhammad Bello and Abdullahi formed the inner chamber of government and military leadership, planning the consolidation of the Islamic state and the perpetuation of a permanent state of jihād that was directed from the emirates and the numerous subemirates that constituted the caliphate. Gidado's library provided the documentation for Last's initial study of the Sokoto Caliphate.[79] This commitment to written texts also included many scholars in Kano and the other emirate capitals, as well as the pilgrims who came to Sokoto, especially after the death of the Shehu in 1817 and the construction of the mausoleum in his honor (plate 12).

Indeed, the rapidity with which jihād spread throughout West Africa after 1804 indicates that 'Uthmān dan Fodio, at least, was already widely respected and successfully could issue flags of leadership and authority for dozens of jihād leaders to undertake revolutionary action in their specific areas. Thus all the Hausa governments were overthrown, although a number of the exiled aristocracies established enclaves of political authority based on walled cities and cavalries in new locations from which the military campaigns of the caliphate could not dislodge them. These enclaves were found at Maradi, Tsibiri, the Ningi hills, and the Jos Plateau, among other places. Because of this resistance, towns had to be walled; the walls of Kano were particularly impressive (plate 13). In addition, frontier fortifications had to be maintained that were encouraged by Muhammad Bello, such as the fortified town (ribāṭ) that he founded at Wurno, north of Sokoto (plate 14). Hence, for Sokoto, there was a period of consolidation after the tawaye rebellions, and the exiled governments of Gobir and Katsina at Maradi, Tsibiri, and Konya continued to be a problem. The tawaye after the death of 'Uthmān dan Fodio and the continuing inroads of Maradi and Gobir raised issues of national security, the result of which was the construction of numerous ribāṭ throughout the hinterland of Sokoto and near all the major cities of the caliphate. Clapperton provides invaluable information on several of these, including Fanisau, near Kano, which he had also visited in 1824. He provides considerable information on the ribāṭ at Magaria, which was later replaced by Wurno, both located in the Rima River valley northeast of Sokoto.[80] According to Last, "The establishing of ribats was an extension of Bello's own practice of living in fortified camps, first at Karindaye, then at Magaria and finally at Wurno where he had his own ribat."[81] Magaria, Wurno, and Karindaye were located on the eastern edge of the Rima valley, Magaria a short distance northeast of Wurno and Karindaye southwest of Wurno. Of the other major ribāṭ, Silame was established on the frontier against Kebbi, standing on a ridge where the Rima River runs in a narrow valley between high escarpments.[82]

Hence the jihād movement was never completely successful in conquering West Africa, and the campaigns to subdue enclaves of resistance and opposition

The Jihād of 'Uthmān dan Fodio

to conversion to Islam lasted the whole of the nineteenth century. This was also the case in the areas of Fuuta Toro, Fuuta Bundu, and Fuuta Jalon and in the emergence of the Caliphate of Hamdullahi after 1817. The two independent states of Kaarta and Segu, controlled by the military, waged annual war on the surrounding regions, including the Muslim states of the Senegal valley. After 1837, however, al-Hājj 'Umar subdued the middle Niger basin from the borders of Fuuta Jalon to the western emirates of the Sokoto Caliphate. Virtually all the interior of West Africa had come under the authority of states established through jihād, thereby reflecting the full impact of the movement. The subsequent respect and deference paid to 'Uthmān dan Fodio, Abdullahi, and Bello are widely acknowledged. All scholarly authorities, including texts written in Arabic and Hausa, attribute intellectual and spiritual leadership to the three, and particularly to the Shehu.

Implications of the Jihād Movement

The long-term implications of the jihād movement are clear. As Last has observed, jihād altered the course of West African history:

> The Islamic reform movement in West Africa gave rise to the largest
> unitary state in nineteenth-century Africa [i.e., the Sokoto Caliphate].
> It inspired a literature greater in quantity and higher in learning than
> any previously seen south of the Sahara. It laid down conditions for
> generating one of the most productive indigenous economies in West
> Africa in the later nineteenth century. Indeed, the movement is as
> central to West African history as is, for example, the French
> Revolution to Europe.[83]

The timing and direction of West African reformist thought paralleled the European world. According to Last, there is a need to "examine the underlying causes of these changes and the ways by which they might have affected West Africa."[84] Moreover, I argue, the events in Africa must be incorporated into conceptions of the Atlantic world during the age of revolutions; however, the extent to which the events in West Africa shaped or did not shape the Americas and Europe and the ways in which the age of revolutions affected the jihād movement are debatable. As I argue here, the transatlantic world and Islamic West Africa were autonomous, largely disentangled in ways that helped define the Atlantic world.

Building on the earlier jihāds, the Sokoto leadership provided the intellectual inspiration and tactical training for future jihādists, who were linked to Sokoto and who sustained the tradition of jihād. The movement continued well after the deaths of the leadership of the Sokoto jihād ('Uthmān dan Fodio in 1817, Abdullahi dan Fodio in 1828, and Muhammad Bello in 1837). Seku Amadou b. Muhammadu Lobbo (1776–1845) of Masina founded Hamdullahi in the inner Niger delta in the region of Mopti in 1818. Amadou had been a student of Sīdī al-Mukhtār, the Qādirī shaykh in the Azawad region northwest of Timbuktu. In 1848 Hamdullahi fell to the forces of al-Ḥājj 'Umar, who had launched a jihād under the banner of Tījāniyya. Al-Ḥajj 'Umar, as he was known after his pilgrimage to Mecca, was originally from Fuuta Toro and settled in Sokoto after he had performed the pilgrimage. In Mecca he accepted the *wird* for the Tījāniyya, which made him the spiritual and political leader of members of the Tijani brotherhood, or *ṭarīqa*, in West Africa and thereby transformed the jihād movement beyond the monopoly of the Qādiriyya. Al-Ḥājj 'Umar married Muhammad Bello's daughter Maryam (d. 1838) and had pretensions to succeed to the supreme leadership of the Sokoto Caliphate, but his ambitious were thwarted. When he was not selected as Bello's successor in 1837, he left Sokoto, returned to the western Bilād al-Sūdān, and started a jihād under the banner of the Tījāniyya.[85] By the time of 'Umar's death in 1864, the Tījāniyya jihād dominated much of the western Bilād al-Sūdān but was exposed to French expansion into the interior from Senegal. 'Umar's career further demonstrates that the Sokoto triumvirate was part of a strong tradition of learned scholarship of Muslim philosophers, political scientists, and intellectuals that continued through the nineteenth century and beyond.

The Mahdist movement in the Nilotic Sudan after 1884, too, owed its inspiration to the Sokoto leadership. Many of the first adherents to the Mahdiyya came from the Sokoto Caliphate, whose citizens migrated eastward in expectation of meeting the Expected Mahdī, who was supposed to herald the end of the world and its subsequent rebirth. Indeed, some of the Sokoto faithful believed that dan Fodio himself was the Mahdī, which he denied. The tradition of a catastrophic end of the world continued; the revised prediction held that the Expected Mahdī would appear at the beginning of the thirteenth century of the *hijra*, that is, 1884, which was precisely when Muhammad Aḥmad was proclaimed Mahdī in the Nilotic Sudan, then under Egyptian rule and informal British influence. The Mahdī established Omdurman, across the Nile from Khartoum, as his capital, and when he died shortly thereafter, his second in command, 'Abdullāhi b. Sayyid Muhammad, a Baqqara cleric from southern Darfur, succeeded Khalifa in the consolidation of the Mahdist state. Subsequently, upon the defeat and death of Khalifa 'Abdullāhi in 1899, a breakaway army under Rābiḥ ibn Faḍallāh moved

The Jihād of 'Uthmān dan Fodio

westward on a path of conquest. The Mahdī had a designated representative in the west, Hayatu, who was a grandson of 'Uthmān dan Fodio. Hayatu hoped to extend Mahdism to the Sokoto Caliphate. However, after Rābiḥ moved through Bagirmi and conquered Borno, the two Mahdists were estranged, and Hayatu was killed.[86] Thus jihād continued to be a guiding force in history in the region that extended across Africa from Senegal to the Red Sea, and this has to be acknowledged in any attempt to understand the contemporary manifestations of jihād that have emerged since the colonial period and the independence of modern states of Africa in the present. The Boko Haram movement in the twenty-first century sustains this tradition, although with significant differences in its justification for jihād. The long arm of history has been just as powerful in relation to the regeneration of jihād as it has been for industrialization and transformations of modern capitalism.

As with the age of revolutions in the Atlantic world and Europe, there were antecedents to these momentous events that came to fruition in the nineteenth century. Before becoming imam of the Sokoto jihād, 'Uthmān dan Fodio had been a disciple of Jibrīl ibn 'Umar, who in the 1790s had advocated jihād, following the model for success of the earlier jihāds in the far western Bilād al-Sūdān, from which many proponents of jihād in the central Bilād al-Sūdān had come.[87] 'Uthmān dan Fodio, by implementing jihād after 1804, provided the leadership, along with his brother, Abdullahi dan Fodio, and his son, Muhammad Bello, for a revolutionary movement that swept aside governments from the upper Niger through the western Bilād al-Sūdān to Lake Chad and ultimately the Nile valley. Although Jibrīl ibn 'Umar had been a proponent of jihād against the Hausa states and the clan leadership of the Tuareg nomads, 'Uthmān dan Fodio, his brother, and his son implemented the jihād.[88] In the context of West Africa, their names are as familiar to scholars as Marx, Lenin, and Trotsky are in Marxist historiography, or Hobsbawm and Genovese in the study of the age of revolutions and the history of slave resistance. Together, the Sokoto triumvirate wrote over one thousand books, pamphlets, and tracts that included poetry, legal texts, exhortations, and manuals of governance that were mostly written in Arabic but included *ajami* (Arabic-script) texts in Hausa and Fulfulde.[89] This wealth of intellectual production in itself was a revolution, deserving comparison with the outburst of literary productivity of the Enlightenment. As the book market of the Sahel demonstrates, scholars in the western Bilād al-Sūdān read the triumvirate's works, just as the dan Fodios and their associates read Maghreb and Songhay texts.[90] The book trade establishes clearly the intellectual background of the jihād movement, which involved a written debate comparable to that of the age of revolution in Europe and the Americas. The many parallels and revealing contrasts are such that it is time to incorporate the jihād movement into the corpus of revolutions that characterized the era from the last quarter of the eighteenth century through the middle of the nineteenth century.

Hobsbawm and Genovese can perhaps be excused for not understanding the momentous events in West Africa, but in fact they should not be, since these events and the transformations that arose have been well known since the late 1950s and 1960s and could easily have been incorporated into broader interpretations.[91] The establishment of the Sokoto Caliphate as a federation that stretched from modern Burkina Faso to the Central African Republic was revolutionary. The caliphate consolidated a region that contained the thirty-three emirates under the dual capitals at Sokoto and Gwandu after 1817, which eventually included forty subemirates under Adamawa, also known as Fombina, whose capital at Yola on the Benue River promoted this expansion. The resulting Sokoto Caliphate was the largest state in Africa since the collapse of Songhay in 1591–92 and remained so until the European conquest between 1897 and 1903, when Sokoto was divided among France, Germany, and Britain, with Britain taking the most populous central portions. Moreover, the Sokoto movement swept the region from modern Mali to the Nile valley, and its reverberations extended more widely, with influences continuing to this day.

The Jihād of ʿUthmān dan Fodio

4 THE ECONOMIC IMPACT OF JIHĀD IN WEST AFRICA

The jihād movement not only had a profound impact on the political integration of West Africa but also resulted in the intensification of economic development and, specifically, led to an increase in the incidence of slavery on a scale that was comparable to that in the southern United States, Brazil, and Cuba at the same time. The evidence demonstrates that the Sokoto Caliphate, in particular, was one of the largest slave societies in history, and that slavery was a central institution, sanctioned in law, political ideology, military commitment, legal enforcement, and economic gain through trade, production, and services. The use of slaves in production was especially noteworthy, including their employment on cotton, grain, and indigo plantations, in the manufacture of woven, dyed, tailored, and embroidered textiles and of leather goods, in the processing of various salts for industry and consumption, and in porterage. As I argue below, slaves probably constituted a quarter to half of the total population of the Sokoto Caliphate well before the middle of the nineteenth century, as was also the case in Fuuta Jalon and Fuuta Toro in the early part of the century. These populations are to be compared with the scale of slavery in Brazil (1,500,000 in 1871), Cuba (365,000 to 375,000 in 1855–59) and the United States (almost 4 million in 1860) during the height of slavery in these countries.[1] An assessment of economic growth that was concentrated in the jihād states provides some idea of the impact of jihād and the emergence of a political economy that bears some resemblance to the "second slavery" of the Americas, as characterized by Dale Tomich.[2] According to Tomich, slavery became more important during the age of revolutions despite the independence of Haiti and the numerous slave uprisings elsewhere, and thereby slavery underpinned the growth of Brazil, the United States, and Cuba, among other countries. I argue here that a similar, parallel expansion in slavery occurred in the jihād states, and that this provides a clarification and extension of Tomich's analysis. Hence the revolutionary significance of jihād extended far beyond the overthrow of established elites, the consolidation of new states, and the transformation of the political order. The new economic order emphasized the control of subjugated populations through slavery.

The new elites were different from those that they replaced, being Fulbe in ethnicity, although they also understood languages other than Fulfulde, particularly Malinke and its dialects, Wolof in the Senegal River valley, and Hausa in the central Bilād al-Sūdān. The jihād governments ruled on the basis of the Sharīʿa, which was interpreted on the basis of Islamic norms that were understood as traditional and therefore justified the implementation of a social order based on slavery according to precedent. Education in Arabic and increasingly in Hausa and Fulfulbe written in *ajami*, that is, in Arabic script, became more widespread, generally following curricula established by the Qādiriyya brotherhood and reinforcing a social hierarchy that was associated with literacy in Arabic. The effect of these changes on society in turn was revolutionary in fundamentally altering social relationships, even if particular governments or some officials deviated from the intentions of the ideals of jihād. The impact of these changes on economic and social structures is explored in this chapter.

Although the jihād movement was a response in part to the transatlantic slave trade and the rippling spread of enslavement that entrapped freeborn Muslims, jihād did not lead to a decrease in enslavement and the number of enslaved persons but, quite the contrary, resulted in the intensification of slavery in West Africa. This apparent contradiction has to be placed in the context of aims of the jihād states to establish strong governments based on a new social order. Enslavement and the use of slaves in the economy allowed the further consolidation and expansion of the jihād states and at the same time established the autonomy of West Africa from the European-dominated Atlantic world. The parallel of the era of jihād with the age of revolutions emanating from Europe extended to the intensification of slavery as an institution; however, whereas changes in the Americas resulted in a shift to more racialized social structures, in West Africa the increase in slavery was related to religious factors that were used to justify social differentiation and economic exploitation. The response of the Islamic world to the growing influence of the European world was withdrawal and the imposition of a different kind of social order. The Eurocentrism that has come to dominate historical interpretation overlooks the corresponding revolutionary change in Islamic Africa and thereby distorts an understanding of the Atlantic world by omitting reference to West Africa, even though West Africa bordered the Atlantic.

Demographic Implications of the Jihād Movement

The incidence of slavery in the Muslim interior of West Africa had been substantial since the period of Songhay dominance in the sixteenth century, and this pattern continued into the period of decentralization that followed the collapse of Songhay in the 1590s.[3] Although the proportion of the population in slavery in the seventeenth and eighteenth centuries is difficult to estimate, it is clear that the jihād states were economically dependent on large slave populations. Estimates for the size of these populations are not especially solid before the end of the nineteenth century, well after the ending of the transatlantic trade in slaves. Nonetheless, the scale of slavery had to have been considerable if reports on the movement of caravans and tribute payments in the form of slaves are considered or estimates of the trans-Saharan trade are taken into account. French studies of caravan traffic in the western Bilād al-Sūdān in the nineteenth century indicate probable levels of slaving, and scattered observations suggest that the level of enslavement during the jihād era was considerable.[4] As with the Saharan trade, the internal trade of West Africa appears to have been on a scale that was comparable to that of the transatlantic slave trade in the late eighteenth century and the first half of the nineteenth century. Indeed, as I argue in chapter 5, it would have been possible to have diverted many slaves to the Atlantic coast if merchants had found it desirable to do so, but they did not. Relatively speaking, the number of slaves who were sent to the Americas was not large.

The questions that I raise here relate to the influence of the jihād movement in determining where the slave population was concentrated and in what ways slavery was manifested in economic and social contexts. Given the scale of slavery, a related question concerns the demography of the traffic in enslaved Africans across the Atlantic, which I will discuss in chapter 5, and why the jihād movement was most influential in Bahia and much less so elsewhere in the Americas, a question that I will address in chapter 6. As the size of the enslaved population in Islamic West Africa demonstrates, the incidence of enslavement in the course of jihād was massive and affected not only those who were actually enslaved but also many other people who were killed in the course of warfare and slave raiding or were driven from their homes and forced into areas that were defensible but in which it was difficult to eke out a living. Anyone who belonged to one of the small societies, often referred to as stateless, that lay along the frontiers of the Sokoto Caliphate was subject to possible enslavement or death during raids that were consciously planned and directed at enslaving non-Muslims or those who were accused of being apostates. Since enslavement was not random but was organized at the highest political levels, with commercial arrangements already secured, intended quotas were set aside for distribution among participants, for use in agriculture or harems, and for sale. Moreover, there is little doubt that the inhabitants of these frontier communities and settlements were aware of this fate. It is virtually impossible to determine how many enslaved people were forcibly incorporated into the jihād states or from where they all came. Nonetheless, the historical context that informs our understanding of enslavement is based on the demographic consolidation of the jihād states, particularly the Sokoto Caliphate, and the great expansion in the number and size of urban centers in the savanna regions of West Africa. The proportion of slaves in the population was considerable, especially in the Sokoto Caliphate in the nineteenth century. Although there are no censuses for any period in the nineteenth century, the size of the slave population can be gleaned from circumstantial evidence, including travelers' observations during the nineteenth century, the scale of the slave trade, court records, estimates of the numbers of slaves who ran away at the time of the British, French, and German conquest after 1897, and documents from the early colonial period.

Estimates made at the end of the nineteenth century and in the first decade of the twentieth century (table 4.1) provide some idea of the size of the slave population in West Africa. As I initially discussed in 1983, perhaps 30 to 50 percent of the population of the western Bilād al-Sūdān was enslaved by the late nineteenth century, and the percentage was even higher near some commercial centers.[5] The areas of the western Bilād al-Sūdān that included Fuuta Jalon, Fuuta Toro, the Umarian state, and other areas of Muslim concentration had a slave population estimated to have been in excess of 1.7 million about 1900. These areas are designated in French colonial terms as Haut-Sénégal-Niger, Guinée, and Sénégal. The area of modern Mali and Niger had an estimated slave population of approximately 822,000, while Guinée, dominated by Fuuta Jalon, had an estimated 687,000 enslaved people. Sénégal, which included Fuuta Toro, had another 330,000 slaves. The Sokoto Caliphate, the largest state geographically and in population, had a slave population of "many millions"—well in excess of 1 million and perhaps more than 2.5 million.[6] Despite weaknesses in the demographic data, the scale of slavery in the jihād states appears to have been roughly the same as that in the Americas in the nineteenth century, and the great expansion in slavery in West Africa can be attributed to the first half of the nineteenth century. The large population

The Economic Impact of Jihād in West Africa

TABLE 4.1. Slave Populations of the Western and Central
Bilād al-Sūdān, ca. 1900

Region	Slave Population	% of Total Population
Haut-Sénégal-Niger	822,000	21
Guinée	687,000	51
Sénégal	330,000	31
Sokoto Caliphate	1,250,000–2,500,000	25–50
Total	3,089,000–4,339,000	25–50

Sources: Martin A. Klein, *Slavery and Colonial Rule in French West Africa* (Cambridge: Cambridge University Press, 1998), 252–56; Paul E. Lovejoy and Jan Hogendorn, *Slow Death for Slavery: The Course of Abolition in Northern Nigeria, 1897–1936* (Cambridge: Cambridge University Press, 1993), 1, 305n. Also see appendix.

of slaves is a general indication of the enormous size of the market for slaves, which continued after the termination of transatlantic slave trading.

Hence the Islamic areas of the western and central Bilād al-Sūdān had slave populations that were roughly the same as the total number of slaves in the Americas at the end of the eighteenth century and more than the total number of slaves in the Caribbean at any time. The Sokoto Caliphate probably had a slave population that matched that of Brazil and may have been less than but nonetheless comparable to that of the United States in 1860. Kano Emirate alone probably had more slaves than Cuba in the middle of the nineteenth century. In sheer numbers, therefore, the enslaved population of Islamic West Africa was of major proportions, and the market for slaves had to have been of such a scale that it influenced both the transatlantic trade and the trans-Saharan trade from western Africa. Moreover, it seems that adult females outnumbered adult males in the slave population of West Africa; this demographic structure would have affected the formation of society. Demographic information collected by French colonial officials at the turn of the twentieth century suggests that about 60 percent of adult slaves were female.[7] Although the sources behind this estimate vary in reliability, there is no reason to question the overall impression that the scale of slavery was substantial.

The concentration of slaves because of the jihād had a significant impact on the demography of West Africa, especially in regard to urbanization and the corresponding development of plantations involving slave labor around the urban centers.[8] On the one hand, major urban complexes were destroyed, and new urban concentrations arose in their place. The capitals of the three largest states in the interior of the Bight of Benin, for example, were destroyed. The Gobir capital of Alkalawa fell to the forces of jihād in 1808 and was evacuated, while new settlements were established at Sokoto and Gwandu thereafter.

JIHĀD IN WEST AFRICA DURING THE AGE OF REVOLUTIONS

Birni Ngazargamu, the capital of Borno, was destroyed in 1810, and the populated district of the middle Komodugu Yo River valley, the western affluent of Lake Chad, was abandoned, with many people being enslaved. The Borno capital was then moved to Kukawa, closer to Lake Chad, and was heavily settled by Kanembu from northwest of Lake Chad, who were among the principal supporters of al-Kānimī, the leader of the reformist movement that came to the rescue of the Sayfawa dynasty. The capital of Oyo, known in Hausa as Katunga, was evacuated in 1835–36, and the capital district around the city to this day remains largely uninhabited, despite its previous density. Ilorin emerged as the new center of population. On the other hand, not all the major centers of states that were overthrown were destroyed or seriously damaged, although the ousted governments were displaced and forced to relocate to outlying areas that then became the centers of reformed and reconstituted polities, all centered in walled towns. Kano, Katsina, Zaria, Daura, Rano, and other places remained intact, with changed governments, and Kano actually expanded considerably, with many new towns founded within a fifty-kilometer radius of the city.

Urbanization accelerated with the establishment of the Sokoto Caliphate in particular. By the middle of the nineteenth century, the two largest cities were Kano, with an estimated population of 30,000 to 80,000 people, and Sokoto, with a population in the range of 50,000 (plate 15).[9] In Hausa terminology any settlement with a wall (*birni*) was considered a town, including frontier fortresses (*ribāt*) and the capitals of the various emirates. All thirty emirates in the Sokoto Caliphate had a capital town, and in addition Sokoto and Gwandu, the twin capitals of the caliphate after 1817, were cities; Sokoto was particularly large. According to the earliest colonial census, there were thirteen towns in Zamfara and Gobir that had populations over 6,000.[10] A town (*birni*) was identified as being walled and was distinguished from villages (*kauye*), hamlets (*unguwa*), and plantations (*rinji, tungazi, gandu*). In Kano emirate alone there were forty to sixty towns and perhaps as many as one hundred, each settlement walled and having a population of 1,000 or more, and many having populations of several thousand. Within fifty kilometers of Kano, there were at least twenty towns with a population of 5,000 or more.[11] The indigo-dyeing industry was concentrated in these towns; some of the largest establishments were at Kura, Rano, Tarai, Burum, Bunkure, Gwarzo, Dawakin Kudu, Garko, Dal, Zarewa, Rogo, and Belli (map 4.1). This heavily urban region continued into northern Zaria Emirate, where such towns as Dan Guzuri, Makarfi, Kudan, and Hunkuyi were also textile centers. Other large towns in Kano Emirate included Bichi, Utai, Sumaila, Madobi,

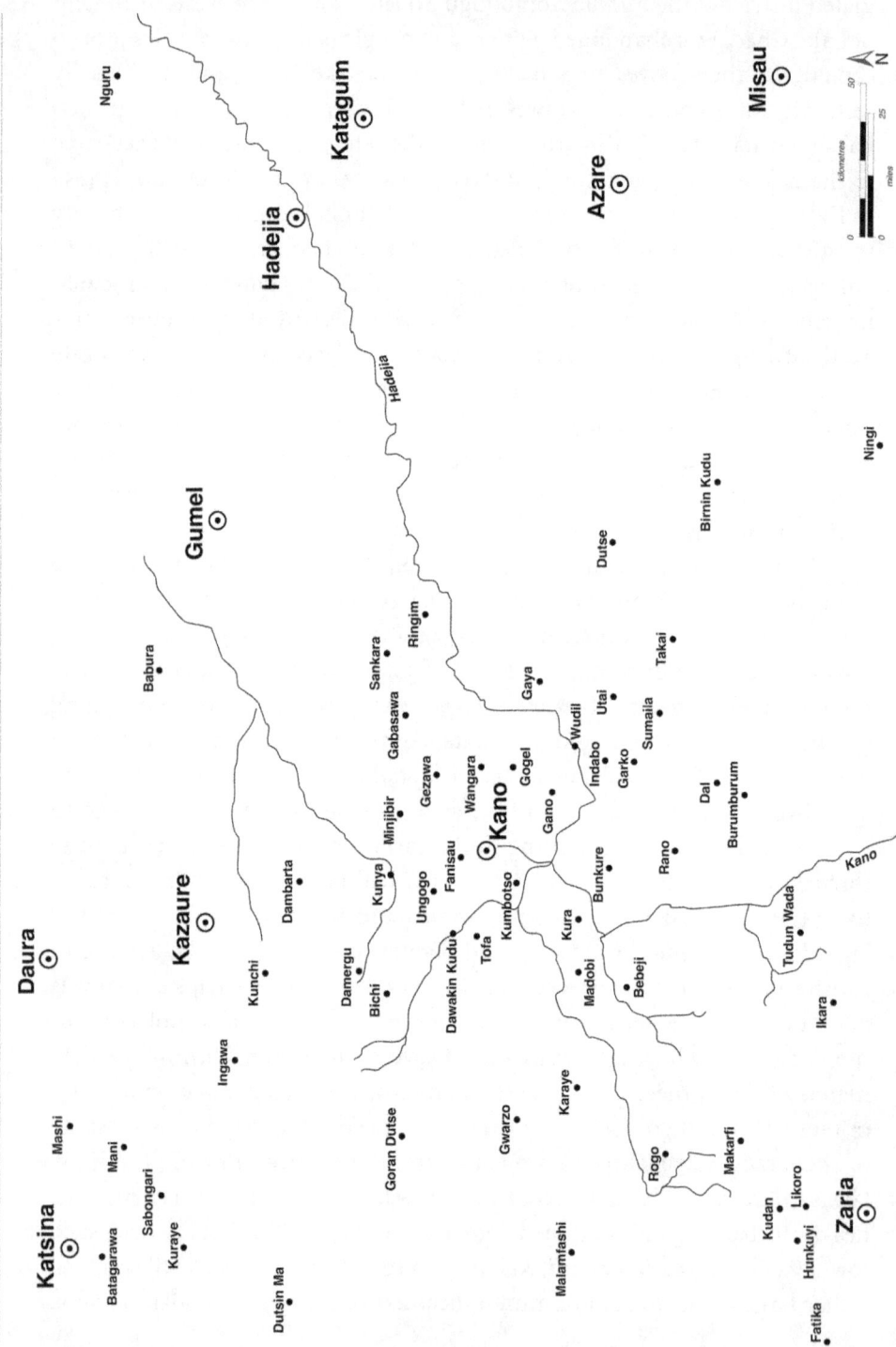

Bebeji, Fanisau, and Kunya. The densely populated region also stretched northward and westward into Katsina Emirate. The city of Katsina had a population of 10,000 to 12,000 people in 1824, declining to 7,000 to 8,000 permanent residents in 1850, but there were another twenty to thirty towns that had several thousand inhabitants each, and the populations of all the towns swelled during the dry season.[12] Moreover, there were at least a dozen towns east and northeast of Kano, including Katagum, Azare, Jema'are, Hadejia, Daura, and Kazaure, as well as forty subemirates in the province of Adamawa.

Besides the many emirates and the two capital districts, there were many subemirates, *ribāṭ* (walled frontier towns), and commercial centers that contained a large population overall. Fombina, with an area of 100,000 square kilometers, had forty subemirates.[13] Zaria had eight fairly large subemirates, including Kajuru, Kadara, Kauru, Kagarko, Doma, Jema'a, Keffi, and Kwatto.[14] Bauchi had ten subemirates in addition to numerous less autonomous districts, including Kirfi, Fali, Ganjuwa, Zungur, Jama'a, Toro, Lere, Lafia, Wase, and Darazo.[15] The capital districts, Sokoto and Gwandu, incorporated the formerly independent territories of Kebbi, Zamfara, and Gobir and also had numerous subemirates within their domains. Finally, the Tuareg federation, which was centered on the town of Agades, in the southern Aïr Massif, had a unique relationship with Sokoto, whether or not it is counted as an integral part of the state. Other towns in the Sahel might also be considered part of the caliphate, although not the independent walled towns of Maradi, Tassawa, and Argungu.

The population of the Sokoto Caliphate cannot be determined with any accuracy. From early tax assessments in the British colonial period and much guesswork, it appears that something like ten to twenty million people may have lived in the Sokoto Caliphate, with perhaps half of the total in the central emirates (Kano, Katsina, and Zaria) and the capital districts (Gwandu and Sokoto) (appendix). Various independent estimates of the proportion of slaves in caliphate society suggest that as much as 50 percent or more of the population was servile,[16] although the percentage of slaves varied from emirate to emirate. By the end of the nineteenth century, for example, apparently most people in the Sokoto area were slaves, and this pattern extended to Gwandu, the twin capital of the caliphate.[17] The Kano, Zaria, Nupe, and Katsina Emirates also had large numbers of slaves, and there were heavy concentrations in Bauchi, Ilorin, Liptako, and the various subemirates of Fombina (Adamawa).[18] Heinrich Barth, for example, who was at Yola in 1853, made the following observations:

Slavery exists on an immense scale in this country, and there are many private individuals who have more than a thousand slaves. In this respect the governor of the whole province is not the most powerful man, being outstripped by the governors of Chamba and Koncha for this reason, that [Emir of Yola] Mohammed Lowel has all his slaves settled in rumde or slave-villages, where they cultivate grain for his use or profit, while the above-mentioned officers, who obtain all their provision of corn from subjected pagan tribes, have their whole host of slaves constantly at their disposal; and I have been assured that some of the head slaves of these men have as many as a thousand slaves each under their command, with whom they undertake occasional expeditions for their masters. I have been assured, also, that Mohammed Lowel receives every year in tribute, besides horses and cattle, about five thousand slaves, though this seems a large number.[19]

These large numbers of slaves are reflected in other estimates and not only demonstrate the concentration of slaves in agricultural activities but also reflect the existence of a mechanism of massive enslavement and an organized structure of labor supply through trade and tribute.

Urban centers had a number of distinctive characteristics that pertained to each of the emirate capitals, the many subemirates, and the semiautonomous towns. They had a central mosque, such as the one in Kano (plate 16), a central market, such as the one at Sokoto in 1850 (plate 17), a palace, wards that were composed of craftsmen, merchants, and residents of foreign origin, and gardens that were protected by the walls that surrounded the town. Pasturage for livestock, including donkeys and often camels, was located outside the town because of the difficulty of moving animals through the limited number of gates. Many people in these towns, perhaps most, also had residences outside the town in nearby villages or on landed estates that were inhabited during the rainy season, when agriculture production was at its peak. Wealthy merchants maintained rural properties where they kept and bred donkeys, mules, and hinnies. Similarly, the aristocracy pastured horses on rural estates, while migrating Tuareg camel herders tethered their herds in rural areas where they maintained agricultural estates when they were not involve in transporting goods during the dry season.

Economic Development of the Jihād States

The consolidation of the jihād states was related to commercial expansion and economic development. The ecological basis of trade and production in the regions extending from the southern Sahara through the Sahel and the savanna to the forests provided the basis for this expansion and development. It can be argued that the potential for such transformation was apparent without the jihād movement, but the foundation of jihād states shaped the way in which change took place. Moreover, in the case of the Sokoto Caliphate, it is unlikely that such extensive economic growth would have taken place without political consolidation. This growth was internal to West Africa and was not related to the phase of the age of revolutions in Europe and the Atlantic world that derived from industrialization in Europe and the modernization of production, finance, and trade in the European-dominated world. There were economies that were achieved in the jihād states, but they were not on the scale or intensity of the changes in the European-dominated world. Nonetheless, the changes are still worth considering in regard to the parallel developments that can be discerned.

The jihād movement in the last quarter of the eighteenth century and the first years of the nineteenth century occurred at a time when there were no severe droughts. Most of the West African savanna and the Sahel had suffered a period of extensive drought that lasted for several years in the late 1740s and early 1750s, but there were no multiyear droughts over wide regions thereafter. Local drought conditions struck specific places each year, but the impact was minimized through the movement of grain from areas of surplus to places of shortage. Hilltop retreats and other sanctuaries from the jihād were vulnerable to famine because of isolation, but the centers of development were not. The fact that there were no prolonged, multiyear episodes of drought similar to the great drought of the mid-eighteenth century was a contributing factor to the economic developments that occurred with the consolidation of the jihād states.[20]

The economic development was related to investments in plantation agriculture, which was a common feature of the areas around towns even before the jihād era. The pattern is apparent in the commercial network across West Africa and in the earliest jihād states. For example, Ayuba ibn Sulaymān Diallo came from a wealthy slave-owning family in Fuuta Bundu; his father tried to ransom him after Ayuba was seized on the south side of the Gambia River in 1731, which reflected his economic position as a slave owner.[21] Muhammad Kabā Saghanughu, who was enslaved in 1777 and taken to Jamaica, where he lived until his death in 1845, came from Bouka, a Mandinka town in the Tinkisso River valley to the east of Timbo, the capital of Fuuta Jalon. His father, 'Abd al-Qādiri, was a "substantial yeoman, possessing 140 slaves, several cows and horses, and grounds producing quantities of cotton, rice, and provisions."[22] At the time, Bouka was one of many Saghanughu communities in West Africa whose inhabitants were not involved in the jihād movement but were nonetheless devout Muslims and members of the Qādiriyya.

Similarly, Abū Bakr al-Ṣiddīq, who was born in Timbuktu around 1790, grew up in the important commercial center of Jenne on the upper Niger River but then studied with his uncles, first at Kong and then at Bouna in northwestern Asante, where his father, Kara Mūsā, died. The family was also involved in trade; al-Ṣiddīq's uncle at Bouna sent slaves, gold, and probably kola nuts, a widely used stimulant in Muslim society, to his wife's father in Katsina, while al-Ṣiddīq's father was involved in the trade of gold and also kola nuts from Asante that were sold north to Jenne.[23] The leading Muslims in Bouna and other towns in northern Asante and along the trade routes across West Africa owned plantations with numerous slaves, and it is likely that Kara Mūsā did, too, just as Kabā's father did. There were many commercial towns that adhered to the tolerant Suwarian tradition of Islam, which advocated peaceful coexistence with non-Muslim states and societies, but that were centers of trade and production.[24] The enslavement of Muslims from these communities was one of the complaints of the jihād leadership, which abhorred such insecurity for Muslims.

The involvement of these Muslims in production and their ownership of slaves continued during the consolidation of the jihād states. The plantation economy was particularly important in the Sokoto Caliphate, where the economic impact of the jihād affected production, land tenure, royal slavery, lineage, and gender relations. The Sokoto Caliphate can be subdivided into the following sectors for purposes of analyzing the development of the plantation economy in the nineteenth century. First, there were the core Hausa provinces, where industrial production, population concentration, and agricultural development were most advanced; second, there were frontier regions in the far west and far east, including the Benue River basin and the area to the west as far as Ilorin, and the distant Cameroon highlands and beyond in the southeast. Finally, there was the desert-side sector in the north. There is an extensive literature on these subjects that covers most parts of the Sokoto Caliphate and also the reconstituted Borno state after 1810, as well as the consolidation of the jihād states of the western Bilād al-Sūdān. Mohammed Bashir Salau has explored slave-based production in various parts of the Sokoto Caliphate;[25] Ahmadou Séhou has documented the plantation sector in one of the subemirates in Adamawa;[26] and similar developments also occurred in Borno under the reform government of Shehu Muhammad al-Kānimī.[27] The various types of land tenure were conducive to such plantation development, as has been documented for Sokoto by Ibrahim Jumare, for Kano by Salau, and for various parts of the Sokoto Caliphate by other scholars.[28] Some lands were attached to political office, while other land was owned by wealthy aristocrats. The caliphate government controlled land allocation and actively promoted agricultural development through the free distribution of fields to slave owners.[29] Usually, immigrant merchants and craftsmen applied to local officials for a land grant, and upon payment of a small gift as *gaisuwa* (greeting or homage) an area of bush was set aside. Only improved land, especially low-lying tracts that could be irrigated (*fadama*) but also manured farms, were salable, although sales may have been rare where unused land was plentiful. In Zaria, and probably elsewhere as well, individuals were not permitted to establish separate, walled communities without specific government approval, but anyone with slaves could obtain enough land to start a plantation.[30] Although plantations usually belonged to individuals, some were owned by dynastic families, and less frequently others were attached to particular offices. Large tracts of land were granted to merchants, craftsmen, and immigrants with resources who were encouraged to settle near caliphate towns and cities through methods of allocation associated with *caffa* and *hurumi*, which involved arrangements for access to land through clientage.[31]

There were several words that referred to plantations in the languages spoken in the Sokoto Caliphate; the terms in Hausa were *rinji* and *gandu*, in Fulfulde *rumde*, and in Nupe *tungazi*.[32] *Gandu* has been more commonly studied in the analysis of twentieth-century agricultural practices, after conditions had changed dramatically from earlier patterns. *Gandu*, however, once referred to farming activities that involved large numbers of slaves, frequently in excess of twenty field hands and occasionally involving hundreds. *Rinji* and *tungazi* have most often been translated as "slave village." Here I prefer to translate the term as "plantation" but the term includes situations that have previously been described as "slave villages." Salau has analyzed one plantation complex at Fanisau, north of Kano City. The complex was centered on one of the large *rinji* owned by the emir of Kano and the surrounding plantations that were owned by merchants who lived in the city.[33]

The characteristics of these agricultural holdings included the prevalence of slave labor, often organized in gangs under an overseer (Hausa: *sarkin gandu* or more simply, *gandu)*, the farming of a common field for the master, the division between large fields and small garden plots (*gayauna*) for slaves, separate housing for slaves, specifically designated times when slaves worked on their own, and well-defined rights with respect to religion, marriage, and other social institutions. Except for the output of slave gardens, masters

The Economic Impact of Jihād in West Africa

controlled the distribution of crops, which were either sold or used within their own households. The main crops included cotton, indigo, and grain, especially bulrush millet and sorghum, but numerous irrigated crops, particularly rice, tobacco, onions, cowpeas, peanuts, rice, wheat, and sugarcane, were also important, and such tree crops as shea nuts and locust beans were gathered, along with kola nuts in Nupe. Absentee ownership was common for the big plantations that belonged to the aristocracy and wealthier merchants. Some estates were attached to political positions, which meant that influential slave officials benefited from plantation output. Many other plantations were quite small, however, and masters and their families often worked in the fields alongside their slaves.[34]

Regional specialization was a significant dimension of production. Cotton and indigo were most extensively cultivated in Zamfara, southern Katsina, northern Zaria, and Kano, although both were grown to some degree elsewhere. Tobacco and shea nuts were cash crops everywhere, but tobacco may have been a major plantation crop only in Katsina and parts of Kano, and shea nuts became most important in the Nupe economy, especially by the middle of the nineteenth century. Crops could be distributed over a distance of several hundred kilometers, particularly along the desert edge and within the textile belt of southern Kano and northern Zaria. Grain, for example, was carried north into the Sahel and the southern Sahara for sale to livestock breeders and salt miners, although because of fluctuations in rainfall, distribution varied from year to year within the Sahel. Cotton and, to a lesser extent, indigo were taken to the numerous dye works of the textile belt, and some cotton at least was carried great distances, even into the Sahel, where it was spun and woven for reexport south to be dyed.[35] Besides the bulk movement of these commodities and the transport of produce from countryside to city, a few items were exported beyond the borders of the caliphate. These included dried onion leaves, tobacco, and prepared indigo. Indirectly, of course, the production of the textile industry also accounted for the export of agricultural commodities, although in the form of finished goods.

British diplomat Hugh Clapperton provided a detailed description of slave production in 1827, which he based on his observations in Kano and Sokoto:

> The domestic slaves are generally well treated. The males who have arrived at the age of eighteen or nineteen are given a wife, and sent to live at their villages and farms in the country, where they build a hut,

JIHĀD IN WEST AFRICA DURING THE AGE OF REVOLUTIONS

and until the harvest are fed by their owners. When the time for cultivating the ground and sowing the seed comes on, the owner points out what he requires, and what is to be sown on it. The slave is then allowed to enclose a part for himself and family. The hours of labour, for his master, are from daylight until mid-day; the remainder of the day is employed on his own, or in any other way he may think proper. At the time of harvest, when they cut and tie up the grain, each slave gets a bundle of the different sorts of grain, about a bushel of our measure, for himself. The grain on his own ground is entirely left for his own use, and he may dispose of it as he thinks proper. At the vacant seasons of the year he must attend to the calls of his master, whether to accompany him on a journey, or go to war, if so ordered.[36]

Nonetheless, Clapperton noted that "the children of a slave are also slaves, and when able are usually sent out to attend the goats and sheep, and, at a more advanced age, the bullocks and large cattle; they are soon afterwards taken home to the master's house, to look after his horse or his domestic concerns, as long as they remain single." Clapperton reported that "the domestic slaves are fed the same as the rest of the family, with whom they appear to be on an equality of footing," and that "when a male or female slave dies unmarried, his property goes to the owner. The children of slaves are sometimes educated with those of the owner, but this is not generally the case."[37] In this description of plantation agriculture, Clapperton implied that slaves were allowed to own property and to bequeath it to their children, but the incentive disguised in this privilege depended on the extent to which the individual slave was acculturated and had conformed to the regimentation of plantation life, since only those slaves who met these standards were allowed to marry in the first place. Clapperton appears to have made at least one significant error in his report, probably because of a cultural misunderstanding. According to his information, slaves worked for their master until midday, but in the context of caliphate society, midday referred to the prayer at 2:00 p.m., when work stopped and slaves were given food. After that, there was another prayer at 4:00 p.m., and usually slaves worked their own gardens from then until dusk. This work schedule shifted the labor obligation decidedly in favor of the master, a far different pattern than Clapperton was led to believe.

Imam Umoru, the learned scholar, writer, and jurist who wrote extensively on caliphate economy and society as he knew it at the end of the century, spent much of his professional career in the merchant communities outside the caliphate, but he knew Kano during the 1870s when he was being educated there. His family, which was actively involved in business between Kano and Asante, apparently owned many slaves. Hence his comments are those of the slave-owning class:

> People have nothing but contempt for slaves in Hausaland. The slaves suffer; people look at slaves as worthless creatures: they do not consider them human beings; and they treat them harshly. . . . When a slave runs away, and is found, he is punished. He is not killed, but he is tied up and humiliated very much; no elder or important person will go to his aid because running away is a grave offense for a slave.[38]

Umoru's comments demonstrate that slave masters could talk about "domestic slavery" to visiting Europeans, but they were prepared to use force to maintain control of the slave population. What difference could it mean to an individual if he was a slave in a society with slaves that was fundamentally committed to the perpetuation of slavery, and where slavery was not only widespread but also economically essential to production?

The emir of Kano had substantial holdings (table 4.2). Among his estates were three *rinji* in the Minjibir area: two at Yokanna and Gasgainu under Jakada Garko and a third at Sawaina under the shamaki, a slave official who managed other plantations for the emir as well. The Yokanna plantation had 351 acres, Gasgainu 1,053 acres, and Sawaina 264 acres. A report from 1936 on the holdings of the emir is the most detailed listing, but it should be noted that the list is not complete, and it is not clear whether all the holdings can be traced to the precolonial period. Nonetheless, field research has identified many that date back to the nineteenth century, and it is likely that most, if not all, did. Most especially, it does not include the large holdings already noted, or the estates that have been studied by Abdulrazak Giginyu Sa'idu and Yusufu Yunusa.

The slave official, the *shamaki*, was responsible for Gandun Nassarawa, Takai, Fanisau, Dorayi ta Gandu, Gandun Bubbugage, and Gandun Falke, among others.[39] In the early colonial period, at least, there were about five hundred slaves at Gandun Nassarawa, which was located just outside the walls of Kano near the gate K'ofar Mata. Particularly large estates were located at Dorayi ta Gandu, Gasgainu, Nassarawa, Shanono, Wasai, Yokanna, Fanisau, and Takai. Gandun Nassarawa was usually referred to simply as "Rinji" before the "Nassarawa," that is, Europeans (Christians), arrived. Although its acreage is not known, Gandun Nassarawa was very large, extending

TABLE 4.2. **Landholdings of the Emir of Kano, 1936**

District	Estate	Official	Acreage	Slaves
Kumbotso	Gandu Rafin Sarki		22.06	
	Ja'oji	Gandun sarki	105.84	
	Dorayi ta Gandu	Shamaki	54.26	
	Shekar Barde	Rajin sarki	4.00	
	Dan Bare	Gandun sarki	13.56	
	Darmana		16.00	
	Ungogo Munchika	Gandun sarki	200.66	
	Minjibir Magarawa	Gandun sarki	88.61	
	Karke	Gandun sarki	78.86	
	Garwa	Gandun sarki	111.95	
	Rimi	Gandun sarki	35.98	
	Yokanna	Jakada	351.00	
	Gasgainu	Jakada	1,058.00	
	Sawaina	Shamaki	264.00	
Kano City	Fuskar Kudu	Gandun sarki	13.95	
	Gwagwarwa	Rafin sarki	1.91	
	Gandun Nassarawa	Shamaki	1,900.00	500
Dawakin Kudu	Giwaran	Shamaki	330.00	
	Garin Dau	Rafin sarki	5.55	
	Gogel	Dan Rimi	152.58	400
	Madarin Taba		—	
Kano North	Fanisau	Shamaki	—	
Gaya	Hungu			
	Fanda			
Others	Gandun Bubbugage	Shamaki	—	
	Gandun Falke	Shamaki	—	
	Chairomawa			
	Fano			
	Garko			
	Takai	Shamaki		
	Tumburawa			
	Durumin Shura			
	Waceni			

(*continued*)

TABLE 4.2. (*continued*)

District	Estate	Official	Acreage	Slaves
	Shanono			
	Chalawa			
	Ruwan Tsa			
	Wasai			
Known Acreage			4,808.77	

Sources: Revenue Survey Assessment, Kanoprof 1708/vol. 1, 5/6/36; Abdulrazak Giginyu Sa'idu, "History of a Slave Village in Kano: Gandun Nassarawa" (B.A. thesis, Bayero University, Kano, 1981); Yusufu Yunusa Collection; Tijani Garba, "Taxation in Some Hausa Emirates, c. 1816–1939" (Ph.D. dissertation, University of Birmingham, 1986), 292.

about three kilometers from the city walls. It included what became the European quarter outside the walls of Kano City.[40] As Sa'idu notes, there was a difference between a *gandu* or *rinji* that was attached to an office and one that was privately owned. The "royal *gandu*" could not be subdivided through inheritance and, by implication, could not be sold.[41] Besides the emir's estate at Dorayi ta Gandu, the officials known as *madaki*, *kaura* and *dagaci*, had an estate there, while the *dagaci* of the Ja'en Fulbe, "the notorious Alhaji Halilu," had another, and there were "nineteen local slaveowners," including the Sarkin Makera, the chief of the Kano blacksmiths.[42] According to Malam Idrisu Danmaiso, who was born around 1900, "most of the towns around Kano had royal farms."[43]

Yunusa, in his discussion of *rinji*, lists the estates of the emir of Kano as Fanisau (Panisau), 8 kilometers north-northeast of Kano; Waceni, 7.5 kilometers north of Kano; Nassarawa, extending from the city wall for about 3 kilometers; Dorayi ta Gandu, 7 kilometers south-southeast of the city; Darmana, 5 kilometers south of the city; Gogel, 24 kilometers southeast of the city, established between 1846 and 1855; Giwaran, 25 kilometers southeast and close to Gogel; Shanono, 88 kilometers west-northwest; Takai, 88 kilometers southeast; Farke [Falke], 54 kilometers northeast; Garko, 64 kilometers south-southeast; Fanda; Chalawa; Ruwan Tsa; Hungu; Durumin Shura; and Gandun Bubbugaje. The three largest were Giwaran, Fanisau, and Gogel, the first two under the slave official *shamaki*, and the last under the *dan rimi*.[44] Yunusa describes the emir's estate at Gogel as having at least four hundred slaves there.[45]

In the north, the desert edge (including parts of the neighboring, independent state of Borno) was a specialized area of production that supplied mineral salts, livestock, various other commodities, and transport services to the Sokoto Caliphate.[46] It was an important market for grain and manufactures and the main source of ostrich feathers for export to North Africa and Europe. It was also a principal outlet to the wider world via trans-Saharan trade routes. In regard to the plantation sector, it was the location of numerous slave estates owned by Tuareg entrepreneurs, and it was the origin of many merchants who subsequently came to own plantations in the savanna. Commercial patterns required the movement of many desert-side traders to the savanna each year, where they established plantations. The Tuareg nomads of the Sahara lived across state boundaries, not within or forming a state themselves, but they carried goods for merchants who were operating across international frontiers and between states. The societies of the Sahara in which the Tuareg were prominent had no state structures, although they recognized a common law and respected a court system that extended beyond political frontiers. The possibility of state enforcement of legal decrees, however, was remote if not impossible. Rather, society operated on the basis of trust, derived from a resort to Islamic law and the intervention of the courts.

Islamic law was enforceable from within the group and required at least tacit approval over a wide region to avoid potential conflict. How does one delimit social boundaries in this case, when Tuareg crossed into the Sokoto Caliphate and maintained extensive agricultural estates farmed by slaves where they could find pasture and water their herds in the dry season? The Tuareg clearly operated between and beyond states and invested heavily in slavery and even raiding for slaves, depending on circumstances and alliances.[47] Barth, who has provided the most detailed observations of caliphate society in the early 1850s, incorporated the contradiction between the ideology of slavery and its reality into his discussion of slavery:

> The quiet course of domestic slavery has very little to offend the mind
> of the traveler; the slave is generally well treated, is not overworked, ...
> and is very often considered as a member of the family. .... However,
> I was surprised at observing so few home-born slaves in Negroland—
> with the exception of the Tawarek, who seem to take great pains to rear
> slaves—and I have come to the conclusion that marriage among
> domestic slaves is very little encouraged by the natives; indeed, I think
> myself justified in supposing that a slave is very rarely allowed to
> marry. This is an important circumstance in considering domestic

slavery in Central Africa; for, if these domestic slaves do not of themselves maintain their numbers, then the deficiency arising from ordinary mortality must constantly be kept up by a new supply, which can only be obtained by kidnapping, or, more generally, by predatory incursions, and it is this necessity which makes even domestic slavery appear so baneful and pernicious. The motive for making these observations in this place [Kano] was the sight of a band of slaves whom we met this morning, led on in two files, and fastened one to the other by a strong rope round the neck.[48]

This was decidedly a slave society, one buttressed by Islam.

These plantations were located at defensive centers (singular: *ribāṭ*) founded as the result of the policies of Muhammad Bello strongly influenced policy even before he became the caliph of the empire upon his father's death in 1817. According to Murray Last,

> The establishment of *ribats* was a part of the policy of stabilising the frontiers and providing strongholds round which settlement could flourish despite the raids of the Kebbawa, the Tuareg, the Gobirawa and their allies in Zamfara. Likewise Bello encouraged the building within the frontiers of walled towns where mosques and schools could be opened and trade and workshops started: with scholars appointed to those towns as Imams, judges, *muhtasib*s (legal inspectors), and teachers, Bello hoped to maintain both the practice of Islam and the military control of the area.[49]

Bello himself always lived in such settlements, first at Karindaye, then at Magaria, and finally at Wurno, and he was responsible for the establishment of dozens of others in the Sokoto area. Indeed, almost every walled town could be classified as a *ribāṭ*, although the tendency was to found new communities away from pre-jihād centers. These in turn became the focal points of each *ribāṭ*, which were started in the neighborhood of the initial settlements. Eventually, large areas were consolidated in this fashion, and the countryside between Sokoto and Wurno in particular became densely inhabited, second only to the closely settled zone around Kano City in population.

Bello's *ribāṭ* at Magaria was one center of plantation agriculture by the 1820s: "This town is a sansan [Hausa: *sansani*], or gathering place for their armies, and is mostly inhabited by the slaves of the great in Saccatoo, who all have houses here, and their slaves, who are employed in raising grain, and tending the cattle, mostly reside here, and in the villages around."[50] Besides grain, there were "a number of plantations of cotton" along the road to Sokoto. Nearby was the estate of Malam Moodie, which had about seventy slaves, including children, and was largely devoted to the production of cotton, rice, and calabashes. Elsewhere, too, plantations were common, even up to the very gates of Sokoto itself, while around Gwandu rice was grown for export to Sokoto.[51]

The estates of the Zaria aristocracy demonstrate the extent of plantation agriculture (table 4.3). In 1900 there were forty-six estates associated with the nine leading families of the aristocracy and another four that were attached to the office of emir. Although the number of slaves on these estates is unknown, research completed in the 1970s indicated that even by that late date there were hundreds of slaves, or by then their descendants, on Biye and Hunkuyi. It is not known when the various estates were established, but certainly this occurred in the course of the nineteenth century and involved large numbers of slaves. Biye had about one hundred slaves.

Many slave owners, particularly those who were not members of the aristocracy, held land under *hurumi* or *caffa* arrangements (table 4.4). These commoners, especially merchants, craftsmen, and livestock herders with holdings

TABLE 4.3. *Rinji* of the Zaria Aristocracy, ca. 1900

Family	Names of Estates
Mallawa	Likoro, Taban Sidi, Bassawa, Magada, Sabon Gari, Dan Damisa, Sakadadi, Farin Kasa, Durum
Bornuawa	Farda, Taban Sani, Taban Yamusa, Nassarawa, Kako, Jigiro, Kohoto, Birnin Yero, Bugan Aba, Surdu, Kaikaiyi
Katsinawa	Guga, Madobi, Tsibiri, Bajimi, Biye, Hunkuyi, Talakawa
Suleibawa	Tgabi, Mazangamo, Kwasallo, Racifa, Dambo
Katsinawa 'Yan Doto	Kufena, Rafin Yashi, Keffin Liman
Dokajawa	Birnin Bawa
Yegwamawa	Kagarko, Bagaldi, Abote, Babu
Katukawa	Keffin Katuka, Keffin Fagaci, Surdu
Torankawa	Musawa, Farin Kasa, Karo
Gidadawa throne estates	Zagina, Dambi, Cigo, Lifita, Kohoto
Total 51	

Source: M. G. Smith, *The Economy of Hausa Communities of Zaria* (London: HMSO,1955), 81.

The Economic Impact of Jihād in West Africa

TABLE 4.4. *Caffa* Compounds in Sarkin Dawaki Tsakkar Gidda District, 1909

Town	Total Compounds	Caffa Compounds	Caffa (%)
Sindininia	151	122	80.8
Dumus	41	28	68.3
Kangari	84	55	65.5
Kwatai	83	54	65.1
Kawo	34	19	55.9
Maichedia	140	74	52.9
Total	533	352	66.0

Sources: E. G. M. Dupigny, Assessment Report, Sarkin Dawaki Tsakkar Gidda District, SNP 7/10 5570/1909, Nigerian National Archives, Kaduna. Also see Paul E. Lovejoy and Jan Hogendorn, *Slow Death for Slavery: The Course of Abolition in Northern Nigeria, 1897–1936* (Cambridge: Cambridge University Press, 1993), 170.

in land, were usually wholly or partially exempt from agricultural taxes, other than the religious tithe.[52] *Hurumi* exemptions arose from the fact that land was acquired from a political official who was responsible for the administration of waste or abandoned land that technically belonged to the state.[53] 'Abdullahi dan Fodio discussed this concept in his treatise on caliphate land law, drawing on Mālikī legal precedents.[54] The right to land could be either communal, as in grazing lands, cemeteries, forest reserves for fuel, and other common lands, or individual, as in the case of farms that were allowed tax exemptions. Official farms attached to political office were also declared *hurumi*, but unlike private farms, they could not be alienated. According to Featherstone Cargill, "'Hurumi' farms were the perquisites of jakadas [tax collectors] and local 'Sarikis' [*sarki* = chief in Hausa]; they paid no taxes, but subsisted the people, to whom they were reserved as sort of official estates."[55]

According to G. P. Bargery, *caffa* involved "attaching oneself to a person of influence for the advantage of his protection, and in return being to a certain extent at his call; volunteering one's allegiance" to that person.[56] By accepting *caffa*, therefore, an individual was subject to "the appropriation, by a privilaged [*sic*] class usually resident in principal towns, of the taxes of certain talakawa [commoners] whose allegiance they claim," that is, officials who had granted land concessions to wealthy commoners for an annual rent.[57] Cargill defined *caffa* as being "under the special protection of some powerful man in Kano, who uses his influence to procure his exemption from taxation in return for an annual present."[58] In both cases these exemptions were associated with absentee farmers, *nomijide*, and dispersed holdings.[59] Often the land appears to have been rented from aristocrats, which is probably the

JIHĀD IN WEST AFRICA DURING THE AGE OF REVOLUTIONS

reason that it was wholly or partially exempted from taxation. According to Arthur H. Festing, *hurumi* and *caffa* were "the system under which villages, hamlets, farms, or individuals pay a little, or a large, sum to some influential 'protector' in Kano (and nothing to the official Revenue) in return for various exemptions."[60]

Hurumi and *caffa* exemptions were numerous and extensive. In Dan Isa Sub-District, immediately outside Kano City, bordering the Challawa River,

> a good many of the farms in the villages belong to farmers living in neighbouring villages. . . . There are 11 villages, all near Kano, the inhabitants of which formerly paid hurmi to various of the Emir's Hakimai. . . . In addition to the above there were formerly a good many individual cases of hurmi and chappa. . . . A large number of the villagers are Nomijide, living in Kano and having farms in the villages. All the villages are near Kano and for most intents and purposes can be treated as part of Kano itself.[61]

In 1908 W. P. Hewby reported from Kano, "With reference to the 'Hurumi' question . . . , nearly every office in the Emirate has a 'Gandu' farm attached to it."[62] These absentee farmers, who were "generally more prosperous" than local residents, farmed 1,968 acres. Similarly, in Mundubawa District several officials and a relative of the emir of Kano had estates that were not subject to taxation.[63] The town of Kafin Madaki, on the border between Katagum and Kano, had 214 compound holders, 56 of whom farmed on lands across the emirate border in Katagum. The *sarki* of Madaki had no "authority over these nomijide."[64]

The numerous "private estates" around Sokoto were held under *hurumi* and *caffa* tenures. Wurno, to the north of Sokoto, which Muhammad Bello developed as a *ribāṭ* and thereafter was a principal residence of the Sarkin Musulmi, was one such concentration of plantations.

> Their origin is as follows—when in the time of [Muhammad] Bello the frontier between the Fillani and Gobirawa was advanced to Wurno all the land was bush; Bello gave his followers grants of land, which they cleared, the land so acquired becomes the property of the clearer; where it has already been cleared and the former occupants are driven out by war it becomes the property of the State.[65]

The merchant Kassara owned one such estate, which was located in the valley known as Rafin Yamulu near Wurno. It had been cleared sometime in the late 1820s. Around 1850 Kassara sold part of the estate to one of Muhammad

Bello's teachers, Malam Mūsā, who already owned plantations at Kuseil and Kalambana, west of Sokoto. Musa apparently paid one million cowries for the land in Rafin Yamulu. He appointed an agent to run his Kuseil and Kalambana estates and then went to live at Yamulu. When he died, the estate was divided among his heirs, with most of the land passing to his only surviving son, Habibi.

> Habibi farms no part of the estate himself; he and his family own some
> 290 acres of which about 80 is of no value as agricultural land. The
> declared yield [in 1908] was 1000 bundles of grain and 300 baskets
> of beans—the rents paid to Habibi and his family [in 1908] amount to
> £6—the gross value of the crop as declared is about £12; probably the
> true gross value is nearer to £25.[66]

Habibi sold two parcels of his land, while Mūsā's nephew, Makoma, who inherited some land, also sold some of his land. The sales were witnessed by the local *alkali* (judge) with "proper deeds of sale" duly registered. One of the purchasers of the land that had been sold actually lived far to the south in Kontagora but "comes yearly to collect his rents."[67] Habibi also rented out a large portion of his remaining land for twenty thousand cowries per year on a lease that began in 1901, before the British conquest, but indicates the types of tenure arrangements that date back to the early nineteenth century. The lease in 1901 was for six years and was about to be renegotiated in 1908.

The investments of merchants and other wealthy commoners, often through *caffa* and *hurumi* arrangements, demonstrate an important characteristic of plantation development in the private sector, specifically, a tendency toward fragmented holdings. Some of the private estates in Zaria Emirate were also substantial. Karo, near the Kano-Zaria border, had close to 250.[68] The wealthiest merchants established slave estates in the countryside around Kano City. This diversified their investments, provided insurance in case of a bad year in trade, and helped feed the large number of dependents employed in commercial activities. The largest had several hundred slaves on plantations, although property was usually subdivided in scattered, smaller farms.[69] According to Imam Umoru, many merchants had significant holdings of slaves located on agricultural land:

> There are slave owners in Hausaland who have purchased 100 and 200
> slaves, and there are some slave owners with 400 or 500 slaves. But, in
> my lifetime, I have heard of only one person who was not an official,

who had 1,000 slaves in Kano: his name was Kaushe. . . . In Hausaland, commoners buy slaves, but they are unable to buy 1,000 of them. Officials have more than 1,000 because they do not buy them: they seize them during war campaigns.[70]

Kundila of Makwarari Ward in Kano, who died in 1901, was a particularly wealthy merchant.[71] He reputedly owned from six hundred to well over one thousand slaves, and most of these worked his lands.[72] Many estates were concentrated in a belt between Utai and Sumaila, southeast of Kano City, through Madobi and Bebeji to the west, and in a pocket between Fanisau and Kunya to the north of the city. Although some landholdings were substantial, there were also smaller farms, called *gona*, which were distinguished from *gandu* or *rinji*, even though the combined acreage of dispersed holdings could exceed the area of a single plantation. Problems of management differed. In the case of *gona*, slaves were sent from one location to another, and they usually lived in the urban compound of the master.

The wealthy Agalawa and Tokarawa merchants often managed dispersed holdings. The Agalawa and Tokarawa lived mainly in Kano and Katsina Emirates and were involved in exporting textiles, salt, leather goods, and other commodities to Asante in exchange for kola nuts. Like other merchants, they identified as Hausa commoners, and because of their success, they were widely respected as an example of the social mobility achieved through caravan trading and plantation investment.[73] According to Ibrahim Tahir, "Much of the Kano countryside contained networks of the slave estates of such men [wealthy merchants]."[74] The fields of Tambarin Agalawa Yakubu, a wealthy kola importer who died in the early 1890s, for example, included Makafi, Gonar Kuka, Allah Tayamu, and Gonar K'ofa within the walls of Kano City, while he owned three other small farms, Kankara, Gonar Kurna, and Gonar Tinshe, outside the walls and two larger farms and a *gandu* at Rijiyar Lemo, just west of the city. Finally, he managed farms at Rantan, near Kura, and probably at several other villages as well. Family tradition credits Yakubu with as many as five hundred slaves, and it certainly seems likely that he owned several hundred in order to farm these lands.[75] Only one of Yakubu's holdings was called a *gandu*. Other merchant-planters followed this pattern. One Agalawa trader who lived in Kano City had farms at Shibdawa in Katsina Emirate, others at Lambu, Garim Malam, and Chiroma in Kano Emirate, and a number of gardens within Kano's walls. Similarly, Madugu K'osai, the famous late nineteenth-century Tokarawa caravan leader, owned Kanyan

The Economic Impact of Jihād in West Africa

Amana, near Fanisau, north of Kano City, on which he kept sixty slaves, and he had farms at Damargu, near Bichi in Kano Emirate, as well.[76] The Dantata family owned Zangon Kaya, just outside Bebeji. The estate was so vast that "you needed a horse to cover its length and breadth in one day," according to one of Tahir's informants.[77] The Dantatas also had large estates in Gora, Madobi, and other places in rural Kano, Paki, and other districts of Zaria, and as far away as Bida. The family of Uba Ringim, of Beriberi origins, had farming "establishments" in eleven villages.

Of course, slavery in the Islamic regions of West Africa was different from slavery in the United States, Brazil, or Cuba in the nineteenth century. First, the legitimacy of enslavement was based on identification with a commitment to Islam as a religion, which did not reduce the essential property component of the master's relationship with slaves but did provide a very different understanding of why individuals could be held in bondage. Second, the status of those who were born into slavery depended on the status of the father, not the mother, as in the Americas. A free man who was a Muslim could have a child by a woman who was a slave, but the child was legally considered free and was expected to be treated as such. Third, the onus of proof in determining whether an individual was legally a slave was placed on the master, not on the individual who was being held in slavery. If an individual could say the prayers in Arabic and otherwise demonstrate knowledge of Islam, the master had the obligation of explaining the claim to enslavement. Hence the legal tradition was based on Islamic law and its extensive literary corpus that placed slavery in the context of Islamic society and governance. Many issues of enslavement were addressed in this legal tradition, such as the fate of captives taken in war, the degree to which race was or was not a factor, the condition of women taken as concubines, and the rights of freeborn Muslims who had been taken captive and faced enslavement. Many other issues, such as the work regime of slaves on plantations and in the household, were largely ignored in this literature.

Besides the crops grown during the rainy season, dry-season cropping patterns also involved slave labor on land that could be irrigated, called *fadama* lands in the Sokoto Caliphate, on which tobacco was grown, as well as onions, whose leaves were dried for export, and other crops. The complexity of the slave economy meant that free labor had to compete with the output of slaves. Moreover, slaves who were trusted were allowed to work on their own account, with weekly, biweekly, or monthly payments in money. This practice was known as *murgu*. Such arrangements particularly favored the urban slave population and enabled marriage, families, and sometimes the purchase of emancipation. While they were working for masters, these slaves expected food and housing, but when they were on their own, they were expected to be self-sufficient, which required them to engage in small-scale cropping, trading, selling services, collecting firewood and thatch, working as stevedores and teamsters, and carding and spinning cotton.

The Textile Industry

Textile production served as a major sector of development. The scale of the economy in Kano and its surrounding towns (Kura, Bunkure, Bebeji, Minjibir, and others) can be assessed by the number of dye pits in the emirate has been estimated at fifteen thousand with perhaps as many as fifty thousand dyers by the end of the nineteenth century, not only in Kano City itself but in many surrounding towns, some of which, like Kura and Bunkure, were substantial manufactories (plate 18). As Colleen Kriger has demonstrated, the textile industry was well established in West Africa long before the expansion of production during the jihād phase.[78] The cotton plant that was indigenous to West Africa had been the basis of local textile production since at least the eleventh century, as noted in early Arabic sources and confirmed by scientific analysis of the variety of cotton that was common in West Africa and formed the basis of local production. Similarly, local silks were indigenous, although by the age of revolutions and the spread of jihād, imported silks from North Africa were also important, the silk usually being unraveled for local weaving.

As with the importance of cotton production in the "second slavery" episode of the Americas in the nineteenth century and the industrial production of textiles in Europe, especially in Britain and then in the United States, cotton was a fundamental ingredient of the expansion of slavery in the jihād states. As in the Americas, indigo was also a plantation crop in West Africa, and its contribution to the expansion of textile production was significant. Indigo was used not only to dye textiles in deep pits but also in a separate, specialized craft, in which raw indigo was beaten into dyed cloth to provide a fine sheen that was comparable to the best muslins from India. Such high-quality textiles were particularly important for the Tuareg nomads and the political elite because of the use of such cloth for turbans.

As Philip Shea has demonstrated, the textile-dyeing industry and the production of locally made cloth in the central Hausa cities and countryside expanded considerably in the nineteenth century. In part, this expansion was related to technological changes involving the use of dye sediments (*laso*) to transform large clay pots into dye pits that were lined with the cement created from the dyeing residue. These *laso* pits enabled greater production of dyed cloth, which was the basis of the textile industry.[79] The observant Barth noted that "the principal commerce of Kano consists of native produce, namely, the cotton cloth woven and dyed here or in the neighboring towns, in the form of tobes or rígona (*sing.* ríga), túrkedí, or the oblong piece of dress of dark-blue color worn by the women; the zenne or plaid, of various colors; and the ráwani baki, or black litham."[80] He elaborated at length on thirty types of "zenne," that is, *zane*, a woman's body cloth or wrapper. Barth considered that the textile industry was the backbone of Kano prosperity in the 1850s:

> The great advantage of Kano is, that commerce and manufactures go hand in hand, and that almost every family has its share in them. There is really something grand in this kind of industry, which spreads to the north as far as Múrzuk, Ghát, and even Tripoli; to the west, not only to Timbúktu, but in some degree even as far as the shores of the Atlantic, the very inhabitants of Arguin dressing in the cloth woven and died in Kanó; to the east, all over Bórnu, although there it comes in contact with the native industry of the country; and to the south it maintains a rivalry with the native industry of the I'gbira and I'gbo, while toward the southeast it invades the whole of Adamáwa, and is only limited by the nakedness of the pagan *sans-culottes*, who do not wear clothing.[81]

Barth understood that the textile market at Timbuktu was supplied chiefly from Kano and estimated that some three hundred camel loads of cloth were taken there each year at the value of sixty million cowries, "an amount which entirely remains in the country, and redounds to the benefit of the whole population."[82]

In some areas cotton and indigo became cash crops comparable to the specialized production that characterized agriculture in the United States. This specialization was especially prevalent in the area of textile concentration south of Kano City and in a belt to the east, south, and west of this core.[83] Again, however, the extent of market orientation was restricted, and the lack of economies of scale meant that independent peasants, often with a few slaves as field hands, competed for the same market. Indeed, indigo was often a specialty of Maguzawa peasants, who produced indigo under cooperative arrangements in order to pay the tax incumbent on non-Muslim populations. Significantly, this communal farming was also called *gandu* and suggests the adaptability of that term.[84] The type of cotton that was harvested, which was indigenous to West Africa, also demonstrates the difference from cash cropping in the Americas.[85] It grew on bushes that produced for several years, albeit with diminishing returns. Although the cost of cotton production was lower than in the Americas, it was still high by the standards of other crops in the caliphate. Nonetheless, labor requirements, despite much lower yields than American varieties, were relatively lower during nonplanting years.

Another difference related to the production of cotton and indigo for the domestic market, not for direct export.[86] Finished textiles were the major export from the caliphate, and there was also a large internal demand. Cotton, however, was not an export crop, except for a limited extent to the desert edge, where it was carded, spun, and woven into narrow strips for reshipment back to the dyeing centers of the savanna. Indigo was exported in small quantities; the Kano variety was particularly well regarded as a dye and commanded a small market. Hence cotton and indigo did supply an export trade, but the crops themselves were primarily consumed domestically. Production was for a regional market that had an export sector, but this regional market contrasts sharply with the usual situation for highly capitalized plantation economies, where export markets are the principal destinations for the cash crop. Clearly, transport was the limiting factor here. Costs within transhumance corridors could facilitate exchange, but outside these desert-side patterns, expenses were too high to enable market growth beyond a fairly low level.

The extensive textile industry across West Africa is a testimony to the autonomy from world markets that was possible. Sometimes it is alleged that European imports of textiles on the coast, which often meant textiles from India and not textiles produced in Europe, undermined local production. This in fact is not true. The market for textiles was insatiable and depended on the ability of people to acquire money to buy cloth and clothing, including elaborately embroidered gowns that used silk that was imported and unraveled to create the beautiful patterns sewn in the cloth. Most of the cloth that was to be found in the jihād states was locally produced and supplemented by cloth that was produced in other parts of West Africa.

The textile-manufacturing centers in the Sokoto Caliphate were particularly noteworthy, as in the textile-dyeing industry of Kano and northern Zaria. The number of artisans required countless numbers of women to card the cotton and spin thread. Most of the female population of the caliphate was involved in some stage of textile production, from growing and picking cotton to weaving. The more finished crafts of embroidery and some of the weaving were left to men. Although slaves were also involved in textile production, the principal characteristic of the industry was the essential role played by freeborn Muslims. Slaves cleaned the huge dye pits, which might be ten meters deep; they carried water and helped prepare the indigo but otherwise played a minor role in production.

Textile production in the Sokoto Caliphate was directed at the very large domestic market and the distant markets of North Africa, Asante, and virtually everywhere merchants of the Hausa diaspora and the Juula diaspora, too, traveled. Some merchants in the Sokoto Caliphate specialized in moving high-value commodities, which always included textiles, without traveling in caravans but providing porterage service that emphasized speed in delivery. In a landscape where there were no natural barriers, but only the Niger and Benue Rivers and Lake Chad as reliable means of water transport, goods had to travel overland. Management of transport was fundamental to the functioning of the jihād states. Camels, which were brought into the caliphate during the dry season, were used extensively to move grain and other bulky commodities about. Specialist long-distance merchants like the Agalawa and Tokarawa merchants of Kano and Katsina bred donkeys but also reared mules and hinnies. They expected to lose a high percentage of animals in the transport of goods to Asante and to Lagos.

The indigo-dyeing industry was particularly extensive; establishments were largest in Kano City and Kura but were also found in such towns as Rano, Tarai, Burum, Bunkure, Gwarzo, Dawakin Kudu, Garko, Dal, Zarewa, Rogo, and Belli and continued into Zaria Emirate and the towns of Dan Guzuri, Makarfi, Hunkuyi, and other places (see map 4.1). In addition to the extensive number of dye pits and many thousand dyers in this region, other craftsmen, including hundreds of cloth beaters, thousands of weavers and tailors, and countless numbers of women who spun and carded raw cotton, contributed to the industrial setting. Much of this development was a nineteenth-century phenomenon and was oriented toward foreign markets.[87] Many immigrants from Borno, Nupe, and elsewhere moved to Kano in the years after the jihād, and a number of technological innovations, including the larger and more durable dye pits mentioned earlier, facilitated the growth of the industry. Such centers as Kudan and Fatika, in northern Zaria, also became famous for their exports of cotton beyond what was consumed by the local dyeing industry.[88] By the end of the nineteenth century these towns were the largest cotton markets in the caliphate. Plantations were scattered on their outskirts, and Kudan, at least, was apparently in the center of an area with many estates. The local dyeing industry, involving several hundred pits between the two towns, used some of the cotton harvest, but most was shipped north.

Tuareg and Borno salt merchants, returning kola traders, and other transporters purchased cotton for resale in Kano Emirate. Some cotton was even taken as far north as Damagaram in western Borno, where it was spun and woven into cloth that was ultimately reexported south for dyeing. In Zamfara both cotton and grain were developed as major cash crops. Kaura-Namoda in the north and Gusau in the south were favorably located on the banks of major river systems, where extensive *fadama* land was available for dry-season farming. This made extensive agricultural development possible, although it was retarded by uprisings in the area in 1817. It seems likely that peasant production was always more significant in Zamfara than elsewhere.

Nonetheless, the popular traditions that credit farmers with growing as much as one thousand bundles of grain in a single year involve quantities that must have been grown under plantation conditions. Grain merchants acquired immense wealth by buying grain in small markets and then storing it for later price rises. Much of this output was ultimately sold to Tuareg and other traders from the desert edge. Cotton supplies, which came especially from southern Zamfara, were sent east to Kano and northwest to Sokoto.[89] The textile belt of Kano, northern Zaria, southern Katsina, and Zamfara was divided into two parts: at the core were the numerous dye works of southern Kano and northern Zaria, while an outlying region of cotton and grain production stretched to the west, south, and east.[90] Other towns outside the center also had pits, and grain and cotton were produced in the heart of the belt. It is clear that a highly integrated economic region had developed by the end of the century.

I argue here that the jihād movement was responsible for this enslaved population, its scale, and its concentration in and near hundreds of cities and areas of agricultural development. The concentration of an enslaved population was directly related to the increase in production, and hence the economic impact of slavery was in many ways comparable to the impact in the Americas. The importance of cotton and the local textile industry later became a fascination of colonial officials, both British and French, whose dreams raised the possibility that the production of cotton in West Africa could feed the looms of England and France and therefore challenge the dependency on the cotton of the US South, which was feeding not only British mills but also emerging textile production in New England.

Although caliphate attempts to adopt sugarcane production and use of a sugar mill were not successful, grain (millets and sorghum) was the basis of the desert-side economy. The production of these commodities for the market was well established in the Muslim regions of West Africa. The very preconditions for the spread of jihād arose from the migrations of merchants and livestock producers, who were closely linked if ethnically distinct, in transporting goods to market, particularly grain, which was moved from areas of surplus to places that had suffered poor harvests. The state itself was involved in grain speculation that arose out of the collection of the tithe, which was always paid in kind, that is, grain. The public tithe was intended to provide a hedge against drought and famine, which periodically affected areas of the countryside, while bumper crops could prevail if conditions were right. Large surpluses could even be harvested in the Sahel, although the risk of drought was greatest there. Not only was grain the staple of the food supply for the population from the Sahara to the forest, but also millet was needed to feed horses, which were essential for the military of the jihād states and equally so for the defensible enclaves of those who resisted jihād.

In this chapter I have demonstrated that the economic impact of jihād in West Africa was transformative, analogous to the emergence of the "secondary slavery" of the Americas. The political integration brought about by jihād contributed to economic development and to the increase in slavery. The jihād states chose to leave the Atlantic slave trade, although, as noted, Islamic West Africa could have fully supplied that trade had it chosen to do so. There was an internal slave trade probably equal in scope to the Atlantic trade, but it was directed within West Africa and to a lesser extent across the Sahara. The size of the enslaved population was comparable to that of the American slave systems, and the economy was also built around plantation agriculture. Plantation agriculture and production for the market were central to this economic development, especially in relation to the growth of staple food crops, including millet and rice, as well as cotton and indigo for the textile industry.

Moslems of Dagombah and Salagha in the Costumes of their Countries

PLATE 1. (*top*) Muslims in Asante, 1820. *Source:* Joseph Dupuis, *Journal of a Residence in Ashantee* (London: Henry Colburn, 1824), facing p. 72

PLATE 2. (*left*) Muslim Fulbe in Senegambia, 1853. *Source:* P. David Boilat, *Esquisses Sénégalaises* (Paris: P. Bertrand, 1853), plate 19

La nouvelle mosquée de Dienné.

PLATE 3. (*top*) Gobarau Mosque in Katsina, Eighteenth Century. *Source:* Wikipedia

PLATE 4. (*bottom*) Jenne Mosque, restored 1906–7. *Source:* Félix Dubois, *Notre beau Niger* (Paris: Flammarion, 1911), 187

Job, Son of Solliman Doiallo, High Priest.

PLATE 5. (*top*) Timbuktu in the 1850s. *Source:* Heinrich Barth, *Travels and Discoveries in North and Central Africa* (New York: Harper and Brothers, 1859), Vol. 3, frontispiece

PLATE 6. (*middle*) Muhammad Kabā Saghanughu, *Kitāb al-ṣalāt. Source:* James Coultart Papers, Baptist Missionary Society Collection, Angus Library, Regent's Park College, University of Oxford

PLATE 7. (*bottom*) Ayuba Sulaymān Diallo of Fuuta Bundu. *Source:* Thomas Bluett, *Some Memoirs of the Life of Job, the Son of Solomon, the High Priest of Boonda in Africa; Who Was a Slave about Two Years in Maryland; and Afterwards Being Brought to England, Was Set Free, and Sent to His Native Land in the Year 1734* (London: R. Ford, 1734), frontispiece

PLATE 8. (top) *Bori* Ceremony. *Source*: A. J. N. Tremearne, *The Ban of the Bori. Demons and Demon-Dancing in West and North Africa* (London: Heath, Cranton and Ouseley, 1914), 391

PLATE 9. (bottom left) ʿAḥmad b. al-Qāḍī b. Yūsuf b. Ibrāhim al-Timbuktāwī. *Hatk al-Sitr ʿAmmā ʿAlayhi Sūdani Tūnus min al-Kufr*, 1813. *Source*: Ms., Bibliothèque Nationale, Tunis

PLATE 10. (bottom right) Shehu al-Kānemī. *Source*: Dixon Denham, Hugh Clapperton, and Walter Oudney, *Narrative of Discoveries in Northern and Central Africa* (London: John Murray, 1826), Vol. 1, frontispiece

PLATE 11. (*top*) Kano Cavalry. *Source:* Wikimedia Commons https://commons.wikimedia
.org/wiki/File:Emir_of_Kano-1911.jpg

PLATE 12. (*bottom*) Tomb of 'Uthmān dan Fodio. Photograph by Ibrahim Jumare, Sokoto

PLATE 13. (*top*) Walls of Kano, 1905. *Source:* The National Archives, Kew, CO 1069 58

PLATE 14. (*bottom*) *Ribāṭ* at Wurno. Photograph by Paul E. Lovejoy

The great Mosque at Kano in 1890

PLATE 15. (*top*) Kano City in 1850. *Source:* Heinrich Barth, *Travels and Discoveries in North and Central Africa* (New York: Harper and Brothers, 1859), Vol. 1, 500

PLATE 16. (*bottom*) Kano Mosque, 1890. *Source:* Postcard, The Great Mosque at Kano in 1890, drawing by Cliff Platt. Lovejoy Collection

PLATE 17. (*top*) Sokoto Market, 1853. *Source:* Heinrich Barth, *Travels and Discoveries in North and Central Africa* (New York: Harper and Brothers, 1859), Vol. 3, 133

PLATE 18. (*bottom*) Kofar Mata Dyeing Center, Kano. Photograph by Paul E. Lovejoy

5 JIHĀD AND THE SLAVE TRADE

Can we say that there was a Muslim factor in the transatlantic migration of enslaved Africans? Is it possible that Muslim governments, especially those established in jihād, adopted a policy or adopted policies that inhibited the sale of slaves to the Atlantic world? Michael Gomez has most thoroughly documented the presence of Muslims in the Americas, demonstrating that Muslims were found in every region of the Americas throughout the whole period of slavery.[1] Although he recognizes the importance of jihād in this migration, he does not specifically identify jihād as an inhibiting factor in the deportation of Muslims. Similarly, Boubacar Barry and other scholars of the Senegambia region have established that the jihād movement was a reaction in part to the perceived injustices of the transatlantic slave trade but have not argued that jihād actually reduced the number of enslaved Muslims sent to the Americas.[2] The focus has been on the presence of Muslims among the enslaved, not on the relative importance of that presence. I argue here that Muslims and indeed people from areas of Muslim domination were far fewer than might have been expected on the basis of the prevalence of slavery in West Africa. The jihād movement was a primary reason that many parts of West Africa, especially away from the coast, were, relatively speaking, unimportant in the peopling of the Americas in the eighteenth and nineteenth centuries. While slavery was being challenged in the Americas in the course of the age of revolutions, Muslims were also confronting the involvement of West Africa in the transatlantic slave trade at the same time.

Since the study of the Atlantic world has focused on western Europe and the Americas and has not explicitly included West Africa, it is not widely recognized that the Muslim states of West Africa helped shape the Atlantic world. I argue here that Muslim attitudes toward the sale of slaves to Christians reduced the number of enslaved Africans who could have gone to the Americas. In Muslim West Africa the jihād movement was an inhibiting factor that reduced the involvement of Muslim regions in the transatlantic trade and forced European buyers to go elsewhere to buy slaves. The pronouncements of

Muslim governments and the behavior of Muslim merchants were not always successful in preventing the deportation of slaves from Muslim areas and even the jihād states, but their actions guaranteed that European and American slavers had to fill their ships in the Bight of Biafra and west central Africa, beyond the range of Muslim influence, and not in West Africa, except in areas near the coast in upper Guinea, on the Gold Coast (before around 1800), and in the Bight of Benin. The British anti-slave-trade patrols after 1807 have often been credited with limiting the flow of slaves from West Africa, and this factor, which can be seen as a product of the age of revolutions, was certainly important. The Muslim factor is not often appreciated, however. Enslaved Africans did come from West Africa, despite the Muslim avoidance of trading slaves to Europeans, but most of the enslaved came from non-Muslim areas near the coast or were more or less carefully screened to prevent enslaved Muslims from reaching the slave ships.

The internal slave trade within West Africa and the transfer of slaves as tribute were substantial and probably at least on the same level of activity as the number of people who crossed the Atlantic from West Africa.[3] Moreover, as I argue below, as many as one million enslaved people were sent north across the Sahara during the same period, some of whom were Muslims. These figures and the likely scale of the internal slave trade demonstrate the availability of an enslaved population for the market. Furthermore, many enslaved Muslims and others from the interior were retained in such places as Ibadan, Lagos, and Asante rather than being sold into the Atlantic trade. In combination, therefore, the Atlantic, Saharan, and internal West African trades were of considerable proportions and thereby underpinned the period of a "second slavery" that was comparable to the intensification of slavery in the Americas.

Theoretically, in terms of the known demography, as I argue here, West Africa could have supplied all the slaves that went to the Americas during the age of revolutions, but this did not happen, even though many slaves did come from there. Discussions of the slave trade usually refer to Senegambia, Sierra Leone, and sometimes the upper Guinea coast as the coastal region whose interior was largely Muslim. Similarly, the regions identified as the Gold Coast and the Bight of Benin refer to areas in which Asante and Oyo, respectively, dominated the interior, but which also connected with areas farther inland where Islam was dominant. The coastal designations reflect the political geography of Africa during the late eighteenth and nineteenth centuries as perceived from the slave ships of the Atlantic. In West Africa, however, the jihād states dominated the region north of the Sierra Leone River from the late eighteenth century and the interior of the Bight of Benin after the first decade of the nineteenth century.

The Transatlantic Trade and the Jihād Movement

There are important implications of considering the jihād movement in West Africa as a historical phenomenon parallel to the transformation of slavery in the Americas in the nineteenth century. First, the Muslim regions of West Africa successfully maintained virtual autonomy from the transatlantic slave trade, with certain relatively specific exceptions. Before British abolition in 1807, virtually all slaves who came from Muslim areas of West Africa went to the Americas from the interior of the western Bilād al-Sūdān, most notably from Senegambia and the upper Guinea coast as far south as Cape Mount. Thereafter, slaves from Muslim areas came largely from the interior of the Bight of Benin and hence from the central Bilād al-Sūdān, where the Sokoto jihād took place. Some slaves continued to come from the western Bilād al-Sūdān along established routes that had been in operation in the eighteenth century and even earlier. Second, a newly enslaved population of considerable numbers was retained internally for deployment in economic development, despite the continued demand for enslaved labor in the Americas and the export of many enslaved persons to other parts of the Islamic world.

The autonomy of Muslim regions is particularly striking when one considers the relative unimportance of slaves from Muslim areas in the Americas in comparison with the origins of slaves from non-Muslim regions. For the transatlantic migration as a whole, less than 10 percent of the enslaved population came from areas where Muslims were politically or economically dominant, and that means that the actual percentage of Muslims would have been considerably less than 10 percent. Nonetheless, we have biographical accounts of Muslims that indicate that despite their relatively low numbers, individual Muslims often stood out, in part because they were usually educated and sometimes well educated. By contrast, two-thirds of all slaves came from Bantu-speaking regions or the Bight of Biafra, where there were no Muslims. Many others came from areas along the West African coast where Islam was relatively unimportant except in regard to trade with the interior regions of Muslim dominance. Those who were enslaved close to the West African coast reflected political and social tensions in the states and societies of the coast and its immediate interior under conditions that often had little if anything to do with Islam.[4]

The slave trade of West Africa with both the Atlantic world and North Africa can be divided into two phases that were separated by a relatively clear break in patterns of trade and society. The first period covered the eighteenth century, while the second corresponded with the consolidation of the Sokoto Caliphate after 1804. Jihād affected both periods, but in the eighteenth century the influence of jihād was confined to the far western Bilād al-Sūdān, while the founding of Sokoto as the capital of an Islamic state in 1809 effectively marked a shift in the trade and politics of West Africa that affected the deportation of slaves to the Americas and North Africa. The stages of involvement in the slave trade affected both the transatlantic and trans-Saharan sectors, in which the jihād movement undermined the deportation of enslaved Africans from West Africa to the Americas while enhancing trade within the Muslim world. Even so, there was a recognizable presence of Muslims in the Americas in both the period before around 1804 and after, just as there was an equally profound presence of West Africans in North Africa and indeed elsewhere in the Ottoman Empire in particular. The second period emerged during the consolidation of jihād in the interior and was also marked by the British campaign to abolish the slave trade. British naval pressure initially focused on the trade along the West African coast and thereby coincidentally reinforced the political aims of the Muslim states of the interior, which wanted to limit involvement in the transatlantic slave trade anyway. The combined impact of Muslim jihād and British abolition further pushed the slave trade from West Africa to west central Africa, the Bantu-speaking region from which approximately half of all Africans who went to the Americas traced their origins for the whole course of the transatlantic slave trade, and from which two-thirds of all Africans came after 1807.

The regional origins of the enslaved in Africa need to be contextualized within Africa, not just through reference to points of coastal departure. From the perspective of the jihād states, most long-distance trade that required caravans was controlled by Muslims who lived in the major cities of the jihād states and used them as their base of operations. The extension of Muslim rule affected Asante, Oyo, and Dahomey, the principal non-Muslim states in West Africa in the late eighteenth and early nineteenth centuries. Just as the destinations of people can be determined in broad outline and therefore projections can be made about cultural, religious, and other influences, from burial practices to foodways, it is possible to assess the influence of jihād and the subsequent political alterations in response to it on the enslavement and sale of captives in West Africa. Specific contexts in West Africa shaped the movement of enslaved Africans to the Americas, but the forces that were unleashed in Africa were also global, influenced to various degrees by events outside Africa as well as regional and local conditions therein.

As is clear in table 5.1, two-thirds of all enslaved Africans came from areas in Africa that had no or very minimal connections with Islam in the century after 1760. Over half (53.1 percent) of all Africans who crossed the Atlantic came from Bantu-speaking areas where Islam was not a factor, except to a limited extent in southeastern Africa, where Muslim merchants operated. Similarly, there were few Muslims or individuals from areas where Muslim merchants were found in the interior of the Bight of Biafra, at least until the very last years of the transatlantic slave trade, when the Emirate of Adamawa founded satellite emirates at Banyo, Ngaundere, Tibati, and other places north of the Cross River. Approximately 15 percent of all enslaved Africans destined for the Americas came from the Bight of Biafra, which suggests that 67 percent of departures had little if anything to do with Islam.

Although one-third of all enslaved Africans came from the region west of the Niger delta where Islam was often significant, many of the enslaved who left had little if anything to do with the Muslim factor. Most of the enslaved population that boarded slave ships at the Bight of Benin, on the Gold Coast, and even along the upper Guinea Coast were not Muslims and did not come from areas where Islam was important in enslavement or trade. The area where Islam was a dominant feature of trade and society was Senegambia, which accounted for only about 4 percent of the total traffic. In my opinion, admittedly based to some extent on conjecture, fewer than 10 percent of Africans taken to the Americas came from Muslim areas, and even fewer were actually Muslims. These projections also call into question the use of the concept "African" since at the time people did not identify with a continental consciousness. Blackness of skin color was a feature of identification within the Muslim world, as reflected in the use of the term "Sūdānī," which specifically referred to Africans south of the Sahara who were black but did not refer to areas of sub-Saharan Africa with which Muslims had no contact. Religion, language, and political association were far more important in distinguishing people from one another. Otherwise, "African" is a convenience of modern scholarship that is meant to refer to the continental origins of people and specifically to the enslaved population that was born in Africa. Europeans and slave owners in the Americas conceived of "nations" and ethnic distinctions among the enslaved population and occasionally recognized that Muslims

TABLE 5.1. Departures from Africa for the Americas, 1761–1860

Decade	Senegambia	Sierra Leone	Windward Coast	Gold Coast	Bight of Benin	Bight of Biafra	West Central Africa	South East Africa	Totals
1761–1770	52,405	42,296	76,521	108,658	110,383	146,542	280,240	1,916	818,961
1771–1780	51,267	36,551	65,186	112,562	109,887	109,997	267,293	2,924	755,667
1781–1790	37,944	31,378	36,067	135,036	113,692	151,242	333,888	28,746	867,993
1791–1800	28,043	51,119	21,176	109,441	93,197	154,642	371,789	19,000	848,407
1801–1810	53,702	42,627	25,241	75,746	95,428	140,385	399,975	50,450	823,554
1811–1820	29,166	22,624	7,190	1,712	74,093	65,870	407,491	77,697	685,843
1821–1830	13,073	43,543	7,867	5,362	59,250	163,525	441,968	121,158	855,746
1831–1840	4,626	43,926	3,155	3,293	73,081	97,829	343,464	116,910	686,284
1841–1850	8,375	21,023	0	0	108,943	27,554	387,008	43,640	596,543
1851–1860	0	4,795	0	0	22,528	2	113,927	30,167	171,417
Totals	278,601	339,882	242,403	551,810	860,482	1,057,588	3,287,043	492,608	7,110,417
Percent	3.9	4.8	3.4	7.8	12.1	14.9	46.2	6.9	

Source: Voyages: The Trans-Atlantic Slave Trade Database, www.slavevoyages.org.

were part of the demographic makeup of the African population, but even then, religious affiliation was often subsumed under such labels as Wolof, Mandinke, Hausa, Fulbe, Nupe, and variations of these terms.

As has been well demonstrated, there were basically two transatlantic migrations, one across the South Atlantic that focused heavily on Brazil but also involved the transport of many people to the Caribbean and even to the mainland of Spanish America and to North America. There was also a North Atlantic migration that populated the Caribbean, the Spanish American mainland, and North America but also sent people to Brazil. It can be argued that this division in part explains the relative absence of Muslims among the enslaved population in much of the overall migration. Although slaves from West Africa, particularly from Bissau and Cacheu on the upper Guinea coast and from the Bight of Benin, were sent to Brazil, the people involved often came from near the coast. Except in specific contexts, not many people came from the Muslim interior. The development of two parallel migrations across the South Atlantic and the North Atlantic explains the relative absence of slaves from Muslim West Africa to some extent, but not entirely. Hence it is appropriate to examine internal factors within West Africa to explain the patterns of migration.

By the late eighteenth century west central Africa and the Bight of Biafra were already the dominant source of slaves for the Americas. Between 1761 and 1789 the proportion of Africans from the Bight of Biafra and west central and southeast Africa was about half of all departures, 52.3 percent in the 1760s and 50.3 percent in the 1770s, but thereafter the proportion rose steadily, reaching 59.2 percent in the 1780s, 64.3 percent in the 1790s, and 71.7 percent in the first decade of the nineteenth century. Thereafter these regions accounted for over 80 percent of all departures (80.3 percent in the 1810s, 84.9 percent in the 1820s, 81.3 percent in the 1830s, 76.8 percent in the 1840s, and 84.1 percent in the 1850s). These proportions are crucial in recognizing the self-imposed withdrawal of Islamic West Africa from participation in the transatlantic slave trade. As noted in chapter 1, the extent of slave resistance near and on-board slave ships in the Senegambia ports may also have reduced the number of European slave ships in the area.[5] This factor combined with the influence of Islam on commercial patterns and the relatively restricted extent of Muslim involvement in the Atlantic slave trade. During the age of revolutions the Bight of Biafra, west central Africa, and southeastern Africa were by far the most important regions of slave supply for the Americas. Changes within West Africa that resulted in the consolidation of Islamic rule were at least as effective in removing the region from transatlantic slavery as British abolition was along the coast, if not more so.

An examination of West Africa reveals how many Muslims are likely to have been included among those who went to the Americas. The analysis attempts to decipher the designations used in the *Voyages: The Trans-Atlantic Slave Trade Database* which are based on the different coastal points of departure but do not indicate from where individuals actually came. The question is how to determine the proportion of the enslaved population transported to the Americas in the period from the middle of the eighteenth century to the middle of the nineteenth century who possibly came from the inland parts of Africa west of the Niger delta. Almost everyone from Senegambia can be included in this category, although it is known that a portion of this population was not Muslim. The region that is designated "Sierra Leone" included Fuuta Jalon and the network of Muslim Juula merchant communities to the east of Fuuta Jalon, and although some Muslims left from this portion of the upper Guinea coast, not everyone was Muslim. Some people from the so-called Windward Coast were also from the Muslim interior, although the term "Windward Coast" is in fact something of a misnomer because it is a nautical term not indigenous to West Africa but instead derives from the geographical observations of European slaving ships. The extent to which people from the far interior left this area is an important consideration in identifying Muslims. Those who came from near the coast, which accounts for almost everyone, including those identified as "Ganga," were not Muslims. Some Muslims came from the interior of the Gold Coast, especially the northern provinces of Asante and even farther north, although those identified as Akan, who accounted for the great majority, were not Muslims. Similarly, some Muslims came from the interior of the Bight of Benin, specifically through Dahomey and Oyo before 1817, but not those usually identified in the Americas as Arara, Mina, or Nagô (although possibly some referred to as Nagô were Muslims). After the uprising at Ilorin in 1817 and the subsequent jihād in Oyo, many enslaved Yoruba, as well as others from farther north who were referred to as Hausa, Tapa (Nupe), and "Borno," can be associated with Islam, even if not everyone was Muslim. Indeed, the designation "Hausa" included many people whose first language was not Hausa but whose enslavement was often a consequence of the jihād.

I estimate that fewer than 10 percent of all the Africans sent to the Americas from the middle of the eighteenth century to the middle of the nineteenth century came from areas affected by jihād, that is, probably no more than 200,000 people out of an estimated departing population of 2,273,000. This assessment depends on the degree to which those identified as Yoruba are considered to have been enslaved as a result of jihād. In my assessment the collapse of Oyo after 1817 was the major contributing factor to the enslavement of those identified in Bahia as Nagô and those in Cuba as Lucumí, and these designations included many people who did not speak Yoruba as a first language. This projection represents a significant proportion of the estimated population that departed from regions west of the Bight of Biafra, but by no means a majority. A closer analysis of the traffic from Senegambia and the upper Guinea coast suggests that the proportion of slaves who were Muslims was considerably less than the aggregate figures might suggest.

The Trade of Senegambia and the Upper Guinea Coast

This section examines what we know about the slave trade from the interior of West Africa to the coast, and where that occurred in the period 1750–1850. The main division in the interior of West Africa was between Muslim regions of the western Bilād al-Sūdān, where dialects of Mande (Mandinka, Juula, Bambara) served as a commercial language, and the interior of the Bight of Benin, where Hausa served a similar function. This linguistic pattern related to historical developments within Africa that are reflected in the artificial "regions" that were perceived from the perspective of slave ships. In effect, the Senegambia of *Voyages: The Trans-Atlantic Slave Trade Database* refers to two relatively distinct areas: first, areas very near the coast, and second, the interior states of Fuuta Toro, Fuuta Bundu, Kaabu, and the Bambara states of Segu and Kaarta, that is, what is often called the western Bilād al-Sūdān. By contrast, "Sierra Leone" refers not just to the river of that name but also to the other trading locations along the upper Guinea coast (Rio Nuñez, Rio Pongo, Îles de Los, the Bullom Shore, Banana Islands, Sherbro, and so on) and also the Muslim interior, especially Fuuta Jalon and the Muslim Juula networks extending inland to Kankan and beyond—that is, the stretch of coast hemmed in by Fuuta Jalon and the routes to the south of Fuuta Jalon that were the main suppliers of kola nuts sent to the western Bilād al-Sūdān. Kola nuts were one of the most important commodities of trade in West Africa, being produced only in the forests of Sierra Leone and areas eastward as far as Asante but consumed largely in the savanna country to the north. Muslims dominated all the routes to the kola-producing zone and therefore the slave trade. Muslims also controlled the gold trade, as well as other commerce in the interior.

There were coastal enclaves that stand out as a feature of the trade with the Muslim interior. European merchants did not venture inland but stayed at the coast, where they dealt through local resident agents. St. Louis on the Senegal River, the island of Gorée, and James Island in the Gambia River served as depots for the trade with the Muslim interior in the Senegambia region. Farther south, settlements were established near the mouths of the many rivers and on the offshore islands as far as Cape Mount on the border of modern Sierra Leone and Liberia. The resident agents, who were of diverse backgrounds, including Portuguese, Jewish, French, Scottish, English, Irish, and even North American and Brazilian, married locally, thereby establishing connections with local kinship networks, and their offspring continued to run the trade. These agents and their descendants were not Muslims, and in fact the women whom they married inherited property and often managed the ongoing family businesses. The status of the women was recognized through their titles as *signares* in French and *donas* in Portuguese. They account for such families as the Caulkers, the Clevelands, and the Lawrences, which retained the names of the foreign merchants and their commercial positions along the coast, including transatlantic connections with Florida, South Carolina, Georgia, Brazil, and the Cape Verde Islands.[6] Fenda Lawrence stands out because she left the Gambia River and moved to Charleston in 1772, apparently with the intention of going to Savannah, along with her slaves.[7] Others of these mixed-race traders, including Elizabeth Cleveland (who went to South Carolina in the 1740s) and the family of John Holman (who went there in the 1790s) also made the move, while other slave traders in the southeastern United States like John Fraser and Stiles Lightbourne had transatlantic families and trade connections.[8] Similarly, Anna Madgigine Jai Kingsley provides another example of a woman who was able to marry into a slave-trading and slave-owning relationship. She was captured in Wolof country in 1806 and taken to Cuba, where she became the slave of Zephaniah Kingsley Jr., who eventually married her.[9] Robert MacNamara, acting governor of the Province of Senegambia until 1777, left property to his common-law wife in his will. MacNamara had apparently resided with her while serving at St. James Fort in the Gambia and then at St. Louis, which further demonstrates that resident Europeans and Americans consolidated commercial arrangements through marriage. African women were useful both in the slave trade and in the management of enslaved populations, whether on the upper Guinea coast or in various places in the Americas. Had the United States not outlawed the trade in 1808, these trade links might have intensified as they did between Lagos, Porto Novo, and Ouidah and Brazil in the South Atlantic.

These individuals can be identified with Ira Berlin's "Atlantic creoles," who have been further studied by Jane Landers in the Americas, but not with respect to the West African coast.[10] The insights of Berlin and Landers help in the analysis of the trade of Senegambia and the upper Guinea coast. These Atlantic creoles were scattered along the coast at such places as St. Louis in the Senegal River, Gorée Island, James Island in the Gambia River, Bissau, Cacheu, Rio Nuñez, Rio Pongo, Îles de Los, the Sierra Leone River, Bunce Island, the Bananas, Sherbro, and the Gallinas. A large percentage of departures from Senegambia and the upper Guinea coast passed through the hands of these coastal agents, as can be seen in table 5.2. The Atlantic creoles of coastal Africa were urbane and educated, traveled widely around the Atlantic, and were innovative, introducing new crops to be produced locally in Africa for the international market, besides trading in slaves who were largely brought from the interior by Muslim merchants and often under the supervision of government agents of Muslim states, such as Fuuta Toro, Fuuta Bundu, and Fuuta Jalon. They made their money as brokers while leaving the major tasks of commercial organization to the Muslim networks.

The places of departure from Senegambia and elsewhere on the upper Guinea coast are reasonably well known for the century after 1760, when approximately 619,000 enslaved individuals left for the Americas. As reflected in table 5.2, the points of embarkation are known for 68.8 percent of departures, that is, about two-thirds of the total number of enslaved who actually left. Hence realistic figures for specific ports would be one-third higher than the recorded estimates in table 5.2. The Senegal River, the Gambia River, the Bissau-Cacheu estuaries, the concentration of Rio Nuñez, Rio Pongo and Îles de Los, and the Sierra Leone River and its outposts to the south as far as Sherbro account for about 90 percent of departures. As can be seen in table 5.2, the Senegal and Gambia Rivers, as well as Îles de Los and the Sierra Leone River, were important only until British abolition of the slave trade in 1807, whereas Gallinas became important during the era of British naval suppression because the barracoons to house slaves could be constructed behind the sandbars that provided some protection from British raids from the sea. As a whole, these points of departure accounted for 292,000 slaves from 1761 to 1807 and 89,000 after 1807, which, as stated, probably represented about two-thirds of actual departures.

The hinterlands on which each of these coastal embarkation points drew were also relatively distinct. The Senegal and Gambia departures drew on the interior as far as the Bambara states which included territory where there was a significant population of Muslims and areas that were heavily influenced

Jihād and the Slave Trade

TABLE 5.2. Departures from Senegambia and the Upper Guinea Coast, Known Places of Embarkation, 1761–1860

Point of Departure	Departures, 1761–1807	Departures, 1808–1860	Departures, 1761–1860	% Known Departures
St. Louis	42,000	5,000	47,000	11.0
Gambia	47,000	1,000	48,000	11.3
Bissau and Cacheu	59,000	26,000	85,000	20.0
Rio Pongo and Rio Nuñez	12,000	18,000	30,000	7.0
Îles de Los	45,000	0	45,000	10.6
Sierra Leone River	84,000	2,000	86,000	20.2
Gallinas	3,000	37,000	40,000	9.4
Subtotal	292,000	89,000	381,000	89.4
Other ports*	25,000	20,000	45,000	10.6
Total: Senegambia and Upper Guinea Coast	317,000	109,000	426,000	
Unspecified Origins	9,000	7,000	16,000	
Estimated Total Departures from Region	412,000	207,000	619,000	

Source: Voyages: The Trans-Atlantic Slave Trade Database, www.slavevoyages.org.
*Other ports include Albreda, Arguim, Banana Islands, Bissagos, Cacandia, Cape Verde Islands, Casamance, Delagoa, Galam, Gorée, Joal, Kissi River, Madeira, Mano, Oibo, Plantain Island, Portudal, Rio Grande, Saloum River, the Scarcies, Sherbro, and Siekere.

by Islam. Many slaves came from the Senegal River valley. Charles O'Hara, governor of the short-lived British Province of Senegambia, was involved in the enslavement of people along the Senegal River from 1767 to 1777, when 17,000 slaves left St. Louis, including an estimated 8,000 people enslaved in Waalo in 1775. The depredations stopped only when O'Hara returned to Britain and the state of Fuuta Toro was established in jihād after 1776.[11] Otherwise, most departures were only marginally related to jihād, other than to demonstrate the insecurity that potentially resulted in the enslavement of Muslims. For example, coastal populations that were enslaved were a significant proportion of the 59,000 leaving from Bissau and Cacheu, and they were not Muslim, although the enslaved brought from Kaabu in the immediate interior included Muslims who were identified as "Mandingo" in the Americas. Nonetheless, there appear not to have been many Muslims, to judge from the demography of the enslaved population in northeastern Brazil, where most of the enslaved from Bissau and Cacheu went.[12] The ports in Rio Nuñez and Rio Pongo and at the Îsle de Los were supplied largely from Fuuta Jalon, and according to contemporary accounts, Fuuta Jalon tried to make sure that no Muslims were in the deported population.[13] Sierra Leone, by contrast, drew on the Muslim commercial networks to the south and east of Fuuta Jalon, and it seems that some Muslims, such as Muhammad Kabā Saghanughu, did find their way to the coast and hence onto slave ships there. Kabā Saghanughu was apparently enslaved in conditions that had little if anything to do with jihād, since he appears to have been captured to the east of his hometown on his way to Timbuktu. His enslavement was reflective more of the state of insecurity of Muslims that prompted jihād. However, again, the non-Muslim population was far more significant in the deported population, as reflected in those who went to the anglophone Caribbean and North America. Similarly, ʿUmar ibn Saʿīd was enslaved in Fuuta Toro about 1770 and at age thirty-seven arrived in South Carolina, where he remained enslaved until his death in 1864 (plate 19).[14] His enslavement was clearly associated with the insecurity in the middle Senegal valley to which the clerical class was subjected and that prompted jihād there.

In the case of Fuuta Jalon, government officials were directly involved in trade to the coast and thereby were in a position to protect freeborn Muslims.[15] The British abolitionist James Watt, who traveled to the Fuuta Jalon capital of Timbo in 1794 to promote the trade of the Sierra Leone Company, was assured that Muslims were not sold into slavery. The representative of Almami Sadu was reported to have claimed that "the people with whom we go to war . . . do not pray to God. We never go to war with people who do God Almighty service."[16] Fuuta Jalon justified its involvement in the slave trade by insisting that those who were being sold were not Muslims, and that the state needed to sell slaves as an expedient way to acquire imports, as long as the state and not individual merchants of the commercial diaspora regulated the trade.[17] Indeed, Roger Botte indicates that the Fuuta Jalon government walked a fine line in its involvement in the slave trade. On the one hand, it wanted to take advantage of the lucrative trade with the Europeans and compete with their non-Muslim neighbors, but at the same time it had to be cognizant of the anti-slave-trade sentiment that existed throughout the region.[18] Hence Muslim merchants were sometimes willing to sell the enslaved to Christians despite moral and religious inhibitions. Yet the interior region of the western Bilād al-Sūdān provided a smaller number of slaves than it was capable of doing, which reveals the combined impact of government policy and the fact that Muslim merchants dominated the trade in slaves from the interior to the coast, as well as the trade in other goods.

The fact that the coastal merchants were largely confined to the coast helps explain why Europeans knew so little about the interior of West Africa until very late in the eighteenth century and even until well into the nineteenth century. The extent of knowledge of the interior was limited because contacts were few and were mediated through coastal agents who themselves lacked such knowledge. This imposed isolation helps explain the intense interest in Europe, especially in Britain, France, Scandinavia, and Germany, whose observers wanted to "discover" the geography of an area of Muslim dominance whose geography had been well known since the days of Ibn Khaldūn, if not centuries earlier. Despite centuries of European trade on the West African coast and in the Niger delta, the degree of European ignorance is astonishing, since the Niger River did not change its course over the centuries, and Lake Chad rose and fell with the extent of precipitation. The relative ease of overland communication and travel in an area that, despite distances, was well supplied with food, water, and accommodation should have made these geographical features common knowledge. There were certainly limitations to the economy and society, as reflected in the spread of the jihād, but the geography did not change.

Hence Muslim commercial dominance relied on coastal merchants who were often closely associated with political authority at the coast, such as the Clevelands of the Banana Islands and other merchant families who were essential in the interface between Atlantic commerce and Muslim networks. A fresh interpretation recognizes that documentary evidence and specialized knowledge of Islamic West Africa can be drawn on to assess the impact of the jihād movement. Clearly, individual Muslims were swept up in the trade, as in the case of Ibrahima ʿAbd al-Raḥmān, who was educated in Timbuktu and Jenne. He was the son of the second *almami* of Fuuta Jalon but was captured in war in 1789 (plate 20). Other examples of Muslims who were part of the commercial and political elite have been cited as evidence that individuals leaked through the sieve of Islamic withdrawal from the transatlantic slave trade. Nonetheless, these exceptions do not alter my conclusion that the jihād movement largely disconnected many parts of West Africa from the European-dominated Atlantic world during the age of revolutions. Scholars of slavery and slave resistance in the Americas, with exceptions, have either overlooked or ignored the jihād as a factor influencing the course of history since Hobsbawm and Genovese published their insights.

Muslims were leaving the Bight of Benin in recognizable numbers during the eighteenth century, especially in the last decades of the century. In his *Infāq al-Maysūr*, Muhammad Bello charged that Muslims were being sold to the "Yoruba" and then to Christians for transport to the Americas.[19] The trade route led through Oyo, from the crossing of the Niger at Raka to the capital at Katunga and southward through the Egbado towns to Porto Novo, where Pierre Tamata served as principal factor for the French until the collapse of the French trade in 1793. Thereafter, Tamata consolidated a Muslim ward in Porto Novo, with its own mosque, that continued to cater to trade from Oyo even though the French were no longer active there. Although the data are not conclusive, it can be stated, as a conservative estimate, that slaves from the Muslim interior constituted at least 10 to 15 percent of the slaves exported from the Bight of Benin in the 1770s and 1780s, and the proportion rose in the 1790s and the first decade of the nineteenth century as the number of slaves from areas close to the coast fell off. During the period from around 1760 to 1810 over 520,000 people left the Bight of Benin, and perhaps 40,000 to 50,000 of these came from the Muslim interior. The port of departure for this period is not known for a significant number of departures, which were often identified only with the "Costa da Mina" or without even that designation. Nonetheless, it is certain that the overwhelming proportion of the these departures were from the single port of Ouidah. In the period from 1811 to 1860 another 340,000 left, and at this time numbers of the enslaved were increasingly a product of the jihād. The four most important points of departure in the Bight of Benin in the century after 1760 were Ouidah, Porto Novo, Badagry before 1800, and then heavily Lagos until the British occupation ended its involvement in 1851. Of the 297,000 people known to have left Lagos, 265,000 departed after 1800 (table 5.3).[20]

The jihād clearly accounted for a significant proportion of slaves leaving from the Bight of Benin in the nineteenth century. The route to the coast continued to pass through Oyo, at least until the early 1830s, but increasing insecurity related to the jihād interfered with the trade. The lower Niger River thereupon became an alternate route to the coast, while other slaves were taken along the major east-west route to Asante, the principal source of kola nuts, the widely consumed stimulant. Slaves sent to Asante were reexported to the ports of the Bight of Benin because the imposition of British abolition after 1807 isolated the Gold Coast castles, which could no longer export slaves.

TABLE 5.3. Departures from the Bight of Benin, 1761–1860

Decade	Bight of Benin	Costa da Mina*	Ouidah*	Porto Novo*	Badagry*	Lagos
1761–1770	110,381	25,524	29,014	8,669	8,451	3,142
1771–1780	109,886	38,733	26,358	10,658	9,894	4,010
1781–1790	113,691	52,867	17,196	19,770	2,650	17,947
1791–1800	93,196	55,914	15,041	6,763	1,321	7,468
1801–1810	95,428	58,583	5,999	2,669	2,481	49,830
1811–1820	74,093	46,427	5,176	1,606	508	43,267
1821–1830	59,250	7,684	10,834	843	3,004	49,503
1831–1840	73,083	2,551	11,354	490	—	43,918
1841–1850	108,943	11,507	8,258	1,673	354	72,753
1851–1860	22,528	1,589	4,981	—	—	5,410
Totals	860,479	301,379	134,211	53,141	28,663	297,248

Sources: Voyages: The Trans-Atlantic Slave Trade Database www.slavevoyages.org for Bight of Benin, Costa da Mina, Ouidah, Porto Novo and Badagry; for Lagos, Kristin Mann, Slavery and the Birth of an African City: Lagos, 1760–1900 (Bloomington: Indiana University Press, 2007), 38.
*Partial figures based on known departures.

At most, 100,000 to 150,000 slaves from the interior, not including northern Yoruba, crossed the Atlantic between the middle of the eighteenth century and the middle of the nineteenth century. This estimate includes those identified as Hausa, Nupe, Borno, Borgu, and other designations that indicate an origin north of the Yoruba country and Asante.[21] At the height of this trade, as reported by Clapperton in 1824, "the greater part of the young Male Slaves [for sale in the central Bilād al-Sūdān] are carried down and disposed of in the Bight of Benin."[22] In the early 1850s Heinrich Barth claimed that the trade along the Niger River below the confluence with the Benue River had fallen "into the hands of the American [i.e., Brazilian] slave-dealers, who have opened a regular annual slave-trade with those regions."[23] Using information gathered in the Sokoto Caliphate during his travels there, Barth devoted a whole chapter in his massive study to the South American slave trade. Other information also demonstrates the continuation of the slave trade from the Sokoto Caliphate, whether or not it was sanctioned by the governments of the various emirates.[24]

Those identified as "northern" Yoruba, that is, Oyo, Ekiti, Yagba, and other Okun Yoruba, were also well represented in the exported population, although it is not possible to estimate the number of northern Yoruba with any accuracy.[25] After the establishment of the Sokoto Caliphate, the proportion of slaves from the far interior in the exported population of the Bight of Benin appears to have fluctuated. In the early 1810s, the first half of the 1820s, and the first half of the 1830s, when total exports from the Bight of Benin were relatively low, perhaps 25 to 40 percent of the exported slaves were captured in the wars associated with the Sokoto Caliphate. In years of peak exports in the late 1810s, the late 1820s, and the late 1830s, the proportion of slaves from the region northeast of the Niger River probably fell to 15 percent of total exports from the Bight of Benin.[26] The impact of the jihād was still considerable, since the numbers of Yoruba were substantial, especially those from the northern Yoruba area that had been part of Oyo.

In 1806 the Bight of Benin supplied Bahia with 8,307 "Gege [Ewe/Fon/Gbe], Usa [Hausa] and Nago [Yoruba] slaves."[27] Although the proportions of the individual categories are not known, the Sokoto wars made it likely that Hausa slaves formed a large share.[28] The importance of the jihād in generating slaves between 1804 and 1810 is further attested in the biographical accounts of slaves who had been captured in the jihād. The concentration of Hausa slaves in Bahia dates from this period. A sample of 177 slaves on four separate slave ships dating to 1821–22 includes 41 Nupe, 34 Hausa, and 1 Fulani; they constituted 43 percent of those whose ethnic origins were identified.[29] This sample of four ships appears to have been typical only for the first half of the 1820s. In the late 1820s and the late 1830s Yoruba slaves went in substantial numbers, and during these periods slaves from farther north declined relatively but were still a substantial proportion of total exports. Patrick Manning, using a different method of projection, has reached a comparable estimate, concluding that 93,000 Hausa and Nupe slaves were exported from the Bight of Benin in the eighteenth and nineteenth centuries. According to Manning's projections, these included 22,200 Nupe slaves between the 1740s and the 1860s and 70,800 Hausa slaves between the 1780s and the 1860s.[30] Given the crudeness of the data and the fact that Manning does not include non-Hausa and non-Nupe slaves, his estimate is approximately consistent with my own.

The overwhelming majority of slaves exported across the Atlantic from the area of jihād were prime adult males.[31] Young adult males constituted "the vast majority of southbound exports" from the Sokoto Caliphate in the nineteenth century, according to David Tambo.[32] Most of these men were seized in war or raids associated with the jihād. It has previously been observed that slave raiding and enslavement through military engagements associated with the jihād were extensive, but the conscious sale of males for export to the

Americas has not been fully appreciated.[33] According to one British officer in Sierra Leone in 1821, "Many natives from Houssa, who have been made prisoners by the Foulahs [Fula, that is, Fulani or Fulbe] and [have] been brought overland to the Gold Coast," were subsequently sold to European slave traders.[34] A collection of 108 biographical sketches of slaves from the central Bilād al-Sūdān in the first half of the nineteenth century supports these observations; 95.4 percent of the exported slaves in the sample were males, and almost all of them were young adults. Moreover, most of these young men appear to have been Muslims.[35] Only five (4.6 percent) were females, three adults and two girls. The preponderance of males among the exported slave population also characterized the northern Yoruba area.[36] This gender ratio corresponds with the information analyzed by Gwendolyn Midlo Hall for Louisiana and Walter Hawthorne for Maranhão in Brazil. Bello's willingness to abolish this trade was consistent with his earlier criticisms of illegal enslavement and sale, while al-Ḥājj 'Umar's criticisms establish that the caliphate leadership was well aware in 1837 that the trade to the coast had not been stopped.[37]

As Clapperton reported from Wawa in Borgu in 1826, "The slaves sold to the sea coast are generally those taken in war or refractory and intractable domestic slaves. Nyffe at present is the place that produces the most slaves, owing to the civil war raging in that country."[38]

Among the many examples of male slaves taken to the coast after the start of the jihād and sold into the transatlantic trade was a man named Dan Kano, who was "born at Brinee Yawoori [Birnin Yauri] and was there about sixteen or seventeen years ago [before 8 April 1821]," when he was seized by Fulani while on a trading expedition "and carried to the Gold Coast," where he was sold to a Portuguese ship, probably at Ouidah or Little Popo.[39] As his name suggests, his mother was apparently from Kano, or at least he otherwise had some connection with Kano. Sergeant Frazer, who was serving in the Second West India Regiment in Sierra Leone in 1821, was born in Hausaland "and resided there a long time, [before being] taken prisoner in Goingia [Gonja], and brought to the Gold Coast, where he was sold." Frazer had been a merchant who dealt in natron from Borno.[40] Similarly, the former slave Pasco, whose birth name was Abubakar, was originally from Gobir and after being taken in war during the jihād sometime before 1815 was "sold to a Gonja trader," who resold him to "a native of Ashantee" who in turn sold him to a trader going to Ouidah, where he was sold to a Portuguese ship.[41] His ship was intercepted, and he was taken to Sierra Leone, where he subsequently became the servant of British diplomat Hugh Clapperton.

Antônio de Menezes Vasconcellos de Drummond published summaries of seven interviews with Hausa slaves in Brazil in 1826. These interviews had been conducted in 1819 by José Bonifácio de Andrada e Silva (1763–1838), poet, naturalist, and Brazilian statesman known as the "Patriarca da Independência" for his decisive role in the independence of Brazil from Portugal in the 1820s. Since the slaves are referred to as "his," it is possible that Andrada was their master. As prisoners of the jihād, they may not all have been Muslims, but it is likely that some of them were, at least nominally. Unfortunately, Andrada's data do not include information on non-Hausa slaves.[42] All had been taken prisoner during the jihād and had passed to the coast at Lagos ("Ico," i.e., Eko, the Hausa name for Lagos). Among these men were François, who came from Kano; Guillaume Pasco, alias Abubakar, who was from Katsina; and Mathieu, who was from Daura. Joseph was originally from Tabarau in Nupe; Bernard was from Gobir; Benoit was from Gaya ("Ghuiah"); and Boniface was from Kebbi.[43] Additional biographical sketches include material from a British officer serving in Sierra Leone in 1821[44] and from Hugh Clapperton's second expedition to the Sokoto Caliphate in 1826.[45]

Of the twenty-three individuals the French consul in Bahia, Francis de Castelnau, interviewed in 1849, twenty-two were Hausa and one was a Fulani cleric from Kano.[46] Most reached the coast at Lagos, although Boué (Bawa), who had come from Zaria, apparently in the 1830s or 1840s, was taken to Asante, where he was sold to "European" slavers, probably Portuguese, most likely at Little Popo, since by this date virtually no slaves were leaving from the Gold Coast for the Americas.[47] So Allah came from Adamawa, and as his name suggests, he was probably enslaved twice, "So Allah" being the Hausa name that was given to a slave in the Sokoto Caliphate (plate 21). The Niger expedition of 1841 recruited former slaves in Sierra Leone to serve as interpreters. The Reverend James Frederick Schön recruited six former slaves who had come from the Sokoto Caliphate in Sierra Leone for the Niger Expedition of 1841, including Kakanda, Yoruba, "Bornu," Hausa, Nupe, and Fulani.[48]

Sigismund Wilhelm Koelle identified many liberated slaves from the interior of the Bight of Benin in 1849–50, including Igala (13), Nupe (303), Borno or Kanuri (36), Buduma (1), Fika (5), Karekare (2), Bede and Ngizim (16), Hausa (8), and an unknown number of Fulani.[49] Abali, who was born in

Kanem, became a soldier in the Borno army but was seized during a raid on Kano in 1844 and was sold south to Lagos. Another slave born in Kano was also a soldier when he was captured in a raid on Gobir in 1844, "where he was bought by slave dealers, and at once carried to the sea by way of Kadzina [Katsina], Zalia [Zaria], Nupe, Ilori [Ilorin], Dsebu [Ijebu], and Eko [Lagos]."[50] Similarly, Habu, renamed Sam Jackson, was born in Kano in the 1820s but was seized in a raid by Gobir sometime in the late 1840s and sold south to Lagos. Or consider Mohammadu from Katsina, who was seized by Fulani while working on his farm and then sold to Gobir, from where he was taken to Damagaram and then sold south to Rabba and Ilorin on his way to the coast, probably at Lagos, in the 1840s.[51] Hausa slaves were underrepresented in Koelle's sample because he was trying to identify as many languages as possible and therefore contacted and enumerated smaller proportions of the larger linguistic communities. Nevertheless, he collected information on the backgrounds of sixty-six individuals.

In the case of eighty-two slaves whose method of enslavement is known, sixty-two (75.6 percent) identified their enslavement specifically with war, Fulani raids, or the jihād.[52] Another twelve slaves (14.6 percent) had been kidnapped, and their seizures may or may not have been related to the jihād. In a few cases war appears to have been related to secondary engagements on the frontiers of the Sokoto Caliphate. Taken together, 90.2 percent of slaves reported that they had been violently seized. The correlation between the high percentage of enslavements through violence and the prevalence of adult males in the enslaved population that was exported is suggestive. Prime males also were common among northern Yoruba exports, although not among Yoruba as a whole. The wars and raids of Nupe and Ilorin appear to have accounted for a significant proportion of these slaves. In some cases captives had been soldiers, and a few were Muslim clerics, who were often involved in the jihād, which also indicates an adult population. As Clapperton reported from Wawa in Borgu in 1826, "The slaves sold to the sea coast are generally those taken in war or refractory and intractable domestic slaves. Nyffe at present is the place that produces the most slaves, owing to the civil war raging in that country."[53]

Hausa, Nupe, and Borno slaves and former slaves constituted a significant portion of the population in Bahia in the first third of the nineteenth century. According to João José Reis, the registers of manumitted slaves between 1819 and 1836 and a sample of urban slaves from 1820 to 1835 suggest that at least 15.8 percent of all slaves and former slaves in Bahia in the mid-1830s had come from the Sokoto Caliphate and Borno. Among those whose ethnic origins are known (2,441 individuals) were 385 individuals from the central Bilād al-Sūdān, of whom 252 were Hausa (10.3 percent), 88 were Nupe (3.6 percent), and 45 were from Borno (1.8 percent). If Yoruba cast into the trade by the wars stemming from the Sokoto Caliphate are included in this total, the proportion of slaves from the area of jihād would have been higher still. Yoruba slaves and freed slaves constituted 28.6 percent of Reis's samples (699 persons),[54] and it seems likely that many, if not most, of these slaves were products of the jihād or its aftermath. In 1848 there were 657 Hausa and 163 Nupe in Sierra Leone; the total population was 13,273.[55] If these numbers are combined with slaves from Borno and elsewhere in areas affected by jihād, which I estimate at approximately 420, it is likely that there were at least 1,240 people from the Sokoto Caliphate and Borno in Freetown, or somewhat less than 10 percent of the liberated slave population.

Among the slaves and former slaves who were tried for their involvement in the 1835 Malês revolt were a number of Muslim clerics. The slave Antonio, for example, was of Hausa origin and had been to Qur'anic school before being captured.[56] Reis has provided the fullest study of these clerics, while Raimundo Nina Rodrigues collected information on Malam Abubakar, who appears to have been the imam of the Muslim community at the time.[57] Crowther met two Hausa men who had been liberated in Brazil at Badagry in 1845. One, Mohama, was a *malam*, with whom Crowther became engaged in a lengthy theological discussion.[58] Castelnau found that some Muslim clerics from the Sokoto Caliphate were learned. In 1848 Muhammad Abdullahi described himself as Fulani from Kano. He had been in Bahia for thirty years, having been taken in battle during a campaign against Maradi, the independent Hausa enclave north of Katsina. According to Castelnau,

> This old man, Mohammed-Abdullad, Filani, who has been in Bahia
> some thirty years, freed himself from slavery by his work, and today
> is a carpenter. He is educated and not only knows how to read and
> write in his language, but also in Portuguese. Moreover, he is very
> intolerant, very fanatical, and he wants to convert me by all means; and
> even though I treated him very well, gave him money, etc. he refused to
> come back to my house, telling another Negro that he did not want to
> go to the house of a Christian dog. He might be seventy years old. He
> was a *marabout* and had made the voyage to Mecca. . . . He makes a lot

of fun of the Hausas, saying that they grow goatee beards in order to look like men. . . . The Hausa Negroes at my house seem to have a great deal of respect for this man and, following his example, start to mutter in chanting the verses of the Koran.[59]

Similarly, the revealing account of the imām of Baghdad, who wrote about his time in Rio de Janeiro in the early 1860s, described the continued presence of Muslims in Brazil even after the suppression of the 1835 rebellion in Bahia.[60] In addition, other accounts have been collected on enslavement in the area of jihād in the first half of the nineteenth century that provide evidence of the impact of the jihād movement.[61] In short, there is no absence of source material, much of which is readily accessible.

Slaves from the area of jihād figured prominently in the transatlantic slave trade from the Bight of Benin after 1810, reflecting the extension of the jihād, including the Muslim uprising of the Ilorin military in 1817, the Owu wars of the early 1820s, the revolts that undermined Oyo in the 1820s, the Nupe wars from 1822 to 1856, and the failed Muslim uprising in Borgu in 1835. The abortive caliphate drive to the coast in 1843 demonstrated the ongoing interest of the caliphate in the south. The jihād clearly resulted in the enslavement of people in areas ever closer to the Bight of Benin. Nonetheless, the numbers of enslaved people from the Yoruba region and the area of the Sokoto jihād were disproportionately small, despite their prominence in Brazil, especially Bahia, as well as the presence in Cuba of people identified as Lucumi and Sierra Leone as Aku or Akoo. The great majority of slaves came from west central Africa, Mozambique, and the Bight of Biafra, not from the Bight of Benin, and by far the greatest number went to Brazil. There was important crossover between Cuba and Brazil, so that Brazilian and Cuban ships, sometimes under the flag of the United States and even owned by Americans, were involved in the trade. Hence the percentage of Yoruba and Muslims was relatively small in the context of the major population movement.

Thus the disruptions of the jihād fed the slave trade after 1804, and Muslim traders were heavily involved. In 1816, according to Simon Cook, editor of John Adams's journal, reports from Lagos noted that Hausa merchants "still came down to that mart, though in smaller bodies" than before 1807.[62] The resident Muslim population included "a number of Haussa Mallams" who in 1820 or 1821 followed their master, Oba Adele, into exile at Badagry. These slaves, who had been owned by Adele's father, were "supporting themselves by trading for slaves which they sell to Europeans."[63] How long these Muslims had been active in the trade is unclear. In Dahomey the accession of Gezo in 1818 ushered in a period of active trade with Muslim merchants. Initially, Dahomey looked to Oyo and its links with the north, but after 1823 attention was directed at the Bariba towns.[64]

The full extent of Muslim commercial involvement in the transatlantic trade is the subject of ongoing study, but by the early 1820s at least one Hausa merchant was trading directly between Salvador and the Bight of Benin. Known by his Portuguese name, Francisco da Rocha lived in Pilar parish in Salvador, Bahia, where he had freed himself from slavery and had married a Hausa woman (Silveira) whom he probably freed, but apparently he did not free her children. Francisco da Rocha carried on an active trade in slaves and other goods with Lagos, even traveling there himself. Details of his affairs are reported in his 1830 will.[65] Although his connections in Lagos are not yet clear, his knowledge of Hausa would have been useful in trade with Muslim merchants from the Sokoto Caliphate.

On the basis of what is known about the Atlantic slave trade, we can conclude that the scale of trade from the interior regions of Muslim dominance was relatively low. Basically, Muslims left West Africa via the Senegambia region as far south as Sierra Leone, where Muslim-dominated trade stretched to the coast or to ports on the Senegal and Gambia Rivers. None of the other rivers penetrated inland far enough to give safe anchorage for ships and allow local merchants to establish warehouses and baracoons and otherwise provide accommodation for caravans that came overland from the interior, particularly the Muslim state of Fuuta Jalon, one of the states of jihād. We also can estimate where people went and when, and in looking at Muslims and people who possibly came from areas of Muslim domination, we can see that the proportion of Muslims in the total migration to the Americas during the era of slavery was very low, certainly not more than 10 percent of the total and probably less, perhaps as little as 5 percent, for the late eighteenth and early nineteenth centuries.

By contrast with the coastal merchants who were tied to the banks of the sea, Muslim merchants traveled hundreds or even thousands of kilometres into the interior, often in caravans of as many as two thousand of them. For example, the merchants of Kano and Katsina went first to Borno and Lake Chad to buy different types of salt and natron, including *ungurnu* (trona), *kanwa* (natron), and *beza* (sodium chloride), to take as far as Salaga, the main market of Asante after around 1800, and before that into the forests of central

Asante. Merchants went to Wasulu, on the northern edge of the kola-production area in the Bandama River valley of modern Côte d'Ivoire. They also crossed the Sahara and because of the pilgrimage to Mecca also might visit India or Mozambique.

Trans-Saharan Connections within the Muslim World during the Jihād Era

The discussion of the number of West Africans removed from Muslim areas has to take into consideration the trans-Saharan traffic in the same period as the transatlantic migration. The number of enslaved who crossed the desert is important in itself but also as an indication of the scale of the slave trade within West Africa and the possible number of people who could have been sent to the Americas but were not. The trans-Saharan trade from West Africa was clearly well established before the jihād movement influenced the selection of individuals who were sent into and across the desert. There were active slave markets in the Sahara, the Maghreb, and the Ottoman Empire well into the nineteenth century and even into the twentieth century, such as the one at Tripoli, even after the slave trade was illegal (plate 22).

There were four principal routes that connected with the northern Sahara terminals: those between Ghadames and Timbuktu, between Ghadames and Kano, between Murzuk and Borno, and from Kufra to Wadai. The main corridor analyzed here is the route from Tripoli through Ghadames and Ghat to Agades, Zinder, Kano, and other cities south of the Sahara. In the nineteenth century the Timbuktu-Ghadames route accounted for some trade to the west of the Kano-Ghadames corridor, and the route south from Murzuk to Borno still carried some traffic even though it was in decline during this period and hence did not serve as an effective alternative to the Ghadames-Kano route. Instead, trade either flowed along the main route between Ghadames and Kano or was directed farther east along the new route between Kufra and Wadai that was developed only in the nineteenth century. For the three routes that passed through Ghadames and Murzuk, Tripoli was the final destination. Some trade flowed to Tunis and Algeria or followed caravan routes overland to Egypt, but most traded goods were exported to markets along the way and ultimately to the port at Tripoli. Benghazi served as the port for the Kufra-Wadai road, and hence to a great extent this eastern route operated separately from the traffic to Tripoli. Approximately 700,000 slaves crossed the Sahara in the eighteenth century and 1,200,000 in the nineteenth century, of whom perhaps 1 million can be traced to the period from around 1776 to 1850.[66]

The major commodities of the northbound trade across the Sahara were slaves, ostrich feathers, ivory, gold, and tanned skins, although textiles, senna, civet, gum arabic, wax, indigo, kola nuts, and other goods were also included. The major import was textiles, but beads, mirrors, paper, spices, perfume, tea, sugar, copper, and many other goods were imported as well. A number of contemporary observers have provided inventories of this trade, often including prices. From 1810 to around 1830 probably 3,000 to 6,000 slaves were exported north each year, as well as commodities and slaves that remained in desert society. Losses on the desert crossing are not included.[67] From around 1830 to around 1870 the average number of slaves increased to 4,000 to 8,000 per year. These figures take account of Graberg di Hemso's estimates for the number of slaves reexported from Tripoli in 1825, when he learned that 2,000 or 2,500 slaves were transferred to Mediterranean shipping, down from a level that he estimated to have been 3,000 to 4,000 a few years earlier.[68] Such figures are consistent with a trans-Saharan volume of 4,000 or more slaves and fit in well with the estimates provided by G. F. Lyon for the transit trade through Murzuk in 1819, when 5,000 to 5,500 slaves passed along the route from Borno.[69] A decade after Graberg di Hemso's report, M. J. E. Daumas estimated that 5,800 slaves were shipped north from the Sokoto Caliphate to Ghadames and Ghat.[70] Some of those slaves probably stayed in the desert, but Daumas's estimate does not include exports north from Borno, so that in the mid-1830s the annual total may have been considerably more than 6,000 per year. Estimates for the 1840s, 1850s, and 1860s are the most complete for the century, and the totals are consistent with the earlier estimates.[71]

These estimates for North Africa indicate that the jihād movement clearly had an impact on the slave population of the Maghreb and the Ottoman Empire. Slaves from sub-Saharan African were easily recognizable in Morocco and in the domains of the Ottoman Empire from Algiers to Egypt.[72] They were often associated with houses connected with spirit possession and organized according to where slaves had come from south of the Sahara, including Timbuktu, Kano, Katsina, and Borno. These practices were known as *gnawa* in Morocco,[73] as *bori* in many other places in the Maghreb, after the Hausa term for spirit-possession practices, and as *zar* in Egypt and other parts of the Ottoman Empire.[74] The Fulbe scholar Aḥmad b. al-Qaḍī b. Abī Bakr b. Yūsuf b. Ibrāhīm condemned the *bori* practices that he witnessed in

Tunis in 1813 and argued that the continuation of such beliefs was sufficient reason to wage jihād in West Africa.[75]

The study of the jihād movement carries the discussion of the age of revolutions into new terrain. The influence of jihād reached North Africa and the Middle East through slavery and pilgrimage. As with the isolation of West Africa from the scholarship on the age of revolutions, Morocco and the Ottoman provinces of North Africa have also been largely ignored in the reconstruction of European history and, by extension, Atlantic history during that age. The Mediterranean lands of Islam were intimately connected with events across the Sahara. Both the dominant *ṣūfī* brotherhoods, the Qādiriyya and the Tījāniyya, were associated with Morocco, and the enslaved population from south of the Sahara was concentrated in agricultural production and urban households in various places from Marrakesh to Cairo. French incursions into Egypt under Napoleon marked the first phase of the challenge to the Ottoman Empire, while the United States and Britain moved to suppress the corsair activities of Muslim potentates in the Mediterranean, first in the "Barbary" wars of 1801–5 and finally in 1815 to end the capture and ransoming of American seamen and travelers. In 1816 Lord Exmouth subsequently attempted to reach a diplomatic agreement with Tripoli, Tunis, and Algiers to terminate corsair activities, and his efforts culminated in several treaties and also the bombardment of Algiers on 27 August 1816. The French occupation of Algiers in 1830 further continued European pressure on the Ottoman Empire. These events in North Africa provide a backdrop for understanding the spread of jihād south of the Sahara in the same period.

Once the Atlantic world is broadened to include the Guinea shores of the Atlantic and the links across the Sahara, additional questions arise that are directed at the place of the Mediterranean in West African history during the age of revolutions. The Congress of Vienna that attempted to restore a balance of power among European states virtually excluded Muslim countries from discussion, thereby delimiting a world that separated Europe, the Americas, and European colonies from North Africa, the Middle East, and large parts of Africa south of the Sahara. Although Muslims in North Africa were not involved in propagating jihād, the interaction across the Sahara was still a factor in West Africa because of the pilgrimage to Mecca, commercial relations that included the dispatch of slaves that had been taken in jihād wars, and the intellectual debate among Muslims relating to the increasing interference of European countries and even the United States in the Mediterranean. These factors are further reasons why the Muslim

JIHĀD IN WEST AFRICA DURING THE AGE OF REVOLUTIONS

interior of West Africa has to be included in a broader discussion of the Atlantic world.

Nonetheless, one impact of the "second slavery" in the jihād states was the increase in the number of the enslaved who were sent to North Africa and the Middle East. On the one hand, the Ottoman provinces looked to sub-Saharan Africa as a source of military recruitment through enslavement of young males, as in the case of Muhammad ʿAlī's regime in Egypt and Yūsuf Qaramanlī's regime in Tripoli after around 1820, mainly in areas east of the jihād states. On the other hand, the availability of slaves from the jihād states facilitated the mobilization of labor for domestic use, porterage, collection of natural products, date-palm production, removal of waste, distribution of firewood, production of thatch and bedding, construction, and house repair. The enslaved sometimes performed corvée labor on behalf of their masters for repair of the walls of towns and cities, palaces, and mosques, often as a levy. Young women often were taken into harems or worked in domestic service throughout the Muslim world from West Africa to the Maghreb and the Hijaz.[76]

Limitations on the Involvement of Muslim West Africa in the Atlantic Trade

There are important reasons that the jihād movement is overlooked. As I am arguing, the Muslim regions of West Africa successfully maintained relative autonomy from the transatlantic slave trade, with certain specific exceptions. Before British abolition in 1807, virtually all slaves who came from Muslim areas of West Africa went to the Americas from the interior of the western Bilād al-Sūdān, most notably from Senegambia and the upper Guinea coast as far south as Cape Mount. Thereafter, slaves from Muslim areas came largely from the interior of the Bight of Benin and from the central Bilād al-Sūdān, although some slaves continued to come from the western Bilād al-Sūdān along established routes that had been in operation in the eighteenth century and even earlier. The autonomy of Muslim regions stands in stark contrast to Igboland and the Bantu-speaking regions of west central Africa when it is recognized that Muslim areas of West Africa could have supplied all the slaves that ended up in the Americas, at least theoretically in terms of the demography of West Africa and the size of the enslaved population that inhabited the areas dominated by Muslims.

Hence in the period of revolution in the Atlantic world, there was a countervailing movement within West Africa that insulated the region from the age of revolutions in the Atlantic world, other than for those Muslims who had the misfortune of being taken to the Americas as slaves. There was a parallel revolutionary movement in West Africa that had far different consequences for the history of slavery and hence for our understanding of the history of this period. While revolutionary forces were undermining slavery in the Atlantic world and otherwise changing the political landscape there, the impact of jihād in West Africa was far different. By the middle of the nineteenth century there were more slaves in Muslim areas of West Africa than in all parts of the Americas at any time in the history of the black Atlantic. Despite the preponderance of slavery in these Muslim regions, which do not include the coastal states of Asante and Dahomey or the Igbo interior of the Bight of Biafra, where slavery was also widespread, it is not recognized in virtually any of the scholarship. West Africa experienced a countervailing historical trajectory from the black Atlantic. The region of West Africa did not become the major source of slaves for the Americas, although we can trace influences and overlap whose significance has not been understood, especially in relation to the roles of Yoruba and Muslims. As I have argued elsewhere, the reasons for this abstention of the Islamic countries of West Africa from the major changes in the Atlantic world were political and religious and were the result of the conscious decisions of the political and commercial leadership. When we do find Muslims concentrated in the Americas, their role in resistance to slavery and their accommodation with slavery have been often dismissed or minimized. Some scholars, notably Michael Gomez, Sylviane Diouf, and a few others, have understood the anomalous place of enslaved Muslims in the Americas and have commented on the Malês uprising in Bahia and the impact of Islam.[77]

In short, the reasons for the autonomy of the West African interior were determined in Africa, not in Europe and certainly not in the Americas. Indeed, the jihād movement itself was in part a response to violations of the embargo against sale of slaves to Europeans, specifically Christians, and the attempt to protect Islamic society and its own ability to control a very large enslaved population, including filtering outside, foreign influence. The attempt to understand slavery and the legitimacy of enslavement can be traced back at least to the days of Aḥmad Bābā of Timbuktu in the early seventeenth century and was a constituent of the curriculum of Islamic education in West Africa from that period on, as has been amply documented.[78] The spread of jihād as a mechanism to safeguard autonomy and thereby sustain a long tradition of opposition to Europe was both legal and customary and was enshrined in literary form. Therefore, it has to be taken into account in understanding broader patterns of history, which ironically did not result in the ending of slavery in West Africa; quite the contrary, jihād increased the incidence of slavery within the region as one of the mechanisms that was employed to retain autonomy and buttress Africa against the economic and political forces emanating from the Atlantic world.[79] An understanding of the jihād movement requires an alternate perspective on assessing the age of revolutions that derives from understanding historical changes in Africa.

Emmanuel Terray has argued that the internal West African trade and the transatlantic trade had no bearing on each other and formed two parallel trading systems that did not interact.[80] Terray contends that as reflected in price structures, the Atlantic and the internal slave markets were supplied neither by the same sources nor in the same way and were therefore largely autonomous. In his analysis Terray recognizes the importance of local and internal demand in determining price but does not take into consideration the impact of noneconomic factors, such as gender preferences and Muslim cultural and religious values, on the determination of price. While acknowledging the potential for noneconomic factors to determine price, David Eltis has also argued that the relatively low numbers of slaves from the West African interior were due to African disinterest in European trade goods and high transportation costs from the interior to the coast.[81] However, African traders of the interior were interested in African coastal products and European trade goods that constituted a substantial trade between the Atlantic shore and interior markets. For example, salt, kola nuts, and dried fish were sent into the interior along with imported textiles from India and Europe, iron bars, firearms, tobacco, and other goods. Interior markets also provided customers for other products, such as metal basins, paper, glassware, and various luxury items. Moreover, as James Searing has pointed out, the transportation of high-cost goods, such as gold, ivory, gum arabic, and slaves, was economically viable, since interior merchants were willing to "purchase cheap and sell dear."[82] In contrast to Terray and Eltis, my analysis has taken into consideration noneconomic factors in the examination of gender ratios in the trans-Saharan and transatlantic slave trades.[83] I argue that the lack of greater participation in the Atlantic slave trade by interior merchants was due to the deliberate attempt by Muslim governments to refrain from participating in the trade and specifically to oppose the sale of slaves to Christians because of long-standing legal, moral, and social traditions.

There were limits on involvement in the slave trade that inhibited inter-action between Muslim merchants and European and American traders at the Atlantic shore. I contend that Islam was an inhibiting factor in the provision of slaves for the Americas. That is, Muslims in West Africa inter-fered with market forces by largely withdrawing from the trade in slaves with Europeans. They did not respond to market demand, although they could have done so. At the time of the age of revolutions in Europe and the Ameri-cas, there was a revolution in West Africa that had a profound impact on the shaping of the Atlantic world. Because of religious and ideological factors, Muslims were not interested in trading slaves to Europeans or for transatlan-tic markets.[84] There were exceptions in Bahia, Jamaica, and North America, but these exceptions demonstrate only that efforts on the part of the Muslim states of West Africa to control the slave trade were not always successful, despite the attempt to boycott the sale of slaves to the Americas. The con-trolled efforts to isolate West Africa from slavery in the Americas coincided with the age of revolutions. How West Africa was situated in history of this period is therefore open to reinterpretation to account for Islam as a factor.[85] Let us consider the limitations that the Muslim factor put on the development of the Atlantic world, which I contend were conscious attempts within West Africa to enforce autonomy.

Islamic law that was applied to commercial relations discouraged trade with non-Muslims except under restricted conditions. Admittedly, individ-ual merchants might find ways to circumvent the law, but slaves were usually moved in considerable numbers and in caravans where it was difficult to ig-nore legal conditions. Islamic law permitted the acceptance of property, such as a house or a slave, as collateral on a loan, but the creditor could not legally receive interest per se. Hence creditors were prohibited from benefiting from the use of mortgaged property. In principle, they could not host visitors in a house being held as collateral or make use of the labor of a slave being used to secure a debt. However, the restrictions against *ribā* (usury) could be eas-ily circumvented, even if such instances are difficult to document. Examples of these types of collateral arrangements can be found in the accounts of Abū-l-Ghayth b. Sayyid Aḥmad b. Sayyid Muhammad al-Wajdāwī 'l-Tuwātī. Al-Ghayth, also known as al-Ḥājj Balghīth, was a Muslim who was origi-nally from Tuwāt but who relocated to Katsina in the early 1820s and was the wealthiest merchant in Katsina by the 1850s. In al-Ghayth's accounts between 1829 and 1845, property in the form of houses and slaves was used to secure debts, although it is not possible to tell whether such collateral was actually

JIHĀD IN WEST AFRICA DURING THE AGE OF REVOLUTIONS

used for personal gain. In one instance al-Ghayth received a slave girl in lieu of a loan of fifteen thousand cowries, the currency of the central Bilād al-Sūdān.[86] The repayment date was specified as the month of Dhū-l-Ḥijja, but until then al-Ghayth was not supposed to collect interest on the loan through the labor of the slave girl, Akakba. Apart from the labor required to compensate for her maintenance, Akakba was not supposed to work either in his household or as a domestic whose services could be rented out. She had value only as a slave, and if she had been rented out as a domestic servant to someone else, the profit of her labor would have benefited the loan provider, but illegally. As the case of Akakba demonstrates, there were well-defined legal structures that governed the operation of trade, and when individuals violated these structures, they were held to account. When issues were in dispute, there was recourse to legal experts who determined how issues were to be resolved. Such legal recourse extended to inheritance rights and the settlement of claims to property in relation to merchants who failed to return home. The legal structures protected wives and kin from arbitrary seizure of property and allowed for redress if such seizure did occur.

Interest could be gained through fictitious sales in at least two ways. In the first scenario, for a secured loan, the debtor could sell the lender an item and immediately buy it back at a higher price to be paid at a later date. The difference between the two prices was the "interest" on the loan, with the lender keeping the "sold" object as security on the loan. In the second scenario, for an unsecured loan, the lender could sell the debtor an object for a set price that included both the loan amount and what amounted to the interest, with the agreement that the total amount be paid at a later date. The lender then immediately would buy back the same object at a lower price that he would pay the debtor. The debtor thereby would end up with a loan (the "lower" price of the object) and later would repay the "higher" price, with the difference between the two prices serving as the interest. Such was the practice revealed in the accounts of al-Ghayth.[87] For example, in one transaction from 1829, Aḥmad b. Ḥamma, a Katsina merchant, bought forty-eight thousand cowries worth of merchandise from al-Ghayth that needed to be repaid two months later along with an additional four thousand cowries.[88]

Another type of legal fiction used to bypass ribā, which was especially useful in long-distance trade, was the so-called sleeping partnership, muḍāraba, analogous to what was known in medieval Europe as a simple commenda. Here, one partner would supply the capital or goods, share in the profits, and maintain the sole liability for any losses. The other partner did the actual work and received a share of the profits but would bear no losses. The provider of capital could demand that a set amount of money be repaid, but only for a part of the profit made from a venture in addition to his initial investment. In this way the capital-providing partner was able to invest in a trading venture while avoiding any accusation that he was receiving interest for a loan.[89] These types of partnerships appear to have been common means of securing capital and managing labor in the nineteenth-century trans-Saharan trade between central Bilād al-Sūdān cities such as Katsina and northern ports such as Ghadames, Tuwāt, and Ghat.[90] The same practices also governed Muslim and non-Muslim systems of credit. For example, both Muslims and non-Muslims permitted the exchange of individuals for security on a loan. However, while Muslims restricted this type of legal fiction to the exchange of slaves, non-Muslims contemplated it even with regard to the exchange of free individuals. Just like their Muslim neighbors, non-Muslim traders in West Africa also depended on granting and receiving credit for successful long-distance commercial transactions.

As Aḥmad Bābā made clear in the early seventeenth century, scholars and clerics in West Africa were concerned about slavery and its impact on the Muslim community.[91] They advocated the protection of Muslims from enslavement and effectively argued for limitations on Muslim involvement in trade with Europeans, that is, with Christians, which implicitly undermined the sale of slaves to the Americas, although the difficulty of enforcement meant that some trade was inevitable. Muslims were sold to the Americas, despite a moral economy that abhorred such injustice. Nonetheless, as I have argued, proportionately fewer slaves were sent across the Atlantic than might have been the case in the absence of such religious and legal restrictions. Even if governments, officials and merchants did not always respect this moral economy, there were limitations on involvement that resulted in the adoption of government policies and were implemented through the self-imposed behavior of merchants.

Slavery was a factor in the jihād movement, specifically in regard to complaints that freeborn Muslims were being enslaved and that such enslavement was illegal under Islamic law and was condemned as a violation of the rights of Muslims. The concern was directed at protecting Muslims, not at opposing slavery, which became a core institution underpinning the society and economy of the Sokoto Caliphate as it expanded in the course of the first half of the nineteenth century. Hence the revolutionary movement of jihād that swept West Africa in the period of the age of revolutions in Europe and the Atlantic world had a far different impact on the course of slavery, but nonetheless the revolutionary dimensions of the jihād were profound and constituted a parallel movement to the forces with which Hobsbawm and Genovese were concerned. The protection of the rights of freeborn Muslims and the insistence on the rule of law were directed at arbitrary government. It is important to note that one of the signs of arbitrary rule was what was considered illegal enslavement and the sale of individuals who were freeborn Muslims to Christians and the transatlantic slave trade. The jihād movement in this sense can be thought of as a distant and indirect reaction to the excesses of the ancien régime in Europe that were being swept aside in the age of revolutions.

I argue here that West Africa could have supplied all the slaves that were destined for the Americas in the period after around 1760, but it did not. The size of the domestic slave population in all parts of West Africa was so substantial that it is not difficult to agree that demographically the slaves were potentially available. Why they stayed there and were not sold into transatlantic slavery is the issue. Instead, about 80 percent of all slaves came from west central Africa, southeast Africa, and the Bight of Biafra. The predominant political influence in West Africa in the eighteenth and nineteenth century was Islamic, culminating in the radical movement of jihād that completely reshaped the map of West Africa. The parallels in chronology and possible interactions have to be absorbed into the scholarly analysis of slavery in the Americas, Africa, and a redefined Atlantic world. The states that emerged out of jihād adopted policies that reduced the sale of slaves into the Atlantic slave trade, which explains why there were not more Muslims in the enslaved populations of the Americas. Hence these states played a significant role in shaping the Atlantic world. Although historians of the slave trade have often credited the success of British patrols in restricting the slave trade from areas of West Africa once central to it, the efforts of the Muslim states to stop the trade further help explain the shift in supply. The huge internal trade, probably equal in scope to the Atlantic trade, shows that West Africa could have engaged in the Atlantic trade had the political leadership chosen to do so. The internal and transatlantic trades were linked together in a way that fundamentally reshapes our understanding of the slave trade. Jihād did result in the enslavement of some Muslims, and the timing of revolts in Brazil and Cuba, combined with the history of West Africa, explains why we find important concentrations of Muslims in Cuba and Brazil despite their small numbers overall. The connection of the Atlantic trade to the large and important slave trade from sub-Saharan Africa to North Africa and the Ottoman Empire fundamentally alters our understanding of the nineteenth-century slave trade.

6 THE REPERCUSSIONS OF JIHĀD IN THE AMERICAS

Chapter 5 analyzed the Islamic factor in the movement of enslaved Muslims across the Atlantic, as well as others of the enslaved who came from the Muslim-dominated interior of West Africa. Although the jihād states and indeed the areas affected by jihād were closely linked with the trans-Saharan world of Islam, they were otherwise only marginally related to the emergence of a "second slavery" in the Americas. Whereas the patterns of Muslim-dominated trade tended to restrict the sale of enslaved Muslims to European slavers but did not prevent their sale, the early phases of jihād in West Africa evinced opposition to the deportation of enslaved Muslims to the Americas. However much the consolidation of jihād rule in Fuuta Jalon and Fuuta Toro may have limited the sale of enslaved Muslims in the Atlantic world, enslaved Muslims still were being sent to the Americas, even if in relatively small numbers.

This chapter explores the impact of enslaved Muslims on the societies of the Americas and specifically identifies two phases in which the repercussions of jihād can be identified. In the first phase, enslaved Muslims were scattered as individuals in a hostile world of racialized slavery. Largely isolated from communities of believers, they personified the complaints of the jihād leaders that the political and legal structures of West African states and societies were not adequately protecting freeborn Muslims from enslavement. The sale and deportation of Muslims were evidence that jihād was necessary as a means of correcting injustices that were anathema to Islam and against the sensibilities of devout Muslims. In the second phase, largely confined to the nineteenth century, Muslims, including recent converts, were able to coalesce as a community in scattered locations, most especially in Bahia, where the influence of jihād ideology played a role in social and political relationships. Moreover, even Muslims who were virtually isolated from other Muslims were sometimes able to engage in political action that in some ways reflected a background in which jihād had been a factor in their lives.

There were few identifiable communities of enslaved Muslims in the Americas because of the relatively low proportion of Muslims among the enslaved population. Muslims were found in virtually all parts of the Americas, and noticeably so in North America among an admittedly small number of African-born persons in the enslaved population. They were also present in Jamaica, the French Caribbean, the Hispanic mainland, and especially Bahia, Pernambuco, and Rio de Janeiro by the end of the eighteenth century. Very few Muslims arrived after the beginning of the nineteenth century except in Brazil, most notably in Bahia, and to a much lesser extent in Cuba. Hence the influence of jihād was restricted. Similarly, West Africans were found in North Africa and the various provinces of the Ottoman Empire, but their presence was also marginal, and the context was very different from that in the Americas. Although the number of the enslaved from sub-Saharan Africa increased in the early nineteenth century, identifiable communities mostly were associated with *bori*, *gnawa*, and *zar*—spirit-possession cults that were anathema to proponents of jihād. There were noticeable communities from south of the Sahara in Tunis, the towns of southern Morocco, Jerusalem, Bosnia, and elsewhere. In contrast with the Americas, where enslaved Muslims were evidence of injustice in West Africa that justified jihād, the presence of sub-Saharan Africans in North Africa was considered proof that jihād was legitimate as a means of purging West Africa of unbelief. As in the Americas, the visibility of Africans in Islamic society was correspondingly dimmed.

In the late eighteenth century the concentration of Muslims in Bahia attested to connections with Porto Novo and Oyo, from which most Muslims came before Lagos became important after 1800.[1] The enslaved also left the cities of the savanna and the Sahel for the Sahara crossing, and hence a string of identifiable people can be followed out of West Africa. With respect to the movement to the Atlantic shores, this enslavement confirmed the charges of Muhammad Bello and other jihād leaders that Muslims were being sold as slaves to Oyo and from there to Christians for transport across the Atlantic. The legitimacy of these complaints can be seen in the presence of Muslims from the interior of the Bight of Benin in Bahia and the development there of a recognizable Muslim community. However, the northward flow across the Sahara of the enslaved reveals the contradictions in how slavery was perceived. In Bahia, the Muslim community included recent converts, as well as Muslims who had been enslaved in the context of jihād, while in the Islamic lands of North Africa, enslaved Africans were basically perceived as apostates or "pagans" whose allegiance to Islam was questionable. An understanding of the movement of enslaved Muslims to the Americas has to take this global context into account.

Enslaved Departures from Senegambia and the Upper Guinea Coast

Less than one-third (32.0 percent) of the total number of Africans who went to the Americas between 1760 and 1860 left from West Africa to the west of the Niger delta (2,273,000 out of 7,110,000), and that portion dropped to 20 percent after 1800. That is, more than two-thirds of Africans destined for the Americas for the period as a whole came from west central Africa, southeastern Africa, and the Bight of Biafra, which were regions not affected by the jihād movement, and during the period of most intense jihād after 1804, the proportion from areas not under the influence of jihād increased to four-fifths. Although the dominance of west central Africa has been recognized as an important feature of the slave trade in this period, the analysis so far has not appreciated why Muslim regions were marginal and underrepresented despite the relative unimportance of Muslims in North America in the eighteenth century and their limited presence in Jamaica, St. Domingue, and elsewhere. The Muslim factor has been recognized as significant in Bahia in the first third of the nineteenth century, culminating in the Malês uprising in 1835. Moreover, the presence of Muslims elsewhere is well documented. Of the total number of enslaved who came from the region to the west of the Bight of Biafra, more than one-third (36.8 percent) went to the British Caribbean and North America. About one-quarter went to Brazil, while 13.6 percent went to Spanish territories, almost entirely to Cuba in the nineteenth century (table 6.1). The population that reached the French Caribbean arrived largely before the influence of jihād had an impact in the interior, and hence there were relatively fewer Muslims in this population. The proportion of Muslims in this demographic profile was much less.

Before the late eighteenth century almost all Muslims who went to the Americas came from the western Bilād al-Sūdān, and most left Senegambia or the upper Guinea coast. By the end of the eighteenth century Muslims were also departing from the Bight of Benin and to a limited extent from the Gold Coast. The "Mandinga" and "Mandingo" identified in the Americas from the sixteenth century through the eighteenth century often were Muslims from the western Bilād al-Sūdān, initially from the region controlled by Songhay, which dominated West Africa in the sixteenth century, including the

TABLE 6.1. Destinations of Enslaved Departures from West Africa (Senegambia through Bight of Benin), 1761–1860

	North America	British Caribbean	French Caribbean	Dutch Americas	Danish Americas	Spanish Americas*	Brazil	Africa**	Totals
1761–1770	43,865	168,453	60,496	33,275	8,419	4,244	71,412	98	390,262
1771–1780	32,866	179,003	69,099	29,259	7,173	777	57,065	211	375,453
1781–1790	13,267	119,830	112,872	16,517	14,016	9,926	67,660	0	354,088
1791–1800	16,316	118,496	22,864	18,092	13,847	33,078	79,950	335	302,978
1801–1810	46,833	84,609	8,631	8,813	6,521	30,566	103,632	3,139	292,744
1811–1820	2,325	1,569	10,283	523	0	35,690	75,725	8,670	134,785
1821–1830	0	1,223	20,699	1,046	0	55,994	26,106	24,028	129,096
1831–1840	0	7,701	368	0	307	81,543	26,081	12,080	128,080
1841–1850	0	215	0	0	0	34,626	79,810	23,690	138,341
1851–1860	126	0	0	0	0	23,440	1,713	2,043	27,322
Totals	155,598	681,099	305,312	107,525	50,283	309,884	589,154	74,294	2,273,149
Percent	6.8	30.0	13.4	4.7	2.2	13.6	25.9	3.3	

Source: Voyages: The Trans-Atlantic Slave Trade Database, www.slavevoyages.org.
Note: The total for these regions does not include 69 slaves sent to Europe.
*Virtually all went to Cuba and other Spanish possessions in the Caribbean by 1790.
**Virtually all went to Sierra Leone.

Gambia and Senegal River valleys, until its collapse after the Moroccan invasion of the middle Niger valley in 1591–92. Despite political collapse, the commercial network and the urban focus of trade between the interior and the coast continued. Indeed, the overland caravan trade facilitated the movement of slaves to the coast, whether or not the slaves were Muslims. The trade in enslaved Muslims led to reforms in the Senegal River valley that attempted to restrict the movement of slaves by protecting the citizens of the various states (e.g., Walo, Kayor) from sale into foreign slavery and also became a justification of jihād in Fuuta Toro and Fuuta Jalon. The designation of Mandinga/Mandingo in the diaspora reflects the political and geographical origins of the Muslim population of the western Bilād al-Sūdān. The term itself derives from Mandinke/Mandinka, which is the ethnic name for people who speak Malinke and are usually presumed to have been Muslim, as they are today. Malinke is one of several "languages" that are dialects of one another, including Bambara, Mandinka, and Juula. These are considered Manding languages, the main differences largely being phonetic. Susu is also closely related. Often identified as Mandingo or Mandinga in the Americas, these languages were spoken over a wide area from the Gambia River valley and Kaabu in the west throughout the headwaters of the Niger and Senegal Rivers in the east as far as the Niger River valley southwest of Timbuktu, while Susu was spoken in the coastal region to the south of the Fuuta Jalon highlands. Moreover, the commercial dialect, Juula, was spoken even more widely, especially to the southeast and east of the upper Niger River. The term "Bambara" is important; it was originally used as a pejorative term to refer to non-Muslims, the Bamana, but now also refers to the language spoken by the majority of the inhabitants of modern Mali. The ethnic/national terminologies for people in the Americas who are called Mandingo/Mandinga and Bambara therefore derive from this common linguistic background.

The largest proportion of enslaved Muslims and other people from Muslim-dominated regions who went to the Americas before 1780 went to British colonies, especially to North America (table 6.2). A significant number also went to the French islands before the uprising in St. Domingue. By no means were all of these people Muslims. A larger proportion of those leaving from the upper Guinea coast for British and French territories actually came from the non-Muslim societies close to the coast, including Balanta and Baga, although others came from Kaabu and its environs. Together, these are the ethnic origins of most of the slaves who left from Bissau and Cacheu for northeastern Brazil between 1760 and 1820 and who left the upper Guinea

TABLE 6.2. Departures from Senegambia and the Upper Guinea Coast for the Americas, 1761–1860

	North America	British Caribbean	French Caribbean	Dutch America	Danish Caribbean	Spanish Americas*	Brazil	Africa	Totals
1761–1770	23,517	41,236	16,553	426	1,868	1,351	9,651	98	94,700
1771–1780	19,788	44,092	10,352	768	0	0	12,828	0	87,828
1781–1790	5,512	18,065	27,866	912	387	2,786	13,768	0	69,296
1791–1800	10,728	30,116	6,005	5,036	1,960	11,438	13,545	335	79,163
1801–1810	27,371	19,042	4,449	2,681	3,328	14,913	23,188	1,357	96,329
1811–1820	2,325	1,242	10,283	0	0	20,955	13,033	3,952	51,790
1821–1830	0	0	17,273	896	0	25,336	6,056	7,054	56,615
1831–1840	0	4,114	0	0	307	39,564	1,043	3,524	48,552
1841–1850	0	0	0	0	0	15,429	11,071	2,897	29,397
1851–1860	0	0	0	0	0	4,795	0	0	4,795
Totals	89,241	157,907	92,781	10,719	7,850	136,567	104,183	19,217	618,4565
Percent	14.4	25.5	15.0	1.7	1.3	22.1	16.8	3.1	

Source: Voyages: The Trans-Atlantic Slave Trade Database, www.slavevoyages.org.
*Virtually all those destined for Spanish America went to Cuba and Puerto Rico after 1781.

coast for Cuba in the nineteenth century. In general, their enslavement had little if anything to do with the jihād movement in the interior. Because of their knowledge of rice cultivation, many of these Africans were sent to rice-producing colonies, such as South Carolina and northeastern Brazil, especially Maranhão. The links between Charleston, South Carolina, and Bunce Island in the Sierra Leone River relied extensively on the slave-trading firms of Henry Laurens and Richard Oswald. Other firms included the Clevelands and the Corkers, who were stationed at the Banana Islands and Turtle Island, off the southern shores of the Sierra Leone Peninsula, while Miles Barber was on Îles de Los until 1793, when he sold his business to a former employee, Thomas Hodgson, and his brother. Other Europeans were at Rio Pongo and supplied British and North American merchants.[2] Thus there was a regular, if relatively small, migration from the far western shores of Africa from the seventeenth century into the nineteenth century. Muslims were caught up in this migration, but those who were recognizable through the ethnic label indicating Mandinka, Mandingo, or similar origins were only a small proportion of arrivals in all colonies in the Americas, no matter which colony. The most striking feature of this trade, other than its relatively small scale, was the concentration of Muslims in North America and to a lesser extent in Jamaica and the French islands.[3]

As noted in chapter 5 (table 5.2), there were 59,000 recorded departures from Bissau and Cacheu in 1761–1807, of whom 56,000, or 95 percent, were destined for Brazil, almost entirely to Maranhão and Para. For the 84,000 enslaved leaving the Sierra Leone River before 1808, 12,000 were destined for North America and 44,000 for the British Caribbean; that is, about two-thirds for British colonies and North America, including 14 percent destined for North America. For Gambia, almost three-quarters who left before 1807 (35,000 out of 47,000) went to the British Caribbean and North America. In addition, 50,000 of the enslaved were sent to the French Caribbean from Senegambia and the upper Guinea coast. Again, these figures represent about two-thirds of total departures, so that realistic estimates would be one-third higher than these figures. Nonetheless, the overall pattern is clear. Besides those identified as Mandingo in British and French colonies or Mandinga in Spanish colonies and Brazil, there were also Wolof, often referred to as Jolof, and Fulbe (Ful, Pullo, Pular, and so on). Sometimes the term "Bambara" was used, as in Louisiana, a term that was current in West Africa and referred either to the Bamana or to anyone who was not considered a Muslim.[4] The term referred specifically to people from the region of Segu and Kaarta, between the Niger River and the Senegal River, who were inhabitants of those states and were often considered legally enslavable, whether or not they were actually Muslims. In almost all cases their origins meant that they left via the Senegal or Gambia River valleys, although some also departed from ports farther south on the upper Guinea coast, and a few were sent south to the trading castles on the Gold Coast.

As can be seen in table 6.3, the gender composition of the enslaved population of the interior of Senegambia and the upper Guinea Coast is indicated in records from Louisiana and Maranhão for the period 1723–1831.[5] The proportion of males from areas of Muslim influence was 68.7 percent, with the highest ratio among males from farthest in the interior, who were known to Muslim merchants and to slave owners in the Americas as "Bambara" and in most cases were Bamana from the states of Segu and Kaarta, which were not considered Muslim states and in the nineteenth century were the targets of the jihād movement. Those identified as "Mande," or Mandinka, are predominant in the two samples, constituting 54 percent and an overall proportion of two males for every female. They came from Kaarta, the Gambia River valley, and areas farther east and were generally known as Mandingo or Mandinga in the Americas.

In the period from 1700 to 1820, almost one-quarter of those who arrived in North America (23.1 percent) came from the upper Guinea coast and Senegambia (table 6.4). From 1761 through 1820, 86,000 Africans arrived in North America from Senegambia and the upper Guinea coast—the trade being concentrated in the Gambia River, at Bunce Island in the Sierra Leone River, and at the barracoons of Rio Pongo, Rio Nuñez, Îles de Los, the Banana Islands, and Sherbro. Many of these arrivals came from rice-producing, non-Muslim areas near the coast, but others came from the western Bilād al-Sūdān, where rice was also produced in some areas. This large percentage characterized all regions of North America, far out of proportion to other parts of the Americas, representing a significant concentration of Africans who were Muslims or who came from areas with a strong Muslim influence, and in any event from places where rice was grown. For immigration to the Chesapeake region before 1700, there were three times as many immigrants from Senegambia and the upper Guinea coast (7,000) than from the Bight of Biafra (slightly more than 2,000), totaling over 25,000 from Senegambia and the upper Guinea coast by the end of the migration, or 30 percent of all arrivals. The greatest number (45,000) went to the coastal Low Country of the Carolinas and Georgia, constituting over half of African immigrants from Senegambia

TABLE 6.3. Ethnic Identification of Africans in Louisiana (1723–1805) and Maranhão (1767–1831)

Ethnicity	Males	% Male	Females	% Female	Unknown	Total
Bamana*	388	88.6	50	11.4	2	440
Fulbe	181	65.6	95	34.4	1	277
Mande**	1,114	66.7	557	33.3	4	1,675
Wolof	346	60.4	227	39.6	1	574
Susu	19	65.5	10	34.5	—	29
Moors	81	72.3	31	27.7	—	112
Total	2,129	68.7	970	31.3	8	3,107

Source: Slave Biographies: The Atlantic Database Network, http://www.slavebiographies.org.
*I.e., "Bambara." **Mandinke (Mandingo/Mandinga).

and the upper Guinea coast and 12 percent of all arrivals in North America. This concentration effectively transferred people from rice-producing areas of West Africa to the area where rice was grown in North America. Those from Senegambia and the upper Guinea coast were also prominent among African immigrants in the northern colonies, accounting for about 30 percent of arrivals, or about 7,000 people. Almost 9,000 enslaved Africans from Senegambia and the upper Guinea coast went to the Gulf region, especially to Louisiana, where they constituted about 40 percent of the population arriving in the region from Africa.

A relatively significant number of the enslaved came from the so-called Windward Coast, but many of these came from areas close to the Gold Coast and were really part of that trade. Others came from near Cape Mount and more appropriately reflected the patterns of the upper Guinea coast. Although Muslims were sometimes found among the deported populations throughout the region west of the Bight of Biafra as far as the Senegal River, the majority of these unfortunate people were probably not Muslims. As the North American profile demonstrates, many Muslims and others from Senegambia and the upper Guinea coast were transported on North American and British ships from embarkation points in the Sierra Leone River and places northward to the Senegal River, especially at the Gambia. People from Senegambia were prominent everywhere in the United States, much more so than virtually anywhere else in the Western Hemisphere, although there were also considerable numbers of Senegambians in the French Caribbean islands and in French Guiana. Senegambia was strongly influenced by Islam, more so than any other region of origin, which means that many enslaved Africans in North

The Repercussions of Jihād in the Americas

TABLE 6.4. Estimated Arrivals in North America from Senegambia and the Upper Guinea Coast, 1701–1820

	Northern Region	Chesapeake Region	Carolinas, Georgia	Gulf Region	Total North America	Estimated total from Africa	Percent from Senegambia and Upper Guinea Coast
1701–1710	0	3,213	0	0	3,213	13,131	24.5
1711–1720	0	1,833	845	134	2,811	12,679	22.2
1721–1730	0	1,913	5,169	4,674	11,756	36,838	31.9
1731–1740	1,267	8,233	3,469	0	12,969	62,181	20.9
1741–1750	2,341	2,252	769	222	5,583	21,144	26.4
1751–1760	1,974	3,523	7,369	0	12,866	42,947	30.0
1761–1770	1,694	3,392	7,367	0	12,453	46,691	26.7
1771–1780	0	1,117	7,889	1,435	10,440	31,185	33.5
1781–1790	0	106	3,308	205	3,619	14,298	25.3
1791–1800	0	0	1,607	0	1,607	14,388	11.2
1801–1810	0	0	6,796	1,121	8,074	72,978	11.1
1811–1820	0	0	95	810	905	4,635	19.5
Totals	7,276	25,582	44,683	8,601	86,296	373,095	23.1
Percent of total from Senegambia and Upper Guinea Coast	8.4	29.6	51.8	10.0			
All arrivals	24,128	115,479	210,173	21,584	373,095		
Percentage of all arrivals in each region	30.2	22.2	21.2	39.8	23.1		

Source: Voyages: The Trans-Atlantic Slave Trade Database, www.slavevoyages.org.

America had been exposed to Islam, more so proportionately than in the rest of the Americas.

Richard Pierpoint, for example, was born in Fuuta Bundu, one of the jihād states, in about 1744. He was enslaved when the Bambara state of Segu invaded his country and subsequently was taken to North America, as were many other Muslim males from the Senegambia region. Pierpoint escaped from slavery in Pennsylvania during the American Revolution, joined British forces, and fought with Butler's Rangers the British regiment that fought in western New York, whereupon he gained his freedom through military service, before moving to Upper Canada after the British defeat in 1784. Pierpoint was granted two hundred acres of land on Twelve Mile Creek in what later became Grantham Township, near St. Catharines and Niagara Falls.[6] On 29 June 1794 Pierpoint was one of nineteen "Free Negroe" veterans of the "late war" to petition Lieutenant Governor John Graves Simcoe for land. At the outbreak of the War of 1812, he helped form an all-black regiment of twenty-seven to thirty men who fought at the Battle of Queenston Heights, which was a defining moment in the maintenance of Canadian independence. Although he later petitioned for aid "to return to his native country," he was given land in Garafraxa Township on the Grand River, near present-day Fergus, where he died, probably in 1838, without heirs. Although it is difficult to attribute motives to Pierpoint's contribution to the war, he clearly welcomed his freedom from slavery and demonstrated his loyalty to the British Crown in return.

Other Muslims from Fuuta Toro, Fuuta Jalon, and the Muslim commercial centers in the interior were to be found in North America, where they continued their identity as Muslims. Bilali Mahomet, who was born about 1760, came from Timbo, the capital of Fuuta Jalon, probably in the 1790s, and after some time in the Caribbean was taken to South Carolina in 1802, where he became an overseer on one of the plantations of Thomas Spalding on Sapelo Island. Among his many achievements, he led a group of armed slaves who defended his master's property during the War of 1812. Through his dress and conduct, he maintained a strong allegiance to Islam, even composing several texts in Arabic that were intended to sustain the literature tradition. His methods of prayer were clearly in the style of the Qādiriyya.[7] This pattern reflects what is known about the slave trade originating in the interior of West Africa, which was composed almost entirely of males. The farther that slaves came from the interior of West Africa, that is, areas where Muslims were prominent, the more likely it was that they were males. This observation even

The Repercussions of Jihād in the Americas

applies to the Bambara region between the upper Senegal River and the Niger River that is sometimes considered to be largely non-Muslim.

There are very few references to Muslim women, which makes the case of Rosalie, the Fulbe woman studied by Rebecca Scott and Jean-Michel Hébrard, unusual.[8] Rosalie struggled to gain her freedom and then to sustain it during her sojourn first in Haiti, then in Cuba, and finally in Louisiana. She lived first in Jérémie in southern Haiti, where she was granted her freedom in 1795 in ambiguous circumstances that left her actual status unclear, although she eventually became the partner of Michel Vincent and mothered Vincent's children. Finally, in 1803, Vincent, Rosalie, and at least one of their children were able to reach Cuba. In the turmoil that continued over the next several years, Rosalie repeatedly had to assert her liberty. As a woman of Fulbe background, she almost certainly had some relationship with the jihād heritage, although there is no evidence that she continued any practices that would have identified her as Muslim. As in many other cases, Rosalie was very likely a Muslim who had no choice but to accept enslavement, often in isolation, and somehow survive.

In Jamaica, Muhammad Kabā Saghanughu was able to preside over a Muslim community on the escarpment overlooking St. Elizabeth Parish, where coffee was grown and livestock breeding was common for some time, although with increasing difficulty. Kabā lived on a coffee estate, Spice Grove, which was adjacent to the livestock pen of Nottingham, owned by the same family, which also owned other nearby property. Kabā's community included the inhabitants of all these estates because of the movement of labor among properties. Moreover, Kabā achieved his own accommodation with unbelievers by joining the Moravian Mission, which relocated from the St. Elizabeth plains below to the Fairfield estate, which was adjacent to Nottingham and Spice Grove, where Kabā lived. His allegiance to the Moravians, who appointed him "Helper," which was a formal position in the Moravian Church. His role with the Moravians provided protection for his community, which may have numbered as many as one thousand in the 1810s. He was able to raise funds to purchase the emancipation of evangelical preacher George Lewis, who himself was from the upper Guinea coast and also may well have originally been a Muslim. Kabā was implicated in the Christmas conspiracy in 1831–32, when the enslaved population staged a massive uprising across Jamaica because it was believed that their emancipation had been declared but was being denied by the planter class and the colonial government. Whether or not Kabā was actually involved is unclear, but at least one of his sons,

Abraham, aged thirty and listed as a cartman at Spice Grove, was convicted of being involved in the uprising. Abraham, along with two others from Spice Grove, African-born Edward Robinson, aged forty and a second driver, and creole-born Richard, aged thirty and a field hand, were all executed.[9] Moreover, Kabā was alleged to have been in possession of a letter in Arabic that was considered at the time a possible *wathīqa* (document) from West Africa. Kabā's wife allegedly destroyed the letter because it was feared that its existence would incriminate Kabā. As in other cases, Kabā's presence in Jamaica reflected the political conditions in West Africa that prompted jihād.

These examples are evidence that Muslims were being enslaved despite the legal pronouncements of such scholars as Aḥmad Bābā in the early seventeenth century and numerous jurists and Muslim leaders thereafter. The fate of these Muslims in diaspora was usually a life of isolation and compromise. It was difficult to practice the rituals of Islam, especially praying five times a day, fasting during Ramaḍān, and even abstaining from eating pork. Kabā explained what he and his small community had to do, which was probably the practice of many Muslims. During Ramaḍān, Kabā pretended to be sick and unable to eat during the day, which nonetheless raised the suspicions of his owner. With respect to prayer, Kabā composed two books in Arabic, *Kitāb al-ṣalāt*, which were texts on prayer—when to pray, how to pray, the consequences of not praying, and manuals for weddings and funerals. Kabā referred to scholarly sources to buttress his exposition, which he wrote from memory since he did not have access to the manuscripts that had circulated in West Africa when he was a student.[10] Kabā could not maintain the autonomy of his community under the pressure of enslavement, and in 1813 he and his followers joined the Moravian Mission at Carmel, located in the plains below the escarpment where Spice Grove, the coffee estate where he lived, was located. At that time he took the name of his deceased master, Robert Peart, as a way of asserting his dignity in the face of the man who married his deceased master's widow, who was determined to subdue the slave population at Spice Grove. In the end, Kabā and his owner reached an accommodation, in part because Kabā became a Helper at the Moravian Mission only a couple of years after Kabā apparently wrote his *Kitāb al-ṣalāt*. Despite his association with the Moravians, Kabā continued to harbor his identity as a Muslim in silence. In letters that he wrote in Arabic to other Muslims in Jamaica in 1834, he insisted that his coreligionists address him by his Muslim name and not by the name he was publicly known, that is, Robert Peart.[11]

Isolated and divorced from the context of jihād, these Muslims nonetheless harbored a connection with Africa that shunned the rocky shores of integration and assimilation. When individuals had to compromise in order to survive, they often did so on terms that reflected their Muslim heritage. Individuals like Richard Pierpoint thought about returning to Africa and their home communities of Muslims. Others, like Kabā Saghanughu, nurtured a community that had to adjust to local circumstances through measures that disguised their heritage but asserted their autonomy. The relatively few women who found themselves in the Americas, such as Rosalie, asserted their identity through marriage in ways that were somewhat similar to the positions of the prominent women on the coast and rivers of Senegambia.

Bight of Benin and Gold Coast Departures

By contrast with the upper Guinea coast, the lower Guinea coast, especially the Bight of Benin, and indeed the Gold Coast as well, sent almost no Muslims to the Americas before the end of the eighteenth century. By far the largest number of enslaved Muslims clearly left Africa in the nineteenth century after the start of the jihād in the Hausa states and Nupe and especially after its spread to Oyo in 1817. Of an estimated 858,000 Africans who left the Bight of Benin from 1761 to the end of the traffic a century later (table 6.5), most went to Brazil, approximately 480,000 (almost 56 percent), about 304,000 before British abolition and 176,000 after. Those who left in the eighteenth century were largely identified as Jeje and sometimes Mina, while those in the nineteenth century were mostly identified as Nagô, with some being Hausa, Nupe or Tapa, and Borno, most of whom were likely to have been Muslims. Significant numbers from the Bight of Benin also went to the French Caribbean before the 1790s and the British Caribbean before 1807, while relatively few went to North America. Approximately 86,000, or just over 16 percent, were sent to the British Caribbean and North America, while 124,000 (23.6 percent) were sent to the French Caribbean. Approximately 7,000 (14.3 percent) were destined for the Spanish colonies, increasingly to Cuba. While some Muslims were clearly in the departing population before British abolition in 1807, the proportion was undoubtedly very small.

Although relatively few of the enslaved from interior regions of Bilād al-Sūdān were Muslims, they became noticeable by the end of the eighteenth century. Ukawsaw Gronniosaw was an early example of someone who came from the Muslim interior; he was taken to North America apparently in the second decade of the eighteenth century, although his memory of Islamic

TABLE 6.5. **Destinations of the Enslaved from the Bight of Benin, 1761–1860**

	North America	British Caribbean	French Caribbean	Spanish Americas*	Brazil	Africa**	Totals All Destinations
1761–1770	1,941	18,934	26,106	775	61,761	—	110,381
1771–1780	1,351	19,342	44,612	—	44,237	—	109,886
1781–1790	510	13,599	42,956	2,734	53,892	—	113,691
1791–1800	—	17,092	7,033	3,065	66,006	—	93,196
1801–1810	1,348	11,620	2,823	922	77,880	—	95,428
Total 1761–1810	5,150	80,587	123,530	7,496	303,776		522,582
Percent 1761–1810	1.0	15.4	23.6	14.3	58.1		
1811–1820	—	327	—	9,016	61,188	3,562	74,093
1821–1830	—	—	500	23,197	19,806	15,747	59,250
1831–1840	—	2,876	368	36,783	24,867	8,189	73,083
1841–1850	—	215	—	19,197	68,738	20,793	108,943
1851–1860	126	—	—	18,646	1,713	2,043	22,528
Total 1811–1860	126	3,418	868	106,839	176,312	50,334	337,897
Percent 1811–1860	0.0	1.0	0.3	31.6	52.2	14.9	
Totals	5,276	84,005	124,398	114,335	480,088	50,334	860,479
Percent of Total Period	0.6	9.8	14.5	13.3	55.8	5.8	

Source: Voyages: The Trans-Atlantic Slave Trade Database, www.slavevoyages.org.

*Virtually all to Cuba.

**Virtually all to Sierra Leone.

***Totals include 2,043 sent to Dutch and Danish colonies.

practice was confused. He claimed to have come from the "City of BOURNOU" and that his mother was the daughter of the king of "Zaara," of which the city of "Bournou" was the chief city.[12] At the time, Birni Ngazargamu was the capital of Borno and was often referred to as the city of Borno. He describes praying before sunrise, which may refer to the Muslim prayer. His mention of merchants whom he says were from the Gold Coast most likely referred to the Muslim merchants who followed the caravan route from the Hausa towns and Borno to the kola-producing region of Asante.[13] On the Gold Coast he was sold to a Dutch ship, which took him to Barbados, where a Dutchman by the name of Vanhorn bought him and took him to New York City. Theodorus Jacobus Freylinghusen, whom he called "Freelandhouse," subsequently purchased him. Freylinghusen was a follower of the Great Awakening of George Whitefield and the Countess of Huntingdon, Selina Hastings, with whom Gronniosaw also became associated. After the death of Freylinghusen, he spent several years in the Netherlands before settling finally in England, where he continued his involvement with the Huntingdonian Connexion. His trajectory took him far from any Muslim origins that he may have had in Borno.

Another example of someone who likely came from a Muslim background in the interior of the Gold Coast was Venture Smith, whose birth name was Broteer, and who left Anomabu on the Gold Coast for New England in 1739. Smith appears to have been of Fulani origin and hence was probably Muslim.[14] He subsequently earned his freedom and that of his wife and children after making a living chopping firewood and working as a carpenter building houses. He had also been a slave on an island in Long Island Sound, where he tended livestock. Once he was free, he engaged in trade on the Connecticut River, purchasing land on its left bank and building a house and several outbuildings. Smith evinced characteristics that suggest a Muslim background, including not drinking and avoiding attending Christian churches, despite his strong sense of morality and his frugality. Although he did not read or write English, he dictated his autobiography, which was published in 1798, and commissioned a tombstone for his grave at the Congregational Church in East Haddam, Connecticut, that stated that he was the son of an African king and had earned his own freedom. Since Smith apparently had little contact with Muslims in New England from the time of his arrival as a boy until his death, he had no chance to engage in the rites of Islam, or at least there is no evidence that he did so, and the extent to which he evinced any ties to Islam was reflected in his sense of morality and his avoidance of Christian observance.

By contrast, Abū Bakr al-Ṣiddīq, who was born in Timbuktu about 1790 and was a devout Muslim, was enslaved in Bouna in 1805, when Asante attacked the town. He had lived in Jenne, Kong, and other places along the Juula commercial routes between the inner Niger delta and Asante before his capture. After his enslavement he was taken to Jamaica, where he first became the slave of a stonemason, Donellan, and then of an absentee landowner named Haynes, who had him baptized as Edward Donellan (variously spelled Donlan or Doulan). In 1823 he was sold to Alexander Anderson, who employed him as a "storeman." Al-Ṣiddīq kept accounts in Arabic since he had learned only to speak English, not to read or write it. In 1834 Anderson was persuaded to free al-Ṣiddīq through the exertions of Dr. Richard R. Madden, special magistrate in Jamaica concerned with the supervision of the Emancipation Act of 1833. Madden arranged for al-Ṣiddīq to travel to Britain and then to participate in an exploratory mission under John Davidson in Morocco for the Royal Geographical Society. Davidson lost his life in the attempt to cross the Sahara, but al-Ṣiddīq appears to have survived and to have returned to Jenne, where he had been educated as a youth.[15]

The influences of the different worlds of radical change, one associated with revolution in Europe and the emergence of Haiti out of the ashes of St. Domingue and the other with the spread of jihād in West Africa, strongly shaped the transatlantic migration of enslaved Africans. Revolution in St. Domingue severed that colony from West Africa and the movement of enslaved persons from the central Bilād al-Sūdān via Oyo's trade with Porto Novo. The impact on French domination of exports from this port is particularly noticeable with respect to the special role of Pierre Tamata, the leading merchant at Porto Novo, in that trade. Tamata was a Muslim of Hausa origin who had been educated in France and served as the principal agent supplying slaves to French traders in the 1780s and early 1790s. Tamata established a clear link between the Muslim community at Porto and the interior of West Africa through the heartland of Oyo.[16] In fact, Tamata's role in the slave trade underscores one of the complaints of 'Uthmān dan Fodio that Muslims were being sold to Christians via Oyo, one of the justifications for the jihād movement.[17]

The Second Phase of Migration to the Americas: Repercussions of the Sokoto Jihād

The uprising of Muslims in Salvador, Bahia, in 1835 marked the principal expression of jihād in the Americas. In Brazil, Muslims were known as Malês, after the Yoruba term *imale*. The capital of Bahia was particularly vulnerable to the influence of jihād. As an urban center, it became home to a large concentration of Muslims (plate 23). Although Muslims had been sent to Bahia before the outbreak of the Sokoto jihād in 1804, they had been largely isolated and were more a reflection of the complaints of Muslims against the established governments in West Africa than agents of the jihād movement. The concentration of Muslims in Bahia after the outbreak of jihād was different in two respects. First, the number of Muslims was significantly greater than anywhere else in the Americas at any other time, which made it possible to develop a sense of community that was virtually impossible elsewhere, except perhaps in the hills of Manchester in Jamaica for a brief period, the sea islands of South Carolina, and perhaps a few other places. Second, the existence of a community of Muslims made it possible to convert others to Islam in ways that to some extent mirrored the expansion of Islam in West Africa. The culmination of this movement was the Malês revolt, which appealed to Muslims who had come from the areas in the interior of the Bight of Benin where jihād had transformed the political landscape and the nature of religious affiliation. Those who supported the revolt included Muslims with various backgrounds, including some who converted to Islam in Bahia. Those who came from the Hausa emirates, Nupe, and Borno had experienced the jihād firsthand, often having been enslaved during jihād campaigns, either by the proponents of jihād or by those who were resisting the jihād. Many others were Yoruba who had been Muslims before leaving Africa, while others had become Muslim in Brazil. Allegiance to Islam provided the common bond among those who resisted in Bahia, a factor that was clearly recognized by the Brazilian authorities.

There were two reasons that Muslims were concentrated in Bahia. First, Bahia experienced renewed growth in sugar production as a result of the collapse of St. Domingue after 1793, which prompted an increased demand for enslaved Africans. A major staple of the Bahian trade was tobacco, which enabled Bahian merchants to focus on the Bight of Benin, while relatively few Pernambuco slaving companies operated there, and virtually no merchants from Rio de Janeiro. Bahian slave dealers were well situated because tobacco production was concentrated in Bahia. This expansion occurred at the same time at which Britain withdrew from the slave trade, thereby preventing similar growth in production in the British Caribbean because of the inability to expand the labor force. Second, the focus of trade in the Bight of Benin, which continued to be a major supplier of enslaved labor for Bahia, shifted to Lagos, which inevitably resulted in the migration of Yoruba war captives and refugees, many of whom were also Muslims as a result of the jihād and the subsequent collapse of Oyo. As a result, according to Stuart Schwartz, "the ratio of Africans in the population rose to new heights as the wave of slaves inundated the captaincy . . . , most of them young adult males."[18] Many of these were Hausa, Nupe, or "Borno" (that is, people from Borno) by the first decade of the nineteenth century. After 1820 increasing numbers of Yoruba swelled the arriving population, thereby changing the composition of the population but not the influence of Islam. Yoruba became the language of communication and thereby seemed to mark an ethnic shift that was in fact less significant than the allegiance to Islam. Most if not all the Hausa, Nupe, and others from farther inland than Oyo were also fluent in Yoruba because they had passed through and sometimes actually had resided for some time in Oyo.

The consolidation of jihād in West Africa, perhaps ironically, considering the importance of the slavery issue in the eyes of Muslims, increased the number of enslaved Africans in the overall population, both among those who remained locally and those who were forced to migrate. It is likely that most of those who were enslaved in this period remained in West Africa, but still a sizable number of them were sent to the Americas, especially to Bahia and Cuba. As Manuel Barcia has demonstrated, there was a pattern common to Bahia and Cuba, the two main destinations of the enslaved from the Bight of Benin.[19] War and specifically the jihād and its ripple effect accounted for the great majority of captives, which confirms my earlier analysis of biographical accounts that indicate the methods of enslavement. João José Reis has also recognized that jihād provided Bahia with enslaved Africans, many of whom were devotees of Islam. Bahia received the largest number of slaves who resulted from the fall of the Oyo Empire, but the pattern in Cuba only confirms the impact of jihād. The influence of the enslaved population that originated in jihād was out of proportion to the total number of enslaved Africans who arrived in Brazil and Cuba in this period, moreover. The British-led abolition movement, which did indeed limit the scale of slave departures from West Africa and thereby pushed the trade farther south to Angola and beyond to Mozambique, combined with the jihād restrictions on the sale of Muslims to non-Muslims and specifically Christian Europeans to shape the Atlantic world of the nineteenth century. Because many of the identified participants in the 1835 uprising in Bahia worked in English households or for British firms, they must have absorbed information relating to British emancipation in 1833, the anti-slave-trade activities centered on Sierra Leone, and the emergence of a Yoruba factor in diaspora identity that influenced the

Muslim uprising there. These linkages indicate that the history of the diaspora has to incorporate Africa, not focus solely on the Americas and the European age of revolutions with regard to resistance and the related efforts to establish reconstituted social, religious, and cultural manifestations of a Muslim homeland.

The increasing importance of Islam as a mobilizing factor in Bahia was evident as early as 1807 in the attribution of resistance to "Hausa" influence in an abortive conspiracy. The Hausa, that is, the Muslim factor, surfaced with some regularity until the revolt of 1835. In 1807, besides the ethnic identification of the conspirators, the seizure of numerous amulets reflected the significance of Islam, since amulets were common in areas of Hausa dominance both before and after the jihād. At least another ten revolts and conspiracies surfaced in Bahia after 1807 (1809, 1814, 1816, 1822, 1824, 1826, 1827, 1828, 1830, and 1831) and were associated with slaves who often were Muslims, in some cases specifically with those described as Hausa.[20] Moreover, in 1807 it was alleged that the Hausa planned to install a governor in Salvador, poison the white population, burn all the religious objects in the churches in the public squares, and then proceed to Pernambuco to free their compatriots there. While these allegations may seem to be far fetched, the rebels were accused of wanting to establish an independent state in the interior and enslave all the blacks who had been born in Brazil.[21]

The revolt of 1814 provides a further example of Muslim involvement in slave resistance. Hausa insurgents attacked the village of Santiago de Iguape in the region where Bahia's largest sugar plantations were located. The slaves planned to gather at one of the plantations and from there march on the town of Maragogipe, located on the Paraguaçu River twenty kilometers from the Baía de Todos os Santos. On 23 March, regular troops and the militia occupied all roads leading to Maragogipe. Three freedmen, identified as Hausa, were in regular contact with the slaves on the plantation and were arrested. The leader was apparently João, reputed to be a *malomi*, or priest, according to police. The word *malomi*, that is, *malam*, is a Hausa term denoting a *mu'allim*, Arabic for a Muslim teacher. This evidence of Muslim involvement and the organizational role of Muslim leaders identified as Hausa represented an even more significant intervention beyond complicity in 1807, which had basically been demonstrated by the existence of the amulets taken from the rebels. According to Reis,

> Malomi João led the revolt from his base in a *quilombo* [maroon].
> His principal agent in Salvador was a slave known as Francisco Cidade,

who, taking advantage of the relative freedom urban slaves enjoyed under the count of Arcos, maintained contacts with Africans through-out the Recôncavo and on the islands in the bay. He collected money and sent it and food to the *quilombo* regularly. On one of his trips to Itaparica Island, he is reputed to have conferred the title "Duke of the Island" upon someone known as David.[22]

Reis suggests that the rebels were adopting Portuguese nomenclature as a means of establishing political and social power, although the title may have been little more than an attempt to interpret a Hausa designation, which could have been *sarki* or *galadima*, for example.

The police identified Francisco Cidade as "president of his Nation's dances, its protector and agent," which Reis has suggested refers to *sarkin bori,* that is, chief of the *bori* spirit possession cult, and indicates that he may have been associated with the spirit-possession cult that was targeted during the jihād. If he was a *sarkin bori*, this would reflect the influence of jihād. Muslims from the interior of the Bight of Benin recognized *bori*, despite its condemnation by the jihād leadership, and it should be noted that *bori* does not indicate an impure form of Islamic practice or an "African" influence but rather only that *bori* was common, as the treatise *Hatk al-Sitr* of Aḥmad b. al-Qāḍī al-Timbuktāwī, written in North Africa in 1813, also demonstrates.[23] The milieu was different from the previous period, when the western Bilād al-Sūdān had been the predominant source of enslaved Muslims. The leaders of the 1814 conspiracy may have had some association with *bori*, or their ad-herence to Sufism may have been interpreted as such. The 1814 revolt was in-fluenced by individuals who were affected by the conditions of jihād, whether or not they were directly associated with the practice of *bori*, the jihād, or both. It is possible that a Hausa *malam* in Bahia catered to a variety of indi-viduals whose understanding of Islam was situational, and indeed this *malam* might have represented the imperfect and incomplete allegiance that prompted the jihād. Unfortunately, little else is known about the uprising. Nonetheless, the influences that were emanating from the Hausa states were still apparent. The same contradictions that empowered the jihād were op-erational in Brazil, only in a context of colonial slavery. In effect, conditions similar to those prevalent in West Africa extended to Bahia.

In the early nineteenth century resistance in Bahia was concentrated within two overlapping groups of slaves and former slaves, those who identi-fied as Yoruba and those who identified as Muslim. The two groups over-lapped because some Yoruba were Muslim and some were not. Muslims from the central Bilād al-Sūdān included Hausa, Nupe, Kanuri, and others associated with Borno and the Sokoto Caliphate. In the case of both groups, Muslims and Yoruba, the personal histories of the slaves and freed slaves who resisted the Bahian slavocracy reveal some similarities that establish important factors in the conspiracies and revolts. Because virtually all the participants had been born in Africa and had arrived in Bahia on the same Portuguese-Brazilian ships, shipmates formed strong allegiances, and the ethnic backgrounds of slaves further consolidated these ties. In some contexts individuals who were on the same ship referred to one another as "Malungo," an Umbundu term for friend or companion, but one that was probably mirrored in Hausa and Yoruba.[24] The ethnic concentrations on ships reinforced the emergence of a community of African-born slaves and former slaves with the potential to revolt.[25] In the case of individuals from the interior of the Bight of Benin, this community was heavily male. With reference to Hausa in Bahia, for example, Francis de Castelnau noted that "bien qu'ils soient assez nombreux à Bahia, il est au contraire très rare d'y rencontrer des femmes de leur nation. Ils viennent à peu près tous par la voie d'Onim [Lagos]" (plate 24).[26]

The departures from the Bight of Benin after 1810 were closely associated with the Sokoto jihād and the reverberations of jihād in Nupe, Oyo, and the broader Yoruba region, as reflected in table 6.5. The departure of Africans who were identified as Yoruba or who came from areas bordering the Yoruba-speaking area also included many people who were enslaved in the jihād, but mostly after 1817. The overwhelming number of Yoruba leaving the port of Lagos left after the outbreak of the jihād in the interior, so that the trade of Lagos featured prominently in the second phase of slave departures, just as Ouidah, Porto Novo and Badagry had figured in the phase before the jihād. Not surprisingly, the movement of people to British colonies and to the United States virtually ceased after abolition of the slave trade in the Anglophone world. Similarly, the movement to French colonies also disappeared, so that virtually all of the enslaved from the Bight of Benin went either to Cuba or Brazil, unless the British Navy captured vessels and diverted people to Sierra Leone and to a lesser extent elsewhere. Of the total number of departures from the Bight of Benin after 1810 (338,000), 107,000 (31.6 percent) went to Cuba and 176,000 (52.2 percent) went to Brazil, especially Bahia. Another 50,000 (14.9 percent) ended up in Sierra Leone. For those destined for Bahia, many remained in the Recôncavo and Baía de Todos os Santos in the vicinity of Salvador, but not all. Some went to the plateau in the hinterland to the west of Salvador and were involved in the search for diamonds.[27]

JIHĀD IN WEST AFRICA DURING THE AGE OF REVOLUTIONS

With the arrival of many Yoruba in Cuba and Brazil after 1820, some of whom who were already Muslims and others who subsequently converted to Islam, the Muslim factor became more pronounced, particularly in Bahia. Islam provided an umbrella for those who had to endure slavery despite the strong pressures of a Catholic Brazilian society, and those who achieved their emancipation continued to strive for some autonomy through their religious allegiance. By the late 1820s enslaved Yoruba, known locally as Nagô, had become the largest part of the Muslim community. By then, Yoruba was the most common language used by Muslims, although many of those who spoke Yoruba were of other origins and also spoke other languages. As the surviving biographies of enslaved Muslims from this era demonstrate, Muslims from Ilorin and enslaved Muslims from elsewhere as far as Borno adopted the Yoruba language once they were in Oyo and its dependencies. Hence the ethnic configuration of the Muslim community was complex, although the allegiance to Islam seems to have been straightforward. The signs of West African Islam included the fact that rebels dressed in white, used amulets, and conversed through Arabic manuscripts and documents. Police seized many of these documents, including scraps of paper used in making amulets. A number of the protagonists admitted to having learned to read and write Arabic in Africa; some admitted to having been Qur'ānic teachers.[28] Their everyday jobs meant that they were employed as stevedores on the docks; as porters of palanquins, which were carriage seats for carrying people up and down the steep slopes of Salvador from the lower, waterside city to the upper city (plate 25); and as caulkers, carpenters, and other craftsmen, which reflected the urban context. Of the Hausa whom Castelnau interviewed, "la plupart sont employés à Bahia comme nègres de palanquin."[29]

We have a reasonably good profile of those who came from Africa, based on biographical information that helps determine the nature of the impact of the jihād in establishing the context of enslavement and the fundamental shift in social and political society that was clearly a factor in shaping resistance in Brazil. The Arabic texts, amulets, and other documents seized after the 1835 revolt included the crude writings of students, as well as more sophisticated passages that were copied from the Qur'ān.[30] The presence of mosques and Qur'ānic schools was noted by authorities at the time, and indeed, the destruction of one mosque in Vitória was a factor in the outbreak of the uprising. As the activities of Muslim clerics make clear, resistance was cast in a religious mold that was transferred directly from Africa to Bahia. Raimundo Nina Rodrigues, himself of African descent, despite the racist overtones of

The Repercussions of Jihād in the Americas

his analysis, concluded in 1900 that the ideology of jihād was the basis of resistance in Bahia.[31]

The evolution of Malês identity reflected the influence of the ideological
and political struggle in Hausa society at the turn of the nineteenth century.
When Hausa slaves began to arrive in sufficient numbers to establish a community and redefine their identity under slavery, they brought with them the
experience of the political turmoil that preceded the jihād in the central Bilād
al-Sūdān. The recognition of Muslims as a community was a controversial
factor underlying this turmoil, and when Gobir and other Hausa states tried
to regulate the activities of Muslims, even enslaving many of them, the violent reaction manifested itself in the form of jihād. Enslavement of Muslims
was challenged. Ironically, the jihād did not end the export of Muslim slaves
to the Americas, but the arrival of newly enslaved Muslims after the outbreak
of the jihād reinforced links between Africa and the Americas. Muslim identity emerged as the dominant loyalty among Hausa and, by extension, among
slaves from neighboring Borno and Nupe and subsequently among Yoruba.
People of other ethnic backgrounds from the interior appear to have been
absorbed into the Muslim community, whether or not they had been Muslims
before leaving Africa.

The influx of Yoruba-speaking people from Oyo and other parts of the
hinterland of the Bight of Benin resulted in what can be labeled the "Yoruba-
ization" of the Muslim community, although the correlation between Yoruba
ethnicity and Islam was never total because many people who were identified
as Nagô were not Muslims. It seems that Yoruba slaves and former slaves
sometimes behaved on the basis of ethnic background and at other times responded as Muslims. In certain contexts there was solidarity on the basis of
Yoruba identity that resulted in a coalition between Muslims and non-Muslim
Yoruba, but on other occasions Yoruba resistance was associated with *orişa*
worship. Hence there were two traditions of revolt in Bahia, one Muslim and
the other based on *orişa*, the first being transethnic and the second being
ethnic.

The ethnic, age, and gender profile of the exported population of the
Bight of Benin reveals the role of religion and ethnicity in the various conspiracies and uprisings in Bahia between 1807 and 1835. These revolts followed
a pattern that suggests strong influences stemming from the jihād that was
under way during the same years. Features of the uprising in 1835 included
the use of a flag, the reliance on amulets, the wearing of white Muslim robes
(known in Bahia as *abadá*), the use of Muslim names, group prayers led by

an imām, and the staging of the revolt at the end of the month of Ramadan.[32] Indeed, the Muslim uprising at Ilorin in 1817 and the subsequent establishment of the emirate of Ilorin in 1823 may well have inspired many Muslims in Brazil. As Pierre Verger has observed, the conspirators in both Ilorin and Bahia used silver rings as a means of identifying sympathizers.[33] The use of signet rings, whether engraved or not, followed the *Sunna* of the Prophet Muhammad.

The 1835 revolt in Bahia seems to have been planned as early as the previous November, after the celebration of the Laylat al-Miʿrāj (believed to be the twenty-seventh day of the month of Rajab), the Muslim holiday commemorating the Prophet's nighttime journey from Mecca to Jerusalem in the heavens, where he received instructions to pray five times a day. The Laylat al-Qadr, which was "the night of power" and "the night of destiny" when the Prophet Muhammad began to receive the revelations that formed the Qurʾān, according to the 97th Sura. After the dispersal of the celebrants, the Bahian authorities destroyed the mosque in Vitória parish, which, of course, was a direct attempt to suppress Islamic observance. The rebels failed to free two Muslim leaders who were in jail—Alufa Pacifico Licutan, who said that his name was Bilal, and Alufa Ahuna, both of "Nagô" origin. There appears to have been a flag or banner that consisted of a red and white handkerchief with a purple border. Another leader, known as Mubakar, alias Tomé, may have been the imām of the Muslim community.[34] According to Nina Rodrigues, the imām of Salvador in the 1890s claimed that the imām at the time of the revolt in 1835 was Abubakar (Mubakar), which is a Hausa name.[35] Although Reis has suggested that Ahuna and Mubakar may have been the same person, this seems unlikely on the basis of the names alone. Other leaders included Sanim, alias Luis, who spoke both Hausa and Yoruba and claimed to be Nupe but was not particularly fluent in Portuguese, and Dandará (a Hausa name), who was known as Eslebão do Carmo.[36] The use of silver rings as a sign of recognition was similar to the practice in the Sokoto jihād. Similarly, ʿUthmān dan Fodio issued flags to those he designated as leaders of particular campaigns of the jihād and potential emirs of new provinces of the Sokoto state. There is no suggestion that the flag that is reported in Bahia had any connection with this practice, however.

Any Muslim initiative on the political level, and particularly an uprising, would of necessity and by definition have had a recognized imām, or spiritual leader. Similarly, if the Muslims who were committed to revolt in 1835 fashioned their action as a jihād, then certain specific actions would have been necessary, including a *hijra* or physical withdrawal of the community from the scene of confrontation, which in the Bahia situation would have been interpreted as removal to a *quilombo* outside Salvador. However, there is no evidence that a withdrawal conceived along these lines actually took place, although there was communication between the Muslims involved in the revolt and *quilombos* in the countryside. In any event, an estimated six hundred Muslims, including slaves and freedmen, many in white dress, ran through the streets of Salvador shooting guns in the early hours of Sunday, 25 January 1835. As Reis has noted, "The rebellion had been planned to come off at a very special moment in the Muslim religious calendar, in fact at the most important time of all—Ramadan."[37] The timing was auspicious because the selected date, Sunday, 25 January, a holiday celebrating the feast day of Our Lady of Guidance, when most of the city was preoccupied, and free and enslaved blacks were able to congregate. The date coincided with the 25th day of the holy month of Ramaḍān, during which Muslims fasted. While the fast was technically broken with a feast on the first day of the month of Shawwāl, three days later, in the context of restrictions enforced in Bahia, Muslims took advantage of the relative lax security of the Christian holy day to hold the ʿĪd al-fiṭr feast three days early and then stage the revolt. The Muslims shouted "Death to the whites" and "Death to the soldiers." For three hours they fought against a larger force estimated at fifteen hundred men. This included police, cavalry, National Guard soldiers, and civilians who possessed swords, knives, clubs, and pistols. The rebels attacked the jail, attempting to free Bilal Licutan, but were unsuccessful. They also tried to take the police station but were again beaten back.[38]

The revolt failed. At least seventy rebels died; perhaps double that number were wounded, while nine persons were killed crushing the uprising. Subsequently, Bahian authorities responded quickly to suppress the Muslim community. There were trials that generated a considerable body of testimony.[39] Of 286 people who were indicted, 260 were men and 26 were women; 160 were slaves and 126 were free; 189 were jailed, and the other 97 included individuals who were indicted later or died during the insurrection and were subsequently identified. Among those who were arrested were 176 slaves, 112 freed persons, and 4 whose status is not known. Of these, about three-quarters (73 percent) were identified as Nagô, although at the time Nagô represented less than a third (30 percent) of the African population resident in Salvador in 1835, which was estimated at 22,000.[40] There were eighteen death sentences, of which only five were actually carried out, on 14 May.[41] The Bahian government sent one ship with 150 "free Africans" on board to Africa at public expense. Of this group, police labeled 120 as "suspected persons." The other 30 were Liberated Africans who had been removed from captured slave vessels by the British Squadron and were residing in Salvador. Slave owners deported another 380 Africans to other provinces of Brazil. Of these, 136 were Nagô. By the end of 1835 at least 700 African freed persons were issued passports to allow their departure from Bahia. Officials facilitated this emigration by streamlining the processing of applications through the bureaucracy.[42]

As Reis has demonstrated, the Malês uprising was multifaceted. It was conceived mainly by enslaved people seeking their freedom but also involved former slaves and attracted people of different faiths, not only followers of Islam but also others who practiced rituals associated with *orisa* and *vodun* but who were willing to unite under the banner of Islam.[43] Although the uprising in 1835 was easily crushed, it is clear that practices associated with jihād in West Africa were fundamental to the rebellion. Muslims obviously had religious and historic connections in Bahia that sustained networks built on the inspirations of jihād. The question is not whether but how jihād informed resistance in Bahia. The preponderance of Yoruba in the uprising related to the collapse of Oyo in jihād and the ability of Muslims to transcend ethnic distinctions based on allegiance to Islam. The factors underlining a sense of identity, a shared cosmology, and tendencies toward resistance made it possible to stage an uprising, whether or not the event itself was proclaimed a jihād.[44]

The Malês uprising is an important legacy for Brazil. It shows that Muslims and Africans did not accept their enslaved and oppressed situation. Moreover, legally, if not in practice, the slave trade to Brazil had been abolished in 1831, and anyone who arrived from Africa after 13 March 1830 was declared to be legally a free person.[45] It is not known whether most slaves and former slaves knew about this law, but it may have been a factor. Moreover, in 1834 slaves in British colonies were emancipated. A number of the key Muslim leaders worked for British residents in Salvador, and they would have heard the discussions among the British in 1832–34 about abolition. There had been a major uprising in Jamaica in 1831–32, the so-called Christmas uprising, in which slaves in Jamaica accused their masters of denying them their emancipation, which they believed had already been made law in Britain. British residents in Bahia would have talked openly about this, which may have been a contributing factor. As I have pointed out, there were numerous revolts and conspiracies in Bahia and other parts of Brazil anyway, so there was a lot of pressure on the slave owners that related to the corruption of the state and the brutality of the slavery system. The Malês uprising occurred in this context. It represented the voices of those who had been illegally enslaved and was a powerful expression of protest. Eventually the legal abolition of the slave trade in Brazil had to be enforced, but not before tens of thousands of Africans had been brought illegally into Brazil as slaves. This shameful part of Brazilian history reveals corruption at the highest levels of government. The authorities in Bahia had arrested the leaders of the Muslim community in November 1834, and they had destroyed the mosque in Vitoría parish. Hence the uprising was an unsuccessful statement about religious freedom, and the repression of Muslims after the uprising was severe.

The Malês revolt stands out because it was an urban revolt, although there were strong links to the plantation districts, which posed the possibility that the uprising could have spread. If the urban uprising had been successful, and, for example, if the prison had been taken and those inside had been freed, the rebels would have been able to seize more guns. Then there would have been danger that the revolt would have achieved its goals. The revolt had a common ideology based on Islam, and those who had come from West Africa knew that jihād had successfully transformed the political landscape there and had established the Sokoto Caliphate. This background provided the inspiration for the events of November 1834 through January 1835. The reverberations of jihād were clearly evident in the Malês uprising.[46]

As for the motives, it is difficult to know. At the trials after the suppression of the revolt, as might be expected, those who were accused did not necessarily tell the truth or reveal their grievances. Freeing the slaves and taking power were feared, although these aims were not necessarily realistic. Even the identity of the imām was carefully concealed, but most certainly the Muslims wanted to negotiate better conditions. They could not have defeated the Brazilian government. They did not have access to enough weapons to do that. If they had been more successful, more slaves might have joined the uprising and might have converted to Islam, however, but that would not have resulted in the creation of a Muslim state. It might have resulted in greater religious tolerance and autonomy for Muslims and perhaps return to Africa for many.

Thirty years after the revolt, an Ottoman scholar, Imām ʿAbd al-Raḥmān al-Baghdādī al-Dimashqī, interviewed Muslims who had been involved in the uprising while he was in Brazil. The imām was in Rio de Janeiro because an Ottoman fleet that he was on ran into trouble in the South Atlantic on a voyage from the Mediterranean around the Cape of Good Hope to the Indian

Ocean. When the fleet stopped in Rio to undergo repairs, Muslims went on board to greet the imām and, initially through a Jewish interpreter, thereby involved the imām in the local Muslim community. Although suspicious at first because of problems of language, the imām nonetheless remained in Brazil for more than two years to instruct the local Muslims in rituals and the norms of Islam. In the course of his stay, he learned about the 1835 Malês uprising and "the reasons why Muslims hide their faith from Christians."[47] He subsequently wrote an Arabic text on his experiences in Brazil, which included a journey to Bahia, Alagoas, and Pernambuco, as well as his involvement with the Muslims in Rio. According to al-Baghdādī's explanation,

> I asked them several times about the reasons for this exaggerated care in hiding, especially since the [Brazilian] state granted all sorts of freedom to individuals. They informed me that a war [ḥarb] had taken place between them [the Muslims] and the Christians. The Sudanese [i.e., Blacks] decided to claim some territories, but the victory went to the Christians. It was clear to them [the Christians] that a group of Muslims [jamā'a] from the black communities [ṭā'ifa] were at the origin of this struggle [fitna]. The Blacks are the ones who testified against each other because, as I mentioned earlier, they belong to different religions. For this reason, the Muslims denied their adherence [ankara] to this religion [in public], fearing retribution. Until now, if the Christians know that somebody is Muslim, they will probably kill him, exile him, or jail him for life. Each time I see Islam corrupted the way I mentioned, such as in my discussion of baptism, burial, and secrecy, a flow of tears drifts from my eyes. I feel sorry for the land of Islam. I remember my country and the long distances that separate us. I do not find any free [capable] person to help me, especially in a country without allies, subjugated by the despised, where bells ring and the temptations of Satan abound.[48]

His account attributes the motives of the Muslims to persecution and claims that the aim was to carve out a territory where Muslims would be autonomous. The sadness that al-Baghdādī expressed related to serious obstacles that he faced in his mission to re-educate the Muslim community in the fundamentals of Islam, including the necessity of fasting during Ramadan, abstinence from eating pork, avoidance of alcohol, and other commitments of Islam. Whether or the "war" (ḥarb) had the characteristics of a jihād is left unanswered. As John Ralph Willis has demonstrated, "The classical jurists . . .

The Repercussions of Jihād in the Americas

distinguished four ways by which the believer could fulfil his *jihād* obligation," and warfare in the land of unbelievers was incumbent if the jihād of self-purification and the injunction to command the good and forbid the bad failed.[49]

There was no explicit attack on slavery as an institution or a demand for emancipation of those being held in slavery. The focus was on the defense of the Muslim community, with an appeal to those Muslims who were enslaved and those who might join the Muslims in revolt. The identity of the rebels as Muslims was obvious in the way they dressed, the wearing of rings as a means of recognition, the use of amulets, and the timing of the uprising in the month of Ramadan. The symbols accorded to breaking the fast relate the uprising to Islam and a community of Muslims more than to a revolt against slavery. The rebels directed punitive actions against other Africans who were not Muslims, as well as mixed-race "browns" who were considered hostile to Africans and who would not join the uprising. The Muslim rebels even distrusted those identified as Mandingo, who were Muslims but were not committed to jihād. The Muslims were betrayed by non-Muslims, whose hostility reveals a cleavage on religious grounds that was reflected in ethnic divisions but was not specifically ethnic. The rallying cry "Death to all whites" implicitly was also ideological because there were no whites who were Muslims. Whites dominated a government that was considered oppressive not just because of slavery but because of the persecution of Muslims, as demonstrated in the incarceration of Muslim leaders and the destruction of the mosque in Vitoría parish.

Muslim Complicity in Resisting Slavery Elsewhere in the Americas

Although the Malês uprising in Bahia stands out as the clearest example of the repercussions of the jihād movement across the Atlantic, especially the jihād of 'Uthmān dan Fodio, there were other reverberations that arose from the presence of Muslims in the Americas. Thanks to the research of a number of scholars, particularly Michael Gomez, Sylviane Diouf, Allan D. Austin, and João Reis, there is considerable information on enslaved Muslims in the Americas, which emphasizes the efforts of Muslims to preserve their autonomy and their moral and spiritual commitment to the maintenance of a sense of honor in the face of the brutality of slavery. Often, too, there is evidence of the desire to return to West Africa and reintegrate into Muslim society despite the obstacles of recrossing the Atlantic and the temptations that sometimes undermined such a return migration.

The plight of Muslims varied according to the specific colonial or post-colonial context in the Americas. In the French islands, and especially in St. Domingue, there were relatively few Muslims. Gomez concludes that the Muslim presence was weak in St. Domingue, probably amounting to less, perhaps much less, than 10 percent of the population in the decade or two before the French Revolution in the 1790s.[50] According to plantation records analyzed by Gabriel Debien, the Muslim population as determined by recognizable names may have been less than 5 percent and perhaps as low as half that proportion.[51] The most prominent individual who probably was of Muslim origin was François Makandal, who became a maroon, headed a conspiracy in the 1750s, and was burned alive at the stake in 1758.[52] However, there was not anything in particular in his activities that linked him to Islam and certainly not to the jihād movement. Sylviane Diouf has argued that the revolutionary hero Boukman was a Muslim on the basis of his name, "book man," but it is hard to see how an English name would have been used in a French colony.[53]

Muslims were visible in Trinidad in the early nineteenth century, where they were known locally as Mandingo even if they were Hausa in origin. There were "Mandingo" at Manzanilla, Quare, and Turue in the 1820s and 1830s, although they likely had had little if anything to do with the jihād movement.[54] In Port of Spain there was a small Muslim community under Muhammad Sisse, who was born in 1788–90 at Niani-Maru on the Gambia River and was probably Jahanke in origin. He was enslaved in 1810, but the British navy captured the French ship that he was on, and along with others so liberated, he served his subsequent apprenticeship in the Third West India Regiment. His compatriots in the regiment included Muhammad Hausa, known as Philip Finlay, and Jackson Harvey, who also retained their commitment to Islam and submitted a petition to colonial authorities to return to Sierra Leone, a request that was granted for them and their wives in 1837.[55] Maureen Warner-Lewis has identified other Muslims, including a woman named Auta.[56] Muhammad Bath was imam for an estimated 140 Muslims in Port of Spain. Bath had been captured in 1804–5 by "Caffres," although where exactly is not known. Under his leadership the Muslim community purchased the freedom of everyone it could identify as being Muslim.[57] Many of these Muslims were successful in returning to Africa.[58] The allegiance of these Muslims focused on Africa and an unwillingness to assimilate to the racialized societies of the postslavery Americas. The consequences were the virtual elimination of Islam in Trinidad until its revival with the immigration of

The Repercussions of Jihād in the Americas

Muslims from the Indian subcontinent. By the end of the nineteenth century Islam was associated with indentured workers from South Asia, not with African Muslims.

As discussed in previous chapters, Muslims were relatively prominent among Africans in North America, and since most Muslims reached North America before 1807, they largely came from the western Bilād al-Sūdān in the eighteenth century. Richard Pierpoint, for example, not only fought with the British during the American War of Independence but also was a soldier in the War of 1812 and helped repulse the US invasion across the Niagara River. His petition to Governor Simcoe, cited earlier, suggests that he was well aware that Simcoe had wanted to abolish slavery in Upper Canada, although in the end the British government allowed Simcoe only to prevent the further arrival of slaves in the colony but not actually to end slavery. Nonetheless, Simcoe's stance on slavery was certainly one reason that Pierpoint was loyal to the British. In North America, however, except possibly in the Sea Islands of South Carolina, especially on Sapelo Island, and in the Mississippi delta, Muslims were not numerous enough to form a community of believers, and as elsewhere, therefore, individuals were essentially isolated from the Islamic background.[59] Muhammad ʿAlī Saʿīd stands out as an anomaly for Muslims in the United States. Saʿīd crossed the Sahara to the Middle East before ending up in St. Petersburg in Russia and then traveled through western Europe before reaching North America, enlisting in the Union army and fighting in the American Civil War, where he was known as Nicholas Said. The role of Muslims in the events of the Americas were varied but nonetheless can be delineated.[60]

Gwendolyn Midlo Hall has identified 2,731 individuals in Louisiana who were Muslims or came from areas that suggest that they might have been Muslim (table 6.6).[61] Of this sample, 2,241 (82 percent) came from the areas of jihād in the western Bilād al-Sūdān, while 490 (18 percent) came from the interior of the Bight of Benin and hence the area of the Sokoto jihād, which reflects the discontinuation of African arrivals after the withdrawal of the United States from the transatlantic slave trade after 1807. The heavy concentration of males is particularly striking, 71.4 percent of those who have been documented, and is especially pronounced among those identified as Hausa (91.4 percent), which corresponds with other information on the movement of enslaved persons from the area of the Sokoto jihād to Brazil.

One feature of these examples was how Muslims maintained their identity through nominal conversion to Christianity. Kabā Saghanughu, despite

TABLE 6.6. Ethnic Origins of Possible Muslims in Louisiana, 1767–1831

Ethnicity	Males	%	Females	%	Unspecified	Total
Wolof	346	60.4	227	39.6	1	574
Moor	81	72.3	31	27.7		112
Bambara [Bamana]	388	88.6	50	11.4	2	440
Fulbe[1]	153	75.0	51	25.0	1	205
Mande[2]	589	67.2	288	32.8	4	881
Susu	19	65.5	10	34.5		29
Hausa	117	91.4	11	8.6		128
Yoruba	240	69.1	107	30.9	1	347
Bargu/Borgu	8		4	0.4		12
Gwari	1					1
Nupe	1					1
Totals	1,943	71.4	779	28.6	9	2,731

Source: Gwendolyn Midlo Hall, "Lousiana Slave Database," *Slave Biographies: The Atlantic Database Network*, http://slavebiographies.org.

[1] Includes 10 identified as "Timbo."

[2] Includes 3 Marka and 1 Soninke.

joining the Moravian Mission and serving as a helper at Fairfield, secretly continued to adhere to his Islamic identity and promoted values and practices that reflected his Muslim upbringing and learning, as reflected in his *Kitāb al-ṣalāt*.[62] That Kabā continued to profess Islam in private is lent credence through his correspondence in Arabic with other Muslims in Jamaica, which Special Magistrate R. R. Madden inadvertently discovered while he was stationed in Jamaica in 1834.[63] In that correspondence Kabā clearly stated that he wanted to be addressed by his Muslim name, not the name that the Christians called him. Ironically, Kabā came to the attention of Madden through a Jewish proprietor who owned a nearby estate named Timbuctoo after the fabled city where Kabā was destined to study law when he was enslaved.

Mahommah Gardo Baquaqua retained his Muslim name but found sanctuary among the Free Will Baptists, first in Haiti and then in upstate New York (plate 26). His association with Africa remained firm, nonetheless, including being on the African Mission Committee of the Baptists and a projected member of a planned mission to Africa that was never implemented. In his correspondence and autobiographical account, he stressed his desire

The Repercussions of Jihād in the Americas

to return to Africa and specifically to Katsina, the home of his mother. It seems possible that he actually did return to the Sokoto Caliphate because of contacts in Liverpool, which at the time had direct steamship links with Lagos and the Niger River. His association with William P. Powell, who worked in the customhouse in Liverpool and was a prominent abolitionist who had helped Baquaqua escape from jail in New York in 1847, suggests that Baquaqua may have secured passage on a steamship of Macgregor Laird's Africa Steamship Company that operated to Lagos and the Niger delta.[64] While it is likely Baquaqua was baptized, as was common among new arrivals from Africa in Brazil, he appears never to have renounced Islam or abandoned his Muslim Hausa name. As with Kabā, the formative impact of the Muslim background stands out, but the impact in transferring the influence of Islam in the Americas was minimal.

The Impact in Cuba

The jihād had a significant impact on the demography of Cuba after around 1820, when many Yoruba arrived in the wake of the decline and collapse of Oyo. Virtually all of those who were identified as Lucumí appear to have been enslaved in the course of the jihad and the ripple effect of the subsequent wars and migrations as refugees fled south from the heartland of Oyo and the destruction of the Owu wars. Nonetheless, the proportion of Muslims in this population appears to have been relatively low. Barcia has identified numerous Muslims as recorded in the Havana Court of Mixed Commission between 1824 and 1835, but he otherwise notes the "almost total lack of references" to Muslims in Cuba, unlike Bahia.[65] The proportion of people who were enslaved as a result of the collapse of Oyo after 1817 or otherwise can be considered to have been enslaved directly or indirectly in the jihād nonetheless was substantial. This is an important issue, as the work of Henry Lovejoy has made clear in his study of Yoruba in Cuba between 1817 and 1850.[66] His work shows clearly, through an analysis of the records of the Courts of Mixed Commission, the way people identified as "Lucumí," and the documentation on the Yoruba cabildo (i.e., brotherhood) of Juan Prieto in Havana. Barcia has argued that Lucumí led or were involved in fifteen insurrections and conspiracies between 1832 and 1843, which he correlates with the collapse of Oyo and the "Africanization of slave resistance in the nineteenth century."[67]

There were Muslims and other individuals who might have been Muslim but whose religious affiliation cannot be established before the influx of Yoruba. According to Gomez, perhaps about 10 percent of Africans arriving in 1790–1800 could have been Muslim, a proportion that doubled for 1808–16 before falling back to 10 percent through 1829, and this included those identified as Wolof, Fulbe, and Mandinke, suggesting that few were Yoruba.[68] Henry Lovejoy's analysis of shipping records and the Court of Mixed Commission that operated in Havana has revealed that many of those who were referred to as Lucumí were of Oyo origin who adhered to *orisa* practices, as did many Yoruba from dependencies of Oyo that were disrupted and destroyed after the 1817 uprising in Ilorin and the subsequent spread of jihād in northern Yorubaland after 1823. The records of shipment and related documents from the Courts of Mixed Commission in Havana and Rio de Janeiro confirm a pattern of migration that saw almost all Muslims, of whatever ethnicity, being sent to Bahia, along with many survivors of Oyo. By contrast, only a few Muslims went to Cuba, although, as Barcia has pointed out, a few did. The Yoruba who went predominantly to Cuba often were not Muslims, although Muslims of Yoruba, Hausa, and other ethnic backgrounds were clearly concentrated in Bahia.[69] However, many Fulani, Nupe, Bariba, Hausa, and Borno in Cuba were identified as Lucumí. This identification inadvertently disguised the presence of Muslims among them.

A comparison of the arrival of Yoruba in Cuba and Bahia reveals the distinctions that underpin religion, ideology, and political background and are fundamental in understanding the continuities and disjunctures between enslavement in Africa and adjustments to the slave societies in the Americas. As Henry Lovejoy's study of Lucumí *cabildos* in Cuba demonstrates, a significant proportion of the Yoruba who came to Cuba in the nineteenth century were from Oyo and the dependencies of Oyo during the period in which jihād undermined the Oyo state from 1817 to 1836. The Oyo *orisa*, Shango, became identified with Santa Barbara, the three *bàtá* drums (hourglass drums of different sizes with tones representing those in the Yoruba language) of Shango became common, and the *bere* festival of Oyo became associated with the Cuban festival of Day of Kings (Día de Reyes).[70] By contrast, there were almost no Muslims in Cuba. Instead, most Muslims taken during the Yoruba wars associated with the jihād were sent to Bahia, thereby setting the stage for the Malês uprising of 1835. The continued conversion of Yoruba in Bahia to Islam was a factor in rallying support for the Muslim cause, but no similar pattern of conversion occurred in Cuba. Thus the impact of jihād during the age of revolutions is discernible in two phases, one that was associated with the symbolic re-creation of the Oyo state in Cuba and the second in spreading notions of jihād in Bahia. Hence there are distinctions not only between the

The Repercussions of Jihād in the Americas

period before 1804 and the period after but also in the nature of transatlantic migration. Geographically, the temporal division distinguishes the upper Guinea coast and Senegambia from the interior of the Bight of Benin. The geographical and temporal divisions reflect the course of jihād, which first affected Senegambia and the upper Guinea coast and only after 1804 spread to the interior of the Bight of Benin, where the expansion and intensity of the movement reached a new level. Virtually every state and government in the region from Lake Chad to Timbuktu was overthrown and replaced by a government committed to the jihād or at least to the implementation of extensive reforms that were similar to the goals of the jihād, as in the case of Borno. In this period the main states that were opposed to the implementation of Islamic reform, namely, the "Bambara" states of Kaarta and Segu, were overthrown and replaced with a new Muslim regime under al-Ḥājj ʿUmar and the Tījāniyya, but by then Senegambia and the upper Guinea coast were no longer major areas of supply for the transatlantic trade. With the imposition of Tījāniyya rule, virtually the whole of the interior of West Africa had fallen to jihād.

The enslaved Muslims in the military at Ilorin who rebelled in 1817 are usually identified as Hausa, while the identification of rebels in Bahia in 1835 has been as Nagô. By applying a methodology that uses ethnicity as a lens, we are led to ask, what does ethnic labeling mean in these circumstances? In both cases there is an important linguistic component; the language that was being spoken did not necessarily identify origins. Ilorin was particularly important because of the role it played in the migration to Cuba and Brazil and also to Sierra Leone, Trinidad, and elsewhere. In Ilorin, identification as Hausa inevitably meant that individuals came from more diverse backgrounds but spoke Hausa and had become Muslim if they had not already been Muslim when they arrived in Ilorin, and whether or not they came from Kano, Katsina, or the distant lands of Adamawa. In Bahia, Nagô identification meant that people spoke Yoruba as the common language, whether or not they also spoke Hausa, Nupe, or other languages. Any attempt to simplify the transformations in identification as a simple, essentialist ethnic label— "Hausa" or "Yoruba"—is doomed to confusion. Both in Ilorin and in Bahia, it is impossibly simplistic to try to determine who were Yoruba and Hausa at the time of the Ilorin uprising of 1817 or in Bahia at the time of the Malês uprising of 1835 without distorting history. The complexity, manipulation, and inaccuracies of accepting "ethnic" labels as anything more than the start of historical inquiry are made clear by Olatunji Ojo, who has observed, "Religion also played a unifying role, bringing in people from outside the Central Sudan. Indeed, it did not take long for brigands of Yoruba origin to be identified as 'Hausa' so as to benefit from opportunities open to the latter," who were called "Gambari" in Yoruba, and who in fact might not even be ethnically Hausa in origin.[71] The comparison of Bahia and Cuba supports Barcia's conclusion for the "*Nagoization* and *Lucumization* of slave rebellion" with "direct links and continuities existing between the Yoruba- and Hausa-speaking people and other West African groups in Bahia and Cuba on one side, and the Bight of Benin and its interior on the other," that resulted in "two near-simultaneous cycles of slave movements that occurred in Bahia and western Cuba. . . . for most of the first half of the nineteenth century."[72]

Assessment of Muslim Influence in the Americas

The difficulty in determining what proportion of the Africans who left West Africa was actually Muslim affects an assessment of the impact of jihād in the Americas. Those who were either Muslim or influenced by events relating to the jihād movement in Oyo, Senegambia, and the Bambara states of Segu and Kaarta cannot always be identified. The actual population movement sets limits on what is in the realm of reality, however, while individual stories amplify the pattern. The collective impact was less than the number of people who left the regions from the Bight of Benin to Senegambia might suggest. The appeal of Islam was restricted only to those who came from areas where Islam was common and was strongest among those who were already Muslims in Africa. There is virtually no evidence that many enslaved Africans ever considered conversion in the Americas, except for some who spoke Yoruba in Bahia. The extensive documentation on the ships of trade in this period and the number of distinguished scholars who have worked on this material are impressive. We know that a minority, but a recognizable minority, of the enslaved came from the interior where jihād was a cause of enslavement, either in its perpetuation or in the resistance that subsequently ensued, but without doubt the number was relatively small.[73]

As demonstrated in this study, the effort to understand the influence of jihād on the migration of enslaved Africans to the Americas can be broken down into two broad patterns, one temporal, which divides the eighteenth century from the nineteenth century, and one geographical, which basically separates the western Bilād al-Sūdān from the central Bilād al-Sūdān. The scholarship that focuses on Muslims in North America and the anglophone and francophone Caribbean largely draws on the life histories of individuals

The Repercussions of Jihād in the Americas

who came from the western Bilād al-Sūdān during the eighteenth century (except Trinidad, which received a recognizable immigration of Muslims in the nineteenth century).[74] This temporal division reflects patterns of historical change in West Africa, the first occurring in the eighteenth century and largely confined to the western Bilād al-Sūdān, and the second focusing on the central Bilād al-Sūdān and the early nineteenth century but with reverberations throughout the western Bilād al-Sūdān. The migrations affecting the Malês uprising in Bahia, the formation of Yoruba culture in Cuba in the nineteenth century, and the establishment of Muslim and Yoruba communities in Trinidad and Sierra Leone have their origins in the jihād movement of the central Bilād al-Sūdān in the early nineteenth century. In both cases the age of revolutions was mirrored in the jihād movement, with some important differences that can be established. There was no clear distinction between "rebellion" and "revolution" as posited by Genovese. There was instead a wider range of responses to slavery in the Americas than the simple dichotomy between "rebellion" and "revolution" that included alternate perspectives associated with Islam and followed a chronology parallel to the era of jihād in West Africa.

While the first phase of Islamic influence largely affected North America and the anglophone and francophone Caribbean, the second phase was connected with Bahia and Cuba. There were important overlaps that need to be explored, especially in relation to St. Domingue. Those who have studied the age of revolutions certainly did not initially envision a contemporary transformative movement in the context of Islam in a part of the world that was an important source of slaves for the Americas and demographically could have been more important but was determinedly not. however, there has been recognition of the parallels, notably in the work of Manuel Barcia. The dialogue in determining what constituted the Atlantic world now concerns definitions of "revolution" and the relevance of contemporary movements and possible influences that may have overlapped. Hence the role of Muslims in slave resistance in the Americas has to be reconceptualized in terms of the dominant historiography. The early contributions of scholars on this subject have demonstrated the way. Stuart Schwartz placed uprisings in Bahia in the context of Hausa immigration, while Barcia has argued that jihād in both Cuba and Bahia was interpreted by participants as "war," not resistance or rebellion.[75] Their insights allow a reassessment of the era that focuses on both revolution and jihād.

These findings demonstrate that the jihād movement of West Africa had direct repercussions on the expression of resistance in Cuba and Bahia. The context of Muslim influence extended to places other than Cuba and Brazil. There was a Muslim disturbance of Aku, that is, Yoruba and often Muslims, in Sierra Leone in the 1830s as well.[76] The efforts of Muslims in Trinidad to return to West Africa in the 1820s and early 1830s should also be seen in this light, as well as the possible role of Muslims in the Christmas uprising in Jamaica in 1831–32.[77] The question raised here is to what extent this widespread Muslim activity challenges a Eurocentric perspective in understanding historical change during the age of revolutions. Expanding the concept of the Atlantic world to include a region where a parallel movement was altering the political, social, and ideological foundation of the political economy relates the age of jihād to the age of revolutions. An examination of available sources reveals a particular confusion over attempts to identify ethnicity with rebellion when religion was the dominant organizational and motivating factor. Those who were enslaved and sent to Brazil and Cuba or ended up in Sierra Leone and who were referred to as Nagô, Lucumí, or Aku or similar names for Hausa, Nupe, and other labels often referred only to language as the principal identifying factor, which is not necessarily the same as ethnicity and confuses allegiance to Islam with ethnicity.

7 SOKOTO, THE JIHĀD STATES, AND THE ABOLITION OF THE ATLANTIC SLAVE TRADE

The literate tradition of Islamic scholarship in West Africa and the surviving biographical accounts of Muslims demonstrate the importance of contemporary testimony in understanding the jihād movement in the context of the age of revolutions. So far, this study has established that the Muslim regions of West Africa were underrepresented in the demography of the transatlantic slave trade, largely because of internal factors within West Africa related to Muslim sensibilities that resulted in the jihād movement of the eighteenth and nineteenth centuries. Moreover, in the Americas the repercussions of jihād were directly related to Muslim resistance in Bahia and reverberations elsewhere in Brazil but were also felt in events in Cuba related to the presence of Yoruba and others, even if they were not Muslims. Nonetheless, the influence of Islam dissipated in Brazil, and Yoruba identity as Lucumí shifted away from the context of jihād in West Africa. Muslims were involved in resistance to slavery elsewhere in the Americas and occasionally had a significant impact as individuals, but they were nonetheless divorced from the tradition of jihād, whatever factors may have prompted their enslavement and subsequent accommodations to slavery in the Americas. As individuals, Muslims sometimes participated in radical attempts to undermine slavery, but not through jihād or identifiable communities. In many ways, as individuals, Muslims were occasionally in the forefront of transformative changes that were divorced from the context of jihād.

In the jihād states of West Africa that were resisting incorporation into a world of transatlantic slavery, the ideology of disengagement was a force in limiting the transfer of the enslaved to the Americas, but at a cost to the social fabric of West Africa, where slavery expanded considerably through jihād. As I demonstrated in earlier chapters, the jihād states opposed involvement in the transatlantic slave trade except under specific conditions. Muslims were nonetheless enslaved and not always ransomed, and some individuals were forcibly deported to a life of slavery in the Americas. This chapter considers the relationship between the jihād states, especially the Sokoto Caliphate, and the British-led international campaign to abolish the transatlantic slave trade and by extension the slave trade in the Mediterranean and elsewhere, although during the age of revolutions there was little attempt to combat the slave trade within Africa, where slavery became much more widespread on levels that were comparable in impact to the second slavery of the Americas in the same period. The inherent contradiction in the ideology and policies of the jihād states with respect to slavery demonstrates an intellectual and political problem that faced Muslims. Although a goal of jihād was to protect freeborn Muslims from enslavement and prevent the sale of anyone who was enslaved to non-Muslims, especially Europeans, jihād promoted enslavement and created the massive slave populations that underpinned the economies and societies of the jihād states.

The legitimacy of enslavement was a topic of considerable debate within Muslim circles, as revealed in the diplomatic exchange between Muhammad Bello and Muhammad al-Kānimī, the heads of state of the Sokoto Caliphate and of Borno, respectively, and the open warfare that erupted between these states in consequence of the failure to reach an acceptable accord over the implementation of religious reform and the course of jihād.[1] Similarly, the little-known diplomatic negotiations between Britain and Sokoto over the slave trade are revealing in regard to Muslim attitudes toward the transatlantic slave trade. Caliph Muhammad Bello, as supreme ruler of the Sokoto Caliphate, and Captain Hugh Clapperton, as the official representative of the British government, formally agreed to an accord on the abolition of the transatlantic slave trade in 1824, which links the era of jihād to the age of revolutions.[2] The correspondence between Bello and al-Kānimī reveals that the controversy over who was considered a Muslim and who was not was a basic issue at the time. The debate highlights an awareness of the contradictions surrounding the reliance on slavery in the construction of society when it was not always clear who could be enslaved and who should be protected from enslavement. The practice of slavery enshrined mechanisms whereby individuals could secure safeguards against abuse and might attain emancipation for their children, if not for themselves. The discourse over slavery in Muslim society in the jihād states emphasized the restrictions on the brutalizing features of slavery. Although the practice of ransoming and the possibility of third-party redemption were not always implemented, they reduced the dangers of enslavement and lifelong servitude. Deathbed acts of

Sokoto, the Jihād States, and Abolition

emancipation, the free status of children born to concubines, the frequency of *murgu* arrangements, whereby the enslaved could work on their own account as long as a regular payment was made to masters, and other features of slavery as governed by Islamic law and customary practice lightened the burden of slavery for many, despite instances of individual abuse. Nonetheless, the ongoing commitment to jihād meant that the enslaved population was regenerated through the capture of new victims in frontier campaigns, often through brutal measures.

The extensive scholarship on Muslim resistance to slavery and the surviving biographical information are useful in analyzing not only the impact of Muslims in the Americas but also the response to the abolition of the slave trade across the Atlantic.[3] The Muslim factor is revealed in an extensive literature of Arabic and *ajami* texts on Yoruba history and the jihād movement that is associated with Sokoto and Gwandu and the leadership of ʿUthmān dan Fodio, ʿAbdullahi dan Fodio, and Muhammad Bello. It is on this basis that a case has been made for a close connection among Yoruba migration, jihād, and the Muslim presence in the Americas.[4] Priscilla Mello, José Cairus, and Alberto da Costa e Silva have specifically analyzed the Muslim background of resistance in Brazil, amplifying the analysis pioneered by João José Reis.[5] Biographical accounts show the range of Muslim influences that derived from the jihād, both in Bahia and elsewhere.[6] These accounts set the context for understanding what the governments of Britain and Sokoto thought that they were doing when the age of revolutions confronted the era of jihād. Often overlooked by those studying the abolition of the slave trade, however, are the negotiations in the 1820s between Bello and Clapperton, which are examined in this chapter.[7]

The initial reaction of the early jihād states was hostile to Muslim involvement in the transatlantic slave trade, as demonstrated earlier. According to Roger Botte,

> L'exemple du Fuuta Jaloo n'autorise aucune généralisation quant au rôle joué par l'islam dans la traite négrière en Sénégambie. D'une part, parce que des sociétés non musulmanes s'adonnent à la traite: le Ngaabu, État négrier en concurrence directe avec le Fuuta Jaloo pour l'hégémonie du trafic en Sénégambie méridionale, est un État animiste; d'autre part parce que, depuis la seconde moitié du XVIIᵉ siècle, des aspirations récurrentes contre la traite (mais non contre l'esclavage domestique) animent des communautés musulmanes.[8]

The initial pronouncements against the slave trade were made after the War of Shurbubba, at the end of seventeenth century, which engaged five king-doms of the Senegal River valley, including Fuuta Toro, Waalo, Wolof, Kajor, and Bawol. Effective or not, similar policies opposing the transatlantic slave trade were enacted under the subsequent jihād regimes.[9] In 1787 C. B. Wad-ström learned that the jihād regime in Fuuta Toro was attempting to combat the sale of enslaved persons to the slave ships on the coast. According to his information, the "marabous [who] are the chief priests among the negroes, and are the only people who can read and write Arabic," had imposed a ban on the slave trade with Europeans.

> The conduct of the present king (late grand marabou) or Almammy, is more interesting to humanity, and evinces the firm manly character of the negroes when enlightened. His understanding having been more cultivated in his youth than that of the other black princes, he has rendered himself intirely independent of the whites. He has not only prohibited the slave-trade throughout his dominions, but [in the year 1787] would not suffer the French to march their captives from Gallam, through his country. He redeems his own subjects when seized by the Moors, and encourages them to raise cattle, to cultivate the land, and to practice all kinds of industry. As grand marabou, he abstains from strong liquor, which, however, is not the general rule among that order; for some who travel with the whites are not scrupulous in this respect. His subjects, imitating his example, are much more sober than their neighbours.[10]

Nonetheless, there was a contradiction inherent in the position of Muslims on slavery. Although there was a willingness to restrict and even prevent the trade in slaves with Christians, thereby limiting the involvement of non-Muslims in shaping society, there was nonetheless an intensification of a "second slavery" within the jihād states that was related to the consolidation of Islam, which ultimately set the stage for the European occupation of the Muslim world, including sub-Saharan Africa.

The attitude of the jihād states to the slave trade has to be understood within the context of West Africa. Muslim leaders were opposed to the slave trade if it was not controlled by Muslims and if the liberties of freeborn Mus-lims were not protected. Muslim governments enacted measures to prevent the sale of slaves to merchants who were not Muslims, and sale to Christians was a particular concern for some Muslim leaders, such as Muhammad Bello.

Muslim governments legally and publicly opposed the sale of slaves to "Christians" on the coast except under strict conditions that were not always easy to enforce. Preventing the sale of freeborn Muslims was the goal of these restrictions, and inevitably the recognition of legal norms that put the onus of proving who was freeborn and who was not on merchants undermined the sale of slaves to non-Muslims. As demonstrated earlier, Aḥmad Bābā expressed his legal opinions on the slave trade in a treatise written in Timbuktu in 1614–15 in which he attempted to distinguish among people on the basis of who could be enslaved and who could not be.[11] The later jihād leaders subscribed to Aḥmad Bābā's approach to slavery, citing him with respect to issues of ethnicity and the status of slaves. However, as the biographical accounts of those who were enslaved demonstrate, many Muslims were enslaved and sold. Moreover, this forced migration had varying impacts in Brazil, Cuba, Jamaica, and the United States, as I demonstrate in this chapter.

The dilemma for Muslims was establishing proof of religious conviction on the part of the slave. If someone was a slave and a Muslim, it did not mean that the person should be free or at some point had been free. However, the burden of proof that a person was not a freeborn Muslim rested with the owner and the merchant, not the person who was enslaved. Anyone who could say the prayers in credible Arabic and knew the basic precepts of Islam had to be taken seriously if the person claimed to have been freeborn. Because the onus of proof rested on the shoulders of the owner, legally and morally, merchants could not easily be flippant and speculative in trading slaves who might be Muslim.[12] During jihād campaigns individuals who joined the jihād were accepted as free if they claimed this status, no matter whether they had been enslaved. In relations with the Atlantic world and its vast markets, therefore, the concern of Muslims was not only economics and profitable exchange but ideological respectability in relation to law and religious obligations as Muslims who were enjoined to protect Muslims. The development of abolitionist strategies and antislavery sentiments among Muslims in the Americas may have had revolutionary overtones in the Atlantic world, but the justification of enslavement in West Africa generally reinforced slavery as an institution in West Africa in light of Muslim attitudes and policies.

The abolition of the slave trade is usually conceived only within a European framework as a product of Enlightenment thinking about the rights of man and the injustices of the state. The scholarly argument usually emphasizes the relation to the duality of economic adjustments of the Industrial Revolution and religious and humanitarian impulses emerging from a society able to provide a critique of itself through new methods of making issues of common concern public. What was happening in Africa, the source of the enslaved population, is virtually left out of the discussion other than to say that the settlement of Freetown provided an outpost of British reform, and the founding of Liberia represented the racial expansion of the United States in the age of revolutions. The protection of Muslims from enslavement, prohibitions on their sale, and efforts to confront the dangers of subsequent abuse are obscured at least as much as the Bourbon reforms are overlooked in analyzing the events that affected the course of abolition in mainland Spanish America.[13] Abolition is seen as a uniquely British phenomenon. The early discussion of abolition as presented by Thomas Clarkson and other abolitionists, such as the sons of William Wilberforce, is selective in who is included and who is not, as Suzanne Schwarz has argued.[14] Clarkson does not even mention the activities of Gustavus Vassa, whose *Interesting Narrative of the Life of Olaudah Equiano*, published in 1789 and reprinted in numerous editions thereafter, was arguably essential to the success of the parliamentary enactment of abolition in 1807. Even the curious double abolition in the French domain, first in 1794 and then in 1848, is usually excluded in this restricted view of slavery and emancipation. Abolition in the United States is tempered by continued American involvement through the domestic American trade, investments in Atlantic commerce, and the use of the American flag to protect slave ships, some of which were actually American owned. Analytically, antislavery and emancipation, sometimes referred to as abolition, are considered sectional issues in the United States leading to the Civil War without much consideration, if any, of the global issues that opposition to slavery raised elsewhere in the world, including Africa.[15]

Nonetheless, the discourse on slavery in Muslim societies was a motivating factor in attempting to restrict the slave trade and thereby helped shape attitudes toward a limited abolition. If the Muslim states of West Africa are incorporated into an Atlantic perspective that considers the whole of the Atlantic world, then there must be allowance for a consideration of alternative arguments against the slave trade other than those of the Quakers, Thomas Clarkson, and William Wilberforce. Humphrey Fisher has raised the interesting question whether there was a "Muslim Wilberforce" in his analysis of the historical causes of the Sokoto jihād "as antislavery crusade." Fisher certainly exaggerates in referring to 'Uthmān dan Fodio as a Muslim Wilberforce[16] because dan Fodio was not against slavery, only the enslavement of freeborn Muslims, but Fisher's comparison is perceptive in highlighting a clash of different worldviews. As Fisher notes, the dialogue over abolition and the critique of slavery have been unnecessarily and inappropriately restricted largely to the English-speaking world. When the criticisms of slavery that were closely associated with the jihād movement and were widespread within the Muslim communities of West Africa are included in the analysis, it is clear that the contradictions that resulted in the second slavery of the Americas and the unrelated second slavery of the jihād states require more sophisticated reflection.

As Fisher has noted, the Muslim leaders of the early nineteenth century addressed issues relating to slavery in their writings, teaching, and political actions; indeed, the slavery issue was "a major grievance stimulating the Sokoto jihād."[17] Among the concerns were the issues of "just" enslavement and the status of Muslims as slaves. This intellectual and political discourse dated back several centuries before the outbreak of the Sokoto jihād and predated the European Enlightenment. Legal scholarship, which derived from the Sharīʿa according to the Mālikī school of law as interpreted by Ibn Abī Zayd al-Qayrawānī (d. 996), considered that slavery arose from a condition of unbelief. The freeborn, who by definition had to be Muslim, could not legally be enslaved, or so it would seem. However, there was considerable room for qualification and doubt, and hence the subject of slavery was much studied. For example, Aḥmad Bābā (1556–1627) examined issues of enslavement and the legitimacy of slavery in Islamic society. In 1615/16 Aḥmad Bābā wrote that "whoever is taken prisoner in a state of unbelief may become someone's property, whoever he is, opposed to those who have become Muslims of their own free will."[18] Since religious identification was not always clear to Muslims, Aḥmad Bābā discussed slavery in terms of ethnicity, thereby attempting to categorize populations according to the legitimacy of enslavement in both religious and ethnic terms.

This intellectual and legal tradition involved a degree of reflection that affected the institution of slavery in West Africa and provides context for the actions of enslaved Muslims, notably in the Ilorin mutiny of 1817 against Oyo, the resistance of Muslim Aku (i.e., Yoruba) in Sierra Leone in 1831–32, and the series of disturbances in Bahia that culminated in the abortive 1835 Malês uprising. Each of these responses to the ordeals and adjustments along the slave route was different, but they all involved Muslims from West Africa. Disjuncture characterized the slave route even as groups of slaves tried to maintain links with the past through reference to a common tradition. The similarities and differences in these responses are suggestive of the complexities of an alternate perspective on abolition.

As I argued in chapter 5, there appears to have been a network of Muslim commerce that stretched to Bahia, as well as an enforced movement of enslaved Muslims along the trade routes of this same network. Bello's own account indicates that the Sokoto government was fully aware of this trade, and Clapperton even thought that "Bello exacts an annual Tribute from the Traders for permission to carry those unfortunate Beings down to the Coast."[19] Clapperton did not explain the apparent contradiction between the caliphate's prohibition and this "tribute," unless he mistakenly confused efforts to restrict the trade to the coast with a general tax on caravans. Whether or not the caliphate was taxing the slave trade, Muhammad Bello revealed a willingness to suppress the transatlantic portion of the trade. This is perhaps not surprising unless it is assumed that he was as ignorant about the transatlantic route as contemporary Europeans were about the course of the Niger.

Often it is thought that British pressure to impose the abolition of the slave trade across the Atlantic was the driving force in suppressing the deportation of enslaved African to the Americas in the nineteenth century even as slavery continued and expanded.[20] This assessment has some validity with respect to the nations of Europe, the Americas, and many parts of the West African coast, but there is at least one important exception to this perspective that requires the insertion of the policies and objectives of African states into the equation. The reservations of the Sokoto Caliphate about the transatlantic slave trade emerge in the virtually unknown efforts of caliphate officials to reach an accord with the British government on the abolition of the transatlantic slave trade in the 1820s, although without reference to the trans-Saharan traffic. The motivation stemmed from Muslim intentions to prevent the sale of slaves to Christians. The Sokoto Caliphate accepted the British challenge to implement abolition and approved a treaty for doing so. Ironically, Britain never approved the agreement, despite British diplomatic efforts to pressure European and American governments to reach such accords and often to force African potentates along the coast to enter into such agreements.

Until now, the relationship of the Muslim states of West Africa to the abolition movement of the transatlantic slave trade and the emancipation of slaves in the Americas has been virtually ignored. How did the British campaign to end the slave trade and the British blockade of the African coast look from the interior of West Africa? How did Muslims in West Africa and in the Americas perceive abolition? There is considerable information that can help elucidate these issues. Information from Muslims who were "liberated" in Sierra Leone after 1807 is one source. The interactions between British

Sokoto, the Jihād States, and Abolition

abolitionist efforts and local developments offer another method of accessing opinions and actions.[21] The reports of R. R. Madden on the Gold Coast, Sierra Leone, Gambia, Jamaica, and Cuba offer still another.[22] The advocacy of Eugène Daumas and Ausone de Chancel in reviving the trans-Saharan slave trade after the French conquest of Algeria provides yet another way of problematizing abolition that goes beyond a narrow Eurocentric perspective.[23]

There are key dates in understanding Muslim involvement in dealing with the abolition of the slave trade and ultimately in undermining slavery in the Atlantic world, although not in the Muslim world, in the early nineteenth century. The American war with the "Barbary states," the British mission to North Africa under Lord Exmouth, the French conquest of Algiers, and further pressure on the Ottoman Empire all influenced events and the implementation of policy south of the Sahara. Exmouth's naval campaign in North Africa and the bombardment of Algiers in 1816 resulted in the release of three thousand slaves and the imposition of a treaty with the dey of Algiers on 24 September 1816.[24] The emancipation of slaves in Algeria in the 1830s and 1840s followed French occupation of Algiers in 1830. With the ouster of Dey Hussein of Algiers, the French consolidated their rule, subsequently reorganizing the territories around Algiers into three *départements* in 1848. Slaves were emancipated in Tunisia in 1846 in concordance with moves in Egypt and elsewhere in the Ottoman Empire to abolish the slave trade.[25] These events were noticed in West Africa. The impetus for abolition came from two sides, from the Atlantic seaboard and across the Sahara, although the Muslim interaction with these global currents of change is not usually considered in the context of the Atlantic world.

The Sokoto Caliphate and Abolition

The Sokoto Caliphate specifically banned the sale of slaves to Christians, and this law predated any possible direct influence from the British abolition movement or the European Enlightenment more generally. In *Infāq al-Maysūr* (1812), Muhammad Bello condemned the "Yoruba" (i.e., Oyo) for selling slaves to Christians: "The people of this land would get captured slaves from our land here and they would sell them to the Christians. . . . I have mentioned this so that you should not purchase a Muslim slave if someone captures such a slave and brings him to you."[26] Moreover, 'Abdullahi dan Fodio interpreted the commercial law on slave sales through verse in order to reach the rank and file of the jihād movement. The fifth chapter of *Kifāyat al-ʿAwāmm fī ʾl-buyūʿ* dealt with the sale of slaves and domestic animals.[27] In

1824 Bello reiterated the prohibition to Clapperton, who learned that "their own Law . . . forbids them to sell their Slaves to Christians."[28] Writing in the 1830s, al-Ḥājj 'Umar Tal was equally clear: "To sell Muslim slaves to the Europeans or to others, is totally prohibited."[29] The Sokoto ban on slave sales implicitly was directed at the transatlantic slave trade, as this evidence establishes, and for religious reasons. Because of this, Muhammad Bello was willing to reach an agreement with Britain to abolish the external slave trade to the coast. Bello was aware that enslaved Muslims from the central Bilād al-Sūdān were being exported from the Bight of Benin in the decades after the beginning of the jihād in 1804, despite the official prohibition on slave sales.

The pronouncements of Shehu 'Uthmān dan Fodio on the illegality of enslaving freeborn Muslims bordered on advocacy of partial emancipation. In *Wathīqat ahl al-Sūdān wa man shā'a Allāh min al-ikhwān*, which is often considered the manifesto of the Sokoto jihād, the shehu decreed that "to enslave the freeborn among the Muslims is unlawful by assent, whether they reside in the territory of Islam, or in enemy territory."[30] In *Bayān wujūb al hijra 'alā l-'ibād*, he cited numerous authorities to support his ruling that fugitive slaves were free if they fled to the side of the jihād, and that free Muslims who had wrongly been enslaved could also claim their liberty. Among the laws that he decreed were "the law concerning giving freedom to slaves of unbelieving Belligerents if they flee to us; . . . the law concerning one who has been found as a slave in the hands of Unbelievers and claims to be a freeborn Muslim but has not emigrated; and the law concerning one who has been brought from a land where the selling of free men is commonplace and claims to be a freeborn Muslim."[31] Muhammad Bello informed "the people of the east," apparently in 1813, that "all those captured by the enemy from among the communities that followed us, and who were sold to the merchants who sold them to you, are free Muslims whose enslavement is forbidden, *ḥarām*. You are to do your utmost to rescue their necks from bondage. May God reward you for that."[32]

In *Ḍiyā' al-sulṭān wa ghayrihi min al-ikhwān fī ahamm ma yuṭlab 'ilmuhu fī umūr al-zamān*, Abdullahi dan Fodio discussed the status of prisoners captured in the jihād, including the categories of persons who were liable to enslavement, ransom, or freedom. At Bodinga in 1813 he outlined the laws on the distribution of booty, including a description of seven categories of spoils.[33] The distribution of slaves, of course, figured prominently in these instructions. According to Abdullahi, prisoners of war should be able "to pay ransom for their freedom and the ransom money would be paid into the booty." It was

Sokoto, the Jihād States, and Abolition

also possible to exchange prisoners, although if "the ransom was in the form of Muslim prisoners of war, then the value of the ransom must be deducted from the imām's fifth," that is, the share belonging to the caliphate.[34] Legally, freeborn Muslims should not have been enslaved. Hence procedures for ransoming attempted to safeguard such captives.[35]

Although the jihād states attempted to enforce restrictions on the sale of slaves to non-Muslims, these measures certainly did not prevent the sale of some Muslims to the Atlantic trade. Indeed, al-Ḥājj 'Umar observed in *Risālat shawq al-ḥabīb ilā as'ilat Ibrāhim al-labīb* in 1837 that the sale of slaves to Christians continued long after the consolidation of the jihād states, even though the sale of slaves had been "totally prohibited." He complained,

> Despite this prohibition, people who pretend to be knowledgeable, let alone the ignorant are still competing in this hated transaction . . . [;] worse still we do not see anyone condemning it, nor is there any one from among the 'ulama or the amirs, trying to put an end to this illegal practice. They act as if it were no longer obligatory upon them to do so.[36]

Nonetheless, it seems certain that overall, the measures were successful in protecting freeborn Muslims. Muhammad Bello's open condemnation of the trade to Oyo ("Yariba") certainly drew attention to a trade in substantial numbers because of the difficulty of hiding the trade. It is difficult to determine how effective these public policies of jihād leaders were in limiting the trade, but there is no question that there was some impact. The movement of caravans of slaves required substantial infrastructure to feed and guard the slaves and to provide protection against brigandage. The government of Fuuta Jalon did engage in the sale of slaves through the resident merchants on Rio Pongo and Rio Nuñez, but indications are that the state controlled the trade precisely to guarantee that there were no Muslims in the enslaved population for sale. As Zachary Macaulay of Sierra Leone learned in 1793, there was considerable opposition in Fuuta Jalon to the sale of slaves to the coast. Macaulay met "a Foulah man, who pretends to be a kind of agent or ambassador for the king of the Foulahs [i.e., Fuuta Jalon] in the rivers of Rockelle and Port Logo [Loko]," which were the main tributaries of the Sierra Leone River. Macaulay reported that "the king had heard of us and wished much to see someone from us, which he more particularly desired, as he understood we were averse to the slave trade, a thing he had also set his heart on destroying." This representative "had taken notice of the coincidence of our views with respect to the abolition of the slave trade with the views of the Foulah nation" and reported that the new almami of Fuuta Jalon would be required "to stipulate that he shall have no power to enslave his subjects" because they were Muslims.[37] Similarly, Fuuta Toro prohibited the trade along the Senegal River in an effort to protect freeborn Muslims, although by no means with the intention of ending slavery, which was vital to the Fuuta Toro economy. Hence at the time of British abolition, the Muslim states were already implementing restrictions on the slave trade.

Heinrich Barth certainly exaggerated when he claimed in the 1850s that the trade along the Niger River below the confluence with the Benue River had fallen "into the hands of the [South] American slave-dealers, who have opened a regular annual slave-trade with those regions."[38] By the 1850s the slave trade from the Bights of Benin and Biafra was largely over, especially after the occupation of Lagos by the British in 1851, but Barth observed that the involvement of the Muslim regions under the Sokoto Caliphate was far from over.[39] If the transatlantic slave trade had not come to an end at the coast, his observation might have turned into a prediction. On the basis of information gathered in the Sokoto Caliphate during his travels there, Barth devoted a whole chapter in his massive report to the South American slave trade. Other information also demonstrates the continuation of the slave trade from the Sokoto Caliphate, whether or not it was sanctioned by the governments of the various emirates.[40] The second slavery of the Americas and the increased incidence of slavery in the jihād states had the potential to become linked in ways that could have sustained an international system of slavery despite ideological and religious differences.

The British Missions to Borno and the Sokoto Caliphate

The first British mission to Borno and Sokoto in 1822–25, as analyzed by A. Adu Boahen, Robin Hallett, E. W. Bovill, and Jamie Bruce Lockhart,[41] was an exercise in European exploration and diplomacy in a context in which Europeans, in this case diplomats from Britain, did not understand local societies very well, even when they learned Hausa and Kanuri or already knew Arabic. According to Boahen, abolition was not the primary reason for British interest in the Sahara and the Bilād al-Sūdān, which may explain why the accord reached by Bello and Clapperton was never ratified in London.[42] The course of the Niger and the establishment of British trade in the interior had precedence over the suppression of the slave trade. The British consul in Tripoli, Colonel Hamer Warrington, took advantage of the policies of Pasha Yūsuf Qaramanlī (1795–1830) to promote expeditions across the Sahara.

Indeed, the preoccupation with "discovery" in relation to the Niger River has often confused analysis of the relations between Sokoto and Britain. Bello provided Clapperton with a map that clearly showed where the Niger flowed if Clapperton had only known how to read it (plate 27). From Bello's perspective, the ports along the Niger River from Raka through Idah were effectively on the Atlantic Ocean because it was well established that merchants could travel down the Niger River and through the delta to Lagos.

In 1822 Tripoli was already deeply involved in the politics of the central Bilād al-Sūdān, even nurturing imperial ambitions. The pasha sought British support to maintain the autonomy of Tripoli from the Ottoman Porte and therefore provided a military escort for the mission of Denham, Clapperton, and Oudney to Borno. The pasha also wanted to obtain slave recruits for his army in the central Bilād al-Sūdān and hopefully a flow of credit and access to military hardware from the British. According to Kola Folayan, Qaramanlī supported al-Kānimī as the first step in establishing an empire south of the Sahara.[43] Major Denham accompanied several expeditions that caught slaves, including one that successfully defeated a Bagirmi force, resulting in the enslavement of many people. British arms are credited with making the difference; Hillman had built the carriages on which the Borno cannon were mounted, and Denham had supervised the manufacture of cartridges for the Borno guns.[44] Otherwise, British support was not especially effective but was nonetheless present. In southern Mandara, for example, the combined Tripoli-Borno force faced a Fulani contingent loyal to the caliphate and was heavily defeated. Denham, who had accompanied this expedition as well, lost even the clothes he was wearing and nearly his life.[45] One unintended result, perhaps, was confirmation that Borno was relying on foreign troops and British weapons, which must not have been welcome news in Sokoto. In both campaigns the Tripoli forces clearly intended to seize slaves, which specifically violated the instructions of the British mission. Their participation in military campaigns in the African interior involving enslavement might have proved embarrassing to the British government, but abolitionists either did not notice or were not yet concerned.

Although the actions of the British mission compromised abolitionist principles, the association with Tripoli guaranteed the safety of travel across the Sahara and provided the necessary introduction to the governments of both Borno and Sokoto. Such participation and support inevitably conflicted with the thrust of British abolitionist thought. The official accounts of the mission indicate that involvement in slaving activities was incidental to the main purpose of the British venture, but Denham, Clapperton, and Oudney were less than candid about what they knew about the intentions of Yūsuf Qaramanlī. They certainly must have known that Tripoli was recruiting a slave army through capture, as Muhammad ʿAlī had done in Egypt through campaigns in the upper Nile. Because of the context, they may well have cast their personal observations in antislavery rhetoric to minimize their complicity. Far from being principled, the British mission supported enslavement out of expediency. The close relationship between the British consulate and the Tripoli government overlooked the inherent contradiction between British abolition policy and Tripoli's intention of military recruitment through slavery. Despite the complicity of the British mission, the topic of abolition was on the agenda of British diplomats and became the subject of formal negotiations. Because Muhammad Bello, in particular, was concerned about the condition of enslaved Muslims in the countries along the routes to the Guinea coast and their sale to the Americas, as expressed in *Infāq al-Maysūr*, the British diplomatic effort unexpectedly encountered a leader receptive to its own sometimes nominal commitment and interest in abolition.

British diplomat Captain Hugh Clapperton was responsible for the British initiative to negotiate a treaty with the Sokoto Caliphate that would acknowledge abolition. In his negotiations with Muhammad Bello in 1824, he reached an accord that not only included abolition but also promoted British commercial interests in the efforts to expand trade with the African interior (plate 28). This little-known diplomatic episode resulted in the drafting of a treaty between Britain and Sokoto that was approved by Bello but never ratified in London for reasons that pertained largely to a British preoccupation with determining the course of the Niger River and a failure to appreciate the political importance of the Sokoto Caliphate. Both the Arabic and the English translations of this draft agreement reveal details of negotiations that demonstrate a commitment to modernization on the part of the Sokoto Caliphate and a tentative but futile effort by British authorities to craft an alternate approach to relations with African authorities that might have avoided eventual conquest and imperial rule. The draft agreement was overshadowed by subsequent distortions in the application of its terms that resulted in an imperial mythology and racist extrapolation of what had been negotiated, then ignored, and finally forgotten. This trajectory is reflected in the distorted historiography that has dominated the study of British and European conquest and a colonialism that reinterpreted slavery and its suppression. The impact of this history on the subsequent independence of African countries, particularly Nigeria, stands in contrast to the events highlighted in 1822–25 and again in 1826–27, when a second mission tried to revitalize that initiative. The British missions were informed by the ideas of the Enlightenment in discussing matters of slavery, the search for scientific and geographical knowledge, and the quest for markets, which meant that the interior of West Africa seemed to be an Eldorado, especially the central Bilād al-Sūdān because of the political events that occurred there after 1804. The debate among Muslims over "just" and "illegitimate" enslavement provided the context for how these ideas were received.

Official discussions between Bello and Clapperton lasted for several months in 1824 and resulted in a preliminary accord that abolished the transatlantic slave trade in exchange for various concessions and a promise of arms, ammunition, and other goods. Clapperton reported,

> I remained with Bello nearly three Months, and from a daily intercourse with this Prince I am thoroughly convinced that he is sincere in his wishes for a friendly footing with England; Indeed I cannot speak too highly of this excellent Man, whom—should he live and the Government here feel disposed to cherish a friendly Relation with him,— would be able, with very little assistance from us, to put an End to that detestable Traffic in Slaves, by opening to him a free and uninterrupted Passage to the Sea Coast, from which he is now no more than ten days distant.[46]

The agreement reached between Clapperton and Bello, as contained in a letter in Arabic from Muammad Bello to King George IV that Clapperton brought back to England, read as follows:

> In the name of God, the merciful and the element [sic]. May God bless our favourite Prophet Mohammed, and those who follow his sound doctrine.
>
> To the head of the Christian nation, the honoured and the beloved among the English people, George the Fourth, King of Great Britain:
>
> Praise be to God, who inspires, and peace be unto those who follow, the right path:
>
> Your Majesty's servant, Rayes Abdallah, [Mr. Clapperton's travelling name], came to us, and we found him a very intelligent and wise man; representing in every respect your greatness, wisdom, dignity, clemency, and penetration.

When the time of his departure came, he requested us to form a friendly relation, and correspond with you, and to prohibit the exportation of slaves by our merchants to Atagher [Idah, i.e., the Niger River], Dahomi [Dahomey, i.e., Ouidah], and Ashantee [Asante, i.e., the Gold Coast]. We agreed with him upon this, on account of the good which will result from it, both to you and to us; and that a vessel of yours is to come to the harbour of Racka [Raka, located on the Niger River] with two cannons, and the quantities of powder, shot, &c. which they require; as also, a number of muskets. We will then send our officer to arrange and settle every thing with your counsel, and fix a certain period for the arrival of your merchant ships; and when they come, they may traffic and deal with our merchants.

Then after their return, the consul may reside in that harbour (viz. Racka), as protector, in company with our agent there, if God be pleased.

Dated 1st of Rahmadan, 1239 of Hejra. 18th April, 1824[47]

The accord stated that Sokoto wanted a "friendly relation" with Britain "on account of the good which will result from it, both to you and to us." The agreement declared henceforth the "prohibition" of "the exportation of slaves by our merchants." The treaty was intended to terminate the trade through intermediary states; Idah on the Niger River, Dahomey, and Asante were specifically mentioned. Bello assured Clapperton that "he was able to put an effectual stop to the slave trade."[48] In 1824 Idah was trading heavily with Bonny, and merchants were traveling to Lagos, by then the main trade center for the Atlantic trade, via the Niger at this time as well. The agreement in effect provided rights of extraterritoriality similar to the agreements between the Ottoman Porte and European countries. In reality, however, the accord was not implemented until 1841, when the "Niger expedition" was consummated. Although most historiography has discussed the 1841 venture as a British-inspired exploration of commercial prospects of the Niger River, in fact the expedition was a continuation of the Clapperton initiative, which is often ignored or misinterpreted in the discussion of the "opening of the Niger."

Bello asked whether "the King of England would send him a consul and a physician, to reside in Soudan, and merchants to trade with his people," given his opposition to the slave trade. The implications of appointing a British consul at a port in Sokoto territory were also clearly understood: "It would be the consul's duty to see that engagement [to abolish the slave trade] faithfully fulfilled." Bello insisted that "a total stop should be put to the Traffic immediately."[49] In return, Bello would provide "a place on the coast to build a town: only I wish a road to be cut to Rakah [on the Niger above the confluence with the Benue], if vessels should not be able to navigate the [Niger] river." According to Clapperton, Bello claimed that "God has given me all the land of the infidels," and hence he had the authority to provide the British with a free port at which to trade. Bello wanted a port on the Niger itself, not the coast, and the "road" that he wanted would have eliminated the existing route from Raka to Porto Novo, Badagry, and Lagos by stopping at the Niger. According to Bello, "Fundah [Panda] is the name of the place where the Quarra [Kwara, i.e., Niger in Hausa] enters the sea, during the rainy season; and . . . . Tagra [Atagara, i.e. Idah], a town on the sea-coast, where many Felatahs reside, is governed by one of his subjects, a native of Kashna [Katsina], named Mohamed Mishnee."[50] Panda, the capital of Koton Karfe, was located north of the confluence of the Niger and Benue, whose flood plain was inundated during the rainy season, creating the "lakes of Nupe" that could give the impression that this was the sea. The combined rivers flowed south through hills whose identity had mystified European geographers for a century or more. When the 1841 expedition established a "model farm" and commercial outpost at Lokoja, the Sokoto Caliphate effectively extended extraterritorial rights as it had proposed to Clapperton. After 1857 the Nupe emirate at Bida effectively provided the recognition that the British required, although this relationship with the Sokoto Caliphate has been virtually ignored in discussions of the expedition or treated as little more than a footnote.

Despite the intention of the Bello-Clapperton accord, could Sokoto, however sincere it may have been, actually have implemented a prohibition? Clapperton thought that this could be achieved with "very little assistance" from Britain. The means would be through "opening to him a free and uninterrupted Passage to the Sea Coast, from which he is now no more than ten days distant; By doing this he would disperse those Gangs of Slave Dealers, who dwell in that short distance from the Bight of Benin, receiving whole Kofilas [qāfila, i.e., caravans] of Slaves from the interior of Soudan." In Clapperton's assessment, "With regard to the Foreign Slave Trade, I should think that through our intercourse with Bello there is a fair opportunity of cramping, if not totally abolishing, this nefarious traffic."[51]

The Bello-Clapperton agreement was tied to military, commercial, and technical concessions. Bello wanted arms and ammunition and regular trade to maintain supplies; he "dwelt much on receiving in return cloth, muskets, and gunpowder."[52] Clapperton promised that Britain would send a ship to "the harbour of Racka [Raka] with two cannons, and the quantities of powder, shot, &c. which they require; as also, a number of muskets."[53] Perhaps because of the northern connection, Raka had sided with Ilorin in the revolt against Oyo in the 1820s and therefore was recognized as a possible port for British ships. Raka was destroyed in the late 1820s, however, and was replaced by a series of other river ports, most notably Raba in the early 1830s, which was the key port until its destruction in 1844–45.

Bello told Clapperton, "Let me know the precise time, and my messengers shall be down at any part of the coast you may appoint, to forward letters to me from the mission, on receipt of which I will send an escort to conduct it to Soudan."[54] Hence, before leaving Kukawa for Tripoli, Clapperton wrote to Bello that he would be at Ouidah in July 1825 and that he expected that messengers would be there to meet him. In fact, Bello never received Clapperton's letter. Given the tension between Borno and Sokoto, this interruption in communication is perhaps not surprising, and in any event Clapperton was unable to reach Ouidah before December 1825. Nonetheless, the Clapperton-Bello exchange demonstrates that Muslim governments might well have had their own reasons for prohibiting the transatlantic slave trade.

Clapperton was instructed to renew the preliminary accords of 1824 during his second expedition in 1826–27, but his mission ended in failure, not because of African objections but because of the inability of Britain to meet its obligations. Clapperton's concerns about whether Bello would live were unwarranted. Bello not only continued to live but reigned until his death in 1837, while Clapperton died in Sokoto in 1827. Although Clapperton could not really have known whether Bello could have stopped the export of slaves from his domains, as a naval officer with experience from Canada to the Sahara, Clapperton was not prone to exaggeration. Moreover, Bello seems to have fully understood the significance of British abolitionist measures. Clapperton believed that "the sultan could easily prevent all slaves from the eastward passing through Haussa and Nyffee."[55] In fact, however, Bello could not prevent the deportation of all Muslims to the Americas, despite his commitment.

The political situation changed by 1826 because Sokoto was at war with Borno, which compromised the British mission. Nonetheless, it is clear that the proposed withdrawal of the Sokoto Caliphate from participation in the Atlantic trade was a result of its own policies and had virtually nothing to do with a British initiative. The caliphate's potential share of a trade it was consciously forgoing is a moot point since Bello had no intention of selling slaves to Christians anyway. Bello assumed primary responsibility for negotiating a treaty of abolition that involved compensation that Britain was not initially prepared to provide. Nonetheless, as the terms of the Niger expedition of 1841 make clear, Britain changed its stance and thereupon negotiated an outpost at Lokoja that was similar to the proposed station at Raka. Until now, scholarship has generally afforded primacy of action to Britain and has overlooked the fact that the 1841 agreement in effect implemented the accord first reached in 1824. This trajectory requires a reconsideration of what is known about policies toward slavery and the slave trade in Islamic Africa.

The British mission also reached an accord with Borno, although this was a far more restrictive agreement. Clapperton's agreement with Bello explicitly associated Sokoto policy with the establishment of diplomatic relations, while the agreement with al-Kānimī of Borno only granted "permission, that merchants seeking for elephant-teeth, ostrich feathers, and other such things, that are not to be found in the country of the English, might come among us." It is clear that al-Kānimī, who was allied with the Ottoman Porte, while Bello was not, was more in line with policies that would be acceptable to Tunisia and its efforts to expand Ottoman influence south of the Sahara. In fact, al-Kānimī informed Dixon Denham, that is, Rayes Khaleel, Dixon's Arabic name,

> that our country, as he himself had known and seen its state, does not
> suit any heavy (rich) traveller, who may possess great wealth. But if a
> few light persons (small capitalists), as four or five only, with little
> merchandise, would come, there will be no harm. This is the utmost
> that we can give him permission for; and more than this number must
> not come. If you should wish to send any one from your part to this
> country again, it would be best to send Rayes Khaleel [i.e., Denham];
> for he knows the people and the country, and became as one of the
> inhabitants.[56]

This letter, dated August 1824, advised the British that all correspondence should be conducted through the British consul in Tripoli or via Cairo. Denham had specifically been told to be careful in his relations with al-Kānimī over the matter of slavery. In October 1823 Sir John Barrow, second secretary to the Admiralty, sent instructions to Denham that the Borno mission was to abstain "most cautiously from any act which might bear the remotest construction of ... appropriation" of the "disgraceful traffic" in slaves.[57]

The peculiarities of British diplomacy in the interior of West Africa in the first third of the nineteenth century reveal several interlocking and contradictory themes governing British actions. The Sokoto Caliphate, as the Muslim state that came to dominate much of West Africa in the period after the formal abolition of the British slave trade in 1807, pursued initiatives that reflect an independence of European and particularly British motivations and require a reassessment of abolition and related critiques of slavery. As I have demonstrated, Muslim areas of West Africa could have supplied most, if not all, of the slaves destined for the Americas in the last century of the transatlantic slave trade, but this did not happen. The reasons had little to do with European intentions or American demand and more with policies and objectives deriving from religious motivations and a perspective on society and economy that was not driven by the quest for sugar, gold, and other marketable commodities of the European-dominated commercial world of the eighteenth and early nineteenth centuries. Without in any way disparaging the driving forces of capitalism and personal and national aggrandizement that underpinned much of the Atlantic world, I argue that the political, intellectual, and economic forces prevalent in the interior of West Africa had another agenda that attempted to sustain a worldview and a degree of autonomy that did not require or seek involvement in the transatlantic world. Dominated by Muslims, this worldview and political economy had specific reasons for opposing and undermining the transatlantic slave trade. Although Muslim leaders in West Africa often were unsuccessful in restricting the flow of the enslaved to the Atlantic world, they nonetheless made efforts to do so. These efforts, often ignored or misunderstood, require careful study in determining alternate perspectives on the global economy that was emerging during the era of slavery and its subsequent suppression in the Americas.

The negotiations between Britain and Sokoto are significant for several reasons. First, the British policy of signing treaties with other countries enforced and expanded British abolition of the slave trade after 1807 in connection with the naval blockade of the West African coast. Because the Bello-Clapperton accord was never formally approved in London, although it was in Sokoto, the impression emerges that only Britain served to champion abolition. Second, the negotiations constituted one of the objects, although seldom appreciated, of British efforts to determine the geography of the West African interior and specifically the course of the Niger River and where it entered the Atlantic Ocean. The purpose was clearly to open a commercial link to the interior that would provide access to the mythical golden trade of the Moors, that is, the Muslim commercial networks. Third, and perhaps most important, the exchange between Bello and Clapperton reflects the policies of the Sokoto Caliphate as the most important Muslim country in West Africa and indeed the largest independent state in Africa in the nineteenth century. In the 1820s the Sokoto Caliphate had little to fear from European encroachment and instead was preoccupied with promotion of its conception of legitimate Islamic government. Some eighty years later conditions would change, and the caliphate would fall to the armies of Britain, France, and Germany, but this future was far from clear in the 1820s.

Debates over slavery and abolition reflect perspectives that are situated in specific historical and cultural contexts. In western European thought, enlightened rationalism legitimized slavery by defining the "nature" of Africans with reference to biblical interpretations, natural science, and sociology as inferior. Ultimately these efforts at correlating the enslavement of Africans and definitions of who constituted the "other" came to be interpreted in racialized forms. Inevitably, the analysis of the abolition of slavery has focused on race and how efforts to end the slave trade appealed to the humanity of reformers in decrying the oppression of slavery but ultimately also reinforced prejudices against people with the physical differences of skin color. The campaign to outlaw the import of enslaved blacks into the Americas and later to free black slaves resulted in new forms of colonial servitude. However, in the Islamic context the practice and discourse of slavery centered on religion, not semantic and racial categories; that is, the Islamic debate concentrated on cultural and social categories rather than on biological distinctions, and in this context it did not oppose slavery as a system but considered how slavery related to the political economy and the moral community.

From this perspective the discussion within West Africa over the legitimacy of enslavement focused on the efforts of Islamic governments to develop their own slavery policies and determine how and to what ends populations could be directed. An African-centered perspective raises questions about the dominance of a "European" tradition of abolition. Muslims, at least, viewed the issue of slavery and the African diaspora across the Atlantic from another perspective, although the Muslim critique also was situated within a context that was only partial as well. Because perspectives on slavery were situated in contexts, the aims and methods of abolition were different. While European abolition was directed at the transatlantic trade, the Islamic debate concentrated on the protection of Muslims and the means of securing redemption, emancipation, and the incorporation of freeborn Muslims and those who converted to Islam.

The questions raised here address the policies of Islamic states toward the transatlantic slave trade, specifically as reflected in efforts to negotiate the abolition of that trade. In the first four decades of the nineteenth century, slaves leaving the Bight of Benin for the Americas included Muslims from the interior, such as those identified as Hausa, Nupe, and Borno (meaning those who came from Borno) and increasingly northern Yoruba as well. The meanings of these terms as designators of ethnicity have to be deconstructed in a methodological fashion that sees ethnicity as a lens through which to view history. What is meant by these terms and how people actually identified themselves and others cannot be envisioned in an essentialist framework that sees "ethnicity" as a substitute terminology for "tribe." Muslims were being enslaved as a consequence of the political context in the central Bilād al-Sūdān, most especially the jihād that led to the consolidation of the Sokoto Caliphate after 1804. How people were identified occurred in that context, where the dominant languages of communication were one means of recognition. Place of origin, social status, occupation, gender, and the identity of parents and the towns and cities where individuals and their parents had lived were contributing factors in identification. Such distinctions were sometimes reflected in facial and body scarification. In the case of Muslims, moreover, familiarity with Arabic prayers and the extent of literacy in Arabic were essential determinants of identity. Fundamentally, the dominant ideological framework related to interpretations of Islamic governance and who should be recognized as a Muslim and thereby protected from enslavement and who should not.

Restrictions on the Caliphate Slave Trade

By the early 1830s, if not earlier, caliphate authorities were inspecting caravans traveling to North Africa. They were looking for Muslims who had been wrongly enslaved. According to an account attributed to a Tuareg caravan "khabir," (i.e., expert) Cheggueun, who supposedly traded between North Africa and the caliphate in the early 1830s, merchants had to establish in public that they were not trading enslaved Muslims. It is claimed that caravans were first inspected in Katsina. Although the actual account of Cheggueun appears to be a fabrication, the details most certainly were based on information derived from firsthand observation. Cheggueun is credited with having observed that each caravan section, "as it passed through the gate ... was searched by the chaouchs of [Emir] Mohammed Omar who had been given the task of ascertaining that we were not carrying off either Fulanis or Negroes who were Muslims or Jews [i.e., craftsmen]." Caravans were searched again at Tassaoua and in Damergu, to the north of Katsina. According to this account, caravans were subject to the decrees of Muhammad Bello of Sokoto. Even in territory "inhabited by black Muslim Touareug, the chiefs had to make sure that the returning caravans do not carry with them Foullanes [Fulani] or black Muslims as slaves."[58] According to the alleged account of Cheggueun,

> The purchase of Fulani, pregnant Negresses, and black Jews [Nègres juifs] is strictly prohibited by the order of the sultan. The purchase of Fulani is forbidden because they claim to be white, pregnant Negresses because the child who is born will be the property of the sultan if he is an idolator and will be free if he is a Muslim; Jewish Negroes because they are all jewellers, tailors, useful artisans or indispensible interme-diaries in commercial transactions; for under the skin, in the Sudan, in the Sahara and along the coast, Jews everywhere have the same instincts and the twin gifts of language and commerce. To prevent cheating, no caravan leaves the Hausa country without the slaves having been closely examined and the same is done at Tassaoua, at Damergu, at Agades, with the Tuareg, where [Muhammad] Bello has wakil (agents) wakil charged with the same task. A merchant who contravenes his orders exposes himself to the confiscation of all his merchandise.[59]

Eugène Daumas and Ausone de Chancel, who recorded this account for pur-poses of promoting French expansion into the Sahara, referred to "Nègres juifs," although in fact there was no Jewish population of merchants and ar-tisans in the central Bilād al-Sūdān; rather, these occupations were almost entirely in the hands of Muslims, including Hausa merchants described as Wangarawa, Beriberi, Agalawa, and other designations that depicted their origins (asali). The reason people with commercial and craft specialization were not supposed to be enslaved was that such people were invariably Muslims, not Jews. Although Daumas and Chancel may have fabricated the travels and adventures of Cheggueun, there is no reason to doubt their ob-servations about the official efforts to protect Muslims from enslavement.

The slave trade from the Sokoto Caliphate continued, nonetheless, which may indicate that official efforts to prevent slaves being sent to the Americas were ineffective. After returning from pilgrimage and settling in Sokoto in the early 1830s, al-Ḥājj ʿUmar Tal issued a condemning report on the exter-nal slave trade of the caliphate. In Risālat shawq al-habīb ilā as'ilat Ibāhīm al-labīb, he described improper practices that resulted in the enslavement of

people through "legal" proclamations. In his view, "No one can be more ignorant and arrogant than sinful and criminal people who legalize enslavement of free people by an act of *fatwā*." By 1835 'Umar had become a close
confidant of Muhammad Bello, even marrying his daughter Mariam.[60] Hence
his comments on the continuation of the transatlantic trade indicate that
Bello's abolitionist policies may have been adopted but were not successfully
being enforced. At least, al-Ḥājj 'Umar did not think so.

Nonetheless, a shift in the slave trade appears to have begun in the 1830s.[61]
Whereas previously there had been an extensive enslaved movement southward, thereafter most enslaved individuals appear to have been sold north.
Hence in 1833 or 1834 a caravan from Ghadames and Ghat purchased three
thousand slaves in Nupe who might otherwise have gone south.[62] By the late
1830s the Nupe wars continued to generate large numbers of captives, with
the result that much of the west bank of the Niger below the confluence of the
Niger and Benue had been depopulated. Throughout the 1830s Muslim traders
from the central Bilād al-Sūdān maintained their position in the trade to the
coast as well. As Samuel Ajayi Crowther reported in 1844, "All the Mohamedans learn to understand and speak the Hausa language and through it the
Koran is explained and interpreted in their mosques throughout Yoruba
[country]. So that from Lagos, Badagry, and Porto Novo, and upwards to the
Niger, where Mohamedans are found, the Haussa [language] is spoken by
them."[63] The use of Hausa reflected not only the extent of Muslim commerce but also the relative ease of communication between the interior
and the coast.

In this context the naval expedition to the Niger in 1841 displayed the
British policy to promote trade. Under the inspiration of Thomas Fowell
Buxton, the expedition attempted to "open" the Niger for "civilization, commerce and Christianity" and thereby sought to establish firm relations with
the non-Muslim governments along the lower Niger and also build a permanent settlement and model farm near the confluence of the Niger and the
Benue. In continuation of the British missions of the 1820s, Buxton hoped to
undermine the external slave trade by encouraging local agricultural production for export, even using slave labor if necessary. The mission's settlement at Lokoja, founded seventeen years after the Bello-Clapperton accord
of 1824, was destined to be the port for Sokoto-British trade. Its location at
the confluence was in the disputed and virtually deserted territory on the
west bank of the Niger, not at the flourishing port that Raka had been in the
mid-1820s. As noted earlier, Lokoja was in fact part of the Nupe emirate

initially centered at Raba and, after its destruction, at Bida. Hence Lokoja was in caliphate territory and effectively fulfilled the position for which Raka had been designated in 1824.[64]

The decline in the southern trade appears to have reflected the collapse of Brazilian demand for adult male slaves from the central Bilād al-Sūdān, especially after official abolition in 1831, when the slave trade to Bahia and other parts of Brazil continued. However, after the Malês uprising in Bahia in 1835, there appears to have been reluctance to import Muslims, if not an outright ban on doing so. Although Hausa and other Muslims had been involved in revolts and disturbances in Bahia before 1835, the Malês uprising was significantly different in its scale and direction. The slaves responsible for this revolt were subjected to extreme repression thereafter. At the public trial that followed the revolt, Muslims revealed, both through their testimony and their denials, that Hausa, Nupe, Borno, and Yoruba Muslims had perpetrated the conspiracy. Many rebels were executed, imprisoned, or deported to the Bight of Benin.[65] The collapse of the Bahian market did not end the trade, however; instead, Spanish slavers from Cuba picked up the slack.[66] Slaves continued to be sent overland to Lagos or purchased on the Niger, but apparently not as extensively as in the previous three decades.

Partial Perspectives and Situated Knowledge

Partial perspectives and situated knowledge are aptly demonstrated in British efforts to establish diplomatic relations south of the Sahara in the wake of the Napoleonic adventure in the Middle East in 1798–1801. The difficulty of incorporating new information is apparent. Despite the clarity of the geographical information, the informed British public was slow to accept the facts of where the Niger River reached the coast of Guinea. The broad details of the Niger flow had been known in Britain and elsewhere in Europe at least since the 1780s, if not earlier. This geographical knowledge had certainly been understood in learned Islamic circles for centuries. For European "scientific" recognition, however, "confirmation" of its course, including its termination in the "sea," required "European" observation, clearly an early manifestation of racism.

The Niger question remained a subject of dispute, although no one doubted that the Sokoto Caliphate and Borno were closer to the Guinea coast than to Tripoli. Reports of the "lakes of Nupe" had been widespread for years, but still there was doubt, even among the members of the British mission in the 1820s.[67] Although Denham remained unconvinced, Clapperton and

Oudney realized that confirmation of the course of the Niger had to be secured in the Sokoto Caliphate, not Borno.[68] Influential English geographers and publicists, especially Barrow, refused to believe the early reports. Hence theories that had no basis in fact still influenced policy until 1830.[69] In studying the abolition of slavery, the racial component of British policy should be highlighted for further discussion. Knowledge had to be processed, and it was done in racialized terms. The fact that it took almost fifty years before the actual geography was recognized in Europe indicates that scientific knowledge was not always cumulative. Denham, who clearly did not understand what he was being told in Borno in 1822, learned that "at eight days' distance only from Yeouri [Yauri, on the Niger], large boats came to a place called Yearban [Yoruba], but it is not on the *bahr kebir* [i.e., great river or sea]. Katungah [Katunga, i.e., Oyo] is the great port, which is at some distance [from the sea]: to both of these places people he called Americans came; they were white, and Christians: they always demand gum arabic and male slaves, for which they will pay as high as sixty to seventy dollars each." Denham was being told that the capital of Oyo, Katunga in Hausa and in Borno, was not itself on the sea, and since he did not understand that the Niger flowed into the Gulf of Guinea, he did not realize that there was a direct river route to the south as well.[70]

Shaykh ʿUthmān dan Fodio was indeed a contemporary of Wilberforce, as Fisher reminds us, and Muhammad Bello was a contemporary of Buxton, both of whom emphasized economic and social development. Abolition and commercial "progress" found proponents in both Britain and the caliphate. Attitudes toward the emancipation of slaves were another matter, however.

Inevitably, seeing events through the distorting lens of European diplomats presents problems, which is one reason that it is fortunate to have so much Arabic and other documentation. The difficulties are compounded when European diplomats are perceived as "explorers" and scientists are referred to simply as "travelers." The incomplete and often inaccurate information of the period can disguise historical change. For example, the ignorance of late eighteenth-century geographers in Britain resulted in a preoccupation with "discovery." Hence the search for the outlet of the Niger River was a "European" search; where the Niger flowed was well known in the hinterland of the Bight of Benin, of course. Similarly, the Enlightenment review of the morality of slavery was conducted within a European world that had created the plantation economies of the Americas but understood little about the lands from where the enslaved population had come. The Islamic debate over slavery concentrated on religion and enslavement in a different world not generally perceived by European outsiders. Identifying the "other," of course, depends on perspective.

British-Sokoto negotiations provide some insight into the relationship of Muslim states to Christian Europe in matters of slavery, however. British abolition came into force in 1808, the same year in which the first phase of the Sokoto jihād reached its conclusion and Borno resistance to the jihād coalesced under al-Kānimī. The issue of slavery was paramount in the clash over jihād; al-Kānimī defended Borno by arguing that nobody should legally have been enslaved, while Muhammad Bello justified the destruction of Borno and its capital at Birni Ngazargamu because he claimed that the inhabitants of Borno were not sufficiently orthodox in their religious observance and had supported resistance to jihād. As the ensuing correspondence between al-Kānimī and Muhammad Bello demonstrates, the issue of slavery was a subject of debate among people other than those influenced by the European Enlightenment.

By ignoring other perspectives, the Eurocentric debate tends to marginalize slaves through the construction of an artificial dichotomy between the abolitionist actions of free Europeans and the resistance of enslaved Africans. Such a discourse over the legitimacy of slavery is perceived largely in racial terms. Of course, former slaves and free blacks were influential in the evolution of abolitionist thought in the Atlantic world, but they are often dismissed as pawns of the movement. Rather than authors of their own thoughts, they are assigned the role of victims whose examples of salvation from the barbarities of slavery inspired the political drive to outlaw the slave trade. The heroes (and heroines) of slave studies who resisted through revolt, flight, or subtler forms of action or inaction are pictured as rebels divorced from their backgrounds when in fact they were involved in warfare that would determine their future.

The European abolition "movement" and its North American counterpart are sometimes assumed to have opposed the institution of slavery in its entirety when in fact the initial aims were directed only against the transatlantic component of the trade in slaves rather than against slavery as an institution. Abolition and the struggle to emancipate slaves advanced in partial stages, geographically specific and variable in time. The British stage involved abolition of the slave trade in 1807, the emancipation of slaves in the Americas and South Africa in 1834, and abolition of the legal status of slavery in India, Ceylon, and Burma only in 1843–44. Hence the debate over slavery tended to be relative. Whether or not opponents of slavery declared themselves ultimately against all forms of slavery everywhere, their actions were directed at particular elements of the slavery curse, not the whole institution. Modern scholarship has tended to concentrate on the partial measures of European abolition without realizing that the focus of research itself reveals a partial perspective isolated from the total setting of the transatlantic world. Muslim reformers, too, took partial steps to combat slavery as an institution, attempting to harness slavery to the development of states that had been founded in jihād.

Sokoto, the Jihād States, and Abolition

8 EMPOWERING HISTORY
Trajectories across the Cultural and Religious Divide

How are we to understand the odyssey of Muhammad Kabā Saghanughu and the execution of his son in Jamaica 1832,[1] the legacy of Richard Pierpoint's military service to the Canadian nation,[2] the contributions of Mahommah Gardo Baquaqua on the abolition lecture circuit in upstate New York, eastern Pennsylvania, and Canada West in the 1850s,[3] or the enlistment of Muhammed ʿAlī (Nicholas) Saʿīd in the Union army in the American Civil War in the 1860s?[4] The path of Muslims in Bahia is far clearer in the ways in which resistance was pursued between 1807 and 1835, when Muslims from the area of the Sokoto jihād were involved in uprisings and conspiracies, most notably in the Malês revolt in 1835 and its specific links to the jihād tradition. The Muslims who returned to West Africa after the 1835 uprising sometimes reached the jihād states, but many remained on the coast and did not choose to return to their original homes in Borno, in Kano, or elsewhere in the interior. Muslims in Trinidad tried to reach West Africa to escape apprenticeship and the ongoing discrimination of postemancipation slavery in the Caribbean, and many succeeded. These responses were part of a pattern of Muslim entanglement in a broader Atlantic world that includes West Africa beyond the European enclaves on the coast. In the jihād states of West Africa, the Muslim regimes and many Muslim merchants and scholars tried to abstain from involvement with Europeans, that is, Christians, and instead promoted the independence of the jihād states, including a heavy investment in slavery. The repercussions of jihād affected those who were forced into diaspora differently from the impact in West Africa. Muslims in diaspora became involved in antislavery activities, while the Muslim leaders in West Africa tempered their attitudes to slavery in the interests of the jihād states.

ʿUthmān dan Fodio was concerned with matters of slavery, particularly the enslavement of free Muslims and encouraging the conversion of the enslaved to Islam. The context is important in understanding the possible motivations and influences underlying the policies of the Sokoto leadership, as well as the actions of enslaved Muslims. Muslims were engaged in an active debate over their identities both as free people and as slaves to Muslims and non-Muslims, possibly even to Christians. Muslim reformers were particularly worried about the justification for enslavement when the status of an individual as a Muslim was in doubt. Needless to say, in the context of war in West Africa and the establishment of jihād states, the preoccupation with this issue suggests that many individuals who were enslaved could claim to be Muslims, whether or not they were actually freeborn, simply by pledging themselves to jihād. The issue pitted those who supported the jihād, defined as Muslims, against those in opposition, whether or not they were Muslims and regardless of how they were otherwise categorized. Even resistance to slavery in diaspora fitted into this perspective, since considerable compromise was required to accept enslavement to non-Muslims.

In challenging an approach that emphasizes the intellectual tradition of the European Enlightenment, the political repercussions of the French Revolution, and British abolition, this book has addressed how Muslims in Africa questioned the legitimacy of slavery in the context of ṣūfī Islam. The transatlantic slave trade was the subject of written and legal debate within West Africa that reflects another perspective on the struggle to confront slavery as an institution. In different ways, this Muslim debate was partial, not specifically centered on the trade across the Atlantic but rather concerned about the fate of enslaved Muslims and slaves who might otherwise have converted to Islam. The Sokoto leadership, at least, could promote abolition of the transatlantic trade on its own terms. There was no need to coerce the Sokoto government or the other jihād states into compliance with British abolitionist policies. Unlike in the Mediterranean, where sea power could be brought to bear, there was no way in which European states could impose abolition of the slave trade or the emancipation of slaves in the jihād states, at least not before French penetration inland from the Senegal River in the mid-nineteenth century and the British, German, and French invasion and conquest of the West African interior in the last decade of the nineteenth century. Despite the removal of more than 100,000 individuals from slave ships, the Royal Navy patrols still had relatively limited impact on stopping the departure of slave ships.

As Donna Haraway has argued, perspectives on knowledge imply the limitations of the viewpoint, which in the context of jihād in West Africa has to be perceived in at least two guises, one emanating from Europe and one originating in the Islamic world.[5] "Situated knowledges," as Haraway has argued, arise out of partial perspectives, whether determined by gender or by other factors associated with the subaltern or the non-European.[6] On the one hand, knowledge is situated within a particular discourse, which may reveal incomplete and inaccurate perspectives. Hence the European debate over the flow of the Niger River affected policy and actions differentially even within the various spheres of British influence. Interpretations of geographical information changed in the 1820s and 1830s, but the course of the Niger did not. On the other hand, Muslims were preoccupied with religious issues that arose from an entirely different tradition within West Africa and the wider Islamic world. Hence debate over matters of slavery assumed a different form arising from a perspective that envisioned the methods for the amelioration of slavery in an Islamic context. The apparent contradiction in a commitment to the abolition of the transatlantic slave trade and the protection of freeborn Muslims while perpetuating massive enslavement reveals an alternate perspective on understanding history and the quest for the ideal society. The genesis of jihād and the ways it is manifested in the contemporary world highlight conceptions of a social order that abhors corruption and social deviance. Jihād in the twenty-first century injects solutions to political problems in a fashion that is neither progressive nor revolutionary but rather is puritanical and restorative, but this jihād phenomenon clearly manifests a continuity with the past that can be traced from the eighteenth century to the present.

Differences in perspective challenge a consideration of the slavery debate beyond the Eurocentric. The Sokoto interest in abolition neither reduced the extent of enslavement nor undermined the incidence of slavery in West Africa. Quite the opposite, slavery developed as a key institution of the Sokoto Caliphate and remained such even under European colonial rule in the early twentieth century. Because Sokoto abolition was directed only at the protection of Muslims and the prohibition of the sale of slaves, especially Muslims, to Christians, slavery continued to flourish and served as the cornerstone of social relationships well into the twentieth century.[7] British policy initially emphasized abolition of transatlantic slavery through the suppression of the slave trade off the West African coast, while the French penetration inland from Senegambia exploited slavery to advance the frontier of expansion. Both British and French officials cooperated with regimes in North Africa and in West Africa whose interests in abolition related to religious issues that were far different from the humanitarian sentiments of the abolitionists of Britain, France, and North America. The Bello-Clapperton accord reveals a new perspective on the course of abolition—the Muslim dimension. The impact of the Islamic discourse on Western thought may have been marginal, but the

JIHĀD IN WEST AFRICA DURING THE AGE OF REVOLUTIONS

effects on diplomatic history were important nonetheless. British policy was as mixed as those of Sokoto and Borno. In these cases abolitionist ideology was employed but its practical application permitted the continuation of slave raiding. The British mission excused its support of enslavement as expedient in the interest of "scientific" observation. For Muhammad Bello and al-Kānimī, abolition was desirable with respect to Muslims but not always under the conditions of war, when enslavement of those who opposed the policies of specific jihād states was tolerated and perpetrated. The French use of "liberated villages" in the nineteenth century as a source of labor recruitment to construct railroads and other public works also reveals a willingness to compromise the human rights of antislavery.

In order to comprehend contemporary events and dangers of the twenty-first century, we cannot ignore history and the continuities from the past. The sudden explosion of such violent movements as Boko Haram in Nigeria and the uprisings inspired by al-Qaeda in northern Mali and southern Algeria onto the world stage should be a warning about the dangers of forgetting history, which can result in a distorted view of events. Are we to respond to the kidnapping of hundreds of schoolgirls, which first came to the attention of the international community in the attack on Chibok, Nigeria, in 2014, the dangers to invaluable historic Arabic documents in Timbuktu, and the destruction of world heritage sites in Syria with ignorance and confusion, or should we try to comprehend the events of our times by reference to the past and the trajectories that emanate therefrom? The description of Boko Haram as occurring in a "remote" part of Nigeria shows a profound ignorance of geography and context; the region has been exposed to jihād for two hundred years. The attacks on the literate and sophisticated tradition of Islam in Timbuktu are misinterpreted as the actions of individuals described as misguided if not crazy fanatics rather than as a continuation of a long-standing struggle between the nomads of the desert and the urban, literate cultures south of the Sahara. The simplified and ahistorical interpretations of the media both in West Africa and globally undermine an understanding of the historical past. To what extent is there a geographical divide between Islam and Christianity in Nigeria, as some pundits would have it, when Boko Haram attacks both Muslims and Christians? Are the Arabic libraries of the Sahara and the Sahel not sacred to Muslims who advocate jihād and a different kind of world? There certainly are spiritual divisions, both among Muslims and among Christians, and indeed among secularist scholars and politicians, but the alleged geographical separation and secular divisions ignore a long history of interaction and entanglement.

In discussing the jihād movement of West Africa in the context of the age of revolutions, it should be clear that revolutions and radical changes are neither inherently good nor inherently bad any more than jihād is something new that has been introduced from outside the region. The jihād movement is a historical phenomenon, and we have to confront the implications for the societies in question and the world at large. In the context of West Africa, as in the European-dominated Atlantic world, there was a period of intensified slavery that can be compared with the "second slavery" that Dale Tomich has described, which has been previously discussed in my analysis of the "transformations in slavery" in Africa, as well as in the scholarship of many other scholars. If one links the analysis of these two phenomena, one in the Americas and one in Africa, into an inclusive common framework, it is no longer possible to sustain a narrow view of the Atlantic world that does not include Africa; rather, we must highlight the fact that the continent of Africa shapes the Atlantic basin and therefore has to be conceptualized within an Atlantic world. The Muslim world and changes therein are usually excluded in the discussion of the abolition movement and its antecedents in the period of the European Enlightenment, at least until the Congress of Vienna in 1814–15. An alternate view to one that focuses only on Europe and the Americas reveals the necessity of reconceptualizing history to include a global perspective that transcends Eurocentrism. The implication for a reconsideration of the abolition movement affects how we analyze the ways slavery was transformed internationally. A broader perspective uncovers currents in the Islamic world of West Africa, North Africa, and elsewhere that deserve attention.

Individuals in the Slave Trade

Fortunately, it has been possible to recover hundreds of biographical accounts of individuals who were enslaved in Muslim areas, many of whom indeed were Muslims themselves. Their stories provide personal testimony to the significance of jihād in the thinking of people. As I have argued in this study, Muslims were underrepresented in the transatlantic slave trade, but numerous accounts of Muslims have survived because of the literacy of many Muslims and their ease at acquiring some fluency in other languages. In some cases Muslims came to the attention of others who wrote down their stories, but many left their own paper trail. Some Muslims were "Liberated Africans" taken to Sierra Leone and elsewhere, and other accounts come from networks that crossed the Sahara. These accounts attest to the precarious life of the jihād period. The overwhelming proportion of accounts chronicle enslavement of males in their late teens and early twenties. Enslavement targeted young men who had military potential and who were the prime male slaves of the Atlantic trade. This profile suggests that the reported accounts of enslavement refer to sale and migration at an age when individuals were fully grown and were well aware of geography and political terrain. The range of these accounts helps empower history, providing voices for a part of the Atlantic world that needs to be understood more clearly.

It is possible to document specific individuals who fit the pattern of a heavily male migration. They left Africa from Senegambia or the upper Guinea coast as far south as the Sierra Leone River. Overwhelmingly this meant that individuals departed from St. Louis in the Senegal River, from James Island and adjacent mainland depots on the Gambia River, and from various rivers to the south, including Bissau and Cacheu, which were heavily patronized by Portuguese and Brazilian ships with connections to the Cape Verde Islands. Fuuta Jalon traded mostly with Rio Nuñez and Rio Pongo, although Îles des Los and the Bullom Shore north of the Sierra Leone River also were sources of slaves. Bunce Island in the Sierra Leone River was a major center of trade because of the safe anchorage of the estuary. To the south of the Sierra Leone Peninsula, the islands of the Bananas, Plantain, and Sherbro were bases of operations for mulatto slave merchants and rice planters. Most of the slaves from these southern points of embarkation were not Muslims, but some Muslims were sold along routes that ended at the coast at these points. Bunce Island seems to have been the southernmost point that connected with Muslim networks to the south and east of Fuuta Jalon, as well as with Fuuta Jalon itself.

The bias in the biographical accounts with respect to gender clearly distorts the analysis. There are almost no accounts of women; the scanty details on women and girls do not allow analysis. There are accounts from Kano in the 1820s of concubines being accused of murdering their masters.[8] One emir of Bauchi was accused of selling his concubines when their breasts started to sag.[9] There are descriptions of mothers being sold with their nursing offspring along the Niger River and the region north of the confluence with the Benue River from the 1840s onward.[10] These few biographical accounts provide trajectories across the cultural and religious divide that has remained largely hidden in the study of the Atlantic world. It is possible to understand, on the one hand, the resistance of women to enslavement and, on the other, efforts to keep mothers and their infant children together. Concubinage was an important feature of society; female slaves generally cost more than males, even though children in Muslim areas were awarded the social status of their fathers.[11]

Most of the accounts that have survived tell of enslavement during jihād. Sometimes the descriptions attribute enslavement to war, although the context makes it clear that the war in question was jihād. In other cases raids by the Fulani account for enslavement, which again in context refers to campaigns associated with the jihād. Those who were enslaved in these situations were very diverse in origin and status. They might have been opponents of the jihād in the core Hausa region or in Borno, and those who were already slaves in these areas would certainly have faced continued enslavement unless they escaped to the jihād camp and claimed freeborn status. Those who were enslaved also included Yoruba and their dependents after the uprising in Ilorin and the subsequent collapse of Oyo as an effective state, even though some of these "Yoruba" may well have already been enslaved or have come from areas outside Oyo. The enslaved further included people who had not converted to Islam, especially from the Jos Plateau, the highlands of Tangale, Tula, and Waja, north of the Benue River between Bauchi and Yola, and the borderlands between Borno and the Hausa emirates. Others came from the Adamawa plateau through one of the many subordinate emirates from Madagali in the north to Rai Buba in the south. Similarly, Fuuta Jalon continued to harass people who were not considered Muslims or who were thought to be unorthodox in their religious practices in areas adjacent to the Fuuta Jalon highlands. Moreover, after 1837 al-Ḥājj ʿUmar specifically targeted the Bamana of Segu and Kaarta because of their supposedly poor allegiance to Islam.

The study of individuals caught up in the slave trade during the era of jihād highlights issues of methodology and questions of identity that inevitably confront the meaning of ethnicity in Muslim regions of West Africa and the corresponding assignment of ethnic designations in Bahia, Cuba, and elsewhere. Fortunately, there are numerous sources for the history of slavery during the era of jihād that shed light on these issues. First, there is Samuel Johnson's *History of the Yorubas*—Johnson himself was of Oyo origin.[12] There are also the many texts by ʿUthmān dan Fodio, ʿAbdullahi dan Fodio, Muhammad Bello, Nana Asmaʾu, Waziri Junaidu al-Bukhārī, Muhammad al-Kānimī, al-Ḥājj ʿUmar, and others who explicitly documented the jihād commitment to the consolidation of an Islamic society and therefore refer to the origins of people and how they were identified.[13] Finally, the firsthand observations by Europeans who traversed the Sokoto Caliphate and other parts of West Africa in the nineteenth century provide numerous biographical accounts of individuals caught up in the events of the time.

Samuel Ajayi Crowther, besides being the first Anglican bishop in West Africa, appointed in 1864, was born in Osogun about 1807 (plate 29). Of Oyo origin, he was enslaved when he was about twelve during the jihād in Oyo. His memoirs and observations are extensive, as are those of others who were associated with the Church Missionary Society in Sierra Leone and subsequently in what became Nigeria.[14] Moreover, his contribution to African studies is particularly noteworthy; he was at the forefront in promoting the adoption of the term "Yoruba" as an ethnic name that included all people who spoke the common language, whether or not they were of Oyo origin and despite the fact that the term was not indigenous but rather was used as the ethnic designation by Hausa and other people in the north who were Muslims.

'Alī Eisami Gazirmabe was captured during the jihād in Borno at the time the metropolitan district (Gazir; hence his last name) was sacked around 1808–10 (plate 30). He was sold as a slave to Katunga, the capital of Oyo, where he was sold again at the time of the Ilorin uprising in 1817. His master feared that he would flee to the Muslim banner and hence sold him to the coast for sale to the slave ships. He was liberated by the British navy and subsequently became known in Sierra Leone as William Harding.[15] Eisami was therefore an eyewitness to two major historical events, the destruction of the capital district of Borno in 1810 and the uprising in Ilorin as perceived from the capital of Oyo in 1817. As William Harding, the name he took upon his conversion to Christianity in Sierra Leone, he provided detailed information on his native Borno, including stories, historical accounts, poetry, and other texts in both Kanuri and English. His accounts were transcribed by German missionary and scholar Sigimund Koelle in 1848–49 and form the basis of modern Kanuri studies.

There are many other accounts that are cited in this study, most notably those collected by José Bonifácio de Andrada e Silva in Brazil and published by Antônio de Menezes Vasconcellos de Drummond in 1819 and those collected by Francis de Castelnau in 1849.[16] The numerous testimonies of those involved in the Malês uprising of 1835 also document the jihād,[17] as do the accounts of some Muslims who were not in Bahia at the time of the revolt, such as Rufino José Maria, whose African name, Abuncare, might be rendered "Abu," short for Abubakar, and "Ncare," perhaps a reference to his home town. Rufino did not participate in the uprising because he was in the south of Brazil at the time, but his origins were connected to jihād.[18]

There are many other accounts of enslavement in the central Bilād al-Sūdān in the first half of the nineteenth century that have provided the basis for the study of the impact of the jihād movement on slavery.[19] The abundant source material, much of which is readily accessible, provides a rich sample of why people were enslaved and what happened to them subsequently, as explored in the numerous examples examined in this book. Although there is considerable disagreement among scholars on interpretation of the causes, course, and impact of the jihād, these sources highlight the jihād as a cause of enslavement. Methodologically, this book has expanded our horizon to include a wealth of biographical material that documents resistance to slavery in the age of revolutions through voices from Africa and thereby supplements the research of Peter Linebaugh, Marcus Rediker, Jane Landers, James Sweet, Rebecca Scott, Jean Hébrard, Walter Hawthorne, and my own work on Kabā Saghanughu, Baquaqua, Saʿīd, Kwage Adamu Dorugu, Guillaume Pasko, and others.[20] Although the focus has been on youths, especially males, because of the limitations of the data, the world of females may become more visible through the analysis of materials on liberated Africans and through baptismal records. In the case of Muslims who were taken to the Americas, the usual practice of ransoming freeborn Muslims was not successful, even if it was attempted, despite the fact that the price for ransoming was usually higher than the purchase price of a slave and was favored under Islamic law and practice. For purposes of historical analysis, the cases where individuals were ransomed are informative.[21]

There are instances, too, of important individuals ending up in slavery and failing to be caught by the ransoming net, such as Muhammad ʿAlī Saʿīd, who was a slave because his father, Barka Gana, was a royal slave whose position as general and governor in Borno depended on his being a slave.[22] Because of Barka Gana's status, his son was well educated; ironically, this increased his appeal as a slave. His subsequent bondage to a merchant in Tripoli, his sale to an Ottoman official in Istanbul, and then his transfer to a Russian diplomat who took him to St. Petersburg after his emancipation constituted an unusual trajectory that reveals the precariousness of individual freedom in the context of jihād. Saʿīd acquired his Christian name through his baptism in the Orthodox Church in Riga (Latvia) in 1853. His autobiography makes it clear that he understood the context of jihād and the role his father had played in the reform government of Borno in the face of Sokoto hegemony, but his personal odyssey took him beyond the orbit of jihād. His subsequent transatlantic odyssey and enlistment in the all-black Thirty-Fourth

Massachusetts Regiment in the American Civil War as Sargeant Nicholas Said (plate 31) demonstrate an expanding consciousness of racial issues that dominated the African diaspora. Although he intended to return to his native Borno and presumably reintegration into Muslim society, he remained in the southern states after the Civil War, married in Alabama, and moved to Brownsville, Tennessee, by 1882.[23]

Similarly, Richard Pierpoint appreciated his free status in British Canada, as did other blacks who had settled in Upper Canada and cherished their free status. He was loyal to Lieutenant Governor John Graves Simcoe, whose tenure in Upper Canada in 1791–1796 was marked by Simcoe's attempt to implement the abolition of slavery; in May 1793 a measure was introduced to free all slaves, although in the end the act was modified from immediate emancipation to gradual abolition. The Legislative Assembly forced a compromise that banned enslaved immigration and freed children born in the province at age twenty-five rather than granting outright emancipation, but nonetheless the Anti-slavery Act was the first measure in the British Empire to limit slavery.[24] Pierpoint, who was Fulbe, wanted to return to his native home late in his life, but his petition to British authorities in 1821 was turned down, and he died in Upper Canada in about 1838. Initially provided with two hundred acres of land in what is now St. Catharines, he subsequently owned land in Garafraxa near Fergus (plate 32).[25]

When a methodology that attempts to interpret ethnicity as a lens into historical reconstruction is applied, it can be demonstrated that ethnicity and identity in the central Bilād al-Sūdān, including Oyo, were very complex indeed. People spoke more than one language and often had to learn new languages; individuals traced their origins to the places they came from through both their maternal and paternal lines. They identified with the city or town where they had lived or near where they had lived, such as Kano, Katsina, Bebeji, Kura, or Zaria, to name only a few of the walled towns that dotted the Sokoto Caliphate alone; there were more in the other jihād states. In the Muslim context and among Yoruba and Hausa specifically, place of origin was essential in establishing identification, and such identity virtually always referred to which town or city a person came from, as well as the person's mother and father.[26] Facial and body scarification was widely practiced as a means of identification, providing protection from enslavement and expressing ritualized forms of community solidarity.[27] Naming practices and changes in names in some instances established pedigrees of assimilation, denoted social status, and confirmed religious belief.[28] When I talk about a methodology through the ethnic lens, my intention is specifically to understand the layering of ethnicity and the complex expressions of identification. Although people identified as Muslims, this included the recognition of origins, which was often apparent on faces and bodies through variations in scarification and hairstyles. They accepted a common bond as Muslims and freeborn and sought to be distinguished from the ways in which the enslaved population was identified.

The Muslims involved in the uprising in Bahia spoke at least Yoruba and Hausa and often Nupe, Kanuri, and other languages, and they knew some Arabic, at least enough to say their prayers in Arabic because prayers could not be spoken in any other language. If they were males and had been Muslims in West Africa before reaching Bahia, they also knew how to read and write at least some Arabic. However, in Bahia, where Yoruba became the lingua franca, they might identify or be identified as Nagô, that is, Yoruba, no matter what other identifications might have been pertinent in their lives or continued to be. ʿAlī Eisami spoke at least Kanuri, Hausa, and Yoruba and wrote his autobiography in English and Kanuri. Similarly, Dorogu, who was enslaved in western Borno but who spoke Hausa as a first language, also knew Kanuri and learned both English and German. He wrote his autobiography in Hausa and provided numerous historical fragments, stories, and poems in Hausa that have been translated into English. Both ʿAlī Eisami and Dorugu had also studied Arabic in Qurʾānic school and knew enough Arabic to say their prayers and carry on rudimentary conversations in Arabic. This multilinguistic ability complicates simplistic efforts to establish ethnicity as a specific and narrowly defined feature. Ethnicity can be confused with the language people spoke as a means of communication in the absence of further analysis.

As discussed in chapter six, two patterns characterized the ways in which the jihad influenced the migration of enslaved Africans to the Americas, the first in the eighteenth century and the second in the nineteenth century. The narratives that originate in Senegambia including Fuuta Jalon largely date to the eighteenth century, while those from the central Bilād al-Sūdān focus on the nineteenth century, although there are exceptions. The temporal division reflects the phases of the jihād movement and the more extensive jihād of the nineteenth century that affected the region that became the Sokoto Caliphate and included the reformed government of Borno. However, the social and political conditions that sparked jihād existed throughout West Africa, and the jihād of the nineteenth century sent reverberations throughout the western

Bilād al-Sūdān. The period of intensified jihād in West Africa after around 1775 coincides with the chronology of the age of revolutions in the wider Atlantic world, but the causes of the jihād were unique to West Africa.

While the first phase of Islamic influence largely affected North America and the anglophone and francophone Caribbean, the second phase was connected with Bahia and Cuba. There were important parallels between the jihād movement and the age of revolutions that need to be explored, especially in relation to St. Domingue. St. Domingue was indeed a revolution, but the events in West Africa were also of such proportions that the impact was just as significant, especially in the central Bilād al-Sūdān between 1804–8 and 1817. They were parallel movements whose various manifestations caused reactions and resulted in changes that were sometimes contradictory and were not always consistent with the course of events more broadly. The historical silence with respect to the jihād movement arises largely from the failure to comprehend an Atlantic world that incorporates large parts of Africa into a common framework. The challenge to Atlantic studies concerns definitions of "revolution" and the relevance of historical events in understanding contemporary movements and possible influences that may have had overlapping precedents.

The forms of Muslim resistance to slavery in the Americas have to be understood in the context of jihād. The early contributions of scholars on this subject have been largely overlooked or misunderstood. The identification of Hausa and Yoruba as ethnic labels indicates an association with Islam in the interior of the Bight of Benin during the period leading to the outbreak of jihād and thereafter to its impact. As Manuel Barcia has demonstrated, the dominant paradigm associates resistance in the Americas with war, both in Cuba and Brazil, not with resistance and revolt. Barcia suggests that the jihād had a dramatic impact on both Cuba and Bahia in the ways in which participants articulated their actions.[29] Henry Lovejoy's analysis of shipping records and the Havana Court of Mixed Commission has revealed that non-Muslims of Oyo origin, including Yoruba from dependencies of Oyo that were disrupted and destroyed after 1817 and the subsequent spread of jihād in northern Yorubaland after 1823, went predominantly to Cuba, while more Muslims of Yoruba, Hausa, and other ethnic backgrounds were sent to Bahia.[30] The timing of enslavement and migration can be seen visually through animated mapping that correlates warfare in the interior of the Bight of Benin with estimates for slave departures from ports between Lagos and Little Popo.[31] The implications of these findings are enormous in challenging a Eurocentric perspective on the "age of revolutions" without reference to the jihād movement of West Africa during the same period. The context of Muslim influence extends to places other than Cuba and Brazil. We can look to the Muslim disturbance in Sierra Leone in the 1830s as well.[32] Efforts of Muslims in Trinidad to return to West Africa in the 1820s and early 1830s should also be seen in this light, as well as the possible role of Muslims in the Christmas uprising in Jamaica in 1831–32.[33]

Just as the revolutions in western Europe and the Americas were constitutional, often republican, in reaction against the *ancien régime* of despotic monarchy, jihād in West Africa was a response to the rule of despotic warlords through the establishment of Islamic governments that were based on religious leadership and consensus among Muslim officials.[34] Rule was conducted according to Islamic law and the precedent of inherited leadership, which relied on regimes with royal slaves. Because of these features, it is essential to determine whether there was an imam in Bahia at the time of the Malês uprising; in the context of jihād and the Islamic community, the recognition of an imam was essential to communal identity and religious observance. In the case of Bahia in 1835, the best evidence comes from Raimundo Nina Rodrigues at the end of the nineteenth century, who learned from the then imam in Bahia who the imam had been at the time of the uprising.[35]

There is an ongoing problem that is exposed in understanding why the jihād movement has been excluded from the history of the age of revolutions and why recognition of its imprint on the demography of transatlantic migration and the history of slave resistance in the Americas has been largely overlooked. A major omission in the scholarship of the African diaspora concerns the genesis of the Yoruba/Nagô/Lucumí/Aku diaspora and its relationship to jihād. Although there may have been exceptions, it appears that most if not all Yoruba in diaspora traced their origins to enslavement in the course of the jihād and the subsequent events after the destruction of the Oyo capital in 1835–36. However, the influence of Yoruba in diaspora finds its genesis in jihād after 1817 in Oyo, and indeed earlier still in 1810 in neighboring and formerly dependent Nupe and earlier yet, in 1804–8, when the governments of Gobir, Zamfara, Katsina, Kano, Zaria, Daura, and Kebbi were toppled. Why has the history of West Africa been relegated to a degree of obscurity penetrated only through specialized analysis that seems not to have affected an understanding of the Atlantic world? For some reason, a curtain of silence has often prevented this situated knowledge from extending into the study of the Atlantic world.

The intellectual community in Europe and the Americas knew so little about West Africa at the beginning of the age of revolutions in the late eighteenth century that its ignorance casts doubt on the extent of learning associated with the Enlightenment. Claims to a global world order were Eurocentric and did not incorporate the lands of Islam, and certainly not West Africa. The uprising in St. Domingue after 1791 and the establishment of Haiti as the first state to abolish slavery completely in 1804 marked a fundamental shift in the nature of slave resistance in the Americas. They coincided with the growth of the abolition movement in Europe, especially Britain and France, and therefore figured prominently in the age of revolutions. The subsequent period of a "second slavery" in the Americas, even as mainland Hispanic America achieved its independence and emancipated its enslaved populations, surely complicates the analysis of the age of revolutions, just as the jihād movement in West Africa and the intensification of slavery there also do. The inclusion of Islamic West Africa in the study of the Atlantic world confronts Eurocentric interpretations that entangle histories.

The biographical accounts of Muslims allow us to see a merging of worlds in which some West African Muslims ended up in slavery in the Americas despite the efforts at prevention. How did they respond? What did they do? Kabā, Baquaqua, and Sa'īd were learned young men when they were exposed to slavery. They endured hardships that were difficult but not insurmountable. There was every reason for them to rely on their faith, attributing their survival to their belief in the justice of Allāh and thereby attempting to practice their religion as conditions allowed. Their approach was different from that of those engaged in syncretism and creolization which emphasize accommodation under slavery. The portrayal of Yoruba and other religious forms of expression that adjusted under slavery, including the African-derived religious practices known as *abakuá, palo monte, candomblé,* and *vodun* or voodoo, demonstrates mixtures and hybrids that reflect adaptations and strategies of resistance. Muslims, too, had to adjust, of course, often by hiding their commitment to Islam. Nonetheless, it seems that often these men intended to adhere to their religion as Muslims. There was no interest in linking their beliefs to Christian saints and symbols. In its simplest form, the practice of Islam required no ornamentation. A place of prayer could be anywhere, and if water was not available for cleansing before prayer, sand could do. Rather than create elaborate renditions of cultural features of religion, Muslims were prone to disguise their religion, abstaining from the consumption of pork and alcohol, engaging in fasting during Ramaḍān as best they could, and praying in private, after sunset and before sunrise. The difficult part of being a Muslim or becoming a Muslim involved learning the prayers, which had to be in Arabic. Those who came from Africa and continued to pray remembered the prayers. How to convey that knowledge to young people when there were no Qur'ānic schools because they were not allowed was a challenge that often led to the disappearance of Islam. Hence the destruction of the mosque in Vitoría parish in November 1834 was a serious blow to the Muslim community in Bahia, but what is astonishing is that there had been a mosque, even if it was not publicly visible, where Muslims could pray.

How does it happen that an important slice of history is not inserted into the Atlantic world and the black Atlantic? The story of Muslims is especially relevant to the United States and Brazil and the Muslim presence was also important in Jamaica and Trinidad. What significance was there to the fact that immigration of Muslims to North America largely ended with the outbreak of jihād in the interior of the Bight of Benin, with the result that very few Yoruba came to North America before recent times? The Muslim presence in all parts of North America, whether Louisiana, South Carolina, and Georgia, the Tidewater, or the northern colonies and states, was similar and important despite the fact that far fewer Africans went to North America than to the Caribbean or Brazil. Hence where Muslims came from in West Africa is an important consideration of the demography of North America before 1808, just as it is for Bahia, especially after 1804. Admittedly, the number of enslaved Muslims resulting from the jihād movement was relatively small in terms of the total number of Africans forcibly sent to the Americas, but Muslims were concentrated in time and place. One of the major points of this book has been exploration of this entanglement. The movement of enslaved Africans was intimately connected with the events of African history. That is, African history was part of the Atlantic world and was not continental but global.

Why does it matter? Because understanding world history is essential. Jihād is a factor of history and affects the period well before 9/11 and the destruction of the World Trade Center in New York, which has become the crudest symbol of jihād in the modern era. This book has addressed the formative jihād of West Africa as a means of understanding the background to the current jihād that rules our lives from the Atlantic to the Indian Ocean and threatens innocent citizens in North America, Europe, the Middle East, southern Asia, and Africa. We are now indoctrinated to worry about the shoes of airline passengers, the danger of young girls being used as mules to carry explosive devices. This current jihād even targets travelers with disabilities through tight screening. In the process we have become indoctrinated to accept a world that is governed by the treat of terrorism.

The relevance of the jihād movement in West Africa today relates to the continuation of jihād as a viable expression of political discontent. This book has analyzed a phase in jihād. The Mahdism that occurred in the late nineteenth century, especially after 1884, was another phase in jihād that erupted in the 1880s in the Nilotic Sudan and then spread across West Africa in the 1890s and continued through the first years of colonial imposition in Nigeria, Cameroon, and elsewhere. This phase of Mahdism was supposedly suppressed by the 1930s, at least in West Africa, but the resurgence of jihād in areas of Nigeria and Cameroon where Mahdism was prominent suggests otherwise. The interconnections with jihād elsewhere in the world today extend from al-Qaeda to northern Mali and the war in the Sahara after the fall of Muammar Gaddafi in Libya, the Arab spring, and the emergence of the Islamic State of Iraq and Syria. Boko Haram is a deadly manifestation that builds on a tradition of Maitatsine in the 1980s. These contemporary forms are different in their Salafist commitment and their rejection of the Sufism that underlay the jihād movement of the eighteenth and nineteenth centuries.

Atlantic History, Jihād, and the Course of History

The inclusion of the jihād movement of West Africa in the discussion of the age of revolutions requires the reconceptualization of Atlantic history and how we discuss slavery during the period. The parameters of Atlantic history need to be broadened to include the areas in Africa that were connected to the Atlantic world through the migration of Africans under conditions of slavery. This wider paradigm means that the events in the coastal states of West Africa that were not Muslim have to be examined in the context of global revolutionary change. Moreover, the South Atlantic that integrated Portuguese, Brazilian, and African influences into a transatlantic sphere of interaction has to be related to the revolutionary changes of the era through an analysis that demonstrates significant differences from the jihād states and their withdrawal from the Atlantic world. How are we to understand global change from the end of the eighteenth century through the middle of the nineteenth century without taking into consideration the crucial flow of labor from Africa to the Americas at the same time as the era experienced revolutionary change, restoration reaction, and Muslim withdrawal? As the history of the jihād movement makes clear, the expansion of slavery not only was a phenomenon of the southern United States, Cuba, and Brazil but also characterized the jihād states. The coastal regions of West Africa that were not subjected to jihād also experienced a second slavery that was tied to the shift from the export of slaves to the export of so-called legitimate commodities, specifically palm oil and other agricultural products. West central Africa also witnessed an increase in the use of slaves domestically, although because Angola was shielded from the measures to suppress the transatlantic slave trade longer than West Africa, the second slavery was much less prominent and occurred later than elsewhere in Africa.

Just as events in the Americas reveal a struggle between resistance to slavery and efforts to sustain what some had thought a dying institution, events in Africa reflect the great expansion in slavery, not its demise, so that the focus on revolutionary change in relation to resistance to slavery has to take into account the origins and destinations of the enslaved population, whether that population remained in Africa or went to the Americas. The West African experience enters the important debate about what Tomich has suggested was a "second slavery" in which slavery in the Americas was anything but a dying institution.[36] Rather, in Tomich's view, slavery increased in the early nineteenth century thanks to a new political order largely imposed by the British after the fall of Napoleon. Hence the parallel in the great expansion of slavery with jihād in West Africa requires an approach that incorporates global Africa.

Debates over slavery reflect perspectives that are situated in specific historical and cultural contexts. In western European thought, enlightened rationalism came to legitimize slavery by referring to natural science and defining the "nature" of Africans as a race as inferior. Inevitably, appeals for the abolition of slavery also focused on race, initially outlawing the import of more enslaved blacks into the Americas and later freeing black slaves but not subsequently allowing or encouraging the migration of free blacks to the Americas, other than a brief experiment with indentured labor. However, in the Islamic context, the debate over slavery related to its legitimacy as centered on religion and not race. The Islamic debate concentrated on cultural and social categories to justify slavery rather than on biological or phenotypic distinctions. Both the European and the Islamic debates claimed universality, although each was dependent on incomplete and culturally filtered bodies of knowledge. Hence the abolition of the slave trade across the Atlantic, and then by extension elsewhere, and the struggle to emancipate slaves, but through a variety of means, such as apprenticeship, emancipation of the womb, and compensation for slave owners for the loss of "property," must be seen as more than products of the European Enlightenment and the concern for the "rights of man" as articulated in the French Revolution and the Christian-based reform movement in Britain that underlay the abolition of the Atlantic slave trade. Such a partial perspective overlooks the concern within West Africa about the legitimacy of enslavement and the assumption that Muslims were freeborn unless proven otherwise, with the burden of proof the responsibility of the master or merchant claiming that an individual was a slave, not on the necessity of the slave providing proof of freedom. The intensification of enslavement in the jihād states, especially in the nineteenth century, parallels the more extensive use of slaves in Cuba, Brazil, and the southern United States. I have argued that the jihād movement has to be included in the discussion of the age of revolutions because of the issue of slavery. There were two countervailing trends in relation to slavery during the age of revolutions: first, the ending of slavery, whether radically, as in St. Domingue, or more gradually, as in British possessions; and second, an intensification of slavery in some places, such as Cuba, the southern United States, Brazil, and, as one must now acknowledge, the jihād states of West Africa.

It is not clear why Atlantic history has emerged as a focus of historical inquiry without incorporating African history more centrally into the nexus of analysis, especially by following individuals from specific contexts in Africa into diaspora. The focus here begins in Africa and thereby provides another perspective on the Atlantic that requires an understanding of the African context in very specific ways.[37] These efforts at historical reconstruction necessitate a correlation of ethnicity as represented in diaspora manifestations of "nation" and "country of origin" with specific locations in Africa and the consequences of historical circumstances. How did people get where they went, and why did they get caught up in the slave trade? How was it that west central Africa, the Bight of Biafra, and southeastern Africa came to supply two-thirds of the enslaved population sent to the Americas in the nineteenth century? The predominant Atlantic focus needs to be informed by the historical context of the slave migration and the resulting impact and response in Africa as well as the adjustments that occurred in the Americas. I argue that a revisionist approach to the study of slavery in Africa and the Americas requires a reconceptualization of Atlantic studies.[38]

Reconceptualizing Slavery and Atlantic History

The scholarly interest in slavery and the African diaspora needs to include an examination of what was happening in different parts of Africa. How this is analyzed historically requires a clear chronology and geographical focus. The relations with Europe clearly should be articulated within an historical discourse that is global. Such a perspective recognizes that planters and other slave owners in the Americas moved between colony and homeland and that their relatives were to be found throughout the empire, even sometimes on the coast of Africa. Similarly, the enslaved population was global, as revealed in the networks of Muslims. In fact, even though the ruptures of slavery isolated individuals from their kin, they still had kin, and it is essential to consider what was happening to those kin and the states and societies from which they came during their period of slavery in the Americas. Does the rupture of their lives mean that West Africa was cut off from the Atlantic world, left behind on the continent and effectively outside what is described as the "Atlantic world"? Did the Atlantic world include West Africa, and if so, how was that manifested? I contend here that an analysis of the jihād movement demonstrates that West Africa was outside the Atlantic world through conscious design, and hence, as Hobsbawm thought in defining the geographical extent of the world that he was analyzing in his examination of the age of revolutions, West Africa and indeed all of Africa and Asia were beyond its influence.

It is now well recognized that the study of slavery in the Americas requires an understanding of specific context in terms of chronology and locality, including whether or not the enslaved population was living on plantations or in urban areas. Moreover, the great expansion in the incidence of slavery in the southern United States, Cuba, and Brazil warrants comparison with earlier periods, such as the conditions in Spanish colonies during the period of Bourbon reforms. Similarly, a study of slavery in Africa during the era of transatlantic slavery calls for a nuanced treatment of time and place. As the demographic analysis presented in this book demonstrates, there were some enslaved Muslims who were sold to coastal merchants and thereby entered the transatlantic slave trade, but the number was relatively few, especially when considering the scale of slavery within the Muslim states of the interior. West central Africa and the Bight of Biafra together accounted for the overwhelming majority of the enslaved migration from Africa, especially in the nineteenth century. In these regions, the influence of Islam was either marginal or non-existent.

Despite the fact that millions of Africans left West Africa, almost nothing was known in Europe about the interior until the end of the eighteenth century. Thereafter, several expeditions sponsored by European governments traveled across the Sahara and inland from the Atlantic to establish relations and undertake geographical, linguistic, and anthropological research on a region of the world that lay behind a curtain of ignorance. European fascination with geography and the interior of West Africa coincided with the age of revolutions. One of the signs of a divided world was the nonrecognition of sources of information unless Europeans actually personally observed places and things. Historically, the Atlantic world was built on an ignorance of Africa, as if it was better not to know too much about the people who were being enslaved. The coastal waters of West Africa were charted and given suitable names as if the lands were unknown and unpopulated. Local knowledge was in fact important, especially in piloting in the few places along the African coast where vessels might actually be able to find anchorage, but knowledge of local societies and states was haphazard and impressionistic. The interior was terra incognita, and this served the intentions of the jihād states of West Africa to maintain autonomy and protected the commercial interests of coastal merchants. While the knowledge of the Senegal River, the Gambia, and the mouths of the various rivers of the upper Guinea Coast, including Rio Pongo, Rio Nuñez, and the Sierra Leone River, exposed the Muslim interior, the boundary was sharply delimited so that Europeans knew almost nothing about the interior. Along much of the West African coast, including the Gold Coast, the Bight of Benin, and the Bight of Biafra, there were virtually no harbors, so that ships had to anchor offshore and rely on local canoes to navigate the rough currents of the coast. Only Bonny, in the Niger delta, and Calabar, on the Cross River, had sufficient anchorage, and both of these ports were largely beyond contact with the Muslim interior until the early nineteenth century.

How communication was managed in West Africa depended on status and occupation. Merchants were inevitably closely associated with Arabic because of links with the Muslim scholars and teachers in the towns of West Africa and the association of respectability with Islamic learning. Merchants one day might retire and dedicate their time to scholarship. Families often singled out one son for education and higher learning in jurisprudence, astronomy, or even history. Normal communication was not done in Arabic, except with respect to religion. Otherwise, a dominant commercial language prevailed over large parts of West Africa: Malinke in the western Bilād al-Sūdān and Hausa in the central Bilād al-Sūdān. Moreover, the factors and landlords on the coast spoke local languages, and sometimes Hausa or Malinke/Juula, and they clearly had to know the appropriate European languages—French,

English, or Portuguese. One of the functions of merchants resident at the coast was to serve as intermediaries who facilitated exchange across linguistic frontiers. Hence, if they did not know the dominant languages of the commercial interior, they had to employ interpreters who did. The linguistic configuration of the interior with respect to trade relied on the two languages, Hausa and the commercial tongue Juula, which was in fact mutually intelligible to Malinke and other Manding languages, with Arabic providing legal and religious texts that were essential in the functioning of Muslim societies and commerce.

Inevitably, appeals for the abolition of slavery in the Americas focused on race, initially outlawing the import of more enslaved blacks into the Americas and later freeing black slaves, while the Islamic debate concentrated on cultural and social categories rather than on biological distinctions. Both the European and the Islamic debates claimed universality, although each was dependent on incomplete and culturally filtered bodies of knowledge. A partial perspective that focuses on Europe and the Americas overlooks the discussion within West Africa over the legitimacy of enslavement and therefore ignores the efforts of Islamic governments to develop their own slavery policies.

In consolidating a field of research that focuses on the Atlantic, even the Black Atlantic, scholars have neglected how Africa fits into the paradigm of world history. While we understand the origins and development of ethnic-based "nations" in the Americas, including European and African ethnic identities, and distinguish between African-born populations and creole/mulatto/mestizo societies that variously emerged in Brazil, the Caribbean, mainland Hispanic America, and North America, there has been a neglect of how the processes of change that were unleashed by the expansion of slavery in the Americas altered and otherwise influenced in the course of history in Africa. The challenge goes beyond the insights of Hobsbawm and Genovese to address the field of Atlantic studies. The focus here expands on the contributions of Paul Gilroy, Ira Berlin, Gwendolyn Midlo Hall, Jane Landers, and others in understanding how the emergence of a black Atlantic related to Islamic West Africa.[39] While transnational and broad in perspective, the influences emanating from Africa and the impact on Africa are transnational and broad in perspective and become factors in analysis. Bernard Bailyn and David Brion Davis, among others, have focused on the expansion and consolidation of European settler control of the Atlantic world, while the study of the jihād movement that has been examined here breaks through a curtain of silence with respect to the relationship of the jihād states to transatlantic African migration.[40] Although Atlantic history has emerged in a form that recognizes that the overwhelming number of people who crossed the Atlantic before the middle of the nineteenth century came from Africa, not Europe, the implications for understanding historical change in Africa have not always been addressed. When African participation is introduced, usually as a contributing factor in slave resistance, sense of community, and commercial involvement, there is seldom an effort to connect these influences with local historical developments in Africa. This study has demonstrated an approach that incorporates Africa into the black Atlantic through an analysis of the extent to which Islamic West Africa attempted to remain outside that world.

The implications of the jihād movement have been apparent to specialists of West Africa for some time. As Murray Last has observed, jihād was as important to West African history as the French Revolution to Europe and, by extension, the Americas. The Islamic reform movement in West Africa gave rise to the largest unitary state in nineteenth-century Africa, the Sokoto Caliphate. It inspired a literature greater in quantity and higher in learning than previously known south of the Sahara. It laid down conditions for generating one of the most productive indigenous economies in West Africa in the nineteenth century.[41] Last realized that the timing and direction of West African reformist thought paralleled the European and Christian worlds, and that the period 1775–1850 witnessed upheavals and new ideas in many parts of the Islamic world, as well as in Europe and the Americas. Last proposed that there is a need to "examine the underlying causes of these changes and the ways by which they might have affected West Africa"—and, as argued here, how the events of West Africa shaped or did not shape events in the Americas and whether or not West Africa can be incorporated into a conception of the Atlantic world that includes Africa.

This study suggests that Atlantic history can be redefined as a focus of historical inquiry by incorporating African history into the nexus of analysis. As in the work of Walter Hawthorne, James Sweet, and other scholars who have attempted to redress this distortion, the focus on individuals has allowed an analysis that begins in Africa in specific historical contexts, as best as can be reconstructed.[42] By following individuals, such as Baquaqua, Kabā Saghanughu, and others, it is possible to cross the Atlantic in a manner that introduces a perspective that requires an understanding of the African context in very specific ways. This study suggests that Atlantic history can be redefined as a focus of historical inquiry that incorporates African history into the analysis. By following individuals, such as Baquaqua, Kabā Saghanughu, and others, it is possible to reconstruct historical change. The correlation of ethnicity as represented in diaspora through designations of "nation" and "country of origin" with historical context provides a more nuanced understanding of Atlantic history. Such an approach to historical reconstruction has profound implications for how Africa can be integrated into Atlantic studies, specifically during the age of revolutions.[43]

Are the various individuals who were Muslims to be considered conscious actors in the events of their times? Did they understand their participation in an age of revolutions? I contend that they did so as much as anyone. Their perspective was foremost one of jihād in West Africa. Did they know about St. Domingue and the emergence of Haiti or the Congress of Vienna and the reaction to revolution? In most cases, they probably did not, or they had a distorted view at best. Did they know about the jihād movement and its ramifications? Probably they knew much more than some scholars have thought. It may be doubtful that Baquaqua knew about the Malês uprising, but those he had to interact with in Pernambuco and Rio de Janeiro did know, and they treated him accordingly. In part because of this experience, Baquaqua ended up promoting abolition in North America. Al-Baghdādī had no idea that there were Muslims in Brazil when he arrived in Rio de Janeiro in 1865, but once he knew, he remained in Brazil and tried to mentor the community. Madden was surprised to find Muslims in Jamaica in 1834. He might not have condoned the involvement of Muslims in the Christmas uprising, but he tried to engage the Muslim community nonetheless.

It is clear that the jihād of West Africa was reflected in the Americas in ways that usually have been overlooked because Eurocentrism has precluded a consideration of other perspectives. But Muslims in Jamaica at the time of emancipation in 1834 and Muslims in the United States from the 1840s through the1860s are reflected in the details of Kabā's life, Baquaqua's odyssey, Sa'īd's participation in the Civil War, and the mission of Martin Delaney to West Africa and then his enlistment of blacks in the Civil War. Are the Muslims in Sierra Leone and Trinidad to be written out of history, or are they to be incorporated into a reassessment of the Atlantic world? In the mid-nineteenth century the Reverend Samuel Ajayi Crowther, Anglican bishop, adopted Muslim nomenclature, "Yoruba," as a common ethnic and linguistic designation that has persisted, supplanting the term "Aku" used in Sierra Leone and ultimately replacing the use of "Lucumī in Cuba and "Nagô" in Brazil. Samuel Johnson consolidated the usage of "Yoruba" in writing his influential *History of the Yoruba*; is Muslim influence to be ignored and misrepresented? The trajectory of abolition did not just include West Africa and flows of influence across the Atlantic but also extended beyond the Sahara and elsewhere in the Muslim world to the Mahdist state in the Nilotic Sudan. These links tie the world together from the central Bilād al-Sūdān to elsewhere in West Africa, so that the Muslim regions of sub-Saharan Africa provide a unique perspective that counters a focus on the European age of revolutions and Atlantic resistance to slavery. The Islamic lands of West Africa, the continuation of slavery under Muslim governance, and the ultimate transition to French, British, and German imperial conquest have to be incorporated into a reconceptualized worldview. Such a view of the Atlantic world, and indeed the black Atlantic, confronts the countries of origin from which the majority of the population in the Americas derived their roots and explains why the demography of migration did not include more people from West Africa. This approach to slavery and the origins of the African population of the Americas reveals historical links that counter the analysis of Orlando Patterson and others who emphasize social death.[44]

The irony, of course, is that West Africa borders the Atlantic, and indeed its shores define the eastern boundary of the Atlantic. Yet the study of the Atlantic world has been largely Eurocentric and has not included Atlantic Africa. Because the jihād movement was a major historical phenomenon in the regions of the broader Atlantic basin and interacted with the transatlantic world, the aim here has been to reconceptualize Atlantic history. Another conception of the Atlantic extends to the expansive beach of the sandy Sahara, as can be seen in the ways in which the Muslim regions of West Africa helped establish the contours of what the Atlantic world became through a consideration of resistance to incorporation and the quest for autonomy. The level of ignorance of jihād in West Africa extends to a wider public. Jihād has meaning today, which calls for an appreciation of the relationship, or lack of relationship, between the "age of revolutions" and the "age of jihād."

A reconceptualization of slavery also requires an understanding that the issue of slavery was a fundamental issue of jihād, which affected the past and extends to the contemporary world. Individuals have been considered "enslavable" if they opposed jihād, and if they protested or attempted to resist. The terror involved in the imposition of such a world order is apparent today; it was less obvious in the past because the victims of jihād were often voiceless. The modern terrorist group in Nigeria, Boko Haram, can be seen as a continuation of the radical Islamic factor of jihād, particularly the manifestations of Mahdism in the 1890s and the first three decades of the twentieth century, with the important difference that the current jihād movement opposes Sufism and champions Salafist conceptions of puritanism. During the colonial conquest the Mahdists were defeated in Borno and retreated to the subemirates of Adamawa from Madagali south to Garoua, where they maintained a reign of terror against defenseless communities in the hills and mountains who were raided for slaves and whose boys were castrated, at a loss of nine boys for every ten who were castrated. The Mahdists were involved in the "manufacture" of eunuchs through raids on communities that were considered pagan well into the 1930s. Madagali, which has since been subjected to the terror that the emirate once perpetrated, was the home base from which Emir Hamman Yaji operated in the 1920s in conducting his reign of terror against non-Muslims who had attempted to escape his outrageous policy of castration.[45] The links with Boko Haram can be found in the continued appeal to the mass of dispossessed young men who have everything to gain in a movement of pillage and self-glorification. Boko Haram attacks "western education" as the symbolic enemy of Islam, but one is met with a typical Hausa response that claims Boko Khalak, that is, "education is *khalak*," lawful, not *ḥarām* or prohibited.

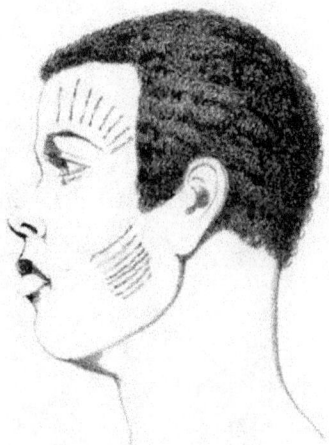

PLATE 19. (*top left*) ʿUmar ibn Saʿīd of Fuuta Toro. Courtesy of the Davidson College Archives, North Carolina

PLATE 20. (*bottom left*) Ibrahima ʿAbd al-Raḥmān, engraving of crayon drawing by Henry Imman, New York, 1828, in *The Colonizationist and Journal of Freedom* (Boston: G.W. Light, 1834, frontispiece)

PLATE 21. (*top right*) So Allah. *Source:* Francis de Castelnau, *Renseignements sur l'Afrique centrale et sur une nation d'hommes à queue qui s'y trouverait, d'après le rapport des nègres du Soudan, esclaves à Bahia* (Paris: Librairie P. Bertrand, 1851), Planche Troisième, Figure Deuxième.

LE MARCHÉ DES ESCLAVES
ET LA CONTREBANDE DES ARMES A TRIPOLI

PLATE 22. (*above*) Tripoli Slave Market. *Source: Le Petit Journal*, Paris, 15 October 1911

PLATE 23. (*opposite page*) Salvador, Bahia. *Source: View of the City of Bahia in the Brazils, South America—pictorial work* (293 mm x 726 mm) by George Johann Scharf (1788–1860). (1826), Legends by Edmund Patten; Drawn on Stone by G Scharf, from a Sketch by Edmund Patten, taken on the Water at a Distance of half a Mile / Published by Edmund Patten June 18th 1826 / Printed by C Hullmande, In: The British Museum, http://collection .britishmuseum.org/resource?uri=http://collection.britishmuseum.org/id/object/PPA136250

A VIEW OF THE CITY OF BAHIA IN THE BRAZILS, SOUTH AMERICA.

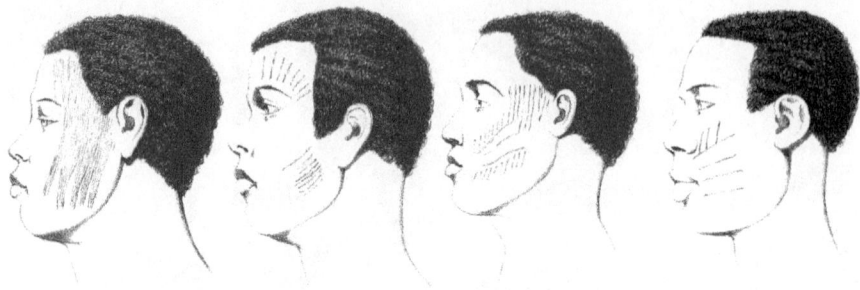

PLATE 24. (*top*) Muslims in Bahia. *Source:* Francis de Castelnau, *Renseignements sur l'Afrique centrale et sur une nation d'hommes à queue qui s'y trouverait, d'après le rapport des nègres du Soudan, esclaves à Bahia* (Paris: Librairie P. Bertrand, 1851), Planche Troisiéme, Figure Première, Deuxième, Trosième and Planche Quatrième, Figure Deuxième.

PLATE 25. (*bottom*) Hausa Porters in Bahia. *Source:* Alcide Dessalines d'Orbigny, *Voyage pittoresque dans les deux Amériques* (Paris: L. Tenré, 1836), facing p. 150, fig. 3

PLATE 26. (*top, opposite page*) Mahommah Gardo Baquaqua. *Source:* Samuel Moore, *Biography of Mahommah G. Baquaqua, a Native of Zoogoo, in the Interior of Africa* (Detroit: Geo. E. Pomeroy, 1854), frontispiece

PLATE 27. (*bottom, opposite page*) Bello's Map of the Sokoto Caliphate. *Source:* Dixon Denham, Hugh Clapperton, and Walter Oudney, *Narrative of Discoveries in Northern and Central Africa* (London: John Murray, 1826), Vol. 2, 330

MAHOMMAH G. BAQUAQUA,
Engraved by J. G. Darby, from a Daguerreotype by Sutton

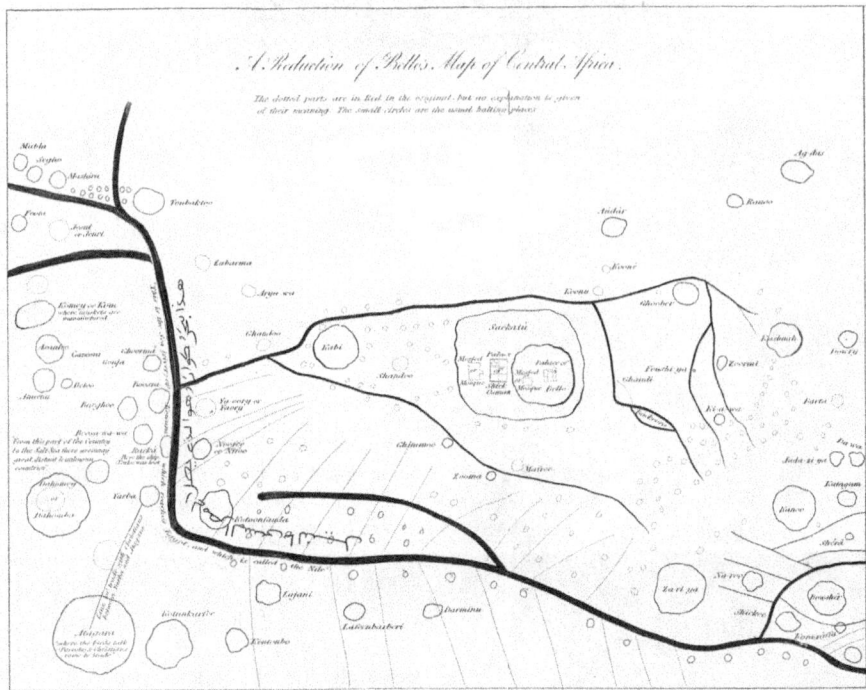

A Reduction of Bello's Map of Central Africa.

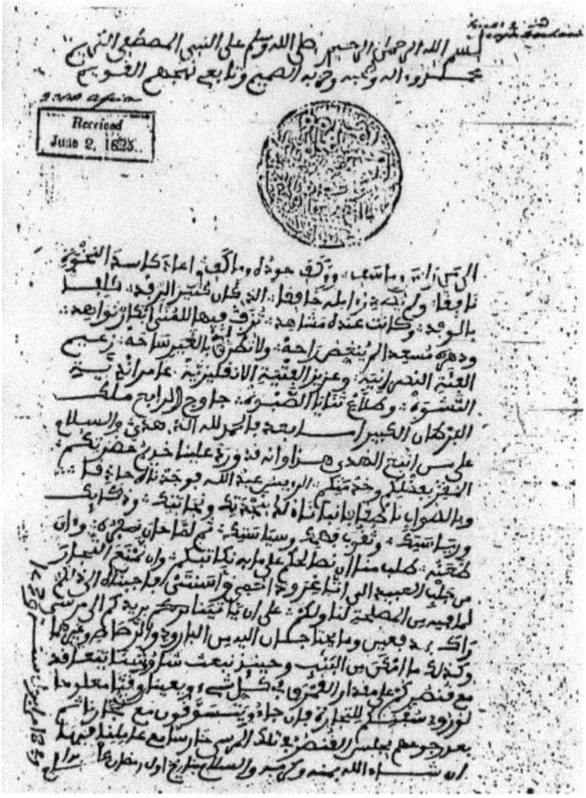

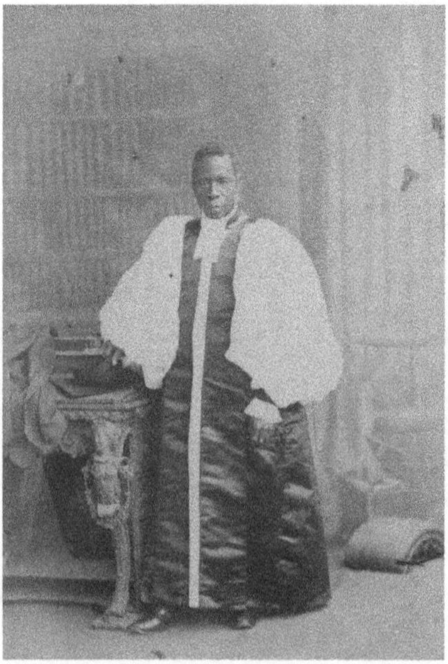

PLATE 28. (*top*) Bello-Clapperton Accord on Slave Trade. *Source:* Jamie Bruce Lockhart and Paul E. Lovejoy, eds., *Hugh Clapperton into the Interior of Africa: Records of the Second Expedition 1825–1827* (Leiden: Brill, 2005), 444

PLATE 29. (*left*) Bishop Samuel Crowther. *Source:* University of Birmingham, Cadbury Research Library, Special Collections, CMS/ACC314/Z1

ALI EISAMI GAZIRMA.

PLATE 30. Ali Eisami (William Harding). *Source:* Basel Mission Archives, Basel,
Switzerland, Basel Mission Holdings, ref. no. QQ-30.005.0115, Rev. Koelle's language teacher

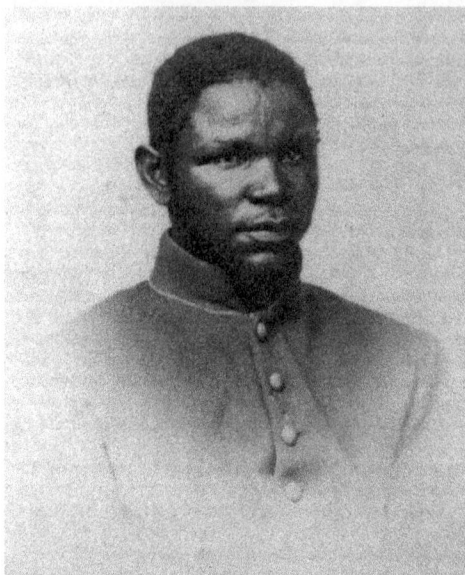

PLATE 31. (*left*) Sergeant Nicholas Said (Mohammed Ali Sa'id). *Source:* Massachusetts Historical Society, Boston, Wolcott Family Civil War carte de visite album, Nicholas Said carte de visite, circa 1863–1866, Photo. 70.93, http://www.masshist.org/database/2692

PLATE 32. (*bottom*) Will of Richard Pierpoint. *Source:* Archives of Ontario, RG 22-235, Lincoln County Surrogate Court Estate Files, Microfilm MS 8416

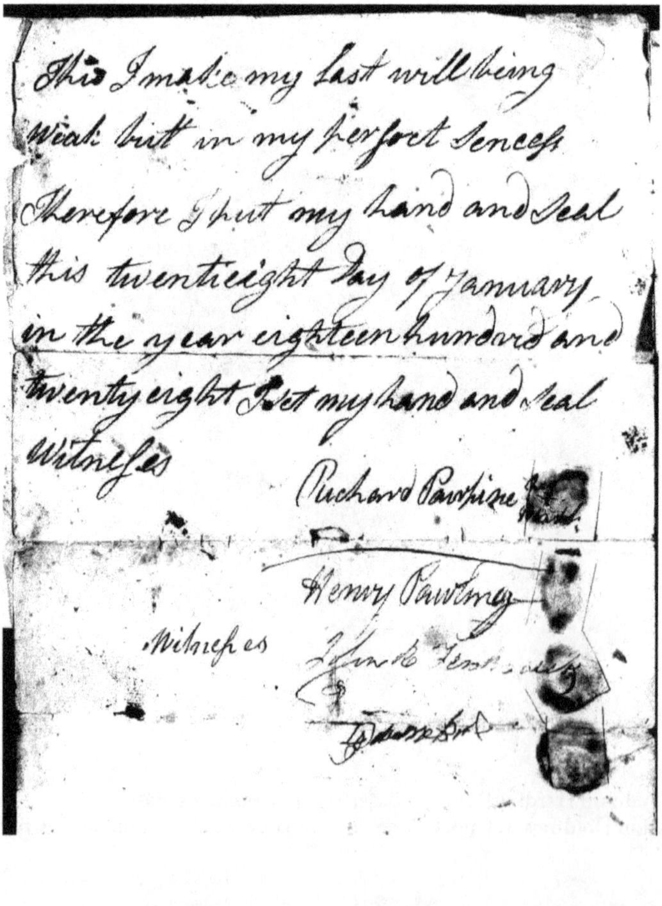

This I make my last will being
weak but in my perfect sences
Therefore I put my hand and seal
this twentieight day of January
in the year eighteen hundred and
twenty eight I set my hand and seal
Witnesses

Richard Pawpine

Henry Pawling

Witnesses

APPENDIX
Population Estimates for the Sokoto Caliphate, ca. 1905–15

Although it is generally accepted that the Sokoto Caliphate was the largest state in Africa at the end of the nineteenth century, there is considerable dispute over the size of its population, the proportion of slave to free inhabitants, and even the number of constituent emirates and districts in the state. According to Modibbo Tukur, the size of the Sokoto Caliphate in 1900 was approximately 150,000 square miles (388,500 square kilometers), although his estimate does not include the parts of Adamawa in Cameroon, whose area has been estimated at 100,000 square kilometers.[1] There were thirty emirates in the caliphate at the end of the nineteenth century, not including the twin capitals of Sokoto and Gwandu.[2] According to Yusufu Bala Usman, these included Daura, Katsina, Kano, Zazzau (Zaria), Bida, Agaie, Lapai, Lafiagi, Shonga, Ilorin, Fombina (Adamawa), Bauchi, Muri (Hammanruwa), Gombe, Kazaure, Katagum, Hadejia, Jama'are, Missau, Jema'a, Kontagora, and nine to the west of Gwandu, including Junju, located in Dendi country, on the left bank of the Niger River, near the confluence with Dallol Mawri; Birnin Gaoure, located in Dallol Bosso; Say, on the right bank of the Niger; Kunari, with its capital at Wuro, located west of the Niger River; Gelajo, located approximately forty kilometers west of Say; Torodi, with its capital at Lamorde, located twenty kilometers west of Kunari; Bitinkogi, with its capital at Lamorde, on the right bank of the Niger River opposite Niamey, the French colonial capital; Yaga, in Burkino Faso, with its capital at Sebba, southwest of Tera and southeast of Dori; and the westernmost emirate, Liptako, also in Burkina Faso, with its capital at Dori.

A number of emirates had autonomous subemirates under them. Fombina had forty subemirates, including Cheboa, Tibati, Ngaoundere, Banyo, Malabu, Rai-Buba, Song, Zummo, Gola, Holma, Pakorgel, Maroua, Bogo, Kobotshi, Laro, Belel, Daware, Mayo-Farang, Sorau, Madagali, Gider, Michika, Moda, Mubi, Uba, Mindif, Binder, Ridadu, Bibemi, Kalfu, Be, Demsa (Cisiga), Vokna, Tola, Agorma, Pette, Wuro Mayo-Najarendi, Mbere, Garoua, and Balala, with the capital at Yola on the Benue River. Zaria had eight fairly large subemirates, including Kajuru, Kadara, Kauru, Kagarko, and Doma, as well as Jema'a, Keffi, and Kwatto, which became separate emirates under British rule.[3] Bauchi had ten subemirates in addition to numerous less autonomous districts, including Kirfi, Fali, Ganjuwa, Zungur, Jama'a, Toro, Lere, Lafia, Wase, and Darazo.[4] Both the capital districts, Sokoto and Gwandu, ruled over the formerly independent territories of Kebbi, Zamfara, and Gobir, which had several subemirates within their domains. The Tuareg federation, centered at Agades in the Air Massif, and Adar, located north of Sokoto, had unique relationships with Sokoto, whether or not they are counted as an integral part of the state. No population estimates are presented for Adar and Agades.

British colonial statistics, as summarized by M. G. Smith, suggest that there were 9 million people in the Protectorate of Northern Nigeria in 1901, of whom 6 million were Muslim.[5] Polly Hill has stated that "the first population 'census' of Northern Nigeria, that of 1911, was no more than an 'informed guess'—the original total of 8.1 million having been later raised to 9.2 million."[6] A second census of the Northern Provinces was conducted in 1921, at which time the recorded population was 10.0 million.[7] Hill rightly points out that these estimates represented serious undercounting because the compilation was associated with tax collection, included estimates on the size of families, and relied on poorly trained and insufficient staff. The 1921 census also included a large population that had never been part of the Sokoto Caliphate.

C. L. Temple also estimated the population on the basis of tax assessment reports up to 1916, and his estimates are included in the table A.1. Smith notes that the population of Northern Zaria was estimated at 200,000 in 1900, and that there were 100,000 slaves in Northern Zaria.[8] According to S. F. Nadel, Bida Emirate had a population of 171,958 in 1921, while Agaie and Lapai had 52,000 people, and there were also 64,600 Nupe in Ilorin Province and 233,000 Nupe in Niger Province.[9] The estimated population of Liptako was 80,000.[10] Scattered returns, of varying degrees of accuracy, can be cited for all the emirates and the capital districts of Sokoto and Gwandu.[11] Estimates for the subemirates of Adamawa, which were located in German Kamerun, were perhaps as high as 400,000. Hence the total estimate for the taxable population was at least 6 million.

TABLE A.1. Population Estimates for the Sokoto Caliphate, ca. 1905–15

Districts[a]	Estimated Population
Sokoto	1,094,000
Gwandu	249,000
Emirates	
Katsina	441,000
Kano	1,788,000
Zazzau	462,000[b]
Daura	47,000
Yola	45,000[c]
Adamawa subemirates	400,000
Bauchi	531,000[d]
Muri	170,000
Gombe	160,000
Bida	24,000
Agaie	29,000
Lapai	33,000
Lafiagi	30,000
Shonga	8,000
Ilorin	200,000
Kazaure	28,000–34,000
Katagum	189,000
Hadejia	115,000
Jama'are	19,000
Missau	90,000
Kontagora	120,000
Liptako	37,000[e]
Western Emirates (Junji, Say, Kunari, Birnin Gaoure, Yaga, Torodi, Bitimi Kogi)	180,000
Total	6,589,000

[a] These population estimates derive largely from O. Temple and C. L. Temple, *Notes on the Tribes, Provinces, Emirates and States of the Northern Provinces of Nigeria* (Lagos: C.M.S. Bookshop, 1922), except for the eight western emirates, whose estimated population was 180,000, according to French colonial sources.

[b] Zazzau includes Zaria, 404,000; Jema'a, 33,000; and Keffi, 25,000.

[c] Yola only, not including the many subemirates.

[d] The Bauchi estimate includes Bauchi itself, 478,000; Wase, 11,000; and Lafia, 42,000.

[e] The estimated population of Liptako was 80,000 according to Paul Irwin, *Liptako Speaks: History from Oral Tradition in Africa* (Princeton, NJ: Princeton University Press, 1981), 15.

NOTES

Introduction

1. An earlier version of the arguments in this book was presented in a paper at the conference "Les résistances à l'esclavage dans le monde atlantique français à l'ère des Révolutions (1750–1850)," McGill University, Montreal, 3–4 May 2013. A revised version of this paper was published as "*Jihād* na África Ocidental durante a 'Era das Revoluções'—Rumo a um Diálogo com Eric Hobsbawm e Eugene Genovese," *Topoi: Revista de História* 15, no. 28 (2014): 22–67. The basic thrust of these arguments expands on *Transformations in Slavery: A History of Slavery in Africa* (Cambridge: Cambridge University Press), first published in 1983 and now in its third edition (2011), and my earlier discussion in 1979 at a conference organized by Michael Craton; see Paul E. Lovejoy, "Indigenous African Slavery," in *Roots and Branches: Current Directions in Slave Studies*, ed. Michael Craton,(Toronto: Pergamon Press, 1979), 19–61, originally published in *Historical Reflections / Réflexions Historiques* 6, no. 1 (1979), 19–61, with commentaries by Igor Kopytoff and Frederick Cooper, 62–83.

2. See Paul Lubeck, "Islamic Protest under Semi-industrial Capitalism: Yan Tatsine Explained," *Africa: The Journal of the International African Institute* 54, no. 4 (1985): 369–89; and William Hansen, "Boko Haram: Religious Radicalism and Insurrection in Northern Nigeria," *Journal of Asian and African Studies* (2015): 1–19.

3. See especially Paul E. Lovejoy and Steven Baier, "The DesertSide Economy of the Central Sudan," *International Journal of African Historical Studies* 8, no. 4 (1975): 551–81; reprinted in *Drought in the Sahel: The Politics of a Natural Disaster*, ed. Michael Glantz (New York: Praeger, 1976), 145–75; Paul E. Lovejoy and J. S. Hogendorn, "Slave Marketing in West Africa," in *The Uncommon Market: Essays in the Economic History of the Atlantic Slave Trade*, ed. Henry Gemery and J. S. Hogendorn (New York: Academic Press, 1979), 213–35; Paul E. Lovejoy, "The Characteristics of Plantations in the Nineteenth-Century Sokoto Caliphate (Islamic West Africa)," *American Historical Review* 85, no. 5 (1979): 1267–92; Lovejoy, "The Internal Trade of West Africa, 1450–1800," in *History of West Africa*, rev. ed., ed. J. F. A. Ajayi and Michael Crowder (London: Longman Group, 1985), 1:640–90; Lovejoy, "The Central Sudan and the Atlantic Slave Trade," in *Paths toward the Past: African Historical Essays in Honor of Jan Vansina*, ed. Robert W. Harms, Joseph C. Miller, David C. Newbury, and Michelle D. Wagner (Atlanta: African Studies Association Press, 1994), 345–70; Lovejoy, "Background to Rebellion: The Origins of Muslim Slaves in Bahia," *Slavery and Abolition* 15, no. 2 (1994): 151–80; Paul E. Lovejoy and David Richardson, "Competing Markets for Male and Female Slaves: Slave Prices in the Interior of West Africa, 1780–1850," *International Journal of African Historical Studies* 28, no. 2 (1995): 261–93; Paul E. Lovejoy, "The Clapperton-Bello Exchange: The

Sokoto *Jihād* and the Trans-Atlantic Slave Trade, 1804–1837," in *The Desert Shore: Literatures of the African Sahel*, ed. Christopher Wise (Boulder, CO: Lynne Rienner, 2000), 201–28; Lovejoy, ed., *Identity in the Shadow of Slavery* (London: Continuum, 2000); Lovejoy, "The Black Atlantic in the Construction of the 'Western' World: Alternative Approaches to the 'Europeanization' of the Americas," in *The Historical Practice of Diversity: Transcultural Interactions from the Early Modern Mediterranean to the Postcolonial World*, ed. Dirk Hoerder, Christiane Harzig, and Adrian Shubert (New York: Berghahn Books, 2003), 109–33; Lovejoy, ed., *Slavery on the Frontiers of Islam* (Princeton, NJ: Markus Wiener, 2004); Lovejoy, "The Urban Background of Enslaved Muslims in the Americas," *Slavery and Abolition* 26, no. 3 (2005): 347–72; Lovejoy, *Ecology and Ethnography of Muslim Trade in West Africa* (Trenton, NJ: Africa World Press, 2005); Lovejoy, *Slavery, Commerce and Production in West Africa: Slave Society in the Sokoto Caliphate* (Trenton, NJ: Africa World Press, 2005); Lovejoy, "The Context of Enslavement in West Africa: Ahmad Bābā and the Ethics of Slavery," in *Slaves, Subjects, and Subversives: Blacks in Colonial Latin America*, ed. Jane Landers (Albuquerque: University of New Mexico Press, 2006), 9–38; Lovejoy, "Internal Markets or an Atlantic-Sahara Divide? How Women Fit into the Slave Trade of West Africa," in *Women and Slavery*, ed. Gwyn Campbell, Suzanne Miers, and Joseph C. Miller (Athens: Ohio University Press, 2007), 259–80; Lovejoy, "Patterns in Regulation and Collaboration in the Slave Trade of West Africa," *Leidschrift* 22, no. 1 (2007): 41–57; Lovejoy, "Transatlantic Transformations: The Origins and Identities of Africans in the Americas," in *Africa, Brazil, and the Construction of Trans-Atlantic Black Identities*, ed. Boubacar Barry, Livio Sansone, and Elisée Soumonni (Trenton, NJ: Africa World Press, 2008), 81–112; Lovejoy, "The Slave Trade as Enforced Migration in the Central Sudan," in *Removing Peoples: Forced Removal in the Modern World*, ed. Claudia Haake and Richard Bessel (London: German Historical Institute, 2009), 149–66; Behnaz A. Mirzai, Ismael Musah Montana, and Paul E. Lovejoy, eds., *Slavery, Islam and Diaspora* (Trenton, NJ: Africa World Press, 2009); Paul E. Lovejoy, "Esclavitud y comercio esclavista en el África Occidental: Investigaciones en curso," in *Debates históricos contemporáneos: Africanos y afrodescendientes en México y Centroamérica*, ed. María Elisa Velázquez (Mexico City: Instituto Nacional de Anthropología e Historia, 2011), 35–58; Lovejoy, "Diplomacy in the Heart of Africa: British-Sokoto Negotiations over the Abolition of the Atlantic Slave Trade," in *Distant Ripples of British Abolition in Africa, Asia and the Americas*, ed. Myriam Cottias and Marie-Jeanne Rossignol (Trenton, NJ: Africa World Press, forthcoming); Paul E. Lovejoy and Suzanne Schwarz, eds., *Slavery, Abolition and the Transition to Colonialism in Sierra Leone* (Trenton, NJ: Africa World Press, 2014); Jennifer Lofkrantz and Paul E. Lovejoy, "Maintaining Network Boundaries: Islamic Law and Commerce from Sahara to Guinea Shores," *Slavery and Abolition* 36, no. 2 (2015): 211–32; and Lovejoy, *Transformations in Slavery*.

4. Dale W. Tomich, *Through the Prism of Slavery: Labor, Capital, and World Economy* (Lanham, MD: Rowman and Littlefield, 2004); Anthony E. Kaye, "The Second Slavery: Modernity in the Nineteenth-Century South and the Atlantic World,"

Journal of Southern History 75, no. 3 (2009): 175–95. Also see Tomich, "The 'Second Slavery': Bonded Labor and the Transformations of the Nineteenth-Century World Economy," in *Rethinking the Nineteenth Century: Contradictions and Movement*, ed. Francisco O. Ramírez (New York: Greenwood, 1988), 103–17; Tomich, "The Wealth of the Empire: Francisco de Arango y Parreno, Political Economy, and the Second Slavery in Cuba," *Comparative Studies in Society and History* 1 (2003): 4–28; Dale W. Tomich and Michael Zeuske, eds., "The Second Slavery: Mass Slavery, World-Economy, and Comparative Microhistories, Part II," special issue, *Review: A Journal of the Fernand Braudel Center* 31 (2008); Dale W. Tomich, "Atlantic History and World Economy: Concepts and Constructions," *Proto Sociology: An International Journal of Interdisciplinary Research* 20 (2004): 102–21; and Michael Zeuske, "Historiography and Research Problems of Slavery and the Slave Trade in a Global-Historical Perspective," *International Review of Social History* 57, no. 1 (2012): 87–111.

1. The Age of Revolutions and the Atlantic World

1. Eric Hobsbawm, *The Age of Revolution, 1789–1848* (New York: Vintage Books, 1996 [1962]), ix.

2. Eugene Genovese, *From Rebellion to Revolution: Afro-American Slave Revolts in the Making of the Modern World* (Baton Rouge: Louisiana State University Press, 1979).

3. David Armitage and Sanjay Subrahmanyam, "Introduction: The Age of Revolutions, c. 1760–1840—Global Causation, Connection, and Comparison," in *The Age of Revolutions in Global Context, c. 1760–1840*, ed. David Armitage and Sanjay Subrahmanyam (Basingstoke, UK: Palgrave Macmillan, 2010), xii.

4. Joseph C. Miller, "The Dynamics of History in Africa and the Atlantic 'Age of Revolutions,'" in Armitage and Subrahmanyam, *Age of Revolutions in Global Context*, 101–24.

5. For a reformulation of this perspective that Africa was involved in the Atlantic world only through the actions of the enslaved who were taken to the Americas, see Wim Klooster, "Slave Revolts, Royal Justice, and a Ubiquitous Rumor in the Age of Revolutions," *William and Mary Quarterly* 71, no. 3 (2014): 401–24.

6. The brilliant insights of Barbara Solow in her analysis of Eric Williams's thesis have been conveniently combined, with additional analysis, in *The Economic Consequences of the Atlantic Slave Trade* (New York: Lexington Books, 2014).

7. David Armitage, "Three Concepts of Atlantic History," in *The British Atlantic World, 1500–1800*, ed. David Armitage and Michael J. Braddick (New York: Palgrave Macmillan, 2002), 11–27 (quotation, 11). See Patrick Griffin, "A Plea for a New Atlantic History," *William and Mary Quarterly* 68, no. 2 (2011): 236.

8. James Sidbury and Jorge Cañizares-Esguerra, "Mapping Ethnogenesis in the Early Modern Atlantic," *William and Mary Quarterly* 68, no. 2 (2011): 181–208; but see Griffin, "Plea for a New Atlantic History," 236–39.

9. On Mahdism, see Muhammad Al-Hajj, "The Thirteenth Century in Muslim Eschatology: Mahdist Expectations in the Sokoto Caliphate," *Research Bulletin*,

Centre of Arabic Documentation (Ibadan) 3, no. 2 (1967): 100–113; R. A. Adeleye, "Rabih Fadlallah, 1879–1893: Exploits and Impact on Political Relations in Central Sudan," *Journal of the Historical Society of Nigeria* 5, no. 2 (1970): 223–42; Muhammad Al-Hajj, "Hayatu b. Sa'id: A Revolutionary Mahdist in the Western Sudan," in *The Sudan in Africa: Studies Presented to the First International Conference Sponsored by the Sudan Research Unit*, ed. Y. Fadl Hasan (Khartoum: Khartoum University Press, 1971), 128–41; Martin Z. Njeuma, "Adamawa and Mahdism: The Career of Hayatu ibn Said in Adamawa, 1878–1898," *Journal of African History* 12, no. 1 (1971): 61–77; Saburi Biobaku and Muhammad Al-Hajj, "The Sudanese Mahdiyya and the Niger-Chad Region," in *Islam in Tropical Africa*, ed. I. M. Lewis (Oxford: Clarendon Press, 1966), 425–39; John E. Lavers, "Jibril Gaini: A Preliminary Account of the Career of a Mahdist Leader in North-eastern Nigeria," *Research Bulletin, Centre of Arabic Documentation* (Ibadan) 3, no. 1 (1967): 16–38; Paul E. Lovejoy and Jan Hogendorn, "Revolutionary Mahdism and Resistance to Colonial Rule in the Sokoto Caliphate, 1905–1906," *Journal of African History* 31, no. 2 (1990): 217–44; C. N. Ubah, "British Measures against Mahdism at Dumbulwa in Northern Nigeria, 1923: A Case of Colonial Overreaction," *Islamic Culture* 50, no. 3 (1976): 169–83; and Asmau G. Saeed, "The British Policy towards the Mahdiyya in Northern Nigeria: A Study of the Arrest, Detention and Deportation of Shaykh Said b. Hayat, 1923–1959," *Kano Studies* 2, no. 3 (1982–85), 95–119.

10. John Ralph Willis, "*Jihād fī sabīl Allāh*—Its Doctrinal Basis in Islam and Some Aspects of Its Evolution in Nineteenth-Century West Africa," *Journal of African History* 8, no. 3 (1967): 398–99. Also see 'Uthmān dan Fodio, *Bayān wujūb al hijra 'alā l-'ibād* (The exposition of obligation of emigration upon the servants of God), ed. and trans. F. H. El Masri (Khartoum: University of Khartoum Press, 1978), 117–20; and 'Uthmān dan Fodio, "Dispatch to the People of the Sudan," in A. D. H. Bivar, "The *Wathīqat ahl al-Sūdān*: A Manifesto of the Fulani *Jihād*," *Journal of African History* 2, no. 2 (1961): 235–43. There are also several works by 'Abdullahi dan Fodio on jihād, including *Ḍiyā' al-sulṭān wa ghayrihi min al-ikhwān fī ahamm ma yuṭlab 'ilmuhu fī umūr al-zamān*, which deals with *hijra*, jihād, and the administration of justice; see Abubaker Aliu Gwandu, "Abdullahi b. Fodio as a Muslim Jurist" (Ph.D. dissertation, University of Durham, 1977), 208.

11. E. Ann McDougall, "On Being Saharan," in *Saharan Frontiers: Space and Mobility in Northwest Africa*, ed. James McDougall and Judith Scheele (Bloomington: Indiana University Press, 2012), 39–57.

12. Paul E. Lovejoy and Steven Baier, "The DesertSide Economy of the Central Sudan," *International Journal of African Historical Studies* 8, no. 4 (1975): 551–81.

13. Paulo F. de Moraes Farias, *Arabic Medieval Inscriptions from the Republic of Mali: Epigraphy, Chronicles, and Songhay-Tuâreg History* (Oxford: Oxford University Press, 2003).

14. Jane Landers, for example, refers to "Muslim converts along the Gambia"; see "The Atlantic Transformations of Francisco Menéndez," in *Biography and the Black Atlantic*, ed. Lisa A. Lindsay and John Wood Sweet (Philadelphia: University of Pennsylvania Press, 2013), 213, citing Donald R. Wright, *The World and a Very Small*

Place in Africa: A History of Globalization in Niumi, the Gambia, 2nd ed. (Armonk, NY: M. E. Sharpe, 2004), 83.

15. Paulo F. de Moraes Farias, "Muslim Oralcy in West Africa: A Neglected Subject," in *Landscapes, Sources, and Intellectual Projects in African History: Symposium in Honour of Paulo Fernando de Moraes Farias*, University of Birmingham, 12–14 November 2015, https://www.youtube.com/watch?v=gQSlo6ThoDg.

16. Charles Stewart, "10,000 MSS, 1850 Authors across 300 Years: A Preview of ALA-V," in *Landscapes, Sources, and Intellectual Projects in African History: Symposium in Honour of Paulo Fernando de Moraes Farias*, University of Birmingham, 12–14 November 2015.

17. Paul E. Lovejoy, "Islamic Scholarship and Understanding History in West Africa before 1800," in *The Oxford History of Historical Writing*, vol. 3, *1400–1800*, ed. José Rabasa, Masayuki Sato, Edoardo Tortarolo, and Daniel Woolf (New York: Oxford University Press, 2012), 212–32.

18. 'Abd al-Rahman al-Sa'di bin 'Abd Allah, *Tarikh al-Sudan*, in *Timbuktu and the Songhay Empire: Al-Sa'di's "Tarikh al-Sudan" down to 1613 and Other Contemporary Sources*, ed. John Hunwick (Leiden: Brill, 1999); Nehemia Levtzion, "A Critical Study of 'Tarikh al-fattash,'" *Bulletin of the School of Oriental and African Studies* 34, no. 3 (1971): 571–93.

19. See John O. Hunwick et al., eds., *Arabic Literature of Africa*, vol. 2, *The Writings of Central Sudanic Africa* (Leiden: Brill, 1995), and vol. 4, *The Writings of Western Sudanic Africa* (Leiden: Brill, 2003); Chouki El Hamel, *La vie intellectuelle islamique dans le Sahel Ouest-Africain (XVIe–XIXe siècles): Une étude social de l'enseignement islamique en Mauritanie et au Nord du Mali (XVIe–XIXe siècles) et traduction annotée de "Fath ash-shakur" d'al-Bartili al Walati (mort en 1805)* (Paris : L'Harmattan, 2002); and Andrea Brigaglia and Mauro Nobili, "Central Sudanic Arabic Scripts (Part 2): Barnāwī," *Sudanic Africa* 4, no. 2 (2013): 195–223. Also see Natalie Zemon Davis, *Trickster Travels: A Sixteenth-Century Muslim between Worlds* (New York: Faber, 2006).

20. See especially Rudolph T. Ware, *The Walking Qu'ran: Islamic Education, Embodied Knowledge, and History in West Africa* (Chapel Hill: University of North Carolina Press, 2014); and Bruce Hall and Charles Stewart, "The Historic 'Core Curriculum' and the Book Market in Islamic West Africa," in *One Thousand Years of Trans-Saharan Book Trade*, ed. Graziano Krätli and Ghislaine Lydon (Leiden: Brill, 2011), 109–174.

21. David Robinson, *Muslim Societies in African History* (Cambridge: Cambridge University Press, 2004), 45.

22. William W. Bascom, *Ifa Divination: Communication between Gods and Men in West Africa* (Bloomington: Indiana University Press, 1969); and Rosalind Shaw, *Memories of the Slave Trade: Ritual and the Historical Imagination in Sierra Leone* (Chicago: University of Chicago Press, 2002), 134–35.

23. Chouki El Hamel, "Constructing a Diasporic Identity: Tracing the Origins of the Gnawa Spiritual Group in Morocco," *Journal of African History* 49 (2008): 241–60; Ehud R. Toledano, "The Fusion of Zar-Bori and Sufi Zikr as Performance:

Notes to Pages 18–20

Enslaved Africans in the Ottoman Empire," in *Medieval and Early Modern Performance in the Eastern Mediterranean*, ed. A. Öztürkmen and E. B. Vitz (Turnhout, Belgium: Brepols, 2014), 216–40; Ismael Musah Montana, "Bori Practice among Enslaved West Africans of Ottoman Tunis: Unbelief (Kufr) or Another Dimension of the African Diaspora?," *History of the Family* 16 (2011): 152–59; and Fremont E. Besmer, *Horses, Musicians and Gods: The Hausa Cult of Possession-Trance* (South Hadley, MA: Bergin and Garvey, 1983).

24. Aziz A. Batran, *The Qadiriyya Brotherhood in West Africa and the Western Sahara: The Life and Times of Shaykh al-Mukhtar al-Kunti (1729–1811)* (Rabat: Institut des Études Africaines, 2001); Louis Brenner, *Muslim Identity and Social Change in Sub-Saharan Africa* (Bloomington: Indiana University Press, 1993), 8; Brenner, "Concepts of Tariqa in West Africa: The Case of the Qadiriyya," in *Charisma and Brotherhood in African Islam*, ed. C. Coulon and D. B. Cruise O'Brien (Oxford: Clarendon Press, 1988), 33–52; and Stewart, "10,000 MSS, 1850 Authors across 300 Years."

25. Willis, "*Jihād fī sabīl Allāh*," 398–99.

26. Hobsbawm, *Age of Revolution*, ix.

27. Genovese, *From Rebellion to Revolution*. Of course, C. L. R. James, *The Black Jacobins: Toussaint L'Ouverture and the San Domingo Revolution*, 2nd ed. (New York: Random House, 1963), drew attention to the European background of the Haitian revolution and thereby influenced both Hobsbawm and Genovese. Likewise, Herbert Aptheker, *American Negro Slave Resistance* (New York: Columbia University Press, 1944) documented the dynamics of slave resistance in the United States, and his pioneering work, often ignored in the literature, helped focus scholarly attention on slave resistance; see Gary Okihiro and Herbert Aptheker, eds., *Resistance Not Acquiesence: Studies in African, AfroAmerican, and Caribbean History* (Amherst: University of Massachusetts Press, 1986).

28. Hobsbawm, *Age of Revolution*, 3.

29. Although Genovese (*From Rebellion to Revolution*, 28–32) discusses Muslim influence on the uprising in Bahia, he seems to have been unaware of the scholarship on jihād in West Africa. Clyde Ahmed Winters, "The Afro-Brazilian Concept of Jihād and the 1835 Slave Revolt," *Afrodiaspora: Journal of the African World* 2 (1984): 87–91, attempted to understand some of this influence. Also see Roger Bastide, *As religiões africanas no Brasil: Contribuição a uma sociologia das interpretações de civilizações* (São Paulo: Livraria Pioneira, 1989), 106, and Pierre Verger, *Flux et reflux de la traite des nègres entre le Golfe de Bénin et Bahia de Todos os Santos du dix-septième au dix-neuvième siècle* (Paris: Mouton, 1968); Verger, *Trade Relations between the Bight of Benin and Bahia, 17th-19th Century* (Ibadan: University of Ibadan Press, 1976); and Verger, *Fluxo e refluxo do tráfico de escravos entre o Golfo do Benin e a Bahia de Todos os Santos, dos séculos XVII a XIX* (São Paulo: Editora Corrupio, 1987). However, these scholars failed to understand the impact in West Africa. For a much better interpretation, see Michael Gomez, *Black Crescent: The Experience and Legacy of African Muslims in the Americas* (Cambridge: Cambridge University Press, 2005), 91–127. Also see Allan D. Austin, *African Muslims in Antebellum America: Transatlantic Stories and Spiritual Struggles* (New York: Routledge,

1997); and Austin, ed., *African Muslims in Antebellum America: A Sourcebook* (New York: Garland, 1984).

30. James H. Sweet, *Domingoes Álvares, African Healing, and the Intellectual History of the Atlantic World* (Chapel Hill: University of North Carolina Press, 2011); Walter Hawthorne, *From Africa to Brazil: Culture, Identity, and an Atlantic Slave Trade, 1600–1830* (Cambridge: Cambridge University Press, 2010); and on biography, especially Hawthorne, " 'Sendo agora, como se fôssemos, uma família' ": Laços entre companheiros de viagem no navio negreiro *Emília*, no Rio de Janeiro e através do Mundo Atlântico," *Revista Mundos do Trabalho* 3, no. 6 (2011): 7–29. Also see Randy Sparks, *Two Princes of Calabar: An Eighteenth-Century Atlantic Odyssey* (Cambridge, MA: Harvard University Press, 2004); Sparks, *Where the Negroes Are Masters: An African Port in the Era of the Slave Trade* (Cambridge, MA: Harvard University Press, 2014); Cassandra Pybus, *Epic Journeys of Freedom: Runaway Slaves of the American Revolution and Their Global Quest for Liberty* (Boston: Beacon Press, 2006); Toyin Falola and Kevin D. Roberts, eds., *The Atlantic World, 1450–2000* (Bloomington: Indiana University Press, 2008); and Toyin Falola and Matt D. Childs, eds., *The Yoruba Diaspora in the Atlantic World* (Bloomington: Indiana University Press, 2004).

31. Jane Landers, *Atlantic Creoles in the Age of Revolutions* (Cambridge, MA: Harvard University Press, 2010), 4.

32. Ibid., 7.

33. Among the many contributions to the study of slave resistance and revolution in the Americas, the study of St. Domingue stands out; see James, *Black Jacobins*, and also, for example, Carolyn Fick, *The Making of Haiti: The Saint Domingue Revolution from Below* (Knoxville: University of Tennessee Press, 1990); Laurent Dubois and John D. Garrigus, *Slave Revolution in the Caribbean, 1789–1804: A Brief History with Documents* (Boston: Bedford/St Martin's, 2006); David Patrick Geggus, *Haitian Revolutionary Studies* (Bloomington: Indiana University Press, 2002); Geggus, ed., *The Impact of the Haitian Revolution in the Atlantic World* (Columbia: University of South Carolina Press, 2001); Laurent Dubois, *Avengers of the New World: The Story of the Haitian Revolution* (Cambridge: Cambridge University Press, 2004); Laënnec Hurbon, ed., *L'insurrection des esclaves de Saint-Domingue (22–23 août 1791)* (Paris: Karthala, 2000); Gérard Barthélémy, *Dans la splendeur d'un après-midi d'histoire* (Port-au-Prince: Henri Deschamps, 1996), revised edition with the title *Créoles–Bossales: Conflit en Haïti* (Paris: Ibis rouge, 2000); Jacques de Cauna, *Haïti, l'éternelle révolution* (Port-au-Prince: Deschamps, 1996); Aimé Césaire, *Toussaint-Louverture: La Révolution française et le problème colonial* (Paris: Présence africaine, 1960; Marcel Dorigny, *Haiti, première république noire* (Paris: Société Française d'Histoire d'Outre-Mer, 2003); and Nelly Schmidt, *L'engrenage de la liberté: Caraïbes—XIXe siècle* (Aix-en-Provence: Université de Provence, 1995). Also see Michael Craton, *Testing the Chains: Resistance to Slavery in the British West Indies* (Ithaca, NY: Cornell University Press, 1982).

34. Paul Gilroy, *The Black Atlantic: Modernity and Double Consciousness* (Cambridge, MA: Harvard University Press, 1993); Ira Berlin, "From Creole to African:

Atlantic Creoles and the Origins of African-American Society in Mainland North America," *William and Mary Quarterly* 53, no. 2 (1996): 251–88; Gwendolyn Midlo Hall, *Slavery and African Ethnicities in the Americas: Restoring the Links* (Chapel Hill: University of North Carolina Press, 2005); and Landers, *Atlantic Creoles in the Age of Revolutions.*

35. Bernard Bailyn, *Atlantic History: Concept and Contours* (Cambridge, MA: Harvard University Press, 2005); Jack P. Green and Philip D. Morgan, *Atlantic History: A Critical Appraisal* (New York: Oxford University Press, 2008).

36. Wim Klooster, *Revolutions in the Atlantic World: A Comparative History* (New York: New York University Press, 2009); and David Brion Davis, *The Problem of Slavery in the Age of Revolution, 1770–1823* (Ithaca, NY: Cornell University Press, 1975).

37. Landers, *Atlantic Creoles in the Age of Revolutions*, 5; and Manuel Barcia, *West African Warfare in Bahia and Cuba: Soldier Slaves in the Atlantic World, 1807–1844* (Oxford: Oxford University Press, 2014).

38. In the 1820s there were ten uprisings in Bahia and five in neighboring Sergipe de El-Rey in which Yoruba slaves and former slaves were involved; see Stuart Schwartz, *Sugar Plantations in the Formation of Brazilian Society: Bahia, 1550–1835* (Cambridge: Cambridge University Press, 1985), 486–87. Also see Schwartz, *Escravos, roceiros e rebeldes* (Bauru: EDUSC, 2001); Schwartz, "Cantos e quilombos numa conspiração de escravos haussás," in *Liberdade por um fio: História dos quilombos no Brasil*, ed. João José Reis and Flávio dos Santos Gomes (São Paulo: Companhia das Letras, 1997), 373–406; João José Reis, "Slave Resistance in Brazil: Bahia, 1807–1835," *Luso-Brazilian Review* 25, no. 1 (1988): 111–44; and Reis, "La révolte haoussa de Bahia en 1807: Résistance et contrôle des esclaves au Brésil," *Annales: Histoire, Sciences Sociales* 61 (2006): 383–418.

39. João José Reis, *Slave Rebellion in Brazil: The Muslim Uprising of 1835 in Bahia* (Baltimore: Johns Hopkins University Press, 1993); Sylviane Diouf, *Servants of Allah: African Muslims Enslaved in the Americas* (New York: New York University Press, 1998); Michael Gomez, "Muslims in Early America," *Journal of Southern History* 60, no. 4 (1994): 671–710; Gomez, *Black Crescent*, 91–127. Both Roger Bastide, *As religiões africanas no Brasil*, 106, and Pierre Verger have suggested that events in Bahia were an extension of jihād. See Verger, *Flux et reflux de la traite des nègres*; Verger, *Trade Relations between the Bight of Benin and Bahia*; and Verger, *Fluxo e refluxo do tráfico de escravos*. Also see Etienne Ignace Brazil, "Os malês," *Revista do Instituto Histórico e Geográfico Brasileiro* 72 (1909): 69–126.

40. Diouf, *Servants of Allah*, 158–59.

41. Barcia, *West African Warfare in Bahia and Cuba*, 161–65. Also see Manuel Barcia, "West African Islam in Colonial Cuba," *Slavery and Abolition* 35, no. 1 (2014): 1–14; and Barcia, "An Islamic Atlantic Revolution: Dan Fodio's *Jihād* and Slave Rebellion in Bahia and Cuba, 1804–1844," *Journal of African Diaspora, Archaeology, and Heritage* 2, no. 1 (2013): 6–18.

42. Humphrey Fisher, "A Muslim William Wilberforce? The Sokoto Jihād as Anti-slavery Crusade: An Enquiry into Historical Causes," in *De la traite à l'esclavage:*

Actes du Colloque international sur la traite des noirs, ed. S. Daget (Nantes: Centre de recherche sur l'histoire du monde atlantique, 1985), 555. Also see Schwartz, "Cantos e quilombos"; and Reis, "Révolte haoussa de Bahia en 1807."

43. Barcia, *West African Warfare in Bahia and Cuba*.

44. For discussion of terminology, see Robin Law, "Ethnicity and the Slave Trade: 'Lucumi' and 'Nago' as Ethnonyms in West Africa," *History in Africa* 24 (1997): 205–19; Paul E. Lovejoy, "The Yoruba Factor in the Trans-Atlantic Slave Trade," in *The Yoruba Diaspora in the Atlantic World*, ed. Toyin Falola and Matt D. Childs (Bloomington: Indiana University Press, 2004), 40–55; and Henry B. Lovejoy and Olatunji Ojo, " 'Lucumí' and 'Terranova,' and the Origins of the Yoruba Nation," *Journal of African History* 56, no. 3 (2015): 353–72.

45. Henry B. Lovejoy, "Old Oyo Influences on the Transformation of Lucumí Identity in Colonial Cuba" (Ph.D. dissertation, UCLA, 2012). Also see H. B. Lovejoy, "Drums of Şàngó: Bàtá Drums and the Symbolic Reestablishment of Ọyọ in Colonial Cuba, c. 1817–1867," in *Şàngó in Africa and the African Diaspora*, ed. Joel Tishken, Toyin Falola, and Akintunde Akinyemi (Bloomington: Indiana University Press, 2009), 284–308; H. B. Lovejoy, "The Transculturation of Yoruba Annual Festivals: The *Día de Reyes* in Colonial Cuba in the Nineteenth Century," in *Carnival— Theory and Practice*, ed. Christopher Innes, Annabel Rutherford, and Brigitte Bogar (Trenton, NJ: Africa World Press, 2013), 33–50; H. B. Lovejoy, "Re-drawing Historical Maps of the Bight of Benin Hinterland, c. 1780," *Canadian Journal of African Historical Studies* 47, no. 3 (2013): 443–63; and *African Diaspora Maps*, www.africandiasporamaps.com.

46. I owe this analysis to Henry B. Lovejoy; see Henry B. Lovejoy, "West Africa Historical GIS and the Liberated Africans Project" (talk presented at Maryland Institute of Technology in the Humanities, University of Maryland, Washington, D.C., 2016); and Henry B. Lovejoy, "Origins and Destinations: Linking West Africa's Historical Geography to the Trans-Atlantic Slave Trade Database" (paper presented at the American Historical Association Annual Meeting, Atlanta, 7 January 2016). The analysis is based on the statistics of the Voyage database, www.slavevoyages.org.

47. R. R. Madden, who was in Cuba in 1835–39, makes no reference to Muslims in that country. Madden was a careful and experienced observer, and hence his silence suggests that he did not meet any Muslims in Cuba. Madden spoke Arabic, had traveled in Egypt and West Africa, and had befriended Muslims in Jamaica when he was stationed there in 1833–34, before his appointment to Cuba. See Madden, *The Island of Cuba: Its Resources, Progress, and Prospects, Considered in Relation Especially to the Influence of Its Prosperity on the Interests of the British West India Colonies* (London: C. Gilpin, 1849).

48. At least twenty letters were exchanged between the jihād leadership and al-Kanemi between 1808 and 1812. Many of the letters are in Muhammad Bello, *Infāq al-Maysūr fī tārīkh bilād al-Takrūr* (1812), ed. Bahija Chadli (Rabat: Institute of African Studies, 1996). Another letter from el-Kanemi to Goni Mukhtar, the leader of the jihād forces in Borno, dated 17 Rabiʿ al-Awwil 1223 (13 May 1808), is in the University of Ibadan Library (Ms. 82/237). See D. Murray Last and M. A. Al-Hajj, "Attempts at

Defining a Muslim in 19th-Century Hausaland and Bornu," *Journal of the Historical Society of Nigeria* 3, no. 2 (1965): 239; Louis Brenner, *The Shehus of Kukawa: A History of the Al-Kanemi Dynasty of Bornu* (Oxford: Clarendon Press, 1973), 39–43; Muhammad N. Alkali, "El-Kanemi's Response to the Extension of Shaykh ʿUthmān Dan Fodio's *Jihād* against Borno," in *The Sokoto Caliphate: History and Legacies, 1804–2004*, ed. H. Bobboyi and A. M. Yakubu (Kaduna: Arewa House, 2006), 1:231–39; and Louis Brenner, "The Jihād Debate between Sokoto and Borno: An Historical Analysis of Islamic Political Discourse in Nigeria," in *People and Empires in African History: Essays in Memory of Michael Crowder*, ed. J. F. Ade Ajayi and J. D. Y. Peel (London: Longman, 1992), 21–43.

49. My discussion of the Bello-Clapperton negotiations was first presented in "Rethinking the African Diaspora: The Making of a Black Atlantic World in the Bight of Benin and Brazil," Emory University, 17–18 April 1998, and was subsequently published as "The Clapperton-Bello Exchange: The Sokoto *Jihād* and the Trans-Atlantic Slave Trade, 1804–1837," in *The Desert Shore: Literatures of the African Sahel*, ed. Christopher Wise (Boulder, CO: Lynne Rienner, 2000), 201–28. The arguments have been expanded in Paul E. Lovejoy, "Diplomacy of Abolition: Negotiations between Muhammad Bello and Hugh Clapperton over the Abolition of the Atlantic Slave Trade," in *Distant Ripples of the British Abolitionist Wave in Africa, the Americas and Asia*, ed. Myriam Cottias and Marie-Jeanne Rossignol (Trenton, NJ: Africa World Press, forthcoming).

50. Paul E. Lovejoy, "Islam, Slavery, and Political Transformation in West Africa: Constraints on the Trans-Atlantic Slave Trade," *Outre-Mers: Revue d'histoire* 89 (2002): 247–82. Also see Paul E. Lovejoy, ed., *Slavery on the Frontiers of Islam* (Princeton, NJ: Markus Wiener, 2004); and Behnaz A. Mirzai, Ismael Musah Montana, and Paul E. Lovejoy, eds., *Slavery, Islam and Diaspora* (Trenton, NJ: Africa World Press, 2009). An exception is the work of Alberto da Costa e Silva, "Sobre a rebelião de 1835 na Bahia," *Revista Brasileira* 31 (2002): 9–33, reprinted in Silva, *Um rio chamado Atlântico: A África no Brasil e o Brasil na África* (Rio de Janeiro: Editora Nova Fronteira, 2003), 189–214. Also see Barcia, "Islamic Atlantic Revolution," 6–18; Barcia, *West African Warfare in Bahia and Cuba*; and Henry Lovejoy, "Old Oyo Influences."

51. I first presented this approach in 1979 at a conference organized by Michael Craton; see Paul E. Lovejoy, "Indigenous African Slavery," *Historical Reflections / Reflexions Historiques* 6, no. 1 (1979): 19–61; reprinted in *Roots and Branches: Current Directions in Slave Studies*, ed. Michael Craton (Toronto: Pergamon Press), 19–61, with commentaries by Igor Kopytoff and Frederick Cooper, 62–83.

52. See, for example, P. E. Lovejoy, "Islamic Scholarship and Understanding History in West Africa before 1800."

53. Yusufu Bala Usman, ed., *Studies in the History of the Sokoto Caliphate: The Sokoto Seminar Papers* (Lagos: Third Press International, 1979); H. Bobboyi and A. M. Yakubu, eds., *The Sokoto Caliphate: History and Legacies, 1804–2004*, 2 vols. (Kaduna: Arewa House, 2006); Ahmed M. Kani and K. A. Gandi, eds., *State and Society in the Sokoto Caliphate: Essays in Honour of Sultan Ibrahim Dasuki* (Sokoto:

Usmanu Danfodiyo University, 1990); Kabiru S. Chafe, *The State and Economy in the Sokoto Caliphate: Policies and Practices in the Metropolitan Districts, c. 1804–1903* (Zaria: Ahmadu Bello University Press, 1999); Seyni Moumouni, *Vie et oeuvre du Cheik Uthmân Dan Fodio (1754–1817): De l'Islam au soufisme* (Paris: L'Harmattan, 2008); I. A. B. Balogun, *The Life and Works of 'Usman Dan Fodio* (Lagos: Islamic Publications Bureau, 1975). Also see the important work of 'Uthmān dan Fodio in Bivar, "*Wathīqat ahl al-Sūdān*."

54. Dale Tomich, *Through the Prism of Slavery: Labor, Capital, and World Economy* (Lanham, MD: Rowman and Littlefield, 2004); Anthony E. Kaye, "The Second Slavery: Modernity in the Nineteenth-Century South and the Atlantic World," *Journal of Southern History* 75, no. 3 (2009): 627. Also see Tomich, "The 'Second Slavery': Bonded Labor and the Transformations of the Nineteenth-Century World Economy," in *Rethinking the Nineteenth Century: Contradictions and Movement*, ed. Francisco O. Ramírez (New York: Greenwood, 1988), 103–17; Tomich, "The Wealth of the Empire: Francisco de Arango y Parreno, Political Economy, and the Second Slavery in Cuba," *Comparative Studies in Society and History* 1 (2003): 4–28; Dale W. Tomich and Michael Zeuske, eds, "The Second Slavery: Mass Slavery, World-Economy, and Comparative Microhistories, Part II," special issue, *Review: A Journal of the Fernand Braudel Center* 31 (2008); Tomich, "Atlantic History and World Economy: Concepts and Constructions," *Proto Sociology: An International Journal of Interdisciplinary Research* 20 (2004); 102–21; and Michael Zeuske, "Historiography and Research Problems of Slavery and the Slave Trade in a Global-Historical Perspective," *International Review of Social History* 57, no. 1 (2012): 87–111.

55. Murray Last, "Reform Movements in West Africa: The Jihād Movements of the Nineteenth Century," in *History of West Africa*, ed. J. F. A. Ajayi and Michael Crowder, 3rd ed. (London: Longman, 1987), 2:1.

56. Omar Jah, "The Effect of Pilgrimage on the Jihād of Al-Hajj 'Umar al-Futi, 1794–1864," in *The Central Bilad al Sudan: Tradition and Adaptation*, ed. Yusuf Fadl Hasan and Paul Doornbos (Khartoum: University of Khartoum Press, 1977), 239. Also see Omar Jah, "Al-Haj 'Umar's Philosophy of Jihād and Its Sufi Basis" (Ph.D. dissertation, McGill University, 1974).

57. Krätli and Lydon, eds., *The Trans-Saharan Book Trade*; and Scott Reese, ed., *The Transmission of Learning in Islamic Africa* (Leiden: Brill, 2004).

58. David Richardson, "Shipboard Revolts, African Authority, and the Atlantic Slave Trade," *William and Mary Quarterly* 58, no. 1 (2001): 69–92.

2. The Origins of Jihād in West Africa

1. Boubacar Barry, "Senegambia from the Sixteenth to the Eighteenth Century: Evolution of the Wolof, Sereer and 'Tukuloor,'" in *UNESCO General History of Africa*, ed. B. A. Ogot (Berkeley: University of California Press, 1992), 5:273–74.

2. Rudolph T. Ware, *The Walking Qu'ran: Islamic Education, Embodied Knowledge, and History in West Africa* (Chapel Hill: University of North Carolina Press, 2014). Also see Lansiné Kaba, "The Politics of Quranic Education among Muslim

Traders in the Western Sudan: The Subbanu Experience," *Canadian Journal of African Studies* 10, no. 3 (1976): 409–21.

3. Thierno Ka, *École de Pir Saniokhor: Histoire, enseignement et culture arabo-islamiques au Sénégal du XVIIIe au XXe siècle* (Paris: Karthala, 2002).

4. Eric S. Ross, "From Marabout Republics to Autonomous Rural Communities: Autonomous Muslim Towns in Senegal," in *African Urban Spaces in Historical Perspective*, ed. Steven J. Salm and Toyin Falola (Rochester, NY: University of Rochester Press, 2005), 246.

5. For an overview, see Nehemia Levtzion, "North-West Africa: From the Maghrib to the Fringes of the Forest," in *The Cambridge History of Africa*, ed. J. D. Fage and Roland Oliver (Cambridge: Cambridge University Press, 1975), 4:204–5. Also see Philip D. Curtin, "The Uses of Oral Tradition in Senegambia: Maalik Sii and the Foundation of Bundu," *Cahiers d'études africaines* 15 (1975): 189–202; and Michael A. Gomez, *Pragmatism in the Age of Jihād: The Precolonial State of Bundu* (Cambridge: Cambridge University Press, 2002), 32–51.

6. Ivor Wilks, "The Juula and the Expansion of Islam into the Forest," in *The History of Islam in West Africa*, ed. Nehemia Levtzion and Randall L. Pouwels (Athens: Ohio University Press, 2000), 97–98.

7. Charles Stewart, "10,000 MSS, 1850 Authors across 300 Years: A Preview of ALA-V," in *Landscapes, Sources, and Intellectual Projects in African History: Symposium in Honour of Paulo Fernando de Moraes Farias*, University of Birmingham, 12–14 November 2015.

8. Barry, "Senegambia from the Sixteenth to the Eighteenth Century," 274. Also see Boubacar Barry, "Traite négrière et esclavage interne en Sénégambie au xviiiᵉ siècle," in *De la traite esclavage: Actes du Colloque international sur la traite des noirs*, ed. Serge Daget (Nantes: Centre de recherche sur l'histoire du monde atlantique, 1988), 2:213–22; M. S. Balde, "L'esclavage et la guerre sainte au Fuuta-Jalon," in *L'esclavage en Afrique précoloniale*, ed. Claude Meillassoux (Paris: Maspero, 1975), 183–220; Walter Rodney, *A History of the Upper Guinea Coast, 1545–1800* (Oxford: Clarendon Press, 1970), 152–70; Roger Botte, "Les rapports Nord-Sud, la traite négrière et le Fuuta Jaloo à la fin du XVIIIᵉ siècle," *Annales: Économies, Sociétés, Civilisations* 6 (1991): 1411–35; Botte, "Révolte, pouvoir, religion : Les Hubbu du Futa-Jalon Guinée," *Journal of African History* 29 (1988): 391–413; Martin A. Klein, "Social and Economic Factors in the Muslim Revolution in Senegambia," *Journal of African History* 13 (1972): 419–41; and J. Boulègue, "L'expression du refus de la traite négrière dans les sociétés sénégambiennes (xviiᵉ–xviiiᵉ siècles)," in Daget, *De la traite à l'esclavage*, 247–52.

9. Boubacar Barry, *Senegambia and the Atlantic Slave Trade* (Cambridge: Cambridge University Press, 1998), 99–102, 148–50; and Lamin Sanneh, *The Jakhanke: The History of an Islamic Clerical People of the Senegambia* (London: International African Institute, 1979), 94–105. Also see David E. Skinner, "Islam in the Northern Hinterland and Its Influence on the Development of Sierra Leone," in *Islam and Trade in Sierra Leone, ed.* Alusine Jalloh and David E. Skinner (Trenton, NJ: Africa World Press, 1997), 1–20; and Walter Rodney, "Jihad and Social Revolution in Futa Djalon in the Eighteenth Century," *Journal of the Historical Society of Nigeria* 4 (1968): 280.

10. Barry, *Senegambia and the Atlantic Slave Trade*, 98–100.

11. Rodney, "Jihad and Social Revolution in Futa Djalon in the Eighteenth Century," 283–84; Bruce Mouser, "Rebellion, Marronage and *Jihad*: Strategies of Resistance to Slavery on the Sierra Leone Coast, c. 1783–1796," *Journal of African History* 48, no. 1 (2007): 27–44; Ismail Rashid, "Escape, Revolt, and Marronage in Eighteenth and Nineteenth Century Sierra Leone Hinterland," *Canadian Journal of African Studies* 34 (2000): 656–83; Rashid, "'A Devotion to the Idea of Liberty at Any Price': Rebellion and Antislavery in the Upper Guinea Coast in the Eighteenth and Nineteenth Centuries," in *Fighting the Slave Trade: West African Strategies*, ed. Sylviane Diouf (Athens: Ohio University Press, 2003), 132–51; and Bronislaw Nowak, "The Slave Rebellion in Sierra Leone in 1785–1796," *Hemispheres* (Warsaw) 3 (1986): 151–69.

12. François-René Granger, the captain of the *Stanislas*, a French slave ship, was on the coast at the time and made a hasty escape. His letter describing the events there circulated widely in the Atlantic press, including the *Herald of Freedom*, Boston, 18 May 1790, and the *Newport Herald*, Newport, RI, 10 June 1790. I thank Bruce Mouser for these references.

13. Although Zachary Macaulay's testimony indicates that an assassination occurred before 1793, the time of his report, he was almost certainly referring to the death of Sori in 1791; see Suzanne Schwarz, ed., *Zachary Macaulay and the Development of the Sierra Leone Company, 1793–4*, vol. 1, *Journal, June–October 1793* University of Leipzig Papers on Africa, History and Culture, series no. 4 (Leipzig: Institut für Afrikanistik, Universität Leipzig, 2000), 61.

14. For the discussion of Fuuta Toro, I am relying especially on David Robinson, "The Islamic Revolution of Futa Toro," *International Journal of African Historical Studies* 8, no. 2 (1975): 185–221; but also see Robinson, "Revolutions in the Western Sudan," in Levtzion and Pouwels, *History of Islam in West Africa*, 131–68; and Moustafa Kane and David Robinson, *The Islamic Regime of Fuuta Tooro* (East Lansing: Michigan State University Press, 1984).

15. This summary draws on Robinson, "Islamic Revolution of Futa Toro," 196–203.

16. See Ross, "From Marabout Republics," 246, citing A.-B. Diop, *La Société wolof: Tradition et changement* (Paris: Karthala, 1981), 229; and Diop, *L'Afrique noire pré-coloniale* (Paris: Présence africaine, 1987), 72.

17. Robinson, "Islamic Revolution of Futa Toro," 205–17.

18. It was alleged that Fatta could not be killed or wounded, but a disgruntled lover, as the story goes, testified that she had seen several wounds on his body that had healed; see Mouser, "Rebellion, Marronage and Jihad," 40.

19. On Jibrīl ibn ʿUmar, see Djibo Hamani, *L'Adar précolonial (République du Niger): Contribution à l'étude de l'histoire des états Hausa* (Paris: L'Harmattan, 1975), 136–41; and A. D. H. Bivar and Mervyn Hiskett, "The Arabic Literature of Nigeria to 1804: A Provisional Account," *Bulletin of the School of Oriental and African Studies* 25 (1962): 104–48.

20. See Aḥmad Bābā, *Miʿraj al-suʿud: Ahmad Baba's Replies on Slavery*, ed. John Hunwick and Fatima Harrak (Rabat: Institute des Études Africaines, Université

Mohamed V, 2000); also quoted in Paul E. Lovejoy, "The Context of Enslavement in West Africa: Ahmad Bābā and the Ethics of Slavery," in *Slaves, Subjects, and Subversives: Blacks in Colonial Latin America*, ed. Jane Landers (Albuquerque: University of New Mexico Press), 33.

21. R. R. Madden, *A Twelvemonth's Residence in the West Indies, during the Transition from Slavery to Apprenticeship* (Westport, CT: Negro University Press, 1970 [1835]), 2:135. For a biography of Kabā Saghanughu, see Maureen Warner-Lewis, "Religious Constancy and Compromise among Nineteenth Century Caribbean-Based African Muslims," in *Slavery, Islam and Diaspora*, ed. Behnaz A. Mirzai, Ismael Musah Montana, and Paul E. Lovejoy (Trenton, NJ: African World Press, 2009), 237–68, although I have reservations about Warner-Lewis's application of the concept of syncretism to Kabā's life. I do not think that he "mixed" Islam and Christianity but rather realized that Islam could not survive under slavery in Jamaica and made a personal and political decision to affiliate with the Moravian Mission at Fairfield.

22. Ivor Wilks, "The Transmission of Islamic Learning in the Western Sudan," in *Literacy in Traditional Societies*, ed. Jack Goody (Cambridge: Cambridge University Press, 1968), 162–97; and Wilks, "The Saghanughu and the Spread of Maliki Law: A Provisional Note," *Research Review* (Institute of African Studies, University of Ghana) 2, no. 3 (1966): 67–73.

23. Yacine Daddi Addoun and Paul E. Lovejoy, "Muḥammad Kabā Saghanughu and the Muslim Community of Jamaica," in *Slavery on the Frontiers of Islam*, ed. Paul E. Lovejoy (Princeton, NJ: Markus Wiener, 2004), 201–2; and Daddi Addoun and Lovejoy, "The Arabic Manuscript of Muḥammad Kabā Saghanughu of Jamaica, c. 1820," in *Creole Concerns: Essays in Honour of Kamau Brathwaite*, ed. Annie Paul (Kingston: University of the West Indies Press, 2007), 313–41. Initially, Daddi Addoun and I failed to identify the location of Bouka, although we speculated on several places. It is now clear that Bouka is located on the Tinkisso River, approximately 150 kms east of Timbo and 200 kms west of Kankan, near Dinguerye.

24. On ransoming, see Jennifer Lofkrantz, "Intellectual Discourse in the Early Sokoto Caliphate: The Triumvirate's Opinions on the Issue of Ransoming c. 1810," *International Journal of African Historical Studies* 45, no. 3 (2012): 385–401; Jennifer Lofkrantz and Olatunji Ojo, "Slavery, Freedom, and Failed Ransom Negotiations in West Africa, 1730–1900," *Journal of African History* 53, no. 1 (2012): 25–44; Lofkrantz, "Protecting Freeborn Muslims: The Sokoto Caliphate's Attempts to Prevent Illegal Enslavement and Its Acceptance of the Strategy of Ransoming," *Slavery and Abolition* 32, no. 1 (2011): 109–27; Lofkrantz, "Ransoming of Captives in the Sokoto Caliphate in the Nineteenth Century," in *Slavery, Islam and Diaspora*, ed. Behnaz A. Mirzai, Ismael Musah Montana, and Paul E. Lovejoy (Trenton, NJ: Africa World Press, 2009), 125–37; and Lofkrantz, "Ransoming Policies and Practices in the Western and Central Bilād al-Sūdān, c. 1800–1910" (Ph.D. dissertation, York University, 2008).

25. Philip D. Curtin, "Ayuba Suleiman Diallo of Bondu," in *Africa Remembered: Narratives by West Africans from the Era of the Slave Trade*, ed. Philip D. Curtin (Madison: University of Wisconsin Press, 1967), 40, which is based on Thomas

Bluett, *Some Memoirs of the Life of Job, the Son of Solomon, the High Priest of Boonda in Africa; Who Was a Slave about Two Years in Maryland; and Afterwards Being Brought to England, Was Set Free, and Sent to His Native Land in the Year 1734* (London: R. Ford, 1734); also citing Francis Moore, *Travels into the Interior Parts of Africa* (London: Edward Cave, 1738), 69. Also see Allan D. Austin, "Job Ben Solomon—African Nobleman and a Father of African American Literature," in *African Muslims in Antebellum America: Transatlantic Stories and Spiritual Struggles* (New York: Routledge, 1997), 51–62; Arthur Pierce Middleton, "The Strange Story of Job Ben Solomon," *William and Mary Quarterly,* 5, no. 3 (1948): 342–50; and Douglas Grant, *The Fortunate Slave: An Illustration of African Slavery in the Early Eighteenth Century* (London: Oxford University Press, 1968).

26. Ayuba b. Suleiman to his father, ca. 1734, British Library, UIN 000070272, "A collection, ms. and printed, illustrative of various alphabets, etc., brought together by Joseph Ames and pasted in a scrap-book," folio 120r. I thank Paul Naylor, British Library and the University of Birmingham, for drawing this letter to my attention and providing a translation.

27. Jane Landers, *Atlantic Creoles in the Age of Revolutions* (Cambridge, MA: Harvard University Press, 2010), 15–19, 38–39, 41, 51–54.

28. See Kenneth Morgan, "Liverpool Ascendant: British Merchants and the Slave Trade at Sierra Leone, 1701–1808," 29–50, 51–68; Bruce Mouser, "'Keep Hur Bottom Well Paid with Stuff': A Letter of Instruction for a Slaving Venture to the Sierra Leone Coast in 1760," 5168; Denise Jones, "Robert Bostock of Liverpool and the British Slave Trade on the Upper Guinea Coast, 1769-93," 69–88, 89–108; Sean Kelley, "The Dirty Business of Panyarring and Palaver: Slave Trading on the Upper Guinea Coast in the Eighteenth Century," 89–108; and Paul E. Lovejoy and Suzanne Schwarz, "Sierra Leone in the Eighteenth and Nineteenth Century," 163–88, all in *Slavery, Abolition and the Transition to Colonialism in Sierra Leone*, ed. Paul E. Lovejoy and Suzanne Schwarz (Trenton, NJ: Africa World Press, 2015). Also see the relationships established by Zephaniah Kingsley and John Faser, two Florida planters who married women from Rio Pongo, which are discussed in Daniel L. Schafer, "Shades of Freedom: Anna Kingsley in Senegal, Florida, and Haiti," in *Against the Odds: Free Blacks in the Slave Societies of the Americas*, ed. Jane Landers (London: Psychology Press, 1996), 130–54; Schafer, *Zephaniah Kingsley Jr. and the Atlantic World: Slave Trader, Plantation Owner, Emancipator* (Gainesville: University Press of Florida, 2013); Schafer, *Anna Madgigine Jai Kingsley: African Princess, Florida Slave, Plantation Slaveowner* (Gainesville: University Press of Florida, 2003); Schafer, "Family Ties That Bind: Anglo-African Slave Traders in Africa and Florida, John Fraser and His Descendants," *Slavery and Abolition* 20, no. 3 (1999): 1–21; and Landers, *Atlantic Creoles in the Age of Revolutions*, 128–29 and notes.

29. Allan D. Austin, ed., *African Muslims in Antebellum America: A Sourcebook* (New York: Garland, 1984), 109ff.

30. Ibid., 265.

31. Robert L. Fraser, "PIERPOINT, RICHARD," in *Dictionary of Canadian Biography*, vol. 7, University of Toronto/Université Laval, 2003-, accessed July 16,

2016, http://www.biographi.ca/en/bio/pierpoint_richard_7E.html; and David Meyler and Peter Meyler, *A Stolen Life: Searching for Richard Pierpoint* (Toronto: Natural Heritage Books, 1999).

32. Also see Vanicléia Silva Santos, "As Bolsas de Mandinga no espaço Atlântico século XVIII" (Ph.D. dissertation, Universidade de São Paulo, 2008).

33. George Truman, John Jackson, and Thos. B. Longstreth, *Narrative of a Visit to the West Indies, in 1840 and 1841* (Philadelphia: Merrihew and Thompson, Printers, 1844).

34. The most scholarly account is Ivor Wilks, "Salih Bilali of Massina," in Curtin, *Africa Remembered*, 145–51. Also see Allan D. Austin, "Salih Bilali of Massina—Tom of Georgia," in Austin, *African Muslims in Antebellum America: A Sourcebook*, 309–408.

35. Rebecca Scott and Jean-Michel Hébrard, "Rosalie of the Poulard Nation: Freedom, Law, and Dignity in the Era of the Haitian Revolution," in *Biography and the Black Atlantic*, ed. Lisa W. Lindsay and John Wood Sweet (Philadelphia: University of Pennsylvania Press, 2013), 248–67; Rebecca J. Scott and Jean M. Hébrard, *Freedom Papers: An Atlantic Odyssey in the Age of Emancipation* (Cambridge, MA: Harvard University Press, 2012). For other examples from Louisiana in the eighteenth century, see Gwendolyn Midlo Hall, *Africans in Colonial Louisiana: The Development of Afro-Creole Culture in the Eighteenth Century* (Baton Rouge: Louisiana State University Press, 1992); and Hall, *Slavery and African Ethnicities in the Americas: Restoring the Links* (Chapel Hill: University of North Carolina Press, 2005).

36. For the extensive enslavement during the period when Charles O'Hara was governor of the British Province of Senegambia, see Barry, *Senegambia and the Atlantic Slave Trade*, 139–40. For a discussion of the short-lived British colony, see Paul E. Lovejoy, "Forgotten Colony in Africa: The British Province of Senegambia (1765–83)," in Lovejoy and Schwarz, *Slavery, Abolition and the Transition to Colonialism in Sierra Leone*, 109–26.

37. There were 51 females in a Fulbe population of 205 in the Louisiana sample (Gwendolyn Midlo Hall, "Lousiana Slave Database"), while there were 46 females out of 92 Fulbe in the Maranhão sample (Walter Hawthorne, "Maranhão Inventories Slave Database"); see *Slave Biographies: The Atlantic Database Network*, http://slavebiographies.org.

38. Schwarz, *Zachary Macaulay and the Development of the Sierra Leone Company, 1793–4*, 1:59, 61.

39. Robinson, "Islamic Revolution of Futa Toro," 202–3.

40. This discussion draws on Jennifer Lofkranz and Paul E. Lovejoy, "Maintaining Network Boundaries: Islamic Law and Commerce from Sahara to Guinea Shores," *Slavery and Abolition* 36, no. 2 (2015):211–32.

41. Philip D. Curtin, *Cross-Cultural Trade in World History* (Cambridge: Cambridge University Press, 1984), 1–14. Also see Curtin, "Pre-colonial Trading Networks and Traders: The Diakhanke," in *The Development of Indigenous Trade and Markets in West Africa*, ed. Claude Meillassoux (London: Oxford University Press, 1971), 228–39; Curtin, *Economic Change in Pre-colonial Africa: Senegambia in the Era of the*

Slave Trade (Madison: University of Wisconsin Press, 1975), 59–91; Abner Cohen, "Cultural Strategies in the Organization of Trading Diasporas," in, Meillassoux, The Development of Indigenous Trade and Markets in West Africa, 266–81; Cohen, *Customs and Politics in Urban Africa: A Study of Hausa Migrants in Yoruba Towns* (London: Routledge and Kegan Paul, 1969). An important difference between Cohen and Curtin is that Curtin recognized the importance of the metropole to the diaspora, whereas Cohen did not. Moreover, Sebouh D. Aslanian's statement that Curtin borrowed the concept from Cohen ten years after Cohen published his seminar article is inaccurate (*From the Indian Ocean to the Mediterranean: The Global Trade Networks of Armenian Merchants from New Julfa* [Berkeley: University of California Press, 2011], 7–8, 232–33). I was a graduate student at the University of Wisconsin studying with Curtin in the late 1960s. A specific section of Curtin's graduate course was devoted to "commercial diasporas," where he compared, among other commercial networks, the fur trade of North America with Muslim networks in West Africa, specifically the Juula and their various subsections—Jahanke, Yarse, Marka, Saghanughu, and others, with such clan names as Kaba, Ture, and Cisse.

42. See Ivor Wilks, "Abu Bakr al-Siddiq of Timbuktu," in Curtin, *Africa Remembered*, 152–69. The principal sources for Abū Bakr's life are Madden, *Twelvemonth's Residence in the West Indies*, 2:183–89; G. C. Renouard, "Routes in North Africa, by Abu Bekr es Siddik," *Journal of the Royal Geographical Society* 6 (1836): 100–103; *Friend of Africa* 1, no. 4 (25 February 1841); 1, no. 10 (August 1841); 2, no. 18 (April 1842); and Charles H. Wesley, "The Life and History of Abou Bekir Sadiki, Alias Edward Doulan, Discovered by Dr. Charles H. Wesley," *Journal of Negro History* 21, no. 1 (1936): 52–55.

43. See the discussion in Wilks, "Abu Bakr al-Siddiq of Timbuktu" 152–60.

44. For other biographical accounts, see Austin, *African Muslims in Antebellum America: Transatlantic Stories and Spiritual Struggles*, 115–25, which is based primarily on Theodore Dwight Jr., "Condition and Character of Negroes in Africa," *Methodist Quarterly Review*, January 1864, 77–90; Dwight, "Remarks on the Sereculehs, an African Nation, Accompanied by a Vocabulary in Their Language," *American Annals of Education and Instruction* 5 (1835): 451–56.

45. Paul E. Lovejoy, *Salt of the Desert Sun: A History of Salt Production and Trade in the Central Sudan* (Cambridge: Cambridge University Press, 1986), 179, 211–12.

46. Besides Curtin, "Pre-colonial Trading Networks and Traders," 228–39, and Sanneh, *Jakhanke*, see Richard Roberts, "Ideology, Slavery, and Social Formation: The Evolution of Maraka Slavery in the Middle Niger Valley," in *The Ideology of Slavery in Africa*, ed. Paul E. Lovejoy (Beverly Hills, CA: Sage, 1981), 171–200; Roberts, *Warriors, Merchants, and Slaves: The State and the Economy in the Middle Niger Valley, 1700–1914* (Stanford, CA: Stanford University Press, 1987); and Paul E. Lovejoy, "The Role of the Wangara in the Economic Transformation of the Central Sudan in the Fifteenth and Sixteenth Centuries," *Journal of African History* 19, no. 2 (1978): 173–93.

47. Lamin Sanneh, "The Origins of Clericalism in West African Islam," *Journal of African History* 17, no. 1 (1976): 49–72; Sanneh, "Futa Jallon and the Jakhanke Clerical Tradition, Part 1: The Historical Setting," *Journal of Religion in Africa* 12, no.

1 (1981): 38–64. Also see Austin, *African Muslims in Antebellum America: A Sourcebook*, 415–20; and Sanneh, *Jakhanke.*

48. Dwight, "Condition and Character of Negroes in Africa," 77–90; Dwight, "Remarks on the Sereculehs," 451–56; and *The African Repository* (1834). Also see the discussion in Austin, *African Muslims in Antebellum America: A Sourcebook*, 115–26.

49. Dwight, "Condition and Character of Negroes in Africa," 77–90. See the discussion in Austin, *African Muslims in Antebellum America: A Sourcebook*, 117.

50. Dwight, "Remarks on the Sereculehs;" also see Austin, *African Muslims in Antebellum America: A Sourcebook*, 417.

51. Dwight, "Remarks on the Sereculehs," 451–56.

52. For the trading currencies of the region, see Marion Johnson, "The Currencies of West Africa: Part I," *Journal of African History* 11, no. 1 (1970): 17–49; Johnson, "The Currencies of West Africa: Part II," *Journal of African History* 11, no. 3 (1970): 331–53; Paul E. Lovejoy, "Interregional Monetary Flows in the Precolonial Trade of Nigeria," *Journal of African History* 15, no. 4 (1974): 563–85; Philip D. Curtin, "Africa in the Wider Monetary World, 1250–1850," in *Silver and Gold Flows in the Medieval and Early Modern Worlds*, ed. John F. Richards (Chapel Hill: University of North Carolina Press, 1983), 231–68; James L. A. Webb Jr., "On Currency and Credit in the Western Sahel, 1700–1850," in *Credit, Currencies, and Culture: African Financial Institutions in Historical Perspective*, ed. Endre Stiansen and Jane I. Guyer (Uppsala, Sweden: Nordiska Afrikainstitutet, 1999), 38–56; and Jan Hogendorn and Marion Johnson, *The Shell Money of the Slave Trade* (Cambridge: Cambridge University Press, 2003), 15–18.

53. Polly Hill, "Two Types of West African House Trade," in Meillassoux, *Development of Indigenous Trade and Markets in West Africa*, 303–18.

54. See Lofkranz and Lovejoy, "Maintaining Network Boundaries"; Ghislaine Lydon, *On Trans-Saharan Trails: Islamic Law, Trade Networks, and Cross-Cultural Trade in Nineteenth-Century Western Africa* (Cambridge: Cambridge University Press, 2009), 284 and 296–308. Also see Lydon, "Contracting Caravans: Partnership and Profit in Nineteenth- and Early Twentieth-Century Trans-Saharan Trade," *Journal of Global History* 3 (2008): 89–113; Bruce S. Hall, "Saharan Commerce and Islamic Law: The Question of Usury (ribā) in the Nawāzil literature of Mali and Mauritania, 1700–1929." *African Economic History* 41 (2013), 1–18. Also see Hall, *A History of Race in Muslim West Africa, 1600–1960* (Cambridge: Cambridge University Press, 2011), 88–90; and John Hunwick, "Islamic Financial Institutions: Theoretical Structures and Aspects of Their Application in Sub-Saharan Africa," in Stiansen and Guyer, *Credit, Currencies, and Culture*, 72–99.

55. Andreas W. Massing, "Baghayogho: A Soninke Muslim Diaspora in the Mande World," *Cahiers d'études africaines* 176 (2004): 887–922; Bruce Hall and Charles Stewart, "The Historic 'Core Curriculum' and the Book Market in Islamic West Africa," in *The Trans-Saharan Book Trade: Manuscript Culture, Arabic Literacy and Intellectual History in West Africa*, ed. Graziano Krätli and Ghislaine Lydon (Leiden: Brill, 2011), 109–74; Charles Stewart, "Southern Saharan Scholarship

and Bilād al-Sūdān," *Journal of African History* 17 (1976): 73–93; and Stewart, "10,000 MSS, 1850 Authors across 300 Years."

56. J. R. Patterson, *Kanuri Songs* (Lagos: Government Printer, 1926), 25.

57. Bivar and Hiskett, "Arabic Literature of Nigeria to 1804," 104–48.

58. J. Haafkens, *Chants musulmans en peul* (Leiden: Editions CLE, 1983), 147; also see Humphrey Fisher, "Singing the Lord's Songs in a Strange Land," *Journal of African History* 25 (1984): 216–17.

59. Ukawsaw Gronniosaw, *A Narrative of the Most Remarkable Particulars in the Life of James Albert Ukawsaw Gronniosaw, an African Prince, as Related by Himself* (Bath: W. Gye and T. Mills, [London, 1770]). His English name was James Albert, and he was associated with the Huntingdonian Connexion.

60. In the various accounts of Gronniosaw, there is little about his origins in Borno; see, for example, Vincent Carretta, ed., *Unchained Voices: An Anthology of Black Authors in the English-Speaking World of the Eighteenth Century* (Lexington: University Press of Kentucky, 1996), 55; and Henry Louis Gates Jr., *The Signifying Monkey: A Theory of African-American Literary Criticism* (New York: Oxford University Press, 1988), 131. For an exception, see Jennifer Harris, "Seeing the Light: Re-reading James Albert Ukawsaw Gronniosaw," *English Language Notes* 42, no. 4 (2005): 43–57. The preoccupation with Gronniosaw's account of the "talking book" has missed the important point that if he had been brought up as a Muslim, he would have been taught the basic tenets of Islam, which included at least some literacy in Arabic and hence awareness of the written word.

61. For a discussion of the trade routes from Borno to Asante in the eighteenth century, see Paul E. Lovejoy, *Caravans of Kola: The Hausa Kola Trade, 1700–1900* (Zaria: Ahmadu Bello University Press, 1980), 51–61.

62. For discussions of Pierre Tamata, see Pierre Verger, *Trade Relations between the Bight of Benin and Bahia, 17th–19th Century* (Ibadan: University of Ibadan Press, 1968), 186–90; John Adams, *Remarks on the Country Extending from Cape Palmas to the River Congo, Including Observations on the Manners and Customs of the Inhabitants, with an Appendix Containing an Account of the European Trade with the West Coast of Africa* (London: John Murray, 1823), 77–87; and A. Akindele and C. Aguessy, *Contribution à l'étude de l'histoire de l'ancien royaume de Porto Novo* (Dakar: IFAN, 1953), 73.

63. John Adams referred to Porto Novo as Ardrah (Allada) because the ruling family had been forced to flee Allada earlier in the century to escape from Dahomey; see *Remarks on the Country extending from Cape Palmas to the River Congo*, 78. In the 1840s, if not earlier, there were Muslim slaves in the Dahomey army; see Robin Law, "Islam in Dahomey: A Case Study of the Introduction and Influence of Islam in a Peripheral Area of West Africa," *Scottish Journal of Religious Studies* 4, no. 2 (1986): 107.

64. For early Muslims in Bahia, see João José Reis, *Slave Rebellion in Brazil: The Muslim Uprising of 1835 in Bahia* (Baltimore: Johns Hopkins University Press, 1993), 93. I also draw on Marcia Smith, "The Malê Uprising in Bahia, 1835: Mini-biographies of Leaders and Others Accused" (unpublished paper, History 5570, York University, 1998).

65. Maria Inês Côrtes de Oliveira, "Retrouver une identité: Jeux sociaux des Africains de Bahia (vers 1750–vers 1890)" (thèse pour le doctorat en histoire, Université de Paris–Sorbonne [Paris IV], 1992), 38; and Verger, *Trade Relations*, 224–25.

66. Peter Morton-Williams, "The Oyo Yoruba and the Atlantic Slave Trade, 1670–1830," *Journal of the Historical Society of Nigeria* 3, no. 1 (1964): 25.

67. Verger, *Trade Relations*, 186–90; and Adams, *Remarks on the Country Extending from Cape Palmas to the River Congo*, 82–87.

68. Adams, *Remarks on the Country Extending from Cape Palmas to the River Congo*, 83.

69. Samuel Johnson, *The History of the Yoruba from the Earliest Time to the Beginning of the British Protectorate* (Lagos: C. M. S. Bookshop, 1937), 217. The Yoruba name for the town was Ogodo/Ogudu, while Raka was the Hausa and Nupe name.

70. Robin Law, *The Oyo Empire, c. 1600–c. 1836: A West African Imperialism in the Era of the Atlantic Slave Trade* (Oxford: Clarendon Press, 1977), 205–7. Clapperton and Lander met Hausa Muslims (malams) and craftsmen, whom they identified as slaves, in Lagos and Badagry; see Richard Lander, *Records of Captain Clapperton's Last Expedition to Africa* (London: Colburn and Bentley, 1830), 2:259; and Richard Lander and John Lander, *Journal of an Expedition to Explore the Course and Termination of the Niger* (London: John Murray, 1832), 24–27, which is confirmed by Samuel Johnson, *History of the Yoruba*, 123, 193–94.

71. Verger, *Trade Relations*, 234. For the identification of Hufon, see Yves Person, "Chronologie du royaume gun de Hogbonu (Porto Novo)," *Cahiers d'études africaines* 15 (1975): 237.

72. As translated by A. Salame in Dixon Denham, Hugh Clapperton, and Walter Oudney, *Narrative of Travels and Discoveries in Northern and Central Africa, in the Years 1822, 1823, and 1824*, 2 vols. (London: John Murray, 1828), 2:454.

73. Adams, *Remarks on the Country Extending from Cape Palmas to the River Congo*, xxxviii.

74. Simon Cook, editor of John Adams's journal, learned about the activities of the Hausa traders from a merchant, whom he does not name but who had "resided, at different intervals, a considerable time at the settlement of Lagos, and at other places on the coast of the Bight of Benin," presumably in the 1810s but perhaps earlier; Adams, *Remarks on the Country Extending from Cape Palmas to the River Congo*, xxxvii–xxxviii.

75. Mervyn Hiskett, *The Sword of Truth: The Life and Times of the Shehu Usuman dan Fodio* (New York: Oxford University Press, 1973), 77.

76. 'Uthman dan Fodio, "Boneji Hausa," as translated in Alhaji Garba Saidu, "The Significance of the Shehu's Sermons and Poems in 'Ajami,'" in *Studies in the History of the Sokoto Caliphate: The Sokoto Seminar Papers*, ed. Y. B. Usman (Zaria: Department of History, Ahmadu Bello University, 1979), 205.

77. Muhammad Sani Zahradeen, "'Abd Allah ibn Fodio's Contributions to the Fulani Jihād in Nineteenth-Century Hausaland" (Ph.D. dissertation, McGill University, 1976), 21.

78. Muhammd Bello, *Miftah al-sadad fi'l-aqsam hadhihi 'l-bilād*, quoting Aḥmad Bābā. I thank John Hunwick for his translation of this manuscript.

3. *The Jihād of ʿUthmān dan Fodio in the Central Bilād al-Sūdān*

1. Murray Last, *The Sokoto Caliphate* (London: Longmans, 1967).

2. Heinrich Barth, *Travels and Discoveries in North and Central Africa* (New York: Harper and Brothers, 1859), vol. 1, map at beginning of volume.

3. Dixon Denham used the term "Soudan." See Dixon Denham, Hugh Clapperton, and Walter Oudney, *Narrative of Travels and Discoveries in Northern and Central Africa, in the Years 1822, 1823, and 1824* (London: John Murray, 1828), 1:198, 204, 398, 406; 2:178; Clapperton also did so, 2:207, although he also used "Haussa" interchangeably, 2:219, 363.

4. The scholarly literature on the Sokoto Caliphate is extensive. Besides Last, *Sokoto Caliphate*, see Mervyn Hiskett, *The Sword of Truth: The Life and Times of the Shehu Usuman dan Fodio* (New York: Oxford University Press, 1973); Murray Last, "The Sokoto Caliphate and Borno," in *UNESCO General History of Africa*, vol. 6, ed. J. F. Ade Ajayi (Berkeley: University of California Press, 1989), 555–99; Last, "Reform in West Africa: The Jihād Movement of the Nineteenth Century," in *History of West Africa*, J. F. A. Ajayi and Michael Crowder, eds., (London: Longman, 1977), 2:1–29; and Joseph P. Smaldone, *Warfare in the Sokoto Caliphate: Historical and Sociological Perspectives* (Cambridge: Cambridge University Press, 1977). Also see Y. B. Usman, ed., *Studies in the History of the Sokoto Caliphate: The Sokoto Seminar Papers* (Lagos: Third Press International, 1979), especially Yusufu Abba, "The 1804 Jihād in Hausaland as a Revolution," 20–33; Usman, "The Transformation of Political Communities: Some Notes on a Significant Dimension of the Sokoto Jihād," 34–58; John E. Lavers, "The Diplomatic Relations of the Sokoto Caliphate: Some Thoughts and a Plea," 379–91; Djibo Hamani, "Adar, the Toureg and Sokoto: Relations of Sokoto with the Hausawa and Toureg during the Nineteenth Century," 392–407; Junaidu b. Muhammad al-Bukhari, "A Contribution to the Biography of the Shaykh Usman Mentioning the Various Places Where He Lived," 463–72; and I. A. B. Balogun, "Uthman Dan Fodio: The Mujaddid of West Africa," 473–92. Also see H. Bobboyi and A. M. Yakubu, eds., *The Sokoto Caliphate: History and Legacies, 1804–2004* (Kaduna: Arewa House, 2006), especially Usman M. Bugaje, "Scholarship and Revolution: The Impact of a Tradition of *Tajdid* on the Sokoto Caliphal Leaders," 2:11–21; Abubakar Gwandu, "The Vision and Mission of Shaykh Abdullahi Fodio," 2:23–39; Al-Amin Abu-Manga, "The Role of the 'Pen' in the Establishment and Consolidation of the Sokoto Caliphate," 2:40–52; Mahmud M. Tukur, "The Teachings of the Sokoto Caliphate," 2:53–80; Ibrahim Ado-Kurawa, "The *Jihād* and the Consolidation of Sudanic Intellectual Tradition," 2:81–99; Mohammed S. Abdulkadir, "The Effects of the Extension of the Sokoto Caliphate on the Igala Kingdom," 1:53–65; and Murray Last, "Innovation in the Sokoto Caliphate," 2:328–47. Also see Ahmed M. Kani and K. A. Gandi, eds., *State and Society in the Sokoto Caliphate: Essays in Honour of Sultan Ibrahim Dasuki* (Sokoto: Usmanu Danfodiyo University, 1990), including I. A. B. Balogun, "Shaikh Uthman Danfodiyo: Founder of the Sokoto Heritage," 207–22; A. R. Mohammed, "The Sokoto Jihād and Its Impact on the Confluence Area and Afenmai," 142–57; and Ibrahim Sulaiman, "Towards a Vision of the Future: A Letter from Sultan Muhammad Bello to the Muslim *Ummah* in Nigeria," 2:396–408. In addition, see A. Abba, "The Establishment of Gombe Emirate, 1804–1882," 1:11–30. For further

works, see Ahmed M. Kani, *The Intellectual Origin of the Sokoto Caliphate* (Ibadan: Imam Publication, 1984); Usman M. Bugaje, "The Tradition of Tajdid in Western Bilad al-Sudan: A Study of the Genesis, Development and Patterns of Islamic Revivalism in the Region, 990–1900 AD" (Ph.D. dissertation, University of Khartoum, 1991); M. S. Zahradeen, "Abdullahi Ibn Fodio's Contributions to the Fulani Jihād in the 19th Century Hausaland (Ph.D. dissertation, McGill University, 1976); Omar Bello, "The Political Thought of Muhammad Bello (1781–1837) as Revealed in His Arabic Writings, More Especially *al-Ghayth al-wabl fi sirat al-imam al-adl*" (Ph.D. dissertation, University of London, 1983); S. Y. Omoiya, "Diplomacy as Veritable Instrument of War: A Study of Ilorin Wars of Survival as an Emirate," *Ilorin Journal of History* 1, no. 2 (2006): 73–85; Seyni Moumouni, *Vie et oeuvre du Cheik Uthmân Dan Fodio (1754–1817): De l'Islam au soufisme* (Paris: L'Harmattan, 2008); John O. Hunwick and R.S. O'Fahey, eds., *Arabic Literature of Africa, Volume 2: Writings of Central Sudanic Africa* (Leiden: Brill, 1995); Bawaru M. Barkindo, ed., *Studies in the History of Kano* (Ibadan: Heinemann, 1983); M. T. M. Minna, "Sultan Muhammad Bello and His Intellectual Contribution to the Sokoto Caliphate" (Ph.D. dissertation, University of London, 1982); Halil Ibrahim Sa'id, "Revolution and Reaction: The Fulani Jihād in Kano and Its Aftermath, 1807–1919" (Ph.D. dissertation, University of Michigan, 1978); and I. A. B. Balogun, *The Life and Works of 'Uthman Dan Fodio* (Lagos: Islamic Publications Bureau, 1975).

5. Yusufu Bala Usman, *The Transformation of Katsina, c. 1796–1903: The Overthrow of the Sarauta System and the Establishment and Evolution of the Emirate* (Zaria: Ahmadu Bello University Press, 1978), 100; although Smaldone (*Warfare in the Sokoto Caliphate*, 21–22) says that the meeting occurred in 1788–89. For the chronology of the Gobir rulers, see Hiskett, *Sword of Truth*, 44–49.

6. Smaldone, *Warfare in the Sokoto Caliphate*, 21–22.

7. Last, *Sokoto Caliphate*, 25; Hiskett, *Sword of Truth*, 94–95; Smaldone, *Warfare in the Sokoto Caliphate*, 30.

8. Djibo Hamani, *L'Adar précolonial (République du Niger): Contribution à l'étude de l'histoire des états Hausa* (Paris: L'Harmattan, 1975), 148–75.

9. The most detailed account of the extensive warfare in Kano territory is M. G. Smith, *Government in Kano, 1350–1950* (Boulder, CO: Westview Press: 1997), 187–201.

10. Usman, *Transformation of Katsina*, 94, 106–109.

11. Ibid., 124.

12. M. G. Smith, "A Hausa Kingdom: Maradi under Dan Baskore, 1854–1875," in *West African Kingdoms in the Nineteenth Century*, ed. Daryll Forde and Phyllis Kaberry (London: Oxford University Press), 93–122.

13. Ibid., 98.

14. M. G. Smith, *The Affairs of Daura: History and Change in a Hausa State, 1800–1958* (Berkeley: University of California Press, 1978), 145–51.

15. The discussion on Zaria is based on M. G. Smith, *Government in Zazzau: A Study of Government in the Hausa Chiefdom of Zaria in Northern Nigeria from 1800 to 1950* (London: Oxford University Press, 1960), 137–78.

16. For the discussion of the jihād in Borno, I am relying primarily on Louis Brenner, *The Shehus of Kukawa: A History of the Al-Kanemi Dynasty of Bornu* (Oxford: Clarendon Press, 1973), especially 28–48.

17. Ibid., 30.

18. Ibid., 32.

19. Ibid., 47–48.

20. Muhammad Bello, *Infāq al-Maysūr fī tārīkh bilād at-Takrūr*, ed. Bahija Chadli (Rabat: Institute of African Studies, [1812] 1996), 69–72, as translated by Yacine Daddi Addoun.

21. Femi James Kolapo, "Military Turbulence, Population Displacement and Commerce on a Slaving Frontier of the Sokoto Caliphate: Nupe, c. 1810–1857" (Ph.D. dissertation, York University, 1999), 236, notes that Clapperton was told that Abd al-Rahman was "a noted chief of banditti [who] with his followers overran Nyffe and held possession of the capital for six months," citing Hugh Clapperton, *Journal of a Second Expedition into the Interior of Africa* (London: John Murray, 1829), 133.

22. Kolapo, "Military Turbulence," 43; Clapperton, *Journal of a Second Expedition*, 133.

23. Some traditions claim he was killed around 1819, but Clapperton's report shows that he was still alive in 1826. He actually died in April 1829; for a brief biography, see Michael Mason, "The Nupe Kingdom in the Nineteenth Century: A Political History" (Ph.D. dissertation, University of Birmingham, 1970), 59–63.

24. Kolapo, "Military Turbulence," 43.

25. See ibid., 44, for a discussion of the set of wars around 1820–24 that led to the succession of Majiya (Kolapo writes Manjiya) to the throne.

26. Ibid., 241.

27. Richard Lander, *Records of Captain Clapperton's Last Expedition to Africa* (London: Colburn and Bentley, 1830), 1:175. Also see Michael Mason, *The Foundations of the Bida Kingdom* (Zaria: Ahmadu Bello University Press, 1979), 29; and Kolapo, "Military Turbulence," 248.

28. Kolapo, "Military Turbulence," 43–46, 236–48.

29. Ibid., 43–49.

30. Robin Law, "The Oyo-Dahomey Wars, 1726–1823: A Military Analysis," in *Warfare and Diplomacy in Precolonial Nigeria*, ed. Toyin Falola and Robin Law (Madison: African Studies Program, University of Wisconsin–Madison, 1992), 9–25. For a more detailed overview, see Jamie Bruce Lockhart and Paul E. Lovejoy, introduction to *Hugh Clapperton into the Interior of Africa: Records of the Second Expedition, 1825–1827*, ed. Jamie Bruce Lockhart and Paul E. Lovejoy (Leiden: Brill, 2005), 35–46.

31. See I. A. Akinjogbin, "Prelude to the Yoruba Civil Wars of the Nineteenth Century," *Odu* 1, no. 2 (1965): 24–46; Akinjogbin, "A Chronology of Yoruba History, 1789–1840," *Odu* 2, no. 2 (1966): 81–86; Robin Law, "The Chronology of Yoruba Wars of the Early Nineteenth Century: A Reconsideration," *Journal of the Historical Society of Nigeria* 5 (1970): 211–22; Peter Morton-Williams, "The Fulani Penetration into

Nupe and Yorubaland in the Nineteenth Century," in *History and Social Anthropology*, ed. I. M. Lewis (London: Tavistock Publications, 1968), 1–24; T. G. O. Gbadamosi, *The Growth of Islam among the Yoruba, 1841–1908* (Atlantic Highlands, NJ: Humanities Press, 1978), chap. 1; Toyin Falola, "The Impact of the Nineteenth-Century Sokoto Jihād on Yorubaland," in Kani and Gandi, *State and Society in the Sokoto Caliphate*, 126–41; J. A. Atanda, "The Fall of the Old Oyo Empire: A Reconsideration of Its Cause," *Journal of the Historical Society of Nigeria* 5 (1971): 477–90; Atanda, "The Yoruba Wars and the Collapse of the Old Oyo Empire," in *Yoruba Historiography*, ed. Toyin Falola (Madison: African Studies Program, University of Wisconsin–Madison, 1991), 105–21; Hakeem Olumide Akanni Danmole, "The Frontier Emirate: A History of Islam in Ilorin" (Ph.D. dissertation, University of Birmingham, 1980); Danmole, "Samuel Johnson and the History of Ilorin," in *Pioneer, Patriot, and Patriarch: Samuel Johnson and the Yoruba People*, ed. Toyin Falola (Madison: African Studies Program, University of Wisconsin–Madison, 1993), 139–49; Danmole, "Emirate of the 'Yarba': Ilorin in the Nineteenth Century," in Bobboyi and Yakubu, *Sokoto Caliphate*, 1:31–52; and Ann O'Hear, "Samuel Johnson and the *Dramatis Personae* of Early Nineteenth-Century Ilorin," in Falola, *Pioneer, Patriot, and Patriarch*, 151–61. Also see Ann O'Hear, *Power Relations in Nigeria: Ilorin Slaves and Their Successors* (Rochester, NY: University of Rochester Press, 1997).

32. Although the jihād is a major factor in the seminal work of Robin Law, *The Oyo Empire, c. 1600–c. 1836: A West African Imperialism in the Era of the Atlantic Slave Trade* (Oxford: Clarendon Press, 1977), Law considers that jihād was only one influence during this period; see Law, "Chronology of the Yoruba Wars of the Early Nineteenth Century"; Law, "The Owu War in Yoruba History," *Journal of the Historical Society of Nigeria* 7, no. 1 (1973): 141–47; and Law, "Making Sense of a Traditional Narrative: Political Disintegration in the Kingdom of Oyo," *Cahiers d'études africaines* 22 (1982): 387–401. Similarly, J. D. Y. Peel argues for the centrality of Islam in the construction of Yoruba identity in the nineteenth century but does not explore the jihād movement as a decisive phenomenon in that development; see *Religious Encounter and the Making of the Yoruba* (Bloomington: Indiana University Press, 2000). By contrast, the jihād is seen as a central factor in my analysis in Paul E. Lovejoy, "The Yoruba Factor in the Trans-Atlantic Slave Trade," in *The Yoruba Diaspora in the Atlantic World*, ed. Toyin Falola and Matt D. Childs (Bloomington: Indiana University Press), 40–55. Also see Toyin Falola, ed., *Yoruba Historiography* (Madison: African Studies Program, University of Wisconsin–Madison, 1991); and Ade Obayemi, "History, Culture, Yoruba and Northern Factors," in *Studies in Yoruba History and Culture*, ed. G. O. Olusanya (Ibadan: University of Ibadan Press, 1983), 72–87.

33. João José Reis, "Ethnic Politics among Africans in Nineteenth-Century Bahia," in *Identity in the Shadow of Slavery*, ed. Paul E. Lovejoy (London: Continuum, 2000), 240–64; Reis, "African Nations and Cultural Practices in Nineteenth-Century Salvador, Bahia" (paper presented at the conference "American Counterpoint: New Approaches to Slavery and Abolition in Brazil," Yale University, 2010); Reis, "Resistência escrava na Bahia: 'Poderemos brincar, folgar e cantar . . .'; O

protesto escravo na America," *Afro-Ásia* 14 (1983): 107–23; Reis, "Um balanço dos estudos sobre as revoltas escravas da Bahia," in *Escravidão e invenção da liberdade*, ed. João José Reis (São Paulo: Brasiliense, 1988), 87–141; João José Reis and Eduardo Silva, *Negociação e conflito: Resistência negra no Brasil escravista* (São Paulo: Companhia das Letras, 1989). Also see Paulo F. de Moraes Farias, "'Yoruba Origins' Revisited by Muslims," in *Self-Assertion and Brokerage: Early Cultural Nationalism in West Africa*, ed. P. F. de Moraes Farias and Karin Barber (Birmingham: Centre of West African Studies, 1990), 109–47; Farias, "Enquanto isso, do outro lado do mar: Os Arókin e a identidade iorubá," *Afro-Ásia* 17 (1996): 139–55; B. J. Barickman, "Reading the 1835 Parish Censuses from Bahia: Citizenship, Kinship, Slavery, and Household in Early Nineteenth-Century Brazil," *Americas* 59, no. 3 (2003): 287–324; Priscilla Mello, "Leitura, encantamento e rebelião o Islã Negro no Brasil sécolo XIX" (Ph.D. dissertation, Universidade Federal Fluminense, 2009); José Cairus, "Jihād, Captivity and Redemption: Slavery and Resistance in the Path of Allah, Central Sudan and Bahia" (unpublished paper presented at the conference "Slavery and Religion in the Modern World," Essaouira [Morocco], 2001); Cairus, "Intrumentum vocale, mallams e alufás: O paradoxo islâmico da erudição na diáspora africana no Atlântico," *Topoi* 6 (2003): 128–64; and Cairus, "Jihād, cativeiro e redenção: Escravidão, resistência e irmandade, Sudão Central e Bahia (1835)" (dissertação de mestrado ao PPGH, Universidade Federal do Rio de Janeiro, 2002).

34. Crowther to Jowett, 22 February 1837, in Frederick Schön and Samuel Crowther, *Journals of the Rev. Frederick Schön and Mr. Samuel Crowther: Expedition up the Niger in 1841* (London: Church Missionary Society, 1854), app. III; and Samuel Crowther and John C. Taylor. *The Gospel on the Banks of the Niger: Journals and Notices of the Native Missionaries Accompanying the Niger Expedition of 1857–1859* (London: Frank Cass, 1968 [1859]), 100, 126–27. For an authoritative account of Samuel Ajayi Crowther, see J. F. A. Ajayi, "Samuel Ajayi Crowther of Oyo," in *Africa Remembered: Narratives by West Africans from the Era of the Slave Trade*, ed. Philip D. Curtin (Madison: University of Wisconsin Press, 1967), 289–316. Also see Jesse Page, *The Black Bishop* (London: Simpkin, Marshall, Hamilton, Kent and Company, 1910); Jean Herskovits Kopytoff, *A Preface to Modern Nigeria: The "Sierra Leonians" in Yoruba, 1830–1890* (Madison: University of Wisconsin Press, 1965), 285; "Bishop Crowther: His Life and Work," *Church Missionary Gleaner* 5 (1878): 10–11; Samuel Crowther, "Letter of Mr. Samuel Crowther to the Rev. William Jowett, Feb. 22, 1837," *Church Missionary Record* 8 (1837): 217–23; "A Liberated African's Account of His Slavery, and Subsequent Course," *Church Missionary Gleaner* 6 (1846): 16–18; and Schön and Crowther, *Journals*, 371–85.

35. Bruce Lockhart and Lovejoy, *Clapperton into the Interior of Africa*, 36–37, 40–50, 55, 57. Also see Lander, *Records of Captain Clapperton's Last Expedition to Africa*; and Richard Lander and John Lander, *Journal of a Narrative to Explore the Course and Termination of the Niger*, 2 vols. (London: John Murray, 1832).

36. Crowther to Jowett, 22 February 1837, in Schön and Crowther, *Journals*, app. III; and Crowther and Taylor, *Gospel on the Banks of the Niger*, 100, 126–27.

37. Brenner, *Shehus of Kukuwa*, 30.

38. Mahmoud Hamman, "The Rise and Fall of the Emirate of Muri (Hamaruwa), c. 1812–1903" (Ph.D. dissertation, Ahmadu Bello University, 1983).

39. Martin Z. Njeuma, "The Establishment of Adamawa Emirate and Its Legacies in Northern Cameroon," in Bobboyi and Yakubu, *Sokoto Caliphate*, 2:164–65.

40. Martin Z. Njeuma, *Fulani Hegemony in Yola (Old Adamawa), 1809–1902* (Yaoundé: Publishing and Production Centre for Teaching and Research, 1978), 68.

41. Ibid., 262–65.

42. Modibbo Tukur, "The Imposition of British Colonial Domination on the Sokoto Caliphate, Borno and Neighbouring States, 1897–1914" (Ph.D. dissertation, Ahmadu Bello University, 1979), 203; S. A. Balogun, "Gwandu Emirates in the Nineteenth Century with Special Reference to Political Relations: 1817–1903" (Ph.D. dissertation, University of Ibadan, 1971).

43. Humphrey J. Fisher, "A Muslim William Wilberforce? The Sokoto Jihad as Anti-slavery Crusade: An Enquiry into Historical Causes," in *De la traite à l'esclavage: Actes du Colloque international sur la traite des noirs*, ed. Serge Daget (Nantes: Centre de recherche sur l'histoire du monde atlantique, 1985), 2:537.

44. Lovejoy, "Yoruba Factor in the Trans-Atlantic Slave Trade," 40–55.

45. Mervin Hiskett, trans., "*Kitāb al-farq*: A Work on the Habe Kingdoms Attributed to Uthman dan Fodio," *Bulletin of the School of Oriental and African Studies* 23 (1960): 558–73.

46. As translated in Abdul Azim Islahi, "Shehu Uthman Dan Fodio and His Economic Ideas," *Munich Personal RePEc Archive*, 2008, 1.

47. See Ismael Musah Montana, "The *Hatk al-Sitr* of al-Timbuktawi on Enslaved Africans' Religious Practices in Nineteenth-Century Tunisia (Translation and Introduction)" (M.A. thesis, York University, 1999), 22–23.

48. Ismael Musah Montana, "Bori Practice among Enslaved West Africans of Ottoman Tunis: Unbelief (Kufr) or Another Dimension of the African Diaspora?," *History of the Family* 16 (2011): 152–59; Montana, "Ahmad ibn al-Qādi al-Timbuktāwī on the *Bori* Ceremonies of Tunis," in *Slavery on the Frontiers of Islam*, ed. Paul E. Lovejoy (Princeton, NJ: Markus Wiener, 2004), 173–98.

49. Muhammad Bello, *Infāq al-Maysūr fī tārīkh bilād at-Takrūr*, 69–72, as translated by Yacine Daddi Addoun. Also see Muhammad Bello, *Infaq al-Maisur* [1812], in E. J. Arnett, *The Rise of the Sokoto Fulani* (Kano: n.p., 1929). Also see Y. A. Quadri, "An Appraisal of Muhammad Bello's *Infaqul-maysur ft tarikhi bilad t-Takrur*," *Journal of Arabic and Religious Studies* 3 (1986): 53–62.

50. For the political context of the Sokoto-Borno debate, see Louis Brenner, "The Jihād Debate between Sokoto and Borno: An Historical Analysis of Islamic Political Discourse in Nigeria," in *People and Empires in African History: Essays in Memory of Michael Crowder*, ed. J. F. Ade Ajayi and J. D. Y. Peel (London: Longman, 1992), 21–43.

51. On Borno, see Muhammad N. Alkali, "El-Kanemi's Response to the Extension of Shaykh ᶜUthman Dan Fodio's *Jihād* against Borno," in Bobboyi and Yakubu, *Sokoto Caliphate*, 1:231–39; Brenner, "Jihād Debate between Sokoto and Borno," 21–43; and Brenner, *Shehus of Kukawa*.

52. For Nupe, see Kolapo, "Military Turbulence"; Femi James Kolapo, "Ethnicity and Identity at the Niger-Benue during the 19th-Century Nupe Jihād," in *Slavery in Africa and the Caribbean: A History of Enslavement and Identity since the 18th Century*, ed. Olatunji Ojo and Nadine Hunt (New York: I. B. Tauris, 2012), 9–37; Kolapo, "Niger River Trade and the Interregnum at Aboh, 1844–1862," in *Repercussions of the Atlantic Slave Trade: The Interior of the Bight of Biafra and the African Diaspora*, ed. Caroline A. Brown and Paul E. Lovejoy (Trenton, NJ: Africa World Press, 2011), 205–20; Kolapo, "The Dynamics of Early 19th Century Nupe Wars," *Scientia Militaria: South African Journal of Military Studies* 31, no. 2 (2003): 1–35; Mason, "Nupe Kingdom in the Nineteenth Century"; Mason, *Foundations of the Bida Kingdom*; Michael Mason, "The Jihād in the South: An Outline of Nineteenth Century Nupe Hegemony in North-eastern Yorubaland and Afenmai," *Journal of the Historical Society of Nigeria* 5, no. 2 (1970): 193–209; Mason, "Population and 'Slave Raiding'—The Case of the Middle Belt of Nigeria," *Journal of African History* 10, no. 4 (1969): 551–64; Mohammed, "Sokoto Jihād and Its Impact"; and Ade Obayemi, "The Sokoto Jihād and the O-kun Yoruba: A Review," *Journal of the Historical Society of Nigeria* 9, no. 2 (1978): 61–87.

53. In *Tanbih al-ikhwan* (1811), 'Uthman dan Fodio noted the complaints of the Gobir government over the number of people who had joined him at Degel. Although slaves are not mentioned in this account, other evidence suggests that enslaved Muslims were part of this exodus.

54. 'Uthman dan Fodio, *Tanbih al-ikhwan*, as translated in Zahradeen, "'Abd Allah ibn Fodio's Contributions to the Fulani Jihād," 190.

55. A Hausa poem describes the incident; see Mervyn Hiskett, "The 'Song of the Shaihu's Miracles': A Hausa Hagiography from Sokoto," *African Language Studies* 12 (1971): 95. Also see Last, *Sokoto Caliphate*, 14–16; and Murray Last, "'Injustice' and Legitimacy in the Early Sokoto Caliphate," in Ajayi and Peel, eds., *People and Empires in African History*, 45–57.

56. Abdullahi dan Fodio, *Tazyīn al-waraqāt*, trans. M. Hiskett (Ibadan: University of Ibadan Press, 1963), 122.

57. Shehu Yamusa, "The Political Ideas of the Jihād Leaders: Being a Translation, Edition and Analysis of (1) *Uṣūl al-siyāsa* by Muḥammad Bello and (2) *Ḍiyā' al-ḥukkām* by Abdallah B. Fodio" (M.A. thesis, Bayero University, Kano, 1975), 270–85.

58. Law, *Oyo Empire*, 258.

59. Sigismund Wilhelm Koelle, *Pollyglotta Africana* (Graz: Akademische Druck-u. Verlagsanstalt, 1963), 115–21.

60. In 1830 the Landers learned that the jihād loyalists had made "an offer of freedom and protection, and other promises of the most extravagant nature" to Hausa and other Muslim slaves in Oyo; Lander and Lander, *Journal of an Expedition*, 2:189–90.

61. Law, *Oyo Empire*, 255–58.

62. Lander and Lander, *Journal of an Expedition*, 2:71. For an earlier discussion, see Paul E. Lovejoy, "Fugitive Slaves: Resistance to Slavery in the Sokoto Caliphate,"

in *Resistance: Studies in African, AfroAmerican, and Caribbean History*, ed. Gary Okihiro (Amherst: University of Massachusetts Press, 1986), 80.

63. For ransoming, see Jennifer Lofkrantz, "Intellectual Discourse in the Sokoto Caliphate: The Triumvirate's Opinions on the Issue of Ransoming, ca. 1810," *International Journal of African Historical Studies* 45, no. 3 (2012): 385–401.

64. The importance of ransoming is especially evident in oral testimonies; see various interviews in the Lovejoy/Maccido Collection, the Yusufu Yunusa Collection, and the Ibrahim Jumare Collection (transcripts and translations on deposit at the Harriet Tubman Resource Centre, York University).

65. In *Nūr al-albāb*, ʿUthman dan Fodio condemned the "impious practices which affect this Hausa country, both those which have particularly disrupted it and those which are a general evil." He claimed that "most of our educated men leave their wives, their daughters and their captives morally abandoned, like beasts, without teaching them what God prescribes should be taught them." He believed that the education of these dependents in Islam was "a positive duty"; see Zahradeen, " 'Abd Allah ibn Fodio's Contributions to the Fulani Jihād," 25. Also see Abdullahi dan Muhammad dan Fodio, *Ḍiyāʾ al-sulṭān wa ghayrihi min al-ikhwān fī ahamm ma yuṭlab ʿilmuhu fī umūr al-zamān*, in Zahradeen, " 'Abd Allah ibn Fodio's Contributions to the Fulani Jihād," 13–14; Abdullahi dan Fodio, *Tazyīn al-Waraqāt*; and Abdullahi dan Fodio, *Ḍiyāʾ al-Ḥukkām* (Yamusa, "Political Ideas of the Jihād Leaders," 270–85). Also see the writings of ʿUthmān ibn Muhammad dan Fodio, including *Al-ajwibah al-muharrarah ʿan al-as'ilah almuqarrarah fī wathīqat al-shaykh al-ḥājj al-maʿrūf bilaqabih Shisummas ibn Aḥmad* (Zahradeen, " 'Abd Allah ibn Fodio's Contributions," 20); *Nūr al-albāb*, *Taʿlīm al-ikhwān bi-al-umūr allati kaffarnā bihā mulūk alsūdān alladhīna kānū min ahl hadhih al-buldān*; *Sirāj al-ikhwān fī ahamm mā yuḥtāj ilayhi fī hadha al-zamān*; *Kitāb al-farq*; *Wathīqat ahl al-sūdān*; and *Tanbīh al-ikhwān*. Finally, see Muhammad Bello, *Infāq al-maysūr fī taʾrīkh bilād al-takrūr*; Muhammad Bello, *Miftāḥ al-sadād*; and al-Qādir b. al-Muṣṭafā (d. 1864), *Rawḍat al-afkār*.

66. Zahradeen, " 'Abd Allah ibn Fodio's Contributions to the Fulani Jihād," 30.

67. H. F. C [Abdullahi] Smith, D. M. Last, and Gambo Gubio, "Ali Eisami Gazirmabe of Bornu," in Curtin, *Africa Remembered*, 206–9.

68. At least twenty letters were exchanged between the jihād leadership and al-Kanemi between 1808 and 1812. Many of the letters are in Bello, *Infāq al-Maysūr* (1812); two are translated by Abdullahi Smith and Muhammad Al-Hajj. Another letter from al-Kānimī to Goni Mukhtār, the leader of the jihād forces in Borno, dated 17 Rabīʿ al-Awwal 1223 (13 May 1808), is in the University of Ibadan Library (Ms. 82/237). See D. M. Last and M. A. Al-Hajj, "Attempts at Defining a Muslim in 19th Century Hausaland and Bornu," *Journal of the Historical Society of Nigeria* 3, no. 2 (1965): 239; and Brenner, *Shehus of Kukawa*, 39–43.

69. Alkali, "El-Kanemi's Response," 231–39; and Brenner, "Jihād Debate between Sokoto and Borno," 21–43.

70. Paul E. Lovejoy, "Jihād e escravidão: As origens dos escravos Muculmanos de Bahia," *Topoi* 1 (Rio de Janeiro, 2000): 11–44, which is a revision of Lovejoy, "Background to Rebellion: The Origins of Muslim Slaves in Bahia," *Slavery and Abolition*

15, no. 2 (1994): 151–80. Also see Lovejoy, "Jihād and Slavery: The Origins of Enslaved Muslims in Bahia," in *Slavery, Commerce and Production in the Sokoto Caliphate of West Africa* (Trenton, NJ: Africa World Press, 2005), 55–80; and Lovejoy, *Slavery on the Frontiers of Islam*.

71. Brenner, *Shehus of Kukawa*, 40.

72. Ibid., 40, citing the original Arabic, identified as UI 82/237.

73. Ibid., 41–42.

74. For Brazil, for example, see João José Reis, *Slave Rebellion in Brazil: The Muslim Uprising of 1835 in Bahia* (Baltimore: Johns Hopkins University Press, 1993). For Cuba, see Manuel Barcia, *The Great African Slave Revolt of 1825: Cuba and the Fight for Freedom in Matanzas* (Baton Rouge: Louisiana State University Press, 2012); and Barcia, *Seeds of Insurrection: Domination and Slave Resistance on Cuban Plantations* (Baton Rouge: Louisiana State University Press, 2008). Specifically for Prieto, see Henry Lovejoy, "Old Oyo Influences on the Transformation of Lucumí Identity in Colonial Cuba" (Ph.D. dissertation, UCLA, 2012).

75. William A. Brown, "Toward a Chronology for the Caliphate of Hamdullahi (Māsina)," *Cahiers d'études africaines* 8, no. 31 (1968): 428–34.

76. David Robinson, "Revolutions in the Western Sudan," in *History of Islam in West Africa*, ed. Nehemia Levtzion and Randall Pouwels (Athens: Ohio University Press, 2000), 141, 147.

77. Last, "Sokoto Caliphate and Borno," 555–99. Also see A. Batran, "The Nineteenth-Century Islamic Revolutions in West Africa," in Ajayi, *UNESCO General History of Africa*, 6:537–54; Mervyn Hiskett, "The Nineteenth-Century Jihāds in West Africa," in *The Cambridge History of Africa*, ed. J. D. Fage and Roland Oliver (Cambridge: Cambridge University Press, 1976), 5:125–69; Sa'ad Abubakar, "The Established Caliphate: Sokoto, the Emirates and Their Neighbors," in *Groundwork of Nigerian History*, ed. Obaro Ikime (Ibadan: Heinemann, 1980), 305–26; Abubakar, "Borno in the Nineteenth Century," ibid., 327–46; and Robinson, "Revolutions in the Western Sudan," 131–68.

78. Beverly B. Mack and Jean Boyd, *One Woman's Jihād: Nana Asma'u, Scholar and Scribe* (Bloomington: Indiana University Press, 2000); Jean Boyd, ed., *Collected Works of Nana Asma'u, Daughter of Usman 'dan Fodiyo (1793–1864)* (East Lansing: Michigan State University Press, 2012).

79. Last, *Sokoto Caliphate*; Last, "Reform in West Africa," 1–46.

80. Besides the information in Clapperton's account, also see Barth, *Travels and Discoveries*, 4:162, 168–69.

81. Last, *Sokoto Caliphate*, 77–78.

82. Silame was first entrusted to Muhammad Bello's son Muhammad Mudi. For a discussion of *ribāṭ*, see John Edward Philips, "Slavery on Two Ribat in Kano and Sokoto," in Lovejoy, *Slavery on the Frontiers of Islam*, 111–24.

83. Last, "Reform in West Africa," vol. 2, 1.

84. Ibid.

85. Omar Jah, "The Effect of Pilgrimage on the Jihād of Al-Hajj 'Umar al-Futi, 1794–1864," in *The Central Bilad al Sudan: Tradition and Adaptation*, ed. Yusuf Fadl

Hasan and Paul Doornbos (Khartoum: University of Khartoum Press, 1977), 239. Also see Omar Jah, "Al-Haj 'Umar's Philosophy of Jihād and Its Sufi Basis" (Ph.D. dissertation, McGill University, 1974).

86. R. A. Adeleye, "Rabih Fadlallah, 1879–1893: Exploits and Impact on Political Relations in Central Sudan," *Journal of the Historical Society of Nigeria* 5, no. 2 (1970): 223–42; and Muhammad Al-Hajj, "Hayatu b. Sa'id: A Revolutionary Mahdist in the Western Sudan," in *The Sudan in Africa: Studies Presented to the First International Conference Sponsored by the Sudan Research Unit*, ed. Y. Fadl Hasan (Khartoum: Khartoum University Press, 1971), 128–41.

87. For a discussion, see Hamani, *L'Adar précolonial*, 136–41.

88. For a selection of texts on jihād, see 'Uthman dan Fodio, *Bayan wujub al hijra 'ala 'l-'ibad (The Exposition of Obligation of Emigration upon the Servants of God)*, ed. and trans. F. H. El Masri (Khartoum: University of Khartoum Press, 1978). For works by Abdullahi dan Fodio, see *Diyā' Ahl al-Rashād fī Ahkām al-Hijrah wa 'l-Jihād wa 'l-Sunnah fī Siyāsat al-'Ibād*, which deals with *hijra*, jihād, and the administration of justice; *Diyā' al-Hukkām fī-mā lahum wa alaihim min al-Ahkām*, written in AH 1219, 1804–5 CE, at the request of Muslims in Kano; *Diyā' al-Mujāhidīn, Humāt al-Dīn al-Rāshidīn* (AH 1226 AH, 1811 CE), which deals with jihād and gives detailed instructions on the code of conduct; and *Tazyīn al-Waraqāt bi-Jam' Ba'd mā li min al-Abyāt* (AH 1228, 1813 CE), which is a history of the jihād movement in Hausaland. For a discussion, see Abubaker Aliu Gwandu, "Abdullahi b. Fodio as a Muslim Jurist" (Ph.D. dissertation, University of Durham, 1977), 208–10, 226.

89. Last, *Sokoto Caliphate*; Last, "Reform Movements in West Africa," 1–46; Last, "Sokoto Caliphate and Borno," 555–99. Also see Batran, "Nineteenth-Century Islamic Revolutions in West Africa," 537–54; Hiskett, "The Nineteenth-Century Jihāds in West Africa"; Abubakar, "Established Caliphate," 305–26; Abubakar, "Borno in the Nineteenth Century," 327–46; and Robinson, "Revolutions in the Western Sudan," 131–68.

90. Graziano Krätli and Ghislaine Lydon, eds., *The Trans-Saharan Book Trade: Manuscript Culture, Arabic Literacy, and Intellectual History in West Africa* (Leiden: Brill, 2011); and Scott Reese, ed., *The Transmission of Learning in Islamic Africa* (Leiden: Brill, 2004).

91. Scholarship on these events appeared as early as Thomas Hodgkin, ed., *Nigerian Perspectives: An Historical Anthology* (London: Oxford University Press, 1960); and especially H. F. C. [Abdullahi] Smith, "A Neglected Theme of West African History: The Islamic Revolutions of the 19th Century," *Journal of the Historical Society of Nigeria* 2, no. 2 (1961): 169–85. Subsequently there was an outpouring of scholarship on the jihād and its leadership.

4. The Economic Impact of Jihād in West Africa

1. Kenneth F. Kiple, *Blacks in Colonial Cuba, 1774–1899* (Gainesville: University Presses of Florida, 1976); Robert Conrad, *The Destruction of Brazilian Slavery, 1850–1888* (Berkeley: University of California Press, 1972), 26, 281; and Gilder Lehrman Institute of American History, "Facts about the Slave Trade and Slavery," based on the

US census, 1860. http://www.gilderlehrman.org/history-by-era/slavery-and-anti
-slavery/resources/facts-about-slave-trade-and-slavery. Also see Herbert Klein, "African Women in the Atlantic Slave Trade," in *Women and Slavery in Africa*, ed.
Claire C. Robertson and Martin A. Klein (Portsmouth, NH: Heinemann, 1997), 29–
38; Manolo Garcia Florentino, *Em costas negras: Uma historia do trafico de escravos
entre a Africa e o Rio de Janeiro, 1790–1830* (São Paulo: Companhia das Letras, 1997);
Hebe Mattos, *Das cores do silencio: Os significados da liberdade no sudeste escravista,
século XIX* (Campinas: EdUNICAMP, 2014); and Flavio dos Santos Gomes, *Historias
de quilombolas: Mocambos e comunidades de senzalas no Rio de Janeiro, século XIX*
(Rio de Janeiro: Arquivo Nacional, 1995).

2. Dale W. Tomich, *Through the Prism of Slavery: Labor, Capital, and World
Economy* (Lanham, MD: Rowman and Littlefield, 2004); Anthony E. Kaye, "The Sec-
ond Slavery: Modernity in the Nineteenth-Century South and the Atlantic World,"
Journal of Southern History 75, no. 3 (2009): 627. Also see Tomich, "The 'Second
Slavery': Bonded Labor and the Transformations of the Nineteenth-Century World
Economy," in *Rethinking the Nineteenth Century: Contradictions and Movements*, ed.
Francisco O. Ramírez (New York: Greenwood, 1988), 103–17; Tomich, "The Wealth
of the Empire: Francisco de Arango y Parreno, Political Economy, and the Second
Slavery in Cuba," *Comparative Studies in Society and History* 1 (2003): 4–28; Dale W.
Tomich and Michael Zeuske, eds., "The Second Slavery: Mass Slavery, World-
Economy, and Comparative Microhistories, Part II," special issue, *Review: A Journal
of the Fernand Braudel Center* 31 (2008); Tomich, "Atlantic History and World Econ-
omy: Concepts and Constructions," *Proto Sociology: An International Journal of
Interdisciplinary Research* 20 (2004): 102–21; and Michael Zeuske, "Historiography
and Research Problems of Slavery and the Slave Trade in a Global-Historical
Perspective," *International Review of Social History* 57, no. 1 (2012): 87–111.

3. This chapter builds on my earlier analysis in *Transformations in Slavery: A
History of Slavery in Africa* in 1983 and extended through later editions, published in
2000 and 2012; references are to the third edition (Cambridge: Cambridge University Press, 2012). See especially 186–217. This chapter also draws on the analysis of
the colonial impact on the plantation economy of the Sokoto Caliphate as discussed
in Paul E. Lovejoy and Jan Hogendorn, *Slow Death for Slavery: The Course of Abolition in Northern Nigeria, 1897–1936* (Cambridge: Cambridge University Press, 1993),
especially 128–36, 165–85.

4. Paul E. Lovejoy and A. S. Kanya-Forstner, eds., *Slavery and Its Abolition in
French West Africa* (Madison: African Studies Program, University of Wisconsin–
Madison, 1994).

5. Lovejoy, *Transformations in Slavery*, 186–96.

6. For the size of the slave population in the area that became Afrique Occiden-
tale Française, see Martin A. Klein, *Slavery and Colonial Rule in French West Africa*
(Cambridge: Cambridge University Press, 1998), 252–56. Klein bases his estimates
largely on the reports of colonial officials, especially the K series in Dakar, which are
summarized in the reports of E. Poulet and E. Deherme; see Lovejoy and Kanya-
Forstner, *Slavery and Its Abolition in French West Africa*. The relative scale of slave

populations in Islamic West Africa is also discussed in Lovejoy, *Transformations in Slavery*, 186–96; and Lovejoy and Hogendorn, *Slow Death for Slavery*, 1–2.

7. Martin A. Klein, "Women in Slavery in the Western Sudan," in Robertson and Klein, *Women and Slavery in Africa*, 69. Also see Lovejoy, *Transformations in Slavery*, 187.

8. For the extent of urbanization, see Paul E. Lovejoy, "The Urban Background of Enslaved Muslims in the Americas," *Slavery and Abolition* 26, no. 3 (2005): 347–72.

9. Alan Frishman, "The Population Growth of Kano, Nigeria," in *African Historical Demography*, ed. Christopher Fyfe (Centre of African Studies, University of Edinburgh, 1977), 212–50. Also see Saleh Abubakar, "Aspects of an Urban Phenomenon: Sokoto and Its Hinterland to c. 1850," in *Studies in the History of the Sokoto Caliphate*, ed. Y. B. Usman (Zaria: Department of History, Ahmadu Bello University, 1979), 125–39.

10. In the British census of 1911, Sokoto Province had thirteen towns with populations over 6,000, the largest being Sokoto with 21,624, Isa with 18,919, and Kaura-Namoda with 13,067, while Bongudu, Gwandu, Moriki, Wurno, Gusau, Jega, Talata Mafara, Gummi, Argungu, and Birnin Kebbi had populations from 6,000 to 10,000. See Garba Na-dama, "Urbanization in the Sokoto Caliphate: A Case Study of Gusau and Kaura-Namoda," in Usman, *Studies in the History of the Sokoto Caliphate*, 140–62. These estimates did not include the large number of people who moved to the towns from the adjacent countryside during the long dry season.

11. Lovejoy, *Transformations in Slavery*, 204.

12. Paul E. Lovejoy, *Caravans of Kola: The Hausa Kola Trade, 1700–1900* (Zaria: Ahmadu Bello University Press, 1980), 65.

13. These included Cheboa, Tibati, Ngaundere, Banyo, Malabu, Rai-Buba, Song, Zummo, Gola, Holma, Pakorgel, Marwa, Bogo, Kobotshi, Laro, Belel, Daware, Mayo-Farang, Sorau, Madagali, Gider, Michika, Moda, Mubi, Uba, Mindif, Binder, Ridadu, Bibemi, Kalfu, Be, Demsa (Cisiga), Vokna, Tola, Agorma, Pette, Wuro Mayo-Najarendi, Mbere, Garwa, and Balala, besides the capital, Yola. For a discussion, see Paul E. Lovejoy, *Slavery, Commerce and Production in West Africa: Slave Society in the Sokoto Caliphate* (Trenton, NJ, Africa World Press, 2005), chap. 1. Also see Ahmadou Séhou, "L'esclavage dans les Lamidats de l'Adamaoua (Nord-Cameroun), du début du XIXᵉ siècle" (thèse pour le doctorat, Université de Yaounde I, 2010).

14. Modibbo Tukur, "The Imposition of British Colonial Domination on the Sokoto Caliphate, Borno and Neighbouring States, 1897–1914" (Ph.D. dissertation, Ahmadu Bello University, 1979), 204.

15. Y. A. Aliyu, "Establishment and Development of Emirate Government in Bauchi, 1805–1903" (Ph.D. dissertation, Ahmadu Bello University, 1974), 479–80; and Tukur, "Imposition of British Colonial Domination," 204.

16. For a summary, see Polly Hill, *Rural Hausa: A Village and a Setting* (Cambridge: Cambridge University Press, 1972), 40, 319. E. A. Ayandele has noted that "without slaves the economy would have collapsed"; see "Observations on Some Social and Economic Aspects of Slavery in Pre-colonial Northern Nigeria," *Nigerian Journal of Economic and Social Studies* 9 (1967): 333.

17. Frederick D. Lugard, *Instructions to Political and Other Officers, on Subjects Chiefly Political and Administrative* (London: Waterloo, 1906), 296, 301; and S. A. Balogun, "Economic Activities and Ties of Gwandu Emirates and Their Neighbors in the Nineteenth Century" (unpublished paper, Kano Seminar, Kano, 1976).

18. Polly Hill, "From Slavery to Freedom: The Case of Farm-Slavery in Nigerian Hausaland," *Comparative Studies in Society and History* 18 (1976): 395–426; Michael Mason, "Captive and Client Labour and the Economy of the Bida Emirate, 1857–1901,"*Journal of African History* 14 (1973): 453–71; Allan Meyers, "Slavery in the Hausa-Fulani Emirates," in *Aspects of West African Islam*, ed. Daniel F. McCall and Norman R. Bennett (Boston: African Studies Center, Boston University, 1971), 173–84; M. G. Smith, *The Economy of Hausa Communities of Zaria* (London: H.M.S.O., 1955), 81–82; Smith, "Slavery and Emancipation in Two Societies," in *The Plural Society in the British West Indies* (Berkeley: University of California Press, 1965), 116–61; Lugard, *Instructions to Political and Other Officers*, 296–302; Irmgard Sellnow, "Die Stellung der Sklaven in der Hausa-Gesellschaft," *Mitteilungen aus des Institut für Orientforschung* 10 (1946): 85–102; Joseph Paul Irwin, *Liptako Speaks: History from Oral Tradition in Africa* (Princeton, NJ: Princeton University Press, 1981); and Jean-Claude Froelich, "Le commandement et l'organisation sociale chez les Fulbe de l'Adamoua (Cameroun)," *Etudes Camerounaises* 45–46 (1954): 5–91.

19. Heinrich Barth, *Travels and Discoveries in North and Central Africa* (New York: Harper and Brothers, 1859), 2:174, 190–91.

20. Paul E. Lovejoy and Steven Baier, "The Desert-Side Economy of the Central Sudan," *International Journal of African Historical Studies* 8, no. 4 (1975): 551–81. Also see Philip D. Curtin, *Economic Change in Pre-colonial Africa: Senegambia in the Era of the Slave Trade* (Madison: University of Wisconsin Press, 1975), app. I; Sèkéné-Mody Cissoko, "Famines et épidémies à Tombouctou et dans la Boucle du Niger du XVIe au XVIIIᵉ siècle," *Bulletin de l'IFAN* 30, no. 3 (1968): 815; and "Kitab Ghunja," as translated in Jack Goody, *The Ethnography of the Northern Territories of the Gold Coast* (London: Colonial Office, 1954), 41.

21. Philip D. Curtin, "Ayuba Suleiman Diallo of Bondu," in *Africa Remembered: Narratives by West Africans from the Era of the Slave Trade*, ed. Philip D. Curtin (Madison: University of Wisconsin Press, 1967), 17, 40.

22. R. R. Madden, *A Twelvemonth's Residence in the West Indies, during the Transition from Slavery to Apprenticeship* (Westport, CT: Negro University Press, 1970 [1835]), 2:135. For a discussion, see Yacine Daddi Addoun and Paul E. Lovejoy, "Muḥammad Kabā Saghanughu and the Muslim Community of Jamaica," in *Slavery on the Frontiers of Islam*, ed. Paul E. Lovejoy (Princeton, NJ: Markus Wiener, 2004), 201–20.

23. Abū Bakr's father, Kara Mūsā, is described as *tafsīr*, which, according to Ivor Wilks, is a grammatically corrupt form of *mufassir*, i.e., someone learned in Qur'ānic exegesis and a common term in West Africa. His paternal greatgrandfather, 'Umar, was a *qa'id*, i.e., a judge, and his maternal greatgrandfather was a *shahid 'lmalik*, i.e., a "king's witness," presumably a jurisconsult. See Wilks, "Abu Bakr al-Siddiq of Timbuktu," in Curtin, *Africa Remembered*, 152–69. Also see Madden, *Twelvemonth's Residence in the West Indies*, 2:183–89; G. C. Renouard, "Routes in North Africa, by

Abú Bekr es Siddík," *Journal of the Royal Geographical Society* 6 (1836): 100–103; and Charles H. Wesley, "The Life and History of Abou Bekir Sadiki, Alias Edward Doulan," *Journal of Negro History* 21, no. 1 (1936): 52–55.

24. Ivor Wilks, "The Juula and the Expansion of Islam into the Forest," in *The History of Islam in West Africa*, ed. Nehemia Levtzion and Randall L. Pouwels (Athens: Ohio University Press, 2000), 97–98.

25. Mohammed Bashir Salau, *The West African Slave Plantation: A Case Study* (New York: Palgrave Macmillan, 2011); Salau, "Ribats and the Development of Plantations in the Sokoto Caliphate: A Case Study of Fanisau," *African Economic History* 34 (2006): 23–43; Salau, "Slavery in Kano Emirate of Sokoto Caliphate as Recounted: Testimonies of Isyaku and Idrisu," in *African Voices on Slavery and the Slave Trade*, vol. 1, ed. Alice Bellagamba, Sandra E. Greene, and Martin A. Klein (Cambridge: Cambridge University Press, 2013), 88–116; Salau, "Slave Trading in Kano Emirate," in *Slavery in Africa and the Caribbean: A History of Enslavement and Identity since the Eighteenth Century*, ed. Olatunji Ojo and Nadine Hunt (London: I. B. Tauris, 2012), 38–64; Salau, "Voices of Those Who Testified on Slavery in Kano Emirate," in *Crossing Memories: Slavery and African Diaspora*, ed. Ana L. Aruajo, Mariana P. Candido, and Paul E. Lovejoy (Trenton, NJ: Africa World Press, 2011), 129–45; and Salau, "Slaves in a Muslim City: A Survey of Slavery in Nineteenth Century Kano," in *Slavery, Islam and Diaspora*, ed. Behnaz A. Mirzai, Ismael Musah Montana, and Paul E. Lovejoy (Trenton, NJ: Africa World Press, 2009), 91–101.

26. Séhou, "L'esclavage dans les Lamidats de l'Adamaoua."

27. See, for example, Abba Tuja Mafama, "Some Aspects of Slavery in Borno" (B.A. paper, Bayero University College, 1977); and J. H. Patterson, Borsari District Report, Borno Province, 21 August 1918, 504p/1918, Arewa House, Kaduna.

28. Ibrahim Jumare, "Land Tenure in the Sokoto Sultanate of Nigeria" (Ph.D. dissertation, York University, 1995); Salau, *West African Slave Plantation*; Salau, "Slaves in a Muslim City," 91–101; and Salau, "Ribats and the Development of Plantations in the Sokoto Caliphate," 23–43.

29. J. S. Hogendorn, "The Economics of Slave Use on Two 'Plantations' in the Zaria Emirate of the Sokoto Caliphate," *International Journal of African Historical Studies* 10 (1977): 372; Paul E. Lovejoy, "Plantations in the Economy of the Sokoto Caliphate," *Journal of African History* 19, no. 3 (1978): 341–68; Lovejoy, *Caravans of Kola*, chap. 5; Mary Smith, *Baba of Karo: A Woman of the Moslem Hausa* (London: Faber, 1955), 37–40; M. G. Smith, *The Affairs of Daura: History and Change in a Hausa State, 1800–1958* (Berkeley: University of California Press, 1978), 32, 43, 268–69, 271, 277–78, 281; M. G. Smith, *Development and Organization of the Fulani Chiefdom of Kaura Namoda, 1809–1903* (Zaria: Papers of the Institute of Administration, Ahmadu Bello University, 1972), 49–50; M. G. Smith, "Slavery and Emancipation in Two Societies," 116–61; Hill, "From Slavery to Freedom," 417–20; Y. B. Usman, *The Transformation of Katsina, c. 1796–1903: The Overthrow of the Sarauta System and the Establishment and Evolution of the Emirate* (Zaria: Ahmadu Bello University Press, 1978); Mason, "Captive and Client Labour and the Economy of the Bida Emirate," 453–71; Sa'ad Abubakar, "A Survey of the Economy of the Eastern Emirates of the

Sokoto Caliphate in the Nineteenth Century" (paper presented at the Third Annual Seminar, Departments of History, Ahmadu Bello University and Abdullahi Bayero College, Sokoto, 1975); Abubakar, *The Lāmībe of Fombina:: A Political History of Adamawa, 1809–1901* (Zaria: Ahmadu Bello University Press, 1979); R. J. Gavin, "The Economy of Ilorin" (paper presented at the University of Birmingham, 1976); Barth, *Travels and Discoveries in North and Central Africa*, 2:159, 163, 174, 190–96; Lugard, *Instructions to Political and Other Officers*, 296–302; Froelich, "Commandement et l'organisation sociale," 5–91; Siegfried Passarge, *Adamaua: Bericht über die Expedition des deutschen Kamerun-Komilees in den Jahren 1893/94* (Berlin: Geographische Verlagshandlung D. Reimer, 1895), 108, 261–62; R. Bruce, "The Gindiri Rinji, 1890–1907" (paper presented at the Kano Seminar, Kano,1976); Bruce, "The Fulani Settlement of Butu, Slavery and the Trade in Slaves," in *Studies in the History of Plateau State, Nigeria*, ed. E. Isichei (London: Macmillan, 1982), 191–205; and David C. Tambo, "The Pre-colonial Tin Industry in Northern Nigeria" (paper presented at the Kano Seminar, Kano, 1976). Extensive data on the plantation system are also contained in the oral testimonies collected during 1975–76 at Ahmadu Bello University, Zaria, under the supervision of Paul E. Lovejoy and Jan S. Hogendorn, which are deposited there, as well as at the Harriet Tubman Resource Centre on the African Diaspora, York University. Relevant collections include those by J. S. Hogendorn (Zaria), Paul E. Lovejoy and Ahmadu Maccido (Zaria), Aliyu Bala Umar (Kano), Yusufu Yunusa (Kano), O. S. Ahmed (Nassarawa), Aliyu Musa (Kano), A. Babangida (Hadejia), and Musa Ahmed (Katagum). For a discussion, see Paul E. Lovejoy and Jan S. Hogendorn, "Oral Data Collection and the Economic History of the Central Savanna," *Savanna* 7 (1978): 71–74.

30. M. G. Smith, *Government in Zazzau: A Study of Government in the Hausa Chiefdom of Zaria in Northern Nigeria from 1800 to 1950* (London: Oxford University Press, 1960), 81.

31. For a discussion, see Lovejoy and Hogendorn, *Slow Death for Slavery*, 168–80.

32. The problem of defining what constituted a plantation is discussed in Paul E. Lovejoy, "The Characteristics of Plantations in the Nineteenth-Century Sokoto Caliphate (Islamic West Africa)," *American Historical Review* 84 no. 5 (1979): 1267–92. Also see M. G. Smith, *Economy of Hausa Communities of Zaria*, 81–82, 102–8; M. G. Smith, "Slavery and Emancipation in Two Societies," 116–61; Mason, "Captive and Client Labour," 453–71; Michael Mason, "Trade and State in Nineteenth-Century Nupe" (paper presented at the Seminar on the Economic History of the Central Savanna of West Africa, Kano, 1976); Hill, "From Slavery to Freedom," 395–426; and Hogendorn, "Economics of Slave Use," 369–83.

33. Salau, *West African Slave Plantation*.

34. The characteristics of these plantations are discussed more fully in Lovejoy, *Slavery, Commerce and Production in West Africa*. For a survey of the plantation sector, see Lovejoy, "Plantations in the Economy of the Sokoto Caliphate," 341–68; and Salau, *West African Slave Plantation*.

35. For a discussion of the development of the regional market, see Paul E. Lovejoy, "Interregional Monetary Flows in the Precolonial Trade of Nigeria," *Journal of*

African History 15 (1974): 563–85; Lovejoy, "The Borno Salt Industry," *International Journal of African Historical Studies* 10 (1977): 465–80; Lovejoy, *Caravans of Kola*, chaps. 3–5; Lovejoy and Baier, "Desert-Side Economy of the Central Sudan," 551–81; Philip Shea, "The Development of an Export-Oriented Dyed Cloth Industry in Kano Emirate in the Nineteenth Century" (Ph.D. dissertation, University of Wisconsin, 1975); Abubakar, "Survey of the Economy of the Eastern Emirates of the Sokoto Caliphate;" Mason, "Trade and State in Nineteenth-Century Nupe"; and Mason, "Captive and Client Labour," 453–71.

36. Hugh Clapperton, *Journal of a Second Expedition into the Interior of Africa* (London: John Murray, 1829), 213–14. For the text of the manuscript, see Jamie Bruce Lockhart and Paul E. Lovejoy, eds., *Hugh Clapperton into the Interior of Africa: Records of the Second Expedition, 1825–1827* (Leiden: Brill, 2005), 311.

37. Ibid.

38. Douglas E. Ferguson, "Nineteenth-Century Hausaland, Being a Description by Imam Imoru of the Land, Economy, and Society of His People" (Ph.D. dissertation, UCLA, 1973), 230.

39. Interview with Shamakin Sarkin Kano, Alhaji Inuwa Bak'indo, 19 July 1980, conducted by Abdulrazak Giginyu Sa'idu, in Sa'idu, "History of a Slave Village in Kano: Gandun Nassarawa" (B.A. thesis, Bayero University, Kano, 1981), 201–7. Gandun Nassarawa was located just outside the walls of Kano City near K'ofar Mata (Mata Gate).

40. Ibid., 107.

41. Ibid., 106–107.

42. Ibid., 113. This description of Dorayi contradicts the analysis of Polly Hill in her study of Dorayi, who argued on the basis of her field research that Dorayi had little contact with Kano City. However, Dorayi was located only a couple of kilometers from the nearest gate into Kano, and the farms and plantations that were located there were clearly managed by owners who lived in Kano. See Polly Hill, *Population, Prosperity, and Poverty: Rural Kano, 1900 and 1970* (Cambridge: Cambridge University Press, 1977).

43. See interview with Idrisu Danmaiso, Hausawa Ward, Kano, 7 August 1975. Danmaiso was born about 1900.

44. Yusufu Yunusa, "Slavery in 19th Century Kano" (B.A. thesis, Ahmadu Bello University, 1976), 35–41, 55–64.

45. Many of the emir's *gandu* were located along rivers. Gogel and Giwaran, for example, were on opposite sides of the Challawa. Of these two estates, Giwaran was the larger; see Yunusa, "Slavery in 19th Century Kano," 59. For information on Gandun Suwaina, located in Minjibir District, twenty-five miles northeast of Kano, see interview with Zubairu, 11 September 1975 (Yunusa Collection). Zubairu was born around 1915. For Darmanawa, which was established early in the nineteenth century by Emir Dabo, see interview with Malam Yunusa Darmanawa, 23 August 1975 (Yunusa Collection). Other estates were located at Hungu and Fanda in Gaya District and Durumin Shura, near Kano, although these three estates may have been established under colonial rule. Other estates were located at Takai, Fanisau, Gogel,

Giwarah, and Shanono. For information on Giwaran and Gandun Gogel, located seventeen miles southeast of Kano city, see interview with Malam Sa'adu, Gandun Gogel, 23 August 1975; interview with Sarkin Bagarmi, Gandun Giwaran (born ca. 1910), 23 August 1975; and interview with Malam Yunusa Darmanawa (Yunusa Collection). For information on the estate at Fanisau, see interview with Galadiman Shamaki Hamidu (born ca. 1905), Fanisau, 3 April 1975. It should be noted that both Clapperton and Barth visited this estate. For information on Ruwan Kuka (Danbatta District) and Wasai, see interview with Galadiman Shamaki Hamidu, Fanisau, 3 April 1975. For Gogel, Gurjiya, Nassarawa, and Gangara, see interview with Malam Bawa, Dambazau Ward, Kano City, 31 July 1975 (Yunusa Collection). Bawa was born sometime before 1890.

46. Lovejoy and Baier, "Desert-Side Economy of the Central Sudan," 551–58; and Paul E. Lovejoy, *Salt of the Desert Sun: A History of Salt Production and Trade in the Central Sudan* (Cambridge: Cambridge University Press, 1986).

47. Lovejoy and Baier, "Desert-Side Economy of the Central Sudan," 551–81; Steven Baier and Paul E. Lovejoy, "The Tuareg of the Central Sudan: Gradations in Servility at the Desert Edge (Niger and Nigeria)," in *Slavery in Africa: Historical and Anthropological Perspectives,* ed. Suzanne Miers and Igor Kopytoff (Madison: University of Wisconsin Press, 1977), 391–411; Benedetta Rossi, *From Slavery to Aid: Power, Labour, and Mobility in the West African Sahel, 1800–2000* (Cambridge: Cambridge University Press, 2015).

48. Barth, *Travels and Discoveries in North and Central Africa,* 1:527–28.

49. Murray Last, *The Sokoto Caliphate* (London: Longmans, 1967), 79–80; and Last, "An Aspect of the Caliph Muhammad Bello's Social Policy," *Kano Studies* 1 (1966): 56–59.

50. Clapperton, *Journal of a Second Expedition,* 192.

51. Ibid., 192, 216–17, 220, 225, 243–45; and Balogun, "Economic Activities and Ties of Gwandu Emirates."

52. Featherstone Cargill, Resident Kano, 27 May 1908, in File 7173, "Kano Province Economic Survey, 1909," in John Paden, "The Influence of Religious Elites on Political Culture and Community Integration in Kano, Nigeria (Ph.D. dissertation, Harvard University, 1968), 1302–4.

53. According to G. P. Bargery, *A Hausa-English Dictionary and English-Hausa Vocabulary* (London: Oxford University Press, 1934), 470, *hurumi* was defined as, first, a compound that was not assessed for tax but had to pay heavy demands made on it by a district head or other "native official"; second, a cemetery; third, common land; fourth, a forest or other reserve; fifth, an official farm that could not be alienated; and finally, any private property.

54. See *Ta'lim al-radi* (1809–10), a tract on land tenure, as translated in Muhammad Sani Zahradeen, "'Abd Allah ibn Fodio's Contributions to the Fulani Jihād in Nineteenth Century Hausaland" (Ph.D. dissertation, McGill University, 1976), 263–66. Also see Frederick Lugard, *Political Memoranda: Revisions of Instructions to Political Officers on Subjects Chiefly Political and Administrative,* 3rd ed., ed. A. H. M. Kirk-Greene (London: Frank Cass, 1970 [1918]), 360.

55. Cargill, 27 May 1908, in Paden, "Influence of Religious Elites," 1302–4.

56. Bargery, *Hausa-English Dictionary*, 146.

57. E. G. M. Dupigny, Assessment Report, Sarkin Dawaki Tsakkar Gidda District, SNP 7/10 5570/1909, Nigerian National Archives, Kaduna.

58. Cargill, 27 May 1908, in Paden, "Influence of Religious Elites," 1302–4. For Zaria, see interview with Malam Ali of Kudan, 8 December 1975, Ahmadu Maccido Collection, tape no. 3. Kudan was in the midst of an important cotton-growing district.

59. According to Bargery, *Hausa-English Dictionary*, 822, a *nomijide*, *nomijidi*, or *nomijiji* was a person "living in the jurisdiction of one, and farming in the jurisdiction of another." *Nomi-* is derived from *noma*, farming, and hence invariably referred to scattered holdings. Dupigny defined a *nomijide* as an "absentee farmer . . . who resides in one town and farms on the lands of another town paying his taxes to the latter and, as a rule, not acknowledging fealty to either town"; Dupigny, Assessment Report, Sarkin Dawaki Tsakkar Gidda District.

60. Arthur H. Festing report, 1907, in W. P. Hewby, Report on Kano Emirate, 10 July 1908, SNP 6/4 c.111/1908, Nigerian National Archives, Kaduna.

61. N. M. Gepp, Assessment Report, Dan Isa's Sub-District, 5 May 1911, SNP 7/12 1035/1911, Nigerian National Archives, Kaduna.

62. W. P. Hewby, Report on Kano Emirate, 10 July 1908, SNP 6/4 c.111/1908. Also see H. Foulkes, Assessment Report, Jaidanawa District, SNP 7/13 4817/1912, Nigerian National Archives, Kaduna.

63. Dupigny, Assessment Report, Sarkin Dawaki Tsakkar Gidda District.

64. Dupigny learned that *nomijide* could not be conscripted to perform labor for the colonial state because they had specific rights in relation to the land. According to Dupigny, "If they were asked to assist in clearing the roads they would only do so if they felt disposed to (the inclination was usually unfavourable) but that there could be no compulsion in the matter." See Dupigny, Assessment Report, Sarkin Dawaki Tsakkar Gidda District.

65. Edward John Stanley, Resident, Sokoto Province, Report No. 36 on Sokoto Province for Half-Year Ending June 30, 1908, Sokprof 2/9 985/1908, Nigerian National Archives, Kaduna.

66. Ibid.

67. Ibid.

68. Mary Smith, *Baba of Karo*.

69. Lovejoy, *Caravans of Kola*, chap. 5.

70. Ferguson, "Nineteenth-Century Hausaland," 233.

71. Yunusa, "Slavery in Kano," 39–40.

72. C. N. Ubah, *Government and Administration of Kano Emirate, 1900–1930* (Nsukka: University of Nigeria Press, 1985), 57, drawing on oral sources. Also see Abdukarim Umar Dan Asabe, "Comparative Biographies of Selected Leaders of the Kano Commercial Establishment" (M.A. thesis, Bayero University Kano, 1987), 84–87; and Yunusa, "Slavery in Kano," 39–40.

73. Paul E. Lovejoy, "The Kambarin Beriberi: The Formation of a Specialized Group of Hausa Kola Traders in the Nineteenth Century," *Journal of African History*

14 (1973): 633–51; Lovejoy, *Caravans of Kola*; and Lovejoy and Baier, "Desert-Side Economy of the Central Sudan," 551–81.

74. Ibrahim A. Tahir, "Scholars, Sufis, Saints and Capitalists in Kano, 1904–1974: The Pattern of Bourgeois Revolution in an Islamic Society" (Ph.D. dissertation, Cambridge University, 1975), 211.

75. Musa na Madabo, Kano, 1 February 1970, tape 14, Lovejoy Collection, 1969–70, Tubman Institute, York University.

76. Muhammadu Kasori, Kano, January 1970, tape 14, Lovejoy Collection, 1969–70; and Miko Hamshak'i, Bako Madigawa, and Audu Ba'are, Kano, January 1970, tape 12, Lovejoy Collection, 1969–70, Tubman Institute, York University.

77. Tahir, "Scholars, Sufis, Saints and Capitalists," 212.

78. Colleen E. Kriger, "Textile Production and Gender in the Sokoto Caliphate," *Journal of African History* 34 (1993): 361–401; Kriger, "Robes of the Sokoto Caliphate," *African Arts* 21 (1988): 52–86; Kriger, "Mapping the History of Cotton Textile Production in Precolonial West Africa," *African Economic History* 33 (2005): 87–116; Kriger, *Cloth in West African History* (Lanham, MD: AltaMira Press, 2006); Kriger, "The Importance of Mande Textiles in the African Side of the Atlantic Slave Trade, ca. 1680–1710," *Mande Studies* 11 (2009): 1–21; Kriger, "Silk and Sartorial Politics in the Sokoto Caliphate, 1804–1903," in *The Force of Fashion in Politics and Society: Global Perspectives from Early Modern to Modern Times*, ed. Beverly Lemire (London: Ashgate, 2010), 143–63; Kriger, "'Guinea Cloth': Production and Consumption of Cotton Textiles in West Africa, before and during the Atlantic Slave Trade," in *The Spinning World: A Global History of Cotton Textiles, 1200–1850*, ed. Giorgio Riello and Prasannan Parthasarathi (Oxford University Press, 2009), 105–26. Also see Ann O'Hear, "The Introduction of Weft Float Motifs to Strip Weaving in Ilorin," in *West African Economic and Social History: Studies in Memory of Marion Johnson*, ed. David Henige and T. C. McCaskie (Madison: African Studies Program, University of Wisconsin–Madison, 1990), 175–88; and O'Hear, "The Economic History of Ilorin in the Nineteenth and Twentieth Centuries: The Rise and Decline of a Middleman Society" (Ph.D. dissertation, Centre of West African Studies, University of Birmingham, 1983), 121–68. O'Hear's research draws on the Lovejoy-Adesiyun Collection of interviews conducted in Ilorin in 1975, on deposit at the Harriet Tubman Institute at York University and the Centre for West African Studies, University of Birmingham.

79. Philip Shea, "Kano and the Silk Trade," *Kano Studies* 11 (1980): 96–112; Shea, "Approaching the Study of Production in Rural Kano," in *Studies in the History of Kano*, ed. Bawuro M. Barkindo (Ibadan: University of Ibadan Press, 1983), 93–115; and especially Philip Shea, "Collection of Notes on Interviews Concerned with the History of Production of Indigo Dyed Cloth in Kano Emirate, Nigeria," in Shea, "Development of an Export-Oriented Dyed Cloth Industry," appendix.

80. Barth, *Travels and Discoveries in North and Central Africa*, 1:510.

81. Ibid., 1:511.

82. Ibid.

83. Shea, "Development of an Export-Oriented Dyed Cloth Industry," 53–140; and Lovejoy, "Plantations in the Economy of the Sokoto Caliphate," 355–59.

84. Hill, *Rural Hausa*, 39.

85. Kriger, "Mapping the History of Cotton Textile Production in Precolonial West Africa," 87–116; and Kriger, *Cloth in West African History*.

86. Shea, "Development of an Export-Oriented Dyed Cloth Industry," 53–140; and Lovejoy, "Plantations in the Economy of the Sokoto Caliphate," 355–59.

87. C. W. J. Orr, Trade Prospects, 26 October 1904, C.O. 446/43 (1907), National Archives, London. Also see Shea, "Development of an Export-Oriented Dyed Cloth Industry;" Shea, "Black Cloth: An Export Oriented Industry in Kano" (paper presented at the Kano Seminar, Kano, 1976); and, for northern Zaria, the numerous interviews conducted in Kudan, Makarfi, Fatika, Hunkuyi, and Zaria in the Lovejoy-Maccido Collection.

88. Ferguson, "Nineteenth-Century Hausaland," 80; and Lovejoy-Maccido Collection.

89. Ferguson, "Nineteenth-Century Hausaland," 80; Na-dama, "Urbanization in the Sokoto Caliphate."

90. This analysis conflicts with that of Polly Hill, who considers that Zaria was outside the core region; see Hill, "From Slavery to Freedom," 406–7.

5. Jihād and the Slave Trade

1. Michael Gomez, *Black Crescent: The Experience and Legacy of African Muslims in the Americas* (Cambridge: Cambridge University Press, 2005). Also see Sylviane Diouf, *Servants of Allah: African Muslims Enslaved in the Americas* (New York: New York University Press, 1998); Behnaz A. Mirzai, Ismael Musah Montana, and Paul E. Lovejoy, eds., *Slavery, Islam and Diaspora* (Trenton, NJ: Africa World Press, 2009); and Paul E. Lovejoy, ed., *Slavery on the Frontiers of Islam* (Princeton, NJ: Markus Wiener, 2004).

2. Walter Rodney, *A History of the Upper Guinea Coast, 1545–1800* (Oxford: Clarendon Press, 1970), 152–70; Rodney, "Jihād and Social Revolution in Futa Djalon in the Eighteenth Century," *Journal of the Historical Society of Nigeria* 4 (1968): 269–84; Boubacar Barry, "Traite négrière et esclavage interne en Sénégambie au xviiie siècle," in *De la traite esclavage: Actes du Colloque international sur la traite des noirs*, ed. Serge Daget (Nantes: Centre de recherche sur l'histoire du monde atlantique, 1988), 2:213–22; M. S. Balde, "L'esclavage et la guerre sainte au Fuuta-Jalon," in *L'esclavage en Afrique précoloniale*, ed. Claude Meillassoux (Paris: Maspero, 1975), 183–220; Roger Botte, "Les rapports Nord-Sud, la traite négrière et le Fuuta Jaloo à la fin du XVIIIe siècle," *Annales: Économies, Sociétés, Civilisations* 6 (1991): 1411–35; Botte, "Révolte, pouvoir, religion: Les Hubbu du Futa-Jalon Guinée," *Journal of African History* 29 (1988): 391–413; Martin A. Klein, "Social and Economic Factors in the Muslim Revolution in Senegambia," *Journal of African History* 13 (1972): 419–41; J. Boulègue, "L'expression du refus de la traite négrière dans les sociétés sénégambiennes (xviie–xviiie siècles)," in Daget, *De la traite esclavage*, 247–52.

3. For the internal African slave trade, see Paul E. Lovejoy, *Transformations in Slavery: A History of Slavery in Africa*, 3rd ed. (Cambridge: Cambridge University Press, 2011), 91–111, 139–64. Also see Jennifer Lofkrantz and Paul E. Lovejoy,

"Maintaining Network Boundaries: Islamic Law and Commerce from Sahara to Guinea Shores," *Slavery and Abolition* 36, no. 2 (2015): 211–32.

4. Lovejoy, *Transformations in Slavery*.

5. David Richardson, "Shipboard Revolts, African Authority, and the Atlantic Slave Trade," *William and Mary Quarterly* 58, no. 1 (2001): 69–92.

6. See, for example, George E. Brooks, "The Signares of Saint-Louis and Gorée: Women Entrepreneurs in Eighteenth-Century Senegal," in *Women in Africa: Studies in Social and Economic Change*, ed. Nancy Hafkin and Edna G. Bay (Stanford, CA: Stanford University Press, 1976), 19–44; Bruce L. Mouser, "Women Slavers of Guinea-Conakry," in *Women and Slavery in Africa*, ed. Claire C. Robertson and Martin A. Klein (Madison: University of Wisconsin Press, 1983), 323; George E. Brooks, *Eurafricans in Western Africa: Commerce, Social Status, Gender, and Religious Observance from the Sixteenth to the Eighteenth Century* (Athens: University of Ohio Press, 2003); E. Frances White, *Sierra Leone's Settler Women Traders: Women on the Afro-European Frontier* (Ann Arbor: University of Michigan Press, 1987); Emily L. Osborn, *Our New Husbands Are Here: Households, Gender, and Politics in a West African State from the Slave Trade to Colonial Rule* (Athens: Ohio University Press, 2011); and James Searing, *West African Slavery and Atlantic Commerce: The Senegal River Valley, 1700–1860* (Cambridge: Cambridge University Press, 1993).

7. For Fenda Lawrence, see Lillian Ashcraft-Esson, "'She Voluntarily Hath Come': A Gambian Woman Trader in Colonial Georgia in the Eighteenth Century," in *Identity in the Shadow of Slavery*, ed. Paul E. Lovejoy (London: Continuum, 2000), 203–21.

8. Bruce Mouser, *American Colony on the Rio Pongo: The War of 1812, the Slave Trade, and the Proposed Settlement of African Americans, 1810–1830* (Trenton, NJ: Africa World Press, 2013).

9. Daniel L. Schafer, *Anna Madgigine Jai Kingsley: African Princess, Florida Slave, Plantation Slaveowner* (Gainesville: University Press of Florida, 2003). Also see Schafer, *Zephaniah Kngsley Jr. and the Atlantic World: Slave Trader, Plantation Owner, Emancipator* (Gainesville: University Press of Florida, 2013).

10. Ira Berlin, "From Creole to African: Atlantic Creoles and the Origins of African-American Society in Mainland North America," *William and Mary Quarterly* 53, no. 2 (1996): 251–88; and Jane Landers, *Atlantic Creoles in the Age of Revolutions* (Cambridge, MA: Harvard University Press, 2010).

11. Rudolph T. Ware III, *The Walking Qur'an: Islamic Education, Embodied Knowledge, and History in West Africa* (Chapel Hill: University of North Carolina Press, 2014), 122–24, for enslavement of Fulbe along the Senegal River in 1773–76. Also see Boubacar Barry, *Senegambia and the Atlantic Slave Trade* (Cambridge: Cambridge University Press, 1998), 139–40.

12. Walter Hawthorne, *From Africa to Brazil: Culture, Identity, and an Atlantic Slave Trade, 1600–1800* (Cambridge: Cambridge University Press, 2010), 52–53, 68–70.

13. Bruce L. Mouser, "Walking Caravans of Nineteenth Century Fuuta Jalon, Western Africa," *Mande Studies* 12 (2010): 19–104.

14. John O. Hunwick, "'I Wish to Be Seen in Our Land Called Afrika': 'Umar b. Sayyid's Appeal to Be Released from Slavery (1819)," *Journal of Arabic and Islamic Studies* 5 (2003): 62–77.

15. Botte, "Rapports Nord-Sud," 1411–35.

16. Bruce Mouser, ed., *Journal of James Watt: Expedition to Timbo, Capital of the Fula Empire in 1794* (Madison: African Studies Program, University of Wisconsin–Madison, 1994), 44.

17. Watt went to Timbo to open trade to the Niger River beyond Fuuta Jalon; see Mouser, "Walking Caravans of Nineteenth Century Fuuta Jalon," 19–104.

18. Botte, "Rapports Nord-Sud," 1411–35; and Botte, "Révolte, pouvoir, religion," 391–413.

19. Muhammad Bello, *Infāq al-Maysūr fī tārīkh bilād at-Takrūr*, ed. Bahija Chadli (Rabat: Institute of African Studies, [1812] 1996).

20. Kristin Mann, *Slavery and the Birth of an African City: Lagos, 1760–1900* (Bloomington: Indiana University Press, 2007), 38, based on a preliminary analysis of the revised *Voyages: The Trans-Atlantic Slave Trade Database*, www.slavevoyages.org.

21. Paul E. Lovejoy, "The Central Sudan and the Atlantic Slave Trade," in *Paths toward the Past: African Historical Essays in Honor of Jan Vansina*, ed. Robert W. Harms, Joseph C. Miller, David C. Newbury, and Michelle D. Wagner (Atlanta: African Studies Association Press, 1994), 351–55, 361–62.

22. Hugh Clapperton to R. Wilmot Horton, 6 June 1825, in *Missions to the Niger*, ed. E. W. Bovill vol. 4 (Cambridge: Cambridge University Press, 1966), 774.

23. Heinrich Barth, *Travels and Discoveries in North and Central Africa* (New York: Harper and Brothers, 1859), 1:516.

24. Macgregor Laird and R. A. K. Oldfield, *Narrative of an Expedition into the Interior of Africa by the River Niger, in the SteamVessels* Quorra *and* Alburkah *in 1832, 1833 and 1834* (London: Richard Bentley, 1837), 2:322–23; and James Richardson, *Narrative of a Mission to Central Africa Performed in the Years 1850–51* (London: Chapman, 1853), 2:203. See the discussion in Lovejoy, "Central Sudan and the Atlantic Slave Trade," 345–70.

25. James Femi Kolapo, "Military Turbulence, Population Displacement and Commerce on a Trading Frontier of the Sokoto Caliphate: Nupe, c. 1810–1857" (Ph.D. dissertation, York University, 1999).

26. Lovejoy, "Central Sudan and the Atlantic Slave Trade," 345–70.

27. Count de Ponte, Governor of Bahia, despatch of 16 June 1807, as quoted in Pierre Verger, *Trade Relations between the Bight of Benin and Bahia, 17th–19th Century* (Ibadan: University of Ibadan Press, 1976), 17.

28. According to Stuart Schwartz, Yoruba, Ewe, and Hausa constituted a third of Bahia's slave population in the early nineteenth century because of recent importation; see *Sugar Plantations in the Formation of Brazilian Society: Bahia, 1550–1835* (Cambridge: Cambridge University Press, 1985), 437, 475.

29. Sierra Leone slave registers, FO 84/9 and FO 84/15, the National Archives, Kew, as cited in David Eltis, *Economic Growth and the Ending of the Transatlantic Slave Trade* (New York: Cambridge University Press, 1987), 358n.

30. See Patrick Manning, *Slavery, Colonialism, and Economic Growth in Dahomey, 1640–1960* (Cambridge: Cambridge University Press, 1982), app. 2. It should be noted that Manning gives slightly smaller totals for Hausa and Nupe exports elsewhere; see 31. See also Manning, "The Slave Trade in the Bight of Benin, 1640–1890," in *The Uncommon Market: Essays in the Economic History of the Atlantic Slave Trade*, ed. Henry A. Gemery and Jan S. Hogendorn (New York: Academic Press, 1979), 127.

31. Hugh Clapperton to R. Wilmot Horton, 6 June 1825, in Bovill, *Missions to the Niger*, 4:774.

32. David C. Tambo, "The Sokoto Caliphate Slave Trade in the Nineteenth Century," *International Journal of African Historical Studies* 9, no. 2 (1976): 204–17.

33. See, for example, Michael Mason, "Population and 'Slave Raiding'—The Case of the Middle Belt of Nigeria," *Journal of African History* 10, no. 4 (1969): 551–64; and Jan Hogendorn, "Slave Acquisition and Delivery in Precolonial Hausaland," in *West African Culture Dynamics: Archaeological and Historical Perspectives*, ed. Raymond Dumett and Ben K. Schwartz (The Hague: Mouton, 1980), 477–93.

34. "Narrative of a Journey from Egypt to the Western Coast of Africa, by Mahomed Misrah: Communicated by an Officer Serving in Sierra Leone, April 8, 1821," *Quarterly Journal*, October 1822, 14.

35. Antônio de Menezes Vasconcellos de Drummond, "Lettres sur l'Afrique ancienne et moderne," *Journal des Voyages* 32 (1826): 290–324 [*sic*; 190–224]); and Francis de Laporte de Castelnau, *Renseignements sur l'Afrique centrale et sur une nation d'hommes à queue qui s'y trouverait, d'après le rapport des nègres du Soudan, esclaves à Bahia* (Paris: P. Bertrand, 1851).

36. According to David Eltis, "The adult male ratios of the Yoruba and Nupe slaves in the 1821–2 Sierra Leone sample [of freed slaves] are exceptionally high"; *Economic Growth and the Ending of the Transatlantic Slave Trade*, 358n.

37. Paul E. Lovejoy, "Diplomacy in the Heart of Africa: British-Sokoto Negotiations over the Abolition of the Atlantic Slave Trade," in *Distant Ripples of the British Abolitionist Wave in Africa, Asia and the Americas*, ed, Myriam Cottias and Marie-Jeanne Rossignol (Trenton, NJ: Africa World Press, 2016).

38. Hugh Clapperton, *Journal of a Second Expedition into the Interior of Africa* (London: John Murray, 1829), 94.

39. Misrah, "Narrative of a Journey," 6.

40. As reported in Misrah, "Narrative of a Journey," 15–16.

41. Richard Lander, *Records of Captain Clapperton's Last Expedition to Africa* (London: John Murray, 1830), 1:204, 206.

42. Drummond, "Lettres sur l'Afrique ancienne et moderne," 203–5.

43. Ibid., 206–16.

44. Misrah, "Narrative of a Journey," 6, 15–16.

45. Lander, *Records of Captain Clapperton's Last Expedition to Africa*, 1:204, 206.

46. Castelnau, *Renseignements sur l'Afrique centrale*.

47. Ibid., 40.

48. William Allen and T. R. H. Thomson, *A Narrative of the Expedition Sent by Her Majesty's Government to the River Niger in 1841, under the Command of Captain H. D. Trotter, R.N.* (London: Richard Bentley, 1848), 2:178–79, 184.

49. Sigismund Wilhelm Koelle, *Polyglotta Africana* (Graz: Akademische Druck-u. Verlagsanstalt, 1963), 1–21; P. E. H. Hair, "Koelle at Freetown: An Historical Introduction," in Koelle, *Polyglotta Africana*, 7*–17*; Hair, "The Enslavement of Koelle's Informants," *Journal of African History* 6, no. 2 (1965): 193–203. Numbers in parentheses include the reported population of each language group.

50. Koelle, *Polyglotta Africana*, 10, 17.

51. Ibid., 17.

52. Lovejoy, "Central Sudan and the Atlantic Slave Trade," 345–70.

53. Clapperton, *Journal of a Second Expedition into the Interior of Africa*, 94.

54. João José Reis, *Slave Rebellion in Brazil: The Muslim Uprising of 1835 in Bahia* (Baltimore: Johns Hopkins University Press, 1993), 102–3.

55. Philip D. Curtin, *The Atlantic Slave Trade: A Census* (Madison: University of Wisconsin Press, 1969), 244. Curtin, who compiled the census from Parliamentary Papers, 1849 [C.1126], includes Nupe under the Bight of Benin and Hausa under the Bight of Biafra, although it is likely that most Hausa slaves traveled through ports in the Bight of Benin, not the Bight of Biafra.

56. João José Reis, "Slave Rebellion in Brazil: The African Muslim Uprising in Bahia, 1835" (Ph.D. dissertation, University of Minnesota, 1983), 146–47; also see Reis, *Slave Rebellion in Brazil*, 102–3.

57. Abubakar is a Hausa name; see Raimundo Nina Rodrigues, *Os Africanos no Brasil* (São Paulo: Companhia Editora Nacional, 1932), 109–10. Nina Rodrigues based his study on notes collected between 1890 and his death in 1906. Also see Verger, *Trade Relations between the Bight of Benin and Bahia*, 300, 307. Reis discusses other clerics who he considers were likely to have been the leader but does not include Abubakar as a candidate; see *Slave Rebellion in Brazil*, 130.

58. Crowther, in his journal entry for 12 June 1846, stated that he and Townsend went to Badagry "to see the extension of Indian corn, beans, groundnuts, and cassava belonging to the Hausa people. Since last month, I have visited many similar plantations. All this cultivation began this year because when we arrived here [in the middle of 1845] there was no sign of cultivation anywhere in or around Badagry"; Church Missionary Society Archives, University of Birmingham, Yoruba Mission, CA2/031 (b), as cited in Mahdi Adamu, *The Hausa Factor in West African History* (Zaria: Ahmadu Bello University Press, 1978), 132.

59. Castelnau, *Renseignements sur l'Afrique centrale*, 46. Also see Verger, *Trade Relations*, 287.

60. Rosemarie Quiring-Zoche, "Bei den Malé Brasilien: Das Reisebuch des 'Abdarraḥmān al-Baghādi," *Die Welt des Islams* 40, no. 2 (2000): 196–273.

61. Paul E. Lovejoy, "Biographies of Enslaved Muslims from the Central Sudan in the Nineteenth Century," in *The Sokoto Caliphate: History and Legacies, 1804–2004*, ed. H. Bobboyi and A. M. Yakubu (Kaduna: Arewa House, 2006), 1:187–216. I am currently completing a biographical database that will form the basis of a study of enslavement in the first half of the nineteenth century.

62. Cook learned about the activities of Hausa merchants from a merchant whom he does not name but who had "resided, at different intervals, a considerable time at the settlement of Lagos, and at other places on the coast of the Bight of Benin." See John Adams, *Remarks on the Country Extending from Cape Palmas to the River Congo, Including Observations on the Manners and Customs of the Inhabitants, with an Appendix Containing an Account of the European Trade with the West Coast of Africa* (London: John Murray, 1823), xxxxvii–xxxxviii. This comment was first published in "The Niger," *Times* (London), 18 May 1816.

63. Robin Hallett, ed., *The Niger Journal of Richard and John Lander* (London: Routledge and Kegan Paul, 1965), 44n. Also see E. Adeniyi Oroge, "The Institution of Slavery in Yorubaland with Particular Reference to the Nineteenth Century" (Ph.D. dissertation, University of Birmingham, 1971), 170–72; and Robin Law, "The Dynastic Chronology of Lagos," *Lagos Notes and Records* 2, no. 2 (1968): 46–54.

64. Robin Law, "Islam in Dahomey: A Case Study of the Introduction and Influence of Islam in a Peripheral Area of West Africa," *Scottish Journal of Religious Studies* 4, no. 2 (1986): 102–3.

65. Mieko Nishida, "Gender, Ethnicity, and Kinship in the Urban African Diaspora: Salvador, Brazil, 1808–1888" (Ph.D. dissertation, Johns Hopkins University, 1992), 43–44; Nishida, "Manumission and Ethnicity in Urban Slavery: Salvador, Brazil, 1808–1888," *Hispanic American Historical Review* 73, no. 3 (1993): 361–91.

66. For Saharan slave-trade estimates, see Lovejoy, *Transformations in Slavery*, 62, 142; Paul E. Lovejoy, "Commercial Sectors in the Economy of the Nineteenth-Century Central Sudan: The Trans-Saharan Trade and the Desert-Side Salt Trade," *African Economic History* 13 (1984): 85–116; Ralph A. Austen, "The Trans-Saharan Slave Trade: A Tentative Census," in Gemery and Hogendorn, *Uncommon Market*, 23–76; and Tambo, "Sokoto Caliphate Slave Trade in the Nineteenth Century," 187–217.

67. For these estimates, see Louis Frank, *La Tunisie* (Paris: Firmin Didot Frères, 1856), 115, for arrivals from Ghadames in Tunis around 1810; UK Consul Warrington for arrivals in Tripoli in 1818, in Bovill, *Missions to the Niger*, 3:541; total number of slaves sent north from Kukawa in 1823, according to Walter Oudney, ibid., 3:568.

68. Jacopo Graberg di Hemso, "Prospetto del Commercio di Tripoli d'Africa, e delle sue relazioni con quello dell'Italia," *Antologia* 30 (1828): 24.

69. G. F. Lyon, *A Narrative of Travels in Northern Africa in the Years 1818–1819 and 1820* (London: John Murray, 1821), 188–89.

70. M. J. E. Daumas and A. de Chancel, *Le grand désert: Itinéraire d'une caravane du Sahara au pays des nègres (Royaume de Haoussa)* (Paris: M. Levy, 1856), 261, 266.

71. For 1845–51, see James Richardson, "Report on the Slave-Trade of the Great Desert," *Anti-slavery and Aborigines' Friend*, ser. 2, 1 (1846): 133–34, 154–55, 181–83; Richardson, *Travels in the Great Desert of Sahara in the Years of 1845 and 1846* (London: Richard Bentley, 1848) 1:9–11; Richardson, *Narrative of a Mission to Central Africa*, 1:144; and Barth, *Travels and Discoveries in North and Central Africa*, 1:515–22; and for 1861–62, see H. Mircher, *Mission au Ghadames (septembre, octobre, novembre, et decembre, 1862): Rapports officiels et documents a l'appui* (Paris: Alger, 1863), 39–54.

72. For Morocco, see Chouki El Hamel, *Black Morocco: A History of Slavery, Race, and Islam* (Cambridge: Cambridge University Press, 2013); for Ottoman domains, see Ehud R. Toledano, ed., *African Communities in Asia and the Mediterranean: Identities between Integration and Conflict* (Trenton, NJ: Africa World Press, 2011); and Toledano, *The Ottoman Slave Trade and Its Suppression, 1840- 1890* (Princeton, NJ: Princeton University Press, 1982).

73. Viviana Pâques, *Religion des esclaves: Recherches sur la confrérie marocaine des Gnawa* (Bergamo, Italy: Moretti & Vitali, 1991).

74. Ismael Musah Montana, "The *Bori* Colonies of Tunis," in Mirzai, Montana, and. Lovejoy, *Slavery, Islam and Diaspora*, 155–67; Montana, "Ahmad Ibn al-Qadi al-Timbuktawi on the *Bori* Ceremonies of Sudan-Tunis," in Lovejoy, *Slavery on the Frontiers of Islam*, 173–98; Montana, "The Trans-Saharan Slave Trade, Abolition of Slavery and Transformation in the North African Regency of Tunis, 1759–1846" (Ph.D. dissertation, York University, 2007); Montana, *The Abolition of Slavery in Ottoman Tunisia* (Gainesville: University Press of Florida, 2013); Montana, "Bori Practice among Enslaved West Africans of Ottoman Tunis: Unbelief (Kufr) or Another Dimension of the African Diaspora?," *History of the Family* 16 (2011): 152–59; Montana, "The *Stambali* of Husaynid Tunis: From Possession Cult to Ethno-religious and National Culture," in Toledano, *African Communities in Asia and the Mediterranean*, 153–66; John Hunwick, "The Religious Practices of Black Slaves in the Mediterranean Islamic World," in Lovejoy, *Slavery on the Frontiers of Islam*, 149–72.

75. Ahmad b. al-Qadi Abi Bakr b. Yusuf b. Ibrahim al-Timbuktawi, *Hatk al-Sitr Ammā Alayhi Sūdāni Tunis min al-Kufr* [Piercing the veil: Being an account of the infidel religion of the blacks of Tunis] (Tunis, 1813), ms., Bibliothèque nationale de Tunisie, Tunis, translated in Ismael M. Montana, "The *Hatk al-Sitr* of Al-Timbuktawi on Enslaved Africans' Religious Practices in Nineteenth-Century Tunisia" (M.A. thesis, York University, 1999); also see Mohammad El-Mansour and Fatima Harrak, *A Fulāni Jihādist in the Maghreb: Admonitions of Ahmad Ibn al-Qādī al-Timbuktī to the Rulers of Tunisia and Morocco* (Rabat: Institute of African Studies, 2000); and Montana, "Ahmad ibn al-Qadi al-Timbuktawi on the *Bori* Ceremonies," 173–89.

76. Khaled Fahmy, "The Era of Muhammad 'Ali Pasha, 1805–1848," in *The Cambridge History of Egypt: Modern Egypt, from 1517 to the End of the Twentieth Century*, ed. M. W. Daly (Cambridge: Cambridge University Press, 1998), 2:139–79; Kola Folayan, *Tripoli during the Reign of Yusuf Pasha Qaramanli* (Ife: University of Ife Press, 1979); Nora Lafi, *Une ville du Maghreb entre ancien régime et réformes ottomanes: Genèse des institutions municipales à Tripoli de Barbarie (1795–1911)* (Paris: L'Harmattan, 2002); John Hunwick and Eve Troutt Powell, eds, *The African Diaspora in the Mediterranean Lands of Islam* (Princeton, NJ: Markus Wiener, 2002); Terence Walz, *Trade between Egypt and Bilad as-Sudan, 1700–1820* (Cairo: Institut Français d'Archéologie Orientale du Caire, 1978); Walz, "Black Slavery in Egypt during the Nineteenth Century as Reflected in the Mahkama Archives of Cairo," in *Slaves and Slavery in Muslim Africa*, ed. John Ralph Willis (London: Frank Cass, 1985), 137–60; Terence Walz and Kenneth M. Cuno, eds., *Race and Slavery in the*

Middle East: Trans-Saharan Africans in Nineteenth-Century Egypt, Sudan and the Ottoman Mediterranean (Cairo: American University in Cairo Press, 2010).

77. However, as Alberto da Costa e Silva has demonstrated in "Sobre a rebelião de 1835 na Bahia." *Revista Brasileira* 31 (2002): 9–33, Reis subsequently largely backed off from his earlier appreciation of the Islamic factor. My critique is made in the context of an extensive scholarship. See, for example, Reis, *Slave Rebellion in Brazil*, and the revised, expanded version, *Rebelião escrava no Brasil: A História do Levante dos Malês em 1835* (São Paulo: Companhia das Letras, 2003). Also see Reis, "Slave Resistance in Brazil: Bahia, 1807–1835," *Luso-Brazilian Review* 25, no. 1 (1988): 111–44; João José Reis and Paulo F. de Moraes Farias, "Islam and Slave Resistance in Bahia, Brazil," *Islam et sociétés au sud du Sahara* 3 (1989): 41–66; Clovis Moura, *Reblioes da Senzala* (São Paulo: Zumbi, 1959); Luis Luna, *O Negro na luta contra escravidão* (Rio de Janeiro: Ed. Leitura, 1967); Raymond Kent, "African Revolt in Bahia," *Journal of Social History* 3 (1970): 334–56; Howard Prince, "Slave Rebellion in Brazil, 1807–1835" (Ph.D. dissertation, Columbia University, 1972); Katia M. de Queirós Mattoso, "Os escravos na Bahia no alvorecer do século XIX: Estudo de um grupo social," *Revista de Historia* 47, no. 97 (1974): 109–35; Verger, *Trade Relations between the Bight of Benin and Bahia*; and Rosemarie Quiring-Zoche, "Glaubenskampf oder Machtkampf? Der Aufstand der Malé von Bahia nach einer islamischen Quelle," *Sudanic Africa* 6 (1995): 115–24. Most of the court records have been published; see "Devassa do Levante de Escravos Ocorrido em Salvador em 1835," *Anais do Arquivo do Estado da Bahia* 38 (Salvador, 1968); "Peças Processuais do Levante dos Malês," *Anais do Arquivo Público do Estado da Bahia* 40 (Salvador, 1971); "Devassa do Levante de Escravos Ocorrido em Salvador em 1835," *Anais do Arquivo Público do Estado da Bahia* 50 (Salvador, 1992); and "Devassa do Levante de Escravos Ocorrido em Salvador em 1835," *Anais do Arquivo do Estado da Bahia* 53 (Salvador, 1996). A final volume was published in 1997.

78. Paul E. Lovejoy, "The Context of Enslavement in West Africa: Ahmad Bābā and the Ethics of Slavery," in *Slaves, Subjects, and Subversives: Blacks in Colonial Latin America*, ed. Jane Landers (Albuquerque: University of New Mexico Press, 2006), 9–38; John O. Hunwick and Fatima Harrak, *Mi'raj al-su'ud: Ahmad Baba's Replies on Slavery* (Rabat: Institute des Études Africaines, Université Mohamed V, 2000).

79. I forcefully argued this perspective in Lovejoy, *Transformations in Slavery* in 1983 (now in its third edition [2011], as well as being translated into Portuguese).

80. Emmanuel Terray, "Reflexions sur la formation du prix des esclaves à l'intérieur de l'Afrique de l'Ouest précoloniale," *Journal des Africanistes* 52 (1982): 120.

81. David Eltis, *The Rise of African Slavery in the Americas* (Cambridge: Cambridge University Press, 2000), 167–71.

82. Searing, *West African Slavery and Atlantic Commerce*, 62–63.

83. Paul E. Lovejoy, "Internal Markets or an Atlantic-Sahara Divide?," in *Women and Slavery: Africa, the Indian Ocean World, and the Medieval North Atlantic*, ed. Gwyn Campbell, Suzanne Miers, and Joseph C. Miller (Athens: Ohio University Press, 2007), 1:259–79.

84. Ibid., 1:259–80; and Lofkrantz and Lovejoy, "Maintaining Network Boundaries."

85. Paul E. Lovejoy, "Islam, Slavery, and Political Transformation in West Africa: Constraints on the Trans-Atlantic Slave Trade," *Outre-Mers: Revue d'histoire* 89 (2002): 247–82. Also see Lovejoy, *Slavery on the Frontiers of Islam*; and Mirzai, Montana, and Lovejoy, *Slavery, Islam and Diaspora*. An exception is the work of Alberto da Costa e Silva, "Sobre a rebelião de 1835 na Bahia," *Revista Brasileira* 31 (2002): 9–33, reprinted in Alberto da Costa e Silva, *Um rio chamado Atlântico: A África no Brasil e o Brasil na África* (Rio de Janeiro: Editora Nova Fronteira, 2003), 189–214. Also see Henry B. Lovejoy, "Old Oyo Influences on the Transformation of Lucumí Identity in Colonial Cuba" (Ph.D. dissertation, UCLA, 2012).

86. This section draws on Lofkranz and Lovejoy, "Maintaining Network Boundaries." For an in-depth discussion of al-Ghayth, see Yacine Daddi Addoun and Paul E. Lovejoy, "Commerce and Credit in Katsina in the Nineteenth Century," in *Africa, Empire, and Globalization: Essays in Honor of A. G. Hopkins*, ed. Emily Brownell and Toyin Falola (Durham, NC: Carolina Academic Press, 2011), 111–24; Abubakar Babajo Sani, *Trade Diplomacy, Banking and Finance in the Trans-Saharan Trade: An Interpretation of Ahmad Abu al-Ghaith's Ledger, a Trade Consul in Katsina, 1824–1870* (Kaduna: Pyla-mak Publishers, 2012). Ghislaine Lydon also describes another type of partnership common in trans-Saharan trade, the *mufāwaḍa*, where partners pooled their investments, one partner was given the discretionary authority to conduct trade, and the gains and losses were divided among the partners in proportion to their original investment; see *On Trans-Saharan Trails: Islamic Law, Trade Networks, and Cross-Cultural Trade in Nineteenth-Century Western Africa* (Cambridge: Cambridge University Press, 2009), 292. Also see Lydon, "Contracting Caravans: Partnership and Profit in Nineteenth- and Early Twentieth-Century Trans-Saharan Trade," *Journal of Global History* 3 (2008): 89–113.

87. Sani, *Trade Diplomacy, Banking and Finance in the Trans-Saharan Trade*.

88. Alhaji Bulgat Tuwat, "Kitab Zima-mun Duyun," AH 1245 AH (1829 CE), KATPROF G/AR3/1, Nigerian National Archives, Kaduna.

89. For more on partnership models, see Lydon, *On Trans-Saharan Trails*, 290–96; and Bruce S. Hall, "Saharan Commerce and Islamic Law: The Question of Usury (*ribā*) in the Nawāzil Literature of Mali and Mauritania, 1700–1929," *African Economic History* 41 (2013): 1–18.

90. Lofkrantz and Lovejoy, "Maintaining Network Boundaries."

91. Lovejoy, "Context of Enslavement in West Africa," 9–38; and Hunwick and Harrak, *Mi'raj al-su'ud: Ahmad Baba's Replies on Slavery*.

6. The Repercussions of Jihād in the Americas

1. On the rise of Lagos as a port in the nineteenth century, see Kristin Mann, *Slavery and the Birth of an African City: Lagos, 1760–1900* (Bloomington: Indiana University Press, 2007).

2. See Kenneth Morgan, "Liverpool Ascendant: British Merchants and the Slave Trade on the Upper Guinea Coast, 1701–1808," in *Slavery, Abolition and the Transition to Colonialism in Sierra Leone*, ed. Paul E. Lovejoy and Suzanne Schwarz

(Trenton, NJ: Africa World Press, 2014), 29–50; and David Hancock, *Citizens of the World: London Merchants and the Integration of the British Atlantic Community, 1735–1785* (Cambridge: Cambridge University Press, 1995).

3. As Michael Gomez has demonstrated, Muslims from the western Bilād al-Sūdān were found in virtually all regions of the Americas; see *Black Crescent: The Experience and Legacy of African Muslims in the Americas* (Cambridge: Cambridge University Press, 2005). For Jamaica, see 50–61; Trinidad, 66–78; St. Domingue, 83–89; Brazil, 91–127; and North America, 145–84.

4. Gwendolyn Midlo Hall, *Slavery and African Ethnicities in the Americas: Restoring the Links* (Chapel Hill: University of North Carolina Press, 2005).

5. These calculations are based on statistics from Louisiana for 1723–1805 and Maranhão for 1767–1831, as found in *Slave Biographies: The Atlantic Database Network*, http://www.slavebiographies.org, including the Louisiana Slave Database, principal investigator, Gwendolyn Midlo Hall, and the Maranhão Inventories Slave Database, principal investigator, Walter Hawthorne. Also see Afro-Louisiana History and Genealogy, 1718–1820 http://www.ibiblio.org/laslave/fields.php.

6. Robert L. Fraser, "PIERPOINT, RICHARD," in *Dictionary of Canadian Biography*, vol. 7, University of Toronto/Université Laval, 2003, accessed July 16, 2016, http://www.biographi.ca/en/bio/pierpoint_richard_7E.html; and David Meyler and Peter Meyler, *A Stolen Life: Searching for Richard Pierpoint* (Toronto: Natural Heritage Books, 1999).

7. See Allan D. Austin, *African Muslims in Antebellum America: Transatlantic Stories and Spiritual Struggles* (New York: Routledge, 1997); Michael A. Gomez, *Exchanging Our Country Marks: The Transformation of African Identities in the Colonial and Antebellum South* (Chapel Hill: University of North Carolina Press, 1998); and B. G. Martin, "Sapelo Island's Arabic Document: The 'Bilali Diary' in Context," *Georgia Historical Quarterly* 77, no. 3 (1994): 589–601.

8. Rebecca Scott and Jean-Michel Hébrard, "Rosalie of the Poulard Nation: Freedom, Law, and Dignity in the Era of the Haitian Revolution," in *Biography and the Black Atlantic*, ed. Lisa W. Lindsay and John Wood Sweet (Philadelphia: University of Pennsylvania Press, 2013), 248–67; and Scott and Hébrard, *Freedom Papers: An Atlantic Odyssey in the Age of Emancipation* (Cambridge, MA: Harvard University Press, 2012).

9. "Minutes of Evidence on the Trials of Persons for Offences Connected with the Revolt, Parish of Manchester," C.O. 137/185, National Archives, London. I thank Sonja Maurer for this reference.

10. Yacine Daddi Addoun and Paul E. Lovejoy, "Muḥammad Kabā Saghanughu and the Muslim Community of Jamaica," in *Slavery on the Frontiers of Islam*, ed. Paul E. Lovejoy (Princeton, NJ: Markus Wiener, 2004), 201–20; and Daddi Addoun and Lovejoy, "The Arabic Manuscript of Muḥammad Kabā Saghanughu of Jamaica, c. 1820," in *Creole Concerns: Essays in Honour of Kamau Brathwaite*, ed. Annie Paul (Kingston: University of the West Indies Press, 2007), 313–41.

11. For further details on Muḥammad Kabā Saghanughu, see Maureen Warner-Lewis, "Religious Constancy and Compromise among Nineteenth Century Caribbean-Based African Muslims," in *Slavery, Islam and Diaspora*, ed. Behnaz A. Mirzai, Ismael

Musah Montana, and Paul E. Lovejoy (Trenton, NJ: Africa World Press, 2009), 237–68.

12. James Albert Ukawsaw Gronniosaw, in *Unchained Voices: An Anthology of Black Authors in the English-Speaking World of the 18th Century*, ed. Vincent Carretta (Lexington: University Press of Kentucky, 1996), 32–34, 55.

13. Most merchants operating between Borno and the interior of the Gold Coast came from Borno, the Hausa cities, or the Muslim centers in the middle Volta basin, not from the Gold Coast or Asante; see Paul E. Lovejoy, *Caravans of Kola: The Hausa Kola Trade, 1700–1900* (Zaria: Ahmadu Bello University Press, 1980), 51–62.

14. Upon reflection, I now consider that Venture Smith came from a Fulani or Fulbe encampment north of Akyem and Akwamu, which he called Dukandarra, which I initially was unable to identify, despite the reference to cattle and horses and other attributes of Fulbe society. See Paul E. Lovejoy, "The African Background of Venture Smith," in *Venture Smith and the Business of Slavery and Freedom*, ed. James B. Stewart (Amherst: University of Massachusetts Press, 2009), 35–55.

15. See Ivor Wilks, "Abu Bakr al-Siddiq of Timbuktu," in *Africa Remembered: Narratives by West Africans from the Era of the Slave Trade*, ed. Philip D. Curtin (Madison: University of Wisconsin Press, 1967), 152–69, which relies especially on G. C. Renouard, "Routes in North Africa, by Abu Bekr es Siddik," *Journal of the Royal Geographical Society* 6 (1836): 102–7; and "The History of Abon Becr Sadiki, known in Jamaica by the name of Edward Donlan," in R. R. Madden, *A Twelve-month's Residence in the West Indies, during the Transition from Slavery to Apprenticeship* (Westport, CT: Negro University Press, 1970 [1835]), 2:183–89.

16. For details on Pierre Tamata, see Pierre Verger, *Trade Relations between the Bight of Benin and Brazil, 17th–19th Century* (Ibadan: University of Ibadan Press, 1976), 186–90; and John Adams, *Remarks on the Country Extending from Cape Palmas to the River Congo, Including Observations on the Manners and Customs of the Inhabitants, with an Appendix Containing an Account of the European Trade with the West Coast of Africa* (London: John Murray, 1823), 82–87. Tamata is also discussed in Jennifer Lofkrantz and Paul E. Lovejoy, "Maintaining Network Boundaries: Islamic Law and Commerce from Sahara to Guinea Shores," *Slavery and Abolition* 36, no. 2 (2015): 211–32.

17. For Oyo trade through Porto Novo, see Peter Morton-Williams, "The Oyo Yoruba and the Atlantic Slave Trade, 1670–1830," *Journal of the Historical Society of Nigeria* 3, no. 1 (1964): 25–45. Badagry became the principal rival for Oyo's trade and hence the ascendancy of Tamata; see Caroline Sorensen, "Badagry, 1784–1863: The Political and Commercial History of a Pre-colonial Lagoonside Community in South West Nigeria" (Ph.D. dissertation, University of Stirling, 1995); and Caroline Sorensen-Gilmour, "Slave-Trading along the Lagoons of South-West Nigeria: The Case of Badagry," in *Ports of the Slave Trade (Bights of Benin and Biafra)*, ed. Robin Law and Silke Strickrodt (Stirling: Centre of Commonwealth Studies, 1999), 84–95. Also see Carlos da Silva, "Ports of Bight of Benin and the Legal Slave Trade to Bahia, Brazil, 1750–1815" (unpublished paper presented at the Canadian Association of African Studies Annual Meeting, Carleton University, Ottawa, 1–3 May 2013).

18. Stuart Schwartz, *Sugar Plantations in the Formation of Brazilian Society: Bahia, 1550–1835* (Cambridge: Cambridge University Press, 1985), 351.

19. Manuel Barcia, *West African Warfare in Bahia and Cuba: Soldier Slaves in the Atlantic World, 1807–1844* (Oxford: Oxford University Press, 2014).

20. See especially João José Reis, "Slave Resistance in Brazil: Bahia, 1807–1835," *Luso-Brazilian Review* 25, no. 1 (1988): 111–44; Reis, *Slave Rebellion in Brazil: The Muslim Uprising of 1835 in Bahia* (Baltimore: Johns Hopkins University Press, 1993), 47–49, 58–59; Reis, "La révolte haoussa de Bahia en 1807: Résistance et contrôle des esclaves au Brésil," *Annales: Histoire, Sciences Sociales* 61 (2006): 383–418; and Stuart Schwartz, "Cantos e quilombos numa conspiração de escravos haussás," in *Liberdade por um fio: História dos quilombos no Brasil*, ed. João José Reis and Flávio dos Santos Gomes (São Paulo: Companhia das Letras, 1997), 373–406.

21. João José Reis, *Rebelião escrava no Brasil: A história do Levante dos Malês em 1835* (São Paulo: Companhia Das Letras, 2003), 73. Also see Bruno Veras, "The Crescent and the Reef: African Muslims in Recife, PE (Brazil) in the 19th century" (paper presented at Université Laval, 26 August 2015).

22. Reis, *Slave Rebellion in Brazil*, 47.

23. Ismael Musah Montana, "Ahmad ibn al-Qādi al-Timbuktāwī on the *Bori* Ceremonies of Tunis," in Lovejoy, *Slavery on the Frontiers of Islam*, 173–98.

24. For Malungo, see Robert W. Slenes, "Malungu, Ngoma vem: África coberta e descoberta do Brasil," *Revista USP* 12 (1991–92): 48–67.

25. See chapter 5.

26. Francis de Castelnau, *Renseignements sur l'Afrique centrale et sur une nation d'hommes à queue qui s'y trouverait, d'après le rapport des nègres du Soudan, esclaves à Bahia* (Paris: Librairie P. Bertrand, 1851), 9.

27. Romulo de Oliveira Martins, "'Vinha na fé de trabalhar em diamantes': Escravos e libertos em Lençóis, Chapada Diamantina-BA (1840–1888)" (M.A. thesis, Universidade Federal da Bahia, 2013).

28. Reis, *Slave Rebellion in Brazil*, 93, 97–98, 103–4.

29. Castelnau, *Renseignements sur l'Afrique centrale*, 9.

30. See Jack Goody, "Writing, Religion and Revolt in Bahia," *Visible Language* 20 (1986): 318–43; Vincent Monteil, "Analyse de 25 documents arabes des Malês de Bahia (1835)," *Bulletin de l'Institute Fondamentale d'Afrique Noire*, ser. B, 29, nos. 1–2 (1967): 88–98; and Rolf Reichert, "L'insurrection d'esclaves de 1835 à la lumière des documents arabes des archives publiques de l'état de Bahia (Brésil)," *Bulletin de l'Institute Fondamaentale d'Afrique Noire*, ser. B, 29, nos. 1–2 (1967): 99–104.

31. Nina Rodrigues published his preliminary analysis of the importance of Islam among slaves in *O Jornal do Commercio* of Rio de Janeiro on 2 November 1900; see Verger, *Trade Relations*, 285–86. For a fuller analysis, see Raimundo Nina Rodrigues, *Os Africnos no Brasil* (São Paulo: Companhia Editora Nacional, 1932), 93–120. For similar conclusions, see Verger, *Trade Relations*, 294–308. For a critique of the conclusions of Nina Rodrigues and Verger, see Reis, *Slave Rebellion in Brazil*, 120–28.

Notes to Pages 185–190

32. Rodrigues, *Os Africanos no Brasil*, 93–120; also see Verger, *Trade Relations*, 294–309; and Reis, *Slave Rebellion in Brazil*, 115, 117. Withdrawal to the fugitive-slave settlements *(quilombos)* that surrounded Salvador should also be noted. Such withdrawal is consistent with the *hijra*, although there is no evidence that rebels perceived the *quilombos* in this manner.

33. Verger, *Trade Relations*, 304; and Reis, *Slave Rebellion in Brazil*, 104. Also see "On the Sunna of Wearing Silver Rings," *Sankore'*, www.siiasi.org; and José Cairus, "Kende Rings" (unpublished paper, n.d.).

34. Reis, *Slave Rebellion in Brazil*, 115, 117–18.

35. Rodrigues, *Os Africanos no Brasil*, 109–10.

36. Reis, *Slave Rebellion in Brazil*, 130, 132–33, 170.

37. Ibid., 115–19. Also see Rodrigues, *Os Africanos no Brasil*, 95.

38. Reis, *Rebelião escrava no Brasil*, 151–57. Also see Dale T. Graden, "Slave Resistance and the Abolition of the Trans-Atlantic Slave Trade to Brazil in 1850," *História Unisinos* 14, no. 3 (2010): 283–84.

39. Many of the court records have been published; see "Devassa do Levante de Escravos Ocorrido em Salvador em 1835," *Anais do Arquivo do Estado da Bahia* 38 (Salvador, 1968); "Peças Processuais do Levante dos Malês," *Anais do Arquivo Público do Estado da Bahia* 40 (Salvador, 1971); "Devassa do Levante de Escravos Ocorrido em Salvador em 1835," *Anais do Arquivo Público do Estado da Bahia* 50 (Salvador, 1992); and "Devassa do Levante de Escravos Ocorrido em Salvador em 1835," *Anais do Arquivo do Estado da Bahia* 53 (Salvador, 1996). A final volume was published in 1997. My analysis is based on Marcia Smith, "The Male Uprising in Bahia, 1835: Mini-biographies of Leaders and Others Accused" (unpublished paper, History 5570, York University, 1998).

40. Reis, *Rebelião escrava no Brasil*, 333–34.

41. Verger, *Trade Relations*, 306–7.

42. Reis, *Rebelião escrava no Brasil*, 482–83, 491–92.

43. Ibid., 271. Reis notes, "I do not deny the hegemony of the Malês in the rebel bloc; I deny their uniqueness. As they held the hegemony of the political movement in 1835, we can say that the *rebellion* was Malê and the *uprising* was African."

44. In addition to the perceptive analysis in Reis, *Slave Rebellion in Brazil*, and in the revised, expanded version, *Rebelião escrava no Brasil*, my critique also draws on Reis, "Slave Resistance in Brazil: Bahia, 1807–1835," 111–44; João José Reis and Paulo F. de Moraes Farias, "Islam and Slave Resistance in Bahia, Brazil," *Islam et sociétés au sud du Sahara* 3 (1989): 41–66; Clovis Moura, *Rebeliões da Senzala* (São Paulo: Zumbi, 1959); Luis Luna, *O Negro na luta contra escravidão* (Rio de Janeiro: Ed. Leitura, 1967); Raymond Kent, "African Revolt in Bahia," *Journal of Social History* 3 (1970): 334–56; Howard Prince, "Slave Rebellion in Brazil, 1807–1835" (Ph.D. dissertation, Columbia University, 1972); Katia M. de Queirós Mattoso, "Os escravos na Bahia no alvorecer do século XIX: Estudo de um grupo social," *Revista de Historia* 47, no. 97 (1974): 109–35; and Verger, *Trade Relations*. Also see Rosemarie Quiring-Zoche, "Glaubenskampf oder Machtkampf? Der Aufstand der Malé von Bahia nach einer islamischen Quelle," *Sudanic Africa* 6 (1995): 115–24.

45. Leslie Bethell, *The Abolition of the Brazilian Slave Trade* (Cambridge: Cambridge University Press, 1970); and Jeffrey D. Needell, "Brazilian Abolitionism, Its Historiography, and the Uses of Political History," *Journal of Latin American Studies* 42, no. 2 (2010): 231–61.

46. This interpretation diverges from the otherwise excellent analysis of Reis, who states that his interpretation "clashes head-on with the opinion of those who saw (or see) the rebellion as a jihād of the sword, a classic Muslim holy war against the infidel of whatever color or origin," although Reis does allow that "the rebellion did of course have its religious side, and for many it was even a holy war, but it was not a classic jihād of the sword." See Reis, *Slave Rebellion in Brazil*, 122, 127.

47. ʿAbd al-Raḥmān al-Baghdādī, *Musalliyat al-gharīb: The Foreigner's Amusement by Wonderful Things*, translated by Yacine Daddi Addoun in *SHADD: Studies in the History of the African Diaspora—Documents*, 2001, http://www.yorku.ca/nhp/shadd/baghdadi/index.asp.

48. Ibid. For Rosemarie Quiring-Zoche's interpretation, see "Glaubenskampf oder Machtkampf?," 115–24; and Quiring-Zoche, "Bei den Malé Brasilien: Das Reisebuch des ʿAbdarrahmân al-Baghâdi," *Die Welt des Islams* 40, no. 2 (2000): 196–273.

49. John Ralph Willis, "*Jihād fī sabīl Allāh*—Its Doctrinal Basis in Islam and Some Aspects of Its Evolution in Nineteenth-Century West Africa," *Journal of African History* 8, no. 3 (1967): 398–99.

50. Gomez, *Black Crescent*, 83.

51. Gabriel Debien, "Les origines des esclaves des Antilles," *Bulletin de l'Institut Fondamental d'Afrique Noire,* ser. B., 23 (1961): 363–87; 25 (1963): 1–41, 215–66; 26 (1964): 166–211, 601–75; 27 (1965): 319–71, 755–99; 29 (1967): 536–58; Debien, *De l'Afrique à Saint Domingue* (Port-au-Prince: Revue de la Société Haitienne d'Histoire et de Géographie, 1982), 7; and Debien, *Les esclaves aux Antilles Françaises (XVIIᵉ–XVIIIᵉ siècles)* (Paris: Société d'Impressions Caron-Ozanne, 1975), 44–45, 67.

52. Gomez, *Black Crescent*, 83.

53. Sylviane Diouf, *Servants of Allah: African Muslims Enslaved in the Americas* (New York: New York University Press, 1998), 152–53.

54. Gomez, *Black Crescent*, 66–67.

55. Ibid., 67–69. Also see Carl Campbell, "John Mohammed Bath and the Free Mandingoes in Trinidad: The Question of Their Repatriation to Africa, 1831–38," *Journal of African Studies* 2 (1975–76): 482–84; and Christopher Fyfe, "Four Sierra Leone Captives," *Journal of African History* 2, no. 1 (1961): 77–85.

56. Maureen Warner-Lewis, *Guinea's Other Sons: The African Dynamic in Trinidad Culture* (Dover, MA: Majority Press, 1991), 5–8, 16–19, 24–27, 48–49, 69–70, 115–16; Warner-Lewis, "Africans in 19th Century Trinidad, Part I," *African Studies Association of the West Indies Bulletin* 5 (1972): 39; and Warner-Lewis, "Africans in 19th Century Trinidad, Part II," *African Studies Association of the West Indies Bulletin* 6 (1973): 13–39.

57. Campbell, "John Mohammed Bath and the Free Mandingoes in Trinidad," 482–84, although, as Gomez points out (*Black Crescent*, 70), Campbell's identification

of the Muslims as Mandingo reflects the terminology of the period, not the actual ethnic origins of the various individuals, many of whom were Hausa.

58. Paul E. Lovejoy and David V. Trotman, "Community of Believers: Trinidad Muslims and the Return to Africa, c. 1810–1850," in Lovejoy, *Slavery on the Frontiers of Islam*, 221–34.

59. For a general discussion of Muslims in North America, drawing on various sources, see Gomez, *Black Crescent*, 145–84. Also see Austin, *African Muslims in Antebellum America*; and Diouf, *Servants of Allah*. For examples of Hausa and other Muslims in Louisiana, see Gomez, *Black Crescent*, 145.

60. Muhammad ʿAlī (Nicholas) Saʿīd, *The Autobiography of Nicholas Said, a Native of Bornou, Eastern Soudan* (Memphis: Shotwell and Co., 1873); "A Native of Bornoo," *Atlantic Monthly*, 1867, 485–95; Allan D. Austin, "Mohammed Ali Ben Said: Travels on Five Continents," *Contributions in Black Studies* 12 (1994): 129–58; and Paul E. Lovejoy, "Muhammad ʿAlī Saʿīd : From Enslavement in Borno to American Civil War Veteran." Paper presented at "Meaning of Blackness II," Universidad de Costa Rica, 2016. According to military records in Massachusetts, it is alleged that he died in Brownsville, Tennessee, in 1882. I thank Dean Calbreath for information that Saʿīd was still alive in 1897 and probably living outside Tennessee.

61. Gwendolyn Midlo Hall, *Africans in Colonial Louisiana: The Development of Afro-Creole Culture in the Eighteenth Century* (Baton Rouge: Louisiana State University Press, 1992).

62. Daddi Addoun and Lovejoy, "Muḥammad Kabā Saghanughu and the Muslim Community of Jamaica," 201–20; and Daddi Addoun and Lovejoy, "Arabic Manuscript of Muḥammad Kabā Saghanughu of Jamaica," 313–41. Kabā had previously come to the attention of historians; see Wilks, "Abu Bakr al-Siddīq of Timbuktu," 152–69.

63. Madden, *Twelvemonth's Residence in the West Indies*, 1:99, 2:133–37.

64. New details on Baquaqua's life are updated on the website *Project Baquaqua*, http://www.baquaqua.com.br.

65. Barcia, *West African Warfare in Bahia and Cuba*, 19; also see table 2.5, "Likely Muslim, Hausa, and Fula Names Found in the Registries of the Mixed Commission Court in Havana, 1824–1835," 68–69.

66. See *Liberated Africans Project*, http://liberatedafricans.org/.

67. Barcia, *West African Warfare in Bahia and Cuba*, 6–7 and "Appendix: Chronology of Slave Movements in Cuba, 1798–1844," 161–65. Also see Henry B. Lovejoy, *Prieto of the Lucumí Nation; Yoruba Identity in Nineteenth-Century Cuba* (Chapel Hill: University of North Carolina Press, 2016).

68. Gomez, *Black Crescent*, 34–36, who cites Laird W. Bergard, Fe Iglesias Garcia, and Marcia del Carmen Barcia, *The Cuban Slave Market, 1790–1880* (Cambridge: Cambridge University Press, 1995), showing the presence of Muslims in Cuba from 1790 through 1869.

69. Henry Lovejoy, "Old Oyo Influences on the Transformation of Lucumí Identity in Colonial Cuba" (Ph.D. dissertation, UCLA, 2012).

70. Henry B. Lovejoy, "Drums of Ṣàngó: Bàtá Drums and the Symbolic Rees-tablishment of Ọ̀yọ in Colonial Cuba," in Ṣàngó in Africa and the African Diaspora, ed. Joel Tishken, Toyin Falola, and Akintunde Akinyemi (Bloomington: Indiana University Press, 2009), 284–308; H. B. Lovejoy, "The Transculturation of Yoruba Annual Festivals: The Día de Reyes in Colonial Cuba in the Nineteenth Century," in Carnival—Theory and Practice, ed. Christopher Innes, Annabel Rutherford, and Brigitte Bogar (Trenton, NJ: Africa World Press, 2013), 33–50. Also see H. B. Love-joy, "Old Oyo Influences on the Transformation of Lucumí Identity in Colonial Cuba."

71. Olatunji Ojo, "Islam, Ethnicity and Slave Agitation: Hausa 'Mamluks' in Nineteenth Century Yorubaland," in Mirzai, Montana, and Lovejoy, Slavery, Islam and Diaspora, 103–24. In 1899 Major Francis C. Fuller, the second British resident officer at Ibadan, described the "Gambari" as "belonging to any tribe beyond the [River] Niger," but they invariably spoke Hausa, no matter what other languages they might have known; see Francis C. Fuller, Journal, 21 January 1899, IbaProf 3/6, Nige-rian Archives, Ibadan. I thank Olatunji Ojo for this reference.

72. Barcia, West African Warfare in Bahia and Cuba, 7.

73. In an assessment of recognizable Muslim names found in the registers of liberated Africans, Daniel Domingues, David Eltis, Philip Misevich, and Olatunji Ojo, "The Nineteenth-Century Transatlantic Islamic Diaspora" (unpublished paper, Harvard University, October 2015), found that a small minority of Africans from the upper Guinea coast from Senegal to Sierra Leone could be identified as Muslims, and an even smaller percentage from the Bight of Benin and Bight of Baifra. Although there are methodological questions concerning the recognition of Muslims on the basis of the recorded names of individuals, the general conclusion supports the ar-gument here, i.e., that there were relatively few Muslims taken to the Americas in the nineteenth century from West Africa.

74. See, for example, Diouf, Servants of Allah; Michael Gomez, "Muslims in Early America," Journal of Southern History 60, no. 4 (1994): 671–710; and Gomez, Black Crescent. Also see the neglected work on Richard Pierpoint, who came from Fuuta Bundu, fought for the British in the American War of Independence, and later formed an all-black regiment that helped prevent the American conquest of Canada in the War of 1812; also see the account of Richard Pierpoint, Meyler and Meyler, Stolen Life.

75. Barcia, West African Warfare in Bahia and Cuba.

76. For the actions of Muslim Aku in Sierra Leone, see John Peterson, Province of Freedom: A History of Sierra Leone, 1787–1870 (London: Faber and Faber, 1969), 93, 212–17; and Christopher Fyfe, A History of Sierra Leone (London: Oxford University Press, 1962), 170, 186–87, 204, 212, 215.

77. For Trinidad, see Lovejoy and Trotman, "Community of Believers," 221–34. For Jamaica and the alleged existence of wathīqat (document) of Kabā Saghanughu, who came from Fuuta Jalon, see Daddi Addoun and Lovejoy, "Muḥammad Kabā Saghanughu and the Muslim Community of Jamaica," 201–20; and Daddi Addoun and Lovejoy, "Arabic Manuscript of Muḥammad Kabā Saghanughu of Jamaica, c. 1820," 313–41.

7. Sokoto, the Jihād States, and the Abolition of the Atlantic Slave Trade

1. On Borno, see Muhammad N. Alkali, "El-Kanemi's Response to the Extension of Shaykh ᶜUthman Dan Fodio's *Jihād* against Borno," in *The Sokoto Caliphate: History and Legacies, 1804–2004*, ed. H. Bobboyi and A. M. Yakubu (Kaduna: Arewa House, 2006), 1:231–39; Louis Brenner, "The Jihād Debate between Sokoto and Borno: An Historical Analysis of Islamic Political Discourse in Nigeria," in *People and Empires in African History: Essays in Memory of Michael Crowder*, ed. J. F. Ade Ajayi and J. D. Y. Peel (London: Longman, 1992), 21–43; and Brenner, *The Shehus of Kukawa: A History of the Al-Kanemi Dynasty of Bornu* (Oxford: Clarendon Press, 1973). At least twenty letters were exchanged between the jihād leadership and al-Kānimī between 1808 and 1812. Many of the letters are in Muhammad Bello, *Infāq al-Maysūr fī tārīkh bilād al-Takrūr* (1812), edited by Bahija Chadli (Rabat: Institute of African Studies, 1996); another letter from al-Kānimī to Goni Mukhtar, the leader of the jihād forces in Borno, dated 17 Rabiᶜ al-Awwil 1223 (13 May 1808), is in the University of Ibadan Library (Ms. 82/237). See Murray Last and M. A. Al-Hajj, "Attempts at Defining a Muslim in 19th Century Hausaland and Bornu," *Journal of the Historical Society of Nigeria* 3, no. 2 (1965): 239; and Brenner, *Shehus of Kukawa*, 39–43.

2. My discussion of the Bello-Clapperton negotiations was first presented in "Rethinking the African Diaspora: The Making of a Black Atlantic World in the Bight of Benin and Brazil" (Emory University, 17–18 April 1998) and was subsequently published as Paul E. Lovejoy, "The Clapperton-Bello Exchange: The Sokoto *Jihād* and the Trans-Atlantic Slave Trade, 1804–1837," in *The Desert Shore: Literatures of the African Sahel*, ed. Christopher Wise (Boulder, CO: Lynne Rienner, 2000), 201–28. I have expanded my arguments in Lovejoy, "Diplomacy of Abolition: Negotiations between Muhammad Bello and Hugh Clapperton over the Abolition of the Atlantic Slave Trade," in *Distant Ripples of the British Abolitionist Wave: Africa, Asia, and the Americas*, ed. Myriam Cottias and Marie-Jeanne Rossignol (Trenton, NJ: Africa World Press, 2016).

3. João José Reis, "Ethnic Politics among Africans in Nineteenth-Century Bahia," in *Identity in the Shadow of Slavery*, ed. Paul E. Lovejoy (London: Continuum, 2000), 240–64; Reis, "African Nations and Cultural Practices in Nineteenth-Century Salvador, Bahia" (paper presented at the conference "American Counterpoint: New Approaches to Slavery and Abolition in Brazil," Yale University, 2010); Reis, "Resistência escrava na Bahia: 'Poderemos brincar, folgar e cantar . . .'; O protesto escravo na America," *Afro-Ásia* 14 (1983): 107–23; Reis, "Um balanço dos estudos sobre as revoltas escravas da Bahia," in *Escravidão e invenção da liberdade*, ed. João José Reis (São Paulo: Brasiliense, 1988), 87–141; João José Reis and Eduardo Silva, *Negociação e conflito: Resistência negra no Brasil escravista* (São Paulo: Companhia das Letras, 1989). Also see P. F. de Moraes Farias, " 'Yoruba Origins' " Revisited by Muslims," in *Self-Assertion and Brokerage: Early Cultural Nationalism in West Africa*, ed. P. F. de Moraes Farias and Karin Barber (Birmingham: Centre of West African Studies, 1990), 109–47; Farias, "Enquanto isso, do outro lado do mar: Os Arókin e a identidade iorubá," *Afro-Ásia* 17 (1996): 139–55; and B. J. Barickman, "Reading the 1835 Parish Censuses from Bahia: Citizenship, Kinship, Slavery, and Household in Early Nineteenth-Century Brazil," *Americas* 59, no. 3 (2003): 287–324.

4. Paul E. Lovejoy, "The Central Sudan and the Atlantic Slave Trade," in *Paths toward the Past: African Historical Essays in Honor of Jan Vansina*, ed. Robert W. Harms, Joseph C. Miller, David C. Newbury, and Michelle D. Wagner (Atlanta: African Studies Association, 1994), 345–70; and Lovejoy, "The Yoruba Factor in the Trans-Atlantic Slave Trade," in *The Yoruba Diaspora in the Atlantic World*, ed. Toyin Falola and Matt D. Childs (Bloomington: Indiana University Press, 2004), 40–55.

5. Priscilla Mello, "Leitura, encantamento e rebelião o Islã Negro no Brasil séc-ola XIX" (Ph.D. dissertation, Universidade Federal Fluminense, 2009); José Cairus, "Jihād, Captivity and Redemption: Slavery and Resistance in the Path of Allah, Central Sudan and Bahia" (unpublished paper presented at the conference "Slavery and Religion in the Modern World," Essaouira [Morocco], 2001); Cairus, "Intrumentum vocale, mallams e alufás: O paradoxo islâmico da erudição na diáspora africana no Atlântico," *Topoi* 6 (2003): 128–64; and Cairus, "Jihād, cativeiro e redenção: Escravidão, resistência e irmandade, Sudão Central e Bahia (1835)" (dissertação de mestrado ao PPGH, Universidade Federal do Rio de Janeiro, 2002).

6. See Paul E. Lovejoy, "Jihād e escravidão: As origens dos escravos Muçulmanos de Bahia," *Topoi* 1 (2000): 11–44, which extends the arguments in Lovejoy, "Background to Rebellion: The Origins of Muslim Slaves in Bahia," *Slavery and Abolition* 15, no. 2 (1994): 151–80; Lovejoy, "Jihād and Slavery: The Origins of Enslaved Muslims in Bahia," in *Slavery, Commerce and Production in the Sokoto Caliphate of West Africa* (Trenton, NJ: Africa World Press, 2005), 55–80; and Lovejoy, ed., *Slavery on the Frontiers of Islam* (Princeton, NJ: Markus Wiener, 2004). The detailed analysis of primary sources that lies behind these various studies is only noted here, but the wealth of documentation provides the context for a dialogue with Hobsbawm and Genovese and implicitly with the scholarship of Atlantic studies and black Atlantic history.

7. For a preliminary discussion, see Lovejoy, "Clapperton-Bello Exchange," 201–28; and the subsequent revision "Diplomacy in the Heart of Africa: British-Sokoto Negotiations over the Abolition of the Atlantic Slave Trade," in Cottias and Rossignol, *Distant Ripples of British Abolitionist Wave in Africa, Asia and the Americas*.

8. Roger Botte, "Les rapports Nord-Sud, la traite négrière et le Fuuta Jaloo à la fin du XVIIIᵉ siècle," *Annales: Économies, Sociétés, Civilisations* 6 (1991): 1411–35.

9. Jean Boulègue, "L'expression du refus de la traite négrière dans les sociétés sénégambiennes, XVIIᵉ–XVIIIᵉ siècles," in *De la traite à l'esclavage: Actes du Colloque International sur la traite des noirs*, ed. Serge Daget (Nantes: Centre de Recherche sur l'Histoire du Monde Atlantique, 1985), 1:247–52.

10. Carl Bernhard Wadström, *Observations on the Slave Trade and a Description of Some Part of the Coast of Guinea* (London: James Phillips, 1789), 33–34.

11. John O. Hunwick and Fatima Harrak. *Mi'raj al-su'ud: Ahmad Baba's Replies on Slavery* (Rabat: Institute des Études Africaines, Université Mohamed V, 2000).

12. On the burden of proof of slavery being on the master or merchant, not the slave, see John Hunwick, "Notes on Slavery in the Songhay Empire," in *Slaves and Slavery in Muslim Africa: The Servile Estate*, ed. John Ralph Willis (London: Frank Cass, 1985), 19, citing al-Maghili and Mahmud b. ʿUmar, the *qadi* of Timbuktu from 1498 to 1548.

13. Rina Cáceres, "La abolición de la esclavitud en Centroamérica" (paper presented at the conference "The Congress of Vienna and Its Global Dimension," Vienna, 18–22 September 2014).

14. Suzanne Schwarz, "'A Just and Honourable Commerce'": Abolitionist Experimentation in Sierra Leone in the Late Eighteenth and Early Nineteenth Centuries" (London: Hakluyt Society Annual Lecture, 2013).

15. But see Cottias and Rossignol, Distant Ripples of the British Abolitionist Wave.

16. Humphrey Fisher, "A Muslim William Wilberforce? The Sokoto Jihād as Anti-slavery Crusade: An Enquiry into Historical Causes," in Daget, De la traite à l'esclavage, 571.

17. Ibid., 551.

18. Lovejoy, "The Context of Enslavement in West Africa: Ahmad Bābā and the Ethics of Slavery," in Slaves, Subjects, and Subversives: Blacks in Colonial Latin America, ed. Jane Landers (Albuquerque: University of New Mexico Press, 2006), 9–38. For the full text, see Hunwick and Harrak, Mi'rāj al-ṣu'ūd'.

19. Clapperton to Horton, 6 June 1825, in Missions to the Niger, ed. E. W. Bovill (Cambridge: Cambridge University Press, 1966), 4:774.

20. See, for example, Seymour Drescher, Abolition: A History of Slavery and Antislavery (Cambridge: Cambridge University Press, 2009).

21. See, for example, Paul E. Lovejoy and Suzanne Schwarz, eds., Slavery, Abolition and the Transition to Colonialism in Sierra Leone (Trenton, NJ: Africa World Press, 2015).

22. R. R. Madden, A Twelvemonth's Residence in the West Indies, during the Transition from Slavery to Apprenticeship, 2 vols. (Westport, CT: Negro University Press, 1970 [1835]); Madden, The Island of Cuba: Its Resources, Progress, and Prospects, Considered in Relation Especially to the Influence of Its Prosperity on the Interests of the British West India Colonies (London: C. Gilpin, 1849); Madden, "Report of Her Majesty's Commissioner on the State of our Settlements on the Western Coast of Africa," C.O. 2/72, Sierra Leone & African Forts, 1841, National Archives, London.

23. Eugène Daumas and Ausone de Chancel, Le grand désert: Itinéraire d'une caravane du Sahara au pays des nègres (Paris: M. Levy, 1860).

24. Yacine Daddi Addoun, "Abolition de l'esclavage en Algérie, 1816–1871" (Ph.D. dissertation, York University, 2010); Ismael Musah Montana, "The Trans-Saharan Slave Trade, Abolition of Slavery and Transformation in the North African Regency of Tunis, 1730–1846" (Ph.D. dissertation, York University, 2007); and Montana, The Abolition of Slavery in Ottoman Tunisia (Gaineville: University Press of Florida, 2013).

25. Daddi Addoun, "Abolition de l'esclavage en Algérie"; Montana, Abolition of Slavery in Ottoman Tunisia; Lawrence C. Jennings, French Anti-slavery: The Movement for the Abolition of Slavery in France, 1802–1848 (Cambridge: Cambridge University Press, 2000), 255. Also see Ehud R. Toledano, ed., African Communities in Asia and the Mediterranean: Identities between Integration and Conflict (Trenton, NJ: Africa World Press, 2011); and Toledano, The Ottoman Slave Trade and Its Suppression, 1840–1890 (Princeton, NJ: Princeton University Press, 1982).

26. I thank Mohamed Kassim for this translation.

27. Shehu Yamusa, "The Political Ideas of the Jihad Leaders: Being a Translation, Edition and Analysis of (1) *Uṣūl al-Siyāsa* by Muhammad Bello and (2) *Ḍiyā' al-Ḥukkām* by Abdallah B. Fodio" (M.A. thesis, Bayero University, Kano, 1975), 270; and Abubaker Aliu Gwandu, "Abdullahi b. Fodio as a Muslim Jurist" (Ph.D. dissertation, University of Durham, 1977), 216.

28. Hugh Clapperton to R. Wilmot Horton, 6 June 1825, in Bovill, *Missions to the Niger*, 4:775.

29. Al-hājj, ʿUmar, *Risālat shawq al-habīb ilā as'ilat Ibāhīm al-labīb*, in Omar Jah, "The Effect of Pilgrimage on the Jihād of Al-Hajj ʿUmar al-Futi, 1794–1864," in *The Central Bilad al Sudan: Tradition and Adaptation*, ed. Yusuf Fadl Hasan and Paul Doornbos (Khartoum: University of Khartoum Press, 1977), 239. Also see Omar Jah, "Al-Haj ʿUmar's Philosophy of Jihād and Its Sufi Basis" (Ph.D. dissertation, McGill University, 1974).

30. A. D. H. Bivar, "The *Wathīqat ahl al-Sūdān*: A Manifesto of the Fulani *Jihād*," *Journal of African History* 2, no. 2 (1961): 240.

31. ʿUthmān dan Fodio, *Bayān wujūb al hijra ʿalā l-ʿibād (The Exposition of Obligation of Emigration upon the Servants of God)*, ed. and transl. F. H. El Masri (Khartoum: University of Khartoum Press, 1978), 117–20.

32. ʿUmar Al-Naqar, *The Pilgrimage Tradition in West Africa* (Khartoum: University of Khartoum Press, 1972), 54, 142.

33. ʿAbdullahi dan Fodio, *Tazyīn al-waraqāt*, trans. M. Hiskett (Ibadan: University of Ibadan Press, 1963), 121–22.

34. ʿAbdullahi dan Fodio, *Ḍiyā' al-Ḥukkām*, in Yamusa, "Political Ideas of the Jihād Leaders," 270–85.

35. For a discussion of ransoming, see Jennifer Lofkrantz, "Protecting Freeborn Muslims: The Sokoto Caliphate's Attempts to Prevent Illegal Enslavement and Its Acceptance of the Strategy of Ransoming," *Slavery and Abolition* 32, no. 1 (2011): 109–27; Lofkrantz, "Ransoming of Captives and Slavery in the Sokoto Caliphate in the Nineteenth Century," in *Slavery, Islam and Diaspora*, ed. Behnaz A. Mirzai, Ismael Musah Montana, and Paul E. Lovejoy (Trenton, NJ: Africa World Press, 2009), 125–37; Lofkrantz, "Intellectual Discourse in the Early Sokoto Caliphate: The Triumvirate's Opinions on the Issue of Ransoming, ca. 1810," *International Journal of African Historical Studies* 45, no. 3 (2012): 385–401; and Lofkrantz, "Ransoming Policies and Practices in the Western and Central Bilād al-Sūdān, c. 1800–1910" (Ph.D. dissertation, York University, 2008).

36. Al-hājj, ʿUmar, *Risālat shawq al-habīb ilā as'ilat Ibāhīm al-labīb*, as cited in Jah, "Effect of Pilgrimage on the Jihād of Al-Hajj ʿUmar al-Futi," 239. Also see Jah, "Al-Haj ʿUmar's Philosophy of Jihād and Its Sufi Basis."

37. Suzanne Schwarz, ed., *Zachary Macaulay and the Development of the Sierra Leone Company, 1793–4*, vol. 1, *Journal, June–October 1793* (Leipzig: Institut für Afrikanistik, Universität Leipzig, University of Leipzig Papers on Africa, History and Culture, series no. 4, 2000), 59.

38. Heinrich Barth, *Travels and Discoveries in North and Central Africa* (New York: Harper and Brothers, 1859), 1:516.

39. Robert Smith, "The Lagos Consulate, 1851–1861: An Outline," *Journal of African History* 15, no. 3 (1974): 393–416. Also see Kristin Mann, *Slavery and the Birth of an African City, 1760–1900* (Bloomington: Indiana University Press, 2007).

40. Macgregor Laird and R. A. K. Oldfield, *Narrative of an Expedition into the Interior of Africa by the River Niger, in the SteamVessels* Quorra *and* Alburkah *in 1832, 1833 and 1834* (London: Richard Bentley, 1837), 2:322–23; and James Richardson, *Narrative of a Mission to Central Africa Performed in the Years 1850–51* (London: Chapman, 1853), 2:203. See the discussion in Lovejoy, "Central Sudan and the Atlantic Slave Trade," 345–70.

41. A. Adu Boahen, *Britain, the Sahara, and the Western Sudan, 1788–1861* (Oxford: Clarendon Press, 1964); Robin Hallett, *The Penetration of Africa: European Enterprise and Exploration in Northern and Western Africa up to 1830* (London: Oxford University Press, 1965); E. W. Bovill, *The Golden Trade of the Moors*, 2nd ed. (London: Oxford University Press, 1970); Jamie Bruce Lockhart, *A Sailor in the Sahara: The Life and Travels in Africa of Hugh Clapperton, Commander RN* (London: Tauris, 2008); and Bruce Lockhart, *Difficult and Dangerous Roads: Hugh Clapperton's Travels in Sahara and Fezzan, 1822–1825* (London: Sickle Moon Books, 2000).

42. Boahen, *Britain, the Sahara, and the Western Sudan*, 55–56.

43. Tripoli troops were engaged in military campaigns in Borno in 1819, in 1820, and again in 1822–24; Kola Folayan, *Tripoli during the Reign of Yusuf Pasha Qaramanli* (Ife-Ife: University of Ife Pres, 1979), 71–72. Also see Folayan, "Tripoli-Bornu Political Relations, 1817–1825," *Journal of the Historical Society of Nigeria* 5 (1971): 463–71.

44. Bovill, *Missions to the Niger*, 3:412.

45. Denham to Warrington, 15 May 1823, in Bovill, *Missions to the Niger*, 4:555–59.

46. Clapperton to Horton, 6 June 1825, in Bovill, *Missions to the Niger*, 4:773.

47. Dixon Denham, Hugh Clapperton, and Walter Oudney, *Narrative of Travels and Discoveries in Northern and Central Africa in the Years 1822, 1823, and 1824* (London: John Murray, 1828), 2:419–20. For the location of Raka, see John Beecroft [Becroft], "On Benin and the Upper Course of the River Quorra, or Niger," *Journal of the Royal Geographical Society* 11 (1841): 186.

48. Denham, Clapperton, and Oudney, *Narrative of Travels and Discoveries in Northern and Central Africa*, 2:367.

49. Clapperton to Horton, 6 June 1825, in Bovill, *Missions to the Niger*, 4:775.

50. According to Clapperton's report; see Bovill, Missions to the Niger, 4:689. Atagara is to be identified with Idah; see Paul E. Lovejoy and Sydney Kanya-Forstner, eds., *Agents, Pilgrims, and Interpreters: French Reconnaissance Reports from the 1890s* (Madison: African Studies Program, University of Wisconsin–Madison, 1997), 144n60.

51. Clapperton to Horton, 6 June 1825, in Bovill, *Missions to the Niger*, 4:773.

52. Denham, Clapperton, and Oudney, *Narrative of Travels and Discoveries in Northern and Central Africa*, 2:367.

53. Clapperton, ibid., 2:420.

54. Bovill, *Missions to the Niger*, 4:695–96. Clapperton wrote to R. Wilmot Horton, 7 June 1825, "I answered that I would acquaint Him so soon as I had rejoined Major Denham at Bornou; from which place I wrote to Bello, mentioning 'July' as the probable period, and name the 'Town of Widdah,' on the sea-coast, as the place to which I gave preference. I then conceived that I should have returned earlier to England" (C.O. 2/13), as quoted in ibid., 4:776–77.

55. Denham, Clapperton, and Oudney, *Narrative of Travels and Discoveries in Northern and Central Africa*, 2:342–43, 348.

56. Ibid., 2:417–18.

57. Jamie R. Bruce Lockhart, *Clapperton in Borno: Journals of the Travels in Borno of Lieutenant Hugh Clapperton, RN, from January 1823 to September 1824* (Cologne: Rüdiger Köppe Verlag, 1996), 26n.

58. Daumas and Chancel, *Grand désert*, 231.

59. Ibid., 244.

60. For a discussion of ʿUmar's residence in Sokoto in the 1830s, see David Robinson, *The Holy War of Umar Tal: The Western Sudan in the Mid-Nineteenth Century* (Oxford: Clarendon Press, 1985), 102–8.

61. Michael Mason, *The Foundations of the Bida Kingdom* (Zaria: Ahmadu Bello University Press, 1979), 34–35.

62. Daumas and Chancel, *Grand desert*, 199–247.

63. S. A. Crowther, Report to the Niger Mission, letter to the CMS, dated January 1855, CMS: The Yoruba Mission: CA2/031(b), as cited in Mahdi Adamu, *The Hausa Factor in West African History* (Zaria: Ahmadu Bello University Press, 1978), 129.

64. Mason, *Foundations of the Bida Kingdom*, 60–61.

65. Pierre Verger, *Trade Relations between the Bight of Benin and Bahia, 17th-19th Century* (Ibadan: University of Ibadan Press, 1976), 285–313; and João José Reis, *Slave Rebellion in Brazil: The Muslim Uprising of 1835 in Bahia* (Baltimore: Johns Hopkins University Press, 1993), 196–204.

66. It is likely that Muslim slaves were taken to Cuba before the collapse of the Bahian trade; see the report of circumcised boys on board the *Prineria* of Havana, as reported for March 1831, in Peter Leonard, *The Western Coast of Africa: Journal of an Officer under Captain Owen; Records of a Voyage in the Ship "Dryad" in 1830, 1831, and 1832* (Philadelphia: Edward C. Mielke, 1833), 2:71.

67. Clapperton wanted to confirm the flow of the Niger to the south; like Oudney, he believed that the Niger flowed into "the lakes of Nupe." The idea can be traced to an Arab report "years before," apparently alluding to early reports to the African Association (Bovill, *Missions to the Niger*, 3:567). For a discussion, see Jamie Bruce Lockhart and Paul E. Lovejoy, eds., *Hugh Clapperton into the Interior of Africa: Records of the Second Expedition, 1825–1827* (Leiden, Brill, 2005), 7–9.

68. Also see the letter written by W. Oudney to R. Wilmot, dated Kukawa, 14 July 1823, in which Oudney wrote that he "suspects very much it [the Niger] ends in the lakes at *Nyffee*" (Bovill, *Missions to the Niger*, 3:567).

69. In 1789 Henry Beaufroy, secretary of the African Association, had been told that "*below Guinea* is the *sea*, into which the river of Tombuctoo disembogues itself.

This may therefore be considered the *prevailing idea* at Houssa and Tombuctoo." Beaufroy's source was a merchant who had lived in Timbuktu "altogether about 12 years" (Bovill, *Missions to the Niger*, 1:4). There is no reason to believe that this was the first source of such information.

70. Denham, Clapperton, and Oudney, *Narrative of Travels and Discoveries in Northern and Central Africa*, 2:91–92.

8. Empowering History

1. "Return of every Slave tried and convicted by a Court Martial during the late Rebellion in Jamaica or in consequence thereof distinguishing in separate Columns Parish of Manchester" (C.O. 137/185, The National Archives, London), which lists the execution of Abraham Peart (aged thirty), Edward Robinson (aged forty), and Richard (age thirty), all of Spice Grove. Peart was listed as a cartman and creole, while Robinson was a second driver and African born, and Richard was a creole and "Field Negro." I thank Sonja Maurer for this reference. Also see Yacine Daddi Addoun and Paul E. Lovejoy, "The Arabic Manuscript of Muḥammad Kabā Saghanughu of Jamaica, c. 1820," in *Creole Concerns: Essays in Honour of Kamau Brathwaite*, ed. Annie Paul (Kingston: University of the West Indies Press, 2007), 313–41.

2. Robert L. Fraser, "PIERPOINT, RICHARD," in *Dictionary of Canadian Biography*, vol. 7, University of Toronto/Université Laval, 2003, accessed July 16, 2016, see http://www.biographi.ca/en/bio/pierpoint_richard_7E.html; also see David Meyler and Peter Meyler, *A Stolen Life: Searching for Richard Pierpoint* (Toronto: Natural Heritage Books, 1999).

3. Robin Law and Paul E. Lovejoy, eds. *The Biography of Mahommah Gardo Baquaqua: His Passage from Slavery to Freedom in Africa and America*, 2nd ed. (Princeton, NJ: Markus Wiener, 2001).

4. Paul E. Lovejoy, "Muhammad ʿAlī Nicholas Saʿīd: From Enslavement to American Civil War Veteran," paper presented at "Meaning of Blackness II," Universidad de Costa Rica, 2016.

5. Donna Haraway, "Situated Knowledges: The Science Question in Feminism and the Privilege of Partial Perspectives," *Feminist Studies* 14, no. 3 (1988): 575–99. Although Haraway's insights are directed at interpretations of gender, I have borrowed her conceptual framework in applying the situational dimensions of perspective to the interpretation of history in relation to Islam.

6. Ibid.

7. Paul E. Lovejoy and Jan Hogendorn, *Slow Death for Slavery: The Course of Abolition in Northern Nigeria, 1897–1936* (Cambridge: Cambridge University Press, 1993); and Benedetta Rossi, *From Slavery to Aid: Power, Labour, and Ecology in the Nigerien Sahel, 1800–2000* (Cambridge: Cambridge University Press, 2015).

8. In 1827 Hugh Clapperton reported from Kano that a merchant from Ghadames had been strangled in his bed. "His female slaves were suspected of being guilty of murder, as two or three similar cases had happened before"; see *Journal of a Second Expedition into the Interior of Africa* (London: John Murray, 1829), 171. Although Clapperton does not state that the female slaves were concubines, it seems

likely that they were. In 1824 Clapperton reported that a merchant from Tripoli, resident in Katagum, "always lay with a dagger, and loaded pistols, under his pillow, lest he should be murdered by his female slaves. He also acquainted me, that almost all the Arabs did the same; for it was chiefly females [slaves] whom they had reason to fear, the master being often strangled at night by the women of the household"; see Dixon Denham, Hugh Clapperton, and Walter Oudney, *Narrative of Travels and Discoveries in Northern and Central Africa, in the Years 1822, 1823, and 1824* (London: John Murray, 1828), 2:407.

9. Mahmood Yakubu, "A Century of Warfare and Slavery in Bauchi, c. 1805–1900" (B.A. thesis, Department of History, University of Sokoto, 1985), 62.

10. Paul E. Lovejoy, "Biographies of Enslaved Muslims from the Central Sudan in the Nineteenth Century," in *The Sokoto Caliphate: History and Legacies, 1804–2004*, ed. H. Bobboyi and A. M. Yakubu (Kaduna: Arewa House, 2006), 1:187–216.

11. Paul E. Lovejoy, "Concubinage in the Sokoto Caliphate (1804–1903)," *Slavery and Abolition* 11 (1990): 159–89.

12. Samuel Johnson, *The History of the Yoruba from the Earliest Time to the Beginning of the British Protectorate* (Lagos: C.M.S. Bookshop, 1937); originally compiled in the 1890s.

13. For Arabic texts, see B. G. Martin, "A New Arabic History of Ilorin," *Research Bulletin* (Centre of Arabic Documentation, University of Ibadan) 1, no. 2 (1965): 20–27; and Abdullahi Smith, "A Little New Light on the Collapse of the Alafinate of Yoruba," in *A Little New Light: Selected Historical Writings of Abdullahi Smith* (Zaria: Centre for Historical Research, 1987), 149–91, especially to the discussion therein of Ahmad b. Abu Bakr Ikokoro, *Ta'līf akhbār al-qurūn min umarā' bilād Ilurin* (1912) and Waziri Junaidu al-Bukhārī, *Ta'nīs al-aḥibba fī dhikr umarā' Gwandu mā'wā al-aṣfiyā'*. Smith's important contribution was also published in *Studies in Yoruba History and Culture*, ed. G. O. Olusanya (Ibadan: University of Ibadan Press, 1983), 42–71. Also see Muhammad b. 'Abdullah, emir of Gwandu, Muhammad b. 'Abdullah, *Risalā Ila Amīr Yoruba 'Abd al-Salam*, in Hakeem Olumide Akanni Danmole, "The Frontier Emirate: A History of Islam in Ilorin" (Ph.D. dissertation, University of Birmingham, 1980), app. 2. For other documentation, see Robin Law, ed., *Contemporary Source Material for the History of the Old Oyo Empire, 1627–1824* (Ibadan: Institute of African Studies, 1993). A revised version (2001) is accessible on line at SHADD, www.harriettubman.ca. The jihād is barely discussed in such classic works of Yoruba history as Robert S. Smith, *Kingdoms of the Yoruba* (London: Methuen, 1969), and Robert S. Smith, *Yoruba Warfare in the 19th Century* (Cambridge: Cambridge University Press, 1964), and, more recently, Toyin Falola's massive study *Ibadan: Foundation, Growth and Change, 1830–1960* (Ibadan: Bookcraft, 2012).

14. For an account of Samuel Ajayi Crowther, see J. F. A. Ajayi, "Samuel Ajayi Crowther of Oyo," in *Africa Remembered: Narratives by West Africans from the Era of the Slave Trade*, ed. Philip D. Curtin (Madison: University of Wisconsin Press, 1967), 289–316. Also see Jesse Page, *The Black Bishop: Samuel Adjai Crowther* (London: Simpkin, Marshall, Hamilton, Kent and Company, 1910); Jean Herskovits Kopytoff, *A Preface to Modern Nigeria: The "Sierra Leonians" in Yoruba, 1830–1890*

(Madison: University of Wisconsin Press, 1965), 285; "Bishop Crowther: His Life and Work," *Church Missionary Gleaner* 5 (1878): 10–11; Samuel Crowther, "Letter of Mr. Samuel Crowther to the Rev. William Jowett, Feb. 22, 1837," *Church Missionary Record* 8 (1837): 217–23; "A Liberated African's Account of His Slavery, and Subsequent Course," *Church Missionary Gleaner* 6 (1846): 16–18; and James Frederick Schön and Samuel Crowther, *Journals of the Rev. James Frederick Schön and Mr. Samuel Crowther* (London: Church Missionary Society, 1854), 371–85. Also see J. F. A. Ajayi, *Christian Missions in Nigeria: 1841–1891* (London: Longmans, 1965); and E.A. Ayandele, *The Missionary Impact on Modern Nigeria: 1842–1914* (London: Longmans, 1966).

15. Ali Eisami Gazirmabe, in Sigismund Wilhelm Koelle, *African Native Literature* (Graz: Akademische Druck- u. Verlagsanstalt, 1968 [London, 1854]), 248–56. Also see H. F. C. [Abdullahi] Smith, D. M. Last, and Gambo Gubio, "Ali Eisami Gazirmabe of Bornu," in Curtin, *Africa Remembered*, 199–216. For accounts of Hausa and Nupe former slaves in Sierra Leone, see Christopher Fyfe, *A History of Sierra Leone* (London: Oxford University Press, 1962), 66, 138, 170, 231, 234, 424 (Hausa), and 170, 231, 289, 293, 320 (Nupe).

16. Antônio de Menezes Vasconcellos de Drummond, "Lettres sur l'Afrique ancienne et moderne," *Journal des Voyages* 32 (1826) : 290–324 [*sic*; 190–224]; and Francis de Castelnau, *Renseignements sur l'Afrique centrale et sur une nation d'hommes à queue qui s'y trouverait, d'après le rapport des nègres du Soudan, esclaves à Bahia* (Paris: Librairie P. Bertrand, 1851). Also see Muhammad Misrah, "Narrative of a Journey from Egypt to the Western Coast of Africa, by Mahomed Misrah Communicated by an Officer Serving in Sierra Leone," *Quarterly Journal*, October 1822, 6, 15–16.

17. Marcia Smith, "The Male Uprising in Bahia, 1835: Mini-biographies of Leaders and Others Accused" (M.A. thesis, York University, 1998); José Cairus, "Intrumentum vocale, mallams e alufás: O paradoxo islâmico da erudição na diáspora africana no Atlântico," *Topoi* 6 (2003): 128–64; Cairus, "Jihãd, cativeiro e redenção: Escravidão, resistência e irmandade, Sudão Central e Bahia (1835)" (dissertação de mestrado ao PPGH, Universidade Federal do Rio de Janeiro, 2002); and Priscilla Mello, "Leitura, encantamento e rebelião o Islã Negro no Brasil século XIX" (Ph.D. dissertation, Universidade Federal Fluminense, 2009). I have also drawn on Rolf Reichert, "L'insurrection d'esclaves de 1835 à la lumière des documents arabes des archives publiques de l'état de Bahia (Brésil)," *Bulletin de l'Institut Fondamental d'Afrique Noire*, ser. B, 29, nos. 1–2 (1967): 99–104; and Reichert, *Os documentos Arabes do arquivo publico do estado da Bahia* (Salvador: Universidade Federal da Bahia, Centro de Estudos Afro-Orientais, 1979). The court transcripts of the trials after the 1835 uprising contain references to other documents; see, for example, *Anais do arquivo do estado da Bahia* 38 (1968): 61–63, and 40 (1971): 42–43; and Vincent Monteil, "Analyse de 25 documents arabes des Malês de Bahia (1835)," *Bulletin de l'Institut Fondamental d'Afrique Noire*, ser. B, 29, nos. 1–2 (1967): 88–98.

18. João José Reis, Flávio dos Santos Gomes, and Marcus J. M. de Carvalho, "África e Brasil entre margens: Aventuras e desventuras do africano Rufino José

Maria, c. 1822–1853," *Revista Estudos Afro-Asiáticos* 4 (2005): 257–302; Reis, Gomes, and Carvalho, *O alufá Rufino: Tráfico, escravidão e liberdade no Atlântico negro (c. 1823–c. 1853)* (São Paulo: Companhia das Letras, 2010).

19. Lovejoy, "Biographies of Enslaved Muslims," 187–216. Through the support of the Social Sciences and Humanities Research Council of Canada, a team of researchers is constructing a biographical database that will form the basis of a study of enslavement in West Africa in the first half of the nineteenth century.

20. Peter Linebaugh and Marcus Rediker, *The Many-Headed Hydra: Sailors, Slaves, Commoners, and the Hidden History of the Revolutionary Atlantic* (Boston: Beacon Press, 2000); Jane Landers, *Atlantic Creoles in the Age of Revolutions* (Cambridge, MA: Harvard University Press, 2010); Rebecca Scott and Jean M. Hébrard, *Freedom Papers: An Atlantic Odyssey in the Age of Emancipation* (Cambridge, MA: Harvard University Press, 2012); Walter Hawthorne, " 'Being Now, as It Were, One Family': Shipmate Bonding on the Slave Vessel *Emilia*, in Rio de Janeiro and throughout the Atlantic World," *Luso-Brazilian Review* 45, no. 1 (2008): 53–77; Hawthorne, *From Africa to Brazil: Culture, Identity, and an Atlantic Slave Trade, 1600–1830* (New York: Cambridge University Press, 2010); James H. Sweet, *Recreating Africa: Culture, Kinship, and Religion in the African-Portuguese World, 1440–1770* (Chapel Hill: University of North Carolina Press, 2003); Sweet, "Mistaken Identities? Olaudah Equiano, Domingos Álvares, and the Methodological Challenges of Studying the African Diaspora," *American Historical Review* 114, no. 2 (2009): 279–306; Sweet, *Domingos Alvares, African Healing, and the Intellectual History of the Atlantic World* (Chapel Hill: University of North Carolina Press, 2011); Luiz R. B Mott, *Rosa Egipcía: Uma santa africana no Brasil* (Rio de Janeiro: Bertrand Brasil, 1993); João José Reis, *Domingos Sodré, um sacerdote Africano: Escravidão, liberdade e candomblé na Bahia do século XIX* (São Paulo: Companhia das Letras, 2008); Reis, Gomes, and Carvalho, *O alufá Rufino*; Mariana P. Candido, "African Freedom Suits and Portuguese Vassal Status: Legal Mechanisms for Fighting Enslavement in Benguela, Angola, 1800–1830," *Slavery and Abolition* 32, no. 3 (2011): 447–59; Roquinaldo Ferreira, *Cross-Cultural Exchange in the Atlantic World: Angola and Brazil during the Era of the Slave Trade* (New York: Cambridge University Press, 2012); Mariana P. Candido, "Aguida Gonçalves da Silva, une dona à Benguela à la fin du XVIIIᵉ siècle," *Brésil(s): Sciences Humaines et Sociales* 1 (2012): 33–54. Also see Robin Law and Kristin Mann, "West Africa in the Atlantic Community: The Case of the Slave Coast," *William and Mary Quarterly* 56, no. 2 (1999): 307–334; and Lovejoy, "Biographies of Enslaved Muslims," 187–216.

21. Jennifer Lofkrantz, "Ransoming of Captives in the Sokoto Caliphate in the Nineteenth Century," in *Slavery, Islam and Diaspora*, ed. Behnaz A. Mirzai, Ismael Musah Montana, and Paul E. Lovejoy (Trenton, NJ: Africa World Press, 2009), 125–37; and Lofkrantz, "Protecting Freeborn Muslims: The Sokoto Caliphate's Attempts to Prevent Illegal Enslavement and Its Acceptance of the Strategy of Ransoming," *Slavery and Abolition* 32, no. 1 (2011): 109–27.

22. Muhammad ʿAlī Nicholas Saʿīd, *The Autobiography of Nicholas Said, a Native of Bornou, Eastern Soudan* (Memphis: Shotwell and Co., 1873); and Saʿīd, "A Native of

Bornoo," *Atlantic Monthly*, 1867, 485–95. For Sa'id's father, Barca Gana, see Denham, Clapperton, and Oudney, *Narrative of Travels and Discoveries in Northern and Central Africa*, 1:210, 268, 272, 375–77. Also see Allan D. Austin, "Mohammed Ali Ben Said: Travels on Five Continents," *Contributions in Black Studies* 12 (1994): 129–58; and Louis Brenner, *The Shehus of Kukawa: A History of the Al-Kanemi Dynasty of Bornu* (Oxford: Clarendon Press, 1973).

23. Lovejoy, "Muhammad 'Alī Nicholas Sa'īd;"; Sa'īd, *Autobiography*.

24. "Simcoe, John Graves," *Dictionary of Canadian Biography*, vol. 5.

25. Fraser, "Pierpoint"; and Meyler and Meyler, *Searching for Richard Pierpoint*.

26. Paul E. Lovejoy, "The Urban Background of Enslaved Muslims in the Americas," *Slavery and Abolition* 26, no. 3 (2005): 347–72.

27. Paul E. Lovejoy, "Scarification and the Loss of History in the African Diaspora," in *Activating the Past: Historical Memory in the Black Atlantic*, ed. Andrew Apter and Lauren Derby (Newcastle: Cambridge Scholarly Publishing, 2009), 99–138. Also see Katrina Keefer, "Scarification and Identity in the Liberated Africans Department Registers, 1814–1815," *Canadian Journal of African Studies* 47, no. 3 (2013): 537–53; and Henry Lovejoy, "Old Oyo Influences on the Transformation of Lucumí Identity in Colonial Cuba" (Ph.D. dissertation, UCLA, 2012). I am currently involved in a research project with Abubakar Babajo Sani, Department of History, Musa Yar'Adua University, Katsina, on the recording of visual images of scarifications and hairstyles in the central emirates of the Sokoto Caliphate, under the auspices of the Canada Research Chair in African Diaspora History and Musa Yar'Adua University.

28. David Eltis, Martin Halbert, and Philip Misevich, eds., *The African Origins Project*, http://www.african-origins.org. Also see Suzanne Schwarz, "Extending the African Names Database: New Evidence from Sierra Leone," *African Economic History* 38 (2010): 137–63; and Henry Lovejoy, "Old Oyo Influences," 17–18, 27–33, 37–38.

29. Manuel Barcia, "An Islamic Atlantic Revolution: Dan Fodio's *Jihad* and Slave Rebellion in Bahia and Cuba, 1804–1844," *Journal of African Diaspora, Archaeology, and Heritage* 2, no. 1 (2013):" 6–18; and Barcia, *West African Warfare in Bahia and Cuba: Soldier Slaves in the Atlantic World, 1807–1844* (Oxford: Oxford University Press, 2014), 99–104.

30. Henry Lovejoy, "Old Oyo Influences."

31. Henry Lovejoy, "Digital History, Slave Databases, and Mapping" (unpublished paper presented at the American Historical Association Annual Meeting, Atlanta, 7 January 2016).

32. For the actions of Muslim Aku in Sierra Leone, see John Peterson, *Province of Freedom: A History of Sierra Leone, 1787–1870* (London: Faber and Faber, 1969), 93, 212–17; Fyfe, *History of Sierra Leone*, 170, 186–87, 204, 212, 215; C. Magbaily Fyle, *A Nationalist History of Sierra Leone* (Freetown: Securicom Printers, 2011); Alusine Jalloh and David E. Skinner, eds., *Islam and Trade in Sierra Leone* (Trenton, NJ: Africa World Press, 1997); and Winston McGowan, "The Development of European Relations with Futa Jallon and the Foundation of French Colonial Rule, 1794–1897" (Ph.D. dissertation, University of London, 1978).

33. For Trinidad, see Paul E. Lovejoy and David Trotman, "Community of Believers: Trinidad Muslims and the Return to Africa, c. 1810–1850," in *Slavery on the Frontiers of Islam*, ed. Paul E. Lovejoy (Princeton, NJ: Markus Wiener, 2004), 221–34. For Jamaica and the alleged existence of *wathiqat* (document) of Kabā Saghanughu, see Yacine Daddi Addoun and Paul E. Lovejoy, "Muḥammad Kabā Saghanughu and the Muslim Community of Jamaica," in Lovejoy, *Slavery on the Frontiers of Islam*, 201–20; and Daddi Addoun and Lovejoy, "Arabic Manuscript of Muḥammad Kabā Saghanughu of Jamaica," 313–41.

34. Sean Stilwell, *Paradoxes of Power: The Kano "Mamluks" and Male Royal Slavery in the Sokoto Caliphate, 1804–1903* (Portsmouth, NH: Heinemann, 2004); Stilwell, "Power, Honour and Shame: The Ideology of Royal Slavery in the Sokoto Caliphate," *Africa* 70, no. 3 (2000): 394–421; Stilwell, " 'Amana' and 'Asiri': Royal Slave Culture and the Colonial Regime in Kano, 1903–1926," *Slavery and Abolition* 19, no. 2 (1998): 167–88.

35. According to the imam of Salvador in the 1890s, the imam at the time of the revolt was Abubakar, which is a Hausa name; see Raimundo Nina Rodrigues, *Os Africanos no Brasil* (São Paulo: Companhia Editora Nacional, 1932), 109–10. Nina Rodrigues based his study on research between 1890 and his death in 1906. Also see Pierre Verger, *Trade Relations between the Bight of Benin and Bahia, 17th–19th Century* (Ibadan: University of Ibadan Press, 1976), 300, 307. Reis discusses other clerics who he considers were likely to have been the leader and perhaps the imam but does not include Abubakar as a possible candidate; see João José Reis, *Slave Rebellion in Brazil: The Muslim Uprising of 1835 in Bahia* (Baltimore: Johns Hopkins University Press, 1993), 130.

36. Dale Tomich, *Through the Prism of Slavery: Labor, Capital, and World Economy* (Lanham, MD: Rowman and Littlefield, 2004); Anthony E. Kaye, "The Second Slavery: Modernity in the Nineteenth-Century South and the Atlantic World," *Journal of Southern History* 75, no. 3 (2009): 627. See also David Eltis and David Richardson, *Atlas of the Transatlantic Slave Trade* (New Haven, CT: Yale University Press, 2010), 189, map 131, for the slave-ship revolts and the percentage of slaves who embarked by African region, 1566–1865.

37. Law and Lovejoy, *Biography of Mahommah Gardo Baquaqua*; Daddi Addoun and Lovejoy, "Muḥammad Kabā Saghanughu," 201–20; Daddi Addoun and Lovejoy, "Arabic Manuscript of Muḥammad Kabā Saghanughu," 313–41; Lovejoy, "Les origines de Catherine Mulgrave Zimmermann: Considérations méthodologiques," *Cahiers des Anneaux de la Mémoire* 14 (2011): 247–63.

38. My critique of Atlantic history was first published in 1997 online as Paul E. Lovejoy, "The African Diaspora: Revisionist Interpretations of Ethnicity, Culture and Religion under Slavery," in *Studies in the World History of Slavery, Abolition and Emancipation* 2, no. 1 (1997): 1–24.

39. Paul Gilroy, *The Black Atlantic: Modernity and Double Consciousness* (Cambridge, MA: Harvard University Press, 1993); Ira Berlin, "From Creole to African: Atlantic Creoles and the Origins of African-American Society in Mainland North America," *William and Mary Quarterly* 53, no. 2 (1996): 251–88; Gwendolyn Midlo

Hall, *Slavery and African Ethnicities in the Americas: Restoring the Links* (Chapel Hill: University of North Carolina Press, 2005); Landers, *Atlantic Creoles in the Age of Revolutions*.

40. Bernard Bailyn, *Atlantic History: Concept and Contours* (Cambridge, MA: Harvard University Press, 2005); Jack P. Green and Philip D. Morgan, *Atlantic History: A Critical Appraisal* (New York: Oxford University Press, 2008).

41. Murray Last, "Reform Movements in West Africa: The Jihad Movements of the Nineteenth Century," in *History of West Africa*, ed. Jacob Ajayi and Michael Crowder, 3rd ed. (London: Longman, 1987), 2:1.

42. Hawthorne, " 'Being Now, as It Were, One Family,' " 53–77; Hawthorne, *From Africa to Brazil*; Sweet, *Recreating Africa*; Sweet, "Mistaken Identities?," 279–306. Also see Law and Mann, "West Africa in the Atlantic Community," 307–34.

43. See P. E. Lovejoy, "African Diaspora."

44. Orlando Patterson, *Slavery and Social Death: A Comparative Study* (Cambridge, MA: Harvard University Press, 1985).

45. J. H. Vaughan and A. H. M. Kirk-Greene, eds., *The Diary of Hamman Yaji: Chronicle of a West African Ruler* (Bloomington: Indiana University Press, 1995); and Nicholas David, "A Close Reading of Hamman Yaji's Diary: Slave Raiding and Montagnard Responses in the Mountains around Madagali (Northeast Nigeria and Northern Cameroon)," Calgary, 2010, http://www.sukur.info/Mont/HammanYaji%20PAPER.pdf.

Appendix

1. Modibbo Tukur, "The Imposition of British Colonial Domination on the Sokoto Caliphate, Borno and Neighbouring States, 1897–1914" (Ph.D. dissertation, Ahmadu Bello University, 1979), 203.

2. There are a number of discrepancies in the list compiled by Yusufu Bala Usman in the spelling of names, including Junju (Junji), Birnin Gaoure (Birnin Ngarne), Torodi (Todori), Bitinkogi (Bitimi), and Yaga (Yaya). Yusufu Bala Usman, "The Transformation of Political Communities: Some Notes on a Significant Dimension of the Sokoto Jihad," in *Studies in the History of the Sokoto Caliphate: The Sokoto Seminar Papers*, ed. Y. B. Usman (Zaria: Department of History, Ahmadu Bello University, 1979), 55.

3. Tukur, "Imposition of British Colonial Domination," 204.

4. Ibid., 204; and Y. A. Aliyu, "Establishment and Development of Emirate Government in Bauchi" (Ph.D. dissertation, Ahmadu Bello University, 1974), 479–80.

5. M. G. Smith, "Slavery and Emancipation in Two Societies," in *The Plural Society in the British West Indies* (Berkeley: University of California Press, 1965), 117, 149.

6. Polly Hill, *Rural Hausa: A Village and a Setting* (Cambridge: Cambridge University Press, 1972), 309. Also see R. Mansell Prothero, "The Population Census of Northern Nigeria," Population Studies 10 (1956), 166.

7. Hill, *Rural Hausa*, 309.

8. Smith, "Slavery and Emancipation in Two Societies," 117, 149.

9. S. F. Nadel, *A Black Byzantium: Kingdom of Nupe in Nigeria* (Oxford: Oxford University Press, 1942), 8–10.

10. Paul Irwin, *Liptako Speaks: History from Oral Tradition in Africa* (Princeton, NJ: Princeton University Press, 1981), 15. According to Martin A. Klein, Dori had 15,300 male slaves and 24,565 female slaves in 1904, for a total of 39,865 slaves, a figure that is consistent with a total population of at least 80,000; see "Women in Slavery in the Western Sudan," in *Women and Slavery in Africa*, ed. Claire C. Robertson and Martin A. Klein (Portsmouth, NH: Heinemann, 1997), 69.

11. The most complete list is to be found in Usman, "Transformation of Political Communities," 55. Also see Tukur, "Imposition of British Colonial Domination," 203, who lists thirty emirates, including Junju, Ngaure, Say, Kunari, Torodi, Mbitimkoji, Yaga, Liptako, Bida, Agaie, Lapai, Fafiagi, Shonga, Ilorin, Gwandu, Daura, Katsina, Kano, Zazzau, Fombina (or Adamawa), Bauchi, Muri (or Hammarwa), Gombe, Kazaure, Katagum, Hadeija, Jama'are, Missau, Kontagora, and Jema'a. However, Jema'a was a subemirate under Zaria, while Tukur considers Gwandu an emirate but does not include Sokoto. He notes that "to these emirates should be added a number of sub-emirates around the metropolises of Sokoto and Wurno, the twin seats of the Caliphs, sub-emirates that were directly under the Caliph himself." Also see Hamidou Diallo, "Les Fulbe de Haute Volta et les influences exterieures de la fin du XVIIIe à la fin du XIXe siècle" (thèse de 3eme cycle, Université de Paris, I, 1979); Y. Georges Madiega, *Contribution à l'histoire précoloniale du Gulma (Haute Volta)* (Wiesbaden: Franz Steiner Verlag, 1982); Boubou Hama, *Histoire traditionnelle des Peul du Dallol Boboye* (Niamey: CRRDTO, 1969); S. A. Balogun, "Gwandu Emirates in the Nineteenth Century with special reference to Political Relations: 1817–1903" (Ph.D. dissertation, University of Ibadan, 1971), 108–57; and Murray Last, *The Sokoto Caliphate* (London: Longmans, 1967), 40–45. My reconstruction is based on a discussion with Dioulde Laya, Niamey, 30 September 1988, who assisted in the identification of the emirates in Niger and Burkina Faso.

BIBLIOGRAPHY

Unpublished Sources

AREWA HOUSE, KADUNA, NIGERIA

Patterson, J.H. Borsari District Report, Borno Province, 21 August 1918, 504p/1918.

NIGERIAN NATIONAL ARCHIVES, KADUNA

Bulgat Tuwat, Alhaji. "Kitab Zima-mun Duyun," AH 1245 AH (1829 CE), KATPROF G/AR3/1.

Cargill, Featherstone, Resident Kano, 27 May 1908, in File 7173, "Kano Province Economic Survey, 1909." In John Paden, "The Influence of Religious Elites on the Political Culture and Community Integration of Kano, Nigeria" (Ph.D. dissertation, Harvard University, 1968), 1302–4.

Dupigny, E. G. M. Assessment Report, Sarkin Dawaki Tsakkar Gidda District, SNP 7/10 5570/1909.

Festing, Arthur H. Report, 1907. In W. P. Hewby, Report on Kano Emirate, 10 July 1908, SNP 6/4 c.111/1908.

Foulkes, H. Assessment Report, Jaidanawa District, SNP 7/13 4817/1912.

Gepp, H. M. Assessment Report, Dan Isa's Sub-District, 5 May 1911, SNP 7/12 1035/1911.

Hewby, W. P. Report, on Kano Emirate, 10 July 1908, SNP 6/4 c.111/1908.

Revenue Survey Assessment, Kanoprof 1708/vol. 1, 5/6/36.

Stanley, Edward John, Resident, Sokoto Province, Report No. 36 on Sokoto Province for Half-Year Ending June 30, 1908, Sokprof 2/9 985/1908.

NIGERIAN NATIONAL ARCHIVES, IBADAN

Fuller, Francis C., Journal, 21 January 1899, IbaProf 3/6.

THE NATIONAL ARCHIVES, LONDON

Clapperton, Hugh to R. Wilmot Horton, 7 June 1825, C.O. 2/13.

Madden, R. R. "Report of Her Majesty's Commissioner on the State of Our Settlements on the Western Coast of Africa." C.O. 2/72, Sierra Leone & African Forts, 1841.

Orr, C. W. J. "Trade Prospects, Northern Nigeria," 26 October 1904. C.O. 446/43 (1907).

"Return of every Slave tried and convicted by a Court Martial during the late Rebellion in Jamaica or in consequence thereof distinguishing in separate Columns Parish of Manchester." C.O. 137/185 (1832).

Ayuba b. Suleiman to his father, ca. 1734, UIN 000070272: "A collection, ms. and printed, illustrative of various alphabets, etc., brought together by Joseph Ames and pasted in a scrap-book." Folio 120r.

Salvador, Bahia View of the City of Bahia in the Brazils, South America—pictorial work (293 mm x 726 mm) by George Johann Scharf (1788–1860). (1826), Legends by Edmund Patten; Drawn on Stone by G Scharf, from a Sketch by Edmund Patten, taken on the Water at a Distance of half a Mile / Published by Edmund Patten June 18th 1826 / Printed by C Hullmande. http://collection.britishmuseum .org/resource?uri=http://collection.britishmuseum.org/id/object/PPA136250.

Muhammad Kaba Saghanughu, *Kitāb al-ṣalāt*. Baptist Missionary Society papers.

Bishop Samuel Crowther

Ali Eisami (William Harding)

Sargeant Nicholas Said

Will of Richard Pierpoint, RG 22235, microfilm MS 8416

al-Timbuktawi ms: Ahmad b. al-Qadi b. Yusuf b. Ibrahim al-Timbuktawi, Hatk al-Sitr Amma Alayhi Sudani Tunus min al-Kufr, 1813. Ms.

Umar ibn Sa'id of Futa Toro

Ahmed, Musa (Katagum), 1975.
Ahmed, O. S. (Nassarawa), 1975.
Babangida, A. (Hadejia), 1975.
Jumare, Ibrahim (Sokoto), 1993.
Lovejoy Collection (Kano, Katsina, Sokoto), 1969–70.
Maccido, Ahmadu (Zaria), 1975.
Musa, Aliyu (Kano), 1975.

Umar, Aliyu Bala Umar (Kano), 1975.
Yunusa, Yusufu (Kano), 1975.

ORAL DATA

Ahmed, Alhaji Ado, Gandun Nassarawa, Kano, 12 July 1980. In Abdulrazak Giginyu Sa'idu, "History of a Slave Village in Kano: Gandun Nassarawa," 207–19. B.A. thesis, Bayero University, Kano, 1981.
Ali, Kudan, 8 December 1975. Ahmadu Maccido Collection, tape no. 3.
Ba'are, Audu, Kano, 1 January 1970. Lovejoy Collection, tape 12, 1969–70.
Bagarmi, Sarkin, Gandun Giwaran, Kano, 23 August 1975. Yunusa Collection.
Ban'indo, Alhaji Inuwa (Shamakin Sarkin Kano), Kano, 19 July 1980, conducted by Abdulrazak Giginyu Sa'idu. In Abdulrazak Giginyu Sa'idu, "History of a Slave Village in Kano: Gandun Nassarawa," 201–7. B.A. thesis, Bayero University, Kano, 1981.
Bawa, Dambazau Ward, Kano, 31 July 1975. Yunusa Collection.
Danmaiso, Idrisu, Hausawa Ward, Kano, 7 August 1975.
Darmanawa, Yunusa, Gandun Gogel, Kano, 23 August 1975. Yunusa Collection.
Hamidu, Galadiman Shamaki, Fanisau, Kano, 3 April 1975. Yunusa Collection.
Hamshak'i, Miko, Kano, January 1970. Lovejoy Collection, tape 12, 1969–70.
Kasori, Muhammadu, Kano, 1 February 1970. Lovejoy Collection, tape 14, 1969–70.
Madigawa, Bako, Kano, January 1970. Lovejoy Collection, tape 12, 1969–70.
Musa na Madabo, Kano, 1 February 1970. Lovejoy Collection, tape 14, 1969–70.
Sa'adu, Gandun Gogel, Kano, 23 August 1975. Yunusa Collection.
Zubairu, Gandun Suwaina, Kano, 11 September 1975. Yunusa Collection.

Websites

African Diaspora Maps. http://www.africandiasporamaps.com.
African Origins Project. http://www.african-origins.org.
Afro-Louisiana History and Genealogy, 1719–1820. http://www.ibiblio.org/laslave.
Arabic Manuscripts from West Africa: A Catalog of the Herskovits Library Collection. http://digital.library.northwestern.edu/arbmss/.
"Facts about the Slave Trade and Slavery." Gilder Lehrman Institute of American History, http://www.gilderlehrman.org/history-by-era/slavery-and-anti-slavery/resources/facts-about-slave-trade-and-slavery.
Islamic Manuscripts from Mali. http://international.loc.gov/intldl/malihtml/malihome.html.
Liberated Africans Project. http://liberatedafricans.org/.
Project Baquaqua. http://www.baquaqua.com.br.
SHADD—Studies in the History of the African Diaspora—Documents. http://tubman.info.yorku.ca/publications/shadd/.
Slave Biographies: The Atlantic Database Network. http://slavebiographies.org.
Voyages: The Trans-Atlantic Slave Trade Database. http://www.slavevoyages.org.

Theses, Dissertations, and Unpublished Papers

Abubakar, Sa'ad. "A Survey of the Economy of the Eastern Emirates of the Sokoto Caliphate in the Nineteenth Century." Paper presented at the Third Annual

Seminar, Departments of History, Ahmadu Bello University and Abdullahi Bayero College, Sokoto, 1975.

Aliyu, Y. A. "Establishment and Development of Emirate Government in Bauchi, 1805–1903." Ph.D. dissertation, Ahmadu Bello University, 1974.

Balogun, S. A. "Economic Activities and Ties of Gwandu Emirates and Their Neighbors in the Nineteenth Century." Paper presented at the Kano Seminar, Kano, 1976.

———. "Gwandu Emirates in the Nineteenth Century with Special Reference to Political Relations, 1817–1903." Ph.D. dissertation, University of Ibadan, 1971.

Brown, William A. "The Caliphate of Hamdullahi, c. 1818–1864." Ph.D. dissertation, University of Wisconsin, 1969.

Bruce, R. "The Gindiri Rinji, 1890–1907." Paper presented at the Kano Seminar, Kano, 1976.

Bugaje, Usman M. "The Tradition of Tajdid in Western Bilad al-Sudan: A Study of the Genesis, Development and Patterns of Islamic Revivalism in the Region, 990–1900 AD." Ph.D. dissertation, University of Khartoum, 1991.

Cáceres, Rina. "La abolición de la esclavitud en Centroamérica." Paper presented at the conference "The Congress of Vienna and Its Global Dimension," Vienna, 18–22 September 2014.

Cairus, José. "Jihad, Captivity and Redemption: Slavery and Resistance in the Path of Allah, Central Sudan and Bahia." Paper presented at the conference "Slavery and Religion in the Modern World," Essaouira (Morocco), 2001.

———. "Jihad, cativeiro e redenção: Escravidão, resistência e irmandade, Sudão Central e Bahia (1835)." Dissertação de mestrado ao PPGH, Universidade Federal do Rio de Janeiro, 2002.

———. "Kende Rings." Unpublished paper, n.d.

Candotti, Marisa. "Cotton Growing and Textile Production in Northern Nigeria from Caliphate to Protectorate, c. 1804–1914: A Preliminary Examination." Paper for the European Conference on African Studies, Leipzig, Germany, 4–7 June 2009.

Chetima, Melchisedek. "Pratiques architecturales et dynamiques identitaires chez les Podokwo, Muktele et Mura (monts Mandara du Cameroun): Une approche à l'ethnicité et au statut social." Ph.D. dissertation, Université Laval, 2015.

Daddi Addoun, Yacine. "Abolition de l'esclavage en Algérie, 1816–1871." Ph.D. dissertation, York University, 2010.

Dan Asabe, Abdukarim Umar, "Comparative Biographies of Selected Leaders of the Kano Commercial Establishment," M.A. thesis, Bayero University Kano, 1987.

Danmole, Hakeem Olumide Akanni. "The Frontier Emirate: A History of Islam in Ilorin." Ph.D. dissertation, University of Birmingham, 1980.

Diallo, Hamidou. "Les Fulbe de Haute Volta et les influences exterieures de la fin du XVIIIᵉ siècle à la fin du XIXᵉ siècle." Thèse de 3eme cycle, Université de Paris I, 1979.

Domingues, Daniel, David Eltis, Philip Misevich, and Olatunji Ojo, "The Nineteenth-Century Transatlantic Islamic Diaspora." Unpublished paper, Harvard University, October 2015.

Farias, Paulo. "Muslim Oralcy in West Africa: A Neglected Subject." Paper presented at the conference "Landscapes, Sources, and Intellectual Projects in African History: Symposium in Honour of Paulo Fernando de Moraes Farias," University of Birmingham, 12–14 November 2015. https://www.youtube.com/watch?v=gQSlo6ThoDg.

Ferguson, Douglas E. "Nineteenth-Century Hausaland, Being a Description by Imam Imoru of the Land, Economy, and Society of His People." Ph.D. dissertation, UCLA, 1973.

Garba, Tijani. "Taxation in Some Hausa Emirates, c. 1816–1939." Ph.D. dissertation, University of Birmingham, 1986.

Gavin, R. J. "The Economy of Ilorin." Paper presented at the University of Birmingham, 1976.

Gwandu, Abubaker Aliu. "Abdullahi b. Fodio as a Muslim Jurist." Ph.D. dissertation, University of Durham, 1977.

Hall, Bruce. "Rethinking the Place of Timbuktu in the Intellectual History of Muslim West Africa." Paper presented at the conference "Landscapes, Sources, and Intellectual Projects in African History. Symposium in Honour of Paulo Fernando de Moraes Farias," University of Birmingham, 12–14 November 2015.

Hamman, Mahmoud. "The Rise and Fall of the Emirate of Muri (Hamaruwa), c. 1812–1903." Ph.D. dissertation, Ahmadu Bello University, 1983.

Hamza, Ibrahim. "Dorayi: A History of Economic and Social Transformations in the 19th and 20th Centuries, Kano Emirate." M.A. thesis, Usmanu Danfodio University, 1994.

Jah, Omar. "Al-Haj 'Umar's Philosophy of Jihad and Its Sufi Basis." Ph.D. dissertation, McGill University, 1974.

———. "The Effect of Pilgrimage on the Jihad of al-Ḥājj 'Umar al-Futi, 1794–1864," in *The Central Bilad al Sudan: Tradition and Adaptation*, edited by Yusuf Fadl Hasan and Paul Doornbos, 233–44. Khartoum: University of Khartoum Press, 1977.

Johnson, James. "The Almamate of Futa Toro, 1770–1836—A Political History." Ph.D. dissertation, University of Wisconsin, 1974.

Jumare, Ibrahim. "Land Tenure in the Sokoto Sultanate of Nigeria." Ph.D. dissertation, York University, 1995.

Kameche, Mohammed. "The Shehu 'Uthman dan Fodio: The Reformer, the Renovator and the Founder of the Sokoto Caliphate, 1774–1817." M.A. thesis, University of Oran, 2009.

Kolapo, Femi James. "Military Turbulence, Population Displacement and Commerce on a Slaving Frontier of the Sokoto Caliphate: Nupe, c. 1810–1857." Ph.D. dissertation, York University, 1999.

Lavers, John E. "Adventures in the Chronology of the States of the Chad Basin." Unpublished seminar paper, Bayero University, Kano, 1992.

Lofkrantz, Jennifer. "Ransoming Policies and Practices in the Western and Central Bilād al-Sūdān, c1800–1910." Ph.D. dissertation, York University, 2008.

Lovejoy, Henry B. "Digital History, Slave Databases, and Mapping." Paper presented at the American Historical Association Annual Meeting, Atlanta, 7 January 2016.

———. "Old Oyo Influences on the Transformation of Lucumí Identity in Colonial Cuba." Ph.D. dissertation, UCLA, 2012.

———. "Origins and Destinations: Linking West Africa's Historical Geography to the Trans-Atlantic Slave Trade Database." Paper presented at the American Historical Association Annual Meeting, Atlanta, 7 January 2016.

———. "West Africa Historical GIS and The Liberated Africans Project." Talk given at the Maryland Institute of Technology in the Humanities (MITH), University of Maryland. Washington, DC, 2016.

Lovejoy, Paul E. "Muhammad ʿAlī Nicholas Saʿīd : From Enslavement in Borno to American Civil War Veteran." Paper presented at "Meaning of Blackness II," Universidad de Costa Rica, 2016.

Mafama, Abba Tuja. "Some Aspects of Slavery in Borno." B.A. paper, Bayero University College, 1977.

Mahadi, Abdullahi. "The State and the Economy: The *Sarauta* System and Its Roles in Shaping the Society and Economy of Kano with Particular Reference to the Eighteenth and Nineteenth Centuries." Ph.D. dissertation, Ahmadu Bello University, 1982.

Martins, Romulo de Oliveira. " 'Vinha na fé de trabalhar em diamantes': Escravos e libertos em Lençóis, Chapada Diamantina-BA (1840–1888)." M.A. thesis, Universidade Federal da Bahia, 2013.

Mason, Michael. "The Nupe Kingdom in the Nineteenth Century: A Political History." Ph.D. dissertation, University of Birmingham, 1970.

McGowan, Winston. "The Development of European Relations with Futa Jallon and the Foundation of French Colonial Rule, 1794–1897." Ph.D. dissertation, University of London, 1978.

Mello, Priscilla. "Leitura, encantamento e rebelião o Islã Negro no Brasil sécola XIX." Ph.D. dissertation, Universidade Federal Fluminense, 2009.

Minna, M. T. M. "Sultan Muhammad Bello and His Intellectual Contribution to the Sokoto Caliphate." Ph.D. dissertation, University of London, 1982.

Montana, Ismael Musah. "The *Hatk al-Sitr* of al-Timbuktawi on Enslaved Africans' Religious Practices in Nineteenth-Century Tunisia (Translation and Introduction)." M.A. thesis, York University, 1999.

———. "The Trans-Saharan Slave Trade, Abolition of Slavery and Transformation in the North African Regency of Tunis, 1759–1846." Ph.D. dissertation, York University, 2007.

Nishida, Mieko. "Gender, Ethnicity, and Kinship in the Urban African Diaspora: Salvador, Brazil, 1808–1888." Ph.D. dissertation, Johns Hopkins University, 1992.

O'Hear, Ann. "The Economic History of Ilorin in the Nineteenth and Twentieth Centuries: The Rise and Decline of a Middleman Society." Ph.D. dissertation, Centre of West African Studies, University of Birmingham, 1983.

Oliveira, Maria Inês Côrtes de. "Retrouver une identité: Jeux sociaux des Africains de Bahia: (vers 1750–vers 1890)." Thèse pour le doctorat en histoire, Université de Paris–Sorbonne (Paris IV), 1992.

Oroge, E. Adeniyi. "The Institution of Slavery in Yorubaland with Particular Reference to the Nineteenth Century." Ph.D. dissertation, University of Birmingham, 1971.

Paden, John. "The Influence of Religious Elites on the Political Culture and Community Integration of Kano, Nigeria." Ph.D. dissertation, Harvard University, 1968.

Philips, John E. "Ribats in the Sokoto Caliphate: Selected Studies, 1804–1903." Ph.D. dissertation, UCLA, 1985.

Prince, Howard. "Slave Rebellion in Brazil, 1807–1835." Ph.D. dissertation, Columbia University, 1972.

Quick, Abdullah Hakīm. "Aspects of Islamic Social Intellectual History in Hausaland: 'Uthmān ibn Fūdi, 1774–1804 C.E." Ph.D. dissertation, University of Toronto, 1995.

Reichmuth, Stefan. "The Early Beginnings of the Ilorin Emirate and the Perils of Its Historiography." Paper presented at the conference "Landscapes, Sources, and Intellectual Projects in African History: Symposium in Honour of Paulo Fernando de Moraes Farias," University of Birmingham, 12–14 November 2015.

Reis, João José. "African Nations and Cultural Practices in Nineteenth-Century Salvador, Bahia." Paper presented at the conference "American Counterpoint: New Approaches to Slavery and Abolition in Brazil," Yale University, 2010.

———. "Slave Rebellion in Brazil: The African Muslim Uprising in Bahia, 1835" (Ph.D. dissertation, University of Minnesota, 1983).

Sa'id, Halil Ibrahim. "Revolution and Reaction: The Fulani Jihad in Kano and Its Aftermath, 1807–1919." Ph.D. dissertation, University of Michigan, 1978.

Sa'idu, Abdulrazak Giginyu. "History of a Slave Village in Kano: Gandun Nassarawa." B.A. thesis, Bayero University, Kano, 1981.

Santos, Vanicléia Silva. "As Bolsas de Mandinga no espaço Atlântico século XVIII." Ph.D. dissertation, Universidade de São Paulo, 2008.

Séhou, Ahmadou. "L'esclavage dans les Lamidats de l'Adamaoua (Nord-Cameroun), du début du XIXᵉ siècle." Thèse pour le doctorat, Université de Yaoundé, 2010.

Shea, Philip. "Black Cloth: An Export Oriented Industry in Kano." Paper presented at the Kano Seminar, Kano, 1976.

———. "Collection of Notes on Interviews Concerned with the History of Production of Indigo Dyed Cloth in Kano Emirate, Nigeria." In "The Development of an Export-Oriented Dyed Cloth Industry in Kano Emirate in the Nineteenth Century," appendix. Ph.D. dissertation, University of Wisconsin, 1975.

———. "The Development of an Export-Oriented Dyed Cloth Industry in Kano Emirate in the Nineteenth Century." Ph.D. dissertation, University of Wisconsin, 1975.

Silva, Carlos da. "Ports of Bight of Benin and the Legal Slave Trade to Bahia, Brazil, 1750–1815." Paper presented at the Canadian Association of African Studies Annual Meeting, Carleton University, Ottawa, 1–3 May 2013.

Smith, Marcia. "The Male Uprising in Bahia, 1835: Mini-biographies of Leaders and Others Accused." Unpublished paper, History 5570, York University, 1998.

Sorensen, Caroline. "Badagry, 1784–1863: The Political and Commercial History of a Pre-colonial Lagoonside Community in South West Nigeria." Ph.D. dissertation, University of Stirling, 1995.

Stewart, Charles. "10,000 MSS, 1850 Authors across 300 Years: A Preview of ALA-V." Paper presented at the conference "Landscapes, Sources, and Intellectual Projects in African History: Symposium in Honour of Paulo Fernando de Moraes Farias." University of Birmingham, 12–14 November 2015.

Tahir, Ibrahim A. "Scholars, Sufis, Saints and Capitalists in Kano, 1904–1974: The Pattern of Bourgeois Revolution in an Islamic Society." Ph.D. dissertation, Cambridge University, 1975.

Tambo, David C. "The Pre-colonial Tin Industry in Northern Nigeria." Paper presented at the Kano Seminar, Kano, 1976.

Tukur, Modibbo. "The Imposition of British Colonial Domination on the Sokoto Caliphate, Borno and Neighbouring States, 1897–1914." Ph.D. dissertation, Ahmadu Bello University, 1979.

Veras, Bruno. "The Crescent and the Reef: African Muslims in Recife, PE (Brazil) in the 19th Century." Unpublished paper presented at Université Laval, 26 August 2015.

Yakubu, Mahmood. "A Century of Warfare and Slavery in Bauchi, c. 1805–1900." B.A. thesis, Department of History, University of Sokoto, 1985.

Yunusa, Yusufu. "Slavery in 19th Century Kano." B.A. thesis, Ahmadu Bello University, 1976.

Zahradeen, Muhammad Sani. "'Abd Allah ibn Fodio's Contributions to the Fulani Jihad in Nineteenth Century Hausaland." Ph.D. dissertation, McGill University, 1976.

Zehnle, Stephanie. "A Geography of Jihad: Jihadist Concepts of Space and Sokoto Warfare (West Africa, ca. 1800–1850)." Ph.D. dissertation, Universität Kassel, 2015.

Arabic Texts

'Abd al-Rahman al-Sa'di bin 'Abd Allāh. *Ta'rīkh al-Sūdān*. In *Timbuktu and the Songhay Empire: Al-Sa'dī's "Ta'rīkh al-Sūdān" down to 1613 and Other Contemporary Sources*, edited by John Hunwick, Leiden: Brill, 1999.

'Abdullahi dan Fodio. *Ḍiyā' al-Ḥukkām*. In Shehu Yamusa, "The Political Ideas of the Jihad Leaders: Being a Translation, Edition and Analysis of (1) Uṣūl al-Siyāsa by Muhammad Bello and (2) *Ḍiyā' al-Ḥukkām* by Abdallah B. Fodio," 270–85. M.A. thesis, Bayero University, Kano, 1975.

———. *Idā' al-nusūkh man akhadhtu 'anhu min al-shuyūkh*. In Mervyn Hiskett, "Material Relating to the State of Learning among the Fulani before Their Jihad," *Bulletin of the School of Oriental and African Studies* 19 (1957): 550–78.

———. *Tazyīn al-waraqāt*. Translated by M. Hiskett. Ibadan: University of Ibadan Press, 1963.

'Abdullahi dan Muhammad dan Fodio. *Ḍiyā' al-sulṭān wa ghayrihi min al-ikhwān fī ahamm ma yuṭlab 'ilmuhu fī umūr al-zamān.* In Muhammad Sani Zahradeen, "'Abd Allah ibn Fodio's Contributions to the Fulani Jihad in Nineteenth Century Hausaland," 13–14. Ph.D. dissertation, McGill University, 1976.

Aḥmad Bābā. *Mi'rāj al-ṣu'ūd.* In *Mi'rāj al-ṣu'ūd: Aḥmad Bābā's Replies on Slavery.* Edited by John Hunwick and Fatima Harrak. Rabat: Institute des Études Africaines, Université Mohamed, 2000.

Aḥmad b. Abū Bakr Ikokoro. *Ta'līf akhbār al-qurūn min umarā' bilād Ilurin.* Unpublished, 1912.

Aḥmad b. al-Qāḍī Abī Bakr b. Yūsuf b. Ibrāhīm al-Timbuktāwī. *Hatk al-Sitr 'ammā 'alayhi Sūdān Tunis min al-kufr* [Piercing the veil; being an account of the infidel religion of the blacks of Tunis]. Tunis, 1813. Manuscript, Bibliothèque nationale de Tunisie, Tunis.

Baghdādī, 'Abd al-Raḥmān al-. *Musalliyat al-gharīb: The Foreigner's Amusement by Wonderful Things.* Translated by Yacine Daddi Addoun. *SHADD: Studies in the History of the African Diaspora—Documents,* 2001. http://www.yorku.ca/nhp /shadd/baghdadi/index.asp.

Bello, Omar. "The Political Thought of Muḥammad Bello (1781–1837) as Revealed in his Arabic Writings, More Especially *al-Ghayth al-wābil fi sīrat al-imām al-'ādil.*" Ph.D. dissertation, University of London, 1983.

Bivar, A. D. H. "The *Wathīqat ahl al-Sūdān*: A Manifesto of the Fulani *Jihad.*" *Journal of African History* 2, no. 2 (1961): 235–43.

Boyd, Jean, ed. *Collected Works of Nana Asma'u, Daughter of Usman 'dan Fodiyo (1793–1864).* East Lansing: Michigan State University Press, 2012.

Daddi Addoun, Yacine, and Paul E. Lovejoy. "The Arabic Manuscript of Muḥammad Kabā Saghanughu of Jamaica, c. 1820." In *Creole Concerns: Essays in Honour of Kamau Brathwaite,* edited by Annie Paul, 313–41. Kingston: University of the West Indies Press, 2007.

El Mansour, Mohamed, and Fatima Harrak. *A Fulāni Jihādist in the Maghrib: Admonitions of Aḥmad Ibn al-Qāḍī al-Timbuktī to the Rulers of Tunisia and Morocco.* Rabat: Institute of African Studies, 2000.

El-Masri, F. H. "A Critical Edition of Dan Fodio's *Bayān wujūb al-hijra 'alā 'l-'ibād* with Introduction, English Translation and Commentary." Ph.D. dissertation, University of Ibadan, 1968.

Hiskett, Mervyn. "An Islamic Tradition of Reform in the Western Sudan from the Sixteenth to the Eighteenth Century." *Bulletin of the School of Oriental and African Studies* 23 (1960): 577–96.

———, trans. "*Kitāb al-farq*: A Work on the Habe Kingdoms Attributed to 'Uthmān dan Fodio." *Bulletin of the School of Oriental and African Studies* 23 (1960): 558–73.

———. "The 'Song of the Shehu's Miracles': A Hausa Hagiography from Sokoto." *African Language Studies* 12 (1971): 71–107.

Martin, B. G. "A New Arabic History of Ilorin." *Research Bulletin* (Centre of Arabic Documentation, University of Ibadan) 1, no. 2 (1965): 20–27.

——. "Unbelief in the Western Sudan: 'Uthmān dan Fodio's Taʿlīm al-Ikhwān." *Middle Eastern Studies* 4, no. 1 (1967): 50–97.

Muhammad b. ʿAbdullah. *Risāla ilā Amīr Yoruba ʿAbd al-Salām*. In Hakeem Olumide Akanni Danmole, "The Frontier Emirate: A History of Islam in Ilorin," app. 2. Ph.D. dissertation, University of Birmingham, 1980.

Muhammad Bello. *Infāq al-Maysūr fī taʾrīkh bilād al-Takrūr*. 1812. Edited by Bahija al-Shadhili. Rabat: Institute of African Studies, 1996.

——. *Miftah al-sadad fiʾl-aqsam hadhihi ʾl- bilād*. John Hunwick ms.

ʿUthmān dan Fodio. *Al-ajwibah al-muharrarah ʿan al-asʾilah almuqarrarah fī wathīqat al-shaykh al-ḥājj al-maʾrūf bi-laqabih Shisummas ibn Aḥmad*. In Muhammad Sani Zahradeen, "ʿAbd Allah ibn Fodio's Contribution to the Fulani Jihad in Nineteenth Century Hausaland." Ph.D. dissertation, McGill University, 1976.

——. *Bayān wujūb al hijra ʿalā l-ʿibād (The Exposition of Obligation of Emigration upon the Servants of God)*. Edited and translated by F. H. El Masri. Khartoum: University of Khartoum Press, 1978.

——. "Boneji Hausa." Translated in Alhaji Garba Saidu, "The Significance of the Shehu's Sermons and Poems in 'Ajami,'" in *Studies in the History of the Sokoto Caliphate: The Sokoto Seminar Papers*, edited by Y. B. Usman. Zaria: Department of History, Ahmadu Bello University, 1979.

Yamusa, Shehu. "The Political Ideas of the Jihad Leaders: Being a Translation, Edition and Analysis of (1) *Uṣūl al-Siyāsa* by Muhammad Bello and (2) *Ḍiyāʾ al-Ḥukkām* by Abdallah B. Fodio." M.A. thesis, Bayero University, Kano, 1975.

Published Primary Sources

Adams, John. *Remarks on the Country Extending from Cape Palmas to the River Congo, Including Observations on the Manners and Customs of the Inhabitants, with an Appendix Containing an Account of the European Trade with the West Coast of Africa*. London: John Murray, 1823.

Allen, William, and T. R. H. Thomson. *A Narrative of the Expedition Sent by Her Majesty's Government to the River Niger in 1841, under the Command of Captain H. D. Trotter, R.N.* London: Richard Bentley, 1848.

Barth, Heinrich. "General Historical Description of the State of Human Society in Northern Central Africa." *Journal of the Royal Geographical Society* 30 (1860): 112–28.

——. *Sammlung und Bearbeitung central-afrikanischer Vokabularien; Collection of Vocabularies of Central-African Languages*. 3 vols. Gotha: Justas Perthes, 1862.

——. *Travels and Discoveries in North and Central Africa*. 3 vols. New York: Harper and Brothers, 1859.

Beaver, Philip. *African Memoranda: Relative to an Attempt to Establish a British Settlement on the Island of Bulama, on the Western Coast of Africa, in the Year 1792. With a Brief Notice of the Neighbouring Tribes, Soil, Productions, &c. and Some Observations on the Facility of Colonizing That Part of Africa, with a View* to Cultivation; and the Introduction of Letters and Religion to Its Inhabitants: But More Particularly as the Means of Gradually Abolishing African Slavery. London: C. and R. Baldwin, 1805.

Beecroft [Becroft], John. "On Benin and the Upper Course of the River Quorra, or Niger." *Journal of the Royal Geographical Society* 11 (1841): 184–90.

"Bishop Crowther: His Life and Work." *Church Missionary Gleaner* 5 (1878): 10–11.

Bluett, Thomas. *Some Memoirs of the Life of Job, the Son of Solomon, the High Priest of Boonda in Africa; Who Was a Slave about Two Years in Maryland; and Afterwards Being Brought to England, Was Set Free, and Sent to His Native Land in the Year 1734*. London: R. Ford, 1734.

Boilat, P. David. *Esquisses Sénégalaises*. Paris: P. Bertrand, 1853.

"Borno Report." Arewa House, Kaduna, 1913.

Bruce Lockhart, Jamie. *Clapperton in Borno: Journals of the Travels in Borno of Lieutenant Hugh Clapperton, RN, from January 1823 to September 1824*. Cologne: Rüdiger Köppe Verlag, 1996.

Bruce Lockhart, Jamie, and Paul E. Lovejoy, eds. *Hugh Clapperton into the Interior of Africa: Records of the Second Expedition, 1825–1827*. Leiden: Brill, 2005.

Castelnau, Francis de Laporte de. *Renseignements sur l'Afrique centrale et sur une nation d'hommes à queue qui s'y trouverait, d'après le rapport des nègres du Soudan, esclaves à Bahia*. Paris: Librairie P. Bertrand, 1851.

Clapperton, Hugh. *Journal of a Second Expedition into the Interior of Africa*. London: John Murray, 1829.

Clarkson, Thomas. *The History of the Rise, Progress, and Accomplishment of the Abolition of the African Slave-Trade by the British Parliament*. 2 vols. London: Longman, Hurst, Rees, and Orme, 1808.

The Colonizationist and Journal of Freedom. Boston: G. W. Light, 1834.

Crowther, Samuel. "Letter of Mr. Samuel Crowther to the Rev. William Jowett, Feb. 22, 1837." *Church Missionary Record* 8 (1837): 217–23.

Crowther, Samuel, and John C. Taylor. *The Gospel on the Banks of the Niger: Journals and Notices of the Native Missionaries Accompanying the Niger Expedition of 1857–1859*. London: Frank Cass, 1968 [1859].

Daumas, M. J. E., and A. de Chancel. *Le grand désert: Itinéraire d'une caravane du Sahara au pays des nègres (Royaume de Haoussa)*. Paris: M. Levy, 1860.

Denham, Dixon, Hugh Clapperton, and Walter Oudney. *Narrative of Travels and Discoveries in Northern and Central Africa, in the Years 1822, 1823, and 1824*. 2 vols. London: John Murray, 1828.

"Devassa do Levante de Escravos Ocorrido em Salvador em 1835." *Anais do Arquivo do Estado da Bahia* 38 (Salvador, 1968).

"Devassa do Levante de Escravos Ocorrido em Salvador em 1835." *Anais do Arquivo Público do Estado da Bahia* 50 (Salvador, 1992).

"Devassa do Levante de Escravos Ocorrido em Salvador em 1835." *Anais do Arquivo do Estado da Bahia* 53 (Salvador, 1996).

"Devassa do Levante de Escravos Ocorrido em Salvador em 1835." *Anais do Arquivo do Estado da Bahia* 54 (Salvador, 1997).

d'Orbigny, Alcide Dessalines. *Voyage pittoresque dans les deux Amériques*. Paris: L. Tenré, 1836.

Dorugu, Kwage Adamu. "The Life and Travels of Dorugu Dictated by Himself." In J. F. Schön, *Magana Hausa: Native Literature or Proverbs, Tales, Fables and Historical Fragments in the Hausa Language*, 7–71. London: Society for Promoting Christian Knowledge, 1885.

Drummond, Antônio de Menezes Vasconcellos de. "Lettres sur l'Afrique ancienne et moderne." *Journal des Voyages* 32 (1826): 290–324 [*sic*; 190–224].

Dubois, Félix. *Notre beau Niger*. Paris: Flammarion, 1911.

Dupuis, Joseph. *Journal of a Residence in Ashantee*. London: Henry Colburn, 1824.

Dwight, Theodore, Jr. "Condition and Character of Negroes in Africa." *Methodist Quarterly Review*, January 1864, 77–90.

———. "Remarks on the Sereculehs, an African Nation, Accompanied by a Vocabulary in Their Language." *American Annals of Education and Instruction* 5 (1835): 451–56.

Frank, Louis. *La Tunisie*. Paris: Firmin Didot Frères, 1851.

Friend of Africa 1, no. 4 (25 February 1841); 1, no. 10 (August 1841); 2, no. 18 (April 1842).

Gronniosaw, Ukawsaw. *A Narrative of the Most Remarkable Particulars in the Life of James Albert Ukawsaw Gronniosaw, an African Prince, as Related by Himself*. Bath: W. Gye and T. Mills, [London, 1770].

Hallett, Robin, ed. *The Niger Journal of Richard and John Lander*. London: Routledge and Kegan Paul, 1965.

Hemso, Jacopo Graberg di. "Prospetto del Commercio di Tripoli d'Africa, e delle sue relazioni con quello dell'Italia." *Antologia* 30 (1828):3–29.

Johnson, Samuel. *The History of the Yoruba from the Earliest Time to the Beginning of the British Protectorate*. Lagos: C.M.S. Bookshop, 1937.

Kanya-Forstner, A. S., and Paul E. Lovejoy, eds. *Pilgrims, Interpreters, and Agents: French Reconnaissance Reports on the Sokoto Caliphate and Borno, 1891–1895*. Madison: African Studies Program, University of Wisconsin, 1997.

Kirk-Greene, Anthony, and Paul Newman, eds. *West African Travels and Adventures: Two Autobiographical Narratives from Northern Nigeria*. New Haven, CT: Yale University Press, 1971.

Koelle, Sigismund Wilhelm. *African Native Literature*. Graz: Akademische Druck-u. Verlagsanstalt, 1968 [London: Church Missionary Society, 1854].

———. *Polyglotta Africana*. Graz: Akademische Druck-u. Verlagsanstalt, 1963 [London: Church Missionary Society, 1854].

Laird, Macgregor, and R. A. K. Oldfield. *Narrative of an Expedition into the Interior of Africa by the River Niger, in the Steam-Vessels* Quorra *and* Alburkah *in 1832, 1833 and 1834*. Vol. 2. London: Richard Bentley, 1837.

Lander, Richard. *Records of Captain Clapperton's Last Expedition to Africa*. 2 vols. London: Colburn and Bentley, 1830.

Lander, Richard, and John Lander. *Journal of an Expedition to Explore the Course and Termination of the Niger*. 2 vols. London: John Murray, 1832.

Law, Robin, ed. *Contemporary Source Material for the History of the Old Oyo Empire, 1627–1824*. Ibadan: Institute of African Studies, University of Ibadan, 1992.

Law, Robin, and Paul E. Lovejoy, eds. *The Biography of Mahommah Gardo Baquaqua: His Passage from Slavery to Freedom in Africa and America*. 2nd ed. Princeton, NJ: Markus Wiener.

Leonard, Peter. *The Western Coast of Africa: Journal of an Officer under Captain Owen; Records of a Voyage in the Ship "Dryad" in 1830, 1831, and 1832*. 2 vols. Philadelphia: Edward C. Mielke, 1833.

"A Liberated African's Account of His Slavery, and Subsequent Course." *Church Missionary Gleaner* 6 (1846): 16–18.

Lovejoy, Paul E., and A. S. Kanya-Forster, eds. *Slavery and Its Abolition in French West Africa*. Madison: African Studies Program, University of Wisconsin–Madison, 1994.

Lugard, Frederick D. *Instructions to Political and Other Officers, on Subjects Chiefly Political and Administrative*. London: Waterloo, 1906.

———. *Political Memoranda: Revisions of Instructions to Political Officers on Subjects Chiefly Political and Administrative*. 3rd ed., edited by A. H. M. Kirk-Greene. London: Frank Cass, 1970 [1918].

Lyon, G. F. *A Narrative of Travels in Northern Africa in the Years 1818–1819 and 1820*. London: John Murray, 1821.

Madden, R. R. *The Island of Cuba: Its Resources, Progress, and Prospects, Considered in Relation Especially to the Influence of Its Prosperity on the Interests of the British West India Colonies*. London: C. Gilpin, 1849.

———. *A Twelvemonth's Residence in the West Indies, during the Transition from Slavery to Apprenticeship*. 2 vols. Westport, CT: Negro University Press, 1970 [1835].

Mahomed Misrah. "Narrative of a Journey from Egypt to the Western Coast of Africa, by Mahomed Misrah: Communicated by an Officer Serving in Sierra Leone." *Quarterly Journal*, October 1822, 6, 15–16.

Mircher, H. *Mission au Ghadames (septembre, octobre, novembre, et decembre, 1862): Rapports officiels et documents a l'appui*. Paris: Alger, 1863.

Moore, Samuel. *Biography of Mahommah G. Baquaqua, a Native of Zoogoo, in the Interior of Africa*. Detroit: Geo. E. Pomeroy, 1854.

Mouser, Bruce, ed. *Journal of James Watt: Expedition to Timbo, Capital of the Fula Empire in 1794*. Madison: African Studies Program, University of Wisconsin–Madison, 1994.

Orbigny, Alcide Dessalines d'. *Voyage pittoresque dans les deux Amériques*. Paris: L. Tenré, 1836.

Passarge, Siegfried. *Adamaua: Bericht über die Expedition des deutschen Kamerun-Komilees in den Jahren 1893/94*. Berlin: Geographische Verlagshandlung D. Reimer, 1895.

Patterson, J. R. *Kanuri Songs*. Lagos: Government Printer, 1926.

"Peças Processuais do Levante dos Malês." *Anais do Arquivo Público do Estado da Bahia* 40 (Salvador, 1971).

Le Petit Journal. Paris, 15 October 1911.

Reichert, Rolf. *Os documentos Arabes do arquivo publico do estado da Bahia.* Salvador: Universidade Federal da Bahia, Centro de Estudos Afro-Orientais, 1979.

Renouard, G. C. "Routes in North Africa, by Abu Bekr es Siddik." *Journal of the Royal Geographical Society* 6 (1836): 100–113.

Richardson, James. *Narrative of a Mission to Central Africa Performed in the Years 1850–51.* 2 vols. London: Chapman, 1853.

———. "Report on the Slave-Trade of the Great Desert." *Anti-slavery and Aborigines' Friend,* ser. 2, 1 (1846): 133–34, 154–55, 181–83.

———. *Travels in the Great Desert of Sahara in the Years of 1845 and 1846.* 2 vols. London: Richard Bentley, 1848.

Sa'īd, Muhammad 'Alī (Nicholas). *The Autobiography of Nicholas Said, a Native of Bornou, Eastern Soudan.* Memphis: Shotwell and Co., 1873.

———. "A Native of Bornoo." *Atlantic Monthly,* 1867, 485–95.

Schön, James Frederick. *Magana Hausa.* London: SPCK, 1885.

Schön, James Frederick, and Samuel Crowther. *Journals of the Rev. James Frederick Schön and Mr. Samuel Crowther: Expedition up the Niger in 1841.* London: Church Missionary Society, 1854.

Schwarz, Suzanne, ed. *Zachary Macaulay and the Development of the Sierra Leone Company, 1793–4.* Vol. 1, *Journal, June–October 1793.* University of Leipzig Papers on Africa, History and Culture, series no. 4. Leipzig: Institut für Afrikanistik, Universität Leipzig, 2000.

———, ed. *Zachary Macaulay and the Development of the Sierra Leone Company, 1793–4.* Vol. 2, *Journal, October–December 1793.* University of Leipzig Papers on Africa, History and Culture, series no. 4. Leipzig: Institut für Afrikanistik, Universität Leipzig, 2002.

Truman, George, John Jackson, and Thos. B. Longstreth. *Narrative of a Visit to the West Indies, in 1840 and 1841.* Philadelphia: Merrihew and Thompson, Printers, 1844.

Vaughan, J. H., and A. H. M. Kirk-Greene, eds. *The Diary of Hamman Yaji: Chronicle of a West African Ruler.* Bloomington: Indiana University Press, 1995.

Wadström, Carl Bernhard. *Observations on the Slave Trade, and a Description of Some Parts of the Coast of Guinea.* London: James Phillips, 1789.

Wesley, Charles H. "The Life and History of Abou Bekir Sadiki, Alias Edward Doulan, Discovered by Dr. Charles H. Wesley." *Journal of Negro History* 21, no. 1 (1936): 52–55.

Winterbottom, Thomas. *An Account of the Native Africans in the Neighbourhood of Sierra Leone, to Which Is Added an Account of the Present State of Medicine among Them.* 2 vols. London: C. Whittingham, 1803.

Published Secondary Sources

Abba, A. "The Establishment of Gombe Emirate, 1804–1882." In *State and Society in the Sokoto Caliphate: Essays in Honour of Sultan Ibrahim Dasuki,* edited by

Ahmed M. Kani and K. A. Gandi, 1:11–30. Sokoto: Usmanu Danfodiyo University, 1990.

Abba, Yusufu. "The 1804 Jihad in Hausaland as a Revolution." In *Studies in the History of the Sokoto Caliphate: The Sokoto Seminar Papers*, edited by Yusuf Bala Usman, 20–33. Zaria: Department of History, Ahmadu Bello University, 1979.

Abdulkadir, Mohammed S. "The Effects of the Extension of the Sokoto Caliphate on the Igala Kingdom." In *The Sokoto Caliphate: History and Legacies, 1804–2004*, edited by H. Bobboyi and A. M. Yakubu, 1:53–65. Kaduna: Arewa House, 2006.

Abubakar, Sa'ad. "Borno in the Nineteenth Century." In *Groundwork of Nigerian History*, edited by Obaro Ikime, 327–46. Ibadan: Heinemann, 1980.

———. "The Established Caliphate: Sokoto, the Emirates and Their Neighbors." In *Groundwork of Nigerian History*, edited by Obaro Ikime, 305–326. Ibadan: Heinemann, 1980.

———. *The Lāmībe of Fombina: A Political History of Adamawa, 1809–1901.* Zaria: Ahmadu Bello University Press, 1979.

Abubakar, Saleh. "Aspects of an Urban Phenomenon: Sokoto and Its Hinterland to c. 1850." In *Studies in the History of the Sokoto Caliphate: The Sokoto Seminar Papers*, edited by Yusuf Bala Usman, 125–39. Zaria: Department of History, Ahmadu Bello University, 1979.

Abu-Manga, Al-Amin. "The Role of the 'Pen' in the Establishment and Consolidation of the Sokoto Caliphate." In *The Sokoto Caliphate: History and Legacies, 1804–2004*, edited by H. Bobboyi and A. M. Yakubu, 2:40–52. Kaduna: Arewa House, 2006.

Achi, Bala. "Arms and Armour in the Warfare of Pre-colonial Hausaland." *African Studies Monographs* (Kyoto) 8, no. 3 (1987): 145–57.

Ackerson, Wayne. *The African Institution (1807–1827) and the Antislavery Movement in Great Britain.* Lampeter: Edwin Mellen Press, 2005.

Adamu, Mahdi. "A General History of the Sokoto Caliphate." In *State and Society in the Sokoto Caliphate: Essays in Honour of Sultan Ibrahim Dasuki*, edited by Ahmad M. Kani and K. A. Gandi. Sokoto: Usmanu Danfodio University, 1990.

———. *The Hausa Factor in West African History.* Zaria: Ahmadu Bello University Press, 1978.

Adeleye, R. A. "Rabih Fadlallah, 1879–1893: Exploits and Impact on Political Relations in Central Sudan." *Journal of the Historical Society of Nigeria* 5, no. 2 (1970): 223–42.

Ado-Kurawa, Ibrahim. "The *Jihad* and the Consolidation of Sudanic Intellectual Tradition." In *The Sokoto Caliphate: History and Legacies, 1804–2004*, edited by H. Bobboyi and A. M. Yakubu, 2:81–99. Kaduna: Arewa House, 2006.

Ado-Sulaiman, Ibrahim. "Towards a Vision of the Future: A Letter from Sultan Muhammad Bello to the Muslim *Ummah* in Nigeria." In *State and Society in the Sokoto Caliphate: Essays in Honour of Sultan Ibrahim Dasuki*, edited by Ahmed M. Kani and K. A. Gandi, 2:396–408. Sokoto: Usmanu Danfodiyo University, 1990.

Ajayi, J. F. A. *Christian Missions in Nigeria: 1841–1891.* London: Longmans, 1965.

———. "Samuel Ajayi Crowther of Oyo." In *Africa Remembered: Narratives by West Africans from the Era of the Slave Trade*, edited by Philip D. Curtin, 289–316. Madison: University of Wisconsin Press, 1967.

Akindele, A., and C. Aguessy. *Contribution à l'étude de l'histoire de l'ancien royaume de Porto Novo*. Dakar: l'IFAN, 1953.

Akinjogbin, I. A. "A Chronology of Yoruba History, 1789–1840." *Odu* 2, no. 2 (1966): 81–86.

———. "Prelude to the Yoruba Civil Wars of the Nineteenth Century." *Odu* 1, no. 2 (1965): 24–46.

Al-Hajj, Muhammad. "Hayatu b. Sa'id: A Revolutionary Mahdist in the Western Sudan." In *The Sudan in Africa: Studies Presented to the First International Conference Sponsored by the Sudan Research Unit*, edited by Y. Fadl Hasan, 128–41. Khartoum: Khartoum University Press, 1971.

———. "The Thirteenth Century in Muslim Eschatology: Mahdist Expectations in the Sokoto Caliphate." *Research Bulletin* (Centre of Arabic Documentation, Ibadan) 3, no. 2 (1967): 100–113.

Alkali, Muhammad N. "El-Kanemi's Response to the Extension of Shaykh ʿUthman Dan Fodio's *Jihad* against Borno." In *The Sokoto Caliphate: History and Legacies, 1804–2004*, edited by H. Bobboyi and A. M. Yakubu, 1:231–39. Kaduna: Arewa House, 2006.

Amosu, Tundonu A. "The Jaded Heritage: Nigeria's Brazilian Connection." *África: Revista do Centro de Estudos Africanos da USP* 10 (1987): 43–51.

Aptheker, Herbert. *American Negro Slave Resistance*. (New York: Columbia University Press, 1944).

Armitage, David. "Three Concepts of Atlantic History." In *The British Atlantic World, 1500–1800*, edited by David Armitage and Michael J. Braddick, 11–27. New York: Palgrave Macmillan, 2002.

Armitage, David, and Sanjay Subrahmanyam. "Introduction: The Age of Revolutions, c. 1760–1840—Global Causation, Connection, and Comparison." In *The Age of Revolutions in Global Context, c. 1760–1840*, edited by David Armitage and Sanjay Subrahmanyam, xii–xxxii. Basingstoke, UK: Palgrave Macmillan, 2010.

Arnett, J. *The Rise of the Sokoto Fulani: Being a Paraphrase and in Some Parts a Translation of the "Infaku'l Maisuri" of Sultan Mohammed Bello*. Kano: n.p., 1929.

Ashcraft-Esson, Lillian. "'She Voluntarily Hath Come': A Gambian Woman Trader in Colonial Georgia in the Eighteenth Century." In *Identity in the Shadow of Slavery*, edited by Paul E. Lovejoy, 203–21. London: Continuum, 2000.

Aslanian, Sebouh D. *From the Indian Ocean to the Mediterranean: The Global Trade Networks of Armenian Merchants from New Julfa*. Berkeley: University of California Press, 2011.

Atanda, J. A. "The Fall of the Old Oyo Empire: A Reconsideration of Its Cause." *Journal of the Historical Society of Nigeria* 5 (1971): 477–90.

———. "The Yoruba Wars and the Collapse of the Old Oyo Empire." In *Yoruba Historiography*, edited by Toyin Falola, 105–21. Madison: African Studies Program, University of Wisconsin–Madison, 1991.

Austen, Ralph A. "The Trans-Saharan Slave Trade: A Tentative Census." In *The Uncommon Market: Essays in the Economic History of the Atlantic Slave Trade*, edited by Henry Gemery and J. S. Hogendorn, 23–76. New York: Academic Press, 1979.

Austin, Allan D., ed. *African Muslims in Antebellum America: A Sourcebook*. New York: Garland, 1984.

———. *African Muslims in Antebellum America: Transatlantic Stories and Spiritual Struggles*. New York: Routledge, 1997.

———. "Job Ben Solomon—African Nobleman and a Father of African American Literature." In *African Muslims in Antebellum America: Transatlantic Stories and Spiritual Struggles*, 51–62. New York: Routledge, 1997.

———. "Mohammed Ali Ben Said: Travels on Five Continents." *Contributions in Black Studies* 12 (1994): 129–58.

———. "Salih Bilali of Massina—Tom of Georgia." In *African Muslims in Antebellum America: Transatlantic Stories and Spiritual Struggles*, 309–408. New York: Routledge, 1997.

Ayandele, E. A. *The Missionary Impact on Modern Nigeria: 1842–1914*. London: Longmans, 1966.

———. "Observations on Some Social and Economic Aspects of Slavery in Precolonial Northern Nigeria." *Nigerian Journal of Economic and Social Studies* 9 (1967):329–38.

Baier, Steven, and Paul E. Lovejoy. "The Tuareg of the Central Sudan: Gradations in Servility at the Desert Edge (Niger and Nigeria)." In *Slavery in Africa: Historical and Anthropological Perspectives*, edited by Suzanne Miers and Igor Kopytoff, 391–411. Madison: University of Wisconsin Press, 1977.

Bailyn, Bernard. *Atlantic History: Concept and Contours*. Cambridge, MA: Harvard University Press, 2005.

Balde, Mamadou S. "L'esclavage et la guerre sainte au Fuuta-Jalon." In *L'esclavage en Afrique précoloniale*, edited by Claude Meillassoux, 183–220. Paris: Maspero, 1975.

Balogun, I. A. B. *The Life and Works of 'Uthman Dan Fodio*. Lagos: Islamic Publications Bureau, 1975.

———. "Shaikh Uthman Danfodiyo: Founder of the Sokoto Heritage." In *State and Society in the Sokoto Caliphate: Essays in Honour of Sultan Ibrahim Dasuki*, edited by Ahmed M. Kani and K. A. Gandi, 207–22. Sokoto: Usmanu Danfodiyo University, 1990.

———. "Uthman Dan Fodio: The Mujaddid of West Africa." In *Studies in the History of the Sokoto Caliphate: The Sokoto Seminar Papers*, edited by Yusuf Bala Usman, 473–92. Zaria: Department of History, Ahmadu Bello University, 1979.

Barcia, Manuel. *The Great African Slave Revolt of 1825: Cuba and the Fight for Freedom in Matanzas*. Baton Rouge: Louisiana State University Press, 2012.

———. "An Islamic Atlantic Revolution: Dan Fodio's *Jihad* and Slave Rebellion in Bahia and Cuba, 1804–1844." *Journal of African Diaspora, Archaeology, and Heritage* 2, no. 1 (2013): 6–18.

———. *Seeds of Insurrection: Domination and Slave Resistance on Cuban Planta-tions*. Baton Rouge: Louisiana State University Press, 2008.

———. "West African Islam in Colonial Cuba." *Slavery and Abolition* 35, no. 1 (2014): 1–14.

———. *West African Warfare in Bahia and Cuba: Soldier Slaves in the Atlantic World, 1807–1844*. Oxford: Oxford University Press, 2014.

Bargery, G. P. *A Hausa-English Dictionary and English-Hausa Vocabulary*. London: Oxford University Press, 1934.

Barickman, B. J. "Reading the 1835 Parish Censuses from Bahia: Citizenship, Kin-ship, Slavery, and Household in Early Nineteenth-Century Brazil." *Americas* 59, no. 3 (2003): 287–324.

Barkindo, Bawuro. "Islam in Mandara, Its Introduction and Impact upon the State and the People." *Kano Studies*, n.s., 1, no. 4 (1979): 24–51.

———. "The Mandara astride the Nigeria-Cameroon Boundary." In *Partitioned Africans: Ethnic Relations across Africa's International Boundaries, 1884–1984*, edited by A. I. Asiwaju, 29–49. London: C. Hurst and Co., 1985.

———. "Mandara-Fombina Relations before 1900." *Kano Studies*, n.s., 2, no. 1 (1980): 84–95.

———, ed. *Studies in the History of Kano*. Ibadan: Heinemann, 1983.

———. *The Sultanate of Mandara to 1902: History of the Evolution, Development and Collapse of a Central Sudanese Kingdom*. Stuttgart: Franz Steiner Verlag, 1989.

Barry, Boubacar. *Senegambia and the Atlantic Slave Trade*. Cambridge: Cambridge University Press, 1998.

———. "Senegambia from the Sixteenth to the Eighteenth Century: Evolution of the Wolof, Sereer and 'Tukuloor.'" In *UNESCO General History of Africa*, vol. 5, ed-ited by B.A. Ogot, 273–74. Berkeley, University of California Press, 1992.

———. "Traite négrière et esclavage interne en Sénégambie au xviiie siècle." In *De la traite à l'esclavage: Actes du Colloque international sur la traite des noirs*, edited by Serge Daget, 2:213–22. Nantes: Centre de recherche sur l'histoire du monde atlantique, 1988.

Barthélémy, Gérard. *Créoles–Bossales: Conflit en Haïti*. Paris: Ibis rouge, 2000.

———. *Dans la splendeur d'un après-midi d'histoire*. Port-au-Prince: Deschamps, 1996.

———. "Le rôle des Bossales dans l'émergence d'une culture du marronage en Haïti." *Cahiers d'études africaines* 37, no. 148 (1997): 839–62.

Bascom, William W. *Ifa Divination: Communication between Gods and Men in West Africa*. Bloomington: Indiana University Press, 1969.

Bassiri, Kambiz Ghanea. *A History of Islam in America: From the New World to the New World Order*. Cambridge: Cambridge University Press, 2010.

Bastide, Roger. *As religiões africanas no Brasil: Contribuição a uma sociologia das interpretações de civilizações*. São Paulo: Livraria Pioneira, 1989.

Batran, Aziz A. "The Nineteenth-Century Islamic Revolutions in West Africa." In *UNESCO General History of Africa*, vol. 6, edited by J. F. Ade Ajayi, 537–54. Berkeley and Los Angeles: University of California Press, 1989.

———. *The Qadiriyya Brotherhood in West Africa and the Western Sahara: The Life and Times of Shaykh al-Mukhtar al-Kunti (1729–1811)*. Rabat: Institut des Études Africaines, 2001.

Baum, Robert. *Shrines of the Slave Trade: Diola Religion and Society in Precolonial Senegal*. New York: Oxford University Press, 1999.

Beckles, Hilary. *Britain's Black Debt: Reparations for Caribbean Slavery and Native Genocide*. Kingston: University of the West Indies Press, 2013.

Beek, Walter van. "Purity and Statecraft: The Fulani Jihād and Its Empire." In *The Quest for Purity: Dynamics of Puritan Movements*, edited by Walter van Beek, 149–82. The Hague: Mouton de Gruyter, 1988.

Bellagamba, Alice, Sandra E. Greene, and Martin A. Klein, eds. *African Voices on Slavery and the Slave Trade*. Cambridge: Cambridge University Press, 2013.

Bergard, Laird W., Fe Iglesias Garcia, and Marcia del Carmen Barcia. *The Cuban Slave Market, 1790–1880*. Cambridge: Cambridge University Press, 1995.

Berlin, Ira. "From Creole to African: Atlantic Creoles and the Origins of African-American Society in Mainland North America." *William and Mary Quarterly* 53, no. 2 (1996): 251–88.

———. *Many Thousands Gone: The First Two Centuries of Slavery in North America*. Cambridge, MA: Belknap Press, 1998.

Besmer, Fremont E. *Horses, Musicians and Gods: The Hausa Cult of Possession-Trance*. South Hadley, MA: Bergin and Garvey, 1983.

Bethell, Leslie. *The Abolition of the Brazilian Slave Trade*. Cambridge: Cambridge University Press, 1970.

Biobaku, Saburi, and Muhammad Al- Hajj. "The Sudanese Mahdiyya and the Niger-Chad region." In *Islam in Tropical Africa*, edited by I. M. Lewis, 425–39. Oxford: Clarendon Press, 1966.

Bivar, A. D. H., and Mervyn Hiskett. "The Arabic Literature of Nigeria to 1804: A Provisional Account." *Bulletin of the School of Oriental and African Studies* 25, no. 1 (1962): 104–48.

Blench, Robert. "The Present in the Past: How Narratives of the Slave-Raiding Era Inform Current Politics in Northern and Central Nigeria." In *Slavery in Africa: Archaeology and Memory*, edited by Paul Lane and Kevin MacDonald, 361–91. London: Oxford University Press, 2011.

Boahen, A. Adu. *Britain, the Sahara, and the Western Sudan, 1788–1861*. Oxford: Clarendon Press, 1964.

Bobboyi, Hamidu, and A. M. Yakubu, eds. *The Sokoto Caliphate: History and Legacies, 1804–2004*. 2 vols. Kaduna: Arewa House, 2006.

Botte, Roger. "Les rapports Nord-Sud, la traite négrière et le Fuuta Jaloo à la fin du XVIIIᵉ siècle." *Annales: Économies, Sociétés, Civilisations* 6 (1991): 1411–35.

———. "Révolte, pouvoir, religion: Les Hubbu du Futa-Jalon Guinée." *Journal of African History* 29 (1988): 391–413.

Boulègue, J. "L'expression du refus de la traite négrière dans les sociétés sénégambiennes (xviiᵉ–xviiiᵉ siècles)." In *De la traite à l'esclavage: Actes du Colloque international sur la traite des noirs*, edited by Serge Daget, 2:247–252. Nantes: Centre de recherche sur l'histoire du monde atlantique, 1988.

Bovill, E. W. *The Golden Trade of the Moors*. 2nd ed. London: Oxford University Press, 1970.

———, ed. *Missions to the Niger*. 4 vols. Cambridge: Cambridge University Press, 1966.

Brazil, Etienne Ignace. "Os malês." *Revista do Instituto Histórico e Geográfico Brasileiro* 72 (1909): 69–126

Brenner, Louis. "Concepts of Tariqa in West Africa: The Case of the Qadiriyya." In *Charisma and Brotherhood in African Islam*, edited by D. B. Cruise O'Brien and C. Coulon, 33–52. Oxford: Clarendon Press, 1988.

———. "The Jihad Debate between Sokoto and Borno: An Historical Analysis of Islamic Political Discourse in Nigeria." In *People and Empires in African History: Essays in Memory of Michael Crowder*, edited by J. F. Ade Ajayi and J. D. Y. Peel, 21–43. London: Longman, 1992.

———. *Muslim Identity and Social Change in Sub-Saharan Africa*. Bloomington: Indiana University Press, 1993.

———. *The Shehus of Kukawa: A History of the Al-Kanemi Dynasty of Bornu*. Oxford: Clarendon Press, 1973.

Brigaglia, Andrea, and Mauro Nobili. "Central Sudanic Arabic Scripts (Part 2): Barnāwī." *Sudanic Africa* 4, no. 2 (2013): 195–223.

Brooks, George E. *Eurafricans in Western Africa: Commerce, Social Status, Gender, and Religious Observance from the Sixteenth to the Eighteenth Century*. Athens: University of Ohio Press, 2003.

———. "The Signares of Saint-Louis and Gorée: Women Entrepreneurs in Eighteenth Century Senegal." In *Women in Africa: Studies in Social and Economic Change*, edited by Nancy Hafkin and Edna G. Bay, 19–44. Stanford, CA: Stanford University Press, 1976.

Brown, Christopher Leslie. *Moral Capital: Foundations of British Abolitionism*. Chapel Hill: University of North Carolina Press, 2006.

Brown, William A. "Toward a Chronology for the Caliphate of Hamdullahi (Māsina)." *Cahiers d'études africaines* 8, no. 31 (1968): 428–34.

Bruce, R. "The Fulani Settlement of Butu, Slavery and the Trade in Slaves." In *Studies in the History of Plateau State, Nigeria*, edited by E. Isichei, 191–205. London: Macmillan, 1982.

Bruce Lockhart, Jamie. *Difficult and Dangerous Roads: Hugh Clapperton's Travels in Sahara and Fezzan, 1822–1825*. London: Sickle Moon Books, 2000.

———. *A Sailor in the Sahara: The Life and Travels in Africa of Hugh Clapperton, Commander RN*. London: Tauris, 2008.

Bruijn, Mirjam de, and Han van Dijk. "Resistance to Fulbe Hegemony in Nineteenth-Century West Africa." In *Rethinking Resistance: Revolt and Violence in African History*, edited by Gerrit Jan Abbink, Mirjam de Bruijn, and Jaas van Walraven, 43–68. Leiden: Brill, 2003.

Bugaje, Usman M. "Scholarship and Revolution: The Impact of a Tradition of *Tajdid* on the Sokoto Caliphal Leaders." In *The Sokoto Caliphate: History and Legacies*,

1804–2004, edited by H. Bobboyi and A. M. Yakubu, 2:11–21. Kaduna: Arewa House, 2006.

Cairus, José. "Intrumentum vocale, mallams e alufás: O paradoxo islâmico da erudição na diáspora africana no Atlântico." *Topoi* 6 (2003): 128–64.

Campbell, Carl. "John Mohammed Bath and the Free Mandingos in Trinidad: The Question of Their Repatriation to Africa, 1831–38." *Journal of African Studies* 2, no. 3 (1975): 467–95.

———. "Mohammedu Sisei of Gambia and Trinidad, c. 1788–1838." *African Studies of the West Indies Bulletin* 7 (1974): 29–38.

Candido, Mariana P. "African Freedom Suits and Portuguese Vassal Status: Legal Mechanisms for Fighting Enslavement in Benguela, Angola, 1800–1830." *Slavery and Abolition* 32, no. 3 (2011): 447–59.

———. "Aguida Gonçalves da Silva, une dona à Benguela à la fin du XVIIIᵉ siècle." *Brésil(s): Sciences Humaines et Sociales* 1 (2012): 33–54.

Caron, Peter. " '. . . Of a Nation Which the Others Do Not Understand': African Ethnicity and the Bambara of Colonial Louisiana, 1719–1760." *Slavery and Abolition* 18 (1997): 98–121.

Carretta, Vincent, ed. *Unchained Voices: An Anthology of Black Authors in the English-Speaking World of the Eighteenth Century*. Lexington: University Press of Kentucky, 1996.

Carvalho, Marcus J. M. de. "Rumores e rebeliões: Estratégias de resistência escrava no Recife, 1817–1848." *Tempo* 3, no. 6 (1998): 49–72.

Cauna, Jacques de. *Haïti, l'éternelle révolution*. Port-au-Prince: Deschamps, 2009.

Césaire, Aimé. *Toussaint-Louverture: La Révolution française et le problème colonial*. Paris: Présence africaine, 1960.

Chafe, Kabiru S. *The State and Economy in the Sokoto Caliphate: Policies and Practices in the Metropolitan Districts, c. 1804–1903*. Zaria: Ahmadu Bello University Press, 1999.

Chetima, Melchisedek, and Gaïmatakwan Kr Dujok Alexandre. "Memories of Slavery in the Mandara Mountains: Re-appropriating the Repressive Past." In *Slavery, Memory, Citizenship*, ed. Paul E. Lovejoy and Vanessa Oliveira, 285–99. Trenton, NJ: Africa World Press, 2015.

Cissoko, Sèkéné-Mody. "Famines et épidémies à Tombouctou et dans la Boucle du Niger du XVIᵉ au XVIIIᵉ siècle." *Bulletin de l'IFAN* 30, no. 3 (1968): 806–21.

Clarence-Smith, William Gervase. *Islam and the Abolition of Slavery*. London: Hurst, 2006.

Cohen, Abner. "Cultural Strategies in the Organization of Trading Diasporas." In *The Development of Indigenous Trade and Markets in West Africa*, edited by Claude Meillassoux, 266–81. London: Oxford University Press, 1971.

———. *Customs and Politics in Urban Africa: A Study of Hausa Migrants in Yoruba Towns*. London: Routledge and Kegan Paul, 1969.

Conrad, Robert. *The Destruction of Brazilian Slavery, 1850–1888*. Berkeley: University of California Press, 1972.

Cottias, Myriam, and Marie-Jeanne Rossignol, eds. *Distant Ripples of the British Abolitionist Wave: Africa, Asia and the Americas*. Trenton, NJ: Africa World Press, 2016.

Craton, Michael, ed. *Roots and Branches: Current Directions in Slave Studies*. Toronto: Pergamon Press, 1979.

———. *Testing the Chains: Resistance to Slavery in the British West Indies*. Ithaca, NY: Cornell University Press, 1982.

Curtin, Philip D. "Africa in the Wider Monetary World, 1250–1850." In *Silver and Gold Flows in the Medieval and Early Modern Worlds*, edited by John F. Richards, 231–68. Chapel Hill: University of North Carolina Press, 1983.

———, ed. *Africa Remembered: Narratives by West Africans from the Era of the Slave Trade*. Madison: University of Wisconsin Press, 1967.

———. *The Atlantic Slave Trade: A Census*. Madison: University of Wisconsin Press, 1969.

———. "Ayuba Suleiman Diallo of Bondu." In *Africa Remembered: Narratives by West Africans from the Era of the Slave Trade*, edited by Philip D. Curtin, 17–59. Madison: University of Wisconsin Press, 1967.

———. *Cross-Cultural Trade in World History*. Cambridge: Cambridge University Press, 1984.

———. *Economic Change in Pre-colonial Africa: Senegambia in the Era of the Slave Trade*. Madison: University of Wisconsin Press, 1975.

———. "Pre-colonial Trading Networks and Traders: The Diakhanke." In *The Development of Indigenous Trade and Markets in West Africa*, edited by Claude Meillassoux, 228–39. London: Oxford University Press, 1984.

———. "The Uses of Oral Tradition in Senegambia: Maalik Sii and the Foundation of Bundu." *Cahiers d'études africaines* 15 (1975): 189–202.

Daddi Addoun, Yacine, and Paul E. Lovejoy. "The Arabic Manuscript of Muḥammad Kabā Saghanughu of Jamaica, c. 1820." In *Creole Concerns: Essays in Honour of Kamau Brathwaite*, edited by Annie Paul, 313–41. Kingston: University of the West Indies Press, 2007.

———. "Commerce and Credit in Katsina in the Nineteenth Century." In *Africa, Empire, and Globalization: Essays in Honor of A. G. Hopkins*, edited by Emily Brownell and Toyin Falola, 111–24. Durham, NC: Carolina Academic Press, 2011.

———. "Muḥammad Kabā Saghanughu and the Muslim Community of Jamaica." In *Slavery on the Frontiers of Islam*, edited by Paul E. Lovejoy, 201–20. Princeton, NJ: Markus Wiener, 2004.

Danmole, Hakeem Olumide Akanni. "Emirate of the 'Yarba': Ilorin in the Nineteenth Century." In *The Sokoto Caliphate: History and Legacies, 1804–2004*, edited by H. Bobboyi and A. M. Yakubu, 1:31–52. Kaduna: Arewa House, 2006.

———. "Samuel Johnson and the History of Ilorin." In *Pioneer, Patriot, and Patriarch: Samuel Johnson and the Yoruba People*, edited by Toyin Falola, 139–49. Madison: African Studies Program, University of Wisconsin–Madison, 1993.

David, Nicholas. "A Close Reading of Hamman Yaji's Diary: Slave Raiding and Montagnard Responses in the Mountains around Madagali (Northeast Nigeria and

Northern Cameroon)." Calgary, 2012. http://www.sukur.info/Mont/Hamman Yaji%20PAPER.pdf.

Davis, David Brion. *The Problem of Slavery in the Age of Revolution, 1770–1823*. Ithaca, NY: Cornell University Press, 1966.

Davis, Natalie Zemon. *Trickster Travels: A Sixteenth-Century Muslim between Worlds*. New York: Faber, 2006.

Debien, Gabriel. *De l'Afrique à Saint Domingue*. Port-au-Prince: Revue de la Société Haitienne d'Histoire et de Géographie, 1982.

———. *Les esclaves aux Antilles Françaises (XVIIᵉ–XVIIIᵉ siècles)*. Paris: Société d'Impressions Caron-Ozanne, 1975.

———. "Les origins des esclaves des Antilles." *Bulletin de l'Institut Fondamental d'Afrique Noire*, ser. B, 23 (1961): 363–87; 25 (1963): 1–41, 215–66; 26 (1964): 166–211, 601–75; 27 (1965): 319–71, 755–99; 29 (1967): 536–58.

Deschamps, Henri. *Créoles—Bossales: Conflit en Haïti*. Paris: Ibis rouge, 2000.

Diouf, Mamadou, and Mara W. Leichtman, eds. *New Perspectives on Islam in Senegal: Conversion, Migration, Wealth, Power, and Femininity*. New York: Palgrave MacMillan, 2009.

Diouf, Sylviane. "Devils or Sorcerers, Muslims or Studs: Manding in the Americas." In *Trans-Atlantic Dimensions of Ethnicity in the African Diaspora*, edited by Paul E. Lovejoy and David V. Trotman, 139–58. London: Continuum, 2003.

———, ed. *Fighting the Slave Trade: West African Strategies*. Athens: Ohio University Press, 2003.

———. *Servants of Allah: African Muslims Enslaved in the Americas*. New York: New York University Press, 1998.

Dobronravin, Nikolay. "Classical Hausa Glosses in a Nineteenth-Century Quranic Manuscript: A Case of Translational Reading in Sudanic Africa?" *Journal of Qur'anic Studies* 15, no. 3 (2013): 84–122.

Dorigny, Marcel. *Haiti, première république noire*. Paris: Société Française d'Histoire d'Outre-Mer, 2003.

Drescher, Seymour. *Abolition: A History of Slavery and Antislavery*. Cambridgte: Cambridge University Press, 2009.

Duarte, Aberlardo. *Negros Muçulmanos nas Alagoas (Os Malês)*. Maceió: Caeté, 1958.

Dubois, Laurent. *Avengers of the New World: The Story of the Haitian Revolution*. Cambridge: Cambridge University Press, 2004.

Dubois, Laurent, and John D. Garrigus. *Slave Revolution in the Caribbean, 1789–1804: A Brief History with Documents*. Boston: Bedford/St Martin's, 2006.

El Hamel, Chouki. *Black Morocco: A History of Slavery, Race, and Islam*. Cambridge: Cambridge University Press, 2013.

———. "Constructing a Diasporic Identity: Tracing the Origins of the Gnawa Spiritual Group in Morocco." *Journal of African History* 49 (2008): 241–60.

———. "The Register of the Slaves of Sultan Mawlay Isma'il of Morocco at the Turn of the Eighteenth Century." *Journal of African History* 51 (2010): 89–98.

———. *La vie intellectuelle islamique dans le Sahel Ouest-Africain (XVIᵉ–XIXᵉ siècles): Une étude social de l'enseignement islamique en Mauritanie et au Nord du*

Mali (XVIᵉ–XIXᵉ siècles) et traduction annotée de "Fath ash-shakur" d'al-Bartili al Walati (mort en 1805). Paris : L'Harmattan, 2002.

El-Masri, F. H. "The Life of Shehu Usuman dan Fodio before the Jihad." *Journal of the Historical Society of Nigeria* 2, no. 4 (1963): 435–48.

Eltis, David. *Economic Growth and the Ending of the Transatlantic Slave Trade*. New York: Cambridge University Press, 1987.

———. *The Rise of African Slavery in the Americas*. Cambridge: Cambridge University Press, 2000.

Eltis, David, and David Richardson. *Atlas of the Transatlantic Slave Trade*. New Haven, CT: Yale University Press, 2010.

Ennaji, Mohammed. *Serving the Master: Slavery and Society in Nineteenth-Century Morocco*. New York: St. Martin's Press, 1999.

———. *Slavery, the State, and Islam*. New York: Cambridge University Press, 2013.

———. *Le Sujet et le mamlouk: Esclavage, pouvoir et religion dans le monde arabe*. Paris: Mille et une nuits, 2007.

Fahmy, Khaled. "The Era of Muhammad 'Ali Pasha, 1805–1848." In *The Cambridge History of Egypt: Modern Egypt, from 1517 to the End of the Twentieth Century*, edited by M. W. Daly, 2:139–79. Cambridge: Cambridge University Press, 1998.

Falola, Toyin. *Ibadan: Foundation, Growth and Change, 1830–1960*. Ibadan: Bookcraft, 2012.

———. "The Impact of the Nineteenth-Century Sokoto Jihad on Yorubaland." In *State and Society in the Sokoto Caliphate: Essays in Honour of Sultan Ibrahim Dasuki*, edited by Ahmed M. Kani and K. A. Gandi, 126–41. Sokoto: Usmanu Danfodio University, 1990.

———, ed. *Pioneer, Patriot, and Patriarch: Samuel Johnson and the Yoruba People*. Madison: African Studies Program, University of Wisconsin–Madison, 1994.

———, ed. *Yoruba Historiography*. Madison: African Studies Program, University of Wisconsin–Madison, 1991.

Falola, Toyin, and Matt D. Childs, eds. *The Yoruba Diaspora in the Atlantic World*. Bloomington: Indiana University Press, 2004.

Falola, Toyin, and Kevin D. Roberts, eds. *The Atlantic World, 1450–2000*. Bloomington: Indiana University Press, 2008.

Farias, Paulo F. de Moraes. *Arabic Medieval Inscriptions from the Republic of Mali: Epigraphy, Chronicles, and Songhay-Tuâreg History*. Oxford: Oxford University Press, 2003.

———. "Enquanto isso, do outro lado do mar: Os Arókin e a identidade iorubá." *Afro-Ásia* 17 (1996): 139–55.

———. "'Yoruba Origins' Revisited by Muslims." In *Self-Assertion and Brokerage: Early Cultural Nationalism in West Africa*, edited by P. F. de Moraes Farias and Karin Barber, 109–47. Birmingham: Centre of West African Studies, 1990.

Ferreira, Roquinaldo. *Cross-Cultural Exchange in the Atlantic World: Angola and Brazil during the Era of the Slave Trade*. New York: Cambridge University Press, 2012.

Fick, Carolyn. *The Making of Haiti: The Saint Domingue Revolution from Below*. Knoxville: University of Tennessee Press, 1990.

Fisher, Humphrey J. "A Muslim William Wilberforce? The Sokoto Jihad as Anti-slavery Crusade: An Enquiry into Historical Causes." In *De la traite à l'esclavage: Actes du Colloque international sur la traite des noirs*, edited by Serge Daget, 2:537–55. Nantes: Centre de recherche sur l'histoire du monde atlantique, 1985.

———. *Slavery in the History of Muslim Black Africa*. London: Hurst, 2001.

Florentino, Manolo Garcia. *Em costas negras: Uma historia do trafico de escravos entre a Africa e o Rio de Janeiro, 1790–1830*. São Paulo: Companhia das Letras, 1997.

Folayan, Kola. "Tripoli-Bornu Political Relations, 1817–1825." *Journal of the Historical Society of Nigeria* 5 (1971): 463–71.

———. *Tripoli during the Reign of Yusuf Pasha Qaramanli*. Ife-Ife: University of Ife Press, 1979.

Fraser, Robert L. "PIERPOINT, RICHARD," in *Dictionary of Canadian Biography*, vol. 7, University of Toronto/Université Laval, 2003–, accessed July 16, 2016, http://www.biographi.ca/en/bio/pierpoint_richard_7E.html.

Frishman, Alan. "The Population Growth of Kano, Nigeria." In *African Historical Demography*, edited by Christopher Fyfe, 212–50. Edinburgh: Centre of African Studies, University of Edinburgh, 1977.

Froelich, Jean-Claude. "Le commandement et l'organisation sociale chez les Fulbe de l'Adamoua (Cameroun)." *Etudes Camerounaises* 45–46 (1954): 5–91.

Fyfe, Christopher. "Four Sierra Leone Recaptives." *Journal of African History* 2, no. 1 (1961): 77–85.

———. *A History of Sierra Leone*. London: Oxford University Press, 1962.

———. "1787–1887–1987: Reflections on a Sierra Leone Bicentenary." *Africa* 57, no. 4 (1987): 411–21.

Fyle, C. Magbaily. *A Nationalist History of Sierra Leone*. Freetown: Securicom Printers, 2011.

Gates, Henry Louis, Jr. *The Signifying Monkey: A Theory of African-American Literary Criticism*. New York: Oxford University Press, 1988.

Gbadamosi, T. G. O. *The Growth of Islam among the Yoruba, 1841–1908*. Atlantic Highlands, NJ: Humanities Press, 1978.

Geggus, David. *Haitian Revolutionary Studies*. Bloomington: Indiana University Press, 2002.

———, ed. *The Impact of the Haitian Revolution in the Atlantic World*. Columbia: University of South Carolina Press, 2001.

Genovese, Eugene. *From Rebellion to Revolution: Afro-American Slave Revolts in the Making of the Modern World*. Baton Rouge: Louisiana State University Press, 1979.

Gilroy, Paul. *The Black Atlantic: Modernity and Double Consciousness*. Cambridge, MA: Harvard University Press, 1993.

Gomes, Flavio dos Santos. *Historias de quilombolas: Mocambos e comunidades de senzalas no Rio de Janeiro, século XIX*. Rio de Janeiro: Arquivo Nacional, 1995.

Gomez, Michael. *Black Crescent: The Experience and Legacy of African Muslims in the Americas*. Cambridge: Cambridge University Press, 2005.

——. *Exchanging Our Country Marks: The Transformation of African Identities in the Colonial and Antebellum South*. Chapel Hill: University of North Carolina Press, 1998.

——. "Muslims in Early America." *Journal of Southern History* 60, no. 4 (1994): 671–710.

——. *Pragmatism in the Age of Jihad: The Precolonial State of Bundu*. Cambridge: Cambridge University Press, 2002.

Goody, Jack. *The Ethnography of the Northern Territories of the Gold Coast*. London: Colonial Office, 1954.

——. "Writing, Religion and Revolt in Bahia." *Visible Language* 20 (1986): 318–43.

Graden, Dale T. "Slave Resistance and the Abolition of the Trans-Atlantic Slave Trade to Brazil in 1850." *História Unisinos* 14, no. 3 (2010): 282–93.

Grant, Douglas. *The Fortunate Slave: An Illustration of African Slavery in the Early Eighteenth Century*. London: Oxford University Press, 1968.

Green, Jack P., and Philip D. Morgan. *Atlantic History: A Critical Appraisal*. New York: Oxford University Press, 2008.

Griffin, Patrick. "A Plea for a New Atlantic History." *William and Mary Quarterly* 68, no. 2 (2011): 236–39.

Gwandu, Abubakar. "The Vision and Mission of Shaykh Abdullahi Fodio." In *The Sokoto Caliphate: History and Legacies, 1804–2004*, edited by H. Bobboyi and A. M. Yakubu, 2:23–39. Kaduna: Arewa House, 2006.

Haafkens, J. *Chants musulmans en peul*. Leiden: Editions CLE, 1983.

Hair, P. E. H. "The Enslavement of Koelle's Informants." *Journal of African History* 6, no. 2 (1965): 193–203.

Hall, Bruce. *A History of Race in Muslim West Africa, 1600–1960*. Cambridge: Cambridge University Press, 2011.

——. "Saharan Commerce and Islamic Law: The Question of Usury (*ribā*) in the Nawāzil literature of Mali and Mauritania, 1700–1929." *African Economic History* 41 (2013):1–18.

Hall, Bruce, and Charles Stewart. "The Historic 'Core Curriculum' and the Book Market in Islamic West Africa." In *The Trans-Saharan Book Trade: Manuscript Culture, Arabic Literacy and Intellectual History in West Africa*, edited by Graziano Krätli and Ghislaine Lydon, 109–74. Leiden: Brill, 2011.

Hall, Gwendolyn Midlo. *Africans in Colonial Louisiana: The Development of Afro-Creole Culture in the Eighteenth Century*. Baton Rouge: Louisiana State University Press, 1992.

——. *Slavery and African Ethnicities in the Americas: Restoring the Links*. Chapel Hill: University of North Carolina Press, 2005.

Hallet, Robin. *The Penetration of Africa: European Enterprise and Exploration in Northern and Western Africa up to 1830*. London: Oxford University Press, 1965.

Hama, Boubou. *Histoire traditionnelle des Peul du Dallol Boboye*. Niamey: CRRDTO, 1969.

Hamani, Djibo. "Adar, the Toureg and Sokoto: Relations of Sokoto with the Hausawa and Toureg during the Nineteenth Century." In *Studies in the History of the*

Sokoto Caliphate: The Sokoto Seminar Papers, ed. Yusuf Bala Usman, 392–407. Zaria: Department of History, Ahmadu Bello University, 1979.

———. *L'Adar précolonial (République du Niger): Contribution à l'étude de l'histoire des états Hausa*. Paris: L'Harmattan, 1975.

Hamza, Ibrahim, Paul E. Lovejoy, and Sean Stilwell. "The Oral History of Royal Slavery in the Sokoto Caliphate: An Interview with Sallama Dako." *History in Africa* 28 (2001): 273–91.

Hancock, David. *Citizens of the World: London Merchants and the Integration of the British Atlantic Community, 1735–1785*. Cambridge: Cambridge University Press, 1995.

Hansen, William. "Boko Haram: Religious Radicalism and Insurrection in Northern Nigeria." *Journal of Asian and African Studies* (2016): 1–19.

Haraway, Donna. "Situated Knowledges: The Science Question in Feminism and the Privilege of Partial Perspectives." *Feminist Studies* 14, no. 3 (1988): 575–99.

Harrak, Fatima. *West African Pilgrims in the 19th Century Morocco: Representation of Moroccan Religious Institutions*. Rabat: Institute of African Studies, 1994.

Harris, Jennifer. "Seeing the Light: Re-reading James Albert Ukawsaw Gronniosaw." *English Language Notes* 42, no. 4 (2005): 43–57.

Hawthorne, Walter. " 'Being Now, as It Were, One Family': Shipmate Bonding on the Slave Vessel *Emilia*, in Rio de Janeiro and throughout the Atlantic World." *Luso-Brazilian Review* 45, no. 1 (2008): 53–77.

———. *From Africa to Brazil: Culture, Identity, and an Atlantic Slave Trade, 1600–1830*. Cambridge: Cambridge University Press, 2010.

———. "Nourishing a Stateless Society during the Slave Trade: The Rise of Balanta Paddy-Rice Production in Guinea-Bissau." *Journal of African History* 42 (2001): 1–24.

———. *Planting Rice and Harvesting Slaves: Transformations along the Guinea-Bissau Coast, 1450–1850*. Portsmouth, NH: Heinemann, 2003.

———. "The Production of Slaves Where There Was No State: The Guinea Bissau Region, c. 1450–c. 1815." *Slavery and Abolition* 20, no. 2 (1999): 97–124.

———. " 'Sendo agora, como se fôssemos, uma família': Laços entre companheiros de viagem no navio negreiro *Emília*, no Rio de Janeiro e através do Mundo Atlântico." *Revista Mundos do Trabalho* 3, no. 6 (2011): 7–29.

Hill, Polly. "From Slavery to Freedom: The Case of Farm-Slavery in Nigerian Hausa-land." *Comparative Studies in Society and History* 18 (1976): 395–426.

———. *Population, Prosperity, and Poverty: Rural Kano, 1900 and 1970*. Cambridge: Cambridge University Press, 1977.

———. *Rural Hausa: A Village and a Setting*. Cambridge: Cambridge University Press, 1972.

———. "Two Types of West African House Trade." In *The Development of Indigenous Trade and Markets in West Africa*, edited by Claude Meillassoux, 303–18. London: Oxford University Press, 1971.

Hiskett, Mervyn. "The Nineteenth-Century Jihads in West Africa." In *The Cambridge History of Africa*, edited by J. D. Fage and Roland Oliver, 5:125–69, Cambridge: Cambridge University Press, 1976.

———. *The Sword of Truth: The Life and Times of the Shehu Usuman dan Fodio.* New York: Oxford University Press, 1973.

Hobsbawm, Eric. *The Age of Revolution, 1789–1848.* New York: Vintage Books, 1996 [1962].

Hodgkin, Thomas, ed. *Nigerian Perspectives: An Historical Anthology.* London: Oxford University Press, 1960.

Hogendorn, Jan S. "The Economics of Slave Use on Two 'Plantations' in the Zaria Emirate of the Sokoto Caliphate." *International Journal of African Historical Studies* 10 (1977): 369–83.

———. "The Hideous Trade: Economic Aspects of the 'Manufacture' and Sale of Eunuchs." *Paideuma* 45 (1999): 137–60.

———. "Slave Acquisition and Delivery in Precolonial Hausaland." In *West African Culture Dynamics: Archaeological and Historical Perspectives,* edited by Raymond Dumett and Ben K. Schwartz, 477–93. The Hague: Mouton, 1980.

Hogendorn, Jan S., and Marion Johnson. *The Shell Money of the Slave Trade.* Cambridge: Cambridge University Press, 2003.

Howard, Allen M. "Trade and Islam in Sierra Leone, 18th–20th Centuries." In *Islam and Trade in Sierra Leone,* edited by Alusine Jalloh and David E. Skinner, 21–63. Trenton, NJ: Africa World Press, 1997.

Hunwick, John O. "Aḥmad Bābā on Slavery." *Sudanic Africa* 11 (2000): 131–39.

———. "Black Africans in the Mediterranean Islamic World." In *The Human Commodity: Perspectives on the Trans-Saharan Trade,* edited by Elizabeth Savage, 5–38. London: Frank Cass, 1992.

———. "Islamic Financial Institutions: Theoretical Structures and Aspects of Their Application in Sub-Saharan Africa." In *Credit, Currencies, and Culture: African Financial Institutions in Historical Perspective,* edited by Endre Stiansen and Jane I. Guyer, 72–99. Stockholm: Nordiska Afrikainstitutet, 1999.

———. "Islamic Law and Polemics over Black Slavery in Morocco and West Africa." In *Slavery in the Islamic Middle East,* ed. Shaun E. Marmon, 43–68. Princeton, NJ: Princeton University Press, 1996.

———. "'I Wish to Be Seen in Our Land Called Afrika': 'Umar b. Sayyid's Appeal to Be Released from Slavery (1819)." *Journal of Arabic and Islamic Studies* 5 (2003): 62–77.

———. "A Note on 'Uthmān B. Fodiye's So-Called 'Ishrīniyya." *Sudanic Africa* 10 (1999): 169–72.

———. "Notes on Slavery in the Songhay Empire." In *Slaves and Slavery in Muslim Africa: The Servile Estate,* edited by John Ralph Willis, 16–32. London: Frank Cass, 1985.

———. "The Religious Practices of Black Slaves in the Mediterranean Islamic World." In *Slavery on the Frontiers of Islam,* edited by Paul E. Lovejoy, 149–72. Princeton, NJ: Markus Wiener, 2004.

———. "A Supplement to *Infāq al-Maysūr*: The Biographical Notes of 'Abd al-Qādir b. al-Mustafā." *Sudanic Africa* 7 (1996): 35–51.

———. "Toward a History of the Islamic Intellectual Tradition in West Africa down to the Nineteenth Century." *Journal of Islamic Studies* 17 (1997): 4–27.

———. *The Writings of Western Sudanic Africa.* Leiden: Brill, 2003.

Hunwick, John O., and R. S. O'Fahey, eds. *Arabic Literature of Africa.* Vol. 2, *The Writings of Central Sudanic Africa.* Leiden: Brill, 1995.

Hunwick, John O., Sydney Kanya-Forstner, Paul Lovejoy, R. S. O'Fahey, and Al-Min Abu-Manga. "Between Niger and Nile: New Light on the Fulani Mahdist Muhammad al-Dādārī." *Sudanic Africa* 8 (1997): 85–108.

Hunwick, John O., and Eve Troutt Powell, eds. *The African Diaspora in the Mediterranean Lands of Islam.* Princeton, NJ: Markus Wiener, 2002.

Hurbon, Laënnec, ed. *L'insurrection des esclaves de Saint-Domingue (22–23 août 1791).* Paris: Karthala, 2000.

Irwin, Joseph Paul. *Liptako Speaks: History from Oral Tradition in Africa.* Princeton, NJ: Princeton University Press, 1981.

Islahi, Abdul Azim. "Shehu Uthman Dan Fodio and His Economic Ideas." *Munich Personal RePEc Archive,* 2008, 1–12.

Jah, Omar. "The Effect of Pilgrimage on the Jihad of Al-Hajj ʿUmar al-Futi, 1794–1864." In *The Central Bilad al Sudan: Tradition and Adaptation,* edited by Yusuf Fadl Hasan and Paul Doornbos, 233–43. Khartoum: University of Khartoum Press, 1977.

Jalloh, Alusine, and David E. Skinner, eds. *Islam and Trade in Sierra Leone.* Trenton, NJ: Africa World Press, 1997.

James, C.L.R. *The Black Jacobins: Toussaint L'Ouverture and the San Domingo Revolution, 2nd ed.* New York: Random House, 1963.

Jennings, Lawrence C. *French Anti-slavery: The Movement for the Abolition of Slavery in France, 1802–1848.* Cambridge: Cambridge University Press, 2000.

Johnson, Marion. "The Currencies of West Africa: Part I." *Journal of African History* 11, no. 1 (1970): 17–49.

———. "The Currencies of West Africa: Part II." *Journal of African History* 11, no. 3 (1970): 331–53.

———. "The Economic Foundations of an Islamic Theocracy The Case of Masina." *Journal of African History* 17 (1976): 481–95.

Jones, Denise. "Robert Bostock of Liverpool and the British Slave Trade on the Upper Guinea Coast, 1769–93." In *Slavery, Abolition and the Transition to Colonialism in Sierra Leone,* edited by Paul E. Lovejoy and Suzanne Schwarz, 69–88. Trenton, NJ: Africa World Press, 2014.

Jumare, Ibrahim M. "The Late Treatment of Slavery in Sokoto: Background and Consequences of the 1936 Proclamation." *International Journal of African Historical Studies* 27, no. 2 (1994): 303–22.

Junaidu b. Muhammad al-Bukhari. "A Contribution to the Biography of the Shaykh Usman Mentioning the Various Places Where He Lived." In *Studies in the History of the Sokoto Caliphate: The Sokoto Seminar Papers,* edited by Yusuf Bala Usman, 463–72. Zaria: Department of History, Ahmadu Bello University, 1979.

Ka, Thierno. *École de Pir Saniokhor: Histoire, enseignement et culture arabo-islamiques au Sénégal du XVIIIe au XXe siècle*. Paris: Karthala, 2002.

———. "Pir Saniokhor: Université Islamique rurale du Sénégal au XVIIe siècle." *Notes Africaines* 199 (2001): 14–16.

Kaba, Lansiné. "The Politics of Quranic Education among Muslim Traders in the Western Sudan: The Subbanu Experience." *Canadian Journal of African Studies* 10, no. 3 (1976): 409–21.

Kane, Moustafa, and David Robinson. *The Islamic Regime of Fuuta Tooro*. East Lansing: Michigan State University Press, 1984.

Kane, Oumar. *La première hégémonie peule: Le Fuuta Tooro de Koli Tengella à Almaami Abdul*. Dakar: Karthala and Presses Universitaires de Dakar, 2004.

Kani, Ahmed M. *The Intellectual Origin of the Sokoto Caliphate*. Ibadan: Imam Publication, 1984.

Kani, Ahmed M., and K. A. Gandi, eds. *State and Society in the Sokoto Caliphate: Essays in Honour of Sultan Ibrahim Dasuki*. Sokoto: Usmanu Danfodiyo University, 1990.

Karaye, Ibrahim Garba, and Philip James Shea. *History of Karaye*. Zaria: Ahmadu Bello University Press, 2013.

Kaye, Anthony E. "The Second Slavery: Modernity in the Nineteenth-Century South and the Atlantic World." *Journal of Southern History* 75, no. 3 (2009): 175–95.

Keefer, Katrina. "Scarification and Identity in the Liberated Africans Department Registers, 1814–1815." *Canadian Journal of African Studies* 47, no. 3 (2013): 537–53.

Kelley, Sean. "The Dirty Business of Panyarring and Palaver: Slave Trading on the Upper Guinea Coast in the Eighteenth Century." In *Slavery, Abolition and the Transition to Colonialism in Sierra Leone*, edited by Paul E. Lovejoy and Suzanne Schwarz, 89–108. Trenton, NJ: Africa World Press, 2014.

Kent, Raymond. "African Revolt in Bahia." *Journal of Social History* 3 (1970): 334–56.

Kiple, Kenneth F. *Blacks in Colonial Cuba, 1774–1899*. Gainesville: University Presses of Florida, 1976.

Klein, Herbert. "African Women in the Atlantic Slave Trade." In *Women and Slavery in Africa*, edited by Claire C. Robertson and Martin A. Klein, 29–38. Portsmouth, NH: Heinemann, 1997.

Klein, Martin A. "The Demography of Slavery in the Western Sudan: The Late Nineteenth Century." In *African Population and Capitalism: Historical Perspectives*, edited by D. D. Cordell and J. W. Gregory, 50–61. Madison: University of Wisconsin Press, 1994.

———. "Ethnic Pluralism and Homogeneity in the Western Sudan: Saalum, Segu, Wasulu." *Mande Studies* 1 (1999): 109–24.

———. *Slavery and Colonial Rule in French West Africa*. Cambridge: Cambridge University Press, 1998.

———. "Social and Economic Factors in the Muslim Revolution in Senegambia." *Journal of African History* 13 (1972): 419–41.

———. "Women in Slavery in the Western Sudan." In *Women and Slavery in Africa*, edited by Claire C. Robertson and Martin A. Klein, 67–88. Portsmouth, NH: Heinemann, 1997.

Klooster, Wim. *Revolutions in the Atlantic World: A Comparative History*. New York: New York University Press, 2009.

———. "Slave Revolts, Royal Justice, and a Ubiquitous Rumor in the Age of Revolutions." *William and Mary Quarterly* 71, no. 3 (2014): 401–24.

Kolapo, Femi James. "The Dynamics of Early 19th Century Nupe Wars." *Scientia Militaria: South African Journal of Military Studies* 31, no. 2 (2003): 1–35.

———. "Ethnicity and Identity at the Niger-Benue during the 19th-Century Nupe Jihad." In *Slavery in Africa and the Caribbean: A History of Enslavement and Identity since the 18th Century*, edited by Olatunji Ojo and Nadine Hunt, 9–37. New York: I. B. Tauris, 2012.

———. "Niger River Trade and the Interregnum at Aboh, 1844–1862." In *Repercussions of the Atlantic Slave Trade: The Interior of the Bight of Biafra and the African Diaspora*, edited by Caroline A. Brown and Paul E. Lovejoy, 205–20. Trenton, NJ: Africa World Press, 2011.

Kopytoff, Jean Herskovits. *A Preface to Modern Nigeria: The "Sierra Leonians" in Yoruba, 1830–1890*. Madison: University of Wisconsin Press, 1965.

Krätli, Graziano, and Ghislaine Lydon, eds. *The Trans-Saharan Book Trade: Manuscript Culture, Arabic Literacy and Intellectual History in West Africa*. Leiden: Brill, 2011.

Kriger, Colleen E. *Cloth in West African History*. Lanham, MD: AltaMira Press, 2006.

———. "'Guinea Cloth': Production and Consumption of Cotton Textiles in West Africa, before and during the Atlantic Slave Trade." In *The Spinning World: A Global History of Cotton Textiles, 1200–1850*, edited by Giorgio Riello and Prasannan Parthasarathi, 105–26. London: Oxford University Press, 2009.

———. "The Importance of Mande Textiles in the African Side of the Atlantic Slave Trade, ca. 1680–1710." *Mande Studies* 11 (2009): 1–21.

———. "Mapping the History of Cotton Textile Production in Precolonial West Africa." *African Economic History* 33 (2005): 87–116.

———. "Robes of the Sokoto Caliphate." *African Arts* 21 (1988): 52–86.

———. "Silk and Sartorial Politics in the Sokoto Caliphate, 1804–1903." In *The Force of Fashion in Politics and Society: Global Perspectives from Early Modern to Modern Times*, edited by Beverly Lemire, 143–63. London: Ashgate, 2010.

———. "Textile Production and Gender in the Sokoto Caliphate." *Journal of African History* 34 (1993): 361–401.

Kurawa, Isa. "The *Jihad* and the Consolidation of Sudanic Intellectual Tradition." In *The Sokoto Caliphate: History and Legacies, 1804–2004*, edited by H. Bobboyi and A. M. Yakubu, 2:81–99. Kaduna: Arewa House, 2006.

Lafi, Nora. *Une ville du Maghreb entre ancien régime et réformes ottomanes: Genèse des institutions municipales à Tripoli de Barbarie (1795–1911)*. Paris: L'Harmattan, 2002.

Landers, Jane. *Atlantic Creoles in the Age of Revolutions*. Cambridge, MA: Harvard University Press, 2010.

———. "The Atlantic Transformations of Francisco Menéndez." In *Biography and the Black Atlantic*, edited by Lisa W. Lindsay and John Wood Sweet, 209–12. Philadelphia: University of Pennsylvania Press, 2013.

Last, Murray. "An Aspect of the Caliph Muhammad Bello's Social Policy." *Kano Studies* 1 (1966): 56–59.

———. "The Book and the Nature of Knowledge in Muslim Northern Nigeria, 1457–2007." In *The Trans-Saharan Book Trade: Arabic Literacy, Manuscript Culture, and Intellectual History in Islamic Africa*, edited by Graziano Krätli and Ghislaine Lydon, 175–212. Leiden: Brill, 2011.

———. "The Book in the Sokoto Caliphate." *Studia Africana* 17 (2006): 39–52.

———. "From Sultanate to Caliphate: Kano, 1450–1800 A.D." In *Studies in the History of Kano*, edited by Bawuro M. Barkindo, 67–91. Ibadan: Heinemann, 1983.

———. "'Injustice' and Legitimacy in the Early Sokoto Caliphate." In *People and Empires in African History: Essays in Memory of Michael Crowder*, edited by J. F. Ade Ajayi and J. D. Y. Peel, 45–57. London: Longman, 1992.

———. "Innovation in the Sokoto Caliphate." In *The Sokoto Caliphate: History and Legacies, 1804–2004*, edited by H. Bobboyi and A. M. Yakubu, 2:328–47. Kaduna: Arewa House, 2006.

———. "Reform in West Africa: The Jihad Movement of the Nineteenth Century." In *History of West Africa*, 3rd ed., edited by J. F. A. Ajayi and Michael Crowder, 2:1–29. London: Longman, 1977.

———. *The Sokoto Caliphate*. London: Longmans, 1967.

———. "The Sokoto Caliphate and Borno." In *UNESCO General History of Africa*, vol. 6, edited by J. F. Ade Ajayi, 555–99. Berkeley: University of California Press, 1989.

Last, Murray, and M. A. Al-Hajj. "Attempts at Defining a Muslim in 19th Century Hausaland and Bornu." *Journal of the Historical Society of Nigeria* 3, no. 2 (1965): 231–39.

Lavers, John E. "The al-Kanimiyyin Shehus: A Working Chronology." *Berichte des Sonderforschungsbereichs* 268, no. 2 (1993): 179–86.

———. "The Diplomatic Relations of the Sokoto Caliphate: Some Thoughts and a Plea." In *Studies in the History of the Sokoto Caliphate: The Sokoto Seminar Papers*, edited by Yusuf Bala Usman, 379–91. Zaria: Department of History, Ahmadu Bello University 1979.

———. "Jibril Gaini: A Preliminary Account of the Career of a Mahdist Leader in North-Eastern Nigeria." *Research Bulletin* (Centre of Arabic Documentation, Ibadan) 3, no. 1 (1967): 16–38.

Law, Robin. "The Chronology of the Yoruba Wars of the Early Nineteenth Century: A Reconsideration." *Journal of the Historical Society of Nigeria* 5 (1970): 211–22.

———. "The Dynastic Chronology of Lagos." *Lagos Notes and Records* 2, no. 2 (1968): 46–54.

———. "Ethnicity and the Slave Trade: 'Lucumi' and 'Nago' as Ethnonyms in West Africa." *History in Africa* 24 (1997): 205–19.

———. *The Horse in West African History.* Cambridge: Cambridge University Press, 1980.

———. "Islam in Dahomey: A Case Study of the Introduction and Influence of Islam in a Peripheral Area of West Africa." *Scottish Journal of Religious Studies* 4, no. 2 (1986):50–64.

———. "Making Sense of a Traditional Narrative: Political Disintegration in the Kingdom of Oyo." *Cahiers d'études africaines* 22 (1982): 387–401.

———. "The Owu War in Yoruba History." *Journal of the Historical Society of Nigeria* 7, no. 1 (1973): 141–47.

———. "The Oyo-Dahomey Wars, 1726–1823: A Military Analysis." In *Warfare and Diplomacy in Precolonial Nigeria*, edited by Toyin Falola and Robin Law, 9–25. Madison: African Studies Program, University of Wisconsin–Madison, 1992.

———. *The Oyo Empire, c. 1600–c. 1836: A West African Imperialism in the Era of the Atlantic Slave Trade.* Oxford: Clarendon Press, 1977.

———. "Slave-Raiders and Middlemen, Monopolists and Free-Traders: The Supply of Slaves for the Atlantic Trade in Dahomey, c. 1715–1850." *Journal of African History* 30 (1989): 45–68.

Law, Robin, and Kristin Mann. "West Africa in the Atlantic Community: The Case of the Slave Coast." *William and Mary Quarterly* 56, no. 2 (1999): 307–34.

Lefebvre, Camille. "Un esclave a vu le monde: Se déplacer en tant qu'esclave au Soudan central (xixe siècle)." *Revista de História* 18, no. 2 (2013): 105–43.

Levtzion, Nehemia. "North-West Africa: From the Maghrib to the Fringes of the Forest." In *The Cambridge History of Africa*, edited by J. D. Fage and Roland Oliver, 4:204–5. Cambridge: Cambridge University Press, 1975.

Levtzion, Nehemia, and Randall Pouwels, eds. *The History of Islam in West Africa.* Athens: Ohio University Press, 2000.

Linebaugh, Peter, and Marcus Rediker. *The Many-Headed Hydra: Sailors, Slaves, Commoners, and the Hidden History of the Revolutionary Atlantic.* Boston: Beacon Press, 2000.

Lofkrantz, Jennifer. "Intellectual Discourse in the Early Sokoto Caliphate: The Triumvirate's Opinions on the Issue of Ransoming, c. 1810." *International Journal of African Historical Studies* 45, no. 3 (2012): 385–401.

———. "Protecting Freeborn Muslims: The Sokoto Caliphate's Attempts to Prevent Illegal Enslavement and Its Acceptance of the Strategy of Ransoming." *Slavery and Abolition* 32, no. 1 (2011): 109–27.

———. "Ransoming of Captives in the Sokoto Caliphate in the Nineteenth Century." In *Slavery, Islam and Diaspora*, edited by Behnaz A. Mirzai, Ismael Musah Montana, and Paul E. Lovejoy, 125–37. Trenton, NJ: Africa World Press, 2009.

Lofkrantz, Jennifer, and Paul E. Lovejoy. "Maintaining Network Boundaries: Islamic Law and Commerce from Sahara to Guinea Shores." *Slavery and Abolition* 36, no. 2 (2015): 211–32.

Lofkrantz, Jennifer, and Olatunji Ojo. "Slavery, Freedom, and Failed Ransom Negotiations in West Africa, 1730–1900." *Journal of African History* 53, no. 1 (2012): 25–44.

Loimeier, Roman. *Islamic Reform and Political Change in Northern Nigeria*. Evanston, IL: Northwestern University Press, 1997.

Lovejoy, Henry B. "Drums of Ṣàngó: Bàtá Drums and the Symbolic Reestablishment of Ọyọ in Colonial Cuba, c. 1817–1867." In *Ṣàngó in Africa and the African Diaspora*, edited by Joel Tishken, Toyin Falola, and Akintunde Akinyemi, 284–308. Bloomington: Indiana University Press, 2009.

———. *Prieto of the Lucumí Nation: Yoruba Identity in Nineteenth-Century Cuba*. Chapel Hill: University of North Carolina Press, forthcoming.

———. "Re-drawing Historical Maps of the Bight of Benin Hinterland, c. 1780." *Canadian Journal of African Studies* 47, no. 3 (2013): 443–63.

———. "The Transculturation of Yoruba Annual Festivals: The *Día de Reyes* in Colonial Cuba in the Nineteenth Century." In *Carnival—Theory and Practice*, edited by Christopher Innes, Annabel Rutherford, and Brigitte Bogar, 33–50. Trenton, NJ: Africa World Press, 2013.

Lovejoy, Henry B., and Olatunji Ojo. "'Lucumí' and 'Terranova,' and the Origins of the Yoruba Nation." *Journal of African History* 56, no. 3 (2015): 353–72.

Lovejoy, Paul E. "The African Background of Venture Smith." In *Venture Smith and the Business of Slavery and Freedom*, edited by James B. Stewart, 35–55. Amherst: University of Massachusetts Press, 2009.

———. "The African Diaspora: Revisionist Interpretations of Ethnicity, Culture and Religion under Slavery." *Studies in the World History of Slavery, Abolition and Emancipation* 2, no. 1 (1997): 1–24.

———. "Background to Rebellion: The Origins of Muslim Slaves in Bahia." *Slavery and Abolition* 15, no. 2 (1994): 151–80.

———. "Biographies of Enslaved Muslims from the Central Sudan in the Nineteenth Century." In *The Sokoto Caliphate: History and Legacies, 1804–2004*, edited by H. Bobboyi and A. M. Yakubu, 1:187–216. Kaduna: Arewa House, 2006.

———. "The Black Atlantic in the Construction of the 'Western' World: Alternative Approaches to the 'Europeanization' of the Americas." In *The Historical Practice of Diversity: Transcultural Interactions from the Early Modern Mediterranean to the Postcolonial World*, edited by Dirk Hoerder, Christiane Harzig and Adrian Shubert, 109–33. New York: Berghahn Books, 2003.

———. "The Borno Salt Industry." *International Journal of African Historical Studies* 10 (1977): 465–80.

———. *Caravans of Kola: The Hausa Kola Trade, 1700–1900*. Zaria: Ahmadu Bello University Press, 1980.

———. "The Central Sudan and the Atlantic Slave Trade." In *Paths toward the Past: African Historical Essays in Honor of Jan Vansina*, edited by Robert W. Harms, Joseph C. Miller, David C. Newbury, and Michelle D. Wagner, 345–70. Atlanta: African Studies Association Press, 1994.

———. "The Characteristics of Plantations in the Nineteenth-Century Sokoto Caliphate (Islamic West Africa)." *American Historical Review* 85, no. 5 (1979): 1267–92.

———. "The Clapperton-Bello Exchange: The Sokoto *Jihad* and the Trans-Atlantic Slave Trade, 1804–1837." In *The Desert Shore: Literatures of the African Sahel*, edited by Christopher Wise, 201–28. Boulder, CO: Lynne Rienner, 2000.

———. "Commercial Sectors in the Economy of the Nineteenth-Century Central Sudan: The Trans-Saharan Trade and the Desert-Side Salt Trade." *African Economic History* 13 (1984): 85–116.

———. "Concubinage in the Sokoto Caliphate (1804–1903)." *Slavery and Abolition* 11 (1990): 159–89.

———. "The Context of Enslavement in West Africa: Ahmad Bābā and the Ethics of Slavery." In *Slaves, Subjects, and Subversives: Blacks in Colonial Latin America*, edited by Jane Landers, 9–38. Albuquerque: University of New Mexico Press, 2006.

———. "Diplomacy in the Heart of Africa: British-Sokoto Negotiations over the Abolition of the Atlantic Slave Trade." In *Distant Ripples of the British Abolitionist Wave in Africa, Asia and the Americas*, edited by Myriam Cottias and Marie-Jeanne Rossignol. Trenton, NJ: Africa World Press, 2016.

———. *Ecology and Ethnography of Muslim Trade in West Africa*. Trenton, NJ: Africa World Press, 2005.

———. "Esclavitud y comercio esclavista en el África Occidental: Investigaciones en curso." In *Debates históricos contemporáneos: Africanos y afrodescendientes en México y Centroamérica*, edited by María Elisa Velázquez, 35–58. Mexico City: Instituto Nacional de Anthropología e Historia, 2011.

———. "Forgotten Colony in Africa: The British Province of Senegambia (1765–83)." In *Slavery, Abolition and the Transition to Colonialism in Sierra Leone*, edited by Paul E. Lovejoy and Suzanne Schwarz, 109–26. Trenton, NJ: Africa World Press, 2014.

———. "Freedom Narratives of Trans-Atlantic Slavery." *Slavery and Abolition* 32, no. 1 (2011): 91–107.

———. "Fugitive Slaves: Resistance to Slavery in the Sokoto Caliphate." In *In Resistance: Studies in African, Afro-American, and Caribbean History*, edited by Gary Okihiro, 71–95. Amherst: University of Massachusetts Press, 1986.

———, ed. *Identity in the Shadow of Slavery*. London: Continuum, 2000.

———. "Indigenous African Slavery." *Historical Reflections / Reflexions Historiques* 6, no. 1 (1979): 19–61.

———. "Internal Markets or an Atlantic-Sahara Divide? How Women Fit into the Slave Trade of West Africa." In *Women and Slavery*, edited by Gwyn Campbell, Suzanne Miers, and Joseph C. Miller, 259–80. Athens: Ohio University Press, 2007.

———. "The Internal Trade of West Africa, 1450–1800." In *History of West Africa*, rev. ed., edited by J. F. A. Ajayi and Michael Crowder, 1:640–90. London: Longman Group, 1985.

———. "Interregional Monetary Flows in the Precolonial Trade of Nigeria." *Journal of African History* 15 (1974): 563–85.

———. "Islamic Scholarship and Understanding History in West Africa before 1800." In *The Oxford History of Historical Writing*, vol. 3, *1400–1800*, edited by José Rabasa, Masayuki Sato, Edoardo Tortarolo, and Daniel Woolf, 212–32. New York: Oxford University Press, 2012.

———. "Islam, Slavery, and Political Transformation in West Africa: Constraints on the Trans-Atlantic Slave Trade." *Outre-Mers: Revue d'histoire* 89 (2002): 247–82.

———. "Jihād e escravidão: As origens dos escravos Muculmanos de Bahia," *Topoi* 1 (Rio de Janeiro, 2000): 11–44.

———. "*Jihad* na África Ocidental durante a 'Era das Revoluções'—Rumo a um diálogo com Eric Hobsbawm e Eugene Genovese." *Topoi: Revista de História* 15, no. 28 (2014): 22–67.

———. "The Kambarin Beriberi: The Formation of a Specialized Group of Hausa Kola Traders in the Nineteenth Century." *Journal of African History* 14 (1973): 633–51.

———. "Methodology through the Ethnic Lens." In *Sources and Methods in African History: Spoken, Written, Unearthed*, edited by Toyin Falola and Christian Jennings, 105–17. Rochester, NY: University of Rochester Press, 2003.

———. "Narratives of Trans-Atlantic Slavery: The Lives of Two Muslims, Muhammad Kabā Saghanaghu and Mahommah Gardo Baquaqua." In *Africa and Trans-Atlantic Memories: Literary and Aesthetic Manifestations of Diaspora and History*, edited by Naana Opoku-Agyemang, Paul E. Lovejoy, and David Trotman, 7–22. Trenton, NJ: Africa World Press, 2008.

———. "Les origines de Catherine Mulgrave Zimmermann: Considérations méthodologiques." *Cahiers des Anneaux de la Mémoire* 14 (2011): 247–63.

———. "Patterns in Regulation and Collaboration in the Slave Trade of West Africa." *Leidschrift* 22, no. 1 (2007): 41–57.

———. "Plantations in the Economy of the Sokoto Caliphate." *Journal of African History* 19, no. 3 (1978): 341–68.

———. "Polanyi's 'Ports of Trade': Salaga and Kano in the Nineteenth Century." *Canadian Journal of African Studies* 16, no. 2 (1982): 245–78.

———. "The Role of the Wangara in the Economic Transformation of the Central Sudan in the Fifteenth and Sixteenth Centuries." *Journal of African History* 19, no. 2 (1978): 173–93.

———. *Salt of the Desert Sun: A History of Salt Production and Trade in the Central Sudan*. Cambridge: Cambridge University Press, 1986.

———. "Scarification and the Loss of History in the African Diaspora." In *Activating the Past: Historical Memory in the Black Atlantic*, edited by Andrew Apter and Lauren Derby, 99–138. Newcastle: Cambridge Scholarly Publishing, 2009.

———. *Slavery, Commerce and Production in West Africa: Slave Society in the Sokoto Caliphate*. Trenton, NJ: Africa World Press, 2005.

———, ed. *Slavery on the Frontiers of Islam*. Princeton, NJ: Markus Wiener, 2004.

———. "The Slave Trade as Enforced Migration in the Central Sudan." In *Removing Peoples: Forced Removal in the Modern World*, edited by Claudia Haake and Richard Bessel, 149–66. London: German Historical Institute, 2009.

———. "Transatlantic Transformations: The Origins and Identities of Africans in the Americas." In *Africa, Brazil, and the Construction of Trans-Atlantic Black Identities*, edited by Boubacar Barry, Livio Sansone, and Elisée Soumonni, 81–112. Trenton, NJ: Africa World Press, 2008.

———. *Transformations in Slavery: A History of Slavery in Africa*. 3rd ed. Cambridge: Cambridge University Press, 2012.

———. "The Urban Background of Enslaved Muslims in the Americas." *Slavery and Abolition* 26, no. 3 (2005): 347–72.

———. "The Yoruba Factor in the Trans-Atlantic Slave Trade." In *The Yoruba Diaspora in the Atlantic World*, edited by Toyin Falola and Matt D. Childs, 40–55. Bloomington: Indiana University Press, 2004.

Lovejoy, Paul E., and Steven Baier. "The Desert-Side Economy of the Central Sudan." *International Journal of African Historical Studies* 8, no. 4 (1975): 551–81.

Lovejoy, Paul E., and J. S. Hogendorn. "Oral Data Collection and the Economic History of the Central Savanna." *Savanna* 7 (1978): 71–74.

———. "Revolutionary Mahdism and Resistance to Colonial Rule in the Sokoto Caliphate, 1905–1906." *Journal of African History* 31, no. 2 (1990): 217–44.

———. "Slave Marketing in West Africa." In *The Uncommon Market: Essays in the Economic History of the Atlantic Slave Trade*, edited by Henry Gemery and J. S. Hogendorn, 213–35. New York: Academic Press, 1979.

———. *Slow Death for Slavery: The Course of Abolition in Northern Nigeria, 1897–1936*. Cambridge: Cambridge University Press, 1993.

Lovejoy, Paul E., and David Richardson. "Competing Markets for Male and Female Slaves: Slave Prices in the Interior of West Africa, 1780–1850." *International Journal of African Historical Studies* 28, no. 2 (1995): 261–93.

Lovejoy, Paul E., and Suzanne Schwarz. "Sierra Leone in the Eighteenth and Nineteenth Century." In *Slavery, Abolition and the Transition to Colonialism in Sierra Leone*, edited by Paul E. Lovejoy and Suzanne Schwarz, 1–28. Trenton, NJ: Africa World Press, 2015.

———, eds. *Slavery, Abolition and the Transition to Colonialism in Sierra Leone*. Trenton, NJ: Africa World Press, 2015.

Lovejoy, Paul E., and David Trotman. "Community of Believers: Trinidad Muslims and the Return to Africa, c. 1810–1850." In *Slavery on the Frontiers of Islam*, edited by Paul E. Lovejoy, 221–34. Princeton, NJ: Markus Wiener.

Lubeck, Paul. "Islamic Protest under Semi-industrial Capitalism: Yan Tatsine Explained." *Africa: The Journal of the International African Institute* 54, no. 4 (1985): 369–89.

Luna, Luis. *O Negro na luta contra escravidão*. Rio de Janeiro: Ed. Leitura, 1967.

Lydon, Ghislaine. "Contracting Caravans: Partnership and Profit in Nineteenth- and Early Twentieth-Century Trans-Saharan Trade." *Journal of Global History* 3 (2008): 89–113.

———. *On Trans-Saharan Trails: Islamic Law, Trade Networks, and Cross-Cultural Trade in Nineteenth-Century Western Africa*. Cambridge: Cambridge University Press, 2009.

MacEachem, Scott. "Enslavement and Everyday Life: Living with Slave Raiding in the Northeastern Mandara Mountains of Cameroon." In *Slavery in Africa: Archaeology and Memory*, edited by Paul Lane and Kevin MacDonald, 109–24. London: Oxford University Press, 2011.

Mack, Beverly B. "Women and Slavery in Nineteenth-Century Hausaland." *Slavery and Abolition* 13 (1992): 89–110.

Mack, Beverly B., and Jean Boyd. *One Woman's Jihad: Nana Asma'u, Scholar and Scribe*. Bloomington: Indiana University Press, 2000.

Madiega, Y. Georges. *Contribution à l'histoire précoloniale du Gulma (Haute Volta)*. Wiesbaden: Franz Steiner Verlag, 1982.

Mahadi, Abdullahi. "The Aftermath of the *Jihād* in the Central Sudan as a Major Factor in the Volume of the Trans-Saharan Slave Trade in the Nineteenth Century." In *The Human Commodity: Perspectives on the Trans-Saharan Trade*, edited by E. Savage, 111–28. London: Frank Cass, 1992.

Mahamat, Adam. "Les eunuques dans le bassin tchadien: Productions et usages." *African Economic History* 41 (2013): 59–72.

Mann, Kristin. *Slavery and the Birth of an African City, 1760–1900*. Bloomington: Indiana University Press, 2007.

Manning, Patrick. *Slavery, Colonialism, and Economic Growth in Dahomey, 1640–1960*. Cambridge: Cambridge University Press, 1982.

———. "The Slave Trade in the Bight of Benin, 1640–1890." In *The Uncommon Market: Essays in the Economic History of the Atlantic Slave Trade*, edited by Henry Gemery and J. S. Hogendorn, 107–40. New York: Academic Press, 1979.

Martin, B. G. "Sapelo Island's Arabic Document: The 'Bilali Diary' in Context." *Georgia Historical Quarterly* 77, no. 3 (1994): 589–601.

———. "Unbelief in the Western Sudan: 'Uthmān dan Fodio's 'Ta'lim al-ikhwān.'" *Middle East Studies* 4, no. 1 (1967): 50–97.

Mason, Michael. "Captive and Client Labour and the Economy of the Bida Emirate, 1857–1901." *Journal of African History* 14 (1973): 453–71.

———. *The Foundations of the Bida Kingdom*. Zaria: Ahmadu Bello University Press, 1979.

———. "The Jihad in the South: An Outline of Nineteenth Century Nupe Hegemony in North-eastern Yorubaland and Afenmai." *Journal of the Historical Society of Nigeria* 5, no. 2 (1970): 193–209.

———. "Population and 'Slave Raiding'—The Case of the Middle Belt of Nigeria." *Journal of African History* 10, no. 4 (1969): 551–64.

Massing, Andreas W. "Baghayogho: A Soninke Muslim Diaspora in the Mande World." *Cahiers d'études africaines* 176 (2004): 887–922.

Mattos, Hebe. *Das cores do silencio: Os significados da liberdade no sudeste escravista, século XIX*. Campinas: Ed. UNICAMP, 2014.

Mattoso, Kátia M. de Queirós. "Os escravos na Bahia no alvorecer do século XIX: Estude de um grupo social." *Revista de Historia* 47, no. 97 (1974): 109–35.

———. *Testamentos de escravos libertos na Bahia no século XIX*. Salvador: Publicação da Universidade Federal da Bahia, 1979.

McDougall, E. Ann. "On Being Saharan." In *Saharan Frontiers: Space and Mobility in Northwest Africa*, edited by James McDougall and Judith Scheele, 39–57. Bloomington: Indiana University Press, 2012.

Meillassoux, Claude, ed. *The Development of Indigenous Trade and Markets in West Africa*. London: Oxford University Press, 1971.

Meyers, Allan. "Slavery in the Hausa-Fulani Emirates." In *Aspects of West African Islam*, edited by Daniel F. McCall and Norman R. Bennett, 173–84. Boston: African Studies Center, Boston University, 1971.

Meyler, David, and Peter Meyler. *A Stolen Life: Searching for Richard Pierpoint*. Toronto: Natural Heritage Books, 1999.

Middleton, Arthur Pierce. "The Strange Story of Job Ben Solomon." *William and Mary Quarterly* 5, no. 3 (1948): 342–50.

Miller, Joseph C. "The Dynamics of History in Africa and the Atlantic 'Age of Revolutions.'" In *The Age of Revolutions in Global Context, c. 1760–1840*, edited by David Armitage and Sanjay Subrahmanyam, 101–24. Basingstoke, UK: Palgrave Macmillan, 2010.

Mirzai, Behnaz A., Ismael Musah Montana, and Paul E. Lovejoy, eds. *Slavery, Islam and Diaspora*. Trenton, NJ: Africa World Press, 2009.

Mohammed, A. R. "The Sokoto Jihad and Its Impact on the Confluence Area and Afenmai." In *State and Society in the Sokoto Caliphate: Essays in Honour of Sultan Ibrahim Dasuki*, edited by Ahmed M. Kani and K.A. Gandi, 142–57. Sokoto: Usmanu Danfodiyo University, 1990.

Mohammadu, Eldridge. "'Kalfu' or the Fulbe Emirate of Bagirmi and the Toorobbe of Sokoto." In *Studies in the History of the Sokoto Caliphate: The Sokoto Seminar Papers*, edited by Yusuf Bala Usman, 336–75. Zaria: Department of History, Ahmadu Bello University, 1979.

Montana, Ismael Musah. *The Abolition of Slavery in Ottoman Tunisia*. Gainesville: University Press of Florida, 2013.

——. "Ahmad ibn al-Qādi al-Timbuktāwī on the *Bori* Ceremonies of Tunis." In *Slavery on the Frontiers of Islam*, edited by Paul E. Lovejoy, 173–98. Princeton, NJ: Markus Wiener, 2004.

——. "The *Bori* Colonies of Tunis." In *Slavery, Islam and Diaspora*, edited by Behnaz A. Mirzai, Ismael Musah Montana, and Paul E. Lovejoy, 155–67. Trenton, NJ: Africa World Press, 2009.

——. "Bori Practice among Enslaved West Africans of Ottoman Tunis: Unbelief (Kufr) or Another Dimension of the African Diaspora?" *History of the Family* 16 (2011): 152–59.

——. "The *Stambali* of Husaynid Tunis: From Possession Cult to Ethno-religious and National Culture." In *African Communities in Asia and the Mediterranean*, ed. Ehud Toledano, 153–66. Trenton, NJ: Africa World Press, 2011.

Monteil, Vincent. "Analyse de 25 documents arabes des Malês de Bahia (1835)." *Bulletin de l'Institut Fondamental d'Afrique Noire*, ser. B, 29, nos. 1–2 (1967): 88–98.

Monteiro, Antônio. *Notas sobre Negros Malês na Bahia*. Salvador: Ianamá, 1987.

Moore, Francis. *Travels into the Inland Parts of Africa*. London: Edward Cave, 1738.

Morgan, Kenneth. "Liverpool Ascendant: British Merchants and the Slave Trade at Sierra Leone, 1701–1808." In *Slavery, Abolition and the Transition to Colonialism in Sierra Leone*, edited by Paul E. Lovejoy and Suzanne Schwarz, 29–50. Trenton, NJ: Africa World Press, 2014.

Morrison, J. H. "Plateau Societies' Resistance to Jihadist Penetration." In *Studies in the History of Plateau State, Nigeria*, edited by E. Isichei, 136–50. London: Macmillan, 1982.

Morton-Williams, Peter. "The Fulani Penetration into Nupe and Yorubaland in the Nineteenth Century." In *History and Social Anthropology*, edited by I. M. Lewis, 1–24. London: Tavistock Publications, 1968.

———. "The Oyo Yoruba and the Atlantic Slave Trade, 1670–1830." *Journal of the Historical Society of Nigeria* 3, no. 1 (1964): 25–45.

Mott, Luiz R. B. *Rosa Egipcía: Uma santa africana no Brasil*. Rio de Janeiro: Bertrand Brasil, 1993.

Moumouni, Seyni. *Vie et oeuvre du Cheik Uthmân Dan Fodio (1754–1817): De l'Islam au soufisme*. Paris: L'Harmattan, 2008.

Moura, Clovis. *Reblioes da Senzala*. São Paulo: Zumbi, 1959.

Mouser, Bruce L. *American Colony on the Rio Pongo: The War of 1812, the Slave Trade, and the Proposed Settlement of African Americans, 1810–1830*. Trenton, NJ: Africa World Press, 2013.

———. "The 1805 Forékariah Conference: A Case of Political Intrigue, Economic Advantage, Network Building." *History in Africa* 25 (1998): 219–62.

———. "A History of the Rio Pongo: Time for a New Appraisal?" *History in Africa* 37 (2010): 329–54.

———. "'Keep Hur Bottom Well Paid with Stuff': A Letter of Instruction for a Slaving Venture to the Sierra Leone Coast in 1760." In *Slavery, Abolition and the Transition to Colonialism in Sierra Leone*, edited by Paul E. Lovejoy and Suzanne Schwarz, 51–68. Trenton, NJ: Africa World Press, 2014.

———. "Rebellion, Marronage and *Jihad*: Strategies of Resistance to Slavery on the Sierra Leone Coast, c. 1783–1796." *Journal of African History* 48, no. 1 (2007): 27–44.

———. "Trade, Coasters, and Conflict in the Rio Pongo from 1790 to 1808." *Journal of African History* 14, no. 1 (1973): 45–64.

———. "Walking Caravans of Nineteenth Century Fuuta Jalon, Western Africa." *Mande Studies* 12 (2010): 19–104.

———. "Women Slavers of Guinea-Conakry." In *Women and Slavery in Africa*, edited by Claire C. Robertson and Martin A. Klein, 320–39. Madison: University of Wisconsin Press, 1983.

Na-dama, Garba. "Urbanization in the Sokoto Caliphate: A Case Study of Gusau and Kaura-Namoda." In *Studies in the History of the Sokoto Caliphate: The Sokoto Seminar Papers*, edited by Yusuf Bala Usman, 140–62. Zaria: Department of History, Ahmadu Bello University, 1979.

Nadel, S. F. *A Black Byzantium: Kingdom of Nupe in Nigeria*. Oxford: Oxford University Press, 1942.

Nagar, 'Umar al-. "The Asānīd of Shehu Dan Fodio: How Far Are They a Contribution to His Biography?" *Sudanic Africa* 13 (2002): 101–10.

———. *The Pilgrimage Tradition in West Africa*. Khartoum: University of Khartoum Press, 1972.

Needell, Jeffrey D. "Brazilian Abolitionism, Its Historiography, and the Uses of Political History." *Journal of Latin American Studies* 42, no. 2 (2010): 231–61.

Nengel, John G. "Echoes of the Sokoto Jihad and Its Legacies on the Societies of the Jos-Plateau." In *The Sokoto Caliphate: History and Legacies, 1804–2004*, edited by H. Bobboyi and A. M. Yakubu, 181–94. Kaduna: Arewa House, 2006.

Nishida, Mieko. "Manumission and Ethnicity in Urban Slavery: Salvador, Brazil, 1808–1888." *Hispanic American Historical Review* 73, no. 3 (1993): 361–91.

———. *Slavery and Identity: Ethnicity, Gender, and Race in Salvador, Brazil, 1808–1888*. Bloomington: Indiana University Press, 2003.

Njeuma, Martin Z. "Adamawa and Mahdism: The Career of Hayatu ibn Said in Adamawa, 1878–1898." *Journal of African History* 12, no. 1 (1971): 61–77.

———. "The Establishment of Adamawa Emirate and Its Legacies in Northern Cameroon." In *The Sokoto Caliphate: History and Legacies, 1804–2004*, edited by Hamidu Bobboyi and A. M. Yakubu, vol. 2:159–75. Kaduna: Arewa House, 2006

———. "The Foundation of Radical Islam in Ngaoundere: 1835–1907." In *Peuples et cultures de l'Adamaoua (Cameroun)*, edited by Hermenegildo Adala and Jean Boutrais, 87–102. Paris: Éditions de l'ORSTOM, 1993.

———. *Fulani Hegemony in Yola (Old Adamawa), 1809–1902*. Yaoundé: Publishing and Production Centre for Teaching and Research, 1978.

———. "Uthman dan Fodio and the Origins of the Fulani Jihad in Adamawa, 1809." *Afrika Zamani* 3 (1974): 51–68.

Nobili, Mauro. "*Risāla min Maryam bt. Fūdī ila al-ibn*: A Brief Contribution to the Study of Muslim Eschatology in Nineteenth Century Nigeria." In *Collectanea Islamica* 1 (2012), edited by Nicola Melis and Mauro Nobili, 71–86. Rome: Aracne: 2012.

Nowak, Bronislaw. "The Slave Rebellion in Sierra Leone in 1785–1796." *Hemispheres* 3, no. 3 (1986): 151–69.

Obayemi, Ade. "History, Culture, Yoruba and Northern Factors." In *Studies in Yoruba History and Culture*, edited by G. O. Olusanya, 72–87. Ibadan: University of Ibadan Press, 1983.

———. "The Sokoto Jihad and the O-kun Yoruba: A Review." *Journal of the Historical Society of Nigeria* 9, no. 2 (1978): 61–87.

O'Hear, Ann. "Ilorin as a Slaving and Slave-Trading Emirate." In *Slavery on the Frontiers of Islam*, edited by Paul E. Lovejoy, 55–68. Princeton, NJ: Markus Wiener, 2004.

———. "The Introduction of Weft Float Motifs to Strip Weaving in Ilorin." In *West African Economic and Social History: Studies in Memory of Marion Johnson*, edited by David Henige and T. C. McCaskie, 175–88. Madison: African Studies Program, University of Wisconsin–Madison, 1990.

———. *Power Relations in Nigeria: Ilorin Slaves and Their Successors.* Rochester, NY: University of Rochester Press, 1997.

———. "Samuel Johnson and the *Dramatis Personae* of Early Nineteenth-Century Ilorin." In *Pioneer, Patriot, and Patriarch: Samuel Johnson and the Yoruba People,* edited by Toyin Falola, 151–61. Madison: African Studies Program, University of Wisconsin–Madison, 1994.

Ojo, Olatunji. "Islam, Ethnicity and Slave Agitation: Hausa 'Mamluks' in Nineteenth Century Yorubaland." In *Slavery, Islam and Diaspora,* edited by Behnaz A. Mirzai, Ismael Musah Montana, and Paul E. Lovejoy, 103–24. Trenton, NJ: Africa World Press, 2009.

Okihiro, Gary, and Herbert Aptheker, eds. *Resistance, Not Acquiesence: Studies in African, Afro-American, and Caribbean History.* Amherst: University of Massachusetts Press, 1986.

Omoiya, S. Y. "Diplomacy as a Veritable Instrument of War: A Study of Ilorin Wars of Survival as an Emirate." *Ilorin Journal of History* 1, no. 2 (2006): 73–85.

"On the Sunna of Wearing Silver Rings." *Sankore'.* www.siiasi.org.

Osborn, Emily L. *Our New Husbands Are Here: Households, Gender, and Politics in a West African State from the Slave Trade to Colonial Rule.* Athens: Ohio University Press, 2011.

Page, Jesse. *The Black Bishop: Samuel Adjai Crowther.* London: Simpkin, Marshall, Hamilton, Kent and Company, 1910.

Pâques, Viviana. *Religion des esclaves: Recherches sur la confrérie marocaine des Gnawa.* Bergamo, Italy: Moretti & Vitali, 1991.

Patterson, Orlando. *Slavery and Social Death: A Comparative Study.* Cambridge, MA: Harvard University Press, 1985.

Peel, J. D. Y. *Religious Encounter and the Making of the Yoruba.* Bloomington: Indiana University Press, 2000.

Person, Yves. "Chronologie du royaume gun de Hogbonu (Porto Novo)." *Cahiers d'études africaines* 15 (1975): 217–38.

———. *Samori: Une revolution dyula.* 3 vols. Paris: IFAN, 1968.

Peterson, John. *Province of Freedom: A History of Sierra Leone, 1787–1870.* London: Faber and Faber, 1969.

Philips, John E. "The Persistence of Slave Officials in the Sokoto Caliphate." In *Slave Elites in the Middle East and Africa: A Comparative Study,* edited by Miura Toru and John Edward Philips, 215–34. London: Kegan Paul International, 2000.

———. "Slavery on Two Ribat in Kano and Sokoto." In *Slavery on the Frontiers of Islam,* Paul E. Lovejoy, ed., 111–24. Princeton: Markus Wiener Publishers, 2003.

Porter, Gina. "A Note on Slavery, Seclusion and Agrarian Change in Northern Nigeria." *Journal of African History* 30, no. 3 (1989): 487–91.

Prothero, R. Mansell. "The Population Census of Northern Nigeria," *Population Studies* 10 (1956): 166–83.

Pybus, Cassandra. *Black Founders: The Unknown Story of Australia's First Black Settlers.* Sydney: University of New South Wales Press, 2006.

────. *Epic Journeys of Freedom: Runaway Slaves of the American Revolution and Their Global Quest for Power*. Boston: Beacon Press, 2006.

Quadri, Y. A. "An Appraisal of Muhammad Bello's *Infaqul-maysur ft tarikhi bilad t-Takrur*." *Journal of Arabic and Religious Studies* 3 (1986): 53–62.

────. "Some Aspects of Muhammad Bello's *Raf' Al-Ishtibah*." *Islamic Culture* 54, no. 4 (1980): 223–27.

Quick, Abdullah Hakim. *In the Heart of a West African Islamic Revival: Shaykh Uthman Dan Fodio (1774–1804)*. Cairo: Al-Falah, 2007.

Quiring-Zoche, Rosemarie. "Bei den Malé Brasilien: Das Reisebuch des ʿAbdarraḥmān al-Baghādi." *Die Welt des Islams* 40, no. 2 (2000): 196–273.

────. "Glaubenskampf oder Machtkampf? Der Aufstand der Malé von Bahia nach einer islamischen Quelle." *Sudanic Africa* 6 (1995): 115–24.

Radtke, Bernd. "Studies on the Sources of the *Kitāb Rimāh Hizb al-Rahīm* of al-Hājj ʿUmar." *Sudanic Africa* 6 (1995): 73–113.

Rashid, Ismail. "'A Devotion to the Idea of Liberty at Any Price': Rebellion and Antislavery in the Upper Guinea Coast in the Eighteenth and Nineteenth Centuries." In *Fighting the Slave Trade: West African Strategies*, edited by Sylviane Diouf, 132–51. Athens: Ohio University Press, 2003.

────. "Escape, Revolt, and Marronage in Eighteenth and Nineteenth Century Sierra Leone Hinterland." *Canadian Journal of African Studies* 34 (2000): 656–83.

Reese, Scott, ed. *The Transmission of Learning in Islamic Africa*. Leiden: Brill, 2004.

Reichert, Rolf. "L'insurrection d'esclaves de 1835 à la lumière des documents arabes des archives publiques de l'état de Bahia (Brésil)." *Bulletin de l'Institut Fondamental d'Afrique Noire*, ser. B, 29, nos. 1–2 (1967): 99–104.

Reichmuth, Stefan. "Imam Umaru's Account of the Origins of the Ilorin Emirate: A Manuscript in the Heinz Sölken Collection, Frankfurt." *Sudanic Africa* 4 (1993): 155–73.

────. "A Sacred Community: Scholars, Saints, and Emirs in a Prayer Text from Ilorin." *Sudanic Africa* 6 (1995): 35–54.

Reis, João José. "Um balanço dos estudos sobre as revoltas escravas da Bahia." In *Escravidão e invenção da liberdade*, edited by João José Reis, 87–141. São Paulo: Brasiliense, 1988.

────. *Domingos Sodré, um sacerdote Africano: Escravidão, liberdade e candomblé na Bahia do século XIX*. São Paulo: Companhia das Letras, 2008.

────. "Ethnic Politics among Africans in Nineteenth-Century Bahia." In *Identity in the Shadow of Slavery*, edited by Paul E. Lovejoy, 240–64. London: Continuum, 2000.

────. *Rebelião escrava no Brasil: A história do Levante dos Malês em 1835*. São Paulo: Companhia das Letras, 2003.

────. "Resistência escrava na Bahia: 'Poderemos brincar, folgar e cantar ...'; O protesto escravo na America." *AfroAsia* 14 (1983): 107–23.

────. "La révolte haoussa de Bahia en 1807 : Résistance et contrôle des esclaves au Brésil." *Annales: Histoire, Sciences Sociales* 61 (2006): 383–418.

────. *Slave Rebellion in Brazil: The Muslim Uprising of 1835 in Bahia*. Baltimore: Johns Hopkins University Press, 1993.

———. "Slave Resistance in Brazil: Bahia, 1807–1835." *Luso-Brazilian Review* 25, no. 1 (1988), 111–44.

Reis, João José, and Paulo F. de Moraes Farias. "Islam and Slave Resistance in Bahia, Brazil." *Islam and sociétés au sud du Sahara* 3 (1989): 41–66.

Reis, João José, Flávio dos Santos Gomes, and Marcus J. M. de Carvalho. "África e Brasil entre margens: Aventuras e desventuras do africano Rufino José Maria, c. 1822–1853." *Revista Estudos Afro-Asiáticos* 4 (2005): 257–302.

———. *O alufá Rufino: Tráfico, escravidão e liberdade no Atlântico negro (c. 1823–c. 1853)*. São Paulo: Companhia das Letras, 2010.

Reis, João José, and Eduardo Silva. *Negociação e conflito: Resistência negra no Brasil escravista*. São Paulo: Companhia das Letras, 1989.

Reyna, Stephen P. *Wars without End: The Political Economy of a Pre-colonial African State*. Hanover, NH: University Press of New England, 1990.

Richardson, David. "Shipboard Revolts, African Authority, and the Atlantic Slave Trade." *William and Mary Quarterly* 58, no. 1 (2001): 69–92.

Roberts, Richard. "Fishing for the State: The Political Economy of the Middle Niger Valley." In *Modes of Production in Africa*, edited by Donald Crummey and Charles Stewart, 175–204. Beverly Hills, CA: Sage, 1981.

———. "Ideology, Slavery, and Social Formation: The Evolution of Maraka Slavery in the Middle Niger Valley." In *The Ideology of Slavery in Africa*, edited by Paul E. Lovejoy, 171–200. Beverly Hills, CA: Sage, 1981.

———. *Warriors, Merchants, and Slaves: The State and the Economy in the Middle Niger Valley, 1700–1914*. Stanford, CA: Stanford University Press, 1987.

Robinson, Charles Henry. *Dictionary of the Hausa Language*. 3rd ed. 2 vols. Cambridge: Cambridge University Press, 1913.

Robinson, David. *The Holy War of Umar Tal: The Western Sudan in the Mid-Nineteenth Century*. Oxford: Clarendon Press, 1985.

———. "The Islamic Revolution of Futa Toro." *International Journal of African Historical Studies* 8, no. 2 (1975): 185–221.

———. *Muslim Societies in African History*. Cambridge: Cambridge University Press, 2004.

———. "Revolutions in the Western Sudan." In *History of Islam in West Africa*, edited by Nehemia Levtzion and Randall Pouwels, 131–68. Athens: Ohio University Press, 2000.

Robinson, David, Philip D. Curtin, and James Johnson. "A Tentative Chronology of Futa Toro from the Sixteenth through the Nineteenth Centuries." *Cahiers d'Études Africaines* 12 (1972): 555–92.

Rodney, Walter. *A History of the Upper Guinea Coast, 1545–1800*. Oxford: Clarendon Press, 1970.

———. "Jihad and Social Revolution in Futa Djalon in the Eighteenth Century." *Journal of the Historical Society of Nigeria* 4 (1968): 269–84.

Rodrigues, Raimundo Nina. *Os Africanos no Brasil*. São Paulo: Companhia Editora Nacional, 1932.

Ross, Eric S. "From Marabout Republics to Autonomous Rural Communities: Autonomous Muslim Towns in Senegal." In *African Urban Spaces in Historical*

Perspective, edited by Steven J. Salm and Toyin Falola, 243–65. Rochester, NY: University of Rochester Press, 2005.

Rossi, Benedetta. *From Slavery to Aid: Power, Labour, and Ecology in the Nigerien Sahel, 1800–2000.* Cambridge: Cambridge University Press, 2015.

Saad, Elias. *Social History of Timbuktu: The Role of Muslim Scholars and Notables, 1400–1900.* Cambridge: Cambridge University Press, 1983.

Saeed, Asmau G. "The British Policy towards the Mahdiyya in Northern Nigeria: A Study of the Arrest, Detention and Deportation of Shaykh Said b. Hayat, 1923–1959." *Kano Studies*, n.s. 2, no. 3 (1982–85): 95–119.

Salau, Mohammed Bashir. "Ribats and the Development of Plantations in the Sokoto Caliphate: A Case Study of Fanisau." *African Economic History* 34 (2006): 23–43.

———. "Slavery in Kano Emirate of Sokoto Caliphate as Recounted: Testimonies of Isyaku and Idrisu." In *African Voices on Slavery and the Slave Trade*, vol. 1, edited by Alice Bellagamba, Sandra E. Greene, and Martin A. Klein, 88–116. Cambridge: Cambridge University Press, 2013.

———. "Slaves in a Muslim City: A Survey of Slavery in Nineteenth Century Kano." In *Slavery, Islam and Diaspora*, edited by Behnaz A. Mirzai, Ismael Musah Montana, and Paul E. Lovejoy, 91–101. Trenton, NJ: African World Press, 2009),

———. "Slave Trading in Kano Emirate." In *Slavery in Africa and the Caribbean: A History of Enslavement and Identity since the Eighteenth Century*, edited by Olatunji Ojo and Nadine Hunt, 38–64. London: I. B. Tauris, 2012.

———. "Voices of Those Who Testified on Slavery in Kano Emirate." In *Crossing Memories: Slavery and African Diaspora*, edited by Ana L. Aruajo, Mariana P. Candido, and Paul E. Lovejoy, 129–45. Trenton, NJ: African World Press, 2011.

———. *The West African Slave Plantation: A Case Study.* New York: Palgrave Macmillan, 2011.

Sani, Abubakar Babajo. *Trade Diplomacy, Banking and Finance in the Trans-Saharan Trade: An Interpretation of Ahmad Abu al-Ghaith's Ledger, a Trade Consul in Katsina, 1824–1870.* Kaduna: Pyla-mak Publishers, 2012.

Sanneh, Lamin O. *The Crown and the Turban: Muslims and West African Pluralism.* Boulder, CO: Westview Press, 1997.

———. "Futa Jallon and the Jakhanke Clerical Tradition, Part 1: The Historical Setting." *Journal of Religion in Africa* 12, no. 1 (1981): 38–64.

———. *The Jakhanke: The History of an Islamic Clerical People of the Senegambia.* London: International African Institute, 1979.

———. "The Origins of Clericalism in West African Islam." *Journal of African History* 17, no. 1 (1976): 49–72.

Schafer, Daniel L. *Anna Madgigine Jai Kingsley: African Princess, Florida Slave, Plantation Slaveowner.* Gainesville: University Press of Florida, 2003.

———. "Family Ties That Bind: Anglo-African Slave Traders in Africa and Florida, John Fraser and His Descendants." *Slavery and Abolition* 20, no. 3 (1999): 1–21.

———. "Shades of Freedom: Anna Kingsley in Senegal, Florida, and Haiti." In *Against the Odds: Free Blacks in the Slave Societies of the Americas*, edited by Jane Landers, 130–54. London: Psychology Press, 1996.

———. *Zephaniah Kingsley Jr. and the Atlantic World: Slave Trader, Plantation Owner, Emancipator.* Gainesville: University Press of Florida, 2013.

Schmidt, Nelly. *L'engrenage de la liberté: Caraïbes—XIXé siècle.* Aix-en-Provence: Université de Provence, 1995.

Schwartz, Stuart. "Cantos e quilombos numa conspiração de escravos haussás." In *Liberdade por um fio: História dos quilombos no Brasil*, edited by João José Reis and Flávio dos Santos Gomes, 373–406. São Paulo: Companhia das Letras, 1997.

———. *Escravos, roceiros e rebeldes.* Bauru: EDUSC, 2001.

———. *Sugar Plantations in the Formation of Brazilian Society: Bahia, 1550–1835.* Cambridge: Cambridge University Press, 1985.

Schwarz, Suzanne. "Commerce, Civilization and Christianity: The Development of the Sierra Leone Company." In *Liverpool and Transatlantic Slavery*, edited by David Richardson, Suzanne Schwarz and Anthony Tibbles, 252–76. Liverpool: Liverpool University Press, 2007.

———. "Extending the African Names Database: New Evidence from Sierra Leone." *African Economic History* 38 (2010): 137–63.

———. *"A Just and Honourable Commerce": Abolitionist Experimentation in Sierra Leone in the Late Eighteenth and Early Nineteenth Centuries.* London: Hakluyt Society Annual Lecture, 2013.

———. "Sierra Leone in the Eighteenth and Nineteenth Century." In *Slavery, Abolition and the Transition to Colonialism in Sierra Leone*, ed. Paul E. Lovejoy and Suzanne Schwarz. Trenton, NJ: Africa World Press, 2015.

Scott, Rebecca J., and Jean Michel Hébrard. *Freedom Papers: An Atlantic Odyssey in the Age of Emancipation.* Cambridge, MA: Harvard University Press, 2012.

———. "Rosalie of the Poulard Nation: Freedom, Law, and Dignity in the Era of the Haitian Revolution." In *Biography and the Black Atlantic*, edited by Lisa W. Lindsay and John Wood Sweet, 249–67. Philadelphia: University of Pennsylvania Press, 2013.

Searcy, Kim. "The Sudanese Mahdī's Attitudes on Slavery and Emancipation." *Islamic Africa* 1, no. 1 (2010): 63–83.

Searing, James. *West African Slavery and Atlantic Commerce: The Senegal River Valley, 1700–1860.* Cambridge: Cambridge University Press, 1993.

Sellnow, Irmgard. "Die Stellung der Sklaven in der Hausa-Gesellschaft." *Mitteilungen des Institut für Orientforschung* 10 (1946): 85–102.

Shagari, Shehu, and Jean Boyd. *Uthman Dan Fodio: The Theory and Practice of His Leadership.* Lagos: Islamic Publications Bureau, 1978.

Shareef, Muhammad. *The Islamic Slave Revolts of Bahia, Brazil: A Continuity of the 19th Century Jihaad Movements of Western Sudan.* Pittsburgh, PA: Sankore', 1998.

———. "More Valuable than Any Other Commodity: Arabic Manuscript Libraries and their Role in Islamic Revival of the Bilad's s-Sudan." *Sankore'*, 2002. www.sankore.org.

Shaw, Rosalind. *Memories of the Slave Trade: Ritual and the Historical Imagination in Sierra Leone.* Chicago: University of Chicago Press, 2002.

Shea, Philip. "Approaching the Study of Production in Rural Kano." In *Studies in the History of Kano*, edited by Bawuro M. Barkindo, 93–115. Ibadan: University of Ibadan Press, 1983.

———. "Big Is Sometimes Best: The Sokoto Caliphate and Economic Advantages of Size in the Textile Industry." *African Economic History* 34 (2006): 5–21.

———. "Kano and the Silk Trade." *Kano Studies*, n.s. 2, no. 1 (1980): 96–112.

———. "Mallam Muhammad Bakatsine and the *Jihad* in Eastern Kano." *History in Africa* 32 (2005): 371–83.

Sidbury, James, and Jorge Cañizares-Esguerra. "Mapping Ethnogenesis in the Early Modern Atlantic." *William and Mary Quarterly* 68, no. 2 (2011): 181–208.

Silva, Alberto da Costa e. *Um rio chamado Atlântico: A África no Brasil e o Brasil na África*. Rio de Janeiro: Editora Nova Fronteira, 2003.

———. "Sobre a rebelião de 1835 na Bahia." *Revista Brasileira* 31 (2002): 9–33.

"Simcoe, John Graves." *Dictionary of Canadian Biography*, vol. 5.

Skinner, David E. "Islam in Kombo: The Spiritual and Militant *Jihad* of Fode Ibrahim Ture." *Islamic Africa* 3, no. 1 (2012): 87–126.

———. "Islam in the Northern Hinterland and Its Influence on the Development of Sierra Leone." In *Islam and Trade in Sierra Leone*, edited by Alusine Jalloh and David E. Skinner, 1–20. Trenton, NJ: Africa World Press, 1997.

———. "Mande Settlement and the Development of Islamic Institutions in Sierra Leone." *International Journal of African Historical Studies* 11, no. 1 (1978): 32–62.

———. "Sierra Leone Relations with the Northern Rivers and the Influence of Islam in the Colony." *International Journal of Sierra Leone Studies* 1, no. 1 (1989): 91–113.

Slenes, Robert W. "Malungu, Ngoma vem: África coberta e descoberta do Brasil." *Revista USP* 12 (1991–92): 48–67.

Smaldone, Joseph P. *Warfare in the Sokoto Caliphate: Historical and Sociological Perspectives*. Cambridge: Cambridge University Press, 1977.

Smith, Abdullahi. "A Little New Light on the Collapse of the Alafinate of Yoruba." In *A Little New Light: Selected Historical Writings of Abdullahi Smith*, 149–91. Zaria: Centre for Historical Research, 1987.

Smith, H. F. C. [Abdullahi]. "A Neglected Theme of West African History: The Islamic Revolutions of the 19th Century." *Journal of the Historical Society of Nigeria* 2, no. 2 (1961): 169–85.

Smith, H. F. C. [Abdullahi], D. M. Last, and Gambo Gubio. "Ali Eisami Gazirmabe of Bornu." In *Africa Remembered: Narratives by West Africans from the Era of the Slave Trade*, edited by Philip D. Curtin, 199–216. Madison: University of Wisconsin Press, 1967.

Smith, M. G. *The Affairs of Daura: History and Change in a Hausa State, 1800–1958*. Berkeley: University of California Press, 1978.

———. *Development and Organization of the Fulani Chiefdom of Kaura Namoda, 1809–1903*. Zaria: Institute of Administration, Ahmadu Bello University, 1972.

———. *The Economy of Hausa Communities of Zaria*. London: H.M.S.O., 1955.

———. *Government in Kano, 1350–1950*. Boulder, CO: Westview Press, 1997.

———. *Government in Zazzau: A Study of Government in the Hausa Chiefdom of Zaria in Northern Nigeria from 1800 to 1950*. London: Oxford University Press, 1960.

———. "A Hausa Kingdom: Maradi under Dan Beskore, 1854–1875." In *West African Kingdoms in the Nineteenth Century*, edited by Daryll Forde and Phyllis Kaberry, 93–122. London: Oxford University Press, 1967.

———. "Slavery and Emancipation in Two Societies." In *The Plural Society in the British West Indies*, 116–61. Berkeley: University of California Press, 1965.

Smith, Mary. *Baba of Karo: A Woman of the Moslem Hausa*. London: Faber, 1955.

Smith, Robert S. *Kingdoms of the Yoruba*. London: Methuen, 1969.

———. "The Lagos Consulate, 1851–1861: An Outline." *Journal of African History* 15, no. 3 (1974): 393–416.

———. *Yoruba Warfare in the 19th Century*. Cambridge: Cambridge University Press, 1964.

Soares, Benjamin. "The Historiography of Islam in West Africa: An Anthropologist's View." *Journal of African History* 55 (2014): 27–36.

Solow, Barbara. *The Economic Consequences of the Atlantic Slave Trade*. New York: Lexington Books, 2014.

Sorensen-Gilmour, Caroline. "Slave-Trading along the Lagoons of South-West Nigeria: The Case of Badagry." In *Ports of the Slave Trade (Bights of Benin and Biafra)*, edited by Robin Law and Silke Strickrodt, 84–95. Stirling: Centre of Commonwealth Studies, 1999.

Sparks, Randy. *Two Princes of Calabar: An Eighteenth-Century Atlantic Odyssey*. Cambridge, MA: Harvard University Press, 2004.

———. *Where the Negroes Are Masters: An African Port in the Era of the Slave Trade*. Cambridge, MA: Harvard University Press, 2014.

Stewart, Charles C. "Diplomatic Relations in Early 19th Century West Africa: Sokoto-Masina-Azaouad Correspondence." In *Studies in the History of the Sokoto Caliphate: The Sokoto Seminar Papers*, edited by Yusuf Bala Usman, 408–29. Zaria: Department of History, Ahmadu Bello University, 1979.

———. "Frontier Disputes and Problems of Legitimation: Sokoto-Masina Relations, 1817–1837." *Journal of African History* 17 (1976): 497–514.

———. "Southern Saharan Scholarship and Bilad al-Sudan." *Journal of African History* 17 (1976): 73–93.

Stilwell, Sean. "'Amana' and 'Asiri': Royal Slave Culture and the Colonial Regime in Kano, 1903–1926." *Slavery and Abolition* 19, no. 2 (1998): 167–88.

———. *Paradoxes of Power: The Kano "Mamluks" and Male Royal Slavery in the Sokoto Caliphate, 1804–1903*. Portsmouth, NH: Heinemann, 2004.

———. "Power, Honour and Shame: The Ideology of Royal Slavery in the Sokoto Caliphate." *Africa* 70, no. 3 (2000): 394–421.

———. "The Power of Knowledge and the Knowledge of Power: Kinship, Community and Royal Slavery in Pre-colonial Kano, 1807–1903." In *Slave Elites in the Middle East and Africa: A Comparative Study*, edited by Miura Toru and John Edward Philips, 81–98. London: Kegan Paul International, 2000.

Sulaiman, Ibraheem. *The African Caliphate: The Life, Work and Teachings of Shaykh Usman Dan Fodio*. London: Diwan, 2009.

———. "Towards a Vision of the Future: A Letter from Sultan Muhammad Bello to the Muslim *Ummah* in Nigeria." In *State and Society in the Sokoto Caliphate: Essays in Honour of Sultan Ibrahim Dasuki*, edited by Ahmed M. Kani and K.A. Gandi, 2:396–408. Sokoto: Usmanu Danfodiyo University, 1990.

Sweet, James H. *Domingos Álvares, African Healing, and the Intellectual History of the Atlantic World*. Chapel Hill: University of North Carolina Press, 2011.

———. "Mistaken Identities? Olaudah Equiano, Domingos Álvares, and the Methodological Challenges of Studying the African Diaspora." *American Historical Review* 114, no. 2 (2009): 279–306.

———. *Recreating Africa: Culture, Kinship, and Religion in the African-Portuguese World, 1440–1770*. Chapel Hill: University of North Carolina Press, 2003.

Tambo, David. "The Sokoto Caliphate Slave Trade in the Nineteenth Century." *International Journal of African Historical Studies* 9, no. 2 (1976): 187–217.

Temple, Olive, and C. L. Temple. *Notes on the Tribes, Provinces, Emirates and States of the Northern Provinces of Nigeria*. Lagos: C.M.S. Bookshop, 1922.

Terray, Emmanuel. "Reflexions sur la formation du prix des esclaves à l'intérieur de l'Afrique de l'Ouest précoloniale." *Journal des Africanistes* 52 (1982): 119–44.

Toledano, Ehud R. "Abolition and Anti-slavery in the Ottoman Empire: A Case to Answer?" In *A Global History of Anti-slavery Politics in the Nineteenth Century*, edited by William Mulligan and Maurice Bric, 117–36. Basingstoke, UK: Palgrave Macmillan, 2013.

———, ed. *African Communities in Asia and the Mediterranean: Identities between Integration and Conflict*. Trenton, NJ: Africa World Press, 2011.

———. "African Slaves in the Ottoman Eastern Mediterranean: A Case of Cultural 'Creolization'?" In *The Mediterranean World: The Idea, the Past and the Present*, edited by Eyüp Özveren, Oktay Özel, Suha Ünsal, and Kudret Emiroğlu, 107–24. Istanbul: Iletisim Yayinlari, 2006.

———. "The Concept of Slavery in Ottoman and Other Muslim Societies: Dichotomy or Continuum?" In *Slave Elites in the Middle East and Africa: A Comparative Study*, edited by Miura Toru and John Edward Philips, 159–76. London: Kegan Paul International, 2000.

———. "Enslavement and Abolition in Muslim Societies." *Journal of African History* 48 (2007): 481–85.

———. "The Fusion of Zar-Bori and Sufi Zikr as Performance: Enslaved Africans in the Ottoman Empire." In *Medieval and Early Modern Performance in the Eastern Mediterranean*, edited by A. Öztürkmen and E. B. Vitz, 216–40. Turnhout, Belgium: Brepols, 2014.

———. "Late Ottoman Concepts of Slavery (1830s–1880s)." *Poetics Today* 14, no. 3 (1993): 477–506.

———. "Ottoman Concepts of Slavery in the Period of Reform (1830s–1880s)." In *Breaking the Chains: Slavery, Bondage, and Emancipation in Modern Africa and*

Asia, edited by Martin A. Klein, 37–63. Madison: University of Wisconsin Press, 1993.

———. *The Ottoman Slave Trade and Its Suppression, 1840–1890*. Princeton, NJ: Princeton University Press, 1982.

———. *Slavery and Abolition in the Ottoman Middle East*. Seattle: University of Washington Press, 1998.

Tomich, Dale W. "Atlantic History and World Economy: Concepts and Constructions." *Proto Sociology: An International Journal of Interdisciplinary Research* 20 (2004): 102–21.

———. "The 'Second Slavery': Bonded Labor and the Transformations of the Nineteenth-Century World Economy." In *Rethinking the Nineteenth Century: Contradictions and Movements*, edited by Francisco O. Ramírez, 103–17. New York: Greenwood, 1988.

———. *Through the Prism of Slavery: Labor, Capital, and World Economy*. Lanham, MD: Rowman and Littlefield, 2004.

———. "The Wealth of the Empire: Francisco de Arango y Parreno, Political Economy, and the Second Slavery in Cuba." *Comparative Studies in Society and History* 1 (2003), 4–28.

Tomich, Dale W., and Michael Zeuske, eds. "The Second Slavery: Mass Slavery, World-Economy, and Comparative Microhistories, Part II." Special issue, *Review: A Journal of the Fernand Braudel Center* 31 (2008).

Tremearne, A. J. N. *The Ban of the Bori. Demons and Demon-Dancing in West and North Africa*. London: Heath, Cranton and Ouseley, 1914.

Tukur, Mahmud M. "The Teachings of the Sokoto Caliphate." In *The Sokoto Caliphate: History and Legacies, 1804–2004*, edited by H. Bobboyi and A. M. Yakubu, 2:53–80. Kaduna: Arewa House, 2006.

Ubah, C. N. "British Measures against Mahdism at Dumbulwa in Northern Nigeria, 1923: A Case of Colonial Overreaction." *Islamic Culture* 50, no. 3 (1976): 169–83.

———. *Government and Administration of Kano Emirate, 1900–1930*. Nsukka: University of Nigeria Press, 1985.

Usman, Yusuf Bala, ed. *Studies in the History of the Sokoto Caliphate: The Sokoto Seminar Papers*. Zaria: Department of History, Ahmadu Bello University, 1979.

———. *The Transformation of Katsina, c. 1796–1903: The Overthrow of the Sarauta System and the Establishment and Evolution of the Emirate*. Zaria: Ahmadu Bello University Press, 1978.

———. "The Transformation of Political Communities: Some Notes on a Significant Dimension of the Sokoto Jihad." In *Studies in the History of the Sokoto Caliphate: The Sokoto Seminar Papers*, edited by Yusuf Bala Usman, 34–58. Zaria: Department of History, Ahmadu Bello University, 1979.

Verger, Pierre. *Flux et reflux de la traite des nègres entre le Golfe de Bénin et Bahia de Todos os Santos du dix-septième au dix-neuvième siècle*. Paris: Mouton, 1968.

———. *Fluxo e refluxo do tráfico de escravos entre o Golfo do Benin e a Bahia de Todos os Santos, dos séculos XVII a XIX*. São Paulo: Editora Corrupio, 1987.

———. *Trade Relations between the Bight of Benin and Bahia, 17th–19th Century*. Ibadan: University of Ibadan Press, 1976.

Voll, John O. "ʿUthmān b. Muhammad Fūdī's Sanad to al-Bukhārī as Presented in *Tazyīn al-Waraqāt." Sudanic Africa* 13 (2002): 111–15.

Walz, Terence. "Black Slavery in Egypt during the Nineteenth Century as Reflected in the Mahkama Archives of Cairo." In *Slaves and Slavery in Muslim Africa: The Servile Estate*, edited by John Ralph Willis, 137–60. London: Frank Cass, 1985.

———. *Trade between Egypt and Bilad as-Sudan, 1700–1820.* Cairo: Institut Français d'Archéologie Orientale du Caire, 1978.

Walz, Terence, and Kenneth M. Cuno, eds. *Race and Slavery in the Middle East: Trans-Saharan Africans in Nineteenth-Century Egypt, Sudan and the Ottoman Mediterranean.* Cairo: American University in Cairo Press, 2010.

Ware, Rudolph T., III. "The *longue durée* of Quran Schooling, Society, and State in Senegambia." In *New Perspectives on Islam in Senegal: Conversion, Migration, Wealth, Power, and Femininity*, edited by Mamadou Diouf and Mara A. Leichtman, 21–50. New York: Palgrave MacMillan, 2009.

———. "Slavery in Islamic Africa, 1400–1800." In *The Cambridge World History of Slavery*, vol. 3, *AD 1420–AD 1804*, edited by David Eltis and Stanley L. Engerman, 47–80. Cambridge: Cambridge University Press, 2011.

———. *The Walking Qur'an: Islamic Education, Embodied Knowledge, and History in West Africa.* Chapel Hill: University of North Carolina Press, 2014.

Warner-Lewis, Maureen. "Africans in 19th Century Trinidad, Part I." *African Studies Association of the West Indies Bulletin* 5 (1972): 27–59.

———. "Africans in 19th Century Trinidad, Part II." *African Studies Association of the West Indies Bulletin* 6 (1972): 13–39.

———. *Guinea's Other Sons: The African Dynamic in Trinidad Culture.* Dover, MA: Majority Press, 1991.

———. "Religious Constancy and Compromise among Nineteenth Century Caribbean-Based African Muslims." In *Slavery, Islam and Diaspora*, edited by Behnaz A. Mirzai, Ismael Musah Montana, and Paul E. Lovejoy, 237–68. Trenton, NJ: Africa World Press, 2009.

Webb, James L. A., Jr. "On Currency and Credit in the Western Sahel, 1700–1850." In *Credit, Currencies, and Culture: African Financial Institutions in Historical Perspective*, edited by Endre Stiansen and Jane I. Guyer, 38–56. Uppsala, Sweden: Nordiska Afrikainstitutet, 1999.

White, E. Frances. *Sierra Leone's Settler Women Traders: Women on the Afro-European Frontier.* Ann Arbor: University of Michigan Press, 1987.

Wilks, Ivor. "Abu Bakr al-Siddiq of Timbuktu." In *Africa Remembered: Narratives by West Africans from the Era of the Slave Trade*, edited by Philip D. Curtin, 152–69. Madison: University of Wisconsin Press, 1967.

———. "The Juula and the Expansion of Islam into the Forest." In *The History of Islam in West Africa*, edited by Nehemia Levtzion and Randall L. Pouwels, 93–116. Athens: Ohio University Press, 2000.

———. "The Saghanughu and the Spread of Maliki Law: A Provisional Note." *Research Review* (Institute of African Studies, University of Ghana) 2, no. 3 (1966): 63–73.

———. "Salih Bilali of Massina." In *Africa Remembered: Narratives by West Africans from the Era of the Slave Trade*, edited by Philip D. Curtin, 145–51. Madison: University of Wisconsin Press, 1967.

———. "The Transmission of Islamic Learning in the Western Sudan." In *Literacy in Traditional Societies*, edited by Jack Goody, 162–97. Cambridge: Cambridge University Press, 1968.

Willis, John Ralph. "Islamic Africa: Reflections on the Servile Estate." *Studia Islamica* 52 (1980): 183–97.

———. *"Jihād fī sabīl Allāh*—Its Doctrinal Basis in Islam and Some Aspects of Its Evolution in Nineteenth-Century West Africa." *Journal of African History* 8, no. 3 (1967): 395–415.

———. "The Torodbe Clerisy: A Social View." *Journal of African History* 19 (1978): 195–212.

Winters, Clyde Ahmed. "The Afro-Brazilian Concept of Jihad and the 1835 Slave Revolt." *Afrodiaspora: Journal of the African World* 2 (1984): 87–91.

Wright, Donald R. *The World and a Very Small Place in Africa: A History of Globalization in Niumi, the Gambia*. 2nd ed. Armonk, NY: M. E. Sharpe, 2004.

Wright, John. *The Trans-Saharan Slave Trade*. London: Routledge, 2007.

Zeuske, Michael. "Historiography and Research Problems of Slavery and the Slave Trade in a Global-Historical Perspective." *International Review of Social History* 57, no. 1 (2012): 87–111.

INDEX

Page numbers with "t" indicate tables. Page numbers with "m" indicate maps.

American slave trade: jihād and, 167–69; Muslim communities on slavery, 194–200; Muslim influence in, 203–5, 248, 317n73. *See also* Atlantic slave trade; Brazil; Christianity; Cuba; Jamaica; slavery and slave trade; United States

amulets, 19–20, 21, 186, 190

Andrada e Silva, José Bonifácio de, 151, 241

Angola, 11

aŋ-bere, 19

Arabic language: in education, 19, 20, 103, 244; elite status and literacy, 25, 53, 209, 227; historical scholarship in, 16, 95–96, 98, 177, 179, 183, 208, 231; in Muslim practices, 6, 61, 126, 189, 244; trade economy and, 253–54

Arara, 140

Are Anakamfo, 84

Armitage, David, 9, 10

Asante, 130, 136, 140, 147

Atiku, Abubakar, 95

"Atlantic creoles," 143

Atlantic slave trade: *vs.* Islamic West Africa trade, 31–34, 132–35; jihād movements and, 31, 62–64, 135–41, 150–52, 164–66; list of destinations from West Africa, 170t; Muslim slaves in, 159–67. *See also* American slave trade; slavery and slave trade; *specific ports and destinations*

Atlantic studies: Atlantic world, defined, 10; on black Atlantic, 24, 27, 30, 159–60, 254, 255; jihād movement and methodology in, 22–25, 32–35, 146, 202, 249–51; map of Atlantic world, 14m; slavery and methodology in, 251–58. *See also* African history; West Africa; *specific regions*

Austin, Allan D., 196

Ayuba ibn Sulaymān Diallo, 48, 49, 76, 111

Ba'awa, 76

Badagry, 64. *See also* Bight of Benin

Al-Baghdādī al-Dimashqī, 'Abd al-Raḥmān, 194–95

Bahia, Brazil: Bight of Benin trade to, 149, 152, 155, 168; ethnic makeup of slave population, 304n28; Hausa population in, 64, 186; jihād movement in, 26, 167, 183–86; Malês uprising (1835), 22, 27–28, 153, 183–84, 191–94, 270n38; Muslim population in, 201, 248; Nagô population in, 29, 141; *oriṣa*, 29–30, 190; slave uprisings in, 186–87, 193, 270n38. *See also* Brazil

Bailyn, Bernard, 24, 254

Bakatsine, Malam, 76

Bamana, 60–61, 171, 174

Bambara (term), 17, 60, 171, 173, 174

Bambara language, 171

Bambara states, 16–17, 60–61, 98, 141

Banī Ḥasan Arabs, 38

Bantu regions, 31, 135, 136, 137, 159

Baquaqua, Mahommah Gardo, 26, 199–200

Barber, Miles, 173

Barcia, Manuel, 25, 28, 185, 200, 245

Bargery, G. P., 122

Barrow, John, 224

Barry, Boubacar, 39, 41, 133

Barth, Heinrich, 68, 109–10, 119–20, 128, 148, 217

Bath, Muhammad, 197

Bauchi, 86, 109

Bawa dan Gima, Katsina, 76–77

Bawa Jan Gwarzo, Gobir, 74

Bayān wujūb al hijra 'alā l-'ibād ('Uthmān), 13, 215

Bebeji, 75, 76, 109, 125

Bede, 151

Bello, Muhammad, 28, 51; abolitionist policies of, 150, 213, 214–15; on animism, 63; Bello-Clapperton accord, 31, 219–24, 225–26; Clapperton and, 30–31, 213, 220; death of, 94; *Infāq al-Maysūr*, 80, 82, 90, 147, 214; jihād by, 78; Magaria plantation of, 97, 120; *Miftaḥ al-sadād*, 66; scholarship by, 100; on slave trade, 65, 90, 92–93, 207, 290n68; on Yamusa succession, 79–80. *See also* Sokoto Caliphate; 'Uthmān dan Fodio

Benue River, 69

Berlin, Ira, 24, 143, 254

Bi Abdur, 80

Bight of Benin: jihād and demographics of, 106; jihād and slave exports from, 147–56, 148t, 168, 180–83, 188; map of, 70m, 71m; Muslim factor in slave trade from, 134–35, 140, 245–46; slave ports of, 63–64, 306n55. See also *specific ports; specific states*

Bight of Biafra: Muslim factor in slave trade from, 134, 135, 169, 174; Muslim population in, 12, 137; slave population from, 31, 139, 141, 154, 165; slave ports of, 253, 306n55

Bilād al-Sūdān: defined, 2, 16, 26; language in, 60–61; map of, 70m; overview of jihād in, 46–49; slave population in, 104–5, 106t, 135; trade economy in, 53–54. *See also* West Africa; *specific states*

Birni Ngazargamu. *See* Borno empire

Bissau. *See* upper Guinea coast

Black Atlantic studies. *See* Atlantic studies

Boahen, A. Adu, 217

Bobboyi, H., 32

Boers, 22

Boko Haram: historical overview of, 1, 3, 15–16, 100; modern interpretations of, 237, 249, 257–58

bori, 19–20, 89, 157–58, 168, 187

Borno empire: British accord with, 224–27; historical overview of, 16, 68; jihād and demographics of, 106–7, 152–53; jihād movements in, 61, 80–82, 90–91; map of, 71m; Rābiḥ ibn Faḍl Allāh and, 13; reforms of, 13; slave trade of, 92–93; textile trade industry of, 131. *See also* Fulbe

Botte, Roger, 145, 208

Bouka, 111–12, 276n23

Bovill, E. W., 217

Brazil: bondage legalities in, 126; migratory path to, 139, 154; national emergence of, 2; slave population in, 102, 141; slave resistance in, 22, 27–28, 186–87, 270n38; Yoruba influence in, 11, 23, 27, 185, 187–88. *See also* American slave trade; Bahia, Brazil

Brenner, Louis, 80, 81, 93

British government: abolitionist movement by, 22, 31, 134, 135, 136, 147, 206–14; Bello-Clapperton accord, 219–24, 225–26; Borno accord and, 224–27; colonialism in Americas, 171, 177, 188; conquest in West Africa, 22, 217; geographical knowledge of, 230–32, 236, 253, 323n67, 323n69; textile industry and, 131. *See also* Clapperton, Hugh

Bruce Lockhart, Jamie, 217

Buduma, 151

Burama, Konde, 41–42

Buxton, Thomas Fowell, 229

cabildos, 201

Cacheu. *See* Upper Guinea coast

caffa, 122–24, 122t

Cairus, José, 208

camels, 58, 59, 110, 130. *See also* pastoralism

Cameroon, 1, 112, 249

Canada, 177

Cañizares-Esguerra, Jorge, 10

caravans and slave regulation, 227–28

Cargill, Featherstone, 122

Caribbean. See *specific islands*

Castelnau, Francis de, 151, 153–54, 188

castration, 258

cattle, 40, 45, 46, 58, 61, 66. *See also* pastoralism

ceddo, 21, 41

Central Bilād al-Sūdān. *See* Bilād al-Sūdān

Chancel, Ausone de, 214, 228

Cheggueun, 227–28

children and slavery, 208, 240

Christianity: conversion to, 198–200; entanglement with Islam, 237, 247. *See also* American slave trade

Christmas uprising (1831–32), 193, 205, 246

Cidade, Francisco, 187

Cisse, Tafsir Abdou, 39

Clapperton, Hugh: Bello and, 30–31, 213, 220; Bello-Clapperton accord, 31, 219–24, 225–26; geographical knowledge of, 230–31; historical record by, 82, 83, 85, 97; on incident with female slaves, 324n8; on jihād and slave exports, 150, 152; servant of, 150–51; on slave trade, 114–15, 148. *See also* British government

Clarkson, Thomas, 211

Cleveland, Elizabeth, 142

clothing, 127–28

Cohen, Abner, 52, 279n41

commercial diaspora, 40, 55, 60, 279n41. *See also* trade economy

concubinage, 91, 239

conversion: to Christianity, 198–200; to Islam, 3, 5, 17, 201

Cook, Simon, 154, 282n74

corvée labor, 159

cotton industry, 127–31. *See also* textile production

Courts of Mixed Commission, 200–201, 245

cowrie shells, 57, 58, 128

Crowther, Samuel Ajayi, 85, 153, 229, 241, 256, 306n58

Cuba: overview of slave resistance in, 12, 22, 23; bondage legalities in, 126; jihād movement in, 28, 29, 200–203; Lucumí in, 29, 141, 200, 201; migratory path to, 154; Muslims in, 29, 200–201, 271n47; slave population in, 102, 141; Yoruba influence in, 27, 189. *See also* American slave trade

cultural identity. *See* ethnic identification

currency exchange, 57–58, 163

Curtin, Philip, 52, 55, 279n41

Dahomey, 64, 69, 84, 136, 140

Dallaji, ʿUmaru, 77

Dambazau, Muḥammadu Dabo, 76

Dambazawa, 76

dan Baskore, 78

Danejawa, 76

dan Kano, 150

dan Kasawa, 77–78

dan Kasawa, Sarkin Katsina, 76

Danmaiso, Malam Idrisu, 118

dan Mari, 78

Dantata family, 126

dan Tunku, Malam Mayaki, 76, 77

Dan Yaya battle (1807), 76

dan Zabuwa, Malam, 76

Daumas, M. J. E., 157, 214, 228

Daura state, 77–78

Davis, David Brion, 24, 25, 254

Debien, Gabriel, 197

Dendo, Malam, 69, 82–83, 285n23

Denham, Dixon, 218, 224, 230

Denyanke dynasty, 42, 44

desert nomads. *See* nomadic peoples

Diouf, Sylviane, 28, 160, 196, 197

divination, 19–20

diwal, 41, 42

Ḍiyāʾ al-sulṭān wa ghayrihi min al-ikhwān fī ahamm ma yuṭlab ʿilmuhu fī umūr al-zamān (Abdullahi), 215

donkeys, 59, 130. *See also* pastoralism

Dorayi, 118, 298n42

Dumyawa, ʿUmaru, 77

Dunama, Galadima, 80

Dunama, Mai, 81–82

Dwight, Theodore, Jr., 56–57

economic development, 10, 102–3, 110–27. *See also* agricultural production; textile production; trade economy

education centers, 39–41, 55–57, 66, 189

Egypt, 22, 54, 214, 219

Eltis, David, 161

emancipation from slavery, 207–8

England. *See* British government

ethnic identification: of Africans, 137–39, 175t, 180, 226–27; historical overview, in jihād states, 6–7; Islam and, 29, 60–61, 140–41; jihād movements and, 45, 202; language and, 25–26, 46–47, 60–61, 85, 140–41, 205, 286n32; in Louisiana, 199t; as methodology, 202–3, 243–44; trade economy and, 52–53. *See also* language; Muslim communities

Exmouth, Lord, 158, 214

fadama land, 113, 126, 131

Farias, Paulo F. de Moraes, 16, 18

Fatta, Mahdī, 42, 45, 275n18

Fellata, 51

Festing, Arthur H., 123

Fika, 151

Finlay, Philip, 197

fiqh, 19, 40, 60

Fisher, Humphrey, 28, 88, 211–12

Florida, United States, 142. *See also* American slave trade

Folayan, Kola, 218

Fombina. *See* Adamawa (Fombina)

Fraser, John, 142

freeborn Muslims: protected rights of, 21, 126, 165; ransoming of, 215–16; slavery and, 6, 30, 41, 62–63, 66, 89–90; ʿUthmān dan Fodio on, 91, 234. *See also* ethnic identification; Muslim communities

French government: in Caribbean, 171; slave trade and, 51, 63, 147, 183; textile industry and, 131

Freylinghusen, Theodorus Jacobus, 182

Ful, 45, 46

Fula, 46

Fulani. *See* Fulbe

Fulani jihād, 26, 41–42, 51, 68, 76, 80. *See also* ʿUthmān dan Fodio

Fulbe: biographical sketches of slaves, 50; jihād movement and, 26, 41–42, 51, 68, 76, 80; language and ethnic identification of, 45, 46, 85; pastoralism and, 45–46, 58, 94–95; slave estates and, 59. *See also* Borno empire; Hausa; Sokoto Caliphate

Mūsā, Mansa, 18
Muslim communities: overview of
geography, 12; in Brazil, 187–90; in
Cuba, 29, 271n47; freeborn *vs.* enslaved
Muslims, 6, 62–63, 66, 126; influence in
American slave trade, 203–5, 317n73;
Islamic practices and revolt in, 194–96;
networks of, 279n41; on slavery as
institution, 196–200, 206–8, 213–14;
slaves in military, 65, 84, 198, 218; trade
networks of, 18, 154–55, 159–66. *See also*
freeborn Muslims; *specific*
brotherhoods; specific groups
mysticism, 19–20, 21

Nadel, S. F., 260
Nafata, 74
Nagô, 29, 140, 141, 202. *See also* Bahia,
Brazil; Yoruba
Namoda, Muhammad, 75
Nana Asma'u, 96
Nāṣir al-Dīn, 36, 39
Ngileruma, Muhammad, 81
Ngizim, 151
Niger, 1, 15–16, 105, 106t
Nigeria: historical overview of jihād in,
15–16, 249; Lagos, 29, 64–65, 130, 147,
188, 217; Maitatsine movement in, 1;
population estimates for, 259–60, 261t.
See also Kano state; Yoruba
Niger River, 229–31, 236
Nina Rodrigues, Raimundo, 153, 189–90,
191, 246
nomadic peoples: caravans and slave
regulations, 227–28; Islam and, 58;
jihād movement and, 39; products of
exchange, 58–59. *See also* pastoralism;
trans-Saharan trade
nomijide, 122–23, 300n59, 300n64
North Africa, 156–59
North America. *See* American slave trade;
Cuba; Jamaica; United States
Nupe: jihād and slave exports of, 149, 152–53;
jihād in, 82–83, 154; population of, 109;
runaway slaves of, 92; slave trade in
Raka, 64–65, 223, 229–30
Nupe language, 244
Nūr al-albāb ('Uthmān), 290n65

O'Hara, Charles, 144
Ojo, Olatunji, 202–3
oriṣa (deity), 29–30, 190

Oswald, Richard, 173
Ottoman Empire slave trade, 156–59
Owu wars (1820s), 84–85, 154, 200
Oyo empire: collapse of, 69, 85, 94, 200;
ethnic identification in, 85; jihād in,
83–85, 136, 147; Muslim slaves in
military, 65, 84; slave trade of, 29–30,
63–65, 90, 140, 289n60

pastoralism, 45–47, 53, 58–59, 94–95. *See also*
nomadic peoples
Peel, J. D. Y., 286n32
Peul, 45
Pierpoint, Richard, 26, 49, 177, 198, 243
Pire religious center, 39, 44
plantations. *See* slave estates and plantations
political revolutions. *See* age of revolutions
Porto Novo, 63–65, 147, 281n63. *See also*
Bight of Benin
Powell, William P., 200
Pula, 46

Qādiriyya *ṭarīqa,* 13; education of, 47; as
model of Islamic rule, 88; Nāṣir al-Dīn
and, 39; overview of jihād and, 5, 16, 20,
36; on tolerance, 40; Toronkawa clan
and, 47. *See also* *ṣūfī* brotherhoods and
Sufism
Qaramanlī, Yūsuf, 217–18
quilombos, 192, 314n32
Qur'ānic schools. *See* education centers

Raka, 64–65, 223, 229–30
ransoming: cases of, 47–48, 66, 242, 290n64;
Islamic law on, 92; price of, 215–16, 242.
See also freeborn Muslims; slavery and
slave trade
Reis, João José, 28, 152–53, 185–87, 191–93,
196, 315n46
religion. *See* Christianity; conversion; Islam
resistance. *See* slave resistance and
revolutions
revolutions. *See* age of revolutions; slave
resistance and revolutions
ribā, 162–63
ribāṭ, 97, 107, 120
rimaibé, 42
rinji, 107, 113, 118. *See also* slave estates
and plantations
*Risālat shawq al-ḥabīb ilā as'ilat Ibrahim
al-labīb* ('Umar Tal), 216, 228–29
river-pebble divination, 19

Rocha, Francisco da, 155
Rosalie, 50
Rufino, José Maria, 241
rumde, 113

Sadu, Almami, 145
Saghanughu clan, 47, 55
Sahara. *See* trans-Saharan trade
Saʻīd, Muhammed ʻAlī, 26, 198, 242–43
Saʻidu, Abdulrazak Giginyu, 116, 118
Saʻīdu, Malam, 76
salafi, 16
salama, 116
Salau, Mohammed Bashir, 112, 113
Ṣāliḥ Bilali, 50
salt trade, 54, 58–59, 131
Salvador, Bahia, Brazil, 155, 183–84, 188, 192.
   See also Malês uprising (1835)
Sankore Mosque, 41
Sanneh, Lamin, 55
sarki, 79, 122, 187
sarkin bori, 187
sarkin gandu, 113
Sayfawa dynasty, 16, 21, 82
Schön, James Frederick, 151
schools. *See* education centers
Schwartz, Stuart, 28, 185, 204
Schwarz, Suzanne, 211
Scott, Rebecca, 50, 178
Searing, James, 161
second slavery theory, 4, 27–28, 34, 102, 134
Segu, 16–17, 60, 98, 141
Séhou, Ahmadou, 112
Sénégal, 105, 106t
Senegambia: geography of, 134, 141–42; jihād
   in, 41–45; Muslim factor in, 3, 137, 140;
   slave resistance from, 139; slave trade
   from, 141–46, 144t, 169–80, 172t, 176t.
   See also West Africa; *specific*
   communities
Sergipe de El-Rey, Brazil, 270n38
Shango, 29, 30, 201
Sharīʻa. *See* Islamic law
shaykh. *See* ʻUthmān dan Fodio
Shea, Philip, 127
Shehu. *See* ʻUthmān dan Fodio
Shisummas ibn Aḥmad, 66
shurfa, 52, 53
Sidbury, James, 10
Sierra Leone: founding of, 22; geography
   and slave trade, 49, 134, 141, 188;
   Muslims in slave trade, 145, 246; Poro

of, 19; slave resistance in, 22, 185;
   Yoruba migration to, 84. *See also*
   Fuuta Jalon
silk industry, 127
Silva, Alberto da Costa e, 208
Sisse, Muhammad, 197
situated knowledge, 235–37
slave estates and plantations: agricultural
   production on, 58–60, 113, 126, 131;
   caffa and *hurumi* arrangements,
   122–24; estates in Kano, 117–18t,
   124–26; land grants of, 112–13; slave
   production of, 113–15; words for, 113.
   See also agricultural production
slave resistance and revolutions: overview
   of West African jihād and, 11–12,
   21–22, 31, 204; in Bahia (1807–1835),
   186, 195–96; Christmas uprising
   (1831–1832), 193, 205, 246; in Fuuta
   Jalon, 42; in Haiti, 2–3, 21–22, 183, 247;
   Ilorin uprising (1817), 69–74, 91–92, 94,
   191; Malês uprising (1835), 22, 27–28,
   153, 183–84, 191–94, 270n38; *quilombos*,
   192, 314n32; scholarship on, 208.
   See also abolition movement; jihād
   movements
slavery and slave trade: abolition movement
   (*See* abolition movement); Atlantic *vs.*
   Islamic West Africa, 31–34, 132–35,
   159–66; Barth on, 119–20; biographical
   accounts of, 47–50, 52–54, 150–52,
   177–79, 181–83, 208, 238–44; Borno-
   Sokoto debate on, 92–93; burden of
   proof of Muslim identity in, 63, 66, 126,
   210, 234–35, 251; children and, 208, 240;
   consolidation of Islam and, 31–35, 92,
   132–35, 139–40, 290n65; corvée labor,
   159; economic development and, 10,
   102–3, 110–27; emancipation from,
   207–8; freeborn Muslims *vs.* enslaved
   status, 6, 30, 41, 62–63, 66, 89–90, 165;
   French policy on, 51, 147, 183; gender
   ratio of, 150, 161, 174, 198, 239, 331n10;
   Islamic law on, 30, 41, 90, 92, 126, 164;
   jihād and demographics of, 104–10;
   jihād and transatlantic deportation,
   31, 62–64, 135–41; men in (*See under*
   men); modern scholarship on, 251–58;
   Muslims on institution of, 196–200,
   206–8; Muslims *vs.* non-Muslims
   as slaves, 50, 135; overview of
   population of, 102, 144t, 148t, 238–39;

102, 155, 157; taxation in, 59; textiles in, 127–29; trans-Saharan slave trade, 156–59. *See also* agricultural production; economic development; slavery and slave trade; trans-Saharan trade
transatlantic slave trade. *See* Atlantic slave trade
transhumance migration patterns, 45, 46, 53, 58, 59
trans-Saharan trade: abolition and, 213–14; caravans and slave regulations, 227–28; jihād movements and, 156–59, 164–66; limits to involvement and autonomy of, 159–62. *See also* nomadic peoples; trade economy; Tuareg; *specific regions*
Trinidad, 32, 84, 197, 205
Tripoli, 81, 156–59, 217–19
Tsagarena, Maremawa Muhammadu, 77
Tsakkar, Dawaki, 122
Tuareg, 58, 61–62, 119, 127, 131. *See also* nomadic peoples; trans-Saharan trade
Tukur, Modibbo, 259
Tukur, Muhammad, 62
tungazi, 113
Tunisia, 214, 224
Ture, Askia Muhammad, 18, 55

'Umar ibn Sa'īd Tal, al-Hājj, 95, 145: on laws against slavery, 215, 216, 228; as leader, 51, 99; reforms by, 67, 150, 202; *Risālat shawq al-ḥabīb ilā as'ilat Ibrahim al-labīb*, 216; Tījāniyya and, 13, 34
'Umar Dallaji, Malam, 77
Umoru, Imam, 115–16, 124–25
unguwa, 107
United States: cotton industry of, 131; independence of, 25; slavery in, 4, 102, 126, 142, 211. *See also* American slave trade
Upper Guinea coast: migratory path from, 139; Muslim factor in slave trade from, 134; slave trade from, 141–46, 144t, 169–80, 172t, 176t
urbanization, 17–18, 107–8. *See also* industrial age and African history
Usman, Yusuf Bala, 32
Usuman, Malam, 76
'Uthmān dan Fodio, 68–101; death of, 69, 96; influences of, 100; jihād and, 13, 15, 68–101; Qādiriyya and, 20; scholarship by, 100; on slavery, 65, 91, 215, 234; works by, 65, 88, 100, 215, 289n53,

290n65. *See also* Abdullahi dan Fodio; Bello, Muhammad; Sokoto Caliphate

Vassa, Gustavus, 211
Verger, Pierre, 191
Voyages: The Trans-Atlantic Slave Trade Database, 34, 140, 141

Waalo, 45, 61
Wabi, Muhammad, 81
Wadström, C. B., 209
Wahhābism, 16
Wangara merchant community, 55, 60
Ware, Rudolph, 39
warfare. *See* jihād movements
Warner-Lewis, Maureen, 197, 276n21
Warrington, Hamer, 217
Wathīqat ahl al-Sūdān wa man shā'a Allāh min al-ikhwān ('Uthmān), 215
Watt, James, 145
West Africa: defining Bilād al-Sūdān, 2, 16, 26; European conquest in, 22; historical context of Islamic conversion in, 3, 5, 17; jihād and demographics of, 104–10; population estimates for, 259–60, 261t; scholarly tradition of, 18–20, 34, 96; slave ship destinations (1761–1860), 170t; slave trade of Atlantic *vs.* Islamic West Africa, 31–34, 132–35, 159–66; urbanization of, 17–18, 107–8. *See also* African history; Atlantic studies; slavery and slave trade; *specific nations and regions*
West central Africa: Muslim factor in slave trade from, 134, 159; slave population from, 139, 169. See also *specific regions*
Western Bilād al-Sūdān. *See* Bilād al-Sūdān
Whitten, Big Prince, 48
Wilberforce, William, 88, 96, 211
Wilks, Ivor, 40, 53–54
Williams, Eric, 10
Willis, John Ralph, 13–15, 195–96
Windward Coast, 140, 175
Wolof language, 46
Wolof states, 44, 45, 61
women: Bahia uprisings by, 192; as concubines, 91, 239; education and, 56; incidents with female slaves, 324n8; slave gender ratio, 150, 161,